THE EXCEPTIONAL
STUDENT IN THE
REGULAR CLASSROOM

FIFTH EDITION

THE EXCEPTIONAL STUDENT IN THE REGULAR CLASSROOM

BILL R. GEARHEART
Professor Emeritus, University of Northern Colorado

MEL W. WEISHAHN
Southern Oregon State College

CAROL J. GEARHEART
University of Northern Colorado

Merrill, an imprint of Macmillan Publishing Company
New York

Maxwell Macmillan Canada
Toronto

Maxwell Macmillan International
New York   Oxford   Singapore   Sydney

Cover photo: Dennis MacDonald/Unicorn Stock Photos

Editor: Ann Castel
Production Editor: Linda Hillis Bayma
Art Coordinator: Raydelle M. Clement
Photo Editor: Gail L. Meese
Text Designer: Anne Flanagan
Cover Designer: Robert Vega
Production Buyer: Pamela D. Bennett

This book was set in Trump by the Clarinda Company and was printed and bound by R.R. Donnelley & Sons Company. The cover was printed by Lehigh Press, Inc.

Macmillan Publishing Company
866 Third Avenue
New York, NY 10022

Macmillan Publishing Company is part of the Maxwell Communication Group of Companies.

Maxwell Macmillan Canada, Inc.
1200 Eglinton Avenue East, Suite 200
Don Mills, Ontario M3C 3N1

Library of Congress Cataloging-in-Publication Data
Gearheart, Bill R. (Bill Ray), 1928-
  The exceptional student in the regular classroom / Bill R. Gearheart, Mel W. Weishahn, Carol J. Gearheart. — 5th ed.
    p.   cm.
  Includes bibliographical references (p.) and indexes.
  ISBN 0-02-341220-8
  1. Handicapped children—Education—United States.
  2. Mainstreaming in education—United States. I. Weishahn, Mel W., 1940- . II. Gearheart, Carol J. (Carol Jean), 1937- .
  III. Title.
  LC4031.G4 1992
  371.9'046—dc20   91-23531
                                                    CIP
Printing: 1 2 3 4 5 6 7 8 9
Year: 2 3 4 5

Photo credits: All photos copyrighted by individuals or companies listed. Ben Asen/Envision, pp. 9, 124; Barbara Clark, *Growing Up Gifted*, Macmillan Publishing Company, p. 417; Cleo Freelance Photo, pp. 57, 400; Tom Hubbard, p. 174; Fritz Locke/Edgar Bernstein, p. 160; Macmillan Pulishing Company/Andy Brunk, pp. 46, 99, 112, 189, 221, 233, 299; Jean Greenwald, p 158; Mary Hagler, p. 28; Jo Hall, p. 23; Bruce Johnson, pp. 281, 288, 395; Lloyd Lemmerman, pp. 275, 292; Tom Morton, pp. 48, 236; David Napravnik, pp. 3, 139, 169, 345; and Tom Tondee, p. 270; Harvey Phillips/PPI, pp. 19, 192, 199, 356; Prentke Romich Company, pp. 267, 268, 269; Charles Quinlan, p. 322; Blair Seitz/R. Maust Photography, p. 101; Ronald Stewart, pp. 212, 215, 220; David Strickler, pp. 76, 89; William Williamson, pp. 205, 206, 207, 208, 209; Gale Zucker, pp. 313, 397.

PREFACE

This fifth edition of *The Exceptional Student in the Regular Classroom* continues with the purpose and focus of the previous editions. Students with disabilities and students who are gifted and talented are enrolled in regular classrooms throughout the nation. Teachers must be informed about the special needs of these students for the sake of the students and for the sake of other students in the class. Most teachers believe in the principle of maximum integration consistent with good educational practice, and teachers now completing teacher training learn about exceptional students as a regular part of the educational program.

We believe that preparation to teach exceptional students requires three general types of knowledge: (a) a history of education for individuals with disabilities and the legislation which governs service delivery; (b) specifics of the nature of exceptionalities and the ways in which characteristics help determine instructional needs; and (c) instructional strategies which are most likely to be effective with students who have special needs.

In this fifth edition, we have attempted to respond to a variety of ideas and suggestions from teachers in regular classrooms and from professors. Chapters 1 through 4 concentrate on information that is applicable for all exceptionalities, while the second section of the text examines eight specific exceptionalities individually.

FEATURES OF THE FIFTH EDITION

The fifth edition builds on the strengths of previous editions, providing a foundation upon which future teachers can develop both confidence and competence. Students will continue to find in the fifth edition:

- A strong focus on the affective nature of teaching, emphasizing the influence of positive personal interactions between teacher/pupil and pupil/pupil on teaching success.
- A wealth of teaching strategies that provide methods coverage in subjects and situations across the entire elementary and secondary curriculum.
- An extensive listing of literature about individuals with disabilities, providing students a vehicle for building a better appreciation of what it means to have a disability.
- A well-planned pedagogical program, including summaries, numerous photographs and illustrations, and a glossary.

NEW FEATURES OF THE FIFTH EDITON

The fifth edition reflects the dynamic nature of special education. Every chapter has been revised and updated to reflect the most current practices:

- We include discussions on collaborative consultation and teacher assistance teams; succinct treatment of the Regular Education Initiative; and new teaching strategies, especially ideas for teaching cross-cultural and bilingual students.

- Information and ideas on how to handle children with health impairments, including students afflicted with the HIV virus, are provided. We have also expanded our coverage on programming for students wtih severe/profound levels of mental retardation.
- Students with behavioral disorders now receive greater attention. We have included new information on depression and suicide, juvenile delinquency, child abuse/neglect, and pupil/parental substance abuse.
- Greater attention is given to the needs of the adolescent student, including strategies for enhancing study skills, listening skills, and self-monitoring abilities.
- More discussion is included on general programming and specific teaching strategies for the gifted and talented pupil.

Many individuals have provided ideas for this edition, and we would like to acknowledge the specific assistance of certain individuals. We offer our sincere thanks to Cliff Baker for continuing, general assistance and to reviewers who were contacted by our editor and were responsible to our publisher: namely Helen C. Botnarescue, California State University-Hayward; Jean M. Ferguson, Western Oregon State College; Joyce Richardson; and J. Barbara Wilkinson, Oklahoma State University.

We appreciate the response to our fourth edition, and we hope that this fifth edition merits continued acceptance. We are even more pleased to see the manner in which regular classroom teachers have accepted students with special needs and are teaching them with increasing skill. We are most happy to be a part of this effort.

Bill Gearheart
Mel Weishahn
Carol Gearheart

A NOTE TO READERS

Because we believe that simple is better than complex (if either will achieve the intended purpose), we use a minimum of technical terms in this text. Certain terms, however, require special comment. For example, we have used *mainstreaming* and *integration* interchangeably in many instances. We would rather not use the word *mainstreaming,* because it has been misused and misunderstood, but it is in common use, so we felt a need to discuss and define it. Integration of students who are disabled means (to us) helping students become as much a part of the mainstream as possible; it requires joint efforts on the part of regular and special educators.

Regular classroom teachers or *regular educators* are the dedicated professionals to whom we have addressed this text. We really mean *educators who are not trained special educators,* but that is very long, so we are using the shorter forms. We ask readers to understand that we are not implying ordinariness. We simply needed short descriptive ways to discuss the teachers who are most important in vitalizing the process of integration.

Our major interest is to help regular classroom teachers better understand and more effectively teach exceptional students. The term *exceptional students* is meant to include all students whose educational needs are not effectively met through use of the usual, or standard, curriculum; thus, they may also be called students who have special needs. In common practice (including most state and federal laws and regulations), such students are identified as hearing impaired, visually impaired, gifted, mentally retarded, and so forth, but these labels can be misleading. Although certain characteristics apply to each exceptionality (that is, all hearing impaired students have some hearing loss), each student is an individual, with unique characteristics and learning abilities. As we discuss the major characteristics associated with the various exceptionalities, remember that these are generalizations.

One other misconception is sufficiently important that we want to guard against it in advance. Because of the manner in which this text is written, we sometimes speak of the exceptionalities in a manner that might lead readers to think that each is always separate and discrete. This, too, is inaccurate. Even though we may discuss the exceptionalities separately, they often overlap. For example, a student with a moderate hearing loss may also be mildly mentally retarded, or a student who is orthopedically impaired may also have a speech impairment. We ask readers to understand and accept this in advance so that we do not need to repeat it every time we consider any particular exceptionality.

CONTENTS

Contents

THE EXCEPTIONAL
STUDENT IN THE
REGULAR CLASSROOM

THE FOUNDATION FOR EDUCATION OF EXCEPTIONAL STUDENTS

PART I (CHAPTERS 1 AND 2) PROVIDES THE FRAMEWORK FOR INFORMED CONSIDERATION OF educational programs for exceptional students. Chapter 1 reviews the philosophical and historical bases for the education of students who have special needs (students who have disabilities and students who are gifted or talented), litigation that has shaped the existing legislation, and litigation that continues to influence the nature of special educational services. Finally, the chapter provides data for students who theoretically require special services, as well as data for students who are actually receiving special services, as reported by the states.

Chapter 2 considers the major legislation that has shaped the development of educational programs for students with special needs during the last half century. It summarizes educational programs and services now available, and it reviews the ways in which students are identified for programs, the means through which educational interventions are implemented, and concerns for appropriate programs for culturally diverse and bilingual populations. An understanding of the content of chapters 1 and 2 is essential to a complete understanding of the rest of this text.

Education of Students Who Have Special Needs

Historical Origins of Present Programs

The Effects of Litigation

The Scope of Special Education

A Philosophy for Education of Students Who Have Disabilities

■ What factors led to concern regarding most special class programs? When and on what bases are special programs justified?

■ When might a student be considered mainstreamed without membership in a regular classroom?

■ How did the basic thrust of the litigation that preceded PL 94–142 differ from that of the litigation that followed it?

■ In your opinion, which disability is the simplest to successfully accommodate in regular classrooms? Which is the most difficult to accommodate in regular classrooms? On what experiences or other bases did you answer these two questions?

■ What type of special educational programming is provided in your state for students called gifted or talented?

■ Can you develop an unambiguous, practical definition of *talented?* How would you differentiate between giftedness and talent?

CHAPTER 1

EDUCATION OF STUDENTS WITH SPECIAL NEEDS

THIS CHAPTER PROVIDES A HISTORICAL ACCOUNT of the development of special educational services plus a statement of philosophy for education of students who have disabilities. It also describes the scope of special education and includes estimates of the prevalence of exceptional students in the United States.

Finally, it discusses the influence of litigation on the development of programs for individuals who have disabilities and considers the Regular Education Initiative, which will affect the manner in which students who have special needs are educated in the future.

EDUCATION OF STUDENTS WHO HAVE SPECIAL NEEDS

Students who have special needs receive much better services in our schools today than they did years ago. Comprehensive services for students who have disabilities are now federally mandated. Gifted and talented students receive increased attention and effort, but not the same emphasis as students who have disabilities. States have responded to the federal legislation in a variety of ways and at differing speeds, but all have responded.

As the quality and quantity of programs and services have increased, other, significant changes have also occurred. The major change relates to the settings in which students who have disabilities receive their education. In earlier programs, almost all students who had disabilities were in separate classrooms or buildings. Now, students with disabilities must be educated in a regular classroom, *whenever this is the most appropriate, effective setting*. Federal law established this principle and led to a need for all teachers to know about education of students who have disabilities. Note the phrase "whenever this is the most appropriate, effective setting," because federal law does *not* require the education of *all* students with disabilities in regular classrooms. Rather, it requires education in the most normal setting possible, given the special needs.

Because education agencies in all states have regulations similar to federal regulations, it might seem that appropriate education of all children and youth who have disabilities is an accomplished fact. This is not the case, however. The concept is legally in place and the regulations exist, but the major determining factor in attaining the goal of appropriate education for most students with disabilities is the regular classroom teacher.

Regular classroom teachers must have the knowledge and skill to help students develop cognitively, emotionally, socially, and physically. More important, they must *believe* in the principle of regular classroom education of students who have disabilities. They must accept such students and genuinely desire to help them in their classrooms.

Education in the least restrictive environment is important. Some students have too many special needs for regular classrooms and require more specialized programs, but when it is possible to educate students who have special needs along with other students, we are certain this is best. Thus, it is important to discuss the word *mainstreaming*, which came into common use in the early 1970s. To some, mainstreaming means the return of *all* students with disabilities to regular classrooms, but this is *not* consistent with the intent of mainstreaming.

The reasons for mainstreaming are many, ranging from evidence of lack of effectiveness of various special educational efforts (Dunn, 1968) to indications that members of various ethnic groups have been improperly placed in special education programs in forms of racial segregation. In addition, special education classes were sometimes used for students who were thought not to fit into existing programs or who could not adjust to particular teachers, regardless of whether the special education programs were appropriate for the needs of the students.

Often, mainstreaming was supported by the knowledge that some students with disabilities, namely students who are visually impaired and physically disabled, had been successfully integrated for many years. This success led to an increased realization that other students with disabilities could be successfully educated in regular classrooms.

If retention in regular classrooms is possible, given the special needs of a student, this is where the student should be. If a separate special program is required, it should be provided. Our concept of mainstreaming is that of maximum integration in regular classes combined with concrete assistance for regular class teachers. The role of special educators is often that of sharing unique skills and competencies with general educators, who also have a great deal to contribute to the education of students who have disabilities.

We wish we could effectively discuss students who have special needs without using the traditional categories of disability, for there is danger in causing bias or self-fulfilling prophecies with the use of categorical labels. We use them, however, because from a practical point of view, they remain the most efficient terms of reference. For example, this book refers to students who have learning problems as a result of less-than-normal ability to hear as *deaf, hard of hearing, hearing handicapped,* or *hearing impaired,* even though some readers might view these terms as as old-fashioned. Other terms are available, but new terms simply become new labels. We believe that although the public has some misunderstandings about deafness or hearing problems, even after decades of efforts to promote better understanding, introduction of new terms for these problems serves no useful purpose.

We also persist with the idea that there is such a thing as mental retardation (mental disability or limited intellectual ability) even though errors have been made in assessments of mental ability, particularly with children who are culturally different from the majority, middle-class population. The major errors that have been made with respect to categorical terminology have been errors in identification of students and presumption that a particular categorical label automatically dictates a particular educational program. Educators are making progress in correcting these errors, although much remains to be accomplished.

HISTORICAL ORIGINS OF PRESENT PROGRAMS

The history of early efforts to assist individuals who have disabilities or to eliminate the disability provides a perspective for consideration of present educational efforts. This section examines the history of programs for individuals with disabilities through four historical eras, as follows:

Early history—before 1800
Era of institutions—1800 to 1900
Era of public school special classes—1900 to 1960/70
Era of accelerated growth—1960 to present

These eras overlap to some extent. In many cases, a new era started in some parts of the nation or world while an older era still existed in others.

All events before 1800 are considered early history. In much of the pre-1800 period, individuals were not recognized as having disabilities unless the disability was severe. This was particularly true with respect to mental retardation, partly because of a lack of any type of universal educational effort.

Early History—Before 1800

The early history of societal involvement with disabled individuals is primarily one of misunderstanding and superstition. It is likely that blindness, deafness, and mental retardation have existed since the beginning of the human race, and early documents clearly refer to abandonment of infants who had disabilities. Roman history repeatedly refers to "fools" kept by the wealthy for entertainment.

It was almost universally held that individuals who were considerably different from normal in appearance or behavior were possessed by demons or evil spirits. Historical writers such as Zilboorg and Henry (1941), Pritchard (1963), and Kanner (1964) provide comprehensive accounts of the manner in which society has related to individuals with disabilities, mainly accounts of inhumanity that developed as a result of fear and ignorance. This section is based on documentation found in the preceding three sources and in Gearheart and Litton (1979).

Most early records refer to individuals with disabilities or defects in ways that make it difficult to determine whether those referred to were mentally retarded, mentally ill, or deaf and unable to communicate. In many societies, a father could determine whether he wanted to keep a newborn infant. If he indicated he did not, it might be thrown off a cliff, left in the wilderness, or left by a roadside. Such infanticide was supported by the common belief that individuals who were different were possessed by demons or evil spirits and that the actions taken were not directed against human infants but against demons. At one time, the Romans even extended this absolute rule of the father over infants to include the possibility that any female infant might be so disposed of. There were, of course, short periods of time during which specific rulers imposed more humane practices, but the foregoing, repugnant as they may seem today, were general practices in much of the "civilized" Western world for centuries.

The Middle Ages and the rise and development of Christianity brought about varied effects, depending on the type of disability, the geographic location, and the specific era. Although the idea of love and concern for others gained headway, individuals with disabilities were variously viewed as fools, nonhumans, or witches (an obvious throwback to earlier demonology). The belief that individuals with mental illness or mental retardation were possessed by demons or evil spirits led to the offering of prayers or the practice of exorcism. On many occasions, the exorcism was rigorous but not nearly so final as later treatment of witches, such as burning at the stake.

Although there were some bright spots, all the more bright for their infrequent appearance, until the 16th century the general picture was bleak. Individuals with disabilities were not accepted as totally human and thus were misunderstood, mistreated, or put to death. Leading philosophers, national governments, and organized churches shared responsibility for this attitude.

Then, slowly and with frequent backsliding, the picture began to change. During the latter part of the 16th century, a Spanish monk, Pedro Ponce de León, was successful in teaching a small group of pupils who were deaf to speak, read, and write. This major breakthrough led to a reversal of the official position of the church that individuals who were deaf could not speak and were uneducable, a position based on the writings of Aristotle. In the following century, Juan Bonet developed an early version of fingerspelling for individuals who were deaf. In 1760, the Abbé de l'Épée opened a school in Paris for individuals who were deaf, and organized education for individuals who were deaf became a reality.

An associate of the Abbé de l'Épée, Valentin Huay, became interested in individuals who were blind. Huay, who had associated with such intellectuals as Voltaire and Rousseau, vowed to improve the lot of individuals who were blind after the traumatic experience of witnessing the exploitation for public entertainment of 10 men who were blind. By 1784, Huay had established a school for individuals who were blind, the National Institution of Young Blind People, also in Paris.

Only a few years later, in 1789, a boy of 11 or 12 years of age was found roaming "wild" in the woods near Aveyron, France. Discovered by hunters, the boy was unable to speak and bore the scars of years of encounters with wild animals. He bit and scratched all who approached, chose his food by smell, and was more animal than human in nearly all respects. This boy, eventually named Victor, was taken to Paris to be observed by students who were studying the development of primitive faculties. There, Phillipe Pinel, a renowned scientist, declared the boy to be an incurable idiot, but Jean Marc Gaspard Itard, who also saw the boy, thought otherwise. Itard obtained custody of Victor and launched an involved program to civilize and educate him, hoping to make him normal. Unfortunately, although the boy showed improvement, he did not become normal in any sense. The record of Itard's work, *The Wild Boy of Aveyron* (Itard, 1801, 1932, 1962), is an important classic in the education of individuals with mental retardation.

Thus, we see that educational programs for individuals with hearing impairments, visual impairments, and mental retardation had their beginnings within less than a half-century, all in or near Paris, France. Perhaps the most fitting comment on the long era brought to a close by the new efforts is that the change, the opening of a new chapter in the history of treatment of individuals with disabilities, was long overdue.

Era of Institutions—1800 to 1900

The manner in which the institutional movement swept Europe and the United States is a reflection of the combination of a critical need on the part of the population of persons with disabilities, an awareness of this need on the part of professionals (both physicians and educators), and changing attitudes among the general population. However, considerable support for institutionalization seems to have come from the fact that such a practice kept undesirable or physically unattractive persons out of the public eye and thus off the public conscience. This attitude, of course, is unacceptable today, but it was a vast improvement over infanticide or the use of prisons as holding centers for individuals with disabilities.

Institutions for individuals with hearing and visual impairments were initiated at about the same time. Institutions for individuals with mental retardation came 50 to 60 years later. The first institutional programs for individuals with disabilities were initiated in Europe, with France, Germany, Scotland, and England leading the way. By 1800, recognized programs for individuals with visual impairment existed in France, England, and Scotland, and programs for individuals with hearing impairment existed in France, Germany, Scotland, and England. Institutions specifically for individuals with mental retardation were not begun until 1831, when the first such program was initiated in France, but multipurpose institutions, such as the Bicetre and Salpetriere in Paris, had housed a variety of societal outcasts—individuals with visual impairment, senility, mental illness, and mental retardation, as well as prostitutes—since the 17th century.

Institutions were *the* way to provide for individuals with disabilities throughout the 19th century, but as the century came to a close, new voices and new ideas began to be heard. For example, in an address to the National Education Association in 1898, Alexander Graham Bell suggested forming an annex to the public schools to provide special classes for individuals with hearing impairment, visual impairment, and mental retardation. In 1902, he further urged that this "special education" be provided so that such children would not have to leave their homes to attend institutions and that the National Education Association actively pursue such educational provisions. As a result, the NEA officially formed a Department of Special Education, thus originating a name that remains to this day (Gearheart, 1974). These efforts by Bell and the actions of the public schools, which soon followed, ushered in a new era.

Era of Public School Special Classes—1900 to 1960/70

Educational efforts designed specifically for students with disabilities originated before 1900, but such efforts were sporadic, met with limited acceptance, and had limited success. The order of introduction of special programs into public schools was reversed compared with that of institutional programs, with public school classes for individuals with mental retardation coming before those for individuals with hearing and visual impairments. Such classes were attempted in New York, Cleveland, and Providence, Rhode Island before 1900, but they tended to be classes provided for "problem children" and probably included more nonretarded students than students with mental retardation.

Early in the 20th century, several cities tried gathering groups of students who had been previously unschooled and who for the most part were mentally retarded. Like the institutions, the schools were interested in a return to normalcy, including normal learning ability, but they were generally unsuccessful. Later in the century, particularly after the appearance of a more adequate way to determine degree of mental retardation (Lewis Terman's revision of the Binet test of intelligence—the Stanford-Binet), classes for students with mild mental retardation were started and were successful enough to warrant continuation.

Day-school classes for students with vi-

This student would not have been in a regular classroom 50 years ago.

sual or hearing impairment were slower in starting, but they did not follow quite so much the start-and-stop pattern that characterized early classes for students with mental retardation, because institutions for students with hearing or visual impairment were more truly schools, and parents were more likely to accept and support residential settings. With the enactment of compulsory school attendance laws in the early part of the century came the problem of providing for *all* minors, including those with disabilities. It should be noted that since most states provided residential schools for students with visual or hearing impairments and students with severe mental retardation, who were often institutionalized at an early age, the real problem was

providing for students with mild mental retardation. Thus, the public schools concentrated on special classes for students with mild mental retardation. However, some of these classes included children whose problems were mostly behavioral, resulting in low academic performance, because no other programs were available.

After about 1920, as special classes for students with mental retardation (later called *educable mentally handicapped* to differentiate them from *trainable mentally retarded*) continued to grow in popularity, there was similar growth in special programs for students with less-than-normal visual acuity (called *visually handicapped, visually impaired,* or *partially seeing*) and classes for those with less-than-normal hearing (called *deaf* or *hearing handi-capped*). In addition, there were special programs for students with speech problems and often special rooms for students with heart problems or orthopedic disabilities. Some classes for students whose major problems were unacceptable or antisocial behaviors were also initiated, but as often as not, if the problems were not too severe, these students were placed in classes for students with mental retardation, and those who could not get along in this obviously special setting were expelled from school.

The close of this era is given a dual date because although there was a considerable increase in the use of service delivery plans other than special classes during the 1960s, many special classes remained in 1970. By calling this the era of special classes, we do not mean that other means of serving students with disabilities were not in use during this time. Many students with physical disabilities, visual impairments, or hearing impairments were integrated with success.

It must also be recognized that a special class may be either a full-time or part-time special class. For example, speech therapy has been conducted for years in small groups of two to four students in totally segregated special settings, often for periods of only 30 to 40 minutes per day, 2 or 3 days per week. Programs for students with visual impairments sometimes consist of segregated special classes at the preschool level, where students learn special skills such as braille, but these same students are almost totally integrated into regular classrooms from second grade on.

In the first 60 to 70 years of the 20th century, special classes were the major means whereby students with disabilities were served. This era represented a definite evolution beyond the institutional era. General educators happily sent problem students to special classes, and special educators ac-cepted a number of students who should not have been so placed. Toward the end of the era, contradictory and inconclusive efficacy studies as well as court cases suggested that special classes were used as dumping grounds, vehicles of segregation, and in some geographic areas, convenient ways to do something for children who were culturally or linguistically different.

As the era came to a close, many educators had negative feelings whenever the phrase "special class" was uttered, particularly when the reference was to self-contained special classes. The misuse of special classes is not questioned by most special educators, but the assumption that special classes are *never* right is just as wrong as the earlier assumption that they were *always* right. The concern must be for evaluation of individual needs and programming that meets those needs. Any other procedure may lead to additional negative results.

Era of Accelerated Growth—1960 to Present

The first half of the 20th century showed improvement and growth in services for students with disabilities, but truly rapid growth, unparalleled in history, began in the 1960s, with the period of most concentrated growth between 1965 and 1980. The changes that took place led to increased acceptance of persons with disabilities as individuals, more positive attitudes on the part of educators regarding their responsibility for education of students with disabilities, and actions of courts and government leaders to attempt to ensure continuing, appropriate education.

Important individual advocates, organized parent groups, and professional groups were catalysts for this change; but the U.S. Congress provided the major impetus for this positive movement. Congress indicated interest by a series of legislation through which it supported better educational programs and services for children and youth with disabilities.

The pattern through which Congress became involved with the education of students with disabilities was similar to that of its entering any new and unfamiliar arena. At first, legislation was limited in scope and funding. Then, as results seemed to warrant further consideration, Congress enacted broader laws in a sequence that culminated in Public Law 94–142: the Education for All Handicapped Children Act of 1975. Individual members of Congress and congressional committees did not, of course, achieve this entirely on their own. Various factors contributed to their actions, including the following:

1. A number of major political figures, including President Kennedy, had personal interest in individuals with disabilities because of such individuals in their immediate families. Twenty years earlier, the existence of family members with disabilities might have been hidden, but increased objectivity, public relations efforts by major organizations concerned with individuals with disabilities, and national concern about minority populations made it socially and politically acceptable to promote such causes.
2. Organizations such as the National Association for Retarded Children (now the National Association for Retarded Citizens) and the United Cerebral Palsy Association had become increasingly active. Leading national figures, particularly those in show business, had supported their efforts and had given the cause of individuals with disabilities unusually high national visibility.
3. Professional organizations, led by the Council for Exceptional Children (but

including many more), had grown in power, recognition, and lobbying expertise.
4. Congress was venturing into new fields of involvement, and this subject appeared to be a fruitful one. Few would criticize efforts to assist individuals with disabilities.

The result of continuing congressional interest, PL 94–142, established the framework for education of students with disabilities as it exists today. Although funding of some of the federal programs designed to encourage better services for individuals with disabilities was reduced as a result of general federal funding cutbacks starting in 1981, it appears that the intent of Congress has mostly been maintained. To a considerable extent, related legislation in the states seems likely to ensure continued educational programs for students who have disabilities.

THE EFFECTS OF LITIGATION

A series of court actions raised important questions about special education classes and services for children and youth with disabilities. This litigation began to appear in earnest in the early 1970s, and although it took many forms, it had several major thrusts. The first may be characterized as litigation that alleged that special education classes (often classes for individuals who were classified educable mentally retarded) led to stigma, inadequate education, and irreparable injury. These lawsuits alleged that special education programs as they existed were a disservice to many students and resulted in a reduction in the numbers of students served by special education in certain parts of the nation.

A second type of litigation involved students who were not served through special education but who were in serious need of such service. These suits led to the initiation of a number of new programs and the addition of students to special education rolls in some areas. Other litigation related to who should pay the cost of private schooling for students with disabilities, recovery (by parents) of attorney fees incident to court proceedings relating to students with disabilities, and the conditions under which students with disabilities can be suspended or expelled from school. Some of these cases are summarized in Table 1–1, and the rest of this section further considers the effect of litigation on programs for students with disabilities.

Much of the special education-related litigation of the 1960s and 1970s was based on the U.S. Supreme Court ruling in *Brown v. Board of Education* (1954), which declared that separate schools for black and white students were unconstitutional. The essence of this decision was that segregation solely on the basis of race deprives minority children of equal educational opportunities, even if various tangible factors appear to be equal (Zirkel, 1978). Parents of children with disabilities later sued school systems in relation to segregated facilities for their children, basing their arguments in part on *Brown v. Board of Education.* Such litigation started in the 1960s but reached previously unheard-of proportions in the 1970s. As noted by Ysseldyke and Algozzine (1982) in a discussion of legal regulation of special education, "Educators today are as much concerned with matters of litigation and legislation as of education" (p. 212). It is certainly unfortunate that educators must spend so much time, effort, and concern on litigation and legislation.

Diana v. State Board of Education, used as a basis for similar suits, alleged that intelligence tests used for placement were culturally biased and that class placement based on these inadequate tests led to inadequate education. This suit also claimed that, as a result, the stigma of mental retardation was suffered by children who were not mentally retarded. In the *Diana* case, the plaintiffs sought relief from existing practices of identification and placement. They also sought compensatory damages.

Diana v. State Board of Education was settled out of court with the following points of agreement: (a) children whose primary language is not English must be tested in their primary language and English, but verbal (as opposed to performance) questions, which by their very nature are unfair to children whose primary language is not English, cannot be used in testing such children; (b) all Mexican-American and Chinese children already enrolled in special education classes must be retested in accordance with the preceding principle; (c) every school district in the state must develop and submit to the court a plan for retesting and reevaluating Mexican-American and Chinese children in classes for students classified as educable mentally retarded, and as a part of this plan, the district must show how it will place back into regular classes children whom this reevaluation indicates were misplaced; (d) school psychologists must develop more appropriate testing devices and measures to reflect Mexican-American culture; and (e) any school district that has a significant disparity between the percentage of Mexican-American children in regular classes and the percentage in classes for students who are educable mentally retarded must submit an acceptable explanation for this discrepancy. The *Diana* case is similar to many filed against the schools. Most were settled in a manner similar to that in the *Diana* case.

Litigation also demanded more special education classes and services in the public schools for students with disabilities. The following description of two cases, one in Pennsylvania and the other in Washington, DC, illustrates this effort. Although the first affected only mental retardation, the second specifically related to all disabilities and, because it was based on the U.S. Constitution, has ramifications for all areas of the United States.

Two major cases appear to have established the right of access to public education for the school-age students classified as trainable mentally retarded. The first, *The Pennsylvania Association for Retarded Children v. the Commonwealth of Pennsylvania*, questioned educational policies of the state of Pennsylvania. The suit alleged that certain policies led directly to practices that denied appropriate education at public expense to children of school age who were mentally retarded. This case was filed on January 7, 1971, by the Pennsylvania Association for Retarded Children on behalf of fourteen specifically named children and all other children similarly situated. This was a typical *class-action suit*, filed to affect the fourteen children named, all others of a similar class now residing in the state, and all children similarly situated who will be living in Pennsylvania in the future.

Pennsylvania, like a number of other states, had compulsory school attendance laws, provided certain types of special classes for children who had disabilities within the public schools and provided residential schools for some children with disabilities. Within the Pennsylvania School Code, children who were trainable mentally retarded could be excluded from public education in two ways. First, if a qualified psychologist or personnel from a mental health clinic certified that a given child could no longer profit from public school attendance, the child could be excluded. Second, because the law provided that the local board of education could refuse to accept or retain children who had not reached the mental age of 5 years, most children classified as trainable retarded were never admitted to the public schools. Even if a child were not excluded under either of these provisions, a third provision permitted the local board to provide

training outside the public schools "if an approved plan demonstrates that it is unfeasible to form a special class."

The Pennsylvania Association for Retarded Children (PARC) set out to establish three main points in their case: (1) children who are mentally retarded can learn if an appropriate educational program is provided, (2) "education" must be viewed more broadly than the traditional academic program, and (3) early educational experience is essential to maximize educational potential. After considerable testimony by the state and a variety of "expert witnesses," PARC won the case.

The Pennsylvania Association for Retarded Children v. Pennsylvania suit, like many suits that followed, was settled on the basis of a *consent decree*, which is an out-of-court agreement, usually formally approved by the court. In this suit, the state was ordered to provide free public education appropriate to the learning capabilities of children with mental retardation and the decree provided the working framework. To make certain that the consent decree was carried out, the court established a time schedule for implementation and appointed two masters to oversee the total process.

Mills v. the Board of Education of the District of Columbia is of unusual significance because it applied to *all* children with disabilities. To a certain extent, it established a principle that tended to lead to the inclusion in future class action suits of all students with disabilities. This case led to a judgment that required the public schools to provide for students with disabilities even if they did not fit the educational mold. As in the Pennsylvania case, the court appointed masters to oversee the operation.[1]

In addition to the preceding litigation, which established the rights of students and parents and the broad framework within

---

[1]From *The Trainable Retarded: A Foundations Approach*, 2nd ed. (pp. 17–18) by B. R. Gearheart and F. Litton, 1979, St. Louis: C. V. Mosby. Copyright 1979 by B. R. Gearheart. Adapted by permission.

TABLE 1–1
Court cases that have greatly influenced special education

Court Case	Summary of Ruling or Settlement
Brown v. Board of Education (1954)	School segregation solely on basis of race deprives children of equal educational opportunities and thus violates the equal protection clause of the 14th Amendment.
Hobson v. Hansen (1967)	Tracking (ability grouping) based on standardized tests that are not relevant to many minority students violates both the due process and equal protection guarantees of the 14th Amendment.
Diana v. State Board of Education (1970)	(Settled through consent decree.) State of California agreed to change its evaluation practices with respect to the language in which students are tested and to eliminate certain test items. It also agreed to develop tests designed to reflect minority cultures and to reevaluate all Mexican-American and Chinese students enrolled in EMR classes.
Pennsylvania Association for Retarded Children v. Commonwealth of Pennsylvania (1972)	(Settled through consent decree.) The state must provide access to free, appropriate public education for children who are mentally retarded. *Education* was redefined to include activities that the state had earlier held were not educational. Other benefits for students with mental retardation were also gained.
Mills v. D.C. Board of Education (1972)	Students cannot be excluded from school because they have been found to be behavior problems, emotionally disturbed, mentally retarded, etc. Students must have a hearing before exclusion or placement in a special program. *All* students have a right to an appropriate education.
Frederick L. v. Thomas (1977)	Philadelphia schools were directed to search systematically for students with learning disabilities. (They had claimed the existing differentiated program provided adequately for such students and that such screening was thus unnecessary.)
Stuart v. Nappi (1978)	Disciplinary expulsion may constitute denial of appropriate education. Due process procedures must be followed.
New York State Association for Retarded Children v. Carey (1979)	Retarded children with hepatitis-B, a disease that can be contained, cannot be placed in separate, self-contained programs, based on existence of the disease.

Court Case	Summary of Ruling or Settlement
Board v. Rowley (1982)	Amy Rowley, a deaf student with excellent speechreading skills, was provided limited instruction by a tutor for the deaf and a speech pathologist, plus amplification equipment. Amy was performing at an academic level above average for her grade and class. Her parents (also deaf) requested a qualified sign-language interpreter for all academic classes. This request was denied. Supreme Court affirmation of this decision supported comparable, appropriate education, but not necessarily maximum opportunity for each student with disabilities.
Roncker v. Walters (1983)	Cost of services may be considered since spending on one student with disabilities may deprive another student with disabilities; however, a proper continuum of placements must be provided.
Smith v. Robinson (1984)	After varying decisions and reversals, the U.S. Supreme Court ruled that parents are not entitled to recover attorney fees. (PL 94–142 amendments now include a provision for some recovery of attorney fees.)
Burlington School Committee v. Department of Education of Massachusetts (1985)	Eight-year-old Michael Panico was enrolled in a private school for students with learning disabilities without school approval. A hearing officer ruled this an appropriate placement, and ordered the parents reimbursed. School officials appealed the ruling. The U.S. Supreme Court eventually ruled that parents may be reimbursed, *if* the court ultimately rules that the placement is appropriate. PL 94–142 provisions were cited.
Honig v. Doe (1988)	Two students who were emotionally disabled were enrolled in the San Francisco Unified School District and received special education services. They were suspended indefinitely during expulsion proceedings. The U.S. Supreme Court held that students with disabilities cannot be expelled for misbehavior that is a manifestation of the disability. Shorter-term suspensions must be used. PL 94–142 does not compel districts to place students with disabilities in regular classrooms, only in the least restrictive setting consistent with their needs and the needs of other students. However, students who are disabled *may* be expelled if their misbehavior is not a manifestation of their disability.

which programs were to be provided, later litigation served to settle more specific questions. For example, *Stuart v. Nappi* (1978) and *Honig v. Doe* (1988) addressed the question of suspension and expulsion of students with disabilities. Other questions, such as who makes the final decision as to how much special service is provided (*Board v. Rowley*, 1982), who pays for private school costs (*Burlington School Committee v. Department of Education of Massachusetts*, 1985), and the conditions under which parents can recover attorney fees incident to litigation of behalf of their child (*Smith v. Robinson*, 1984), have shaped the direction of special education programs in our schools. Now, before continuing with other issues, let us consider the children toward whom this litigation and legislation was directed.

THE SCOPE OF SPECIAL EDUCATION

The scope of special education differs in various areas of the United States. For all practical purposes, *special education* is defined on a state-by-state basis in relation to two factors: (a) specific legislation defining special education for purposes of state reimbursement to districts providing such programs or services and (b) legislation relating to mandatory education of students with disabilities.

There is some national acceptance of a common definition of special education, but because education is primarily a state function, a degree of variation continues. Two national groups have, in effect, defined special education, and with the exception of students who are gifted, talented, or creative, there is growing agreement among the states. The two national definitions are primarily operational in nature and are provided by the Council for Exceptional Chil-

dren (an organization of professionals who work with exceptional children) and the division of the federal government responsible for programs for students with disabilities (the Office of Special Education).

The Council for Exceptional Children has 17 divisions or affiliates, 7 of which relate to recognized categories of exceptionality. These 7 exceptionalities are (a) gifted, (b) behaviorally disordered, (c) communication disordered, (d) learning disabled, (e) mentally retarded, (f) physically handicapped, and (g) visually handicapped. Thus, in addition to the three areas of disability having well-established historical bases, special education now includes education of students who are gifted, students with behavioral disorders and learning disabilities, and students with physical disabilities. In this text, the term *disability* refers to all recognized categories of disability, and the term *exceptional* includes all categories of disability and giftedness.

Federal agencies and offices that monitor special education programs have one major function: to be certain that the dictates of federal legislation are followed. In a related subfunction, these agencies provide reports to Congress relative to existing services for students with disabilities. These reports have used essentially the same terminology as the Council for Exceptional Children, reporting on the same categories of disability. Thus, the scope of special education—at least the part of special education related to disabilities—has been defined in practice by these two organizations. It has been further defined in terms of the services that may be required by students with disabilities through the regulations of PL 94–142 and the states. The major differences between state definitions of special education involve terminology with respect to the various disabilities, but the range of students served is essentially the same. There are, however, other differences related to the quality of services; differences that, we hope, will be reduced in the direction of better services in all states.

Although specialized educational provisions for students who are gifted are not mandated by federal law, as is the case with students who are disabled, there is a steadily growing interest in such programming in most of the nation. Classroom teachers should plan for students who are gifted or creative, because they will sooner or later make their presence known.

Target Populations

At the federal level, PL 94–142 and subsequent amendments spell out the target populations for services for students with disabilities. State laws and regulations further define these populations on a state-by-state basis, and the targets are the same (although given varying names in the various states). Whatever the terminology, it may be said that the intent is that *all* children and youth with disabilities be provided a free, appropriate education by some agency of the state, usually the public schools. As for students who are gifted or talented, most states provide some sort of statement of intent to provide services, although there is no national mandate similar to PL 94–142.

Because of the national mandate, it might seem that the numbers of students served in the various states would represent the total population of students with disabilities, that is, if all *must* be served and if state officials are conscientious and law abiding. There is, however, serious question as to whether this is the case. For example, one state (A) reported only 0.38% of its total student population in public school programs for students with mental retardation. Another state (B) classified 3.26% of its total student population in the same category.

Yet, it is highly unlikely that one state really has nearly ten times more students with mental retardation than the other. It is also unlikely that state A is ignoring such a large group of students. Probably, state A is classifying students differently from state B, and information gathered by various investigators over the years seems to support this conclusion.

Tables 1–2 and 1–3 provide two different types of data about the prevalence of exceptional students in schools. Table 1–2 presents information regarding prevalence as it has been presented for the past 30 or 40 years. This information is based on U.S. government agency estimates, which in turn are based on estimates provided by recognized authorities. These prevalence estimates are reasonably good, given the variable nature of definitions of many of the exceptionalities. The prevalence ranges probably reflect ranges in how severe disabilities must be in order to qualify.

Table 1–3 provides information regarding the prevalence of disabled students receiving services in the public schools, as reported by the states. Note the great differences between the percentages of students served in the various states under the percentage range heading in the right-hand column. The states reporting the largest percentage of students served in some category are not necessarily providing the most effective educational efforts with students who have special needs, nor are the states reporting the smallest percentage of students served in a category necessarily providing the least effective efforts with students who have special needs, because when the states total the conditions (that is, all areas of disability served), the range of differences between the states is much smaller than the range of differences reflected by category.

TABLE 1-2

Target population of exceptional children (theoretical prevalence
of exceptional children in the United States)

Exceptionality	Percentage of Population
Learning disability	2.0–4.0
Speech disability	2.0–4.0
Mental retardation	1.0–3.0
Emotional disturbance	1.0–3.0
Hearing impairment (including deafness)	0.5–0.7
Multiple disabilities	0.5–0.7
Orthopedic and other health impairments	0.4–0.6
Visual impairment (including blindness)	0.08–0.12
Giftedness and talent	2.0–3.0

Note: Based on U.S. government agency estimates and estimates by recognized authorities.

The Regular Education Initiative (REI)

The Regular Education Initiative (REI) is an effort initiated and led by special educators (not by regular educators, as the title might seem to imply) that strongly recommends restructuring the relationship between special education and regular education. It came into focus within the leadership of special education following an article written by Madeleine Will, assistant secretary for the Office of Special Education and Rehabilitative Services of the U.S. Depart-

TABLE 1-3

Exceptional children, ages 6–17, identified and receiving services

Exceptionality	Percentage of National Public School Enrollment	Percentage Range (as reported by the 50 individual states)
Learning disability	4.55	2.06–7.66
Speech disability	2.31	1.16–4.08
Mental retardation	1.20	0.38–3.26
Emotional disturbance	0.85	0.07–2.16
Hearing impairment (including deafness)	0.13	0.02–0.21
Multiple disabilities	0.18	0.00–1.84
Orthopedic and other health impairments	0.21	0.04–0.55
Visual impairment (including blindness)	0.05	0.02–0.10
Giftedness and talent	No comparable data on a national basis	

Note: Based on 1988–89 data, from the 12th Annual Report to Congress on the Implementation of the Education of the Handicapped Act (1990) Washington, DC. These data reflect children served under Chapter One of the Elementary and Secondary Act, and the Education of the Handicapped Act.

ment of Education (Will, 1986). Will advocates "a shared responsibility" between regular and special education. Will's proposal has led to considerable debate within the field of special education, because special educators have applied differing interpretations to her words and have varying perceptions as to the readiness of regular educators to assume the responsibilities inherent in such a proposal.

As a result of the REI proposal, much reexamination of the relationships that exist between regular and special education have taken place, primarily on the part of special educators, not regular educators. This reexamination is certainly a major positive influence of the REI. For example, on January 23, 1987, a number of concerned special education leadership personnel met at Florida Atlantic University to take a closer look at the REI, and, as a result, developed a comprehensive list of assumptions that members of the group felt must be met for success. These assumptions related to student

Although this student has a visual impairment, he enjoys archery.

rights, support from the education community, partnership, attitudes, student grouping, curriculum, instruction, classroom structure, and assessment (Heller & Schilit, 1987). Participants lauded the purpose of Will's call but said: "[I]t is important to acknowledge that special education cannot seek institutional solutions to individual problems without changing the nature of the institution. . . .[T]he nature of school organization is what must fundamentally change" (Heller & Schilit, 1987, p. 6). They felt that a successful initiative requires involvement of regular educators as full partners—involved "as a primary architect and not merely as the recipient of a well intended action" (p. 6). In addition, the Division for Learning Disabilities (of the Council for Exceptional Children) Position Paper expressed hope that "services to students with specific learning disabilities will not be diluted or diminished by remedial or compensatory programs for students with problems in learning due to other causes" (McCarthy, 1987, p. 75), and, more generally, that populations to be served will be clearly defined.

On the other hand, some special educators advocate merger of special and regular education, in effect, eliminating separate special education programs (Stainback & Stainback, 1987). For some time, there has been general concern about the dual system of education that exists and the resultant segregation of some students (Lilly, 1988; Wang & Wahlberg, 1988). It can be argued that the dual system inhibits the integration of students who are supposed to be mainstreamed to the greatest extent possible. Still, some special educators, perhaps many, agree with Keogh (1988) in her concerns about the ability of regular educators to take over the education of students they have already failed to teach. We believe that the REI is essentially a statement of philos-

ophy, not a receipe for educational programming. Only time (perhaps many years) will tell about final acceptance and implementation of this philosophy.

A PHILOSOPHY FOR EDUCATION OF STUDENTS WHO HAVE DISABILITIES

Whatever the prevalence of students with disabilities in schools, it is essential to serve the needs of those students. We believe that it is important to establish principles upon which to base such service. To this end, we have developed the following statement of a philosophy for education of students who have disabilities and certain related principles:

We believe that students with disabilities have the right to an education that will permit them to develop their abilities to the fullest possible extent. We believe that if the students have unique needs, educational programs should be modified and specialized to meet these needs, and that the public, tax-supported educational systems of the nation should adapt existing educational programs and services to make this possible.

We believe that educational planning should emphasize learning strengths and abilities, and that labeling according to disability should be avoided whenever possible. We believe that children and youth should be taught in regular classrooms whenever possible, but the most important consideration in *all* planning should be their ultimate educational, social, and physical well-being.

The following principles, closely related to our philosophy, are of great importance:

1. Early intervention is highly desirable. In most cases, classification at early ages can be avoided.
2. Minority or low socioeconomic status may present unusual problems in as-

sessment, and educators must take special care when this may be a factor.

3. Some disabilities may be more appropriately viewed as symptoms, rather than specific disorders, and may exist at one time in life and not at another.

4. Even in the case of a specific, irreversible disability, the need for special educational services may vary from full-time, special class service at one time in a student's life to little or no service at another time.

5. A wide variety of services and the total spectrum of service delivery capabilities are essential.

6. Services for a broad age range, preschool through high school, are essential.

7. Career education and transition-related efforts are essential for many students with disabilities, and for some individuals, efforts must extend many years into adulthood.

8. A broad, flexible assessment program should include provisions for initial and ongoing assessment and formal and informal evaluation.

9. Parents must be involved in both assessment and program planning. A certain amount of involvement is required by law and regulation, but in many instances, even more involvement will be of great benefit.

10. When properly applied, the concept of the least restrictive environment will effectively unite the skills of regular educators and special educators, thus providing maximum assistance to students who have disabilities.

SUMMARY

This chapter reviewed the history of treatment of persons with disabilities, emphasizing the changes that have occurred since the beginning of the 20th century. About midcentury, parents and special education professional groups began to advocate more comprehensive services for children with disabilities. Parents found powerful allies in certain members of the U.S. Congress, which enacted legislation encouraging school districts to establish a complete range of programs and services for students with disabilities. Court decisions supported the right of all students to appropriate education, including education in the most normal setting possible.

In 1975, Congress passed Public Law 94–142, formalizing what litigation, and the actions of more progressive states had been advocating. With PL 94–142 came several important requirements, but perhaps the most important was that of education in the least restrictive environment consistent with appropriate education. Other aspects of PL 94–142 and the legislative enactments that have amended it have expanded or clarified this basic requirement. This chapter also summarized the authors' philosophy for education of students who have disabilities.

- In what ways are the rights of students with disabilities different from the rights of nondisabled students? How can such differences be justified?

- What placements other than the regular classroom might be inferred by the "most appropriate, least restrictive environment"?

- In what circumstances might a residential school be an appropriate, viable placement for students with disabilities?

- Given that the IEP is not a contract in the legal sense, what is it?

- How and when must parents of students with disabilities be involved in the assessment, planning, and program implementation process?

- What are the responsibilities of regular classroom teachers in program planning and placement?

- What problems are inherent in the assessment of students from culturally diverse backgrounds? How have court decisions influenced such potential problems?

THE LAW AND SERVICES FOR EXCEPTIONAL STUDENTS

A VARIETY OF FEDERAL AND STATE LEGISLATION provides the framework for services to exceptional children and youth. Table 2–1 is a summary of significant federal legislation. This table outlines some major legislative events, beginning with PL 89–10, the Elementary and Secondary Education Act, which was enacted in 1965.

Public Law 94–142, enacted in 1975 and titled the Education for All Handicapped Children Act, was technically an amendment to an earlier law. For several years following the passage of PL 94–142, most government publications referred to PL 94–142 as the Education for All Handicapped Children Act. Then, beginning in the early 1980s, particularly following the passage of PL 98–199, which included another series of amendments to the original act, authors began refer to PL 94–142 as the Education of the Handicapped Act (EHA). In 1990, Public Law 101–476 amended EHA and renamed it the Individuals with Disabilities Education Act (IDEA).

This chapter discusses primarily PL 94–142, subsequent amendments, and the system for provision of educational services that has evolved out of this landmark legislation. However, the chapter also considers education of students who are gifted and talented, as well as the challenge of providing appropriate services where cultural and language differences are involved.

PUBLIC LAW 94–142

Public Law 94–142, the Education for All Handicapped Children Act, was enacted in 1975. It was the culmination of a great deal of support for the rights of all children with disabilities. In its statement of purpose section, PL 94–142 states that it was designed to assure that:

all handicapped children have available to them . . . a free appropriate public education which emphasizes special education and related services designed to meet their unique needs, to assure that the rights of handicapped children and their parents or guardians are protected, to assist states and localities to provide for the education of all handicapped children, and to assess and assure the effectiveness of efforts to educate handicapped children.

PL 94–142, as amended by PL 101–476, specifically directs service to children with certain disabilities, including mental retardation, hearing impairments including deafness, speech or language impairments, vi-

TABLE 2-1
Significant federal legislation relating to education of exceptional children and youth

Year	Legislation
1965	Elementary and Secondary Education Act (PL 89–10) provided assistance to local education agencies to better serve students who were educationally deprived.
1965, 1966, 1967	A variety of amendments to the Elementary and Secondary Education Act expanded efforts on behalf of children and youth identified as disabled.
1968	Handicapped Children's Early Education Assistance Act (PL 90–538) established funding for experimental preschool programs.
1970	Gifted and Talented Education Assistance Act (PL 91–230) provided federal assistance for programs for students who were gifted and talented and students with learning disabilities. These were amendments to the Elementary and Secondary Education Act.
1973	Vocational Rehabilitation Act Amendments (PL 93–112) included Section 504—the Bill of Rights for the Handicapped.
1974	Education of the Handicapped Amendment to the Elementary and Secondary Education Act (PL 93–380) established procedural safeguards and the concept of the least restrictive environment. This set the stage for the passage of PL 94–142.
1975	Education for All Handicapped Children Act (PL 94–142) was the culmination of all federal efforts that preceded it. PL 94–142 established the principle of free, appropriate education in the least restrictive environment for all children with disabilities, parents' rights, as well as rights to due process, appropriate assessment, and fair hearing and appeal.
1978	Gifted and Talented Children's Act (PL 95–561) provided funds to state educational agencies to assist in planning and improving programs for students who were gifted or talented.
1983	Amendments to EHA (PL 98–199) emphasized planning for transition of secondary students and provided incentives for the establishment of services for children from birth to age 3.
1986	Amendments to EHA (PL 99–457) provided for services to children with disabilities, ages 3 to 5, even in states that did not provide public education for other children of these ages. It also provided new incentives for early intervention programs for infants and toddlers (birth through age 2).
1990	Amendments to EHA (PL 101–476) renamed the act the Individuals with Disabilities Education Act (IDEA). It substituted the term *disabilites* for handicapped throughout, amended the definition of disabilities (formerly handicapping conditions), and made a number of other modifications. It did, however, retain the basic thrust of PL 94–142. Changes were primarily terminological.

Note: The Americans with Disabilities Act of 1990 (PL 101–336) is parallel to and in some ways a result of education-related legislation. Eventually, all businesses with 15 or more employees will be covered by this law, which relates to employment and accommodation. Employers may not use disability as a basis for hiring or firing, and they must provide specialized equipment as needed by workers who have disabilities (for example, workers who are blind). With respect to accommodations, the law requires such things as elevators, ramps, and large doorways. Although not an education law, it has potentially great importance to some students with disabilities.

sual impairments including blindness, serious emotional disturbance, orthopedic impairments, autism, traumatic brain injury, other health impairments, or specific learning disabilities. The law clearly provides for all special programs and services required by students between 3 and 21 years of age who are disabled. PL 94–142 was limited in application to children who were 3 to 5 years of age, but amendments in 1986 (PL 99–457) provided that children of 3 to 5 years of age be served, even in states that do not provide public education for other children that young.

Services to be provided, as indicated in the rules and regulations for the act,[1] include (a) audiology, (b) counseling services, (c) early identification, (d) medical services, (e) occupational therapy, (f) parent counseling, (g) physical therapy, (h) psychological services, (i) recreation, (j) school health services, (k) social work services, (l) speech pathology, and (m) transportation (*Federal Register*, August 23, 1977). This specific list of services, according to comments in the rules and regulations, was not intended to be exhaustive but was included to indicate the broad scope of services encompassed in the intent of the law.

Public Law 94–142 was passed in an attempt to correct a number of known problems in educational programs for children and youth with disabilities. In one of the earlier analyses of PL 94–142, Ballard and Zettel (1977) indicated four major purposes:

1. To guarantee free, appropriate education to children and youth with disabilities

2. To assure that decision making with regard to special programs and services is accomplished fairly
3. To establish clear auditing and management procedures for special education programming at local, state, and national levels
4. To use federal funds to assist state and local governments in carrying out the provisions of the law

In a book-length analysis of the law and its influences on education of children and youth with disabilities, Turnbull (1986) considers six primary principles of special education law:

1. Zero reject—the right of every child to receive an appropriate, publicly supported education
2. Nondiscriminatory evaluation—the right to an accurate, meaningful evaluation so that proper educational planning and placement may be accomplished
3. An individualized educational program (IEP) established specifically for the special needs of each student
4. Placement in the least restrictive environment that will permit an appropriate education—opportunity to associate with nondisabled students when possible
5. Due process of law—a system that permits parents and advocates to challenge educational planning when that seems necessary
6. Parent participation in planning and implementation of the educational program

Turnbull's first principle—the right of every child to receive an appropriate, publicly supported education—is the basic intent of all of the laws that have led to the present status of education of children with disabilities. Principles 2 to 6 provide the guidelines through which we are to accom-

---

[1]The rules and regulations for PL 94–142 and all federal laws are not part of the actual legislation. They are guidelines for implementation, spelled out after the legislation is enacted into law and usually developed with input and assistance from professionals in the field.

plish the basic principle of appropriate, publicly supported education. The following sections discuss Turnbull's principles 2 to 6.

Protection in Evaluation Procedures

The various court cases that preceded the passage of PL 94–142 established the minimum basic requirements for nonbiased, meaningful evaluation procedures. The rules and regulations for PL 94–142 outline the following minimum evaluation procedure requirements:

State and local educational agencies shall insure, at a minimum, that

(a) Tests and other evaluation materials:
   (1) Are provided and administered in the child's native language or other mode of communication, unless it is clearly not feasible to do so;
   (2) Have been validated for the specific purpose for which they are used; and
   (3) Are administered by trained personnel in conformance with the instructions provided by their producer.
(b) Tests and other evaluation materials include those tailored to assess specific areas of educational need and not merely those which are designed to provide a single general intelligence quotient
(c) Tests are selected and administered so as best to ensure that when a test is administered to a child with impaired sensory, manual, or speaking skills, the test results accurately reflect the child's aptitude or achievement level or whatever other factors the test purports to measure, rather than reflecting the child's impaired sensory, manual, or speaking skills (except where those skills are the factors which the test purports to measure).
(d) No single procedure is used as the sole criterion for determining an appropriate educational program for a child; and
(e) The evaluation is made by a multidisciplinary team or group of persons, including at least one teacher or other specialist with knowledge in the area of suspected disability.
(f) The child is assessed in all areas related to the suspected disability, including, where appropriate, health, vision, hearing, social and emotional status, general intelligence, academic performance, communicative status, and motor abilities. . . .

Comment. Children who have a speech impairment as their primary handicap may not need a complete battery of assessments (e.g., psychological, physical, or adaptive behavior). However, a qualified speech-language pathologist would (1) evaluate each speech impaired child using procedures that are appropriate for the diagnosis and appraisal of speech and language disorders, and (2) where necessary, make referrals for additional assessments needed to make an appropriate placement decision. (*Federal Register*, August 23, 1977, pp. 42496–42497)

The various states have promulgated regulations consistent with the preceding minimum requirements but more specific in many cases. The federal evaluation requirements are a base, but the states have made their regulations consistent in terminology with their own laws and other regulations.

Individualized Education Programs

As a result of PL 94–142, all students who are placed in special educational programs must have an individualized education program (IEP). To a considerable extent, the requirement of an IEP for each student is the result of unacceptable past practices in special classes for students with disabilities, in which different students were placed in a class but all received essentially the same educational program. The rules and regulations of PL 94–142 indicate that the IEP must include the following:

1. A statement of the present levels of educational performance
2. A statement of annual goals, including short-term instructional objectives

3. A statement of the specific educational services to be provided to this handicapped student and the extent to which such student will be able to participate in regular educational programs
4. The projected date for initiation and anticipated duration of such services
5. Appropriate, objective criteria and evaluation procedures and schedules for determining, on at least an annual basis, whether instructional objectives are being achieved. (*Federal Register*, August 23, 1977, p. 42491)

6. A statement of the needed transition services for students beginning no later than age 16 and annually thereafter (and, when determined appropriate for the individual, beginning at age 14 or younger), including, when appropritate, a statement of the interagency responsibilities or linkages (or both) before the student leaves the school setting. (PL 101–476, Oct. 30, 1990, 104 Stat. 1103)

In addition to the preceding requirements, which should be considered *minimum* re-

Regular classroom teachers, parents, teachers, and others are involved in developing the IEP.

FIGURE 2-1
Major components of an individualized education program (IEP)

1. IEP development checklist and procedural checklist.

2. Identification and background information. This should include the student's name; parents' names, address, telephone numbers; sex; birth date; and primary language.

3. IEP committee members. These should include the names and functional titles of IEP committee members.

4. Assessment information. This is all information (obtained by school personnel through formal or informal assessment procedures) that was considered in developing the IEP. This information should *always* include a definitive statement of present level of academic functioning in pertinent areas and information about nonacademic areas (such as social skills) if the information in any way applies to targeted learning problems or concerns.

5. Other information. This may include medical information, health history, information from community agencies, and historical information about school attendance and academic performance. When this information is included, the source must be fully documented.

6. Prioritized statement of goals. This is a statement of academic and social performance goals to be attained by the close of the school year and how they are to be evaluated.

7. Statement of short-term objectives. These are specific objectives, indicated on a monthly or quarterly basis. These objectives must be consistent with annual goals and should include at least the following: (a) who will provide the required services, (b) where the services will be provided, (c) special materials or media required, and (d) any special information, such as reinforcers to be used.

8. Educational services provided. Examples include occupational therapy or speech therapy services, resource room instruction, and instruction in a special vocational setting.

9. Educational placement recommendations. These should include settings (for example, resource room and regular classroom), time spent in each placement (for example, 2 hours each day in a resource room and the remainder in a regular classroom), and rationales (for example, rationales for such placement).

10. A statement of needed transition services for all students age 16 and older. This ususaly will include a description of interagency responsibilities and linkages. In individual cases, transition services statements may be necessary at younger ages.

11. Time frame for special services. Time frames should include significant dates, including at least (a) service initiation dates (may be different dates for different services), (b) duration of services, (c) approximate dates for evaluations, and (d) approximate dates for additional conferences when applicable.

12. Signatures. These should include IEP conference participants' or IEP developers' signatures and parents' signatures indicating acceptance or rejection of various aspects of the program.

Note: For a detailed description and analysis of IEP development and implementation (including samples of IEP forms in use in various states) see Strickland and Turnbull (1990), *Developing and Implementing Individualized Education Programs,* 3rd ed.

quirements, many states have others, usually developed by state education department personnel with input from special educators from local educational agencies.

The major components of an IEP (as shown in Figure 2–1) reflect the kind of information that is most often found in such documents. It is the responsibility of special educators to see that the legal requirements of the state are fulfilled; regular classroom teachers are not absolutely required by federal regulations to know the details of IEP development. On the other hand, regular classroom teachers are involved in IEP planning meetings and certainly may be involved in implementing IEPs for students with disabilities. Therefore, it is prudent for all teachers to understand the basic requirements for and the purposes of this important management tool. A careful review of the 12 basic components of an IEP should provide a basic concept of the information actual IEPs contain.

IEPs range from 2 to 10 or 12 pages, but their value is not always related to their length. It is not as much a question of length as of the nature of the information and planning provided and the degree to which the information truly reflects an *individualized* program. If assessment is planned with care, assessment tools are appropriate and administered properly, and assessment information and other related information are considered thoughtfully by professionals and parents, a meaningful program can be developed.

The IEP form—the paper on which the IEP is recorded—provides a structured format with which to record both the basis for educational deliberations and the long-range program through which teachers plan to assist the student. The format is important in that it is a reminder to consider a variety of factors and to be as specific as possible in planning. It may also be important as a legal instrument, in case of controversy, to provide evidence concerning whether school officials have followed the requirements of the law. See Table 2–2 for a list of facts and commonly accepted fallacies concerning IEPs.

Education in the Least Restrictive Environment

Public Law 94–142 requires that special classes, separate schooling, or other removal of children with disabilities from the regular educational environment occurs only when the nature or severity of the handicap is such that education in regular classes cannot be achieved satisfactorily, but it is important to note that the law first mandates a "free, appropriate education." The "least restrictive environment" must be determined on the basis of each student. What is appropriate for one student might be totally inappropriate for another.

Ballard and Zettel (1977) note that the requirement of the least restrictive educational environment "is not a provision for mainstreaming. In fact, the word is never used" (p. 183). They further note that the concept of the least restrictive environment "does not mandate that all handicapped children will be educated in the regular classroom" and that "it does not abolish any particular educational environment, for instance, educational programming in a residential setting" (p. 183). Ballard and Zettel were leading advocates for students with disabilities and strongly supported the concept of the least restrictive environment, but they were well aware that by 1977 there were many misunderstandings about the least restrictive environment and the idea of mainstreaming.

In a discussion of four basic requirements and guarantees of PL 94–142, Haring (1990) said this about the least restrictive

Commonly Accepted Fallacy	Fact
PL 94–142 and the principle of mainstreaming dictate that all students with disabilities be enrolled in the regular class for all, or at least part, of the school day.	Students with disabilities should be enrolled in regular classes for as much of the school day as appropriate, given their needs. This may mean that they are in regular classes for all of the day, in a special class for all of the day, or anywhere on the placement continuum between these extremes.
If the parent says *no* to a proposed plan that includes some special class programming, the school has no alternative but to retain the student in regular classes.	The parent(s) must be a part of all deliberations regarding the educational programming and may say *no* to a given plan. The school may decide to go along with the parent's stand, but when this does not work out, in certain clear-cut cases, school officials have the responsibility to initiate an appeals procedure in which outside authorities are involved in final determinations about placement.
The IEP is a contract, and if the student does not reach the educational goals described in the IEP, the teacher and other school authorities may be liable to lawsuit for breaking or not living up to the contract.	The IEP is an educational management plan or tool. It does require good faith efforts to achieve the goals and objectives listed in the IEP, and the parent(s) can ask for revisions, but federal regulations specifically note that the IEP does not constitute a guarantee that the student will progress at a specified rate or achieve specific academic levels.
If a student does not reach the goals and objectives outlined in the IEP, the teacher will be blamed by the administration at teacher evaluation time.	As noted above, the IEP is recognized in the federal regulations as a plan, not a contract. The local school district can establish whatever means of teacher evaluation it deems feasible, but a strong NEA stand on this issue makes such use of the IEP highly unlikely.
Mainstreaming is less costly than providing services in a special class setting.	Mainstreaming may be either more costly or less costly than education in a special class setting. This depends on the needs of the student under consideration. In most cases, *given the provision of proper support services,* it will cost the same or perhaps slightly more.
Mainstreaming students with disabilities will detract from the educational progress of other students.	There is little question that many students are limited in their understanding of the extent and nature of differences between individuals in society. Through mainstreaming they may learn to better understand and appreciate human differences while recognizing important similarities. If regular classroom teachers are assisted through special materials and alternative teaching strategies, *all* students may benefit academically. If such assistance is not provided or if students who should be in special programs are placed in regular classes, other students may suffer academically.

environment: "School districts must offer a continuum of placement options from the most restrictive (residential institutional care) to the least restrictive (full-time placement in a regular classroom) and must not assign a student to a more restrictive setting unless it can be demonstrated that the more restrictive setting will result in greater gains than a less restrictive setting" (p. 15). Consideration should also be given to closeness to a student's home, and if academic integration is not practical or must be limited, integration in other classes or school activities should be provided as possible.

The actual statement from the rules and regulations of PL 94–142 appears in Figure 2–2. In addition to the general statement about the least restrictive environment, there is a requirement that local educational agencies have available for use when needed a continuum of placements, *including* special classes and special schools. (The continuum of placements mentioned here is discussed later in the chapter.) The first question involves what is most appropriate. It is first a matter of meeting a student's individual, educational, and social needs. Then, if these needs can be met in any of two or three placements, the rule is to use the least restrictive setting.

The Right to Due Process

PL 94–142 and related regulations detail precisely how the law must be implemented. Most of its legal requirements are the responsibility of local special education personnel or state officials, but certain aspects of the law and related regulations are important to regular classroom teachers. One of the more important areas is the assurance of due process in all of the proceedings involved with identifying students who require special educational services and with planning and implementing those services.

Before the passage of PL 94–142, due process was primarily limited to matters involving identification, evaluation, and placement. PL 94–142 extended due process to include any matter relating to the provision of free, appropriate education and specifically provided parents the right to, and a specific procedure whereby they might, present concerns or complaints. Specifically, the law requires or provides for:

1. Notification in writing before evaluation (in language parents can understand)
2. Parental consent before initiating evaluation
3. The right to an interpreter or translator when needed
4. A school district outline of all anticipated evaluation
5. The right of the parent to inspect all educational records
6. The right of the parent to obtain an independent evaluation
7. Written notice when a change of placement is planned or when the district refuses to make a change in placement
8. Parental consent to changes in placement
9. A specific procedure for an impartial due process hearing in cases of disagreement, including the following:
   a. The right to a specific, timely notice of hearing
   b. Limitations on who can serve as the hearing officer (to prevent bias)
   c. The right of the parents to legal counsel or other representative
   d. The right to require witnesses to attend and the right to confront and cross-examine witnesses
   e. The right to present evidence
   f. The right to appeal to the state educational agency if either party is aggrieved by the results of the first hearing
   g. The right to bring civil action if either

FIGURE 2–2
**Rules and regulations for PL 94–142 regarding least restrictive
environment**

General

Each public agency shall insure:

That to the maximum extent appropriate, handicapped children, including children in public or private institutions or other care facilities, are educated with children who are not handicapped, and

That special classes, separate schooling or other removal of handicapped children from the regular educational environment occurs only when the nature or severity of the handicap is such that education in regular classes with the use of supplementary aids and services cannot be achieved satisfactorily.

Continuum of Alternative Placements

Each public agency shall insure that a continuum of alternative placements is available to meet the needs of handicapped children for special education and related services.

The continuum required under [the first paragraph] of this section must:

(1) Include the alternative placements listed in the definition of special education (instruction in regular classes, special classes, special schools, home instruction, and instruction in hospitals and institutions), and

(2) Make provision for supplementary services (such as resource room or itinerant instruction) to be provided in conjunction with regular class placement.

Placements

Each public agency shall insure that:

(a) Each handicapped child's educational placement:

(1) Is determined at least annually,

(2) Is based on his or her individualized education program, and

(3) Is as close as possible to the child's home:

(b) The various alternative placements included are available to the extent necessary to implement the individualized education program for each handicapped child;

(c) Unless a handicapped child's individualized education program requires some other arrangement, the child is educated in the school which he or she would attend if not handicapped; and

(d) In selecting the least restrictive environment, consideration is given to any potential harmful effect on the child or on the quality of services which he or she needs.

Note: Federal Register, August 23, 1977, p. 42497.

party so desires after the state educational agency review and decision

The rules and regulations describe the provisions in detail, along with other related procedural matters.

In addition, each state is required to outline its specific regulations, which must be consistent with the requirements of PL 94–142. In actuality, the due process hearings provide additional protection for students in that school districts also have the right and the responsibility to appeal parental decisions that are in violation of the educational rights and needs of students; however, the fact that the law provides parents the right of due process has received most of the attention of those commenting on this aspect of the law.

Parental Consultation and Involvement

Although no major section of PL 94–142 separately considers parental consultation and involvement, this consideration may be found throughout the regulations. We feel certain that this was a major intent of the law, as may be seen from the following provisions:

1. The native language of the parents must be used, with an interpreter or a translator provided as needed. Communications must be in the native language.
2. Parental permission is required to initiate assessment.
3. Parents must be informed about a conference in which assessment results are considered.
4. Because parents should be involved in the IEP meeting, the meeting time must be established far enough in advance to permit opportunity for parents to attend, and the meeting must be in a convenient place at a convenient time. If parents cannot attend, the public agency must use other methods to obtain parental participation (such as a conference phone call).
5. School records must be made available to parents.
6. Parents may ask for amendment of records they feel are inaccurate.
7. Parents may ask for independent evaluation of their child.
8. An involved, detailed procedure for appeals of educational decisions is provided by the law and must be fully explained to parents.

The intent of PL 94–142 regarding parents is clear: Parents can play a significant role in the education of their children. The law and regulations guiding implementation of the law indicate rights and responsibilities. Thus, the law makes it necessary for educators to do all possible to involve parents in planning for children with special needs and demands increased sensitivity on the part of educators to the potential value of help from the parents. It does not mean that parents should dominate such planning, however. Stories about parents who attempt to do this reflect perhaps 1% or 2% of all parents of exceptional children. More often, it is necessary to *encourage* parents to provide information and ideas, and it is the responsibility of educators to do this. Educators must ask parents to provide information in both initial planning and continued program evaluation. This is clearly the intent of the law, and in most instances, the results have been positive, leading to better, more effective, more appropriate programs.

Implementation

PL 94–142 is relatively straightforward; its intent is clear, and its language is no more confusing than that of most other laws relating to education. However, educators must work for its successful implementation. As most teachers well understand, saying that something should be done is in most cases much simpler than actually doing it. The following paragraphs consider a topic that is important to implementation of the law, the critical need for cooperation and joint planning by regular and special educators.

If special educational provisions are to be effective with students who have special needs (regardless of classifications or degrees of severity), regular and special educators must plan and work together for the benefit of the students. Although no major section or subsection of PL 94–142 separately considers cooperation between regular and special educators, this is clearly the intent of the law.

As noted, parental involvement and consultation are of great importance, but it may be possible to develop and implement an effective program if parents flatly refuse to cooperate. This is not possible if a regular class teacher with primary responsibility for a given student and special educators do not truly work together on behalf of the student. It is also important for the administration to be supportive, accepting the assumptions inherent in PL 94–142.

The key player in this scene is the regular class teacher. The law recognizes this in a variety of places. For example, the law requires that each state have a "Comprehensive System of Personnel Development," which includes training for both regular and special educators. The rules and regulations also provide that a teacher must be involved in IEP meetings. The rules further indicate that the first-choice teacher for a child who is being considered for initial placement in special education is the child's regular teacher. Finally, and probably of most importance, the law directs that the student be in the least restrictive educational environment consistent with appropriate programming, which means the regular classroom for most students with mild disabilities, and for many with more severe disabilities.

The law also indicates that there are to be services from various special education specialists, as dictated by the individual needs of the student. It would seem logical that cooperation and joint planning would result in better educational programming, but, in addition, studies such as that reported by Pfeiffer (1982) have demonstrated it. In Pfeiffer's investigation of the team decision-making process, superior decisions (in both placement and educational program-

ming for children with disabilities) were made through the group process. Pfeiffer notes, "Quite clearly, the group decision-making process facilitated a significant reduction in erroneous placement decisions" (p. 69).

Many factors known to influence the involvement of teachers in other aspects of the school come into play here. The attitudes and actions of administrators have considerable influence. Extra duty assignments, time provided for meetings and cooperative planning, and the general tone of cooperation in any given school influence the involvement of teachers in all activities. However, one factor under the direct control of regular class teachers is of considerable importance. Individuals are more likely to participate in a given process if they feel comfortable with their knowledge as it relates to that process. Therefore, regular class teachers must make the effort to become informed about the IEP process.

ADVANTAGES AND DISADVANTAGES OF MAINSTREAMING

There are both advantages and disadvantages to what has happened in regular classrooms as a result of the concept of the least restrictive educational placement for students with disabilities. Every teacher knows that an additional student with behavior problems or one requiring a good deal of additional, individualized planning and attention means a busier, perhaps more trying, school day. As one teacher said, "Too much is just too much." We agree. In fact, that is why we—and the law—have never indicated that all students with disabilities should be in regular classrooms. Yet, if this concept is properly implemented, there can be benefits to students without disabilities and to teachers.

One major advantage of educating students with disabilities in regular classrooms is that all students then have a broader range of experiences with individuals who are different from themselves. They can gain respect for and appreciation of human differences while recognizing inherent similarities. Students must be exposed to differences if they are to reach their full personal potential.

Perhaps today's adults were disadvantaged to some extent because when they were in school, they did not have the opportunity to know classmates with disabilities or differences. This disadvantage may be observed in many ways. For example, why do adults today express so many misconceptions about individuals with disabilities? Could it be that they have had little opportunity to learn about such differences? Is it that they never sat next to a braille-reading classmate or a classmate in a wheelchair? If the less-than-desirable attitudes often reflected by society are an indication of lack of experience with different persons, then integrated classrooms may be of great benefit to *all* students.

There are also certain obvious advantages to teachers. Most evidence indicates that today's teachers are in general the best prepared and the most competent ever. The trend to include as part of every teacher's professional preparation specific coursework and skills or competencies for working with students who have disabilities greatly increases the ability of teachers to work with such students and special educators. After many years of separation, general and special educators are beginning to assume cooperative teaching roles. Each discipline has unique skills and competencies, and both are seeking insights and specific suggestions about how best to meet the needs of all students. Regular classroom teachers now have opportunities for cooperative learning experiences for themselves and their students, including those who present special challenges.

Teachers must have challenges to grow personally and professionally. A student with special needs presents one such challenge. We have had considerable experience with regular classroom teachers who express concern when they are informed that they will have a student with a disability in their classroom. It has been encouraging, however, to see these same teachers grow personally and professionally, and at the end of the year, they indicate this has been one of the most exciting and challenging experiences of their teaching career. Often, such teachers ask if they may have another student with special needs the following year.

What initially may seem a serious threat often turns into a positive growth experience. Very often, the methods and instructional techniques used with students who have special needs may be used with other students, and the challenge of working with students of different abilities—intellectual, physical, or both—may keep teachers from teaching *at* students. With minimal help, regular teachers may learn to serve as facilitators to provide each student with opportunities to reach his or her fullest potential.

As for students with disabilities whose unmet needs led to present programming practices, certain questions remain as to how and to what extent students with moderate and severe disabilities should be integrated with nondisabled students. Public Law 94–142 requires special classes and even residential settings as available alternatives, implying that some students may require such separate settings. Many students with severe disabilities require separate settings. Placement of students with mild or moderate disabilities is a different matter.

If students with disabilities are to have opportunities to reach their maximum potential and become contributing members of society, educators must provide them with equal educational opportunities, or education with their nondisabled peers in the least restrictive environment. When this is possible and educationally appropriate, it is the best way to prepare them to live as successful adults in an integrated society.

THE CONTINUUM OF EDUCATIONAL SERVICES

Public Law 94–142 requires a continuum of educational services for students with disabilities, ranging from the least restrictive (in regular classes with some consultive or collaborative assistance from special education personnel) to the most restrictive (a special day school or residential facility). A simplified representation of this continuum (Figure 2–3) includes the major placement alternatives.

Instruction in Regular Classes with Consultive or Collaborative Assistance

When various prereferral intervention strategies do not provide the desired results, a student should be referred for special education assistance. When it is determined that the student is eligible for and should have

such assistance, the principle of the least restrictive environment dictates that instruction in a regular classroom be the first alternative considered. This placement alternative might involve a wide combination of services. Classroom intervention may prove to be quite successful. Depending on the situation, special educators may do such things as provide special materials, assist a teacher in developing special materials, provide assistance in task analysis (leading to modified instructional ideas), develop student contracts, or in some instances, do demonstration teaching. Such assistance may be relatively indirect or direct. Whenever the regular classroom teacher can be assisted in providing appropriate instruction in a regular class setting, this is the placement of choice. (See Table 2–3 for the percentage of students with disabilities served in regular classes in 1987–88.)

Primary Placement in Regular Classes with Regularly Scheduled Assistance in Another Setting

When a full-time program in a regular class is not effective, the next alternative to be considered is part-time assistance in a resource room or special class. The original

TABLE 2–3
Percentage of students with handicaps, ages 3–5, 6–11, 12–17, and 18–21, served in six educational environments, school year 1987–88

Environment	3–5	6–11	12–17	18–21
Regular class	40.1%	39.7%	18.0%	12.9%
Resource room	14.1	35.7	45.8	35.2
Separate class	28.5	20.6	28.6	32.7
Separate school	14.8	3.4	5.5	14.7
Residential facility	0.5	0.4	1.1	2.9
Home/hospital	2.0	0.3	1.1	1.6

Note: From the Twelfth Annual Report to Congress on the Implementation of the Education of the Handicapped Act (1990).

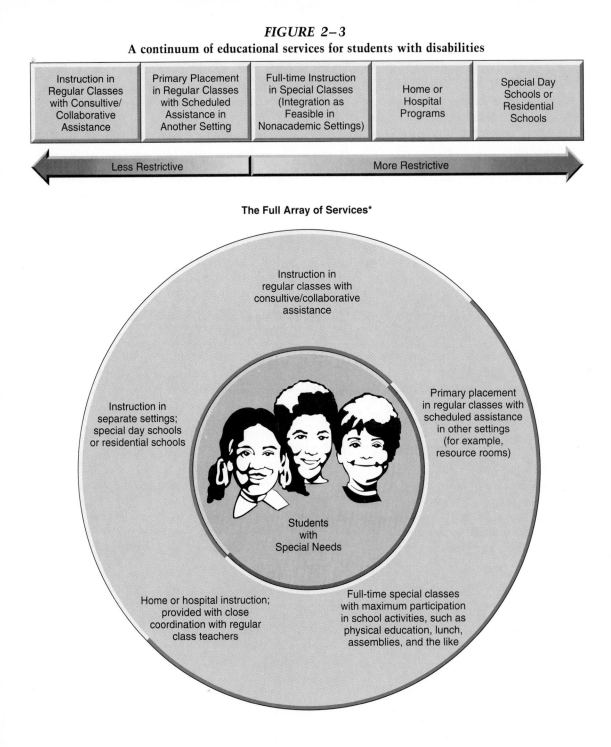

FIGURE 2–3
A continuum of educational services for students with disabilities

Instruction in Regular Classes with Consultive/ Collaborative Assistance	Primary Placement in Regular Classes with Scheduled Assistance in Another Setting	Full-time Instruction in Special Classes (Integration as Feasible in Nonacademic Settings)	Home or Hospital Programs	Special Day Schools or Residential Schools

Less Restrictive ← → More Restrictive

The Full Array of Services*

Instruction in regular classes with consultive/collaborative assistance

Instruction in separate settings; special day schools or residential schools

Primary placement in regular classes with scheduled assistance in other settings (for example, resource rooms)

Students with Special Needs

Home or hospital instruction; provided with close coordination with regular class teachers

Full-time special classes with maximum participation in school activities, such as physical education, lunch, assemblies, and the like

* Beginning with instruction in regular classes — at the top of the circle — each placement clockwise involves more restriction/less contact with age peers in the regular class.

38

plan for a student may be full-time instruction in a regular class (with consultive or collaborative assistance), but after a reasonable period of time, it may become clear that this is not sufficient. After reevaluation, and with the consent of the parents, part-time assistance in a resource room or special class may be implemented. In other cases, it may be evident from the beginning that this level of special assistance is required. *In all cases, remember that movement within the continuum after the original program is implemented may be necessary.* Whenever possible, such movement should be in the direction of a less restrictive setting, with a student spending more time with his or her peers; however, the major determinant must be the overall appropriateness of the educational program.

Full-time Instruction in a Special Class

Full-time instruction in a special class may be the most appropriate, effective program for some students. This is true more often in the case of severe disabilities, but even here, some time may be spent with non-disabled students in school activities such as assemblies or athletic events, or in other nonacademic areas. In each of the previous placement alternatives, the primary responsibility for a student's educational program remains with the regular class teacher, supported by the special educator in whatever manner is indicated in the IEP. In the full-time special class alternative, the special class teacher will have full responsibility for the student, but continuing contact between the regular class teacher and the special educator is important. Therefore, the special educator must maintain a continuing, realistic understanding of the regular class setting and the requirements for a student to function in that setting.

Home and Hospital Programs

Home- and hospital-based programs may be provided in a variety of ways, depending on existing resources, age of the student, the special needs, and related factors. For example, programs for a homebound student may be provided via telephone or electronic hookup in which the student actually participates in class proceedings. Instruction may be provided by a full-time teacher of the homebound, or by a regular class teacher on a contract basis. (Usually, regular class teachers who provide after-school instruction receive extra pay for such responsibilities.) In a few cases, other students may carry home assignments and materials. Then, they or a parent of the homebound student may return them.

Hospital programs may be carried out in a similar manner; however, some large hospital and children's clinic programs have teaching staffs whose members work with regular class teachers.

Special Day Schools and Residential Schools

These alternatives are being used less today than, for example, 50 years ago, even though more of the nation's students with severe disabilities are in educational programs. Such programs serve students with profound hearing impairments, blindness, severe levels of mental retardation, severe emotional disturbance, and in a few cases, multiple disabilities. These placements are alternatives of last resort, but both the law (PL 94–142) and common sense dictate that they be available for use when no other alternative is effective.

Other Alternatives

In some cases, students may be served by an itinerant teacher who is in their building only part of the day, or perhaps only certain days of the week. In terms of the continuum of educational placement alternatives shown in Figure 2–3, this service is probably more similar to the primary placement in regular class with part-time assistance in the resource room alternative. In addition, many students need and receive clinical service from a speech-language pathologist, and a somewhat lesser number need and receive the help of a physical therapist. In the following section, we will review some of the major means whereby students who are in the regular class at least part of the time receive assistance from special educators.

SERVICES PROVIDED BY SPECIAL EDUCATORS

Services for students determined to be eligible for special education assistance are normally provided cooperatively by regular educators and special educators. In a few cases, students are placed in full-time special education classes, but this is the exception to the rule.

Collaborative Consultation

Collaborative consultation (also called consultation and collaboration, or consultive collaboration) has received considerable attention and acceptance as the means whereby regular and special educators cooperatively plan for and provide effective programming for students with special needs. In fact, there may be more unanimity with respect to the potential effectiveness of this process than with respect to any other major process related to the regular education/special education interface. The only major concern expressed about this process is difficulty in implementing what Phillips and McCullough (1990) call the collaborative ethic. This difficulty is not a reflection on its potential value, but rather witness to the fact that all endeavors that require cooperative professional relationships require that the participants accept the underlying ethic.

Collaborative consultation is a model, strategy, or process. Donaldson and Christiansen (1990) call it a decision-making model. Phillips and McCullough (1990) view it as a consultation model that promotes collegial consultation with a problem-solving orientation. Idol, Paolucci-Whitcomb, and Nevin (1986) describe it as "an interactive process that enables people with diverse expertise to generate creative solutions to mutually defined problems" (p. 1). We believe that each of these views has merit and we attempt to characterize this model/strategy/process with the caution that it is considerably more complex than can be described here.

As a strategy, collaborative consultation borrows from psychology and leadership/management orientations, assuming a triadic model. This model includes (a) a consultant (the special educator), (b) a mediator or consultee (the regular education teacher), and (c) a target learner (the student). It involves and promotes collegial consultation, as opposed to expert consultation, thus encouraging co-ownership of both the problem (the needs of a given student) and the process whereby the problem may be solved (the special program, as outlined in the IEP, specific intervention strategies, ongoing program evaluation and redirection, and so on).

Phillips and McCullough (1990) indicate that to enhance the potential for success of such a consultation model, it is necessary to "seek to create a permanent, multidisciplinary, collaborative ethic as well as alternative student support systems" (p. 301). They further suggest that general and special educators must be co-consultants, each contributing from his or her background and expertise.

Idol, Paolucci-Whitcomb, and Nevin (1986) accurately observe that the origin of collaborative consultation in education was a model in which the two professional participants were called mediator (the teacher) and consultant. In this original model, the consultant was a psychologist, and thus was undoubtedly viewed as an expert, no matter how the relationship existed in theory. In the regular education/special education application, we suggest that the terminology co-consultants be substituted, expressing a relationship for maximum effectiveness. For ideas from special educators to be of maximum value, there must be continuing input from regular educators. Such information might easily change the ideas that were originally considered by the special educators. The reverse is also true. Professionals must consider a variety of options until there is agreement; parity must be maintained.

Individual and Small-Group Instruction

A special educator may provide instruction in addition to collaborative consultation. This instruction is often provided in a resource room setting by a teacher who may or may not be called a resource room teacher. Resource room programs vary considerably from state to state, and within states. For example, in some instances, a resource teacher may serve a student on a temporary basis while carrying out additional assessment and planning instructional strategies to be implemented primarily in the regular class.

In the more typical plan, a student spends a planned time in the resource room, receiving individual or small-group instruction consistent with his or her needs. This separate placement must be approved by the parent(s), and to be truly effective, it must include considerable communication between the resource room teacher and the regular classroom teacher. The resource room teacher must have the time, materials, and specific training required to discover effective ways to teach students with special needs. Special class teachers have two functions: (a) to discover and initiate strategies that will help the student experience success in the resource room and (b) to develop concrete ideas that will assist the regular classroom teacher. In addition to instruction in a resource room and collaborative consultation between the regular classroom teacher and the resource room teacher with respect to a targeted student's work in the regular class, a resource room teacher may provide unofficial assistance to other teachers in order to prevent the need for future special education assistance for certain children.

Students may perform in different ways or at different levels in regular classrooms as compared to individual or small-group settings. In recognition of this possibility, a resource room teacher may work at times with students in regular classrooms. Such work permits greater insight into interventions that may be required in regular classes.

Instruction in special classes may be provided by special educators. At times, a student may be assigned to a special class on a part-time basis; however, this may not then be too different from some resource room settings. The more typical setting for a special class is one in which students are enrolled full-time, with limited contact with other students. Such placement alternatives are not ordinarily utilized. They must be deemed absolutely necessary by a multidisciplinary committee that makes such placement decisions. As with other placements, the parent(s) must agree and the least restrictive placement should be considered. Special day schools and residential schools are more restrictive versions of the special class setting. However, in such settings, the students and special class teachers lose essentially all contact with a normal school setting.

PREREFERRAL INTERVENTION

Historically, when a teacher felt the need for assistance with a given student, the next step was referral for further evaluation. Data gathering (including, but not limited to, various formal and informal assessments), compilation, and analysis should provide additional ideas for interventions that would lead to more success in the classroom. In practice, however, referral often means nearly automatic identification, classification, and placement in some type of special education program. This practice, plus specific encouragement in PL 94–142 to educate students in regular class programs whenever possible, has led to a variety of attempts to initiate what is normally called prereferral intervention, prereferral consultation, or prereferral procedures.

The intervention or consultation takes somewhat different forms in the various states. In most cases, it is directly related to regulations promulgated by state-level special education leadership. Some states have mandated prereferral activities, and as a result, both state education agencies and various commercial publishers have developed prereferral checklists, manuals, and other assistance for schools in implementing prereferral activities. However, Strickland and Turnbull (1990) note that even though such guidelines or even specific requirements exist, "procedures often are designed primarily for documentation purposes rather than for the purpose of substantive intervention to maintain the student in the regular program" (p. 60). They note that with direct referral programs (no provision for prerefer-

ral), a referring teacher may sincerely want to gain information that will help a student remain in the regular class, but systems tend to place students in special education classes, regardless of the original intent.

A variety of formats have been established to promote the principle of prereferral. Strickland and Turnbull outline three possible models: (a) the teacher-assistance team, (b) the resource consultation model, and (c) the special education teacher as part-time consultant model. The teacher-assistance-team approach involves the appointment of a group of individuals responsible for providing recommendations and strategies to be implemented by classroom teachers. In most cases, to be successful, such teams must be administratively appointed, provide release time and training, and be composed of individuals who believe in prereferral intervention. The actual makeup of such teams, which may also be called educational management teams or instructional strategies teams, varies from district to district. Such teams should have continuity, however. That is, the team composition should not change each semester.

The resource consultation model involves appointment of an individual who has a high degree of consultation skill in addition to broad knowledge of alternative educational strategies. In this model, consultation should be the primary responsibility of the resource person. As compared with teacher-assistance teams, this model has the disadvantage of becoming a one-on-one situation (teacher and consultant) as opposed to team interaction. Its strength lies in the full-time commitment of the consultant.

Special education teachers were the first prereferral intervention specialists, and they may prove every bit as effective as either of the other two resources cited. The disadvantage of this model is that the assignment often is added on to an already too-busy schedule. In addition, special education teachers may not have the necessary consultation skills.

Whatever model or combination of models is in place in a given school, the success of prereferral strategies relies on the support and belief in the process by all involved, including administrators, regular classroom teachers, and consultants or special education teachers. However, all must also recognize that prereferral strategies do not work for all students. Thus, some students must be referred for further evaluation.

REFERRAL AND ASSESSMENT CONSIDERATIONS FOR SPECIAL EDUCATION SERVICES

When prereferral intervention does not lead to success, regular class teachers must refer students for further assessment and consideration for more specialized programming. Sometimes, referrals come from parents, physicians, or professionals in other community agencies, but usually regular class teachers first recognize a need for assistance and initiate the referral procedure. The flowchart in Figure 2–4 outlines the procedure.

Teacher Responsibilities

Specific referral procedures vary from district to district, but usually, a regular classroom teacher completes a special referral form. In addition to the student's name, age, grade, and sex, most referral forms ask questions about (a) grade level in academic areas (usually, grade equivalent on a standardized achievement test), (b) data on behavior (such as relations with other students and teachers), (c) specific reading strengths and deficits (such as word attack skills, memory for words, and ability to read orally), (d) ability (relative to others in

class) in class discussion and interaction, (e) specific strengths and deficits in arithmetic/mathematics, (f) strengths and weaknesses in nonacademic areas, (g) unusual family data that might be pertinent, and (h) a summary of any methods or approaches that have been unusually successful or unsuccessful for the student.

Students should be formally referred when appropriate, but overreferral should be avoided. Since parents must be contacted to gain information and obtain permission for further assessment, the matter of referral must not be approached lightly. If a student is referred when there is no need, the parents may become upset, and many people will spend time and effort needlessly.

In cases where there is an apparent (or verified) problem with hearing or vision, or where classroom adaptations are required due to physical problems, the major question is not classification of disability (although there may be multiple disabilities), but rather the best way to provide the most effective educational program, given the disability. However, whether the problem is mental retardation, behavior disorder, or learning disability, the matter of classification is important for effective planning, and both schools and parents must consider the various legal requirements.

Testing and Classification

Some people have questioned the necessity of testing and classification of students, and various lawsuits have led to changes in the manner in which testing and classification take place. Yet, testing and classification continue, given today's education system and funding mechanisms.

H. Rutherford Turnbull III (1986) is a lawyer, an advocate for children with disabilities, a parent of a child with disabilities, and a leading national authority on the law and disabilities. He believes there must

FIGURE 2–4
The referral assessment staffing IEP placement process

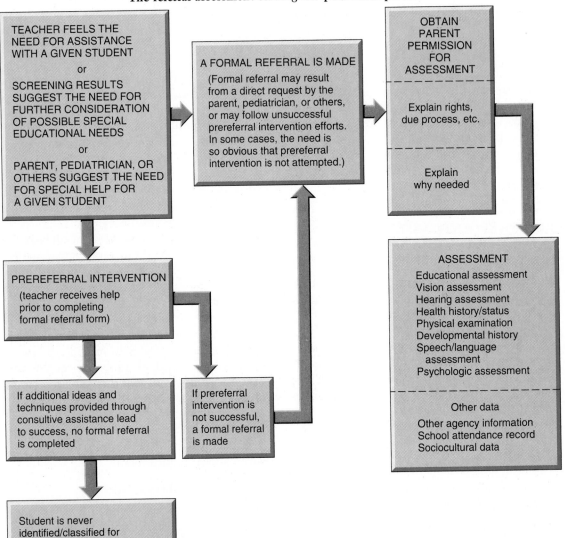

TEACHER FEELS THE NEED FOR ASSISTANCE WITH A GIVEN STUDENT

or

SCREENING RESULTS SUGGEST THE NEED FOR FURTHER CONSIDERATION OF POSSIBLE SPECIAL EDUCATIONAL NEEDS

or

PARENT, PEDIATRICIAN, OR OTHERS SUGGEST THE NEED FOR SPECIAL HELP FOR A GIVEN STUDENT

A FORMAL REFERRAL IS MADE

(Formal referral may result from a direct request by the parent, pediatrician, or others, or may follow unsuccessful prereferral intervention efforts. In some cases, the need is so obvious that prereferral intervention is not attempted.)

OBTAIN PARENT PERMISSION FOR ASSESSMENT

Explain rights, due process, etc.

Explain why needed

PREREFERRAL INTERVENTION

(teacher receives help prior to completing formal referral form)

If additional ideas and techniques provided through consultive assistance lead to success, no formal referral is completed

If prereferral intervention is not successful, a formal referral is made

ASSESSMENT

Educational assessment
Vision assessment
Hearing assessment
Health history/status
Physical examination
Developmental history
Speech/language assessment
Psychologic assessment

Other data

Other agency information
School attendance record
Sociocultural data

Student is never identified/classified for special education purposes

Note: Adapted from *Special education for the 80's* by B. R. Gearheart, 1980, Columbus, Ohio: Merrill. Copyright © 1980. Reprinted by permission of the author.

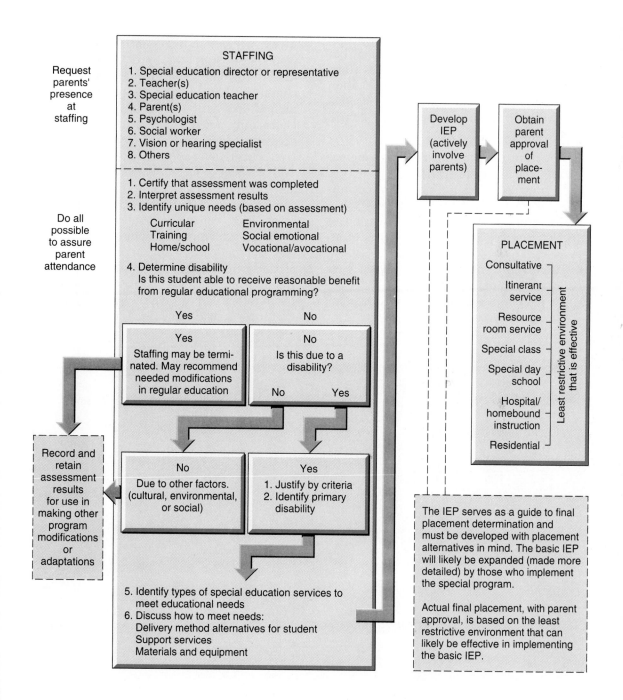

Request parents' presence at staffing

Do all possible to assure parent attendance

STAFFING

1. Special education director or representative
2. Teacher(s)
3. Special education teacher
4. Parent(s)
5. Psychologist
6. Social worker
7. Vision or hearing specialist
8. Others

1. Certify that assessment was completed
2. Interpret assessment results
3. Identify unique needs (based on assessment)

Curricular	Environmental
Training	Social emotional
Home/school	Vocational/avocational

4. Determine disability
   Is this student able to receive reasonable benefit from regular educational programming?

Yes   No

Yes
Staffing may be terminated. May recommend needed modifications in regular education

No
Is this due to a disability?

No   Yes

Record and retain assessment results for use in making other program modifications or adaptations

No
Due to other factors. (cultural, environmental, or social)

Yes
1. Justify by criteria
2. Identify primary disability

5. Identify types of special education services to meet educational needs
6. Discuss how to meet needs:
   Delivery method alternatives for student
   Support services
   Materials and equipment

Develop IEP (actively involve parents)

Obtain parent approval of placement

PLACEMENT

Consultative
Itinerant service
Resource room service
Special class
Special day school
Hospital/homebound instruction
Residential

Least restrictive environment that is effective

The IEP serves as a guide to final placement determination and must be developed with placement alternatives in mind. The basic IEP will likely be expanded (made more detailed) by those who implement the special program.

Actual final placement, with parent approval, is based on the least restrictive environment that can likely be effective in implementing the basic IEP.

be "procedures to protect children from improper testing, misclassification, and inappropriate placement" (p. 73). He adds that this is the focus of current legislation, but he also indicates that "testing, classification, and placement in special education programs must be continued" (p. 72). Reasons listed by Turnbull and others include the following:

1. To permit the planning and implementation of appropriate services
2. To provide a basis for funding to encourage more and better programming
3. To permit more accurate evaluation of the effectiveness of various types of efforts
4. To provide a focal point for advocacy efforts of parents and others
5. To provide a common denominator for professional groups

6. To provide a more meaningful basis for preventive or early intervention efforts

Misclassification, inappropriate testing and placement, and other problems must be dealt with, but ignoring the presence of a condition that can properly be classified as mental retardation or hearing impairment is certainly not the answer to assisting students who have problems requiring innovative educational interventions.

According to federal guidelines, although classification means use of the traditional categories of mental retardation, learning disabilities, behavior disorders, and so on, there is a growing trend across the nation to use a cross-categorical or noncategorical classification system at the state level. This trend is classification without traditional terminology. To receive the special funding that fuels special education services for chil-

Appropriate assessment is essential and is required by PL 94–142.

dren with special needs, all states require some type of classification. However, because it is sometimes difficult to differentiate between mental retardation and learning disabilities, especially when dealing with young children and mild levels of disability, the two categories and mild behavior disorders are sometimes combined in the classification of educationally disabled or some similar terminology. Sensory disabilities (the areas of vision and hearing) and physical disabilities are likely to be classified in a more straightforward manner, since there is less chance for confusion or misclassification.

We believe that classification is justified only if it permits some educational provision and assistance that would not be provided without the classification. Most special educators whom we know hope that many students with mild disabilities can be served in regular classes without ever attending separate, special service programs. However, the more severe a learning problem, the more likely that help from outside the regular classroom is needed. For students with severe learning problems, comprehensive, careful identification and classification procedures are essential.

Of course, some day, the system called public education may provide appropriate, individualized educational programming for all students now called exceptional without need for classification according to exceptionality and identification of specialized services by type and extent. However, until that time, it will be necessary to identify and classify such students according to some established system.

Following Formal Referral

Figure 2–4 shows graphically what happens after formal referral. Parents must give permission for assessment, and they must be told their rights under due process procedures. If they give permission (and most do,

if the situation is explained properly), the various parts of the interdisciplinary assessment are completed. A conference is held (parents must be invited, and efforts must be made to get them to attend). If a student's problems result from a disability, then a classification is agreed upon, and the matter goes to a group that must develop an IEP. Parents must be involved in the IEP development and must sign the IEP.

The content of an IEP commonly determines both the type and extent of special services provided a student and whether the student receives any services outside regular classes. Parents must approve any placement outside regular classes. The range of possible services that should be available to meet a student's needs is the continuum of educational services.

The Placement Decision

Determination that a student requires a specialized program should follow identification and classification of special needs. Then, a decision must be made as to where to place this student on the continuum of services. The rule is, of course, the least restrictive placement required to meet the needs of the student.

What should be considered in making this decision? Logically enough, these variables relate to, in order of importance, the student, parents, teachers, and administration.

Students. For a student, the variables include (a) chronological age, (b) type and degree of impairment or disability, (c) age at onset of disability (congenital or acquired), (d) level of academic achievement, (e) measured intellectual ability, (f) social maturity and skills, (g) presence of multiple disabilities (need for related noneducational services), (h) ambulation or mobility (particularly when considering orthopedic and other health disabilities and visual impairment), (i) success of past and present educational programs, (j) speech and language ability, and (k) wishes of the student and the student's parents.

Parents. Before the passage of PL 94–142, parents were primarily passive consumers of educational services and had limited input. They were occasionally involved in program and placement decisions, but generally, they were receivers of information from professionals. For example, they were told their child would be assigned to a particular room. Today, as a result of federal legislation that came about because of parental demands and litigation, parents are participants in educational decision making. This is evidenced not only by mandatory participation in due

process procedures but also by parental involvement in the development of IEPs.

Teachers. After preliminary placement determinations based on specific student characteristics, the next step is consideration of existing programs and services relative to the needs of a student. In most cases, some intervention by the school staff is effective. Where this is not the case, the possibility of initiating new programs or obtaining services by contract or some tuition arrangement with another school district must be considered.

There is little question that regular class teachers have major influence on the success of students. Some teachers readily accept the challenge of serving students with disabilities, whereas others have considerable difficulty making the adjustments nec-

Can you find the students with disabilities?

essary to be effective with such students. Among the most important variables are the following:

1. Professional preparation or in-service education concerning students with disabilities (not a prerequisite but highly desirable)
2. Previous experience with students who have disabilities (not a prerequisite but highly desirable)
3. Willingness to work cooperatively with resource personnel and parents (resource personnel must be readily available)
4. Willingness to accept variations in scheduling, teaching assignments, and classroom structure
5. Ability to assess individual learning needs, set goals and objectives, plan and implement teaching strategies, and evaluate student progress
6. Acceptance of the basic premise that *all* students have the right to the most appropriate education in the least restrictive environment

Administration. Administrative commitment to serve all students regardless of learning abilities or disabilities is important. Administrative staff from the superintendent to the principal must have real commitment to developing the most appropriate, least restrictive alternative.

A very high correlation exists between administrative commitment to the concept of serving students with disabilities in regular classrooms and the attitudes of teachers and students. In other words, if the principal is sincerely interested in serving all students, the commitment has a positive influence on the attitudes of teachers toward such students. If, however, the principal's attitude toward students with disabilities is essentially negative, often, teachers also ex-

hibit this attitude. The commitment must go beyond a willingness to merely comply with federal and state regulations. It must acknowledge the inherent abilities and potential of all students.

CULTURAL DIVERSITY, LANGUAGE DIVERSITY, AND SPECIAL EDUCATION

Problems generated by difficulties in conducting meaningful assessment of students who are culturally or linguistically different from the majority, middle-class, Anglo population were major factors in the court cases that gave impetus to the passage of PL 94–142. The Executive Committee of the Council for Children with Behavioral Disorders outlined three major factors that may lead to misdiagnosis of students from different backgrounds (1989). Although their focus was behavioral disorders, the factors apply to other disabilities as well. The factors are (a) language differences between the student and others in the social or educational environment, (b) faulty perceptions and lowered expectations on the part of classroom teachers, and (c) increased likelihood of referral for evaluation and assistance of students from culturally diverse backgrounds.

Unacceptable assessment practices remain a major concern; however, they are only one aspect of the problem. Even if students are properly identified, significant questions remain as to how to organize and deliver the programs for the students. For example, how similar (or different) must educational programs be for two students, age 12 and learning disabled: one is of Hispanic background and his first language is Spanish, and the other is of Anglo background, and his language is English? Educators must remain acutely aware of individual needs, especially with respect to cultural and language differences, and learn more about how to meet such needs.

Baca and Cervantes (1989) provide a challenging discussion and analysis of the unusual problems of identifying and then providing appropriate educational programs for bilingual, exceptional children in their text, *The Bilingual, Special Education Interface* (2nd edition, 1989). They provide a useful discussion of assessment procedures, plus theoretical and operational guidelines for bilingual special education, including a number of school district policy suggestions that may help shape a more meaningful program for students who are from different language or cultural backgrounds.

Wood (1989) lists the following major broad categories of culturally different populations in the schools: (a) Asians or Pacific Islanders, (b) Black Americans, (c) Hispanics, and (d) Native Americans. We would add at least two other groups, which overlap these four categories but also include students not included in these four: (e) Students from migrant families and (f) Students from very low socioeconomic families, primarily from inner-city locations. We believe that the last two categories include a significant number of Anglo students whose cultural background is just as unique and who have special needs just as great as those of students who are more commonly referred to as minority students.

Collier (in Baca & Cervantes, 1989) suggests that educational planning for bilingual exceptional children consider such factors as social maturity in both the native and second culture, level of competence in both languages, and degree of acculturation and cultural identity. She also suggests that intellectual ability be measured in both languages.

The challenge involved in providing the most effective educational programs for different exceptional populations is great. Regular classroom teachers should ask for and expect assistance from special educators and other consultants in the local educational agency.

Although we attempt to avoid closing any discussion on a negative note, we feel it may be valuable to list five difficulties associated with identification and programming for students from different populations who are also suspected to have disabilities or to be gifted:

1. Given existing definitions and assessment techniques, it is possible to identify some students as mentally retarded or learning disabled when the problems relate more to cultural or language differences than to what most authorities recognize as mental retardation or learning disabilities.
2. Given existing definitions and assessment techniques, it is possible to identify some students as behaviorally disordered because of misunderstanding of cultural origins of their behavior, inappropriate assessment techniques, or a school organization that does not deal with their needs.
3. Because of the cost and bad public relations associated with mistakes in identification and placement of students from different cultural, ethnic, or linguistic backgrounds, school officials may decide to not search with any real diligence among the minority populations for students in need of special services.
4. Identification procedures in existing programs for students with gifts or talents undoubtedly lead to not finding many potentially gifted or talented students among minority populations.
5. Special education programs have traditionally been viewed as ways to take care of "kids with special problems."

Thus, there is a tendency to substitute special education programs for other programs to assist students who have special needs but are obviously not mentally retarded, learning disabled, or emotionally disturbed. This tendency is encouraged by the fact that programs for students with disabilities receive substantial state funding, whereas many other programs do not.

The problems associated with providing the best possible program for culturally diverse exceptional students are many, but with increased attention, good programs are growing in number. As a concept, cultural pluralism has been accepted by most national educational groups and much of the nation. The multicultural education program this concept demands must become part of special education.

SPECIAL PROVISIONS FOR STUDENTS WHO ARE GIFTED AND TALENTED

This discussion of legislative provisions for educational programs for students who are gifted and talented has been left to the end of the chapter because there is little to report. Table 2–1 includes two federal laws that relate directly to education of students who are gifted or talented—PL 91–230 and PL 95–561. These two laws have been beneficial in providing additional, more effective programs for students who are gifted and talented, but their impact has been far less than that of PL 94–142. The reasons are twofold: (a) laws relating to students with disabilities *require* expanded, appropriate programs, whereas laws relating to students who are gifted or talented merely *encourage* such programs, and (b) laws relating to students with disabilities provide massive amounts of money for programs, whereas laws relating

to students who are gifted and talented provide minimal dollars that tend to be spent by state agencies, not at the local level. Only in cases where students who are gifted and talented also have disabilities (for example, students who are gifted and also orthopedically handicapped or blind) has PL 94–142 directly affected students who are gifted or talented. However, PL 94–142 has had one important indirect effect on programs for students who are gifted and talented. It has led at least some parents of such students to pressure their legislators for better programs, an effort that has had different degrees of success in different states.

PL 91–230 (1970) mandated that the U.S. commissioner of education study the needs of gifted and talented students of the nation and report to Congress. As a result of this report (often called the Marland Report), additional attention was focused on the unmet needs of such students, and important momentum was gained. Later, federal efforts led to the development of the National/State Leadership Training Institute on the Gifted and Talented (NSLTIGT), which has played an important role in developing training programs at local and state levels and in increasing public interest in education of gifted and talented children.

Another positive step was taken when the Office of Gifted and Talented was established in the Department of Education to focus efforts on behalf of students who are gifted and talented. For the first time, a federal office and federal employees were located in Washington, with access to congressional committees and full-time responsibility to monitor and encourage programs for such students.

PL 95–561, the Gifted and Talented Children's Act, provided a modest amount of federal financial assistance to plan, develop, and improve programs for gifted and talented children and youth. It was part of the slow but continuing encouragement from the federal level for state and local agencies to develop better opportunities for students with gifts or talents. However, it made no serious attempt to mandate appropriate programs or provide educational guarantees for students with gifts or talents parallel to the programs provided for students with disabilities.

Who, then, speaks for students who are gifted and talented? How are their educational needs met, and who governs and monitors programs established on their behalf? The laws, regulations, and policies of the states and the District of Columbia determine whether there are special programs, which students are served, the qualifications of teachers who teach such students, the percentage of the state's educational resources committed to this task, and all other related questions. Therefore, there is much variation between states. Sometimes, there is also confusing or misleading information about state practices and policies.

The National/State Leadership Training Institute on the Gifted and Talented has provided a center of focus for efforts to promote more effective programs through better trained leadership in the field. Individual universities have provided unique contributions, too. However, despite these efforts, viable programs are not available in many areas of the nation. The special needs of gifted and talented students are not recognized in those areas, or if they are recognized, they are not met. In any given school district, whether programs provide for the special needs of such students appears to depend on local interest and the ability of interested persons to influence the local administration and school board.

It is difficult to generalize about pro-

grams for students who are gifted and talented; however, the following statements reflect the current situation:

1. During the 1980s, there was a slow but steady increase in the number of states that had specific legislation related to education of students with gifts and talents.
2. Special reimbursement for local education agencies to provide programs for such students is apparently an incentive to some school districts (in states that provide for such reimbursement), but not to others. Therefore, reimbursement alone (as it is presently structured and funded) does not appear to be sufficient for all students who are gifted and talented.
3. Apparently, an increased number of school districts support the concept of early identification of students who are gifted or talented.
4. Definitions designed to guide identification of such students vary widely.
5. The scope and quality of programs for students who are gifted and talented vary widely.

SUMMARY

This chapter outlined the major provisions of PL 94–142, the federal law that mandates integrating students with disabilities with their nondisabled peers. It emphasizes (a) the right of due process of law, (b) protection in the process of evaluation, and (c) an individualized education program (IEP). The chapter also provided a summary of significant federal legislation relating to exceptional children and youth, including those who are gifted or talented.

This chapter included a discussion of the continuum of educational services that must be provided so as to have a variety of settings and programs to meet the educational needs of students with disabilities. Also considered was the great need for collaboration and consultation between regular and special educators in meeting the educational needs of exceptional students.

Finally, problems inherent in special education programming for culturally diverse and bilingual students were discussed. A review of special education provisions for students who are gifted and talented concluded the chapter.

PART II

EFFECTIVE INSTRUCTION AND AFFECTIVE SENSITIVITY

CHAPTER 3 CONSIDERS CERTAIN PRINCIPLES AND STRATEGIES FOR EFFECTIVE INSTRUCTION, most of which apply to all exceptionalities. Chapter 4 addresses affective aspects of teaching—feelings and expectations—and interactions. Possibly, this is the most important single chapter in the text, particularly for teachers who have not been fully aware of the motivational power of good personal interaction in the teaching-learning process.

- What are the advantages of an informally arranged classroom as compared with a traditionally arranged classroom?

- How does curriculum-based assessment differ from formal assessment?

- What are the advantages and disadvantages of learning centers?

- How do preferred learning styles influence instructional approaches?

- What are the major types of peer systems? What are the potential advantages and disadvantages of each type?

- What are advance organizers? How may they be used to facilitate the learning of students with disabilities?

- In what ways may all students profit from teacher presentation alternatives designed for students with special needs?

- What grading alternatives might be considered for use with students who have disabilities? Could these alternatives also be used with nondisabled students?

CHAPTER 3

EFFECTIVE
INSTRUCTION

EFFECTIVE INSTRUCTION IS ACHIEVED THROUGH interaction of a host of variables. Polloway, Patton, Payne, and Payne (1989) indicate that effective instruction involves precursors to teaching, teaching behaviors, and follow-ups to teaching. They outline nearly 40 components of effective instruction classified in these three major areas, as shown in Figure 3–1. These components apply to all students, but they are particularly important in application to students with disabilities. This chapter reviews concepts and strategies generally applicable to students with special needs.

GENERAL GUIDELINES

The general guidelines that follow are adapted from recommendations provided by Wallace and Kauffman (1986). They provide a yardstick against which teachers may measure their own teaching strategies and procedures. The first five principles are sequential; that is, teachers should start at principle 1 in planning instruction for students with disabilities and continue with principles 2, 3, 4, and 5 in the sequence given. Principles 6 and 7 are general, applying throughout the teaching process.

1. *Base initial teaching strategies on assessment information.* This objective means more than the use of test results obtained by a psychologist or educational diagnostician. It includes the results of careful observation, tests given by the teacher, information from school records and parents, and all other available sources. The goal is to establish an overall picture of the student, which will provide a beginning point for planning instructional strategies.
2. *State instructional goals and specific perfor-* *mance objectives and allocate sufficient time to carry them out.* Appropriate goals providing general parameters for instructional planning should come first. Specific instructional objectives, stated in terms of student performance, should follow. In some cases, subobjectives must be added. The purpose is to know where we are heading and to have a means to determine the extent to which we have achieved what we are trying to accomplish. This strategy is important in the education of all students but is particularly important with students with learning problems.[1]
3. *Analyze the student's performance of specific tasks to pinpoint learning problems more precisely.* Careful analysis of the manner in which a student completes learning tasks permits more precise information as to what the student can and cannot do. Error analysis provides guidance as to what must

---

[1]Specific performance objectives may not be regularly used by regular educators, but the IEP may require them, and they are essential to plan for instruction for students with special needs effectively.

FIGURE 3–1
Components of effective instruction

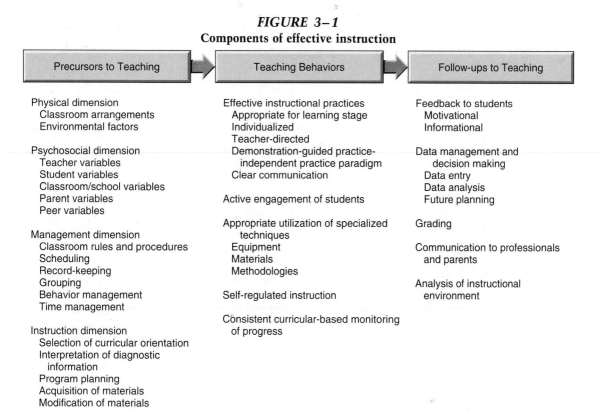

Precursors to Teaching	Teaching Behaviors	Follow-ups to Teaching

Physical dimension
  Classroom arrangements
  Environmental factors

Psychosocial dimension
  Teacher variables
  Student variables
  Classroom/school variables
  Parent variables
  Peer variables

Management dimension
  Classroom rules and procedures
  Scheduling
  Record-keeping
  Grouping
  Behavior management
  Time management

Instruction dimension
  Selection of curricular orientation
  Interpretation of diagnostic
    information
  Program planning
  Acquisition of materials
  Modification of materials

Effective instructional practices
  Appropriate for learning stage
  Individualized
  Teacher-directed
  Demonstration-guided practice-
    independent practice paradigm
  Clear communication

Active engagement of students

Appropriate utilization of specialized
  techniques
  Equipment
  Materials
  Methodologies

Self-regulated instruction

Consistent curricular-based monitoring
  of progress

Feedback to students
  Motivational
  Informational

Data management and
  decision making
  Data entry
  Data analysis
  Future planning

Grading

Communication to professionals
  and parents

Analysis of instructional
  environment

Note: From *Strategies for Teaching Learners with Special Needs* (4th ed.) by E. A. Polloway, J. R. Patton, J. S. Payne, and R. A. Payne, Copyright © 1989, Merrill, Columbus, Ohio. Reprinted by permission of Macmillan Publishing Company.

be taught next. Analysis may lead to modification of initial plans or may verify them. In any event, it is an essential step in the instructional process.

4. *Present a new set of tasks, designed to help the student overcome performance deficits.* In expanding on this step in the process, Wallace and Kauffman (1986) suggest the following: (a) organize tasks for efficient presentation, (b) be directive—tell, don't ask, (c) get student attention before attempting to start the task, (d) provide sufficient time for student response, (e) if the student does not respond, repeat and simplify the directions given, (f) cue responses (with a word, gesture, or other signal), (g) use prompts, (h) provide a model for the student to follow, (i) present only those tasks essential to the concept being taught, (j) present tasks in logical sequence, and (k) provide opportunity for practice until mastery is achieved.

5. *Provide feedback on task performance.* Such feedback should be unambiguous, immediate, and corrective (reinforce correct responses, which should reduce incorrect responses).

6. *Structure the learning environment for success.* Later sections of this chapter will provide more information on this topic.

7. *Monitor student performance and keep records of progress.* This objective would include keeping a log of teaching activities,

maintaining a chart of student progress, and testing what is being taught. Though such record-keeping does take time, we believe it may *save* time, in the long run, for those one or two students who may be having significant difficulties.[2]

Secondary School Instructional Strategies

We include this section titled "Secondary School Instructional Strategies" as a result of feedback from secondary school teachers who said that most special education teaching ideas are grade school ideas. Teachers in secondary schools said they needed more strategies related to their problems and the secondary school setting. Some of their frustration relates to the fact that secondary-level teachers often teach so many students each day that they have little time to get to know any one student. Also, if they use some version of the lecture approach to instruction and students do not have the skills and knowledge base assumed by the teacher, both the students and the teacher feel failure and frustration. We believe that most of the ideas presented in this text can be applied at the secondary level, especially if teachers are willing to make adaptations.

Special Technology

Many technological devices may be valuable to students with special needs, especially students with hearing or visual impairments or students with physical disabilities. These are more fully discussed in chapters 5, 7, and 8 as they apply with respect to

students who have these specific special needs. As for the role of regular classroom teachers with respect to these devices, certain generalizations apply in most instances. First, teachers should not hesitate to ask questions about the use of or potential problems with any technological equipment or device. Second, most such devices can, and should be, openly discussed with students who have special needs. (In most cases, earlier discussions with the parents, school nurse, or a specialist should take place. The importance of this step varies with the device.) Third, it may be appropriate to discuss certain equipment with the class as a whole, particularly with younger children (this might apply to hearing aids, prostheses, wheelchairs, and so forth). Students with special needs should be important contributors to such discussions. Fourth, in some few cases (such as a student with a pacemaker or requiring other very special treatment), written, emergency instructions should be on file, approved in writing by both the parents and a physician.

In a discussion of social issues in technology, Alcorn (1986) says that technological devices were created by the human race in an attempt to manipulate natural law to our advantage. Such devices are good if they lead to positive results; they are bad if misused or inappropriately used. As technology has been used to assist individuals with hearing or visual impairments, it has permitted students to learn more effectively. For students with physical disabilities, it has meant more active participation in school programs. In some cases, it has made the difference between participation in a regular classroom and education at home or in a hospital-like setting. The role of teachers is to enhance the opportunities made possible by the existence of such technology.

---

[2]Abbreviated and adapted from *Teaching Students with Learning and Behavior Problems*, 3d ed. (pp. 126–147) by G. Wallace and J. Kauffman, 1986, Columbus, OH: Merrill. Used with permission of Macmillan Publishing Company.

Good Pedagogy

Teaching practices that appear to be particularly helpful with students who have special needs are, for the most part, general practices rather than special techniques; it can be said that they are simply good pedagogy. This chapter considers a number of good general practices. To be of maximum value, such practices must be systematically integrated with other elements of the instructional process.

PLANNING FOR INSTRUCTION

Planning for instruction includes task analysis of listening skills, self-management skills, concept analysis skills, study skills, preparation for examinations, and critical thinking skills. Informal assessment includes curriculum-based assessment, anecdotal records, and interviews. Organization includes scheduling, classroom arrangement, planning and preparation of learning centers, grouping, and consideration of peer systems.

Task Analysis

Teachers often experience considerable frustration when students do not successfully complete assigned tasks or assignments. To minimize such frustration and failure, teachers may find it helpful to divide a task into smaller steps. Each step then becomes a separate goal or objective. Many teachers routinely use this approach without thinking of it as task analysis and without actually writing the parts—they simply do it as they plan their assignments.

Task analysis is based on the assumption that a student may not be able to accomplish a given task or assignment because of an inability to accomplish one or more of its parts. The following nonacademic anal-

ogy roughly illustrates this concept. A person has a flat tire on an automobile trip. Like some individuals, this individual has difficulty changing the flat tire to resume the trip. Is it sufficient to simply state that the person cannot change the flat tire? No, it is more helpful to analyze the necessary steps of the tire change to determine the actual problem. Does the person know how to use the jack? Should the person loosen the nuts on the wheel before or after using the jack? Is the automobile on a level surface? Is the problem related to the spare tire?

The process of changing an automobile tire may be divided into several steps. To be able to change a tire, one must understand each of the steps that must be taken and the order in which they must be taken. In total, these steps make up the task of changing the tire. A lack of ability in or understanding of just one of these steps may make it impossible for the person to change the tire and resume the trip.

Nearly every learning situation can be divided into as many components as necessary to understand the whole. Often, the essential subskills can be identified and taught to allow the completion of the larger task or assignment. In more difficult situations, teachers may find it helpful to record the subskills.

The following list of steps is an example of task analysis directed to the objective of alphabetizing the following words, each of which has been placed on a separate card: *stop, ask, dinner, name, boy.*

1. The student can write the alphabet in the correct order.
2. Provided a stack of 26 flash cards, each containing a different letter of the alphabet, the student can place the cards in alphabetical order.
3. Provided a stack of 26 flash cards, each

containing a word beginning with a different letter of the alphabet, the student can place the cards in alphabetical order with the help of an alphabet chart.

4. Provided a stack of 26 flash cards, each containing a word beginning with a different letter of the alphabet, the student can place the cards in alphabetical order without the help of an alphabet chart.

5. Provided a stack of 15 flash cards, each containing a different letter of the alphabet, the student can place the cards in alphabetical order with the help of an alphabet chart.

6. Provided a stack of 15 flash cards, each containing a different letter of the alphabet, the student can place the cards in alphabetical order without the help of an alphabet chart.

7. Provided a stack of 15 flash cards, each containing a word beginning with a different letter of the alphabet, the student can place the cards in alphabetical order with the help of an alphabet chart.

8. Provided a stack of 15 flash cards, each containing a word beginning with a different letter of the alphabet, the student can place the cards in alphabetical order without the help of an alphabet chart.

9. The student can alphabetize the following words, each of which has been placed on a separate card: *stop, ask, dinner, name, boy.*

Task analysis may help teachers identify (a) what steps are necessary to accomplish the task, (b) where students are having difficulty with a task, (c) what should be taught next, and (d) what adaptations may assist students with task accomplishment (Bigge, 1991). As mentioned, many teachers routinely use this approach to instruction without thinking of it as task analysis. Good teachers continually use an analytic

or diagnostic approach to instruction to enhance the success of both the students and themselves.

Listening Skills. Assisting students in the development of listening skills may be one of the most overlooked areas in planning for students with special needs. Reading and written expression are major areas of curriculum. Often, a teacher first recognizes that a student (who may be later identified as having a learning disability or mild mental retardation) has special needs as a result of lack of achievement in reading or written expression. Standardized achievement tests attempt to measure achievement in various aspects of reading or written expression, and teachers assign grades or provide other types of evaluation with respect to reading and written expression, but they often overlook listening.

Why is listening important? Listening is the foundation of all of the other language arts. Language arts authorities suggest that in most school programs, more classroom time is spent listening than in any other activity. According to Rakes and Choate (1989): "Through listening activities, students build language skills, expand vocabularies, enrich experiences, learn concepts, understand the mechanics for specific tasks, develop readiness skills for particular lessons, appreciate the joys of spoken and written language, and even relax. Listening is a set of learned skills, incidentally acquired by some students but mastered only through direct instruction by many" (p. 30).

Measurement of listening skills is best accomplished through nonstandardized measures, for example, some variations of informal reading inventories (IRIs). Many standardized tests do not even attempt to measure listening skills. Although measuring listening skills is not so simple as measuring other skills, teachers can learn to look for indications of underdeveloped listening skills, use informal means to verify their existence, and then proceed to help students listen more efficiently. One of the more obvious descriptions of poor listeners is "inattentive." Another is "distractible." Yet, many students with poor listening skills are not so easily recognized.

Rakes and Choate provide a simplified format for determining if students have special listening needs and a series of practical suggestions for remediation in the classroom. In addition to the more typical focus on attention and recognition of auditory stimuli and auditory memory (following directions, remembering general information, recalling in sequence, and listening critically), they suggest a listening area that is not always a major concern of educators. This area, auditory appreciation, relates to skills involved in comfortable listening as well as interactions with other people and good literature.

Wallace, Cohen, and Polloway (1987) believe that "although listening is the most used language arts skill, it is the least taught skill. Teachers assume that children listen, and that if speaking is taught, listening will follow" (p. 67). Wood (1989) believes listening is a skill that must be taught and many slow students prefer to learn from listening rather than from reading. If this is the case, then listening skills are unusually important to many students with special needs.

Since listening skills provide much of the basis for reading and the other language arts, and a great deal of formal school time is spent in listening activities, evaluation of the listening skills of students with special needs and planned listening activities (when indicated) are essential. An awareness of the importance of listening skills is essential. Two resources provide practical consideration of listening skills, how they may be assessed on an informal basis, and activities that may assist in the development of useful skills: (a) Rakes and Choate (1989, pp. 30–55) and (b) Wallace, Cohen, and Polloway (1987, pp. 67–100). See Figure 3–2 for a recorded guided activity to promote listening skills.

Self-Management Skills. Academic achievement appears to be closely related to self-management skills. Students with good self-management skills tend to do well in school, to persist with assignments, and to seek assistance from teachers and peers when appropriate. Many low-achieving students, however, do not have the self-management skills that are obvious prerequisites to learning. When given a task, low-achieving students tend to use their poor organizational strategies consistently regardless of whether they are effective. In other words, they impulsively and hurriedly complete the assignment without the prerequisite organization. Students who do not possess the necessary self-management skills must be taught how to search for useful information, order this data, and organize it for learning and retention.

An environment that encourages students to develop self-management skills generally results in greater independence, increased task completion, and ultimately greater achievement. Teachers should be alert for students who do not have the necessary organizational strategies and should provide specific instruction in this area.

When assisting a student who does not have self-management skills, the teacher must serve as a model, actually demonstrating the skill. The teacher should talk while the student watches the strategy. The

FIGURE 3-2
A recorded guided activity to promote listening skills

1. Prerecord a lesson involving information new to the class and pertinent to topics that you will read or discuss in the near future in the instructional sequence. Adjust the time and length of the recording for the grade level.

2. Tell the students that they must listen carefully, remembering all they can about the lesson.

3. After playing the audiotape, ask the students to tell what they heard. Write their contributions on the board as the students give them, with no comments by or questions from you.

4. Direct the students to listen for additions and corrections, and play the audiotape again.

5. Make additions and corrections on the board as necessary.

6. Ask the students to organize the information on the board into some logical sequence and to indicate the major parts and sub-parts of the presentation. Establish some type of outline (number and letter designations) for this purpose.

7. Ask the class for ideas of how you might have organized and presented this information to make it easier to understand and remember.

8. Conclude the lesson with a discussion of the total lesson. Target the information and concepts that you wish to emphasize.

teacher should identify a series of steps (organizational skills) through which to proceed. Then, the teacher should ask the student to perform the task while instructing himself or herself aloud with assistance from the teacher. The student should verbally follow the steps with statements such as, "First, I must do this, and then this, and this." In the next step, the student should perform the task, still speaking aloud but without assistance from the teacher. In the next step, the student should whisper to himself or herself the necessary tasks. In the final step, the student should subvocalize the tasks. Essential to the success of

teaching self-management skills are (a) teacher modeling through talking, (b) student self-talk, and (c) praise from the teacher.

Concept Analysis Skills. The ability to develop concepts, or to conceptualize, is considered the highest level of human language and thought (Johnson & Myklebust, 1967). Authorities vary in their definitions of concept development, but most agree that conceptualization includes classifying experiences into groups according to some common denominator. Writers in various education fields agree that concept development is highly important. Authorities in the areas of mental retardation and learning disabilities seem to agree that conceptualization is more difficult for students with these disabilities. Conceptualization is also difficult for students with visual and hearing impairments. The reasons for the difficulties vary among the four areas. It is agreed, however, that teachers must help students with disabilities develop conceptual skills.

Unruh, Gilliam, and Jogi (1982) provide some practical guidelines for helping students develop skills of concept analysis. The following guidelines should be of value in developing new concepts or broadening underdeveloped concepts:

1. Concepts used in teaching concept analysis skills should not be abstract. The concepts should be defined by specific, observable, essential characteristics. Red, circle, dog, and six are examples of concepts that meet these criteria. Each concept should have a unique set of shared essential, relevant characteristics that are not shared by other concepts presented.
2. Concepts cannot be taught through a single example. Students must use as many examples of the concepts as available when attempting an analysis. Although every instance of a concept cannot be presented, several instances or examples of the concept must be presented if it is to be analyzed successfully.
3. Each example of the concept should exhibit both essential and non-essential characteristics of that concept.
4. The essential, relevant characteristics of the concept should not be varied in positive examples (those that represent the concept). Furthermore, the non-essential, irrelevant characteristics should always be varied when negative examples are presented (those examples that do not represent the concept).
5. Both positive and negative examples of the

concept should be presented to make sure the student has successfully analyzed the concept presented.[3]

Unruh, Gilliam, and Jogi suggest three steps to follow when using these guidelines:

1. Help the student (as necessary, considering the student's basic disabilities) discover the characteristics that are the same in the examples of the concept under consideration. Discuss these common characteristics and verify that the student understands them.
2. Help the student to discover nonessential characteristics in both the positive examples and negative examples. Discuss and verify the student's understanding of nonessential characteristics.
3. Make certain the student is fully aware that the essential characteristics are not shared by the negative examples. Present a new set of examples, including both positive and negative examples, and ask the student to point out which characteristics are essential to the concept and which are nonessential.

This procedure can be followed using words, pictures, or actual objects. For example, the teacher might use words to teach the concepts of verbs or plural nouns. Pictures or real objects can be used to teach the concepts of dishes, furniture, or the spatial arrangement of one thing above another. Pictures can be used to teach the concepts of transportation or helping. Many

[3]From "Developing Concept Analysis Skills" by D. Unruh, J. Gilliam, and A. Jogi, 1982, *Directive Teacher*, 4(2), p. 27. Copyright 1982 by National Center, Educational Media and Materials for the Handicapped, Ohio State University. Reprinted by permission.

students master most concepts necessary to reach established educational goals with little difficulty; however, when there is a need to teach a certain specific concept, this procedure is of value.

Study Skills. Many, perhaps most, students with learning problems have not developed all of the study skills necessary for success in the academic setting. Some school districts are so convinced of the need to systematically teach study skills that they have initiated systemwide programs as part of secondary school mainstreaming. Smith and Smith (1989) provide a description of such a program in the Mesa, Arizona, schools. This program involves a teacher training phase, a synchronized teaching phase, and a follow-up phase. The training phase includes in-service sessions on multisensory teaching, alternative teaching strategies, note-taking skills, organization and time management, memory skills, listening skills, reading in content areas, vocabulary development, and test taking. The synchronized teaching schedule divides the school year into one-month periods, emphasizing skills one at a time and reinforcing them in classwork when possible. This prevents confusion that might result from trying to learn too many skills at one time and provides maximum reinforcement of new learning. The follow-up phase provides evaluation of effectiveness and helps teachers incorporate instruction of study skills into their specific content areas.

Whatever the approach to teaching study skills to students with special needs and whether regular classroom teachers or special educators teach the skills, they should assess the skills informally to make students aware of and responsible for their study patterns. Teachers may construct an easily administered checklist or questionnaire of study skills (see Figure 3–3). After

FIGURE 3–3
Questionnaire to help teachers assess study skills

	Almost always	Sometimes	Very seldom
1. Do you listen to directions or instructions provided in class?	☐	☐	☐
2. Do you take notes regarding assignments?	☐	☐	☐
3. Do you ask questions when you don't understand?	☐	☐	☐
4. Do you pay attention to class lectures and discussions?	☐	☐	☐
5. Do you keep up with assigned readings?	☐	☐	☐
6. Do you feel disorganized most of the time?	☐	☐	☐
7. Do you participate in class discussions?	☐	☐	☐
8. Do you find it difficult to complete assignments in class?	☐	☐	☐
9. Do you feel adequately prepared most of the time?	☐	☐	☐
10. Do you find the vocabulary too difficult?	☐	☐	☐

students complete the questionnaire, discuss the answers. The objective of this activity is to provide information to each student about his or her study skills and general classroom behavior so that both student and teacher can develop a plan of specific strategies to enhance the skills. Students must understand their desirable and undesirable behaviors and assume responsibility for them.

Teachers may need to take time to teach some of the essential skills related to their subject areas, including time scheduling, note taking, and outlining. Encourage students to use index cards to record their assignments, and check these cards periodically to make necessary revisions. Teachers may also find it necessary to use outlines and advance organizers to give students structure for note taking. Additional skills include using the dictionary and reviewing reading materials.

The question of what should be considered study skills is open to differences in interpretation, but authorities agree that study skills are important and may require direct instruction. Hoover (1988) has written a book on teaching study skills to students with disabilities. Other authors, such as Devine (1987), have developed texts that relate specifically to teaching study skills, but they target all students. Hoover and Devine accept a broad interpretation of study skills, while Sheinker and Sheinker (1989) emphasize skimming, summarizing, note taking, and outlining.

Preparation for Examinations. In addition to not having adequate study skills, many students with learning problems do not have good skills in preparing for and taking examinations. Teachers may want to provide direction and instruction in this area with some of the following suggested methods:

1. Help students understand examination directions and terms such as *define, list, compare, contrast,* and *defend.*
2. Teach students to watch for cue words, such as *never, all,* and *always.*
3. Tell students what you expect. Is your emphasis content, organization, spelling, grammar, mechanics, or creative expression?
4. Provide students with a copy of a previous test, talk about it, and use it as a teaching tool.
5. With objective tests, encourage students to read all questions carefully and answer first the questions whose answers they know immediately. Then, students may consider more carefully the remaining questions.
6. With essay examinations, encourage students to outline their answers before writing.
7. Encourage students to answer all questions unless there is a penalty for incorrect answers.
8. Encourage students to write clearly and distinctly.
9. Encourage students to leave sufficient time to reread their answers, paying attention to such things as punctuation and spelling.

Some of these suggestions are not appropriate for all courses, but these methods generally provide students with the assistance they need to be more successful when taking examinations.

Critical Thinking Skills. A major objective in planning for students with special needs is to help them improve their thinking skills. Development of study skills involves critical thinking skills, but study skills represent just one specific type of thinking. The focus here is a need to plan activities that promote the development of thinking skills, emphasizing activities that work for students with special needs.

Tiedt, Carlson, Howard, and Watanabe (1989) introduce certain assumptions for teaching critical thinking. These assumptions relate to learning through language skills (listening, speaking, reading, and writing) and include the following: (a) children want to learn, (b) children learn more effectively when self-motivated, (c) children learn from each other (they do not require adult instruction), (d) children naturally apply discovery methods, making and testing hypotheses as they learn language, and (e) children like to play with language, showing both humor and creativity. In a discussion of thinking as a major goal of education, Costa (1987) observes: "Many educators are forming a new understanding of what is a basic skill. We are realizing that there is a prerequisite to the 'basics'—the ability to think" (p. 17).

McTighe (1987) suggests teaching *for* thinking, *of* thinking, and *about* thinking. In teaching *for* thinking, he recommends a variety of questioning techniques, including those requiring basic recall: (a) interpretation, and (b) judgment, hypothesizing, or analogical reasoning. In addition, he suggests "interpretive reading and discussion, writing, laboratory experiments, problem solving, debates, simulations" (p 26). McTighe believes that the previous activities provide opportunities to practice thinking. To McTighe, teaching *of* thinking means direct instruction that can help students develop specific thinking skills, for example, how to compare. To teach comparing (or any thinking skill), first define the skill and illustrate it in simple examples that are familiar to all students. One emphasis might be that comparisons involve finding similarities and differences. Then, develop a series of steps to use when comparing in the class setting and outline

them on the board. After it is certain that all students understand how to apply these steps in simple comparisons (such as comparing a football to a basketball or an automobile to an airplane), present a lesson that involves more complex comparisons and help the class work through these comparisons. For example, after studying the Civil War and the Revolutionary War, compare the two. In working through such comparisons in class, involve all students. Devise a similar procedure for whatever thinking skills you want to target.

The third approach suggested by McTighe, thinking *about* thinking, involves helping students develop metacognitive abilities (discussed in more detail in Chapter 10). Such abilities are also a part of the recommendations made by Sheinker and Sheinker (1989).

There is a resurgence of interest in the direct teaching of thinking skills, and such teaching works with students who have special needs. Such instruction can take place in a group setting where students with special needs learn cooperatively with other students. We suggest the following two books on this topic: (a) *Teaching Thinking in K–12 Classrooms: Ideas, Activities, and Resources* (1989) by Tiedt, Carlson, Howard, and Watanabe and (b) *Thinking Skills Instruction: Concepts and Techniques* (1987) by Heiman and Slomianko, editors.

Informal Assessment

In most cases, teachers have little difficulty in identifying students who have learning problems. Specifying a problem, however, may be more difficult because of the likelihood of overlapping problems. The basic difficulty may be intellectual, social, or emotional, or it may be the result of inadequate instruction, lack of opportunity to learn, or some combination of factors.

Through a combination of formal and informal assessment, teachers can more precisely define the nature of problems.

McLoughlin and Lewis (1990) recognize three basic types of informal assessment: (a) curriculum-based assessment; (b) observation, work sample analysis, and task analysis; and (c) procedures using informants. Gearheart and Gearheart (1990) discuss the following types of informal assessment: (a) curriculum-based assessment, (b) systematic (direct) observation, (c) checklists, (d) error analysis, (e) task analysis, (f) work sample analysis, (g) interviews, (h) questionnaires, (i) inventories, and (j) diagnostic probes and diagnostic teaching.

Informal assessment has received a great deal of attention in the past 10 to 15 years, and many school districts have assessment personnel, special education specialists, or content specialists (in areas such as reading, language arts, or mathematics) who can help teachers carry out effective informal procedures. Texts such as Salvia and Hughes (1990) or Howell and Morehead (1987) provide detailed instructions for those who cannot find within-district assistance.

Curriculum-Based Assessment. Curriculum-based assessment (sometimes called curriculum-based evaluation) is informal assessment directly related to classroom curriculum. Salvia and Hughes (1990) effectively state the rationale for curriculum-based assessment: "The fundamental problem with using published tests is the . . . content. If the content of a test—even content prepared by experts—does not match the content that is taught, the test is useless for evaluating what a student has learned from school instruction" (p. 8). The eight steps in the Salvia and Hughes curriculum-based assessment model are (a) specify reasons for assessment, (b) analyze curric-

ulum, (c) formulate behavioral objectives, (d) develop appropriate assessment procedures, (e) collect data, (f) summarize data, (g) display data, and (h) intrepret data and make decisions. As conceptualized by Salvia and Hughes, the steps in this model are both interactive and dynamic. That is, decisions at any one step may affect decisions at other steps, and decisions may be modified as instruction and continuing assessment take place.

In its most simplified form, curriculum-based assessment might include the following steps:

1. List skills in targeted material, making certain that all essential skills are listed.
2. Arrange skills in logical order.
3. Develop a written objective for each skill listed.
4. Develop items and prepare materials to test for each objective.
5. Give the test as a pretest, before teaching the targeted material.
6. Evaluate pretest results. Determine which students have already mastered which skills and whether teaching of prerequisite skills is required. (The question of prerequisite skills may have to be further investigated before proceeding.)
7. Initiate instruction, based on information obtained in step 6.
8. After completion of instruction, readminister the test to determine which students have mastered which skills.
9. Modify instruction as indicated, and repeat the procedure.

Anecdotal Records. Anecdotal records are another form of informal assessment for identifying problems. Anecdotal records help teachers clarify the events leading to behavioral or learning problems by providing factual descriptions of events. A factual record should describe (a) the antecedent (the event that occurred immediately before the behavior), (b) the behavior (quoting the student and using action verbs), and (c) the consequences of the behavior. In describing behavior, teachers should attempt to use quantitative statements. It may not be sufficient to state, "He is always out of his seat" or "He never turns in his assignments." Preferred statements are "During a 50-minute period, he was out of his seat four times" or "During the last 3 weeks he turned in only two of the nine assignments."

Anecdotal records are commonly used to describe disruptive student behavior and can help teachers analyze more accurately what is actually happening. Often, teachers develop anecdotal records before discussing a problem with a resource person or school counselor.

Interviews. A third informal assessment technique is the interview, which is a useful means for learning a student's perspective. The steps in interviewing are (a) establish rapport by being sincere and honest and showing interest; (b) present reasons for the interview; (c) formulate open-ended questions, avoiding questions calling for only a *yes* or *no* response; (d) listen to the student in an accepting environment to gain information and insight into the problem, rather than offer suggestions or point out what you think is wrong; and (e) terminate the interview with a goal or a plan of action. Preferably, the plan should be established by the student with the teacher's input, including an agreed time when the student and teacher can meet again to modify or evaluate the plan.

Organization

Teachers teach and students learn within a framework of schedules, student groupings, and various physical environments. Students learn through interactions with teachers, other students, and instructional materials. Educators must plan and manage these variables to provide the best possible learning situations for students with special needs.

Planning for any student must relate to the special needs of that student, but certain factors in the total instructional environment are likely to require adaptation, or at least special planning. When teachers plan and organize well, students are more secure in the school environment, and teachers are more satisfied with their own efforts. The educational environment is a major determinant in how effectively a student learns.

Scheduling. A concern of many regular classroom teachers is scheduling resource services. Students with disabilities may be required to leave regular classrooms one or more times each day to receive assistance from resource or itinerant teachers, speech or language specialists, or physical or occupational therapists. The most common problems identified by regular classroom teachers are generally related to (a) the optimum time for resource services, (b) completion of work missed while the student was in the resource program, (c) the leaving and returning of students on time, (d) the transition to and from the resource room, and (e) lack of continuity in programming.

A student who attends a resource room obviously misses some of the activities in the regular classroom. There is generally no single best time for the student to be absent, but the advantage of receiving intensive instruction or therapy for a short time outweighs the need for continuous regular classroom attendance. Therefore, the issue involves which activity should be missed. It is tempting to send a student to the resource room during noncore activities, such as art, music, or physical education. However, such activities may be the activities in which the student finds his or her greatest success. Often, a student is sent to the resource room during practice or seatwork periods, but this time may be crucial to the student's success in the regular classroom.

The relative advantages and disadvantages of missing particular regular classroom activities must be carefully weighed, and each student's needs must be considered. Of course, the scheduling needs of resource personnel must also be considered. Often, the decision of the optimum time to be absent from the regular classroom is "the least of several evils." Close communication and cooperative planning between resource personnel and the regular teacher can help alleviate this problem.

The question of whether a student should be expected to complete regular assignments made while the student was attending resource services relates to the question of the time when the student is absent. Expecting completion of a missed assignment may place an unnecessary burden on a student who already has difficulty completing assignments. This problem should also be discussed with the resource teacher.

Resource teachers and the regular classroom teachers must respect each other's schedules. Once a schedule has been agreed to by a regular teacher and resource personnel, every effort must be made to send and return the student on time. Failure to follow the schedule can be extremely frustrating to the teachers and the student and can adversely affect the quality of a student's instruction. This matter may seem trivial, but 10 minutes of tardiness multiplied by 180 school days can amount to a considerable problem for both a student and the teachers.

The movements of a student to and from a resource room should be closely supervised. Some students abuse this "free time" unless teachers take specific efforts to ensure that the students take only a minimum of time in moving between rooms. It is unreasonable for either teacher to accompany a student; thus, the student must assume this responsibility. A system of reinforcement should be used to encourage the student to be on time.

The final area of concern involves a possible discontinuity between the regular and special programs and possible disagreement about the responsibility of the resource teacher. Regular teachers may believe that resource teachers should provide tutorial help for subjects with which the student is having difficulty in their class. This may be part of the assignment, but for the most part, resource teachers must devote time to interventions directed at remediation or compensatory-skill development. This potential problem may be circumvented by close communication between the resource teacher and regular classroom teacher and an understanding of the educational objectives.

Continuity can also be accomplished by the regular classroom teacher's sending seatwork with a student to be completed during free times; however, this work must be carefully supervised so that the student does not become caught between the two teachers and their expectations. Some teachers use help notes to communicate areas requiring assistance and thereby facilitate cooperation. Help notes may be placed in the teacher's mailbox or carried by the students. Communication is essential to assure cooperation.

Classroom Arrangement. This text emphasizes that students learn in different ways and at differing rates. Students also learn more or less effectively in different settings—some students do well in tradition-ally arranged classrooms (rows of desks with the teacher at the front of the room), whereas others learn more readily in infor-mal classrooms. Classroom arrangements are based on many variables, including the age or grade level of the students, the sub-ject or subjects being taught, and philoso-phy and approach of the teacher to instruc-tion.

Traditional arrangement, which is not used as frequently now as it was in years past, has been termed a teacher-centered environment. It emphasizes certain teacher behaviors (such as lecturing, directing, questioning, authoritative control, and vi-sual supervision of students) and certain student behaviors (such as listening and note taking). It also implies that all stu-dents learn the same way.

Informal classroom arrangement (Figure 3–4) provides a more student-centered en-vironment. Such arrangement uses a variety of work areas and learning centers, a direct instruction area, a manipulative work area, and individual study carrels. Yet, it still al-lows for occasional large-group instruction. Informal arrangement allows students to move to several areas in the classroom freely within the class structure and to

FIGURE 3–4
Informal classroom arrangement

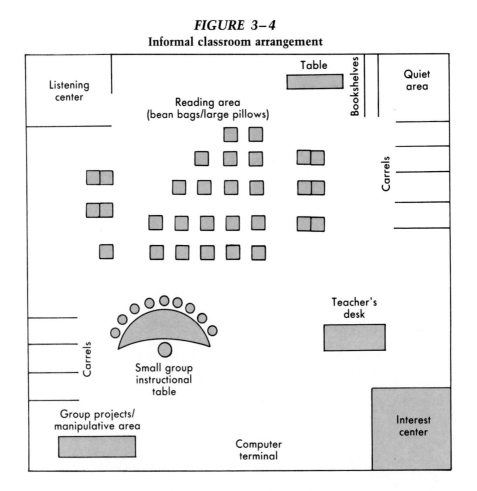

work independently or as a group. A student who is easily distracted may also use a study carrel until he or she is able to work more effectively in a large group.

There may be considerable noise, movement, and general activity in an informally structured classroom, and teachers must establish clear expectations and rules governing the use of each area. The teacher should be cautious when using an informal structure, because some students with learning or behavior problems may need a structured learning environment. Some teachers have experienced considerable success by introducing only one or two special areas to a classroom at a time, adding more centers as the students demonstrate ability to complete their assigned tasks and fulfill their responsibilities.

No one classroom organization is appropriate for all teachers and classes. The best arrangements effectively unite the teacher and learner characteristics with the objectives of the curriculum.

Learning Centers. Although there is considerable misunderstanding of the purpose and instructional usefulness of learning centers, they do provide alternatives to traditional instruction and can be organized to meet individual needs.

Although it is not our purpose to advocate learning centers for all teachers, we think that many teachers do not fully understand how learning centers can enhance teaching effectiveness and ultimately increase the performance of students. To fully understand the potential of learning centers, teachers should first identify how they view themselves. If they view themselves as disseminators of information, then they will have considerable difficulty with learning centers. If, however, teachers view themselves as orchestrators or facilitators, who serve as guides and direct learning,

then they will readily understand the advantage of instructional alternatives such as learning centers.

Learning centers may be used for skill development, independent study, reinforcement, practice, follow-up of teacher-introduced concepts, enrichment, or substitute assignments. Following are significant advantages of learning centers:

1. They provide alternatives to pencil-and-paper seatwork.
2. They allow students to work at their own rate.
3. They provide opportunities to learn through various modes.
4. They can provide instruction in a student's preferred learning style.
5. They allow teachers time to work with other students.
6. They help develop responsibility and self-discipline through accomplishment and success.
7. They provide immediate self-evaluation.

One of the most common problems associated with learning centers is the time to develop them. Initially, development takes extra time and effort, but once developed, learning centers may be modified easily and used in subsequent years (or at the secondary level with more than one section of the same course). Some teachers seek assistance from students in setting up special interest centers, and in some instances, students with high ability help teachers develop them. Other teachers have had considerable success with jointly establishing and sharing centers with teachers in the same grade or content area.

There are essentially four types of learning centers:

1. *Skills centers.* A skills center can include practice sheets, drill cards in

mathematics, sentence completion activities, and dictionary skills.

2. *Discovery and enrichment centers.* Such a center might include science activities, brainteasers, or advanced mathematics activities.

3. *Listening centers.* Such a center may provide lessons on tape, supplemental instruction in another mode, or leisure listening.

4. *Creativity centers.* Such a center may include art, music, crafts, mathematics, or language arts activities.

A learning center has several essential components, varying, of course, depending on the objectives and topics, the age of the students, and the teacher. Each learning center should have clearly stated objectives to structure the activities. Understandable directions should specify what should be done, where and which materials should be used, and how the work is to be evaluated. Samples of student work should be provided to give additional direction and serve as motivators. If media are to be used, instruction in their use should be provided.

The teacher should be certain to introduce each center in such a way that students fully understand the directions, use of the media, the available activities, the evaluation procedures, and the return of materials. A schedule should be established to inform students when they may use the center and how many may use it at one time. There must also be a record keeping procedure so that the teacher knows who uses the center, for what purpose, and for how long. If the teacher carefully demonstrates use of the center and periodically monitors the use, many problems may be avoided.

Some individuals believe that learning centers lack sufficient structure and may not provide enough teacher involvement to be advantageous for students with learning problems. We believe that if carefully planned and designed, learning centers can be effective, allowing students the freedom to work at their own pace and skill level while learning through a variety of sensory modalities. Although there are some disadvantages, we believe that the advantages far outweigh the disadvantages.

Grouping. Students with special needs are more likely to require small-group instruction in basic academic subjects than are other students. Although most teachers, particularly in elementary school, are familiar with grouping procedures, several general practices should be considered. The following discussion briefly considers grouping by instructional level and specific skills. It also considers heterogeneous grouping.

Grouping should always be considered temporary. Because student learning rates are not static, built-in provisions should allow students to move to higher or lower groups as their needs dictate. The practice of assigning students to a group at the beginning of the school year and leaving them there for the duration of the year can impose serious educational limitations.

Grouping students by instructional level is probably the most common method. It is based on the desire to reduce the range of abilities by dividing a class according to learning ability, rate, and style. Students in a group are generally expected to progress through learning materials at about the same rate. Although grouping does reduce the number of students being taught at one time, it does not accommodate differing skill needs that must be addressed. An alternative to instructional-level grouping is skill-specific grouping.

Skill-specific grouping challenges teachers because it takes longer to organize initially, but once it is organized it more directly addresses individual student needs. In a skill-specific arrangement, students are grouped on the basis of short-term objectives established after initial testing to determine the skills needed. Group size varies depending on how many students need instruction in a specific skill. As students move from initial acquisition of a skill to mastery of it, they move on to a different group. This arrangement also allows students to interact with different peers throughout the year. Thus, students may avoid the stigma of continued placement in a low group.

With the skill-specific system, teachers develop a master list or chart of target skills. Such a list may also originate from basal material or a commercial publisher. Teachers should analyze the tasks involved with a specific skill and then provide instruction in tasks that help the student meet the designated objective. A chart or file system that cross-references students and specific skills to be developed helps a teacher know precisely what to teach next and which students to place in a particular skill group.

Instructional-level and skill-specific groupings emphasize placing students with similar abilities and skills together to form homogeneous groups. Heterogeneous grouping is another grouping procedure. It is used in certain activities, such as checking comprehension, completing social studies projects, or reviewing math. With heterogeneous grouping, students with varying abilities and skill levels are placed in the same group. Teachers may use this grouping to ask specific questions, at various levels of comprehension, about a subject the group has studied. The teacher may ask a student with low ability, "What was the main character's name?" and a student with high ability, "What would be another title for

this story?" or "If you were the author, how would you have written the story?" Although the teacher should be careful not to confuse a student with low ability by presenting information that interferes with learning a new concept, heterogeneous grouping is an excellent way for students with learning problems to be a part of a different group.

Johnson and Johnson (1975) describe in detail the relative advantages of cooperative learning experiences and mixed-grouping procedures. Carefully planned grouping procedures can maximize the teacher's effectiveness and provide specific instructional assistance to students. Each teacher must develop a system to promote cooperative learning and enhance student performance.

Peer Systems: Buddies, Advocates, and Tutors. Johnson-Dorn, Stremel-Campbell, and Toews (1984) advocate the use of peer systems in their report on integration of children and youth with severe disabilities. Similar systems have also been found to be effective with students who have mild or moderate disabilities. In peer systems, regular education students work with students who have disabilities to assist in academic learning, social learning, the building of friendships, or understanding on the part of nondisabled students. Johnson-Dorn et al. define peer buddy systems as those in which "a peer buddy is assigned to 'accompany' the student with handicaps during integrated activities" (p. 31). This role is not conceptualized as direct tutoring, though it may involve modeling or general assistance with social behaviors.

The peer advocate system is one in which "a peer watches out for or offers support to a student with handicaps" (Johnson-Dorn et al., 1984, p. 32). This system includes such functions as accompanying a student with a disability on a shopping trip, serving as a source of information to the teacher on the conduct of the student (and others) in activities that the teacher cannot directly observe, or speaking to other students on behalf of the student with the disability. This advocacy role is more likely to be appropriate in middle school or high school, and it relates primarily to severe disabilities.

Peer tutors are students who interact with other students for some specific learning objective. Peer tutoring is not a new concept. It has been widely used with considerable success. In one-room schoolhouses, in which one teacher provided multigrade instruction, older or more able students often taught younger or less able students in certain subjects for specific parts of the school day. The term *peer tutoring* is used here to refer to both cross-age tutoring, in which older students provide instruction to younger children, and same-age tutoring.

Peer tutoring has many benefits for both students with special learning problems and students who are achieving adequately. Often, regular classroom teachers say that they do not have sufficient time to provide the instructional assistance needed to help students with disabilities without neglecting other students in their classroom. In such cases, peer tutoring can help, if used properly.

Students with disabilities may also be peer tutors for younger children. In several programs, students with low skills have instructed younger children (Delquadri, Greenwood, Whorton, Carta, & Hall, 1986). Although there may be considerable advantage to using students with disabilities as tutors—and we hope that teachers consider this method—the following discussion involves students with disabilities as recipients of peer tutoring.

Peer tutoring is most effective when a

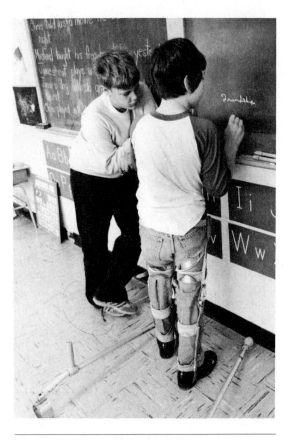

Peer tutoring can be highly effective.

teacher introduces the new concepts to be learned and a tutor provides the necessary review. The teacher should maintain full responsibility for the program and monitor it by periodically observing sessions. Tutors must also report the performance of learners on a routine basis. Probably, the most common form of peer tutoring occurs when the teacher spontaneously asks one student to help another, but such assistance may or may not be helpful. Benefits are likely to result from a carefully planned program with (a) precise instructional objectives, (b) careful selection of the tutors, (c) specific tutor training, and (d) careful pairing of the tutor and student tutored.

The selection of tutors depends on the nature of the program, the subject, and the age of the students. According to Ehly and Larsen (1980), teachers can choose any of the following as tutors: (a) all students who volunteer, (b) students who excel in school, (c) well-behaved students who have some academic difficulties, and (d) students who meet the criteria established for the proposed program. Students selected as tutors should have good skills in listening, prompting, modeling, and reinforcing. Above all other criteria, sincerity, genuineness, and commitment are perhaps the most important. The amount and nature of training for a tutor depend on the teacher's time, the materials available, and objectives of the tutoring program.

A teacher inexperienced in the use of peer tutoring may think that a considerable amount of time is required for training before implementation. This is often true, but careful planning usually results in significant benefits. When deciding which students to place in a tutoring program, inexperienced teachers may feel that many students need extra time and instruction. Some students, however, have needs so great that they require special assistance from the teacher, an instructional aide, or special education personnel. A peer tutoring program should not be used as a substitute for a carefully planned program delivered by a competent professional. Students who would not be good candidates to receive peer tutoring include students with severe behavior problems and students who are aware of their academic deficiencies and might openly reject assistance from peers, feeling that such assistance calls further attention to their learning difficulties.

Pairing the tutor with the student to be tutored must be carefully considered. The requirements of the program and the specific objectives influence this decision. The final decision concerning pairing is best made by a teacher who is well acquainted with the students and can predict how well they will cooperate. Of course, pairings are not final and should be changed as needed.

These suggestions are not intended to serve as instructions for establishing a peer tutoring program but as an overview of some of the components. We recommend that new teachers consult the following before beginning a peer tutoring program: Ehly and Larsen (1980); Haisley, Christine, and Andrews (1981); Harris and Aldridge (1983); and Johnson-Dorn, Stremel-Campbell, and Toews (1984).

BUILDING AND MAINTAINING MOTIVATION

Authorities in educational psychology disagree on many topics, but they seem to agree that motivation has considerable influence on learning. Mehring and Colson (1990) discuss three motivation theories and the implications of each. They also outline six factors associated by various authorities or in research with linkage between motivation and academic success. These factors are (a) anxiety, (b) self-concept, (c) teacher expectations, (d) the learning process, (e) the goal structure, and (f) incentives for learning.

Anxiety can have a variety of effects on learning. Highly anxious students often engage in failure-avoiding strategies because they cannot emotionally handle failure. Such efforts then take the place of efforts and attention that might lead to learning. Anxious students may not attend to many academic tasks because they are preoccupied with worry and feelings of inadequacy. They may have unusual difficulty in learning material that is not well organized, and when given a choice, may choose easier tasks (in which success is more certain) to avoid negative evaluations.

A student with low self-concept may avoid learning activities and begin a cycle of self-perpetuated failure. Combs and Avila (1985) indicate that the problems of some students may be caused entirely by lack of good self-concept. Obviously, self-concept may be closely related to anxiety.

Chapter 4 discusses teacher expectations extensively. Such expectations are critical to learning, and they may be especially critical to students with disabilities.

The learning process has many dimensions, but Mehring and Colson mention several factors in the learning process that have considerable effect on motivation: (a) interest (learner curiosity); (b) relevance, or meaningfulness, of the learning task; (c) expectancy of success (does the student feel that task is possible and under his or her control?); and (d) satisfaction. As discussed in Mehring and Colson (1990), goal structure refers to three basic structures: (a) cooperative, (b) competitive, and (c) individualistic. It is important to note, "All three goal structures are effective under certain conditions and are relevant to specific goals and objectives of a lesson" (p. 7).

Incentives for learning certainly affect motivation, and teachers must plan incentives with individual students in mind. Intrinsic interest may be sufficient, but extrinsic rewards are often necessary, particularly when a student has a history of failure. Too many external rewards, however, may undermine or reduce the likelihood of building natural interest in the subject under consideration.

The authors of most basic educational psychology texts provide lists of techniques to promote motivation. Curriculum guides provided by various major public school districts include suggestions based on what educational psychologists have said and the personal experience of consultants. The list in Figure 3–5 is a composite from the above sources, plus the experience of the authors. The most important thing to remember is to regularly consider and plan for motivation-building activities as part of the teaching-learning process.

Preferred Learning Styles

Most teachers would agree that students have individual needs, likes and dislikes, accomplishments and failures, and strengths and weaknesses. Students also have different preferred ways of learning, and although teachers generally agree that students learn in different ways, they do not always attempt to assess and accommodate these differences. Often, students are expected to fit into a pattern of learning that emphasizes learning through reading and listening.

The concept of different learning styles is not new to educators or psychologists; however, in recent years there has been renewed interest in this important area of learning. Dunn and Dunn (1978) define learning styles as "ways of identifying patterns by which individuals conceptualize information from their environment most efficiently" (p. 36). Each student has a learning style that differs from that of his or her peers, and teachers need to be aware of these unique styles. Dunn and Dunn group factors influencing an individual's learning style into four areas: (a) environmental elements, (b) the individual's emotionality, (c) socialized needs, and (d) physical needs.

Environmental elements have different effects on students. Noise is important in terms of a student's ability to tolerate sounds while learning. Some students are able to block out extraneous noises, whereas others need a quiet environment. Lighting may also affect students in differ-

FIGURE 3–5
Planning to enhance motivation

1. Determine what motivates, and then, initiate a lesson by providing a reason to be motivated.

2. Specify exactly what should be accomplished. Establish clear, specific goals in the simplest possible terms.

3. Relate new learnings to past learnings.

4. Be certain that students are at the proper level of readiness for what they are about to undertake.

5. Make every effort to make learning relevant to students. Use familiar materials in examples.

6. Use humor, suspense, and exploration to arouse and maintain curiosity.

7. Do the novel, unusual, or unexpected at times. Be somewhat unpredictable, but not in a manner that is inconsistent with goal achievement.

8. Use praise, both verbal and written. Look for actions or accomplishments to praise.

9. Use a variety of teaching techniques, such as games, simulations, and group projects. Remain alert to the possibility that some techniques may require special adaptations for students with disabilities.

10. Carefully monitor student responses. Be ready and willing to adjust both type and rate of instruction.

11. Set objectives that challenge but do not intimidate.

12. Show respect for both effort and accomplishment.

13. Speak of what you expect students to do or learn in a positive way. Indicate expectation of success.

14. Avoid trick questions or questions that might be interpreted as punishment. Ask questions to find out what students know, not what they do *not* know.

15. Suspend judgment when students respond to questions. Use exploratory questioning and obtain responses from various members of a group.

16. Use positive reinforcement.

17. Maintain your role as teacher (that's your professional responsibility), but whenever possible, also be a friend.

ent ways—some students prefer a brightly lit area, whereas others prefer subdued light. Some students prefer an easy chair when tackling a difficult learning task, whereas others prefer a straight-back chair and desk. Although teachers may not be able to modify all aspects of the environment significantly, they should consider its effects. If a student's difficulty seems to be related to an environmental problem, attempts should be made to adapt or modify conditions as necessary.

Elements in the emotional realm include persistence, motivation, responsibility for learning, and need for structure. Some students need well-defined guidelines and structure, whereas others are more creative and respond better when given considerable freedom in carrying out assignments. Teachers should recognize these elements and make adjustments to accommodate each student's needs.

The sociological dimension involves the ability of a student to learn from or with others. Some students prefer to work alone, but others choose to work in pairs, in small groups, or with an adult. Few prefer to work the same way all of the time. Therefore teachers should consider varying their instructional approaches to fit individual learning styles and preferences.

Elements in the physical dimension include a student's best time of day for active involvement and learning (early birds or night owls), mobility needs (to move or change positions), and preferred perceptual strengths. Students vary considerably in the ways that they learn. Some students learn better by listening to a teacher (auditory learners). Other students prefer to read or see the material (visual learners), and still others learn more readily by touching and interacting with the material (tactile and kinesthetic learners).

Nearly all students learn better when they are actively involved in the instructional process and are using all of their senses. This multisensory learning approach is preferable to a more limited sensory approach such as lecturing. If it is not practical to offer multisensory instruction, it is often advantageous to present new material through a student's strongest perceptual mode while reinforcing through the other senses. By teaching to a student's strength, the teacher can increase the student's attention, success, and achievement, whereas focusing on the student's weakest perceptual mode may have the opposite effect.

Teachers can assess student learning styles by using a questionnaire (see Figure 3–6). The questionnaire may be administered orally in a personal interview with one student at a time or be given to a small group of students. The statements on the questionnaire should be short, direct, and simply stated. Teachers may add other statements to learn the preferred general learning climates of students.

To assess a student's perceptual strengths, the teacher should observe the student's behaviors. Visual learners may close their eyes or look at the ceiling when they try to recall a visual image or picture. Auditory learners may subvocalize or move their lips when they are attempting to memorize information. Tactile or kinesthetic learners may use their fingers to count off items or write in the air with their fingers. Analysis of these behaviors is subjective, of course, and such behaviors may or may not indicate preferred learning style. However, observation at least provides preliminary information on which the teacher may base continued observation and assessment.

Another informal assessment procedure that may provide insight into the perceptual strengths and preferred learning styles

FIGURE 3–6
Questionnaire to assess preferred learning styles

	True	False
Environmental Statements		
1. I like to have it quiet when I'm working.	☐	☐
2. I work best when there is a little noise in the classroom.	☐	☐
3. I prefer rock music in the background when I am studying.	☐	☐
4. Music of any kind makes it difficult for me to work.	☐	☐
5. I can study when people are talking.	☐	☐
6. I prefer bright light when studying.	☐	☐
7. I learn best in the morning.	☐	☐
8. I learn best in the afternoon.	☐	☐
9. I like to study while sitting in a comfortable chair.	☐	☐
Emotional and Social Statements		
1. I prefer to work with the teacher.	☐	☐
2. I learn best when I work alone.	☐	☐
3. I need specific rules and directions about what I should do.	☐	☐
4. I prefer to work in a small group.	☐	☐
5. I prefer to work in a traditional instructional situation.	☐	☐
6. I like to work with one friend.	☐	☐
7. I need a lot of reinforcement to complete a task.	☐	☐
8. I have a lot of difficulty completing assignments.	☐	☐

of students involves presentation of three lists of words and numbers as follows:

1. Tell the students that you will give them a test to determine whether they are visual, auditory, or tactile-kinesthetic learners.
2. Write a list of five to seven words on the blackboard while the students are watching. Use everyday words, such as *toothpaste, soap, salt, comb,* and *milk* (the number of words you should use depends on the age of the students).
3. Allow the students to view the list of words for approximately one minute.
4. Erase the list, and then ask the students to write down the words.
5. Ask for a volunteer to repeat the list of words. Volunteering may be an additional indication of strong visual learners.
6. Ask the students to score their papers.
7. Dictate orally a different list of similar words, such as *automobiles, bicycles, birds, pencil, paper,* and *shoes.* Dictate the list a second time; neither you nor the students should be writing at this time. Then, ask the students to write down the words.
8. Use the same process of correction you did as with the written presentation in steps 5 and 6.
9. Dictate a different list of words of approximately the same length and ask the students to write the words while you are dictating them. When you are

finished dictating, ask the students to copy the list; they may look at their initial lists if they wish. Next, ask them to turn their papers over and re-write the words from memory. Follow the correction procedures used with both earlier lists.

10. Repeat all nine of these steps using a series of numbers, such as 8, 6, 4, 3, and 9, instead of words. Present the numbers visually, auditorily, and tac-tile-kinesthetically.

When this process is completed, ask the students to total their scores of the word and number parts for each of the three tests. Explain to the students that there may be some relationship between their scores on the three types of tests and the ways they learn. Teachers who observe def-inite patterns may want to note these ob-servations for future planning. This infor-mal method is for general assessment of students' preferred learning styles and is not intended to be precise, but an informal assessment such as this may provide in-sight into the reasons that some students perform better in some situations than in others. Dunn and Dunn (1978), Carbo (1983), and R. Dunn (1983) describe more formal assessment procedures.

The characteristics of learning styles ap-ply to gifted students as well as students who have learning problems. A study re-ported by Dunn and Price (1980) indicates, "Gifted elementary students are somewhat different from non-gifted elementary stu-dents on 6 of the 18 learning style vari-ables" (p. 35). Some of the results of this study were not anticipated by the investiga-tors—for example, the fact that such a high percentage of the gifted preferred tactile-kinesthetic to auditory learning. Although the investigation was only preliminary, it

demonstrates that teachers must consider learning styles when planning for gifted stu-dents, just as they do with students who have learning problems. In practice, gifted students seem to be doing very well in school, so teachers are more likely to over-look consideration of learning style. This tendency, of course, is more reason to keep learning styles in mind when dealing with exceptional students.

Teacher Interest and Enthusiasm

Teachers should demonstrate a sincere in-terest and enthusiasm for topics. Nearly all teachers can recall a college professor who was extremely enthusiastic about the con-tent of a course and whose enthusiasm spread to the students. Studies of effective teaching nearly always emphasize instruc-tor's knowledge and enthusiasm among the most important factors influencing student performance.

Success

In any educational program, it is essential that all students meet with some success, particularly students with special learning problems, because they likely have had con-siderable failure. This failure syndrome must be broken through systematic coun-terconditioning efforts by teachers. Careful planning to provide instruction at a level commensurate with the ability of students is of the utmost importance.

Occasionally, a student's failure may re-sult more from instructional methods than from inadequate skills on the part of the student. Therefore, teachers should watch for opportunities to provide success. Suc-cess may be encouraged, for example, by de-creasing the amount of written work re-quired, making certain that language or other assignments are on the appropriate reading level, encouraging group projects, allowing students to choose among a variety of carefully planned activities, using learning contracts, and a myriad of other techniques.

Fernald (1943) worked with students who had experienced considerable academic difficulty and systematically planned positive reconditioning before actually starting a remedial program. She described four conditions to carefully avoid:

1. Avoid calling attention to emotionally loaded situations.
2. Avoid using methods that experience suggests are unlikely to be effective.
3. Avoid conditions that may cause embarrassment.
4. Avoid directing attention to what the student cannot do.

These principles can be applied to almost all remedial situations, and they are particularly important for a student who has failed many times over a period of several years.

In addition to these specific suggestions, teachers should question their teaching methods to increase the likelihood of their students meeting with success. For instance:

1. Do I emphasize and build on the student's strengths rather than weaknesses?
2. Do I ask the student to perform tasks that are clearly too difficult for him or her to perform?
3. Do I systematically plan for small increments of successful performance?
4. Do I permit my students to make mistakes?
5. Do I provide genuine feedback?
6. Do I look for positive rather than negative aspects of a student's work?
7. Do I provide a sufficient amount of assistance and encouragement to students with learning problems?
8. Do I take special opportunities to provide positive reinforcement?
9. Do I structure honest experiences of success for my students?
10. Do I identify areas of the student's interest and capitalize on them?
11. Do I allow low-achieving students to perform tasks given to high-achieving students?

Another dimension of providing success is to encourage students to assume responsibility for succeeding. Often, students who have experienced considerable failure blame external factors for their difficulties. Students must be taught that they have much control over their own success or failure. They must enter into learning activities believing they will be successful. Joint planning between teachers and students can greatly assist students in understanding that they *can* achieve and be successful. Contracting, for example, gives students responsibility for succeeding, and realistically established contracts, with input from the teacher, may give students opportunities to assume responsibility and achieve much-needed success. As students achieve success, they gain confidence and come to view themselves as successful. "Nothing succeeds like success" should be the motto of every teacher.

PRESENTATION ALTERNATIVES

Teachers should systematically consider alternative ways of providing meaningful instruction. The following suggestions are relatively easy to implement and do not require substantial time. They effectively promote teacher enthusiasm while providing an effective instructional environment.

Study Guides

A study guide may provide direction for students with learning problems and should be of some value to all students. A guide can include statements of objectives, assignment requirements, suggested readings or media to be used, and evaluation criteria used in the course. It can provide direction regarding time, resources, and peer teaching opportunities. Learning contracts can be established in combination with a guide. A teacher and a small group of capable students can develop a study guide cooperatively and then share it. Once developed, a study guide may be used in subsequent courses.

Topic Outlines

A topic outline is less formal than a study guide and takes less time to develop, so a topic outline can be considered a condensed study guide. It provides a general flow of course content and may help students organize their lecture notes. Like a study guide, a topic outline can be developed by students.

Technical Vocabularies and Glossaries

Technical vocabularies or glossaries can be tremendous aids for nearly all students. Effectively used, they may eliminate many of the problems resulting from inability to understand the content of a lecture because students do not understand the vocabulary. These aids can be used in peer teaching and tutoring situations. Alternatively, vocabulary information can be tape recorded and made available. A technical vocabulary or glossary may be written, typed, or recorded by students.

Advance Organizers

Advance organizers are easy to develop with a minimum of teacher time. An exam-ple of an advance organizer is an outline of key points or topics to be learned. Another example is presentation of questions to students before presentation or independent study of the material. Advance organizers give direction and structure and tell students what is important.

Summaries of Concepts

A summary is an overview in one or two paragraphs about a topic. It may be provided in advance to clearly establish the importance of the concepts to be studied. Alternately, many teachers assign a section of a chapter or unit of study and ask the students to summarize their findings, sharing this summary in turn with other groups who have similarly prepared summaries. Different summaries may be assigned to individuals who then collectively overview the lesson. Students who have difficulty with detailed reading may be required only to develop a list of key words or concepts.

Media

Tape recordings of portions of a textbook or chapter summaries may be helpful for students who have reading problems. A tape or multimedia presentation may also be developed to overview a course or specific units of study. Naturally, commercially available films and media can also be used. More capable individual students or a group of students may help develop media presentations. School district or building media specialists are often pleased to assist in the development of media presentations.

Special Texts

Although special modified or adapted texts are generally not popular with students, some individuals may profit from their use. An abridged text is one alternative. Another alternative is a distillation of the material in key concepts or a two- to three-page chapter synopsis. The preparation of such abstracts can be excellent training for academically advanced students in a class.

Alternative Responding

Typically, students respond with written reports, oral presentations, and examination answers. Alternatives include tape-recorded responses, drawings, and peer interpretations of examinations and recording of responses.

Modified Lectures

Many teachers have found that suspending a lecture after a specified time encourages independence and responsibility by students. Students may then be assigned group projects related to the topic being studied. After completing the projects, each group may provide a report to the rest of the class.

Computers

Microcomputers are of value as part of the instructional arsenal for all students, including those with disabilities and gifts or talents. The only question remaining is how to use computers effectively with exceptional students. For the most part, computers can and should be used in the same ways and for the same purposes as they are used with other students. However, there are some unique usages, especially for students with disabilities.

In a review of the value of microcomputers, Hagen (1984) notes that computer applications can "bring speech to the nonvocal, telephone use to the deaf, grade II Braille or voice to the blind, and environmental control to the physically handicapped" (p. 1). He continues, saying that microcomputers "can remove the paper and pencil blockage for the learning disabled and improve the quality of life for the mentally handicapped. All of these dramatic uses . . . can be accomplished without

knowing one word of programming" (p. 1). We agree with Hagen's glowing account. Microcomputers are tremendous tools for teachers of exceptional children and youth.

Other computer applications promise much as they become widely available. Reports in the popular press and on television feature modifications that make it possible for quadriplegics to control computers through mouth-held typing sticks or breath-controlled devices sometimes called sip-and-puff switches. An eye-tracking system developed for jet fighter pilots measures the reflection of light from the retina of the eye, which permits a person to execute a command by merely looking at it on the computer screen.

But there is another side to the story of the magic of microcomputers. They are of great value in the uses cited by Hagen, but they are misused when they become substitutes for real teaching. Microcomputers can be of value when used for drill and practice, but because of the nature of some of the existing software, it is possible for a student to give an answer that the teacher would have accepted but that is not accepted by the computer because it is not exactly the answer that the software developer wanted. With some software, especially in areas other than mathematics or spelling, synonyms for a desired answer are simply wrong as viewed by the computer.

In a similar situation, where a teacher might be delighted to reward an answer that is almost correct, a computer cannot do so. This is particularly unfortunate for students with disabilities and may also distress gifted students, whose answer may be more creative or more complex than the software is programmed to recognize.

Unfortunately, especially with some subjects, there has been a rush to provide software quickly to meet the burgeoning demand, and the quality has been questionable. Teachers must, therefore, carefully evaluate all software before putting it to use. What the publisher says it will do is not enough. Though it may do most of what it is supposed to do, it may also have side effects. These words of caution are not intended to indicate that microcomputers should not be used with exceptional students. We think they *should* be used, but they must be used with care and caution.

Materials must be carefully evaluated. They may be of particular value in relieving teachers of drill and practice yet providing high-level motivation to students. They may be of almost miraculous value in some applications with students who are hearing and visually impaired. They may also have unique applications for students with learning disabilities.

There has been considerable emphasis on becoming computer literate, that is, learning to use computers with some degree of skill. Unfortunately, however, there has been too little emphasis on evaluating materials for their effectiveness relative to specific educational goals.

In addressing instructional design flaws in computer-assisted instruction (CAI), Vargas (1986) concluded her consideration of this problem as follows: "Computers have the flexibility to teach effectively. They will do so, however, only if CAI programs adopt those features shown to be necessary for learning: a high rate of relevant responding, appropriate stimulus control, immediate feedback, and techniques of successive approximation. Until program developers heed the findings of relevant research in instructional design, the computer revolution in education will remain just one more bright technological future waiting to begin" (p. 744).

One of the major challenges for those who use computers in instructional settings is tapping more of the broad potential. Un-

questionably, computers have powerful motivational value, and this value has been utilized with exceptional students. Computers also are of value in drill and practice applications, just as they are with nondisabled students. Yet, if these are the only applications used with exceptional students, educators are missing important opportunities to use the technology to benefit students. A Council for Exceptional Children publication, *Beyond Drill and Practice: Expanding the Computer Mainstream* (Russell, Corwin, Mokros, & Kapisovsky, 1989), addresses this issue effectively. This handbook targets general learning problems and does not attempt to address computer applications unique to hearing impairment, visual impairment, or physical disabilities. Its emphasis is learner-centered software as contrasted with drill-and-practice software and on materials that can both teach content and provide for improvement in learning strategies. The concern of the authors and teachers who contributed to this handbook was to develop procedures whereby the interactive nature of computers could help students become more effective, active learners. The authors suggest that this may be accomplished through use of simulations, interactive games and tutorials, problem-solving software, and word processor programs or graphics packages.

Russell et al. also say that learner-centered software is characterized by four major features: (a) it offers students "choices in selecting the goal of an activity, the strategies to reach the goal, or both" (p. 4); (b) it "provides feedback that is informational rather than judgmental" (p. 4); (c) it "allows, emphasizes, or encourages prediction and successive approximation" (p. 5); and (d) it "encourages learning within a meaningful context for students, building on students' intrinsic motivation" (p. 6). The authors suggest several reasons for using learner-centered software, but one of the more interesting is, "We need to create opportunities to be surprised by what our special education students can do, and they need opportunities to surprise themselves" (p. 7).

These concepts undoubtedly represent the best in what may be expected from use of computers with students who have special needs. They fit present knowledge about learning and helping students develop effective learning strategies. This does not mean that computers should not be used for motivational purposes or drill and practice. It means that educators must continue to expand the use of computers and other available technology to more effectively teach exceptional students.

CLASSROOM CONTROL

McDaniel (1986) compiled a list of 10 principles for teachers who want to "modify their own behaviors in ways that will yield effective group management and control" (pp. 63–67). Briefly consider McDaniel's list (which was meant for all teachers, not only those of exceptional students). This specific list deserves consideration because it is an excellent compilation of principles that McDaniel aptly describes as "traditional and modern, practical and theoretical, pedagogical and psychological" (p. 63):

1. *Focusing.* If you do not have the attention of students, little learning will take place. Trying to teach over the noise of students who are talking to each other or running around the room is essentially useless. To maximize learning, focus the attention of the students on the learning activities.
2. *Direct instruction.* Tell the students what to do, how to do it, and when it should be done. To *keep* students on task, consider topic interest, relevance, and individual needs.
3. *Monitoring.* Monitoring means regular, planned checking to see what students are doing and whether they need assistance or encouragement. It is student accountability, and as students learn they are accountable, classroom control is more easily achieved.
4. *Modeling.* McDaniel emphasizes modeling with respect to using a soft, low-pitched voice, and suggests that soft reprimands (for example) keep a problem private and discourage loud denials or protests. This point is particularly important with students who are frustrated or those with behavior disorders, who have low tolerance for criticism.
5. *Cueing.* As discussed by McDaniel, cues are nonverbal reminders of rules or expectations. Cues may involve facial expressions, raising one's hand, pointing, or clearing one's throat. Some cueing is done automatically, without deliberate planning. Other cueing must be learned, and students must learn what cues mean. It is possible that students with learning disabilities or below-average intelligence will have more difficulty with cues than the rest of a class, and some direct instruction regarding the meaning of specific nonverbal reminders may be required.
6. *Environmental control.* Grouping, scheduling, organization of classroom furniture, and noise control are examples of environmental control.
7. *Low-profile intervention.* This involves intervening to prevent trouble, catching off-task behavior before it becomes a serious problem, and other, less-direct kinds of intervention. This principle overlaps, and is consistent with, principles 3–5.
8. *Assertive discipline.* Chapter 11 discusses this principle in some detail.
9. *I-messages.* McDaniel points out that there are at least two different types of

I-messages. For the assertive-discipline advocate, it is a matter of indicating that "I want you to_____ " or some such absolutely clear message regarding your expectation. For the humanistic-discipline advocate, the *I*-message principle suggests that you communicate how the student's behavior affects you. It is a matter of communication of feelings. The *I*-message principle requires teachers to communicate clearly and consistently.

10. *Positive reinforcement.* This principle is much discussed in the popular press and is applicable in various realms of life. See chapter 11 for further discussion.

McDaniel's 10 principles provide a starting point for the development of better classroom discipline (control) and are valuable as applied to teaching exceptional students. Various aspects of these principles are woven into the fabric of much of the remainder of this text.

Morsink, Soar, Soar, and Thomas (1986) indicate that "few studies have been made with handicapped students from which inferences about teacher effectiveness can be drawn" (p. 34). However, they note two: (a) the importance of direct instruction and (b) contingent praise for appropriate social behavior. Until the compilation of more definitive research in this area, it would seem wise to use the aspects of effective instruction that seem to apply to most other students and be guided by continuing observation and common sense.

Student-Centered Problems

Throughout, this text emphasizes that many factors contribute to poor student performance in school. Among the more common are educational materials, the environment, the teacher, and the peer group.

At times, however, the primary problem involves the student. This section identifies several student-centered problems that interfere with performance. Among the more common problems are limited attention to tasks, negative school attitudes, minimal reading ability, poor comprehension, slow learning ability, poor spelling, poor written expressive ability, high rate of absenteeism, withdrawn or passive behavior, unusually high activity level, and failure orientation. Although these characteristics apply to students, we believe that teachers can greatly reduce the effects of these behaviors and problems by offering specific alternatives to students who have these difficulties. The following suggestions are viable alternatives.

Limited Attention to Academic Tasks. Many students have a relatively short attention span, appear to be disinterested, demonstrate poor organizational ability, and fail to see the relevance of subjects. These characteristics may be related to a variety of causes, but the following teaching techniques may be of value:

1. Show the relevance of the subject to the student's life.
2. Teach the student the following listening formula:
   a. Focus your attention on the speaker.
   b. Ask yourself what you should be learning from the speaker.
   c. Listen carefully and attempt to relate what the speaker is saying to what you already know about the topic.
   d. Review in a way that works best for you, such as discussion with a classmate or reading.
3. Consider contracting with the student to provide structure and reinforcement.
4. Use outlining to divide tasks into small units.

Does this practice promote positive school attitudes?

5. Give short, sequential assignments, one at a time, as they are completed.
6. Use high-interest materials.
7. Pair the student with a peer who can stay on the task for a longer time.
8. Provide immediate feedback on work completed.
9. Provide systematic rewards, such as free time or special interest projects (reading, listening to tapes, photography).
10. Change activities frequently. Know when to accelerate or decelerate assignments and activities.

Negative School Attitude. A negative attitude may result because a student perceives the subject matter as irrelevant or to disguise an inability to succeed. Often, students who have experienced considerable failure in school attempt to compensate for their failure through apathy or consistent noninvolvement. The following suggestions may help overcome such an attitude:

1. Provide alternative assignments. Relate the alternative assignments to the content of the course while focusing on the interests of the student. For example, if the primary assignment for a unit of study concerning the Civil War is to describe the major battle sites, a possible alternative for a student interested in automobiles or transportation might be to describe how supplies were transported to battle sites. For a student interested in music, an alternative assignment might be to describe the influence of music on the morale of soldiers during the Civil War.
2. Provide for small successes and attainable goals.
3. Teach to the personal interests of students.
4. Incorporate relevant information into instruction.
5. Find areas in which students can experience success and capitalize on them.
6. Look for areas in which students feel

good about themselves, such as music, drama, or athletics, and advocate increased involvement in those areas by contacting the music teacher, coach, or other teacher to generate interest. Follow through by reinforcing the student.

7. Arrange brief conferences with students to listen to their problems and communicate that you care about them.

8. Conduct an open class discussion with various students to identify why they do or do not like school. As other students mention positive aspects, an apathetic student may discover or realize similar interests.

Minimal Reading Ability. Many students have difficulty with reading. The following suggestions may help overcome this difficulty:

1. Minimize tedious reading assignments.
2. Be certain that the students understand the purpose of reading assignments.
3. Divide large assignments into small assignments.
4. Use topical outlines, advanced organizers, and glossaries.
5. Use few timed tests and tightly timed assignments or provide additional time.
6. Tell the students in advance about an interesting part of the reading and ask them to find it.
7. Maintain a chart that shows reading progress.
8. Consider tape-recorded materials and presentations using other media.
9. Provide summaries of key concepts to be read.
10. Consider peer teaching and group projects.

Poor Comprehension. Many students have difficulty comprehending what they read or hear. The following suggestions may help overcome this difficulty:

1. Provide direct instruction in needed areas.
2. Provide a summary before directed reading.
3. Divide assignments and tasks into small parts.
4. Control the number of verbal directions.
5. Alternate activities.
6. Maintain realistic performance expectations.

Slow Learning Ability. Many students learn slowly. The following suggestions may help overcome this difficulty:

1. Introduce a few concepts at a time.
2. Provide review frequently.
3. Provide concrete illustrations or examples whenever possible.
4. Consider peer teaching and tutoring.
5. Present new material in varied contexts.
6. Teach to student strengths.
7. Consider multisensory instruction.
8. Simplify explanations, materials, and techniques.
9. Chart the progress of students or have the students chart their own progress.
10. Establish realistic short-range goals.
11. Consider task analysis as an approach to instruction.
12. Try not to underestimate a student's capacity to learn. Watch your expectations.
13. Assess a student's work habits and teach study skills.
14. Call attention to work that is well done.

Poor Spelling. Many students have poor spelling ability. The following suggestions may help overcome this difficulty:

1. Establish realistic goals.
2. Have the students chart their own progress in spelling.

3. Have the students keep a record or note-book of errors.
4. Encourage the use of a dictionary.
5. Emphasize whole word or visual aspects of spelling words.
6. Relate spelling as much as possible to each student's personal interests.
7. Contract with students for the mastery of common words.

Poor Written Expression. Many students have difficulty expressing themselves in writing. The following suggestions may help overcome this difficulty:

1. Attempt to change a student's attitude by providing experiences that lead to success in writing.
2. Initially encourage a student's productivity—not structure, spelling, grammar, punctuation, or capitalization.
3. Provide free-writing opportunities in which students select their own topics. Ask them to write as much as they can for 10 minutes, encouraging them *not* to stop or correct.
4. Consider nonverbal and dramatic activities before writing. Discuss these activities before the students write about them.
5. Provide a wide range of interesting writing topics, such as firsthand experiences, unusual pictures, films, or music.
6. Encourage each student to keep a personal diary or journal.
7. Provide opportunities for the students to record their ideas on a tape and to hear the tape played back before they begin to write.
8. Have the students write captions for cartoons related to something of interest.

High Rate of Absenteeism. For various reasons, many students miss school frequently. The following suggestions may help overcome this difficulty:

1. Be willing to negotiate makeup work.
2. Reinforce good attendance with appropriate rewards.
3. When a student returns after an absence, attempt to involve him or her immediately in class activities.
4. Meet with students and discuss with them the reasons for their high rate of absenteeism.
5. Contact parents and attempt to work closely with them.
6. Make classroom activities interesting and relevant.

Withdrawn or Passive Behavior. For various reasons, many students refuse to take an active part in class. The following suggestions may help overcome this difficulty:

1. Provide opportunities for self-expression through drama or role playing that involves aggressive or assertive roles.
2. Structure group participation to emphasize the strengths of withdrawn or passive students.
3. Reward participation in group activities or projects.
4. Try to become aware of the students' interests and develop conversations and projects around these interests.
5. Put the students in charge of special projects, such as preparing lab materials, taking roll, and handing out and collecting materials.

Unusually High Activity Level. Unusually active students may have difficulty in a classroom environment. The following suggestions may help overcome this difficulty:

1. Discuss with the student the release of tension and restlessness and agree on appropriate outlets.
2. Allow the student to move around, sharpen a pencil, or get a drink when necessary.

3. Send the student on errands.
4. Establish short-term goals and shorten assignments.
5. Provide a change of activity to help focus the student's attention.
6. Reward accomplishments frequently and as soon as possible.
7. Build expectations gradually.
8. Be aware of tension as it is building and provide assistance or a change of pace.
9. Do not accept destructive actions.

Failure Orientation. Some students are so accustomed to failure that they expect it. The following suggestions may help overcome this difficulty:

1. Discuss with the student what he or she needs to do to function well in the classroom.
2. Work out a success plan to help the student cope with problems.
3. Be committed to continue with or change plans, but not to give up.
4. Try to accept and understand the student's feelings without being overly judgmental.
5. Reinforce small successes.
6. Help the student achieve self-discipline and self-control.
7. Deal with immediate problems and mutually work out short-range plans.
8. Formulate realistic expectations.
9. Assist the student in coping with failure.

Managing Inappropriate Behavior

An often verbalized concern about teaching students with special needs is managing inappropriate behavior. Some teachers appear to have few problems in this arena, but others seem to have many. Kameenui and Simmons (1990) believe that teachers must not interpret the various individual acts or elements of a student's behavior as indepen-

dent, isolated, or neutral events. They emphasize that teachers must interpret behavior in relation to the context in which it occurs. They agree that teachers must maintain order to teach effectively but suggest that teachers think of all behavior as providing potentially valuable information. A student's behavior can be viewed as communication; the question is whether the teacher is able to interpret what the student is saying.

Consistent with this point of view, Kameenui and Simmons (1990) suggest five assumptions designed to provide teachers with a "foundation for managing children within the broader context of instruction" (p. 471):

1. A child's inappropriate behavior is not random or evil.
2. Inappropriate behaviors are learned and predictable.
3. A learner's inappropriate behavior is the learner's best effort to be intelligent.
4. There is no place for ridicule or humiliation of children in the process of managing behaviors.
5. A teacher's mere presence influences how children behave.

Teachers must work to attain and maintain order and structure in their classrooms. They must manage student behavior so as to maximize student learning.

Consistency

When teachers are asked what factors most contribute to successful classroom learning, they tend to mention such qualities as teacher's open and honest communication, knowledge of subject matter, sincere interest in and caring about young people, enthusiasm, and consistency. The quality most frequently mentioned is consistency. Clear expectations for the students, care-

fully planned classroom rules and procedures, and natural consequences are closely
related to consistency. Unquestionably, the
teacher is the most critical influence on
classroom atmosphere, and the degree of
consistency in a classroom depends on the
teacher. When the teacher establishes certain expectations for performance and behavior, both the students and the teacher
must adhere to them. Posting these expectations or writing them on the chalkboard
can provide continuity. The teacher should
also allow students to discuss and possibly
modify these expectations so that they may
feel some ownership, but when the expectations are finally established, they must be
followed by everyone.

MONITORING AND RECORDING STUDENT PERFORMANCE

At times, recording student performance
may be considered informal assessment.
Whatever it is considered, monitoring and
recording are essential to modifications in
educational procedures and approaches. Unfortunately, too often, the monitoring and
recording of achievement or other progress
culminates in little more than a letter grade
or a number recorded in a grade book.
Teachers may be so involved with instruction that the progress of students is only ca-
sually or subjectively assessed. A monitoring system can provide important
information about general performance and
skill development and can provide direction
for program modification.

The performance of students can be recorded in many ways, including anecdotal
records, grades, numerical values, charts,
and graphs. Often, teachers think they do
not have time enough to use precise measurement systems themselves. However,
they may use several other approaches,

such as the help of volunteers, parents,
aides, older students in another grade (such
as Future Teachers of America); peers; or
the students themselves. Student self-monitoring can provide considerable reinforcement, meaning, and purpose to learning activities.

Figure 3–7 is an example of a recording
system teachers can use. Without such a
chart, the teacher might not be fully aware
of the value of a new approach to instruction and practice. In this instance, the chart
provided feedback that assisted the teacher
in evaluating a new approach. (It should be
noted that a new approach might also result
in *more* errors, and it would be just as important to learn this, too.)

Measurement and charting procedures
are particularly helpful for students with
behavior problems. For detailed information
about precise charting procedures, see Alberto and Troutman (1990), Walker and
Shea (1991), or Wallace and Kauffman
(1986).

Grading Alternatives

Regular classroom teachers are faced with
the difficult task of fairly evaluating the
progress of all students in their classes.
Teachers are often concerned about
whether they should alter their established
grading practices for students with special
needs. We believe that if a student with disabilities is appropriately placed and instruction is provided at a level commensurate
with the student's ability, it is not necessary to significantly alter the usual grading
practices. Certain alternatives, however,
may be appropriate for all students.

Cumulative Point System. All assignments
are given a predetermined number of
points, and students are offered several options for earning the points that determine

FIGURE 3–7
Student-performance recording system

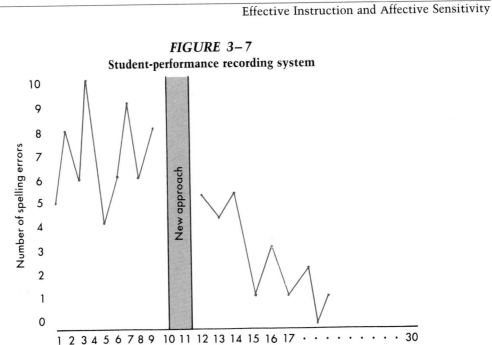

the final grade. This system gives the students the responsibility to do as many assignments as they choose. Some optional assignments may be modified to give a student with special learning problems additional opportunity to succeed.

Contracted Alternatives. Students select the grade they want to earn and negotiate the nature of the assignments and the expected quality of the work. This approach gives students the opportunity to select assignments with teacher guidance and generally encourages greater commitment. A student with learning problems can be given reinforcement at structured intervals to help ensure success.

Alternative Assignments. Giving credit for extra or alternative work related to course objectives but completed in a different format is often helpful for students with spe-

cial needs. This approach gives a student with learning problems options for completing course requirements in manners appropriate to his or her needs.

Other Alternatives. Several other alternatives that relate to the administration of examinations should be given serious consideration.

1. When scoring a student paper, be careful not to limit yourself to negative aspects. Attempt to point out something the student did well.
2. Consider providing prompts to students who do not understand an examination. With prompts, you are not giving answers, but merely rephrasing questions to help students better understand.
3. Accept that students make errors and provide feedback about what they did in-

correctly. Use a test as a teaching tool, not as punishment.

4. Consider giving a free grade. At the beginning of the term record an A in every student's folder or your grade book. This procedure may have a positive effect for a student who has never received an A. It serves as a strong motivational tool, and a student may work diligently to maintain higher grades.

5. Consider giving a test more than once if you really want to know what students do or do not know and how much they have learned.

6. Consider an advance-warning system. When 3 or 4 weeks remain in the term, meet with students and tell them what their final grades will be. If a grade is low, give the student several alternatives to earn a higher grade.

7. Consider joint planning with students for the relative value of course assignments. A student may want, for example, a special project to determine half of a term grade and examinations and class participation to determine the other half.

8. Allow sufficient time for teacher-student discussions of evaluation alternatives and self-evaluation by students.

Teachers should be willing to evaluate the purposes underlying their grading procedures. Grading should not be merely entering grades in a record book. It should be a teaching tool to assist students in achieving goals and objectives.

Mastery Learning/Mastery Teaching

Mastery learning was apparently first suggested by Benjamin Bloom and discussed in a text on mastery learning in 1971 (B. S. Bloom, in J. H. Block). The concept has been expanded, modified, and applied by a number of authors, including Madeline Hunter (1982) and others who have worked with Dr. Hunter. More recently, it has been recommended as a potentially valuable approach for use with students with disabilities (Cicchelli & Ashby-Davis, 1986; Stainback, Stainback, & Forest, 1989; Wood, 1984, 1989).

According to Wood (1989), "Mastery learning methods require mastery at the end of a particular unit of instruction, whereas nonmastery methods allow students to move into a subsequent unit of instruction regardless of their performance at the end of the preceding unit" (p. 156). Cicchelli and Ashby-Davis (1986) view mastery learning as highly Skinnerian (behaviorist) "in that it breaks down a complex behavior into a chain of component behaviors and ensures student mastery of each link in the chain" (p 155). Salvia and Hughes (1990) indicate that there are two different paradigms of instruction, equal opportunity to learn and mastery learning. They say, "In equal opportunity to learn paradigms, all students are given equal exposure to material, and levels of mastery are allowed to vary" (p. 16). In contrast, "in mastery learning all students are expected to learn the same objectives to the same levels of proficiency, and the time and procedures required to attain mastery are allowed to vary" (p. 16).

Stainback, Stainback, and Forest (1989) indicate that mastery learning strategies may also be called outcome-based educational strategies. This is appropriate terminology if a student truly masters the material before moving on. Stainback et al. suggest five steps to mastery learning:

1. Define objectives for each student (different students in a group may have different objectives, which is consistent with the concept of IEPs).

2. Teach the skill or concept in each objective by whatever teaching strategy is most appropriate.
3. Evaluate mastery of the targeted skill or concept through use of a criterion-referenced test.
4. Provide additional instruction as required for each student who has not met his or her individual objective.
5. Retest as required to assure mastery.

Bloom (1971) originally suggested a similar process. Bloom referred to feedback and corrective procedures, and since that time, many instructional systems have been derived from this concept.

Cummings (1980) provides valuable guidelines for mastery teaching in her book *Teaching Makes a Difference*, although she does not specifically label her approach mastery teaching. Cummings believes that teachers make instructional decisions in four major areas, which in turn have a profound influence on student achievement:

1. *Objective selection.* Has the level of complexity of the objective been identified, and is it appropriate to the level of difficulty of the learner?
2. *Teaching to the objective.* Have the student and teacher behaviors that will lead to the objective been identified?
3. *Monitoring and adjusting.* Has the student behavior been monitored to determine whether learning has taken place, and are appropriate adjustments being made, based on student responses?
4. *Principles of learning.* Are known principles of learning being utilized (that is, principles relating to motivation, rate and degree of learning, retention of learning, and so on)?

Mastery teaching, or teaching that follows mastery learning concepts and principles,

has much to offer in instruction for students with special needs. It requires planning time, but apparently, it often pays good dividends when implemented.

PUTTING IT ALL TOGETHER

Effective teachers are able to plan for instruction, to build and maintain motivation, and use a variety of presentation alternatives, as appropriate to the student and the nature of the learning task.

They develop a variety of means whereby they can maintain control of the learning environment, without being authoritarian. They discover and use a wide range of both formal and informal procedures to monitor and record student performance. Their effectiveness is the result of an integration of all of these practices. Although we believe that no list of "instructional tips" can assure success, such ideas can be of value as a teacher reviews what he or she has been doing, and plans for tomorrow, next week, and the rest of the school year. Figure 3-8 provides such a list, presenting ideas shared with the authors by successful teachers. We suggest that they may provide a starting point for increased success in the instructional process.

SUMMARY

This chapter included two sets of instructional principles: one relating to instruction and the other relating to classroom control. A wide variety of specific instructional strategies were reviewed, including those related to listening skills, study skills, critical thinking skills, scheduling, classroom arrangement, grouping, and motivation. Sections on the use of special technology and the creative use of computers in instruction of exceptional students provided insight into these important areas.

FIGURE 3-8
Instructional tips from effective teachers

While not all-inclusive, the following checklist provides a starting point for teaching success. The ideas are not ranked, and the groupings might be considered arbitrary.

Teacher Attitude

1. Show that you are interested in students and that they belong in your classroom.
2. Employ active listening: avoid judging, moralizing, or pulling rank.
3. Treat students as individuals, not as subjects to be taught.
4. Maintain an open-door policy before and after school.
5. Be enthusiastic; show a positive attitude.
6. Model empathy and social responsibility.

Building and Maintaining Interest

1. Continually attempt to show relevance to real-life settings and problems.
2. Make learning as active as possible; involve your students.
3. When there is a choice of several different ways to teach a given skill or subject, use the most interesting, attention-holding way.
4. At times (and within limits) be a ham, an entertainer.
5. Encourage students to direct their own learning whenever possible.
6. To the extent practicable, give students a choice of topics and approaches.

Teaching Methodology

1. Attempt to make your classroom psychologically safe.
2. Use objectives that are challenging but obtainable.
3. Use objectives that are adjusted for individual students.
4. Consider peer teaching and small-group methodologies.
5. Make certain students know what they are to do and how to proceed.
6. Make certain students know how well they achieved their goals and objectives.
7. Emphasize the positive in providing feedback to the entire class, small groups, and individuals.
8. Systematically *plan* successful experiences for individual students.
9. Anticipate possible disruptive behavior and have an alternative plan.
10. Change activities as often as possible within the limits of good instructional practice.

Note: We have collected these tips from successful teachers over the years. Each idea has been suggested by many teachers as a factor in their personal success. These ideas do not represent a formula for success—they are just as presented, teaching tips from successful teachers.

Pedagogical practices relating to task analysis, informal assessment, and monitoring and recording student performance (including grading alternatives) were discussed. The goal of each strategy reviewed in this chapter was to provide a meaningful learning environment for students with disabilities. To accomplish this goal, teachers were urged to strive for instructional flexibility.

■ What is the difference between a student with a disability and a disabling situation?

■ How may teachers evaluate their interactions with students?

■ Can you provide several examples of student-materials interaction? How may any potential negative results of such interactions be minimized?

■ What are the major advantages of cooperative learning? What are the disadvantages?

■ How may racial or ethnic minority group membership influence teacher expectations?

■ How may talk in the teachers' lounge influence the behavior and academic progress of students?

■ What are the major influences on the self-perception of students who have disabilities?

CHAPTER 4

FEELINGS, EXPECTATIONS, AND INTERACTIONS

FEDERAL LAW AND RELATED LAW AND REGULA-
tions in the various states require the
least restrictive educational placement
for students with disabilities. For most,
this means placement in regular classrooms. Recognize, however, that physical presence in a regular classroom
does not mean actual integration. For a
student to truly become a part of a
class, there must be acceptance on the
part of the teacher and a majority of
the students in the class. Also recognize that information and teaching
strategies alone do not necessarily lead
to effective instruction. Without positive feelings, informed but optimistic
expectations, and good personal interactions, students with disabilities do
not receive appropriate instruction.
This chapter emphasizes the necessity
of positive interactions with students
who have disabilities. The same principles apply to students who are gifted or
talented. We believe that this is at
least as important as mastery of teaching strategies.

THE IMPORTANCE OF POSITIVE PERSONAL INTERACTIONS

Positive personal interactions are important
to all students, but they are crucial for students who have disabilities. Personal interactions might be considered major hidden
factors in success or lack of success in
school. One of the more effective ways to
illustrate the potential impact of personal
interactions (positive or negative) is
through the use of true anecdotes. Therefore, this chapter begins with the story of a
high school student who was experiencing
difficulties in school and his personal life.
This anecdote illustrates the manner in
which a biology teacher's awareness of the
student's potential role *outside* the classroom made a major difference in the student's life.

A TEACHER WHO REALLY CARED

Mel, a teenage student in a midwestern state,
was in many respects just like any other high-
school student. He had grown up in a small,
rural community of some five hundred people,
where he had enjoyed all the activities of his
peers. He was active in Boy Scouts, he enjoyed
hiking and swimming in the creek and particularly liked competitive athletics. He excelled in
some areas of athletics and might have been
called a standout athlete in his community. He
definitely had promise and was well known and
liked by almost everyone.

As Mel was about to enter high school, there
was a family move to the city, and for the first
time he had to break into a new group, namely,
the boys who were involved in competitive
sports. He tried to become a part of this group
but was not accepted. This nonacceptance was

a new experience and was devastating until he saw that there was another group that would accept him. This accepting group was a group of troublemakers whose like can be found in almost any school or community. To be accepted, all that was necessary was to do one better (or worse) than the next guy. If another member of the group fought someone 6 feet tall, you only needed to fight someone taller. If another member stole something worth $20, you had to steal something worth $30. The rules were clear and simple and acceptance was assured if you played by the rules.

Another sure way to be accepted was to become a thorn in the side of teachers, counselors, and school administrators. Even if part of the group was not enrolled in school, this type of behavior was very visible and highly respected. Mel wanted to be the best and he quickly moved in that direction, finding solid acceptance with his new friends. Drinking and street fighting became a routine part of his life and he was a regular troublemaker in school. Teachers came to know his problem behavior and most concluded that he was a loser. His

records indicated his problems, and through coffee-room talk, even teachers who had not had Mel in their classes knew what to look for. Mel's school attendance became sporadic, and he was suspended at various times, permitting him to spend more time with his out-of-school friends. Mel was on his way down.

At this point in his life, Mel might have been considered "behavior-disordered." The school counselor suggested that he should think about what type of work he could do at age 16; the assumption was that he would quit school after his 16th birthday. But then an outside influence intervened. At about the same time as the possibility of quitting school became more realistic, Mel got to thinking about something he had noticed over the 18 months he had been in high school. As he walked down the halls, he noticed that one teacher (Mr. S.) often had a group of students, primarily boys, gathered around him in the hall outside his classroom door. Mel was curious about what was going on. Mr. S., who taught biology, would sometimes greet Mel as he walked down the hall, and if he was not engaged in conversations with

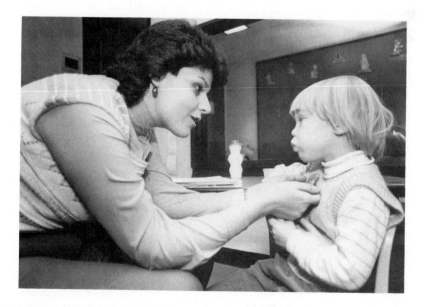

Respect earns respect.

other students, would ask how Mel was doing. Mel was intrigued by this unteacherlike behavior, and would stop and talk if he was alone. He couldn't do this in front of his friends because it might be seen as fraternizing with the enemy.

Before long Mel found ways to spend more time in that group around Mr. S.'s door. At first he was a little uneasy, particularly when Mr. S. looked him straight in the eye in a friendly, nonjudgmental manner, engaging in person-to-person conversation. Mr. S. did not leave his role as a teacher, but somehow came across as a teacher who was also a friend.

Several weeks after deciding that maybe Mr. S. was all right—for a teacher—Mel took something out of another student's locker just as he was entering the wing of the school that included Mr. S.'s room. As he passed Mr. S., he got a look that made him wonder if his behavior had been seen. He avoided Mr. S. for some time, then stopped by when no one else was there.

After a few moments of conversation, Mr. S. said, "I see that you're pretty fast with your hands," at which point Mel thought, "Here it comes, he's just another teacher." But Mr. S. followed quickly with, "Are you fast with your feet, too?" Before Mel could reply, he continued, "Track is going to start in a couple of weeks; are you interested in going out?" Mel wanted to go out, but athletic participation was not acceptable in his group, so he replied that as far as he was concerned, track was for sissies, and left.

In the next few days, Mel saw Mr. S. a number of times, who told him he should think more about going out for track. Then he was given a handout telling when track tryouts were to be held and other such details. Mr. S. didn't give up easily, and somehow Mel found himself in that wing of the school with greater frequency. Just before the day for tryouts, Mr. S. said, "Why don't you come out for three days? If you don't like it, quit, but promise me you'll give it a try for three days." And Mel did try out.

Mel found success in track, which led him to give both football and basketball a serious try. He made the team in all three sports and be-

came a different person. His grades improved in the remainder of high school, and after graduation he entered college, in part on the strength of a track scholarship. While in college, Mel worked part-time, making deliveries for a laundry. One of his stops was a school for students with disabilities. He became interested in these students and changed his major from physical education to special education in his junior year. Mel completed his undergraduate degree and became a teacher of students with disabilities.

Mel continued to teach students with disabilities, later completed a master's degree, and still later a doctorate in special education. Now, 30 years after a teacher took time to encourage a teenage boy to believe in himself, Mel is involved in teaching teachers. He regularly emphasizes the importance of advocacy for students, along with the importance of teaching basic skills and content in the subject areas. He maintains that "good personal interaction is what teaching is all about."[1]

Unfortunately, our experience has been that not all teachers are like Mr. S. in the preceding vignette. Let's take a look at the other side of the coin.

THE POOR SCHOLAR'S SOLILOQUY[2]

No, I'm not very good in school. This is my second year in the seventh grade and I'm bigger and taller than the other kids. They like me al-

---

[1]"Mel," in this vignette, is Dr. Mel Weishahn, one of the authors of this text. He is sorry today for all the problems he caused his parents but will be forever grateful for Mr. S., a teacher who cared. He believes that student advocacy, *really caring*, is of prime importance for all teachers.

[2]From "The Poor Scholar's Soliloquy," 1944, *Childhood Education*, 20, pp. 219–220. Copyright 1944 by the Association for Childhood Education International. Reprinted by permission.

right though even if I don't say much in the classroom because outside I can tell them how to do a lot of things. They tag around me and that sort of makes up for what goes on in school.

I don't know why the teachers don't like me. They never have very much. Seems like they don't think you know anything unless you can name the book it comes out of. I've got a lot of books in my room at home—books like *Popular Science Mechanical Encyclopedia*, and the Sears' and Ward's catalogues—but I don't very often just sit down and read them through like they make us do in school. I use my books when I want to find something out, like whenever Mom buys anything secondhand I look it up in Sears' or Ward's first and tell her if she's getting stung or not. I can use the index in a hurry.

In school though we've got to learn whatever is in the book and I just can't memorize the stuff. Last year I stayed after school every night for two weeks trying to learn the names of the Presidents. Of course, I knew some of them like Washington and Jefferson and Lincoln, but there must have been thirty altogether, and I never did get them straight.

I'm not too sorry though because the kids who learned the Presidents had to turn right around and learn all the Vice Presidents. I am taking the seventh grade over but our teacher this year isn't so interested in the names of the Presidents. She has us trying to learn the names of all the great American inventors.

I guess I just can't remember names in history. Anyway, this year I've been trying to learn about trucks because my uncle owns three and he says I can drive one when I'm sixteen. I already know the horsepower and number of forward and backward speeds of 26 American trucks, some of them Diesels and I can spot each make a long way off. It's funny how that Diesel works. I started to tell my teacher all about it last Wednesday in science class when the pump we were using to make a vacuum in a bell jar got hot but she said she didn't see what a Diesel engine had to do with our experiment on air pressure so I just kept still. The kids seemed interested though. I took four of

them around to my uncle's garage after school and we saw the mechanic, Gus, tear a big truck Diesel down. Boy, does he know his stuff!

I'm not very good in geography either. They call it economic geography this year. We've been studying the imports and exports of Chile all week, but I couldn't tell you what they are. Maybe the reason is I had to miss school yesterday because my uncle took me and his big trailer truck down state about 200 miles and we brought almost 10 tons of stock to the Chicago market.

He had told me where we were going, and I had to figure out the highways to take and also the mileage. He didn't do anything but drive and turn where I told him to. Was that fun! I sat with a map in my lap and told him to turn south, or south-east or some other direction. We made 7 stops, and drove over 500 miles round trip. I'm figuring now what his oil cost and also the wear and tear on the truck—he calls it depreciation—so we'll know how much we made.

I even write out all the bills and send letters to the farmers about what their pigs and beef cattle brought at the stockyards. I only made three mistakes in 17 letters last time, my aunt said, all commas. She's been through high school and reads them over. I wish I could write school themes that way. The last one I had to write was on "What a Daffodil Thinks of Spring," and I just couldn't get going.

I don't do very well in school arithmetic either. Seems I just can't keep my mind on the problems. We had one the other day like this:

"If a 57 ft. telephone pole falls across a cement highway so that 17 3/5 feet extend from one side and 14 9/17 feet from the other, how wide is the highway?"

That seemed to me like an awfully silly way to get the width of a highway. I didn't even try to answer it because it didn't say whether the pole had fallen straight across or not.

Even in shop I don't get very good grades. All of us kids made a broom holder and a bookend this term and mine were sloppy. I just couldn't get interested. Mom doesn't use a broom anymore with her new vacuum cleaner, and all our books are in a bookcase with glass doors in the parlor. Anyway I wanted to make an end gate for my uncle's trailer, but the shop teacher said that meant using metal and wood both, and I'd have to learn how to work with wood first. I didn't see why, but I kept still, and made a tie rack at school and the tail gate after school at my uncle's garage. He said I saved him ten dollars.

Civics is hard for me, too. I've been staying after school trying to learn the "Articles of Confederation" for almost a week, because the teacher said we couldn't be good citizens unless we did. I really tried because I want to be a good citizen. I did hate to stay after school, because a bunch of us boys from the south end of town have been cleaning up the old lot across from Taylor's Machine Shop to make a playground out of it for the little kids from the Methodist home. I made the jungle gym from old pipe, and the guys made me Grand Mogul to keep the playground going. We raised enough money collecting scrap this month to build a wire fence clear around the lot.

Dad says I can quit school when I am fifteen and I am sort of anxious to because there are a lot of things I want to learn how to do, and as my uncle says, I'm not getting any younger.

I TAUGHT THEM ALL[3]

Naomi J. White

I have taught in high school for ten years. During that time I have given assignments, among others, to a murderer, an evangelist, a pugilist, a thief, and an imbecile.

The murderer was a quiet little boy who sat on the front seat and regarded me with pale blue eyes; the evangelist, easily the most popular boy in school, had the lead in the junior play; the pugilist lounged by the window and let loose at intervals a raucous laugh that star-

tled even the geraniums; the thief was a gay-hearted Lothario with a song on his lips; and the imbecile, a soft-eyed little animal seeking the shadows.

The murderer awaits death in the state penitentiary; the evangelist has lain a year now in the village churchyard; the pugilist lost an eye in a brawl in Hong Kong; the thief, by standing on tiptoe, can see the windows of my room from the county jail; and the once gentle-eyed little moron beats his head against a padded wall in the state asylum.

All of these pupils once sat in my room, sat and looked at me gravely across worn brown desks. I must have been a great help to these pupils—I taught them the rhyming scheme of the Elizabethan sonnet and how to diagram a complex sentence.

ABOUT SCHOOL[4]

This poem was handed to a high-school English teacher the day before the writer committed suicide.

He always wanted to explain things,
    but no one cared.
So he drew.

Sometimes he would just draw
    and it wasn't anything.
He wanted to carve it in stone
    or write it in the sky
    and the things inside him that needed saying.

And it was after that he drew the picture.
It was a beautiful picture.
He kept it under his pillow
    and would let no one see it.
And he would look at it every night
    and think about it.
And it was all of him and he loved it.

---

[3]From "I Taught Them All" by Naomi J. White, 1937, *The Clearing House*, 12, pp. 151, 192. Copyright 1937 by The Clearing House. Reprinted by permission.

[4]Original source unknown.

When he started school he brought it with him.
Not to show anyone, but just to have it with
    him
    like a friend.

It was funny about school.
He sat in a square brown desk
    like all the other square brown desks
    and he thought it would be red.

And his room was a square brown room
    like all the other rooms.
And it was tight and close. And stiff.

He hated to hold the pencil and chalk
    with his arm stiff and his feet flat on the
    floor,
    stiff,
    with the teacher watching and watching.

The teacher came and spoke to him.
She told him to wear a tie like all the other
    boys.
He said he didn't like them
    and she said it didn't matter.
After that he drew. And he drew all yellow
    and it was the way he felt about morning.
And it was beautiful.

The teacher came and smiled at him.
"What's this?" she said.
"Why don't you draw something
    like Ken's drawing?

Isn't it beautiful?"
After that his mother bought him a tie
    and he always drew airplanes and rockets
    like everyone else.

And he threw the old picture away.
And when he lay out alone looking at the sky,
    it was big and blue, and all of everything,
    but he wasn't anymore.

He was square and brown inside
    and his hands were stiff.
And he was like everyone else.
All the things inside him that needed saying
    didn't need it anymore.

It had stopped pushing. It was crushed.
Stiff.
Like everything else.

PAIN IN SCHOOL IS having an indifferent
teacher[5]

My unhappy experience was when I was—
well—just last year. I worked on a project for
about two weeks 'cause my parents didn't think
I was doing enough extra projects for school. So,
they wanted me to do one. So I did it. Then,
when I brought it to school (these were the last
few days) my teacher told me that—well—she
didn't really tell me—but she didn't pay very
much attention to my project. I made a map.
And it just sat in the back of the room for a few
days and I finally brought it home. I never got a
grade on it, or anything.

PAIN IN SCHOOL IS learning to feel embarrassed

While in the second grade a question was asked
and I raised my hand with much anticipation
because I knew the answer and I was the only
one who had any idea of the correct answer.

   I was wrong and the teacher proceeded to tell
me how dumb I was to think that I could do
better than her more well-versed students. This
tirade went on for about ten minutes while she
told me to go to the head of the class and talk
about why I had made such a "stupid" answer.
At the end of this she told me my zipper was
down which gave me much more embarrassment.

PAIN IN SCHOOL IS traveling a lonely road
with a hurt that takes many years to heal

"I am sure you will be better off in the service.
The service can teach you a trade. Maybe you
can finish high school while in the service."

---

[5]From *Pain and Joy in School* by E. Schultz, C.
Heuchert, and S. Stampf, 1973, Champaign, IL.: Research Press. Copyright 1973 by Research Press. Used
with permission.

Seventeen years old and my world had just completely collapsed around me. I had just been told by my counselor that I would be better off in the service than in school.

He was polite, very sympathetic but he was still saying "Sorry, boy, you are too dumb for school!" Even today I would like to tell him to stick his advice in his ear! My work in school had not been good, but I felt much of that was due to the fact that I did more playing than studying.

When I left school that day I wondered what I would tell my parents. What could I tell myself? How could I fight a gnawing, cancerous emotion of worthlessness? I wondered how I could face my buddies. I remember having an overwhelming urge to run, to hide, to get away. But, where does a seventeen-year-old boy hide? The only hiding place I could find was the service. That day, I enlisted in the Navy before I went home. There was only one paper to be signed before I left for the service, that was a parental permission paper for men under eighteen years of age—they signed!

The hurt I felt that day almost twelve years ago has actually helped me today. When I am working with a boy who is called stupid, can't read, maybe he feels like he isn't worth much, I can go a little further than just sympathizing with him, I can feel what he feels. . . .

Some refer to such feeling as sensitivity. Call it what you will, but I can simply tell my students to "move over, brother, you have company. I've been down this road before once by myself. It's a lonely road, let me travel with you."

CIPHER IN THE SNOW[6]

Jean E. Mizer

It started with tragedy on a biting cold February morning. I was driving behind the Milford Cor-

---

ners bus as I did most snowy mornings on my way to school. It veered and stopped short at the hotel, which it had no business doing, and I was annoyed as I had to come to an unexpected stop. A boy lurched out of the bus, reeled, stumbled, and collapsed on the snowbank at the curb. The bus driver and I reached him at the same moment. His thin, hollow face was white even against the snow.

"He's dead," the driver whispered.

It didn't register for a minute. I glanced quickly at the scared young faces staring down at us from the school bus. "A doctor! Quick! I'll phone from the hotel . . ."

"No use. I tell you he's dead." The driver looked down at the boy's still form. "He never even said he felt bad," he muttered, "just tapped me on the shoulder and said, real quiet, 'I'm sorry. I have to get off at the hotel.' That's all. Polite and apologizing like."

At school, the giggling, shuffling morning noise quieted as the news went down the halls. I passed a huddle of girls. "Who was it? Who dropped dead on the way to school?" I heard one of them half-whisper.

"Don't know his name; some kid from Milford Corners," was the reply.

It was like that in the faculty room and the principal's office. "I'd appreciate your going to tell the parents," the principal told me. "They haven't a phone and, anyway, somebody from school should go there in person. I'll cover your classes."

"Why me?" I asked. "Wouldn't it be better if you did it?"

"I didn't know the boy," the principal admitted levelly. "And in the last year's sophomore personalities column I note that you were listed as his favorite teacher."

I drove through the snow and cold down the bad canyon road to the Evans place and thought about the boy, Cliff Evans. His favorite teacher! I thought. He hasn't spoken two words to me in two years! I could see him in my mind's eye all right, sitting back there in the last seat in my afternoon literature class. "Cliff Evans," I muttered to myself, "a boy who never talked." I thought a minute. "A boy who never smiled. I never saw him smile once."

The big ranch kitchen was clean and warm. I blurted out my news somehow. Mrs. Evans reached blindly toward a chair. "He never said anything about bein' ailing."

His stepfather snorted. "He ain't said nothing about anything since I moved in here."

Mrs. Evans pushed a pan back off the stove and began to untie her apron. "Now hold on," her husband snapped. "I got to have breakfast before I go to town. Nothing we can do now anyway. If Cliff hadn't been so dumb, he'd have told us he didn't feel good."

After school I sat in the office and stared bleakly at the records spread out before me. I was to close the file and write the obituary for the school paper. The almost bare sheets mocked the effort. Cliff Evans, white, never legally adopted by stepfather, five young half-brothers and sisters. These meager strands of information and the list of D grades were all the records had to offer.

Cliff Evans had silently come in the school door in the mornings and gone out of the school door in the evenings, and that was all. He had never belonged to a club. He had never played on a team. He had never held an office. As far as I could tell, he had never done one happy, noisy kid thing. He had never been anybody at all.

How do you go about making a boy into a zero? The grade-school records showed me. The first and second grade teachers' annotations read "sweet, shy child"; "timid but eager." Then the third grade note had opened the attack. Some teacher had written in a good, firm hand, "Cliff won't talk. Uncooperative. Slow learner." The other academic sheep had followed with: "dull"; "slow-witted"; "low (IQ)." They became correct. The boy's IQ score in the ninth grade had been listed at 83. But his IQ in the third grade had been 106. The score didn't go under 100 until the seventh grade. Even shy, timid, sweet children have resilience. It takes time to break them.

I stomped to the typewriter and wrote a savage report, pointing out what education had done to Cliff Evans. I slapped a copy on the principal's desk and another in the sad, dog-eared file. I banged the typewriter and slammed

the file and crashed the door shut, but I didn't feel much better. A little boy kept walking after me, a little boy with a peaked, pale face; a skinny body in faded jeans, and big eyes that had looked and searched for a long time and then had become veiled.

I could guess how many times he'd been chosen last to play sides in a game, how many whispered child conversations had excluded him, how many times he hadn't been asked. I could see and hear the faces and voices that said over and over, "You're a nothing, Cliff Evans."

A child is a believing creature. Cliff undoubtedly believed them. Suddenly it seemed clear to me: when finally there was nothing left at all for Cliff Evans, he collapsed on a snowbank and went away. The doctor might list "heart failure" as the cause of death, but that wouldn't change my mind.

We couldn't find ten students in the school who had known Cliff well enough to attend the funeral as his friends. So the student body officers and a committee from the junior class went as a group to the church, being politely sad. I attended the services with them, and sat through it with a lump of cold lead in my chest and a big resolve growing through me.

I've never forgotten Cliff Evans nor that resolve. He has been my challenge year after year, class after class. I look up and down for veiled eyes and bodies slumped into a seat in an alien world, "Look, kids," I say silently, "I may not do anything else for you this year, but not one of you is going to come out of here a nobody. I'll work or fight to the bitter end doing battle with society and the school board, but I don't want to have one of you coming out of here thinking himself a zero."

Most of the time—not always, but most of the time—I've succeeded.

We believe that all teachers who work with young people should devise some system for recalling the *absolutely profound influence* they have on their students. Teachers have the potential to greatly enhance or seriously limit their students' feelings of self-worth, achievement, and behavior. After reading the last vignette, "Cipher in the Snow," a teacher we know placed a drawing of a large zero under the glass cover of her desk, to be clearly visible every school day, and pledged that each day it would remind her of her influence so that none of her students would be a "zero" in her class.

Teachers must recognize that all students need to be acknowledged as individuals in their own right and to know that significant others in their lives care about what they do and how they feel. It is easy to become trapped in an atmosphere that is primarily mechanical, that emphasizes achievement, test scores, and rules and regulations. We fully appreciate the tremendous demands on today's teachers, but a perspective that recognizes the worth of every individual is essential to the achievement of basic educational goals. Throughout, this text emphasizes that the teacher is the single most important factor in the successful mainstreaming of students with disabilities. There is little question that teachers have a profound influence on the students' behavior and achievement. We want to encourage every teacher to be aware of this influence and to make certain that it is a *positive* influence.

STUDENT WITH DISABILITIES OR DISABLING SITUATION?

Problems with specific students (perhaps only one or two in a classroom) are a major factor in teacher dissatisfaction. Such problems are among the reasons that teachers leave the teaching profession. These problems are *real* and cannot be ignored or forgotten. Sometimes, the problem *is* Jimmy Smith or Mary Jones. The problem is attrib-

utable directly to a student. At other times, the problem has multiple sources, and they are difficult to isolate and identify.

Students with disabilities have certain limitations imposed *as a result of their disabilities.* By the very nature of a condition, the teacher can predict a need for certain modifications or adaptations of curriculum, materials, teaching strategies, or a combination of these factors. Students with impaired vision, for example, must have modified materials to participate fully in regular classrooms. Students with hearing impairments need adapted approaches and the specialized services of support personnel, and students with orthopedic or other health impairments may need to have architectural barriers removed and special equipment provided if they are to be educated in regular classrooms.

With another group of students, teachers cannot clearly establish the reason for school difficulties, and it is not educationally sound to assume that in every case internal factors are the major cause. In many cases, the failure or difficulty is the result of a number of interacting external factors, or *disabling situations.*

If a student is having difficulty in reading or math, for example, or is withdrawn or acts out in class, the teacher must consider a number of variables that may be influencing the student's poor achievement or unusual behavior. These variables include (a) the student, (b) the materials being used, (c) the environment, (d) the teacher or teachers, and (e) the student's peers. The influence of these variables is depicted in Figure 4–1. Although the student may be the primary cause of the problem, more commonly the interaction of several factors produces a disabling situation. To determine if this is so, teachers must learn to analyze the interactions among various factors.

FIGURE 4-1
Ingredients of a disabling situation

Student-Materials Interactions

The appropriateness of educational materials may greatly influence a student's achievement or behavior. Although this influence may seem obvious, often, not enough time and effort are given to observation, planning, and evaluation of educational materials. For example, the reading materials required for a particular subject may not be appropriate to the actual reading level of the student; the student may be "required" to read a text or some other material that is far beyond his skill level. Teachers should administer an informal reading inventory to determine whether students have sufficient skills to successfully read assigned materials. The readability of the materials being used must also be assessed. Studies have indicated that intermediate texts for third to sixth grades may have readability levels anywhere from second to tenth grades. When the readability level of a particular textbook is far beyond the instructional reading level, it is not safe to assume that the problem is exclusively with the student. Such a case may be a disabling situation for the student. There is also evidence that students have preferred learning styles—auditory, visual, tactile, and kinesthetic—and that if assessment is made of the preferred learning channel or style and materials are matched to this preferred channel, the students' learning rate and achievement can be increased.

Student-Environment Interactions

Poor student-environment interactions occur when a student is highly distracted by a noisy or visually distracting classroom. As a result, this student may not be able to attend to tasks or assignments. Most students can filter out distractions, but some cannot. For example, the last time you studied for an examination, did you seek an area free of auditory distractions (such as a quiet corner of the library) or were you able to listen to hard rock and sit at a table with your friends who were laughing and having a good time? Some individuals have little or no difficulty studying among considerable distractions, whereas others prefer a relatively quiet atmosphere. If you prefer an environment that is free of distractions but were unable to get away from them and as a result did poorly on the examination, who or what should be blamed? In this instance, you might feel that you could not concentrate because there were so many distractions. This situation is similar to that of a student who is distracted by extraneous visual or auditory signals in a classroom environment. In such a case, is it safe to assume that the problem lies within the student? In all likelihood, it is not. The difficulty undoubtedly involves a disabling situation and interactions between the student and environmental factors.

The five-point interaction matrix (Figure 4-1) should be considered when the teacher analyzes the needs of any student. It is not safe to assume that failure of a student is primarily the fault of the student. Rather, it may result from a disabling situation related to inadequacies in the environment, educational materials, instructional techniques, or interactional patterns in the classroom. This situation may be particularly true with a student who is exhibiting only mild problems and for whom there is no known reason for the difficulty. Objectively consider which factors are contributing to a particular student's difficulty and make the necessary adjustments to correct the situation.

So far, the discussion has focused on interactions between a student and the educational materials and educational environment. The remaining two factors, teacher-student and student-student interactions, are discussed next.

Student-Student Interactions

Probably, all teachers understand that some of any student's difficulties are the result of interactions with peers. In fact, many teachers label students' difficulties as "problems with peers." In some cases, such difficulties can be reduced by changing seating, by some specific program of behavior management, or simply by modification of the teacher's attitude. Student-environment interactions, discussed earlier, can be the key to reducing negative interactions between students. Interactions with peers, *combined* with other factors, may best explain the problems under consideration and provide meaningful bases for intervention.

Teacher-Student Interactions

There is little question that teachers have profound influences on the students' behavior, achievement, and feelings of self-worth. The ways in which the teacher interacts with a student can either seriously impede

or greatly facilitate the student's success in school. Such interactions should be considered with all students, but they have even more implications for students who are not achieving or who are apathetic, nonconforming, or acting out in the classroom. In addition, teachers should consider such interactions with students who are identified as disabled.

The nature and quality of the interactions between a teacher and student can be strongly influenced by the expectations of the teacher. The teacher's expectations may be too low, and the teacher may expect only minimal achievement or little acceptable behavior. In contrast, the teacher's expectations may be too high, and the teacher may pressure a student to achieve beyond his or her capabilities, resulting in discouragement, behavior problems, or failure. Expectations are not in themselves bad if teachers are willing to modify their initial expectations as a result of additional information and experience. However, adjustment of expectations does not always occur. Some teachers form inappropriate initial expectations and do not change them even when they obtain disconfirming information. To some extent, everyone forms expectations on the basis of preconceived information or as a result of initial interactions, but teachers must maintain a flexible attitude concerning these expectations and be willing to change them.

The concern about the expectations or biases of teachers is that they may become self-fulfilling prophecies. The teacher who expects particular behaviors from a student may observe and react to the initially expected behaviors. As a result, the student may fulfill the expected role. The following anecdote illustrates this principle:

A discussion among teachers in the teachers' lounge centered on the unacceptable, disruptive behavior of a number of children from the Jones family. Teachers who had previously taught students from this family said that they *all* were troublemakers and in general were the most disruptive members of their classes. As a result of this discussion, Mr. Carlson, the sixth grade teacher, had a preconceived notion about the behavior of Jimmy Jones, a new arrival in his classroom. Mr. Carlson was ready and waiting for disruptive behavior from Jimmy. Whenever Jimmy was the least bit disruptive (even though his behavior was not significantly different from that of other students), Mr. Carlson saw his prophecy as fulfilled: "I knew Jimmy was going to be a problem, and I'm going to stop it before it gets started." Mr. Carlson was so certain that he would observe disruptive behavior that he interpreted minor problems as disruptive. If this situation continued, Jimmy might also fulfill his prophecy—by becoming disruptive.

In this illustration, the prophecy was initiated by a conversation in the teachers' lounge, but expectations concerning a particular student may also be influenced by information contained in the student's cumulative file. Although the discussions in faculty lounges are professional and in the best interests of students in the majority of cases, they can be demeaning and damaging at times. Discussions may concern poorly achieving students or extreme behavior problems. Teachers must vent their feelings, of course, and often the teachers' lounge is the most logical place to do so, but teachers should consider the influence that such discussions may have on other teachers and the possible effect on the students being discussed.

In one particular teachers' lounge where negative comments about students' behavior had become a serious problem, the faculty decided to post a readily observable sign: "If it's not good, don't bother!" When asked what the sign meant, they were quick to say, "If you don't have something

positive to say about students (or any other matter), don't say it. If it is necessary to discuss a particular student, attempt to do so outside the teachers' lounge." This concern may seem trivial compared with other problems in schools, but we believe that often teachers' attitudes and interactions with students are influenced by talk in the teachers' lounge.

TEACHER EXPECTATIONS AND STUDENT BEHAVIORS

Student behaviors include both social behavior (interactions with teachers and other students) and academic achievement. Acceptable, appropriate social behavior and achievement are major educational goals. Yet, teachers should remember the common phrase "what you see is what you get" and substitute *expect* for *see*. To a considerable extent, what teachers expect *is* what they get. This process has been demonstrated over and over again, in educational research studies and classrooms.

The classic research study on teacher expectations was conducted by Rosenthal and Jacobson (1968). The main purpose of the Rosenthal-Jacobson study was to determine if favorable expectations of teachers could be responsible for significant IQ test score gains of students. A group-administered test (with which the students were unfamiliar) was given to all students who would be returning to one elementary school the next fall. The test, the Harvard Test of Inflected Acquisition, was interpreted as a test that would predict with near absolute certainty the students who would show an academic spurt, or demonstrate late blooming. The test in actuality was Flanagan's Test of General Ability (1960), which yielded scores in verbal ability and reasoning and a total IQ score. On completion of the testing, 20% of the students selected to participate in the study were randomly assigned to an experimental group, and were labeled late bloomers. Teachers were given a list of the children in their classrooms who might exhibit marked intellectual growth. From this information, the teachers erroneously assumed that the other children (those who were not identified) did not have the potential for marked intellectual growth.

The findings of this study indicated a significant expectancy advantage in favor of the students who were identified as late bloomers. In other words, the students who were identified as most likely to show an academic spurt did spurt as evidenced by mean gains in total IQ measurements.

This study has been considerably debated and is not unanimously accepted by professionals (Jose & Cody, 1971; Kester & Letchworth, 1972; Mendels & Flanders, 1973). Numerous other studies have examined the influence of teacher-student interactions, however, and these studies have established that teachers' expectations do have the potential to impede or facilitate students' achievement and social behavior (Brophy, 1983; Dusek, 1985; Dusek & Joseph, 1983; Harris & Rosenthal, 1985; Hersh & Walker, 1983).

An interesting experience concerning the effects of intelligence test data on achievement was once shared with us. Although

Realistic expectations and individualization are essential to successful mainstreaming.

this experience cannot be scientifically documented, it provides an interesting dramatization of a self-fulfilling prophecy.

The setting was a large urban junior high school. In an attempt to establish a sense of community and to increase the interaction of students to a level that might be expected in a smaller school, several pods were established. Approximately 100 students were assigned to a pod, with roughly four homerooms in each pod. By design, each pod was established to serve as a school within the larger school.

Several weeks after school began, teachers received a random listing of students assigned to their pod. Preceding each student's name was an assigned number, with numbers ranging from 50 to 150. It was assumed by some teachers that the numbers were the results of group intelligence tests, and accordingly, many teachers established groups on the basis of the number.

After several weeks, it was learned that the numbers were not IQ test results, but locker numbers. The ironic side effect was that the students with high locker numbers tended to be doing very well in their classes and teachers highly valued their interactions; students with relatively low locker numbers were not doing as well.

This may be an extreme example of the influence of student data, but it further illustrates our concern. In all fairness, however, we must say that further investigation of this real-life situation revealed that a number of teachers were quick to question the "IQs" on the student listing. Our concern is for the potentially damaging effects of teachers who could not objectively observe and evaluate their students even after several weeks.

Teachers' expectations can definitely influence student behavior. As mentioned, students who are viewed negatively by their teachers and others tend to behave inappropriately. This inappropriate behavior may promote negative self-evaluations and fur-

ther negative evaluations by others. There is further evidence that students with poor self-concepts may actually attempt to avoid academic situations (McCandless, 1973). In addition to behaving in accordance with negative self-images, such students most likely perform poorly, thereby reinforcing both the negative self-concepts and the negative teacher expectations.

We close this introduction to our consideration of the profound influence of teacher expectations with a short story provided by Rosella Reeves (1989). This story is not about the effect of expectations on students with disabilities. It's about the influence of teacher expectations *on every student in the classroom*. It is also about the influence of expectations *on the teacher*.

STAGES OF INSIGHT: A SHORT STORY[7]

Rosella Reeves

I did my student teaching in a heterogeneously-grouped first grade class. The school was in a low socio-economic area, and the teacher was a veteran master.

When I arrived in February, I observed the most advanced group of first graders I had ever seen; some were reading on a third or fourth year level and most were at least on grade level. Textbooks were only one resource in this classroom; they were supplemented by many and varied materials. Much independent reading was done. Writing instruction included composing sentences and writing creative stories and poems. There was an abundance of math manipulatives. The children could multiply and divide as well as add and subtract. The scientific method of problem solving was used in science projects. The class listened to classical re-

---

[7]From "Stages of Insight: A Short Story" by Rosella Reeves, 1989, *Kappa Delta Pi Record, 25*, pp. 12–13. Copyright 1989 by Kappa Delta Pi. Reprinted by permission.

cordings and recognized many famous paintings. The painting easel was in daily use by the children. The absence rate in the class was low because the children were afraid they would miss something exciting. The children were well-disciplined, interested, and mature.

I taught from February through May; the critic teacher was concerned that I hadn't seen the procedures for starting a first grade in September. She asked that I copy or construct some of her games and charts. In private conferences I was instructed in detail on how to start a first grade class and was given advice on good materials to purchase.

I experienced success as a student teacher. The supervising teacher wanted to be sure that I developed confidence and experienced self-esteem in my practice teaching. She told me that it is impossible for a teacher to help instill self-confidence and self-esteem in children if she hasn't developed these characteristics herself. I was given maximum positive feedback in the classroom and volunteered as hostess to visitors and mistress of ceremonies for a school talent show. I was also a regular solo teacher when the critic teacher found it "necessary" to be out of the classroom on a regular basis. This solo teaching gave me increased opportunities to make decisions independently. I left the student teaching environment feeling confident and excited about starting to teach in my own classroom.

My horizons were enriched and broadened by my observation and practice experiences in this class. Groups of student teachers from the university, classroom teachers, and instructional supervisors were regular observers in this class while I was there. It was a rare privilege to be exposed to a situation where children who had not come from an enriched background were experiencing such a high level of success in school.

When I arrived in the following September as a first year teacher, I was informed by some colleagues that I had been assigned to teach a "not-ready" class. I had never heard of such a class. All the first year pupils in the school had been given a readiness test. My class was composed of children who had fallen below the passing mark on the readiness test.

I was told by some colleagues that with the not-ready class I probably wouldn't need all those materials from student teaching. I was depressed and concerned that I would be unhappy teaching such a class after having completed student teaching in an enriched situation. My fear was that I might be teaching a few letter sounds, color words, number words, and other readiness skills for an entire year.

After some thought, I called my former critic teacher to apprise her of the situation and to get some advice. She made me feel much better by reminding me that I hadn't seen her class in the fall when they were beginners and much less "advanced" than when I saw them in February; that even though her class had not been grouped according to scores on a readiness test, they were from a low socio-economic area and lacking in many experiences usually thought to be necessary for success in school. She said there was no reason I couldn't use the many materials I had collected during student teaching and indeed, have a situation much like the one I had experienced in her classroom. I was told to keep an open mind, ignore negative comments about what to expect from the children, expect that everybody in the class could learn to some degree, and realize that even in this so-called homogeneous group there would be differing levels of ability. The critic teacher also suggested that I work with the children in small groups to determine what they already knew and didn't know, and use this information to group them for instruction. Then, I was to start teaching, using all the materials I had.

That first year, I taught everything as if I expected everybody in the class to be a successful learner. There was some concern in the school about whether my intensive teaching was geared too high for the class. The supervisor visited the class more often than was usual to determine if the children were really understanding what I was teaching. She became very enthusiastic about the amount of teaching material I had as well as the progress and understanding of the class as a whole. The supervisor later commented that if an experienced teacher had looked at the test scores and cumulative folders of this class, she probably would have said, "Forget it!"

There was additional surprise and doubt in the school toward the end of the year when I suggested that a few members of the "not-ready" class be tested for the school system's advance program. The surprise intensified when one or two of the children tested actually passed the test and were admitted to the advance program the next year.

My first year of teaching was stressful and hard at times, but it was also invaluable to me in the formation of a positive attitude toward people with a label. My motivation to teach was improved because I knew if I could successfully teach that class, I could teach anywhere. Because of the experiences I had then, I have never been able to stand before a class without wondering if I am getting maximum effort from each child. I tried to exhibit belief in each child, enrich his learning environment, and communicate to him my expectations for his success. If a child really tried for an entire year and still didn't experience success, I was ready to consider help from a special education class; I wanted to be sure that I wasn't responsible for having a child labeled "special education" who had just not been applying himself in class.

I believe that most children can learn in a regular classroom if they have a teacher who is a builder. A builder:

- has awareness. The educator who has awareness knows that he may be contributing to a child's learning problems if he and the child come from different backgrounds; this educator will seek to gain experiences that will help him successfully teach all children.
- has belief and expectation. The educator who has belief in a child and high expectations for a child to learn, will emphasize what the pupil is doing right and minimize what he is doing wrong; the educator will use this approach to help the child build self-esteem and independence.
- observes learning styles and laws of learning.

A teacher who determines a child's learning style and observes the laws of learning will know if a child learns best from a visual, auditory, or kinesthetic approach, or from a combination of these and will teach each child moving from the concrete to the abstract.
- is interesting. The interesting teacher will be colorful and interested in many things, and will provide an interesting, enriched program.
- provides repetition and involvement. The effective educator will provide repetition in teaching and practice work for the purpose of achieving mastery and will concentrate on getting pupils involved in whatever is happening in class.

The Influence of Labels

When a teacher refers a student for further evaluation and that student is eventually classified as disabled, the teacher should have learned a good deal about the student's strengths as well as weaknesses. Objectivity should overcome possible tendencies to expect too little and thus begin the cycle of self-fulfilling prophecy. When a student arrives with a label, the teacher may respond with unreasonably low expectations. Students labeled disabled may be stereotyped on the basis of the teacher's preconceived attitude or experience with individuals who have disabilities. Although a stereotype may reflect either positive or negative expectations, it generally reflects a negative attitude about a population as a whole. The labels "mentally retarded," "emotionally disturbed," and "learning disabled" have negative connotations and often result in low levels of expectation.

In a series of related studies, teachers were shown videotapes of children labeled learning disabled or mentally retarded, or unlabeled. The teachers had lower expectations for labeled students than for unlabeled students with *identical* behaviors (Coleman & Gilliam, 1983; Foster, Algozzine, & Ysseldyke, 1980; Minner, 1982; Simpson, 1981; Taylor, Smiley, & Ziegler, 1983). The influence of such labels is obvious. Just as success breeds more success, failure and negative thinking are powerful forces for continued failure. An effect of labeling is that it is often difficult to remove the label. Just as removing a paper label from a jar may be difficult and tedious, and often part of the label remains, so removing a label from a student is also difficult, and some of the label often stays with the student.

Achievement Test Results and Tracking

There is considerable evidence that achievement test scores may negatively influence teachers' expectations. Beez (1972) found that teachers who expected high performance from students tended to teach more, and teachers who expected low performance tended to teach less. He demonstrated this tendency by randomly assigning a group of students to high and low achievement groups, using falsified achievement scores. At the end of a term, teachers were asked to rate the students using a five-point scale (with five being high and one being low) in the following areas: social competency, achievement, and intellectual ability. Average teacher ratings indicated that the "high" groups were significantly higher in all three areas. One can only wonder how the "low" group might have fared if the students had been given the falsified, high achievement scores.

Two related studies (Beez, 1970; Rubovits & Maehr, 1971) conducted in tutoring settings reported that teachers' expectations were influenced by student data. In these studies, students enrolled in teacher-preparation programs served as tutors for students who were identified as high or low

achievers. The tutors were provided with falsified psychological information that would predict high or low student performance. The results indicated that the tutors attempted to teach more to the students for whom they had high expectations and less to those identified as having lower potential, when in fact the groups did not differ in performance potential. These studies also noted that the tutors interacted more negatively with students in the low group.

Good (1970) indicated that teachers interact more often with high-achieving than with low-achieving students and that their interactions with high achievers are more facilitative and positive than with low achievers. Other studies have indicated that students of different achievement levels are exposed to different verbal interactions. Students in low groups receive less praise and more negative comments or criticisms than their classmates in high groups (Morrison & McIntyre, 1969).

Another result of low achievement scores may be some sort of grouping, or tracking, based on inferred ability. Although an important historic court case relating to the Washington, DC, schools, *Hobson v. Hanson* (1967), rejected the claims of the school district that tracking was beneficial to all and ordered it to end the practice, some versions of tracking remain today. (In *Hobson v. Hansen*, the court concluded that tests used to make the track placements reflected economic and social backgrounds, not ability, and resulted in de facto segregation of black children.) Ability/achievement level grouping is intended to promote more homogeneity and thus permit more effective instruction. Although this practice may be viable in providing instruction, caution must be exercised in its use. Grouping must be flexible, and it should reflect the particular subject being studied. A given student may be placed in the low reading group but belong in a high group in another subject.

A general problem related to grouping is a type of spread phenomenon. A student is placed either in a high group for all activities regardless of achievement in that subject or all low groups on the basis of achievement in one particular subject. Teachers must make every effort to maintain flexibility when grouping students for instructional purposes.

Racial or Ethnic Minority Group Membership

Membership in racial or ethnic minority groups may contribute to lowered expectations by teachers. It may also lead to different patterns of personal interaction and differences in both the quantity and the quality of verbal interaction. Although much greater awareness of these factors has developed in the past 20 to 30 years, differences in attitude, interaction, and expectation exist on the part of some teachers. Earlier studies indicated that white students were held in higher esteem than black students by white teachers (Leacock, 1969) and that the quantity and quality of verbal interaction was influenced in a negative direction by minority group membership (Jackson & Cosca, 1974). More recent studies have led to similar results (Dusek & Joseph, 1983; Sorenson & Hallinan, 1984). As indicated earlier in this discussion, regardless of studies and statistics, the responsibility of teachers is clear. Teachers must recognize all students as worthy individuals and expend all possible effort to make each student an integral part of the class, with status equal to that of all other students.

Other Characteristics

A number of other student characteristics lead to negative attitudes, lower expecta-tions, and less desirable interactions. Among the more common are gender; speech and language characteristics; physical attractiveness; and personality (Brophy, 1983; Dusek, 1985; Guttman & Bar-Tai, 1982; Harris & Rosenthal, 1985; Levine & Wang, 1983; Rosenthal & Rubin, 1978; Smith, 1980). The crucial factor is whether the teacher firmly believes that students with a particular characteristic are less able to complete assigned tasks. Often, expectations stem from preconceived notions or misinformation rather than from actual experience. For instance, if the teacher firmly believes that girls tend to be higher achievers than boys in language arts and are more capable in general than boys, the teacher's male students most likely receive greater criticism, are given less praise, and experience greater rates of failure.

The first step in attempting to avoid this type of situation is for teachers to recognize that their preconceived attitudes and expectations can significantly influence the behavior, achievement, and self-concepts of students. Some school faculties have addressed this concern by conducting in-service meetings or open discussions concerning characteristics that may negatively influence the expectations of teachers. In this way, teachers recognize that their feelings are not unique and that their colleagues share similar feelings. Often, a student characteristic identified by a colleague seems quite trivial or humorous, although it is very real to the teacher identifying it. By sharing their feelings, teachers may come to recognize the absurdity of some of their feelings about student characteristics and learn to overcome such feelings.

One other type of interaction between teachers and students must be considered—the interaction between teachers and students with physical impairments. Rather than rejective interactions, teachers may demonstrate pitying or oversolicitous attitudes. These attitudes are revealed by such comments as "Isn't it wonderful that a blind student can do so well!" or "I think, because she's in a wheelchair, she deserves a B." Such attitudes and interactions may defeat the very purpose of regular classroom placement. To set a student up as someone so special that he or she becomes the class pet may do serious disservice to that student. Teachers must be aware of the influence of their attitudes, be they negative, pitying, or positive.

Brophy and Good (1974) identified several specific behaviors by teachers that may communicate low expectations to students:

1. Waiting less time for lows (low-achieving students) to answer
2. Staying with lows in failure situations (persisting in such a manner as to call attention to failure)
3. Rewarding inappropriate behavior of lows (praising marginal or inaccurate responses)
4. Criticizing lows more frequently than highs
5. Praising lows less frequently than highs
6. Not giving feedback to responses of lows
7. Paying less attention to lows
8. Calling on lows less often
9. Differing interaction patterns with highs and lows
10. Seating lows farther away
11. Demanding less from lows

By recognizing these variables, teachers may begin to understand the bases of their perceptions and consider modifying their interactions (if such modifications are needed) by maintaining flexible and open attitudes about all students.

MONITORING AND EVALUATING INTERACTIONS

The influence of teacher expectations on the students' behavior and achievement appears to be well established. Educators must go beyond the mere identification of attitudes and expectations, however, and make specific efforts to change their biases. The first step in changing expectations is to analyze interactions with students. Teachers can assess their interactions in a number of ways. Some methods are informal and do not require specific instruments or extensive training. Other methods are the product of research studies and provide very specific information concerning interactions.

Informal Techniques

The available informal techniques are limited only by individual ingenuity, but certain approaches appear to be in common use. These techniques are described here, but teachers are encouraged to modify these informal procedures to fit their individual needs. Note, however, that such modification is not acceptable with standardized or formal techniques.[8]

Time Analysis. The time analysis technique can provide information concerning teacher interactions with students. The checklist and set of directions in Figure 4–2 is an example of this technique. The teacher may add any number of questions to increase the time analysis findings, depending on the specific purpose of the analysis. The time analysis technique is simple to use and interpret and can provide consid-

---

[8]Our thanks to Clifford Baker, who provided a number of informal techniques presented in this discussion.

FIGURE 4–2
Time analysis for teachers

1 Students	2 How Is Time Spent?	3 Pleasurable or Nonpleasurable?
Most Time 1. 2. 3. 4. 5.		
Least Time 1. 2. 3. 4. 5.		

Column 1. List the five students in the class with whom you spend the most time. List the five with whom you spend the least time.

Column 2. Identify what you do with the child during that time—how is the time spent?

Sample Key
XH = extra academic help
BM = behavior management
L = listening to the student
T = talking to the student
PL = playing with the student

Column 3. Write "P" if the time spent is pleasurable and "NP" if it is nonpleasurable.

Analyze the Results. Answer the following questions:
1. At what kinds of activities do you spend most of your time?
2. Is most of your time spent with these 10 students pleasurable?
3. What is different about the students with whom you spend the most time?
4. Do the students with whom you spend more time need you more?
5. What are the differences between the students with whom the time is pleasurable and the students with whom the time is nonpleasurable?

erable information concerning how the teacher spends time and the nature of the interactions.

Teacher-made Checklists. The teacher may develop a checklist to fit almost any situation. The items on a checklist can involve verbal or nonverbal behaviors or general classroom procedures. Such checklists seem to be popular with teachers, and therefore we provide two examples (Figures 4–3 and 4–4). Figure 4–3 is for elementary students, and Figure 4–4 is more appropriate for secondary students. These are merely examples, and teachers are encouraged to modify the lists or add statements of particular interest or concern. Students should not be asked to sign their names, since this may inhibit their openness and sincerity.

The teacher should analyze the results by averaging the responses and plotting the averages to get a picture of teacher interactions. Checklists may be administered several times during the year to measure changes.

Peer-Teacher Observers. A trusted colleague can come into the classroom and observe the teacher in action. The colleague should keep running notes on the teacher's interactions during a period of several days. Often, it is helpful if the observing teacher has a checklist or an indication of specific behaviors to be recorded; otherwise, at the end of the period only very general comments may be shared. The teachers may later change roles if this is agreeable to both.

FIGURE 4–3
Teacher-made interaction checklist for elementary students

	Always 3	Seldom 2	Never 1
1. I can get extra help from the teacher when I need it.	☐	☐	☐
2. The teacher praises me when I do well.	☐	☐	☐
3. The teacher smiles when I do something well.	☐	☐	☐
4. The teacher listens attentively.	☐	☐	☐
5. The teacher accepts me as an individual.	☐	☐	☐
6. The teacher encourages me to try new things.	☐	☐	☐
7. The teacher respects the feelings of others.	☐	☐	☐
8. My work is usually good enough.	☐	☐	☐
9. I am called on when I raise my hand.	☐	☐	☐
10. The same students always get praised by the teacher.	☐	☐	☐
11. The teacher grades fairly.	☐	☐	☐
12. The teacher smiles and enjoys teaching.	☐	☐	☐
13. I have learned to do things from this teacher.	☐	☐	☐
14. When something is too hard, my teacher makes it easier for me.	☐	☐	☐
15. My teacher is polite and courteous.	☐	☐	☐
16. I like my teacher.	☐	☐	☐

FIGURE 4–4
Teacher-made interaction checklist for secondary students

	Always 5	Some-times 4	Often 3	Seldom 2	Never 1
The teacher					
1. is genuinely interested in me	☐	☐	☐	☐	☐
2. respects the feelings of others	☐	☐	☐	☐	☐
3. grades fairly	☐	☐	☐	☐	☐
4. identifies what he or she considers important	☐	☐	☐	☐	☐
5. is enthusiastic about teaching	☐	☐	☐	☐	☐
6. smiles often and enjoys teaching	☐	☐	☐	☐	☐
7. helps me develop skills in understanding myself	☐	☐	☐	☐	☐
8. is honest and fair	☐	☐	☐	☐	☐
9. helps me develop skills in communicating	☐	☐	☐	☐	☐
10. encourages me and provides time for individual help	☐	☐	☐	☐	☐
11. is pleasant and has a sense of humor	☐	☐	☐	☐	☐
12. has "pets" and spends the most time with them	☐	☐	☐	☐	☐
13. encourages and provides time for questions and discussion	☐	☐	☐	☐	☐
14. respects my ideas and concerns	☐	☐	☐	☐	☐
15. helps me develop skills in making decisions	☐	☐	☐	☐	☐
16. helps me develop skills in using time wisely	☐	☐	☐	☐	☐

Videotapes. The teacher may arrange to have his or her teaching videotaped. The teacher should view the videotape alone, noticing interactions with different students. Next, if desired, the teacher can also view and discuss the videotape with a colleague. It may be necessary to tape several sessions so that typical patterns of behavior and interaction are recorded. Also, it may be helpful to arrange for a series of taping sessions, for example, once every two or three months. Nearly every school district has videotaping equipment, and local instructional media personnel may be able to assist with the taping.

Role Playing. A procedure that is particularly appropriate with elementary students is role playing. Young children are very honest and open, and they are quick to role-play typical classroom situations. For role playing to be most effective, it is advisable for the regular teacher to switch classes with another teacher so that the students are not inhibited by the presence of their own teacher. The students may be asked to act out the roles of a good teacher and a poor teacher. Other role questions include the following:

1. How does your teacher act when he is happy or sad?
2. How does your teacher look and what does he say when interrupted?
3. How does your teacher look and what does he say when asked to repeat the directions for an assignment?
4. How does your teacher look and what does he say when you make a mistake?
5. How does your teacher look and what does he say when you misbehave?
6. How does your teacher look and what does he say when you do something well?

Teachers may add other situations about which they are most interested in obtaining feedback. The role playing may be taped on a video or audio recorder so that the teacher receives a firsthand evaluation. Again, it may be helpful for the teacher to exchange classes with a colleague so that the students will not be inhibited by their own teacher's presence. Although the initiation of such role playing may require different introduction and presentation at the elementary level than at the ssecondary level, it works at both levels with just a little innovation.

Formal Techniques

Formal teacher-student observational systems may provide a more reliable, descriptive picture of teacher-student interactions than informal systems. Thus, some teachers prefer to use formal techniques. There are several widely recognized techniques, with those developed by Galloway (1968) and Flanders (1965) among the most used. Other formal observational systems have been reported by Fink and Semmel (1971) and Soar, Soar, and Ragosta (1971). Any of

these systems may prove valuable in gathering data about teacher-student interactions to provide a basis for further planning and decision making.

CHANGING EXPECTATIONS

Teachers are generally willing to change their inappropriate interactions and teaching behaviors once they are made aware of them. Brophy and Good (1974) suggest a deliberate and tactful strategy to help teachers with this important area, using the following steps: (a) collection of specific data; (b) identification of explicit problems from the data; (c) identification of students with whom the teachers are interacting positively; (d) encouragement of the teachers to explain differences in their behaviors; (e) suggestions for changes in the behaviors of the teachers, leading to agreement about explicit treatment behaviors; and (f) reobservation of the teachers in the classrooms.

Dworkin (1979) based specific strategies on successful performance demonstrated by students. Dworkin's program involved a demonstration of teaching techniques, selection of curricular priorities, and planning of sessions with each teacher. Central to this study was the assumption that the success of students is related to the expectations of teachers. The purpose of the study was to examine changes that occur in expectations of teachers as a result of specific strategies. The study demonstrated that expectations of teachers can be changed from negative to positive. The implications of the research are that teachers can bring about positive changes by working through the strengths of students and that when students demonstrate positive performance, teachers can become committed to applying these strategies. It is assumed that observation of a student's progress can significantly influence a teacher's expectations and behaviors. The initial step in changing expectations from negative to positive is for teachers to recognize that they have differing expectations and that if they are sincerely motivated to change their interactive style, instruments and procedures can assist them in making the change. They must begin, however, with self-examination and analysis of all of the variables that contribute to the success or failure of a particular student.

THE QUALITY OF STUDENT INTERACTIONS

Students with disabilities are placed in (or remain in) regular classrooms in the belief that such placements will lead to a variety of positive results. In addition to teacher-student interactions, there are continuous student-student interactions. If physical placement in regular classrooms is to lead to the desired results, there must be *positive* interactions, and several authorities believe that without active teacher efforts, the results are more likely to be negative interactions or rejection.

In a discussion of factors contributing to the development of successful mainstreaming, Salend (1984) notes that non-handicapped students can facilitate the mainstreaming process through positive interactions and can "aid their handicapped peers' adjustment and ability to function in the mainstream by serving as role models, peer tutors, and friends and by providing assistance to physically disabled and sensory impaired students" (p. 411). However, he cautions that peer contributions may be negatively affected by their attitudes.

At times, students may prove to be forces for improvement in the quality of interaction, but for the most part, teachers must provide the impetus. Salend (1984) suggests that all possible effort be expended

before students are mainstreamed to increase their social skills, and that teachers employ specific strategies to promote positive attitudes (toward students with disabilities) on the part of nondisabled students. Whatever process or strategy is used—films, books, or discussions—the first requirement is that teachers accept students with disabilities as valued individuals. Various researchers have established that teacher acceptance can be attained through appropriate teacher education (Donaldson, 1980; Idol-Maestas, 1981; Salend & Johns, 1983; Tymitz-Wolf, 1982).

Measuring the Status of Students with Disabilities

For several years, researchers have attempted to measure the social development and interactions of students with disabilities and students without them (Asher & Taylor, 1982; Bruininks, Rynders, & Gross, 1974; Bryan, 1974; Goodman, Gottlieb, & Harrison, 1972; Iano, Ayers, Heller, McGettigan, & Walker, 1974; Sheare, 1978; Siperstein, Bopp, & Bak, 1978; Strain, 1982). The most commonly used sociometric technique is peer nomination, which requires students to name classmates who fit a particular criterion (e.g., "In working on a project I would like to work with _____ ") (Cartledge & Milburn, 1986). A student's score is the total number of nominations received from classmates. See Figure 4–5 for an example of the nomination method. The directions for administration of this nomination questionnaire are as follows:

1. The teacher explains to the class, "Today I am going to ask you to indicate on your paper the name of a classmate with whom you would like to share certain activities. We all work better when we have the opportunity to work with someone we get along with well. I am

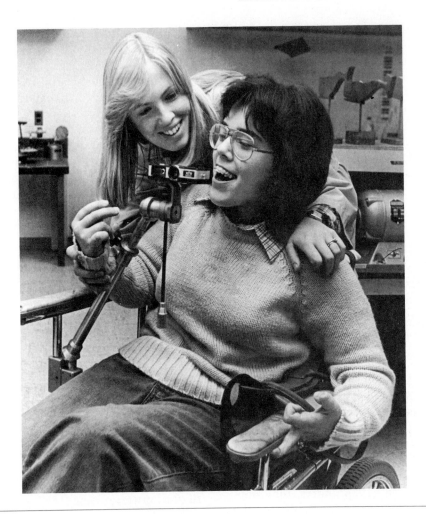

Learning is a pleasure.

gathering this information to find out who in this class would work well together. I hope you will be completely honest. No other student will know whom you have chosen."

2. Hand out preference forms with questions similar to those indicated.
3. Give the following instructions:
   a. At the top of this form, write the names of three classmates you would like to work with in school if you had a choice.
   b. In the middle of your paper, write the names of three classmates that you would like to be with during breaks. You may write down any or all of the three names used previously.
   c. Next, write the names of three classmates you would like to sit near in school if you had a choice. You may

FIGURE 4-5
Peer nomination preference form

Questionnaire

Name:

In working on a project I would like to work with:

1. _____

2. _____

3. _____

During breaks, I would like to be with:

1. _____

2. _____

3. _____

I would like to sit next to:

1. _____

2. _____

3. _____

I would not like to work with:

1. _____

2. _____

3. _____

write any or all of the names previously used.

d. At the bottom of this form, write the names of classmates with whom you would not like to work.

After the students have made their choices, the teacher can add up the results. Any reasonable status categories may be used to determine the sociometric status of any specific student, for example,

Star. One who was chosen 14 or more times by classmates.

Above average. One who received from 9 to 13 choices.

Below average. One who was chosen between 3 and 8 times.

Neglected. One who was chosen fewer than 3 times.

These status numbers are based on an average classroom enrollment of between 28 and 35 students and should be changed proportionately depending on the size of the class. The use of both positive and negative nomination criteria generally permit more accurate status distinction.

A second method, the rating scale technique, can also be used to measure the sociometric status of students. With this procedure, students are provided a list or classroom roster and are asked to rate each classmate on a numerical scale according to particular criterion. A student's score on the rating scale is the average of all ratings from classmates. The criterion may be the degree to which students would like to play or work with each classmate. They may rate their classmates on a scale from 1 (wouldn't like to) to 5 (would much like to) scale. For ease of administration, the teacher can simply prepare a class roster with the range of numerical values printed next to each name, such that students can circle their ratings.

One advantage of the rating scale technique over the nominating method is that evaluations are obtained for all students in a class rather than only students nominated by others. This factor is important because students with disabilities may not be chosen on a positive nomination measure.

A third method of sociometric assessment is the paired comparison technique. With this technique, students are presented one at a time with all possible pairings of classmates and must choose the most preferred peer for each pairing. Each student obtains a score that reflects the total number of times he or she is selected by classmates. Although regularly mentioned in summaries of sociometric measurements,

this method has one serious drawback. It takes a great deal of time in preparation and administration. For example, Vaughn and Langlois (1983) report that it took 20 to 30 hours to complete this procedure in a class of 40 preschool children.

There are many ways to obtain sociometric data and various measures to assess different dimensions of social status. The nomination method measures friendship, and the rating scale can be used to obtain information about general acceptance. Sociometric assessment should be supported by other information, such as behavioral observations and teachers' ratings, to have maximum value.

Certain potential limitations of sociometric measures should be noted. Preferences for same-sex and same-race peers, recent negative experiences, and other similar factors may reflect influences that are either beyond the control of the teacher, or influences that are temporary and not appropriate for long-term, concerted efforts on the part of the teacher. Like other information, sociometric information must be considered as only one part of the total picture.

The use of sociometric information should not stop with the assignment of sociometric status; it should be meaningfully extended. For example, it may help to determine the number of mutual choices (two students who chose each other). It may also be interesting to determine whether students with disabilities were chosen in academic or social areas. Teachers should devise their own methods of analysis for their own situations.

Sociometric information is not the only way to analyze classroom interactions. Most teachers are keenly aware of social interactions in their classrooms. Naturally, they should be aware of their roles as models and the ways in which they interact with students. At times, however, even though teacher interactions with students with disabilities are positive, the students without disabilities do not reflect accepting, empathic, and objective attitudes. In such instances, teachers should structure cooperative learning experiences and open class discussions.

Enhancing Interactions Between Students with Disabilities and Their Peers

Information concerning the effects of mainstreaming on the attitudes of nondisabled students is contradictory and confusing. Several studies have demonstrated that the placement of students with disabilities in regular classrooms may result in greater prejudice, stereotyping, and rejection (Goodman, Gottlieb, & Harrison, 1972; Gottlieb & Budoff, 1973; Gottlieb, Cohen, & Goldstein, 1974; Iano et al., 1974; Panda & Bartel, 1972). But there is also evidence that the placement of students with disabilities in regular classrooms may positively influence the attitudes of their nondisabled peers (Esposito & Reed, 1986; Sheare, 1978; Wechsler, Suarez, & McFadden, 1975).

Based on this contradictory evidence, it is quite clear that if a student's status is low and his or her interactions with peers are not positive, the teacher must make specific efforts to modify the situation. This improvement may be gained in three general ways: (a) by structuring a cooperative learning atmosphere; (b) by providing detailed information and awareness of the potential of all persons; and (c) by providing students with opportunities to discuss, question, and clarify their beliefs and attitudes about persons with disabilities. The following sections consider ways in which teachers may use these specific approaches.

Cooperative Learning. There are at least three major emphases that a teacher may

build into classroom learning situations. These are (a) positive goal interdependence (cooperation), (b) negative goal interdependence (competition), and (c) no goal interdependence (individualistic efforts) (Johnson & Johnson, 1975). A case may be made for the value of each of these emphases as it applies to students in general, but if mainstreaming is to be truly effective, considerable cooperative learning must take place. Students with disabilities must actually interact with nondisabled students, not simply be in the classroom physically. In addition to increasing the likelihood of acceptance of students with disabilities, cooperative learning may help students with disabilities increase their self-confidence by perceiving themselves as achievers.

Evans (1984) summarized the dynamics of cooperative learning situations as part of a discussion of fostering peer acceptance of students with disabilities. His summary (Figure 4–6) provides ample evidence of the importance of cooperative learning to acceptance of students with disabilities.

Developing and using cooperative learning methods requires teachers to believe that cooperation can be as effective as competition. It also requires information about various learning structures that can be used to promote cooperative learning. There are several, research-based, practical cooperative learning structures. We will review the following: (a) cooperative goal structuring (Johnson & Johnson, 1986; Johnson, Johnson, Nelson, & Read, 1978), (b) MAPS and the circle of friends (Forest & Lusthaus, 1990; Polloway et al., 1989; Stainback, Stainback, & Forest, 1989), (c) the teams-games-tournament approach, (DeVries & Slavin, 1978), (d) the jigsaw approach (Aronson, 1978), (e) the student teams achievement divisions approach (Slavin, 1978), and (f) the small-group teaching approach (Sharon & Sharon, 1976). In addition, we

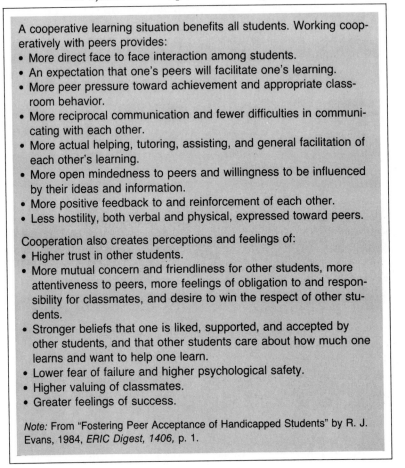

FIGURE 4–6
The dynamics of cooperative learning situations

A cooperative learning situation benefits all students. Working cooperatively with peers provides:

- More direct face to face interaction among students.
- An expectation that one's peers will facilitate one's learning.
- More peer pressure toward achievement and appropriate classroom behavior.
- More reciprocal communication and fewer difficulties in communicating with each other.
- More actual helping, tutoring, assisting, and general facilitation of each other's learning.
- More open mindedness to peers and willingness to be influenced by their ideas and information.
- More positive feedback to and reinforcement of each other.
- Less hostility, both verbal and physical, expressed toward peers.

Cooperation also creates perceptions and feelings of:

- Higher trust in other students.
- More mutual concern and friendliness for other students, more attentiveness to peers, more feelings of obligation to and responsibility for classmates, and desire to win the respect of other students.
- Stronger beliefs that one is liked, supported, and accepted by other students, and that other students care about how much one learns and want to help one learn.
- Lower fear of failure and higher psychological safety.
- Higher valuing of classmates.
- Greater feelings of success.

Note: From "Fostering Peer Acceptance of Handicapped Students" by R. J. Evans, 1984, *ERIC Digest, 1406*, p. 1.

will address the use of rap sessions and buddy systems.

Cooperative Goal Structuring. Johnson et al. (1978) and Johnson and Johnson (1986) describe a process called cooperative goal structuring as a way to promote social integration of students with disabilities through cooperative learning. Cooperative goal structuring involves establishing a goal that can be achieved only if *all* group members work toward the goal. A review of research

(*Research Brief T1, Social Integration of Handicapped Students: Cooperative Goal Structuring,* 1988) provided by the ERIC Clearinghouse on Handicapped and Gifted Children concludes that this process has application at all grade levels, with students who have various mild and moderate handicaps. The research brief concludes that as a result of use of this process for 2 weeks (ten 45-minute sessions) students with disabilities participated more often and students without disabilities looked at and spoke to their peers with disabilities more often. Co-operative goal structuring is most effective when teachers provide specific instruction in cooperation, make certain that all students understand that the goal is a cooperative (group) effort, and then reward individuals based on group results or products. The steps involved in setting up this process follow:

1. The teacher specifies the instructional objectives in such a way that all group members will master the assignment.
2. The size of the groups is determined. With low-achieving or young students, two or three per group may be best; with older students, four may be preferable.
3. Students are assigned to groups on the basis of a pretest. Generally, one high-achieving student, two average students, and one low-achieving student should form the group.
4. The classroom is arranged so that group members are close together and different groups are some distance from each other.
5. Each group is given appropriate instructional materials.
6. The teacher explains the task and the expected, cooperative goal structure. Each student must understand the task. The teacher should also specify a group goal (completion of the assignment) and the criterion for success (90% correct). The criterion may be based on the combined score of all group members.
7. All group members are taught the following skills: helping, tutoring, teaching, and sharing. The teacher should be certain to observe the interactions of the group and intervene if necessary.
8. Evaluation should be based on the group products. If a low-achieving student is having considerable difficulty, the teacher may need to modify the student's responsibility by using improvement scores, assigning less material, or using different material.

The McGill/Map Action Planning System (MAPS)[9]. MAPS is a specific approach developed by Marsha Forest and Judith Snow of the Canadian Association for Community Living. MAPS is based on a planning system developed at McGill University. It was designed to help school personnel more successfully integrate new students with disabling conditions into regular classrooms with age-appropriate peers. (Forest & Lusthaus, 1990; Polloway et al., 1989; Stainback et al., 1989). Its primary use has been to facilitate integration of students who have, prior to this class placement, always been in a special school, special class, or an institutional setting. Although usually used with students at the secondary level, it can be applied with adaptations at any level. Its essential elements are as follows:

1. An integration consultant or resource teacher visits the school where the student to be integrated will attend, to speak with students in the class that the new student will attend. The consultant talks with the students, asking about their perceptions of individuals with disabilities. As a result of this meeting, the class knows of the coming of a new class member and the unique needs of that member. In addition, a potential circle of friends (called by some a peer network) is set up. When possible, those who will be part of the circle meet with school counselors, teachers, a consultant, and

---

[9]In different publications, the *M* in MAPS may stand for McGill University or for the word *Map*. In a text of which Forest is coauthor, it is for McGill. In an article of which McGill is coauthor, it is for Map. In each case, the system and the acronym are the same.

others as appropriate to talk over and prepare in writing a list of things that they can do to make the coming of the new student more effective and pleasant for all.

2. A meeting is held after the new student has been in the class for a few weeks to review what is happening and what more can be done to make the setting work. This meeting normally involves the students in the circle of friends, the integrated student, parents, teachers, and consultants. In a case study relating to May, a 12-year-old with Down syndrome, seven questions were asked and discussed:

What is May's history?
What is your dream for May? (asked of the parents)
What is your nightmare?
Who is May? (her personal traits)
What are May's strengths, gifts, and talents?
What are May's needs?
What would an ideal day for May look like? (Stainback et al., 1989, pp. 51–56)

The circle of friends directly involved with the integrated student is not set; that is, some may wish to discontinue being part of any meeting and planning sessions. Those who participate must want to participate. Some new individuals may wish to join. If students who will be in the class in the fall get to meet the new class-member-to-be in spring, they may plan contacts over the summer.

There can be many variations of MAPS, and in general, MAPS is used with students with severe disabilities. However, the circle of friends aspect of MAPS is generally applicable with all levels of disability. Gaylord-Ross (1989) notes: "One should not assume that every student with severe disabilities

will need this degree of formalization (MAPS) in order to build meaningful relationships. The implementation of a MAPS program . . . should be based upon the unique needs of each individual" (p. 29).

Circle of Friends. Unlike the MAPS system, the circle of friends concept is as applicable at the levels of mild and moderate disabling conditions as it is at severe levels. The concept involves informing nondisabled students about the needs of a given student and formally asking them if they would like to be part of making that student feel welcome in the class setting. Participation in the circle must be voluntary, and the grouping should not be static or fixed. When properly carried through, such a structure can lead to expanded understandings on the part of nondisabled students, in addition to more effective programming for students with disabilities.

Forest and Lusthaus (1989) caution that the system is not a buddy system or a "chance for students to do a good deed for the day" (p. 47). It is a flexible, informal network, emphasizing true friendship and acceptance. They note that, for example, peer tutors can become friends, but they need not be. Circles should meet on some regular basis and be facilitated by a "warm and caring teacher who will promote the reciprocal nature of real friendship" (Forest & Lusthaus, 1989, p. 50). The existence of the circles framework makes legitimate the anxieties, questions, and fears of students and teachers, and it provides the possibility of involvement by peers without disabilities in a friendly, caring, support role.

Teams-Games-Tournament. The teams-games-tournament structure involves four or five students assigned to a team to maximize heterogeneity of ability levels, gender, and race. Following an instructional presentation by the teacher, the student groups are assigned worksheets covering academic material.

Teammates study and quiz each other to be certain that all members are prepared. Then, students are assigned to three-person tournament tables. The highest-scoring three students in past tournaments are assigned to Table 1, the next three to Table 2, and so on. Questions are asked during the tournament about the material presented by the teacher and studied by the teams. Each student's score is added to an overall team score, thereby allowing all students an opportunity to contribute to the score for their team.

Jigsaw. The jigsaw approach also assigns students to heterogeneous teams. Learning material is divided into several sections according to the number of team members. Each student is responsible for studying one section with one member from each of the other teams. After the students have studied thoroughly, they return to their teams and teach their respective sections. On completion of their study, each team member is quizzed on all aspects of the unit.

With the jigsaw approach, the grading or scoring procedure is different from that of the team-games-tournament approach in that the quiz scores contribute to individual rather than group grades. Group members are rewarded for their contributions because each member assists other team members in the learning of the various sections. Slavin (1978) has developed a modification of the jigsaw approach that emphasizes team scores rather than individual scores.

Student Teams Achievement Divisions. Like the teams-games-tournament and jigsaw approaches, the student teams achievement divisions approach uses four or five heterogeneously grouped students. The pri-

mary difference is that the games and tournaments are replaced by 15-minute quizzes that students take after studying with their teams. The quiz scores are converted into team scores, which serve to create achievement divisions.

Achievement divisions are formed with six students in each division, and their performance is compared with past quiz scores. With this procedure, the students' scores are compared with those of students of similar ability. Students in each division do not interact with other divisions and are not aware of other division assignments. A bumping procedure is used to change weekly division assignments and to maintain equality. This approach to cooperative learning allows equal opportunities for contributions to the team score.

Small-Group Teaching. Small-group teaching is similar to the other cooperative arrangements except that it is relatively low in group reward interdependence. In this approach, learning is accomplished through group inquiry, discussion, and information gathering by students. Students choose subtopics provided by the teacher and then form small groups of two to six members. If needed, the groups may further subdivide the assignments into individual responsibilities. After completing their respective assignments, the individual students prepare for a group presentation that is evaluated by the entire class and the teacher. This promotes task interdependence and helps build the self-confidence of *all* students.

Rap Sessions. Rap sessions may be held to bring students together to discuss such things as the nature of a disability, the degree of a disability, the ways in which a disability affects learning, levels of realistic expectation, prognosis, and cause of a disability. The type of disability and the comfort that the teacher and student with a disability feel about the topic should be considered when determining who is included in the rap session. For some reason, people often have more negative feelings about intellectual disabilities than about physical disabilities. Generally, it is a good idea to include the student with a physical impairment (hearing, vision, or health impairment) in the rap session, but occasionally, it may be best to discuss the problems in an open manner without the student present. These sessions may be handled by the resource teacher, a regular classroom teacher, or both.

If rap sessions are handled properly, they can do much to help students without disabilities understand students with disabilities and enhance interactions between students. The success of rap sessions, of course, depends on the disability, age of the students, and classroom climate. It may be a good idea to talk with students with disabilities and their parents before rap sessions. Rap sessions may do more harm than good if not handled properly. Informal rap sessions may be helpful but should not take the place of planned, systematic efforts to provide specific information.

Buddy Systems. With buddy systems, the most important factor is the compatibility of the two students. This situation must be handled very carefully, and the teacher must observe closely to be certain the student with a disability is gaining independence. The wrong buddy could lead to increased dependence. The responsibilities of a buddy usually depend on the particular disability—auditory, visual, health-related, intellectual, or emotional. The buddy or helper may be rotated every few weeks to give more students the opportunity to assume responsibility.

The consideration of group learning strategies in the preceding sections provides a brief overview of such programs. It is of great value when properly implemented, and a solid research base indicates that cooperative learning has consistent, positive influences on interethnic relationships and mutual concern among students (Slavin, 1980).

Thus far, most of our suggestions emphasize interaction and cooperative working relationships—approaches believed to greatly facilitate interaction among all students. Some evidence, however, indicates that contact alone does not necessarily result in positive attitude changes. This research indicates that students also need specific information and that with specific information and awareness of the potential of individuals with disabilities, individuals without disabilities change their attitudes significantly (Cleary, 1976; Gronberg, 1983; Prillaman, 1981; Scheffers, 1977).

UNDERSTANDING STUDENTS WHO HAVE DISABILITIES

The next several sections review ways in which teachers can provide specific information to help students without disabilities better understand the abilities of individuals with disabilities.

Books and Films About Individuals Who Have Disabilities

Many trade books about individuals with disabilities are valuable in helping students without disabilities better understand peers who have disabilities. (See Appendix A for an extensive annotated list of such books.) Such materials may be read to a class or placed on the classroom reading shelf or in the school library. Films about individuals with disabilities also may be of interest and value. Reading such books and viewing such films can serve as starting points for rap sessions and in-service sessions. In most cases, such books and films provide insights into the problems of individuals with disabilities and feelings that they may have about themselves.

As new materials are available (either books or films), teachers may wish to consider using them; however, not all are equally valuable and appropriate. Rudman (1984) provides criteria for selecting books that portray persons with special needs. These criteria may also be valuable in film selection. The following list summarizes her criteria. Books (and films) about individuals with special needs should:

1. Portray persons in a balanced way, having individual talents and temperaments
2. Show persons of various races, social classes, and economic backgrounds
3. Show individuals as capable of helping themselves and others, not as objects of pity
4. Show individuals as coping with disability, not as receiving some miracle cure because they are good persons
5. Use accuracy in describing settings and situations (i.e., not describe institutions as either torture chambers or ideal havens)
6. Not pair specific disabilities or physical attributes with specific personality traits or mental abilities
7. Not show tragedy or violence as a specific by-product of disability
8. Show persons with disabilities as capable of loving relationships

In-Service Sessions

Brief in-service sessions are appropriate for students with physical disabilities. If the student uses special equipment (braille typewriter, hearing aid, or wheelchair, for example), other students may not understand its use and purpose. In an in-service session, the student can explain the use of and actually demonstrate how the equipment operates. Often, the curiosity and lack of understanding of other students about special equipment may distract them from their own work. Once the special equipment is demonstrated and its use is explained, the distraction is usually alleviated.

For example, a visually impaired student can demonstrate magnification devices and explain their value and use. The student may also explain the rationale for using a regular typewriter, braille materials, or large-type materials. Other aids and appliances, such as tape recorders, tape players, talking book machines, arithmetic aids, and embossed or enlarged maps, may also be demonstrated. Units of study on the eye or ear may be presented by the regular classroom teacher or the special education resource teacher in cooperation with a student who is visually or hearing impaired.

The age and willingness of a student with a disability to participate are factors to consider when planning an in-service session. If a student is unwilling, the special education teacher (vision specialist or hearing specialist) may conduct an in-service session. Regardless of who participates, the session must be handled so that the student is not made to seem too "special." If the presentation implies that the student is someone super or someone to feel sorry for, the very purpose of the session may be defeated.

Panel of Individuals with Disabilities

Many teachers have had considerable success by inviting guest speakers who are disabled or panels of persons with disabilities to share their experiences. Such presentations should emphasize ways in which these individuals modify or adapt to everyday living situations. Such individuals may also discuss their interests, hobbies, and work experiences. Students should be encouraged to ask questions of the guests. It is important that the teacher invite individuals who will assist in the development of positive attitudes.

Special Materials

Special materials have been developed to help students without disabilities better understand and accept the differences and similarities of their classmates with disabilities. Such materials are similar to values education and clarification materials but have been designed specifically to provide information about individuals with disabilities and to promote positive attitudinal changes. It appears that attitudes of the general public toward individuals with disabilities are changing slowly in a positive direction. Although some telethons and other fund-raising projects continue to emphasize the differences of people with disabilities, many other efforts emphasize the inherent similarities in the general needs of all people.

Because attitudes, beliefs, and behaviors toward differences are based on values learned from important others, such as family members, or from meaningful experiences, students without disabilities should have opportunities to participate in discussions, interviews, and presentations by adults and students with disabilities and to view films, filmstrips, and other media about individuals with disabilities. Teachers should provide specific information concerning differences between students with and without disabilities, and this content should be part of every student's education.

Interaction is a basic need; therefore, educators must design instruction to help students relate to others in their environment.

TEACHING SOCIAL SKILLS

Teachers must encourage positive interactions; however, students with disabilities must share the responsibility. In what arena are such students most likely to be deficient? A host of researchers, authors, and observers indicate that it may be the arena of social skills (Asher & Hymel, 1981; Asher, Oden, & Gottman, 1981; Gresham, 1982).

In a commonsense definition, Cartledge and Milburn (1986) indicate social skills to be "socially acceptable learned behaviors that enable the person to interact with others in ways that elicit positive responses and assist in avoiding negative responses from them" (p. 7). Important social behaviors include greeting others, sharing, asking for assistance when needed, initiating conversations, giving compliments, following game and classroom rules, talking about such things as current movies and television shows, showing a sense of humor, helping classmates, and knowing current slang words. Unacceptable social behaviors include not responding to peer social initiations, misinterpreting the approach behaviors of peers, and entering games or group activities uninvited.

Since many students with disabilities do not have the social skills necessary to interact positively with their peers, it is imperative that teachers assess students' social skills and begin remediation of deficits. Training in social skills may occur before and after placement in a regular classroom. Gresham (1982) categorizes training in social skills under three major headings (a) manipulation of antecedents, (b) manipulation of consequences, and (c) modeling. Manipulation of antecedents involves having nondisabled students initiate social interactions with statements such as "Come with me," "Let's play a game," and "Come on." By design, these initiations establish occasions for increased interaction. Other examples are sociodramas and cooperative games.

The training approach used most often is manipulation of consequences. This approach involves having the teacher socially reinforce the student with a disability when the student interacts or cooperates with nondisabled peers. This procedure is also used to reinforce students without disabilities when they are interacting or working positively with a student who has a disability.

The third general approach used to teach social skills is modeling. Modeling can be used in film or live formats. With film or videotape presentations, a student observes other students modeling desirable social behaviors. The most practical approach for regular classroom teachers appears to be live modeling, in which a student observes models in natural environments.

Cartledge and Milburn (1986) believe that instruction in social skills "involves many of the same procedures as teaching academic concepts; that is, the exposure of the child to a model of imitation, eliciting an imitative response, providing feedback about the correctness of the response, and structuring opportunities for practice" (p. 115). Regular classroom teachers should consult with special education resource personnel for assistance with specific approaches, but awareness of these principles will involve teachers in informal instruction throughout the school day. For teachers interested in continued study in this area, we suggest the various social skills

curricula described by Cartledge and Milburn (1986); Goldstein, Sprafkin, Gershaw, and Klein (1980); Jackson, Jackson, and Monroe (1983); Milburn and Cartledge (1976); and Stephens (1978).

TEACHER-PARENT INTERACTIONS

In the publication *What Works: Research About Teaching and Learning* (1986), the U.S. Department of Education provides a synthesis of research findings that indicate how to improve the effectiveness of schools. This report emphasizes the importance of parents in education, noting, "Parents are their children's first and most influential teachers" (p. 7). Relating to all students, this conclusion may be even more significant with respect to students who have special needs. A number of other publications provide guidance with respect to parent-teacher relationships, and many school districts provide guidelines for such scheduled events as parent-teacher conferences.

For students who have special needs, effective communication with parents (regular, scheduled conferences, emergency conferences, regular reports of pupil progress, notes, or phone calls) requires somewhat more attention than does communication for other students. Regular classroom teachers and special education personnel who work with such students must collaborate in reporting, and each must keep the others fully informed. In most instances, all involved should know the content of communication before it takes place. Normally, IEP development and reporting are governed by school policies, but written procedures should establish guidance for all other communication. To make teacher-parent interactions maximally effective, all school personnel involved must be fully aware of the need to collaborate and willing to take the time required to make such collaboration effective.

SUMMARY

This chapter emphasized the role of classroom teachers in promoting positive interactions between exceptional students and their peers. It suggested that teachers examine their feelings and expectations to be cer-tain that they contribute to student success. A number of anecdotes illustrating potential negative—or positive—influences of teachers, along with specific strategies to promote positive feelings, were provided. The chapter emphasized that the motivation for positive relationships must come from teachers. Then, it will spread throughout classes, and sometimes even throughout schools.

PART III

TEACHING EXCEPTIONAL STUDENTS

PART III, THE FINAL EIGHT CHAPTERS OF THIS TEXT, INCLUDES BASIC INFORMATION ABOUT students who are often considered according to eight different classifications. These classifications relate to hearing impairments, speech and language disorders, visual impairments, orthopedic and health impairments, mental retardation, learning disabilities, behavior disorders, and giftedness or talent. At times, these classifications are nebulous, and some, like orthopedic and health impairments, include multiple conditions. These classifications are described in federal and state laws and regulations, and most are used (perhaps in some slightly modified form) in all states. Therefore, they may provide the least confusing way to communicate information about exceptional students enrolled in regular classrooms.

- What types of behavior indicate possible hearing impairment?

- Why is it sometimes difficult to identify a young student with a mild hearing loss?

- What environmental and instructional modifications are necessary to provide successful hearing experiences for students with hearing impairment?

- Why do students with hearing impairment tend to avoid interactions with hearing students? How can teachers change this situation?

- What are the three major communication systems used by individuals with severe hearing impairment? Why not have and use just one system to reduce potential confusion?

- Is it essential for regular classroom teachers to know how to sign?

- To what extent should hearing individuals exaggerate gestures when communicating with students who have hearing impairment?

- How may regular classroom teachers facilitate the speechreading skills of students with hearing impairment?

CHAPTER 5

TEACHING STUDENTS WHO ARE HEARING IMPAIRED

NEARLY 20 YEARS AFTER THE PASSAGE OF PL 94–142 and subsequent efforts relating to mainstreaming, many persons who are deaf say they would rather be in segregated settings (Commission on the Education of the Deaf, 1988). Although there are a variety of reasons for such statements, both parents and teachers should ask certain critical questions. Parents should ask about their own motivations and attitudes. Do they really support the concept of integration with a hearing world? Are they cooperating with school personnel and supporting school programs in every reasonable way possible? Teachers must ask, Is my classroom a place in which a student with a hearing impairment wants to be? This questioning leads to many related questions: Is the student accepted and included? and Are the student's needs being met without causing unacceptable feelings of differentness?

This text, especially in Chapter 4, emphasizes the need to promote feelings of acceptance. Students must feel that they are integral parts of a class, or the effectiveness of instruction is significantly reduced. Note that there is more likelihood that parents of students with hearing impairment, particularly the more severe impairment, do not so readily accept education in the mainstream as do parents of students in other categories of disability. We believe, however, that if the full continuum of educational placements is available and appropriate placements and programming are provided, parental and student satisfaction with programs for students with hearing impairment will greatly increase.

THE IMPORTANCE OF HEARING TO EARLY LEARNING

Listening is an important learning tool from the time a child is born. An infant learns to discriminate between loud and soft, high and low, and disturbing and pleasant sounds. An infant also learns to determine the direction, distance, and meaning of sounds. In addition, an infant analyzes the human voice and differentiates his or her own babbling and crying from the sounds of others. Sometime between the ages of 12 and 24 months, as a result of previous language experiences, the child begins to learn to speak and to develop language skills. Obviously, if the child has a hearing impairment, speech and language development may be delayed.

Underdeveloped speech and language skills are the greatest limitations imposed by hearing impairment. Delayed speech and language influence a child's ability to develop communication skills, such as reading, writing, listening, and speaking. As a result, these skills develop at a slower rate than those of the normally hearing child. A student with a hearing impairment has the most difficulty in the language arts areas, such as reading, spelling, and writing, because of their relationship to speech and language development. The extent of difficulty depends on the student's command of the language, degree of hearing loss, and age at the onset of loss. A student may have no trouble understanding concepts but have difficulty learning the label or language used to describe concepts. For example, the concept of buoyancy may be understood, but the student may have difficulty in writing, saying, or spelling the word *buoyancy*. A student with a hearing impairment may have much less difficulty with science, math, or other non-language arts programs. Math, with the exception of story problems, is conceptual in nature. Science may also be thought of as conceptual.

In contrast, the reading process involves associating meaning with sounds and written symbols. A hearing impairment that delays language development seriously limits associations between sounds and written symbols; therefore, reading may be an area of considerable difficulty for such a student, particularly for a young child who is in the process of acquiring reading skills. Such a child *can* learn to read; however, a very well-planned program must be offered—a program that reflects close cooperation between regular teachers and the special education resource or itinerant teachers. Although language development is important to success in school, the student with a hearing impairment is able to learn and profit from instruction in regular classrooms.

In addition to academic difficulties that may result from a hearing loss, two other limitations may be imposed by impaired hearing. The first limitation is characterized by inability to hear music. Such a limitation cannot be overcome, but must be compensated for in a manner that is acceptable to the individual. A second limitation may be imposed by society. Such societal limitations, characterized by negative or demeaning interactions with others, including parents, teachers, siblings, and friends, may lead to self-imposed social limitations and restrictions. Teachers may play important roles in reducing this type of limitation.

THE NATURE OF HEARING IMPAIRMENT

In instances where a hearing impairment has been identified, regular classroom teachers can use a number of methods and techniques. To better understand these methods and techniques, various other aspects of programs for students with hearing impairment are considered here as they are administered in the public schools.

Types of Hearing Impairment

There are two major types of hearing impairment, and different degrees of hearing loss are associated with these two types. One type of hearing impairment affects the loudness, or intensity with which a person hears speech. This type of loss, known as a conductive hearing loss, is caused by interference with the transmission of sound from the outer ear to the inner ear. The interference may be caused by some type of blockage, such as a foreign object, or by a malformation. If detected early, some types of conductive losses are correctable by surgery. A student with this type of loss generally can profit from the use of a hearing aid, because the aid magnifies sounds at all frequencies.

The other type of loss, a sensorineural loss, affects the frequency, intelligibility, and clarity of the sounds the person hears. A sensorineural loss is associated with damage to the sensory end organ or dysfunction of the auditory nerve. This type of hearing loss is not as amenable as a conductive loss to correction by use of a hearing aid because the problem is related to nerve damage. No matter how much the sound is amplified, the nerve damage prevents the sound from reaching the hearing area of the brain.

An analogy to a radio roughly illustrates the two types of hearing loss. By turning the volume down, it is possible to simulate a hearing loss affecting the loudness with which one hears sounds. If one can hear the sounds, one can understand them; they are not distorted. This is similar to a conductive loss. The tuning dial, which controls the frequency of signals, illustrates sensorineural loss. If the radio is not tuned in correctly, the sounds are not clear and are difficult to understand. Often words are not complete. The sentence "He sat at his desk" may sound like "e a a iz de."

Measurement of Hearing

An instrument known as a pure-tone audiometer is used to measure hearing acuity (sharpness or acuteness of sensory discrimination). An audiometer produces sounds at varying intensities (loudness) and frequencies (pitch). When administering an audiometric examination, an audiologist systematically presents a series of carefully calibrated tones that vary in loudness and pitch. The results are charted on a graph called an audiogram, which provides an indication of the person's ability to hear each tone at each of the presented frequencies. An audiometric evaluation assists in determining the extent and type of hearing loss so that the proper remedial or medical steps may be taken.

The unit of measurement used to express the intensity of sound is the decibel (dB), and the freqency is expressed in hertz (Hz). If an individual has a hearing loss, it is indicated in decibels; the more significant the loss, the larger the number. For example, a 60-dB loss is greater than a 25-dB loss. The following common environmental sounds expressed in intensity (decibels) may be of assistance in understanding the nature of hearing loss:

Decibels	*Sounds*
0	Threshold of hearing
20	Very quiet conversation
40	Outdoor minimum sound level in a city
60	Average restaurant sounds or normal conversation
80	Loud radio or tape deck music in a home
100	Riveting machine or air hammer at 30 feet
140	Threshold of pain

In addition to information concerning the extent of the loss in decibels, it may be helpful to have information concerning the frequency at which the loss occurs. The audiogram in Figure 5–1 indicates a severe hearing loss in an 11-year-old student. The numbers on the left side of the audiogram indicate the decibels, or loudness of the sound. The zero indicates the degree of loudness necessary for an average person to hear sound, and the other numbers indicate increasing loudness of sound. The lines on the audiogram indicate the degree of hearing loss in each ear at various frequencies. The numbers across the top of the audiogram indicate the frequency in hertz of the sounds. The sounds that are most critical for interpretation of speech (speech range) fall between 500 and 2000 Hz.

The portion of an audiogram shown in Figure 5–2 represents the sounds of speech at the various frequencies. As shown in this

FIGURE 5–1
Audiogram (○, right ear; ●, left ear)

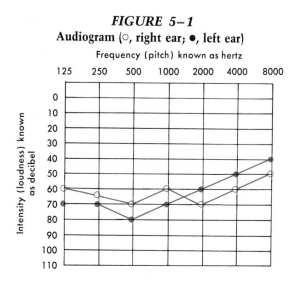

Frequency (pitch) known as hertz

Intensity (loudness) known as decibel

Severity of Hearing Impairment

Often, attempts to systematically classify hearing acuity in relation to actual hearing efficiency or functional ability do not account for a number of outside factors, such as motivation, intelligence, social maturity, and family background. These variables may influence the functional ability of individuals. Two individuals with the same measured hearing loss do not necessarily have the same type or degree of difficulty in academic or social settings.

One type of classification emphasizes how a student might react to language instruction based on the age of onset of the hearing loss. If the hearing loss occurs at birth or at an early age, before speech and language are developed, it is classified as congenital, or prelingual, deafness. If the loss occurs after the development of speech and language, it is classified as acquired, or postlingual, deafness. These definitions emphasize language acquisition, how the student will learn language most effectively.

figure, many of the voiceless speech sounds *(f, th, s)* are in the higher ranges. A student who has a high-frequency (2000 to 4000 level) loss misses those sounds when spoken, and since much of speech is imitation, the student may leave these sounds out of his or her speech.

FIGURE 5–2
Sounds of speech at various frequencies

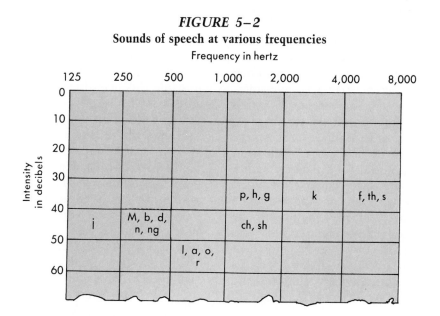

Frequency in hertz

Intensity in decibels

Although it is difficult to classify degrees of hearing impairment on the basis of severity, it is necessary to have a classification system that provides insight into the degree of loss and the potential implications. The following system is commonly used by educators:

Degree	Decibels
Mild	27–40 dB
Moderate	41–55 dB
Moderately severe	56–70 dB
Severe	71–90 dB
Profound	91+ dB

A person who has a hearing loss between 27 and 40 dB has a mild hearing loss and is likely to have difficulty with faint or distant speech. Students with mild losses may need favorable seating; may benefit from speechreading, vocabulary, or language instruction, or a combination of these; and may need speech therapy.

A hearing loss in the 41 to 55 dB range is usually classified as moderate. An individual with such a hearing loss most likely can understand conversational speech at a distance of 3 to 5 feet. Such a student probably needs a hearing aid, auditory training, speechreading, favorable seating, speech conversation, and speech therapy. The extent of services provided by the resource teacher or consultant may vary considerably, depending on the student's actual achievement in the regular classroom.

An individual with a moderately severe hearing impairment has a hearing loss in the 56 to 70 dB range. For a student with a moderately severe loss, conversation must be loud to be understood. The student's speech is probably defective, and he or she may have a limited vocabulary. This student may have difficulty in group and classroom discussion, can use all the services usually provided students with mild and moderate losses, and, in addition, requires specific assistance from the resource teacher or consultant.

A person who has a hearing loss between 71 and 90 dB has a severe loss and may not be able to hear a loud voice beyond a distance of 1 to 2 feet. Such a student may be able to distinguish some environmental sounds. The student has difficulty with consonant sounds but not necessarily vowels. Such a student needs all of the services required by students with less severe losses and may need to learn many of the techniques used with students who are deaf.

An individual with a hearing loss of more than 91 dB has a profound impairment. Although this individual may be able to hear some loud sounds, he or she probably does not rely on hearing as the primary learning channel. Likely, this student needs all of the previously mentioned services and possibly more intensive services from the resource teacher or consultant for the hearing impaired. A student with a profound hearing impairment requires special assistance, with emphasis on speech, auditory training, and language; however, the student may attend regular classes on a part-time basis or attend classes that do not require a significant emphasis on language skills.

Considerable caution must be exercised in using this classification system, because students with nearly identical losses may function differently. In addition to using caution with classification systems, educators must also exercise care in predetermining the extent of special education services needed in relation to the degree of loss. Experts in this field do not agree on the relative importance of various degrees of loss. In any individual case, a variety of other information must be carefully considered. Characteristics of need may include defective speech, with substitutions, omissions, or distortions; reading problems; immature language patterns; lower levels of abstraction; and perhaps fewer interpersonal relationships (Marsh, Price, & Smith, 1983). Some students with severe losses are readily served in regular classrooms, whereas other students with moderate loss need extensive special education services for the majority of the school day.

IDENTIFICATION OF STUDENTS WITH HEARING IMPAIRMENT

Although not always recognized by the regular classroom teacher, a student's learning or behavior problems may result from a hearing loss. The teacher can misjudge the student as being mentally retarded or emotionally disturbed or as having some type of specific learning disability. In other instances, the teacher may feel the student's problems are caused by some failure in the teacher's methods. Until the teacher recognizes that the student's problem may be the result of a hearing loss, a great deal of time can be wasted on fruitless remedial measures. Therefore, it is important for regular classroom teachers to be aware of some common behaviors that may indicate hearing loss.

Behavioral Indications

Following are the most common behaviors and medical symptoms that may indicate hearing loss.

Lack of Attention. One such behavior is apparent lack of attention. If a student does not pay attention, it is possible that he or she cannot hear what is being said. Another possibility may be that the student hears sounds but they are so distorted that they are difficult to understand. Consequently, the student tunes them out or does not make the effort to attend to them. Occasionally, the opposite behavior is observed.

A student may be abnormally attentive—always paying close attention in an attempt to determine what is happening in the classroom. Although this is less frequently seen than inattentive behaviors, it does occur.

Lack of Speech Development. Immature, unusual, or distorted speech may be the result of hearing loss. Distorted speech may be an indication of the way the student is hearing—in a distorted manner.

Difficulty in Following Directions. An unusual amount of difficulty in following oral directions is another possible indicator of hearing impairment. A student who has little difficulty with written directions and considerable difficulty with oral directions may have a hearing loss. Also, a student who often loses his or her place in oral reading assignments could have difficulty hearing what the others are reading. Another indication may be that the student asks the teacher and others to speak louder. Some students with mild losses give inappropriate answers to questions, and this too may be an indication of hearing impairment.

Best Work in Small Groups. If a student seems to work best in small groups or in relatively quiet working areas, this may be an indication of a hearing loss. Greater success with tasks assigned by the teacher at a relatively close distance or in an uncluttered auditory area (as compared with tasks assigned at a distance or in a noisy situation) may also be an indication.

Dependence on Classmates for Instructions. Teachers should be aware of a student who watches classmates to see what they are doing before he or she starts working. The student may not have fully heard or understood the directions given and may be looking for cues from classmates or the teacher.

Turning or Cocking of Head. A behavior that may indicate that a student has a hearing loss is an unusual amount of cocking the head to one side. The student may need to turn one ear toward the speaker to hear more adequately. In addition, the student with a hearing loss may make frequent requests for repetitions.

Acting Out, Stubborn, Shy, or Withdrawn Behavior. Have you ever tried to listen to a speaker who was talking so softly you had difficulty hearing? You could see the speaker's lips move but were unable to hear what was being said. Remembering that frustrating experience may help the teacher understand why a student with a hearing loss may seem stubborn, disobedient, shy, or withdrawn. If a student is unable to hear, personality and behavior problems may arise. The student may compensate for inability to hear by acting out in the classroom. Other students with hearing impairment may compensate by withdrawing, acting stubborn, or being shy.

Use of Gestures. Although rare, some students with hearing loss rely on gestures to communicate when speech would be more effective. This is more common with younger children, because they have not developed the necessary language and communication skills.

Disparity Between Expected and Actual Achievement. A possible indication of hearing loss is disparity between expected and actual achievement. Obviously, there may be many reasons that a student does not achieve in a manner consistent with

his or her ability, but teachers should be aware that one of the reasons may be hearing loss.

Reluctance to Participate in Oral Activities. A less extreme behavior sometimes characteristic of a student with a hearing impairment is reluctance to participate in oral activities. Another possible characteristic is an apparent lack of a sense of humor. A student who often fails to laugh at a joke may not be hearing the joke.

Medical Indications

So far, this chapter has been concerned only with behavior that may indicate that a student has a hearing loss. There are also medical indications of hearing loss that should not be ignored by teachers. These include frequent earaches, fluid running from the ears, frequent colds or sore throats, and recurring tonsillitis.

It is advisable to be aware also of students with allergies. An allergy can produce swollen tissues in the nose and ears, leading to faulty hearing. Signs to watch for include dark circles under the eyes, red eyes, frequent sneezing, and a chronic runny nose. These physical characteristics must be brought to the attention of the school nurse and the parents, who should be urged to contact their physician. Teachers should also be aware of otitis media, an inflammation of the middle ear that, without treatment, can cause a conductive hearing loss. This condition is particularly common among children with hearing problems.

Early detection is of vital importance. It has been estimated that 1 out of 10 persons in the United States has a hearing loss. Hearing loss affects more people than cancer, tuberculosis, blindness, multiple sclerosis, and kidney disease combined (House Ear Institute, 1985).

PROCEDURES FOR REFERRAL

Should the teacher suspect a hearing loss, he or she must compile a list of the specific behaviors noted and refer the student immediately to the school nurse, speech specialist, or audiologist. Any of these professionals will conduct a preliminary screening; and if the results indicate the need, the student will be referred to an otologist (a physician who specializes in diseases of the ear).

It is essential that teachers monitor the referral process. Occasionally, for a variety of reasons, action is extremely slow or no action is taken. In such an unfortunate situation, the classroom teacher may have to ask pertinent questions to determine the status of the referral.

A referral does not automatically mean that a hearing loss is present. For example, assume the teacher observes some behavior that makes him or her suspect that a student has a hearing loss. The teacher refers the student to the nurse, speech pathologist, or audiologist, who concludes that a hearing loss is present. The student is then referred through the parents to an expert for a more extensive examination. The otologist may find an accumulation of wax or some other obstruction in the ears, infected tonsils or adenoids, or some other abnormality that may be medically corrected. In this instance, hearing can be restored and the student returned to school without any educational modifications or adaptations. However, many referrals do not result in medical correction, and as a result, a hearing aid may be recommended. Now what happens to the student? Should the student be placed in a special class, or continue in regular classes? If the student is to be retained in a regular classroom, in which classroom should the student be retained?

These are some of the questions considered in staffing procedures.

PLACEMENT CONSIDERATIONS

The following student characteristics are not criteria for placement, but they are normally discussed in staffing procedures:

1. The ability to exchange ideas through spoken, written, and read language (including expressive and receptive auditory-oral communication skills)
2. Social and emotional maturity nearly equal to that of the other students in the classroom, as well as minimal disparity between listening age and academic skills
3. The ability to profit from large-group instruction when new information is presented
4. Independence, self-confidence, and determination to succeed
5. A chronological age close to that of the regular class students (McCartney, 1984)

In addition to the characteristics of a student, other factors, such as availability of sound amplification, presence of support staff, counseling or remediation if necessary, rate of speech and type of voice of the teacher, visibility of the teacher's lip movements, acceptance and understanding level of the teacher, use of visual aids, quality of lighting, degree to which the other students will extend consideration and respect, and the wishes of the parents, must be considered prior to placement.

Such factors relate to a student, parents, and other students. An additional factor is the working relationship between regular class teachers and resource personnel, who must establish and maintain a working relationship that enhances the education of the student. Regular class teachers must feel free to ask without reservation for assistance whenever needed. Resource teachers must be allowed to observe in regular classrooms at any time, not in a judgmental manner but as team members. If the working relationship between regular classroom teachers and resource teachers is one of mutual respect and understanding, recognizing that there are no authoritative experts and that neither is self-sufficient, they will be well on the way to the critical factor: open communication for the benefit of the student.

Advantages of Regular Classroom Placement

Following are some of the advantages offered by regular classroom placement:

1. An opportunity to continue relationships with hearing classmates, which reinforces the feeling that the student with a hearing impairment is more like than not like other students. The student with a hearing impairment will maintain or gain a feeling of belonging.
2. An exposure to a greater variety of language styles.
3. The necessity of keeping speech and language patterns at an intelligible level. Often, when students with hearing impairment are grouped together in the same class, they do not develop or maintain a high level of speech and language. A regular classroom provides normal, age-appropriate speech, language, and social models.
4. The necessity of establishing a wider variety of communication techniques. A student who is hearing impaired may have to modify his or her communication skills if he or she is not understood by classmates. This may necessitate a reexamination of the student's communication skills.
5. An opportunity for a student with a hearing impairment to compete academically with hearing classmates. The aca-

demic pace is faster, and general achievement expectations are raised. However, in the interests of professional objectivity, note that this may be the major reason why some students *cannot* participate with success in regular classrooms.
6. Preparation to function in a hearing world. All individuals interacting with a student who is hearing impaired must remember that the ultimate objective is for the student with the hearing impairment to function as independently as possible in a hearing society.

In addition, an advantage of regular classroom placement is that hearing students have an opportunity to become acquainted with someone who is different. This must be seen as positive, particularly when students must learn to relate with and understand people of different ethnic backgrounds or races or with persons who have disabilities. Placement or retention in a regular classroom works well for some students with hearing impairment and is essentially unsuccessful with others. As noted, we believe that retention in a regular classroom is the best choice, *if it is effective in meeting the educational goals of the student.*

Obtaining Complete Information

Complete information should be obtained before taking a student with a hearing impairment into a class. Be certain that there is sufficient information concerning (a) the nature of the loss, (b) the amount of residual hearing, and (c) how the student communicates. A few brief private sessions with the student should be arranged so that a comfortable relationship and communication process can be established. Because the speech of a student who is hearing impaired may be defective, such sessions may familiarize the teacher with the student's speech patterns. The teacher may also find it helpful to discuss the student's speech needs with the speech specialist or special education resource person. Most of the information concerning the student can be obtained from special education resource personnel in the school or school district.

By nature of professional preparation and experience, a resource teacher or consultant generally has very good understanding of medical aspects of impairment, audiology, and speech therapy. A resource teacher or consultant may serve as a liaison between the disciplines and regular teachers, interpret the exact nature of hearing loss in relation to medical and audiological evaluations, and provide specific suggestions related to the characteristics of hearing efficiency for a particular student. It is hoped that information concerning the individual's functional ability is emphasized rather than medical or quantitative information. In addition, the resource teacher may interpret a student's development of language and its influence on learning.

Another valuable source of information is the parents of a student. Brief conferences with the parents before actual placement and on an ongoing basis thereafter can provide considerable information about a student who has a hearing impairment. The information, support, and participation of the parents in their child's educational program are known to be primary determinants of successful mainstreaming programs. (Marsh et al., 1983).

WHAT TEACHERS SHOULD KNOW

When a classroom teacher has a student who has a hearing impairment, the teacher should be familiar with certain basic information.

Hearing Aids

A hearing aid is not a complicated piece of equipment. The aid helps compensate for hearing loss by amplifying sound. It cannot replace the natural ability of an ear, and a student who wears an aid should not be expected to hear normally. Limitations in the use of an aid may be imposed by damage to the ear, by the nature of speech sounds, or by the hearing aid itself. Misunderstandings of what a hearing aid can do are common. Many individuals believe, for example, that a hearing aid is like eyeglasses: you simply put them on and you will see—or hear—better. This is not true.

There are basically three parts to a hearing aid: (a) a microphone, which picks up sound and converts the sounds to electrical impulses; (b) an amplifier, which makes sounds louder by increasing the electrical impulses; and (c) a speaker or receiver, which reconverts the electrical signals back into sound and directs them to the ear mold.

There are many types of hearing aids, but hearing aids are generally classified on the basis of where they are worn. The first type is a body aid, which is strapped to the body with a wire connected to the ear mold. These sturdy, compact aids are generally worn by young children. Often, the controls are on the young child's back so that he or she will not play with them. The second type, an ear-level aid, may be mounted in eyeglasses, fit behind the ear, or fit entirely in the ear. Aids are also classified as monaural (one ear) or binaural (both ears).

Care and Maintenance. Even though the parents or a student have examined a hearing aid prior to the student's coming to school, the aid may not adequately function in school. The teacher can check several things if a student seems not to be hearing well because of a hearing aid malfunction.

Although it is not the primary responsibility of the regular classroom teacher to troubleshoot hearing aid problems, it is helpful to be aware of a few minor factors that may cause malfunctions so that the resource teacher or the parents can be alerted. The following suggestions are related to hearing aid malfunctions:

1. Make sure the battery is not dead. Keep a fresh battery at school (changed at least monthly, even though it may not have been used) so that the child does not have to go without the hearing aid on the day the battery goes dead. Often, the resource teacher has an extra supply of batteries and can assist in determining whether other problems might exist.
2. Determine if the battery is installed properly, with the positive and negative terminals in the proper position.
3. Check the cord to see if it is worn or broken or if the receiver is cracked.
4. Be sure the plug-in points are not loose. Check both the hearing aid and the receiver.
5. Check the ear mold to make sure it is not obstructed by wax and that it is inserted properly. An improperly fitted ear mold can cause irritation and feedback (squeaky or squealing sounds that annoy the student wearing the aid and are sometimes heard by other students). Possibly, the student is outgrowing the aid, so the parents or the resource teacher should be informed.
6. Examine the tube to determine if condensation has built up. If it has, blow through the tube until it disappears.

Regular teachers should be aware of some additional considerations with respect to the proper care and maintenance of hearing aids.

1. Do not allow the hearing aid to get wet.
2. Serious damage may result from leaving the hearing aid in extremely hot or cold places.
3. Always turn an aid off before removing it from the ear. Removing the aid without turning it off causes a squeal. Whenever an aid is taken off, it should be placed in a safe, padded box.
4. If a student repeatedly removes the aid, this may be an indication that the aid is not working correctly or does not fit properly and causes discomfort. Naturally, if this occurs, the teacher should contact the resource teacher or consultant.
5. Do not allow a student to wear a hearing aid microphone too close to the receiver, or the aid will make unusual noises. If the student has a unilateral loss (one ear), the receiver should be worn on the side opposite the hearing aid.
6. Do not take an aid apart to attempt to repair it. This should be done by a hearing aid dealer.

Assessing Effectiveness. The resource teacher or consultant can assist in evaluating many aspects of hearing aid problems and hearing aid effectiveness. They can evaluate routinely all aspects of hearing aid operation by checking and replacing worn-out batteries and troubleshooting for any other problems. Many teachers obtain a tester for use in the building or make arrangements for assistance from a local hearing aid dealer.

A more important role of the resource teacher is to assess hearing aid effectiveness in the classroom situation, particularly if a student has just recently been fitted with an aid. The resource teacher can appraise the effectiveness of an aid by evaluating changes in the ways a student handles everyday situations. The resource teacher should look carefully for (a) changes in social interactions, (b) changes in voice quality and articulation, (c) increased language skills, (d) reactions to sound and amplification, and (e) increased educational achievement. In addition, the resource teacher should observe whether the student is turning the volume down or completely turning it off. Such actions may be indications of an improperly fitted aid. Systematic longitudinal evaluation of a student's hearing aid effectiveness is important, and routine procedures should be established to provide hearing aid maintenance.

Increasing Understanding. Often, hearing students are curious about how a hearing aid works. In cooperation with the resource teacher, consultant, parents, and the student with a hearing impairment, the teacher may present information about the operation of the hearing aid. A brief unit of study may be conducted on the anatomy and physiology of the ear and the basic principles of acoustics. Hearing students can be given an opportunity to listen to a hearing aid (a stethoscope may be used so they do not have to put the ear mold in their ears). This type of experience may provide understanding of amplification devices and problems associated with them.

Auditory Trainers

A conventional hearing aid amplifies all sounds, including background noises, and this often poses a serious problem. Background or environmental sounds may mask or cover up what the teacher is saying. One way to accommodate this problem is the use of an auditory trainer. An auditory trainer is similar to a hearing aid and has the same basic three parts, but in addition, the teacher wears a microphone around the neck that sends the teacher's voice directly to the student wearing the auditory trainer. When the teacher speaks, his or her voice is received by the student as if the teacher were standing right next to the student's ear. Some auditory trainers use a wireless microphone that transmits an FM radio signal to a combination hearing aid–FM receiver, bypassing environmental sounds and bringing desired sounds directly to the ear.

Audio Loop Systems

Many hearing aids have a telecoil (T) setting which, when activated, responds to magnetic controls. In this system, a loop of wire is fixed around the inside periphery of a building (classroom, church, theatre). The loop can be connected to the amplifier of a microphone being used by the speaker (teacher, minister, actor), and the changing magnetic fields from the loop of wire can be received and converted back into sound by the induction coil in a hearing aid. This direct system reduces the amplification of background noises and allows receivers to concentrate directly on the words spoken into the microphone.

Cochlear Implants

Since 1985, when the Food and Drug Administration approved cochlear implants for children, increasing numbers of school-age children have undergone the cochlear implant procedure. Candidates for cochlear implants are usually profoundly deaf and have not benefited from the usual amplification devices available. Extensive training is required to make efficient use of cochlear implants. Usually, audiologists and speech-language specialists are involved. The teacher with a student who has had an implant must collaborate with these professionals in any special training pertinent to the regular classroom.

A cochlear implant consists of a microphone, transmitter, processor, and receiver. The microphone is attached externally at ear level and picks up sounds, which are transformed into electrical currents and amplified by a battery-operated processor. This energy is sent to the transmitter, which is located behind the ear and held in place by a magnetic process. The electrical current is transformed into magnetic signals to the receiver, which is a small disk planted beneath the skin behind the outer portion of the ear. Two electrodes are attached to this receiver—one is placed in the scala tympani and the other is grounded in the eustachian tube. As current flows between the two electrodes, the nerve cells of the cochlea are stimulated, so the sensation of hearing occurs.

Variations of this process include use of a percutaneous plug, which provides direct input of electrical energy. Such variations are often referred to as *hardwired*. Some implants have multiple channels to allow for more variation in the sounds that are transmitted. Others use an extra cochlear electrode, which is mounted on the round window rather than the cochlea. Whatever the type of cochlear implant, a cooperative effort with an audiologist or a speech-language specialist is essential.

Methods of Communication

Development of language and communication skills is the primary emphasis of educational programming for students with hearing impairment. There has been considerable controversy concerning the most effective and efficient method of communication for such students. Three methods have been advocated: (a) the manual method, (b) the oral method, and (c) total communication. Each of these methods is briefly discussed in the paragraphs that follow.

Manual Communication. American Sign Language (ASL) is a set of gestures representing words or concepts (Figure 5–3). It is generally used by the adult deaf population and has been called the mother tongue. Fingerspelling, or manual alphabet, is another form of manual communication. In finger-

spelling, various finger positions represent individual letters of the alphabet that are used to spell out words (Figure 5–4).

Oral Communication. The oral-aural method of communication makes use of oral and auditory training and speechreading. This method encourages the use of residual hearing while the presentation of material emphasizes the student's visual and auditory attention. Of course, use of amplification is stressed. The oral method emphasizes speechreading and oral speech as the primary means of communication. Gestures and other movements are generally not used other than those ordinarily used by hearing individuals to supplement conversation.

Cued speech is used to augment oral programs, especially speechreading. It includes eight hand shapes in four specific positions to represent phonetic elements that are not readily visible (Cartwright, Cartwright, & Ward, 1984; Schwartz, 1984). The cued speech system was deliberately designed so that it cannot be used as an independent or total form of communication (Quigley & Paul, 1984).

Total Communication. A third approach, called total communication, combines the manual and oral-aural methods according to the abilities, interests, and needs of the student who has a hearing impairment. The total communication method teaches the student to become skillful in speechreading and oral speech. Signing and the manual alphabet are both used, the information conveyed by signs supplemented by the manual alphabet when necessary, as for proper names.

Because of differences between sign languages and English, there has been a proliferation of methods that purport to code English in sign. The most common meth-

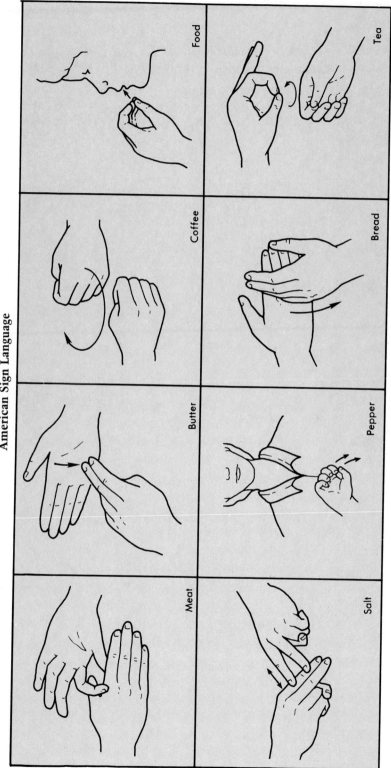

FIGURE 5–3
American Sign Language

FIGURE 5-4
Manual alphabet used by the deaf of North America

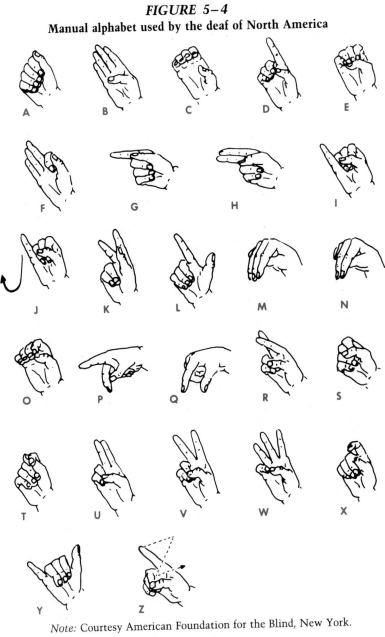

Note: Courtesy American Foundation for the Blind, New York.

ods are Seeing Essential English (Anthony, 1971), Signed English (Bornstein, 1974), and Signing Exact English (Gustason, Pfetzing, Zawolkow, & Norris, 1972).

There exists some controversy between advocates of ASL and advocates of coding English in sign. The main point in dispute is whether it is more effective to use ASL as the primary tool for teaching students with hearing impairments and subsequently teach English (reading and writing) as a second language, or to bypass the necessity of learning two languages in favor of one coded-English system or a combination of coded-English systems. If the latter procedure is followed, a student can use one form of English for signing, reading, and writing.

Although manually coded English systems in some form are widely used in the United States (Quigley & Paul, 1984) and ASL was for a time about the only form of sign language used, there still is only "limited information on the educational effectiveness of the various communication forms" (p. 231).

Facilitating Speechreading

Most students with hearing impairment have some remaining, or residual, hearing, and special efforts must be made to facilitate speechreading because the students may not hear all of the sounds in the environment. Students must learn to closely observe lips, facial gestures, body gestures, and other environmental clues to fully understand what their teachers and classmates are saying. Regular classroom teachers should take the following steps:

1. Allow students with hearing impairment to sit where they can make the most of what they hear and see. Sometimes, young children need guidance in this area. Remember, students with hearing impairment listen with their eyes as well as their ears. Such students should be within 5 to 10 feet of the speaker. Do not, however, have the students sit so close that they must look up constantly. To aid students in becoming more proficient speechreaders, change the seating arrangement from time to time to give the students practice in watching different speakers in the classroom from different positions. Seating arrangements may depend on the classroom organization. If the class is small, arranging the desks in a semicircle and seating a student with a hearing impairment on the end facilitates speechreading. In a lecture situation, placing the student near the front of the room and off to one side allows the student to readily read the speech of classmates and teachers. Seating arrangements must remain flexible to ensure that the student can observe and participate in class activities. The teacher should observe the student to notice whether he or she seems to be straining or missing important concepts; if so, modification in the seating arrangement may be necessary. It may also be helpful to ask the student periodically if he or she would like to move.

2. Seating should be arranged so that a student does not have to look into a light source. Do not stand in front of windows, for this makes speechreading difficult. Do not stand in a dark area or an area where there are shadows. Generally, speechreading is easier when the light source is behind the student.

3. Try to face the group when speaking, and when members of a class are speaking, encourage them to face the student who has a hearing impairment. When writing on the chalkboard, turn to face

the class before speaking. Stay in one place as much as possible when giving oral examinations or while lecturing, so that when the student looks up, you are in the same general location. Some teachers have found it helpful to reserve several seats for the student who has a hearing impairment, with one seat as home base. Oral examinations requiring written responses may also cause considerable difficulty for such a student. If the student is writing a response while you are giving another item, the student may miss several items. Overhead projections and transparencies work extremely well in such cases for all students, and visual aids in general are effective with students who are hearing impaired.

4. Call attention to visual aspects of a particular concept to be learned. Phonetic analysis, as an example, may not be helpful. Generally, instruction that emphasizes visual clues is preferred.

5. Do not exaggerate your gestures, for exaggerated gestures may cause considerable confusion. Use gestures as usual, but keep your hands and any objects away from your face whenever possible. Beards and mustaches sometimes distract attention from the lips or make them difficult to see.

6. Provide a good pattern of speech for a student with a hearing impairment. Distinct articulation is more helpful than speaking louder. Speech patterns should not, however, be exaggerated.

7. Ask questions of the student occasionally to make certain he or she is following the discussion. When presenting a new word or asking a question, repeat it if the student does not understand it the first time, looking directly at the student. If the student seems to miss the term or request, rephrase what you

originally said and ask a question; for example, "This is a stapler. How could you use a stapler?" or "Who would use a stapler often?"

8. Certain words are not easily understood through speechreading; therefore, encourage the student to ask questions or have statements repeated if he or she does not understand.

9. When presenting isolated words, as in spelling lessons, use the words in context. You may also give spelling tests by providing the contextual words of sentences on a sheet of paper, leaving blank spaces for the spelling words. With this method, a student has the necessary contextual clues. Remember, many words appear alike on the lips and sound alike, for example, *beet* and *bead*. Other examples are *meal* and *peal*, *safe* and *save*, and *pie* and *buy*.

10. When presenting new vocabulary words, present the multiple meanings for these words. Some words have more than five meanings. This can be difficult for a student with a hearing impairment because the student's vocabulary may not be sufficient to understand the multiple meanings.

11. Chewing movements should be avoided as much as possible. If students are allowed to chew gum, this may make speechreading difficult, since students with hearing impairment may not be able to differentiate between chewing and speech.

12. When referring to an object in the room, it may be beneficial to point to it, walk over to it and touch it, or actually manipulate the object. This may put the object into the context of the discussion and support what is being discussed. When speaking directly to a student or calling for the student's attention, call the student's name or

speak directly to him or her. In nearly all instances, instruction that combines both visual and auditory cues is more effective.

13. Do not seat a student with a hearing impairment close to audiovisual equipment that has a fan or motor noise.

14. If you use pictures with verbal presentations, initially describe the material and then show the illustration. This allows the student to focus on one major stimulus at a time.

Facilitating Desirable Speech Habits

An essential component of educational programming for students with hearing impairment is speech training. A student's ability to monitor language may be seriously limited by the impairment, thereby limiting the student's expressive language abilities.

Often, the speech specialist working with the student has clearly established goals and objectives related to the student's speech patterns and general articulation. Regular classroom teachers play important roles in facilitating good speech habits. Reinforcement of therapy goals and objectives in the classroom is essential if carryover and maintenance in everyday situations are to be expected. The following suggestions may facilitate carryover and maintenance:

1. Encourage the student to participate in oral discussions and expect the student to use complete sentences when speaking. Be careful, however, not to emotionally load the situation. If proper speech is insisted on and the student is demeaned in front of the entire class for incorrect usage or incomplete sentences, the student may be discouraged from participating in any oral discussion. Be careful not to nag the student. Often, the correction of a mispronounced word may be accomplished by a brief confer-

ence at the end of the period or day. Some teachers have had success with keeping a list of words with which the student has had difficulty and then giving them to the student with the correct pronunciation without comment. Also encourage the student to participate in conversation, reading, storytelling, and creative dramatics.

2. Encourage the student to use the dictionary to aid in pronunciation of difficult words. This practice naturally depends on the age and reading level of the student.

3. Don't be afraid to talk with the student about the hearing loss. Students with hearing impairment need to be told when they are speaking too loudly or too softly. Since a student with a hearing impairment may not be able to monitor his or her own speech sounds, the teacher can do a great deal to keep the student from developing dull or expressionless speech habits.

4. Praise and encourage a student who has correctly pronounced a previously difficult word. Children need a great deal of encouragement and success if they are to accomplish this very difficult task.

5. Provide a relaxed language environment. The more relaxed and casual the speech and language styles of teachers and students, the better the opportunity for language acquisition.

Facilitating Social Interactions

One criterion by which mainstreaming may be judged is the extent to which a student with a disability is accepted, chosen as a friend, and liked by other students (Cartwright et al., 1984). There are indications that the social interaction between hearing students and students with hearing impairment is much less than that among hearing students (Schlesinger, 1985). Such research

For students with hearing impairment, pictures can aid vocabulary development.

seems to place responsibility for increased and positive interaction on the student with a hearing impairment. Part of the poor interaction may be attributed to lack of communication skills of the student with a hearing impairment or to insufficient social skills, such as ability to initiate and continue conversations or discuss playground or after-school activities. Other factors may include the teachers, the environment, and the hearing students.

Teachers. When the regular classroom teacher maintains a supportive climate within the classroom, it is possible for some students with hearing impairment to become dependent on the teacher for positive and rewarding social interactions (Kretschmer & Kretschmer, 1978; Schlesinger, 1985). Teachers must be aware of their influence and the possibility that they are fostering overdependence. They should recognize that overdependence may in fact

be negatively influencing the attitudes of the hearing students and limiting the interactions between the hearing students and the students with hearing impairment. Teachers should encourage and develop procedures to enhance such interactions. Resource or itinerant personnel may have specific suggestions to assist in this area.

Environment. The physical and instructional environment of a classroom is another factor that may discourage interactions among students. The teacher may want to change seating arrangements periodically to enhance interactions between hearing students and students with hearing impairment.

Hearing Students. If the objective is to increase interactions with hearing students, then systems must be developed to foster and enhance these interactions. As mentioned, educators may too quickly assume that the problems lie exclusively with the student who is hearing impaired. Quite logically, if there appears to be a breakdown, part of the problem may rest with the hearing students. As a result, specific efforts must be initiated to help hearing students better understand students with hearing impairment. Perhaps a self-fulfilling prophecy is at work here for not only hearing students but also students who are hearing impaired. Students may think, "I don't relate to _____ because I don't know how; so, I guess I can't," and it becomes a self-perpetuating circle involving all of the students. It is the responsibility of regular classroom teachers to design specific interventions to facilitate communication and interactions by helping hearing students become more proficient at communication skills. Suggestions relating to this topic were included in chapters 3 and 4. This topic is also discussed in "Hearing Students and Communication," presented later in this chapter.

SUGGESTIONS FOR REGULAR CLASSROOM TEACHERS

Students with hearing impairment may find success in regular classrooms if some modifications and adaptations are made. These relate to room arrangement, awareness on the part of teachers, and alternate teaching strategies that do not require substantial teacher time.

Classroom Acoustics

Regular classroom teachers certainly do not have responsibility for the construction of classrooms; however, several factors will improve the acoustics of a room. Hard surfaces such as glass, chalkboards, and tiled floors reflect sound and produce extraneous sound. Soft, porous materials such as fabric, paper window shades, and cork absorb sound. Use of porous materials can reduce

noise. If a classroom has a large expanse of chalkboard, portions of it can be used as bulletin boards. Papers taped to it will reduce some noise. Similarly, posters, corkboard, and curtains on the classroom rear wall reduce the amount of reflected sound. Carpets covering all or part of the floor reduce the sound in a room. Desks arranged in staggered fashion allow for the bodies of the students to further reduce reflected sound. Noise and distance are natural enemies of sound amplification. Extraneous noises interfere with the sounds being attended to (primarily voice in a classroom), and distances increase the possibility of interference by extraneous sounds.

Preferential Seating

The appropriate seating of a student with a hearing impairment depends partially upon the type of hearing loss. If the student has a bilateral loss with binaural amplification, seating should be arranged so that the teacher's voice is not directed above the student. Generally, a second row in the center is best. If the student has different levels of loss in each ear, the second-row placement is helpful but should be off center so that the better ear is angled toward the teacher. However, the teacher does not do all of the talking in a classroom, so some experimentation may be required. Different seats for different classes or activities may be the best solution.

Awareness of Student Fatigue

Students with hearing impairment may experience fatigue more easily than other students, and teachers should be aware of this potential problem. Such fatigue may be particularly noticeable in young children near the end of the day, but this is a factor for all students who are hearing impaired. Such fatigue should not be interpreted as boredom, disinterest, or lack of motivation. The fa-

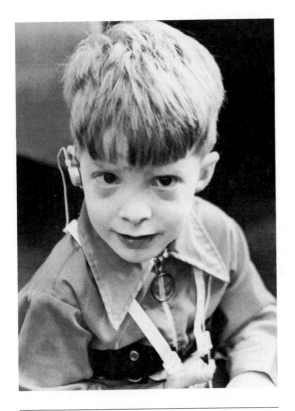

To maintain this degree of attention, teachers must be aware of the fatigue factor.

tigue results in part from the continuous strain of speechreading, the use of residual hearing, and the constant watching required to keep up with various speakers while participating in classroom activities. It may be helpful to vary the daily schedule so that the student is not required to attend to academic subjects for an extended period of time. Shorten lesson periods or alternate written and oral work with rest periods. However, the student should be expected to complete all assignments. The teacher should also be aware that the student with a hearing impairment may hear better on some days than on others. Also, some students experience tinnitus (hearing noises

within the head), which can result in nervousness or irritability.

Preteach-Teach-Postteach

The preteach-teach-postteach strategy assumes that the resource teacher and the regular class teacher have a cooperative, mutually respectful working relationship. The regular classroom teacher informs the resource teacher of the lessons or concepts to be taught, and they are presented first to the student with a hearing impairment in a one-to-one or small-group setting. The student then attends the regular classroom, and the unit of study is taught by the regular classroom teacher. After the class, the regular classroom teacher reports to the resource or itinerant teacher by means of a short note, checklist, or personal discussion indicating problems or areas that may need to be retaught in the one-to-one or small-group setting. Ultimately, it is anticipated that the preteaching and postteaching phases may be shortened or eliminated except where the regular classroom teacher or the student specifically requests it (Reynolds & Birch, 1982).

Classmates as Helpers

The use of a listening helper or buddy can be of considerable assistance to a student who has a hearing impairment. This peer may sit next to the student who is hearing impaired to ensure that the student turns to the correct page or takes notes, or this peer may provide other appropriate assistance in adjusting to a new class or school or participating in activities such as physical education. The buddy may clarify something the teacher has said by repeating it while facing the student who is hearing impaired or by writing it down.

At the upper elementary and secondary levels, a listening helper or buddy may assist in note taking by making a carbon copy of class notes. This allows the student who has the hearing impairment to concentrate fully on what the teacher is saying.

The listening helper or buddy may be rotated weekly or monthly, or a few classmates may volunteer for an extended period of time. Some caution must be exercised so that the helper or buddy provides assistance only when needed. Otherwise, the very purpose of the integrated educational experience may be defeated. If the helper provides assistance when it is not necessary, the student with a hearing impairment may become overly dependent on classmates—a dependency that must be carefully avoided.

Demonstration and Team Teaching

If teachers fully appreciate the potential of true integration, they may realize the value of demonstration and team teaching. The presence of two adults in a classroom is valuable for several reasons. First, a model for working cooperatively is provided for all of the students. In addition, the special educator may learn more about large-group instruction and the limitations imposed in modifying and adapting materials, curricula, and teaching strategies. Regular classroom teachers can increase their competency in working with students who are hearing impaired by observing the special educator.

Team teaching involves the regular classroom teacher and the special educator in cooperatively planning the lessons, including the modifications or adaptations necessary to meet the needs of all of the students. Then, they team teach, or co-teach, the lesson, sharing full responsibility. The team approach may be for a specific unit of study or may be ongoing for a semester or an entire year in a content area such as math or social studies.

Demonstration teaching usually involves the special educator in demonstrating a particular strategy or method of meeting the needs of the student who is hearing impaired, for example, in preparing for the use of a captioned film. This arrangement allows the classroom teacher to learn new competencies.

Variations in the roles of the teachers are possible and should be mutually agreed upon. Sometimes, the special educator assumes the role of an aide or tutor and provides assistance to students having problems with a particular concept or assignment, or the classroom teacher may assume this role. Whatever the roles assumed or approaches used, the goal is the same: full integration of the student who is hearing impaired.

Media and Equipment

Audiovisual equipment and personnel can be of particular value to the teacher who has a student with a hearing impairment in the class. Overhead projectors can greatly enhance the student's achievement. As the teacher lectures, he or she may put important notes or key vocabulary words and phrases on the overhead projector. An overhead projector allows the teacher to maintain eye contact with students while writing. When using slides or films, the teacher should be certain there is sufficient light to enable the student to see faces clearly as the narrator or teacher makes comments. In general, supplementary diagrams and pictures should be used as often as possible. Often, the complete narrative script to a filmstrip or audiotape accompanies the materials and, if available, should be given to the student who is hearing impaired.

Many educational films have been captioned so that they can be used in regular classrooms. The resource teacher or consultant may provide the teacher with a detailed listing of materials that are available free of charge. Use of these modified and adapted instructional materials does not interfere with the education of normally hearing students. In fact, it facilitates their achievement as well.

Previewing New Materials or Assignments

Whenever possible, the teacher should briefly discuss topics with the student who has difficulty hearing before the actual class presentation. This goal may be accomplished by providing the student with an outline of the material to be discussed. Communicating with resource teachers and employing the preteach-teach-postteach strategy should be given consideration. Allowing the student with a hearing impairment to preread assignments is also helpful. Another possibility worthy of consideration is providing on the board or a piece of paper a list of key vocabulary words that deal with the new material. When giving an assignment, write it on the board in addition to giving it orally. The student's listening helper may check to see that the student has the correct assignment.

Curricular Considerations

Students with hearing impairment may have difficulty in reading textbooks in curricular areas such as science, social studies, and literature. The teacher may de-emphasize the use of textbooks and focus on hands-on experiences, particularly in content areas like science. When that is not feasible, books that address the topics with simpler reading levels are alternatives. Easier reading materials combined with captioned films, vocabulary lists presented before verbal presentations, study guides that focus on critical concepts, and visual representations help students who have hearing impairment learn along with their hearing peers. Close collaboration with the resource person is essential. Materials that visually display organization help students note relationships. Visual displays, such as the one shown in Figure 5–5, may be as simple or complex as the subject requires.

Computers may also enhance the learning of a student who is hearing impaired. Software can allow the student to repeat in-

FIGURE 5–5
A visual display showing relationships

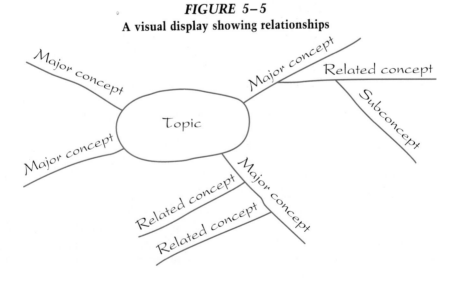

formation previously presented through a lecture, simulate experiments, examine graphics, or practice computation. A word processor allows easy correction and modification of written materials.

Guidelines for adapting written materials for classroom use include:

1. Focus on specific, basic information first.
2. As needed, include related, inferential information to accomplish instructional goals.
3. Expand to include general information.
4. Use technical vocabulary as necessary, but whenever possible, use simpler words.
5. Use coordinating conjunctions, such as *but, so,* and *for,* whenever possible.
6. Relate new information to known information.
7. Avoid the use of negatives *(not, without)*; qualifications *(very, quite, somewhat)*; inferentials *(since, because, however)*; comparatives *(more than, nearer than)*; passive voice; long, involved sentences; and idiomatic expressions.

Interpreter-Tutors

Students enrolled in a total communication program may use interpreter-tutors to help them in their regular classrooms. The interpreter-tutor is usually located just outside the direct line of sight from the student to the teacher, slightly facing the student, thereby allowing the student to directly speechread the teacher or the interpreter.

The interpreter repeats what the teacher is saying through signs, fingerspelling, and nonvocalized speech. He or she may paraphrase or modify what the teacher is saying if the student is not familiar with the words or concepts being used. Interpreter-tutors are not teachers, but they must be experts in total communication. In some states,

they must pass proficiency examinations and be certified.

Using an interpreter is a new experience for many teachers. Initially, it seems unusual to both the teacher and the hearing students. In fact, for the first several days or until the hearing students become comfortable, they may be seriously distracted by the signs, gestures, and expressions of the interpreter.

The following general suggestions may be helpful when using an interpreter:[2]

1. Be aware that you and the interpreter may have to adjust and modify the pace of instruction periodically. Occasionally the interpreter may ask you to stop momentarily, repeat, or slow down. Teamwork between the teacher and interpreter is vital to the student.
2. Be certain there is good lighting wherever the interpreter stands.
3. In using demonstration and visual aids, allow extra time for students to see what is being demonstrated as well as to see what is being said. With hearing students the teacher can turn her back to the class and simultaneously elaborate a point as she demonstrates. With students with hearing impairments this is not possible, since they must turn their attention from the interpreter to the chalkboard to see what the teacher is demonstrating and then turn back again so they will not miss the explanation. The best solution to this problem is first, to be more explanatory as new points are put on the board and second, to pause while maintaining eye contact with the students.
4. When using an overhead projector, slides, videotapes, or films, it is sometimes necessary either to reduce the lighting or to turn off the lights completely in the classroom. In such situations it is important to provide a small lamp or spotlight to focus on the inter-

[2]Adapted from *Guidelines for Interpreting for the Hearing Impaired*, p. 3, 1982. Greeley, Colorado: Office of Resources for the Disabled, University of Northern Colorado.

preter while discussion or explanation takes place.

5. Because sign language does not contain signs for every word in the English language, the interpreter must fingerspell special vocabulary using the manual alphabet. The interpreter may also be asked by the student to pause and define the term. It is most helpful to write special vocabulary on the board or give a list to the interpreter before class so that neither the interpreter nor the student misunderstands the concept.

6. Question-and-answer periods may pose problems. If the student is unable to vocalize her question, she must sign the question to the interpreter and the interpreter then vocalizes the question to the teacher.

7. The interpreter cannot interpret more than one speaker at a time. During discussions, remind the other students to speak one at a time.

8. To establish rapport, speak directly to the student, not to the interpreter.

Some caution must be exercised to avoid dependency between the interpreter-tutor and the student: an interpreter-tutor is used only when necessary.

Students who do not have good speechreading skills and thus might not be able to participate in regular classrooms may be able to do so with the assistance of interpreter-tutors. It is imperative that every method that may help a student make maximum progress be fully investigated.

Hearing Students and Communication

As mentioned, hearing students often do not understand the nature of hearing impairment or how a hearing aid functions. Although many hearing students who have classmates who are hearing impaired learn some of the signs or the manual alphabet, it may be helpful to provide systematic instruction to the hearing students. Unless such instruction is provided, the hearing students often express frustration when at-

tempting to communicate with their classmates who have hearing impairment. Instruction in signing may be offered occasionally after school or during special Saturday morning programs. Such an elective course may be offered on an ongoing basis and may initially be taught by resource or itinerant teachers or in cooperation with students who are hearing impaired. Hearing students who have gained proficiency may be encouraged to share in the instruction or serve as teaching assistants or peer tutors. There is little question that efforts to help hearing students understand and communicate better with their classmates who are hearing impaired can greatly facilitate interactions. In addition, many regular classroom teachers also learn how to sign.

These suggestions to regular classroom teachers are certainly not all-inclusive, but they do represent areas of great concern. It would be helpful to review and discuss them with the resource or itinerant teacher periodically. Ingenuity and creativity in modifying and adapting curriculum, materials, and teaching strategies can make mainstreaming successful for everyone.

The most important consideration is teacher attitude. The teacher is the single most important variable. The teacher must be understanding but not pitying and should treat a student who has a hearing impairment as nearly as possible like any other student in the classroom, being fair and truthful, not lenient, in reporting the progress of the student. The student should be treated as a student who is able, who is an individual, and who, incidentally, has impaired hearing.

SPECIALIZED INSTRUCTION AND ASSISTANCE

A number of special skills should be routinely provided by resource personnel. The specific skills vary, depending on the grade level of the students. At the primary level, the resource teacher may have responsibility for reading instruction or may supplement the material presented in the student's regular class. The reading material used by the resource teacher may be the same as that used in the regular class except that the resource teacher spends considerably more time on comprehension, questioning, and related language activities. At the intermediate level, the resource teacher probably supplements regular classroom instruction by emphasizing phonetic and comprehension skills and by introducing new vocabulary words before their introduction in class. Students who are hearing impaired also may need to be taught words that are popular with their classmates.

In addition to supplemental instruction, the resource teacher may work in a number of other areas, such as individual and small-group auditory training, vocabulary development, comprehension, questioning, speechreading, and speech correction.

At the secondary level, the resource teacher or consultant may be involved in team teaching or demonstration teaching, provide adapted or modified materials, or be part of the preteach-teach-postteach strategy. If activities are planned far enough in advance, captioned films, slide-tape presentations, and other tangible materials may be provided.

Sometimes, the resource teacher or consultant is an integral part of routine classroom activities. This person may have specific instructional responsibilities to hearing students with instructional needs similar to those of students with hearing impairment. The exact nature of the special educator's role depends on the age or grade level of the students, the number of students, and the extent of hearing impairment. Generally, the role involves tutoring

or supplemental instruction, the introduction of new materials or skills, and instruction in specialized skills that relate to hearing impairment.

Depending on the geographical area to be served (one or more schools), resource or itinerant teachers may be responsible for the in-service education of regular classroom teachers in one or several buildings. Often, the resource or itinerant teacher is called on to acquaint a building staff with the rationale underlying integrated placement of students who have hearing impairment. The nature of an in-service session may be general and relate only to the philosophy of integrated education, or it may be specifically related to techniques for modifying and adapting curriculum, materials, and teaching strategies.

Although it is not necessary for regular teachers to know the manual alphabet, they often are interested in learning it. In this instance, the resource or itinerant teacher may conduct in-service programs for teachers or students or arrange for classes to be taught by another person.

Another role often assumed by the resource teacher is providing selected journal articles, readings, or topics of special interest in relation to a particular student's problem or to specific teaching techniques. The orientation and in-service efforts of the resource personnel are ongoing responsibilities that must be taken seriously. How resource personnel "sell" themselves, the program, and the students with hearing impairment has a tremendous influence on the effectiveness of the program.

The resource teacher, due to his or her specialized preparation and experience, may assist regular teachers in counseling the student and the student's parents. This counseling may be routinely academic, such as parent-teacher conferences, or relate to specific problems imposed by hearing impairment, such as interpersonal relationships, language and speech problems, or vocational interests.

The resource teacher assists in planning and implementing work-study, vocational education, and vocational-rehabilitation services for students in secondary schools. The resource or itinerant teacher may be responsible for actually initiating these services or may contact others to initiate them. As mentioned, the roles and responsibilities of resource personnel vary considerably. The key to successful resource services is communication between regular teachers and resource personnel.

SUMMARY

This chapter reviewed the importance of hearing to early learning, types of hearing impairment, how hearing impairment is measured, and both behavioral and medical indications of hearing impairment. Referral procedures, placement variables, and the advantages of regular class placement were considered. A variety of information about hearing aids, their care and maintenance, and assessment of their effectiveness was reviewed.

A discussion of the major methods of communication employed by students who are severely hearing impaired was provided, along with information about how classroom teachers can facilitate speechreading, desirable speech habits, and quality interactions between students with hearing impairment and their peers. A variety of practical suggestions, such as preferential seating, use of classmates as helpers, and previewing new materials before class, were presented. Finally, the role of resource teachers and consultants was outlined, stressing the importance of cooperative efforts between educators who work together to teach students with hearing impairment.

- How do the language development theories proposed by Bruner, Chomsky, Piaget, and Skinner differ? How is it possible to substantiate such theories? What differences in remedial procedures are inferred by the acceptance of each theory?

- How different must a student's speech be to be considered a disability? How does this interpretation apply to linguistic differences that are likely to be found in students from culturally diverse populations?

- What must teachers know about pragmatics to be able to effectively assist students who have communication problems?

- Why has the major focus of speech specialists shifted away from articulation disorders? How do students with minor articulation disorders overcome such disorders?

- Why has stuttering held such historical interest for speech-language professionals? Which of the present causal explanations appears to be most logical?

- Which speech or voice disorders may be so potentially serious that they require immediate referral? What are the possible prognoses for these disorders?

CHAPTER 6

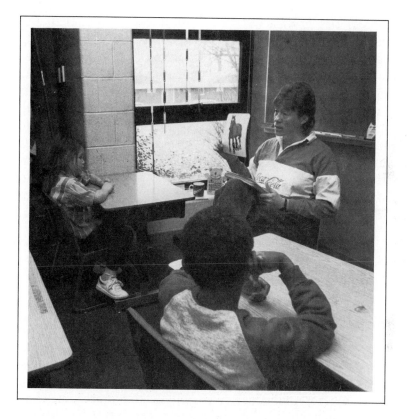

TEACHING STUDENTS WHO HAVE SPEECH OR LANGUAGE DISORDERS

THE MAJOR CONCERNS OF THIS CHAPTER ARE speech disorders, language disorders, and speech or language variations that may lead to social or learning difficulties if not understood and appropriately managed. This chapter focuses on speech and language as they are involved in communication, an essential, central element in education.

The intelligence of humans and the complex language that developed because of such intelligence are the bases for almost unbelievable advances and accomplishments in such areas as technology and medicine. It would appear that without speech, language, and communication skills, such advances could not have taken place. It follows, then, that individuals with impaired speech, language, or communication abilities will not likely function effectively in a world dependent on fast, accurate communication.

COMMUNICATION

Communication is a process that involves two or more individuals in the transmission of thoughts or ideas between them. In the simplest form, this involves individual A transmitting an idea to individual B. To do this, individual A must convert the idea into some type of symbol system. This is often referred to as encoding. After receiving the message, individual B must decode it, or convert the symbols back into the idea. The four major elements of language and their normal relationship in the communication process are illustrated in Figure 6–1. The expressive skills most used by humans are speaking and writing. The receptive skills are listening and reading. The

FIGURE 6–1
Integrative process

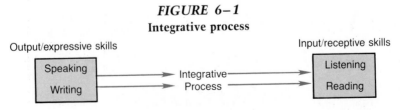

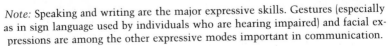

Note: Speaking and writing are the major expressive skills. Gestures (especially as in sign language used by individuals who are hearing impaired) and facial expressions are among the other expressive modes important in communication.

process through which communication takes place may be called an integrative process.

This chapter starts consideration of communication with speech, one aspect of the complex language system. However, note that despite all of the advances involving computers and sound-production equipment, technology cannot produce really natural-sounding human speech. This marvelous technology, through which people can shop, pay bills, cook meals, fly aircraft, and correct both grammar and spelling when typing, cannot be programmed to produce a version of the English language that includes the richness and variation of speech that is developed simply and naturally by a four-year-old child. What, then, is speech? According to Bernstein and Tiegerman (1989), "Speech is . . . the oral verbal mode of transmitting messages and involves the precise coordination of oral neuromuscular movements in order to produce sounds and linguistic units" (p. 3). They note that although speech is the primary mode of communication, it is not the only mode. People also communicate through writing, drawing, and manual signing.

Language is the code or system in which people normally communicate. According to Bernstein and Tiegerman, "Language encompasses complex rules that govern sounds, words, sentences, meaning, and use. These rules underlie an individual's ability to understand language (language comprehension) and his ability to formulate language (language production)" (p. 4). They further note that language can produce an infinite number of sentences, in a wide variety of settings. Most people cannot explicitly state all of the language rules, but their usage indicates knowledge of most of them.

Two additional statements, from an American Speech-Language-Hearing Association (ASHA) committee report, add further

meaning to the Bernstein and Tiegerman description. The first, the core definition provided by the ASHA Committee on Language (1983) is "Language is a complex and dynamic system of conventional symbols that is used in various modes for thought and communication" (p. 44). The second, one of the statements made in expansion of this core definition, is "Effective use of language for communication requires a broad understanding of human interaction including such associated factors as nonverbal cues, motivation, and sociocultural roles" (p. 44).

When PL 94–142 was passed in 1975, the label for students with difficulties in speech, language, or communication was "speech impaired." Recognition that this label did not reflect the scope of the problems that students experience led Congress to change the label to the more inclusive "speech or language impaired." The definition, modified to reflect this thinking, is "a communication disorder such as stuttering, impaired articulation, a language impairment, or voice impairment which adversely affects educational performance" (U.S. Government Accounting Office, 1981, p. 36). Language, the fundamental ability that affects all interactions with others, is complex and not fully understood. However, what is understood is that impairments in language abilities likely lead to impairments in the learning process.

THEORIES OF LANGUAGE DEVELOPMENT

Noam Chomsky (1957, 1965) formulated a theory to explain how native speakers of a language learn all of the variations of the language without having heard them or having learned the rules that govern them. He theorized that there is an inborn capacity to learn language and that human infants have a plan in the brain that enables them to internalize the knowledge necessary to generate words and sentences. According to Chomsky, a baby is predisposed to learn language, and this innate ability is activated when exposed to linguistic input, such as the mother speaking to the baby. This innate ability contains the general principles for forming sentences and applying these principles to the child's native language. Through an explanation of brain structures, Chomsky accounts for the ability of young children to acquire language almost effortlessly, learn the rules governing the language without ever having them explained, and generate an infinite number of sentences never heard.

Chomsky (1965) also developed the concepts of deep structure and surface structure, which are two levels of the communication process. A thought, idea, or feeling that is to be shared with a listener is generated in the brain (deep structure), and through application of morphological and syntactic rules of language, a word, phrase, sentence, or series of sentences is generated (surface structure). The surface structure may be modified in a variety of ways to meet the expectations of the interaction or to clarify to the listener the original idea. Chomsky provided a view relating to the language acquisition process in which the child was active rather than passive; however, his view of language development is regarded as incomplete. Chomsky's concepts served as an impetus to further language research, especially in natural settings, examining both normal and disordered language.

Benjamin F. Skinner (1957) developed a theoretical explanation for a variety of types of learning and applied the principles of imitation, practice, and selective reinforcement to the acquisition of language. He suggests that a child gradually, and with increased precision, imitates the vocal symbols and sequences of symbols heard. Parents and caregivers serve as models of appropriate utterances, which the child imitates. The parents and caregivers act as reinforcers by rewarding the child's attempts at imitation and as shapers of the child's utterances by continued modeling and reinforcement.

Skinner based his theory on animal learning and principles of operant conditioning. According to Skinner and other behaviorists, children learn language because their verbal behavior is rewarded by others in the environment. From Skinner's theory, a systematic approach to training techniques has been developed. It incorporates the principles of modeling, imitation, shaping, and reinforcement. Many programs for children with language disabilities are based on these principles.

Critics of this theory believe that the rate of language acquisition is much too rapid to depend on environmental conditioning alone. Also, children apply rules, inappropriately at times, and produce utterances they have never heard ("I wented" or "I goeses"). Furthermore, parents and caregivers do not correct all grammatical errors, but children learn the appropriate structures.

Jean Piaget (1952, 1954, 1962) suggests that language is cognitively based and that unless certain cognitive levels are achieved, language learning cannot proceed. It is generally accepted that attainment of object permanence must be achieved before expression of words with stable meanings. Bloom (1970) suggests that the meaning of a child's utterance is far more advanced than is the child's knowledge of syntax. A child can convey multiple meanings by using the same words, for example, "Daddy hat." In one situation, the child may be indicating the father's ownership and in another indicating the desire for a ride in the car. According to Bloom, children express meanings before they are able to use syntax, and the meanings that they convey are dependent on their cognitive knowledge. He also indicates that children use language to talk about what they know, which is related primarily to their sensorimotor experiences. This implies that children mean more than they are able to say through the use of syntactically correct utterances.

How children figure out the ways in which words, word order, and inflections convey meaning is not fully explained, nor is the ability of children to use increasingly more complex forms and structures to encode meaning. Further, the fact that children with normal intelligence sometimes do not learn to speak or do so at a level much below their cognitive abilities seems to indicate that abilities other than purely conceptual ones are involved in the process of language learning.

Jerome Bruner (1974, 1975) suggests that children learn language to socialize and direct the behavior of others. In social interaction, children develop the framework for understanding and formulating content and form. The functions of speech acts, the contexts in which they are performed, and the intents of utterances are critical. In general, children learn to talk because they have a reason, and they acquire language only after they learn other forms of communication (such as reaching for a bottle, or leading caregivers to a sink and pointing, indicating the desire for a drink). Language is learned in social interactions in which children are active participants and are able to benefit from the language behaviors of others. This theory partially explains the role of linguistic input, the relationship between gestures and language, and the manner in which children learn complex social devices used by others to make their intentions known.

It does not explain how communicative intentions are linked to appropriate linguistic structures in the process of language acquisition.

Each of the theories regarding the development of language may be viewed as describing an aspect of language development, even though no theory provides a complete model. Yet, taken together, the theories illustrate the complexity of language. Language theories may serve as a starting point for teachers who have students about whom they have suspicions relating to speech and language disabilities.

COMPONENTS OF SPEECH

In order to further understanding of speech and the language process, this chapter considers the major components of speech and language. The theoretical views of language development remain unproven and subject to debate, but the components of speech and language skills described by the American Speech-Language-Hearing Association (ASHA, Committee on Language, 1983) are much less ambiguous. They provide insights that relate to the disorders of speech and language that regular classroom teachers may encounter. Phonology, morphology, syntax, semantics, and pragmatics form the foundation of language. All are rule governed and essential to the normal development of language. Brief definitions and some examples of disorders of each of the components follow. Figure 6-2 illustrates how they are interrelated.

Phonology is the sound system of oral language. The English language consists of 46 sounds, or phonemes, which are either vowels or consonants. These basic units are combined into meaningful sequences. For example, the sounds of *j*, *a*, and *m* combined form the word *jam*. In this case, each letter stands for a single phoneme; how-

A variety of games and activities assist language development.

ever, in the word *this, th* is pronounced as one sound and is a phoneme. Errors may occur through mispronunciations, omissions, or substitutions.

Morphology refers to the smallest units of language that represent meaning. In general terms, morphology relates to the structure of words, to the stems and the suffixes or prefixes that modify the meaning of a stem in some fashion. Morphemes can be words that stand alone, like *took, was,* or *that,* or be parts of words like *un,* which added to the word *able,* for example, changes the meaning. Similarly, the *s* in *chairs* and the *es* in *dishes* modify the meaning of the stems. Errors may be related to incorrect usage of morphemes, for instance, *goed* and *mostest.*

Syntax refers to the relative subordination of words and clauses. In English, these are often determined by word order. A variety of rules govern word order. If the rules are not followed, the result is either a string of words with no meaning or doubt about the meaning. The sentence "The boy bit the dog" has a significant change in meaning if just two words are transposed, namely, *boy* and *dog.* Examples of syntactic errors (violation of rules) include "My teacher gave a talk on the moon" and "The paper said he died last week due to a reporting error." The rules governing morphology and syntax combined make up the rules of grammar.

Semantics encompasses the meanings assigned to words, groups of words, and sen-

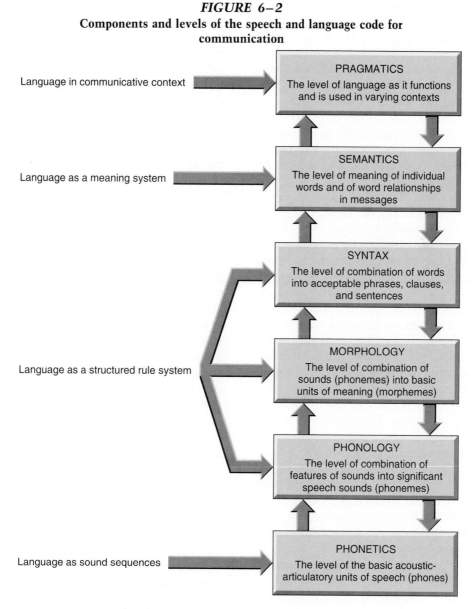

FIGURE 6–2

Components and levels of the speech and language code for communication

Language in communicative context → PRAGMATICS
The level of language as it functions and is used in varying contexts

Language as a meaning system → SEMANTICS
The level of meaning of individual words and of word relationships in messages

SYNTAX
The level of combination of words into acceptable phrases, clauses, and sentences

Language as a structured rule system → MORPHOLOGY
The level of combination of sounds (phonemes) into basic units of meaning (morphemes)

PHONOLOGY
The level of combination of features of sounds into significant speech sounds (phonemes)

Language as sound sequences → PHONETICS
The level of the basic acoustic-articulatory units of speech (phones)

Note: Reprinted with permission of Merrill, an imprint of Macmillan Publishing Company, from *Language Assessment and Intervention for the Learning Disabled,* 2nd ed. (p. 23) by E. Wiig & E. Semel. Copyright © 1984, 1990 by Bell & Howell Company.

tences. Phonology, morphology, and syntax form the structures of the language system, while semantics refers to the meanings of those structures. Knowledge of semantics is reflected in vocabulary usage, concepts that are developed, and word associations. For example, in the group of words *man, in, lives, the, house,* and *white,* each word has some element of meaning. By grouping the words *the man lives* and *in the white house,* a greater degree of meaning is reflected. And finally, by putting the words together in a sentence, *The man lives in the white house,* additional meaning is attached. Understanding either the lesser meaning attached to the string of words or the more involved meaning of the sentence depends upon understanding of the individual words, appropriate word order, and the concept conveyed in the sentence. Semantic errors may be as simple as misunderstanding the meaning of a word (for example, confusing the noun *judge* in isolation with the verb) or as serious as complete misinterpretation of sentences.

Pragmatics refers to the use of language in varying situations. This includes modifying the choice of words based on the information level of the receiver, on the setting, or on the purpose of communication. For example, simple words might be used with a 3- or 4-year-old, while more enriched vocabulary would be appropriate for a 14-year-old. At the college level, more complex vocabulary and sentence structure might be appropriate for a presentation to a class and more informal language would be used in the cafeteria. Pragmatics also includes the intention of the speaker, whether it be to provide information, gather information, share an observation, or something else. A speaker must be aware of characteristics of listeners, including such aspects as level of understanding, interest, and ability to respond.

In summary, pragmatics refers to ability of a speaker to conform to the rules of communication that involve modifying language according to the situation, the characteristics of listeners, the intent of communication, or some combination of these. In our culture, examples of errors include asking personal questions upon just being introduced to a person or using incomplete and incoherent sentences when giving an oral presentation.

The components just reviewed as separate entities are interrelated. Effective communicators have a command of all of the components even though they may not be able to verbalize many of the rules governing them. Individuals with disabilities in this area are at a disadvantage in communicating their thoughts and ideas effectively. When speech and language are underdeveloped or defective, academic problems almost always result, especially in reading. In the case of serious problems, there is an apparent correlation with problems in thinking, because it appears that for the most part, humans think with words.

SPEECH DISORDERS

Teachers regularly ask, How different must a student's speech or language be to be considered a disorder? or When is it appropriate to refer a student? Some questions that teachers might ask in making such determinations have been identified by Culatta and Culatta (1985). The questions and some interpretive thoughts related to them are:

1. *Is the student easily understood?* If your answer is no, a referral is in order.
2. *When I compare this student to others in the class, does this student sound strange?* If the answer is yes, analyze why. Is it because the 6-foot-tall male sounds like an 8-year-old girl? Or does

an 8-year-old girl have a nasal or hoarse voice? Disorders of articulation are easy to identify and may be reason for a referral, but voice problems may be more serious, because they may indicate need for medical attention.

3. *When I observe the student, are there physical characteristics that seem different?* If the answer is yes, again try to identify what they are. Some examples of what to look for are unusual or unnecessary movements of the mouth, lips, tongue, nose, arms, legs, or head and unusual postural changes during speaking.

4. *When the student speaks, even though I can understand what was said, does the student sound out of place or unable to judge what is appropriate for the situation?* If yes, it may be that the student is unaware that good speakers judge situations and adjust their speaking style. It may also be that the student has some desire to resist conformity. The former may indicate a problem meriting referral, whereas the latter may indicate a problem that is unrelated to speech or no problem at all.

5. *Do I enjoy listening to the student?* If no, why not? If it is because the message is not desirable, that is not a speech problem. However, if it is because of the quality of the voice (such as hoarseness, pitch, or unpleasant tone), a referral may be in order.

6. *Does it sound as though the student is damaging or has damaged his or her vocal mechanisms?* Does it sound as though the student is straining? Does speaking induce coughing or wheezing?

7. *Does the student appear embarrassed or seem to experience physical discomfort when speaking?* While a teacher cannot judge the inner feelings of a student, some behavioral indicators may lead the teacher to believe the student is experiencing discomfort. The student may blush when required to speak or be reluctant to participate in class discussions. For this to be a problem, it must be beyond the normal shyness or anxiety that many students experience when speaking in front of a class or similar activities in which attention is focused on them.

A different set of questions that teachers might answer in relation to how different a student's speech must be to be considered a speech disorder are:

1. *Does the speech interfere with communication?*
2. *Does the speech cause the speaker to be maladjusted?*
3. *Does the speech call undue attention to itself at the expense of what the speaker is saying?*

These questions focus on the effects of speech rather than the physiology of speech production. A speech-language specialist is concerned with helping students produce speech in the most normal manner possible and use it effectively in normal communication so that listeners can concentrate on *what* the students are saying, not on *how* they are saying it. This generalization also applies to language disorders, which are often related to speech disorders.

Speech, language, and hearing problems are interrelated and may affect learning. This interrelationship is illustrated in Figure 6–3, and it explains why regular classroom teachers may discuss referral with a speech-language pathologist, teacher of the learning disabled, or teacher of the hearing impaired. If a student is identified as having a speech or language disorder, the IEP should indicate the services to be provided and who is responsible for providing them, as well as who is responsible for providing

FIGURE 6–3
Disorders of speech, language, and hearing and how they interrelate

LANGUAGE DISORDERS
DELAYED LANGUAGE: marked slowness in the onset and development of language skills necessary for expressing ideas and for understanding the thoughts and ideas one hears or reads.
LEARNING DISABILITIES: something interfering with a child's ability to understand the message that his eyes and ears receive.
APHASIA: loss of speech and language abilities following brain damage sometimes resulting from a stroke or head injury.

HEARING DISORDERS
CONDUCTIVE: occur in the outer or middle ear. Speech and other sounds may be heard faintly, often muffled.
SENSORINEURAL: occur in the inner ear or auditory nerve and cause one to hear speech sounds faintly and sometimes in a distorted way; words may sound slurred or lacking in clarity.
MIXED: a combination of conductive and sensorineural losses.

SPEECH DISORDERS
ARTICULATION: difficulties with the way sounds are formed and strung together; characterized by substituting one sound for another (wabbit for rabbit), omitting a sound (han- for hand), and distorting a sound (shlip for sip).
STUTTERING: interruptions in the flow or rhythm of speech; characterized by hesitations, repetitions, or prolongations of a sound, syllable, word, or phrase.
VOICE: inappropriate pitch (too high, too low, never changing, interrupted by breaks); loudness (too loud or not loud enough); or quality (harsh, hoarse, or breathy).

CAN HAVE ACCOMPANYING SPEECH OR HEARING PROBLEMS
CAN HAVE ACCOMPANYING SPEECH OR LANGUAGE PROBLEMS
CAN HAVE ACCOMPANYING LANGUAGE OR HEARING PROBLEMS

Note: From public information materials of the American Speech-Language-Hearing Association. Reproduced by permission.

suggestions and assistance to the regular classroom teacher. Speech disorders may be divided into three broad categories: (a) articulation disorders, (b) stuttering and other speech-flow disorders, and (c) voice disorders. Other speech problems are related to cerebral palsy, hearing loss, and cleft lip or cleft palate.

Articulation Disorders

Articulation errors were once the focus of speech-language pathologists, but the focus shifted because of two major factors: (a) it was increasingly recognized that many young children outgrew minor articulation problems with no specialized assistance and

(b) it became obvious that some of the more serious speech disorders required more time and effort from specialists. This shift does not mean that teachers should not refer students if the only obvious difficulty is an articulation problem. Nor does it mean that speech-language pathologists never serve young children who have only articulation problems. In many cases, a combination of evaluation by a speech-language pathologist followed by management suggestions implemented by a regular classroom teacher and the parent proves most effective. The need for regular classroom teachers to understand and properly play this partnership role is a theme of this chapter.

Articulation errors are those involving omissions, substitutions, distortions, or additions when pronouncing (articulating) words. The following are examples of articulation errors:

Substitution. wun for *run,* dat for *that,* wabbit for *rabbit,* thum for *some*
Omission. pay for *play,* cool for *school,* ift for *lift,* day for *daddy*
Distortion. shled for *sled*
Additions. buhrown for *brown,* cuhow for *cow,* puhlease for *please,* sawr for *saw*

Certain generalizations applicable in nearly all cases of articulation-error therapy may be used as guidelines for remedial efforts. First, *the student must hear the error.* In most cases, the letter or letters are pointed out to the student in writing or print so that there can be no question as to what letter or letters are in question. Then, the student must learn to hear the sound as properly articulated by the teacher or speech-language pathologist. Often, the student must learn to listen for the sound in initial, medial, and final positions and then must learn to differentiate between the sound properly articulated and the sound as

he or she articulates it. This may be done with a tape recorder. The teacher may deliberately mispronounce the sound, and on the playback the student may learn to discriminate the incorrect sound from the correct sound in varying phonetic contexts. After this stage, recordings of both the student and the teacher may be made to assist the student in recognizing the varying sounds. Other methods or materials may be used; however, learning to *hear* errors is an absolute prerequisite to any further work with articulation problems. This is sometimes called auditory training.

When absolutely certain that a child can hear the difference between accurate and inaccurate articulation of the sounds in question, it is necessary that the child learn to produce the correct sound. This may be accomplished through games, exercises, behavior shaping (using approximations of the right sound and slowly approaching the correct articulation), or any method that seems appropriate to the age and interests of the child.

Many young children see little reason to change their speech patterns. This is true with all speech correction but perhaps most often with articulation problems. The children seem to get by, and unless they are embarrassed by the reactions of others, they may not care. In some instances, teachers must make them care enough to hear articulatory differences and then motivate them to learn to make the correct sound. Reward systems may be of considerable value in accomplishing this step.

A third step is to have the student incorporate the newly learned, accurately articulated sound in familiar words. Even though the student learns to hear the difference between accurate and inaccurate articulation and to produce the required sound, until the sound is regularly used in language, the student has not overcome the problem. When an individual has had months or years of practice in saying a sound incorrectly, it takes much repetition to develop new speech habits and patterns. Here again, motivation is highly important, and with young children, games are often valuable.

In addition to the preceding overall rules for remediation, one general rule must be carefully observed by regular classroom teachers. If a student is being seen by a speech-language pathologist, the teacher should consult with the specialist to be certain that any special efforts in the classroom are complementary, not contradictory, to the specialist's efforts.

Stuttering and Other Speech-Flow Disorders

Most speech authorities agree that stuttering has been and remains the most elusive of the speech disorders (Conture, 1990; Van Riper & Emerick, 1990). This is true in terms of both cause and treatment, and although new theories and treatments are advocated with some regularity, there seems to be no best theory or treatment.

Stuttering is just one disorder that may be described as a breakdown in the normal flow of speech. Other disorders receive much less attention, and all can be described as relating to difficulties in one or more of the five generally recognized dimensions of speech flow. Those dimensions are (a) sequence, or the order of sounds (for example, the word *cavalry* is often pronounced as *calvary*); (b) duration, or the length of time any phonetic element is produced (a duration problem may lead to confusion through decreased intelligibility and is usually just one part of a more complex problem); (c) rate, or the speed of articulation of speech sounds, syllables, or words (like duration, rate is not often a problem except as combined with other speech prob-

lems); (d) rhythm, or the pattern of phonetic elements (when rhythm is faulty, intelligibility and thus comprehension of speech are endangered); and (e) fluency, or the smoothness of articulation of sounds (the extreme example of disfluency is stuttering; other types of disfluency, as in some regional speech-flow patterns, are accepted as normal in some parts of the nation and are at least acceptable in others).

Stuttering, the most recognized of the speech-flow disorders, has been explained by speech experts through various theories. There are many such theories, falling into two major groups: organic and behavioral. Organic theories propose a variety of neurological causes for stuttering, ranging from older theories involving a lack of cerebral dominance to those that liken stuttering to epileptic seizures. In many of these theories, the fact that stutterers do not always stutter is accounted for by postulating a constitutional weakness that tends to give under pressure.

Nonorganic theories about the cause of stuttering may be grouped according to three major points of view, each dictating a somewhat different treatment, as may be seen from the accounts that follow. Each of these descriptions is a generalization of two or three closely related theories.

1. Stuttering is a result of the fact that important individuals in a student's early life label normal disfluencies "stuttering." In response, the child focuses on these disfluencies, attempting to eliminate them. Overreaction, fear, tension, and anxiety lead to maintaining these disfluencies long beyond the time when they would normally be abandoned. Thus, they become actual stuttering.

2. Stuttering is the result of an unusual need of the child to be understood. When the child tries to maintain the at-

tention of listeners, normal disfluencies that might otherwise be overlooked by both speaker and listener lead to more and more frustration. As the speaker struggles (because of internal drives, not outside influence) to become more fluent, tension and frustration lead to continued disfluency.

3. Stuttering is the result of a need to satisfy anal or oral desires, infantile tendencies, or high levels of hostility. In turn, these are the result of inadequate or unsatisfactory relationships with parents. Various psychoanalytic theories of child-parent conflict explain these conflicts.

Various combinations of theories have been constructed to form additional theories, but for nonspecialists, these three are the thrust of stuttering theories. Although various authorities may insist that their approach is based on a specific theory and think that recognition of the cause is highly important, all therapies are notable for their high rate of failure in practice.

Fortunately for the student and the teacher who wants to help the student, certain recommendations are generally applicable to stuttering. These should be followed unless the speech specialist specifically dictates other recommendations. These four relatively simple recommendations involve an attitude that the teacher and others who deal with the stutterer should adopt:

1. Do not mention the stuttering. Try to reduce the student's awareness of this problem.
2. Minimize settings and situations that appear to cause increased stuttering.
3. Minimize conflict of all types as much as possible.
4. Encourage speaking when all is going

well, and immediately minimize demands to communicate when stuttering becomes pronounced.

Primary, or beginning, stutterers may overcome the problem if those around them have accurate information and the right attitude. For secondary, or confirmed, stutterers, major goals may include acceptance of stuttering as part of the language pattern and learning to stutter more gracefully.

Though the lack of agreement among speech authorities about stuttering has been emphasized, there is general agreement on a number of observations about stuttering that help provide a better total perspective on this complex disorder. Nine such observations follow:

1. Stutterers rarely, if ever, stutter while singing.
2. Stutterers rarely stutter while speaking in unison or in synchronization with a rhythmic beat.
3. Stutterers rarely stutter while alone or while swearing.
4. Stuttering cannot always be induced, even in those who otherwise stutter regularly.
5. Stutterers tend to stutter on the same words when reading and rereading the same passage. They may not stutter on these same words in other sentences.
6. Stutterers tend to be able to predict their stuttering.
7. Time pressure seems to be a factor in causing or increasing stuttering.
8. Stutterers can learn to hear how their speech flows and understand what normal fluency means. They just cannot attain such fluency.
9. Many cases of stuttering (more than 75% by some estimates) simply disappear without any identifiable, provable reason.

Given this information, the regular classroom teacher should be able to manage the stutterer until the results of evaluation are received. At that point, the speech-language pathologist should offer specific recommendations to follow. Teachers should make every attempt to obtain prompt assistance with students who stutter and should resist the temptation to try out the various quick cures that regularly appear in newsmagazines and Sunday newspapers.

Voice Disorders

Voice disorders are not nearly so common as articulation disorders (Van Riper, 1990). However, they require immediate attention by classroom teachers. That is, teachers must make prompt referrals to speech-language pathologists if voice disorders are suspected. If a speech-language pathologist is not available, referral to a school nurse or parent is in order.

Voice disorders are generally considered to include disorders of pitch, intensity, quality, and flexibility. For the most part, these problems do not have the same kind of direct effect on the learning of basic skills as, for example, serious articulation problems have. In fact, unless they are very different from the norm, they are often accepted as part of the uniqueness of an individual. The following descriptions of these four voice disorders are presented so that teachers may have an overall view of voice disorders and a base from which to consider referral, to either the speech-language pathologist or, through the parents, a physician.

Pitch problems seldom cause any serious difficulty for a speaker, with the exception of a high, falsetto voice in an older teenage or adult male. For girls and women, various levels of pitch are accepted, with low voices often regarded as sexy and high ones as feminine. Despite a number of recent soci-

etal changes in concepts of masculinity and femininity, there is a stubborn persistence of the belief a man should have a voice that is of low or medium pitch. Therefore, a boy with a high-pitched voice that apparently is continuing into his upper-teenage years may benefit from therapy to help him lower the pitch. Sometimes pitch can be lowered, and sometimes it cannot. The matter is usually a sensitive one, but if assistance can be provided, it may help greatly in the social arena.

Voice intensity, loudness or softness, is not often a problem in and of itself, but very loud speech may mean that the individual does not hear his or her own voice distinctly and should serve as a cue to recheck the possibility of a hearing problem. The teacher should also note that if a child speaks indistinctly (as opposed to too softly) and is asked to speak up, the result may be even more unsatisfactory than before. In speaking up, many students with indistinct speech give voice to very loud vowel sounds, which even further drown out the weaker consonant sounds. Therefore, the teacher or speech-language pathologist must work on more precise consonant production.

Of the four major voice disorders, voice quality is the most common. Three types of quality problems are (a) breathiness, (b) harshness, and (c) nasality. Harshness or breathiness may be caused by vocal abuse (such as occurs at a hard-fought football game) or may be the result of infection or inflammation of the vocal cords. These temporary problems usually go away after a few days of vocal rest.

A more serious problem occurs as a result of continued vocal abuse, causing growths to develop on the vocal cords. Benign growths are fairly common among singers and, to some extent, among those who do a great deal of public speaking.

These, too, may go away with vocal rest or with therapy to assist in more normal voice production. However, growths may be malignant. Thus, the advice to seek prompt medical attention is applicable to older students and, of course, to adults. Malignant growths cause the same type of voice quality as do benign growths, but the only way to be sure is referral to a qualified specialist.

A speech-language pathologist should determine whether problems relating to nasality are likely to be longterm. Hypernasality (excessive nasal quality) may be a result of unrepaired cleft palate, and remedial action may be possible. In other cases, some reduction of unpleasant speech resulting from nasality may be attained through speech therapy.

The teacher should be alert for voice disorders and should be particularly alert for rapid changes in voice quality, especially hoarseness or breathiness. If the teacher is in doubt, an immediate referral to a specialist or physician is in order.

The fourth voice disorder is flexibility disorder. The most common flexibility problem is exhibited by the monotone speaker. This problem may result from many different causes, such as physical tiredness, emotional difficulties, voice pitch too near the top or the bottom of the vocal range, or a hearing problem. If a voice is very unpleasant because of a flexibility disorder and the problem persists, referral to a speech-language pathologist is the proper course of action. Seldom does the regular classroom teacher possess the technical knowledge and skill to assess and attempt to remediate this type of problem on his or her own.

In summary, most voice problems may be of a minor nature and may be properly overlooked. An exception is the case of unusual voice changes, particularly those typified by hoarseness, harshness, or breathiness. If these persist, even for a few weeks, referral is recommended.

Other Speech Problems

Three other speech problems, with three specific causes, deserve mention: (a) speech problems directly related to cerebral palsy, (b) speech problems related to hearing loss, and (c) speech problems related to cleft lip or cleft palate. Problems related to cerebral palsy can run the gamut from mild to severe. In some cases, they may result in speech that is almost unintelligible, although perhaps as many as one third of all individuals with cerebral palsy have essentially no speech problem. The best general rules to follow with a student whose cerebral palsy leads to speech problems are to provide sufficient time for the student to respond to questions or participate in class discussion and to make every attempt to learn to decode the student's speech. When a student with cerebral palsy is assigned to a new teacher, a few short one-to-one sessions between the student and teacher can help much toward early understanding of the student's speech. Practical communication is the goal, and speech therapy must be left to the speech-language pathologist except as the specialist provides specific instructions for assistance in the regular classroom.

Problems related to hearing loss may lead to a variety of speech difficulties, depending on various factors, but the major determining factor is the time of onset of the hearing loss. Some speech problems and some language problems are to be expected with students who are hearing impaired, but with proper assistance, such problems can be minimized. Remember that when a student has continued speech or language problems, the possibility of hearing impairment must be fully investigated. In a somewhat similar manner (although for different reasons), students who have mental retardation usually have some difficulties with language and vocabulary development. They may or may not lead to difficulties viewed as speech disorders.

Cleft lip and cleft palate problems vary in their effect on speech, depending on the depth of the cleft and the success of surgical procedures. Since midcentury, most children born with a facial cleft of any severity have been treated surgically during the first few months of life. A cleft lip after surgical treatment seldom causes any serious problem, but a cleft palate is often not completely corrected surgically. The effects of cleft palate commonly include articulation errors and problems with nasality. The correction of these physiologically based speech problems should be left to the speech clinician. As a result of the related problems, students with a cleft palate may avoid speaking and may eventually become retarded in vocabulary and overall language development.

Other less common problems include those related to faulty dentition or abnormal laryngeal structure. In many instances, such students can be helped, but medical assistance and the best efforts of a speech-language pathologist are required for maximum improvement. It is obvious that regular classroom teachers play significant roles in the implementation of speech programs for such students.

LANGUAGE DISORDERS

The speech-language pathologist will assess the student to determine whether or not the student's syntactic and semantic production and comprehension are similar to that of the student's peers. This may be accomplished through the use of standardized tests. An analysis of the student's spontaneous language provides additional informa-

tion regarding pragmatic production and communicative comprehension. This type of analysis of strengths and weaknesses in language may lead to the discovery of disorders broadly classified as (a) delayed language (including impairment of language development) and (b) impairment of acquired language (aphasia).

Delayed Language

Delayed language (also called delayed speech) means simply that an individual is unable to use language in the manner normally expected of that age. This inability may be related to some other known disability, for example, hearing impairment, learning disability, or mental retardation. In such cases, there is usually agreement as to how to proceed, and a joint effort is required among all professionals of different disciplines working with the child and parents.

One of the more common causes of delayed language is a lack of need for the child to talk. If parents attempt to anticipate a child's every need, so that speech is not required for basic need fulfillment, the attempts may delay language development. Or if parents literally believe that children should be seen and not heard, they may delay speech and language. Fortunately, children usually play with other children in the neighborhood and thus have opportunities and needs to speak to be a successful part of the group.

The term *delayed speech* is often used to refer to the speech patterns of children who have hearing impairment or mental retardation, but these conditions are not the same as delayed speech or delayed language in children who have adequate hearing and normal or above-normal mental ability. Parents who might become overly concerned with the fact that their young child seldom speaks and wonder if something is basically wrong should consider the case of Albert

Einstein, who did not speak until after his third birthday. The situation is somewhat different, however, if the child comes to school at the age of 5 years and still has seriously delayed language. This condition may require special attention, and planning should start with a complete physical checkup to eliminate the possibility of physiological defects. If there are no such disabilities and the child's intellectual level appears to be at least normal, then the environmental background should be reviewed.

Impairment of Acquired Language

Impairment of acquired language (aphasia) is more often associated with adults and is known to follow head injuries, strokes, and brain lesions (Shames & Wiig, 1990). Thus, aphasia is thought to be a matter of brain injury that leads to a loss of previously functional ability to speak or comprehend the spoken word.

Childhood (developmental) aphasia is a general term used for a language dysfunction in children that many authorities believe is caused by a brain dysfunction in the auditory mechanism for processing speech (Berko Gleason, 1989; Owens, 1988). Most authorities describe several specific types of aphasia, but as is the case with stuttering, there is considerable disagreement among these authorities as to the causes and in some cases, the treatment. What the teacher is likely to observe is a child who appears to be trying desperately to find the language to respond to a question, to participate in a discussion, or to ask a question.

LINGUISTIC VARIATIONS

Exceptional students from culturally diverse backgrounds present challenges to teachers in relation to assessment and teaching. Spoken language may be different with respect to morphology, syntax, semantics, and pragmatics, and the differences

likely affect writing production and the predictive aspects of reading. All languages or dialects are created equal from a linguistic point of view, in that they all "communicate ideas, intentions and feelings of speakers to listeners. From a sociocultural point of view, however, there are clearly differences" (Hammill & Bartel, 1990, p. 51). Standard English is prerequisite for a variety of occupations, and students whose speech is limited will find that their opportunities are also limited.

Fletcher (1986) notes: "Linguistic variation can occur in many different forms in American English. Typically, the recognition of any linguistic variation is made by comparing it to Standard American English" (p. 181). She also notes that speakers of a standard dialect (standard English) assign a status of correctness to that style and substandard or deviant status to the other styles.

Research has not yet provided information relating to the differences or similarities in learning style, values, or other factors related to the learning of disabled and nondisabled students from culturally diverse populations. In general, what is known about nondisabled students is superimposed on students with disabilities (Gaylord-Ross, 1989). However, cultural values affect socialization and greatly influence the childhood years. The socialization process accomplished prior to school entrance significantly influences students as they enter school systems and may be demonstrated in attitudes, behaviors, and communication patterns that teachers find difficult to understand. Examples of the effects of the socialization process that students from culturally diverse backgrounds may demonstrate in school include:

1. Lack of apparent interest in achievement in academic areas.
2. Apparent shyness.

3. Reluctance to ask for assistance or to welcome it when provided.
4. Poor self-esteem due to lack of acceptance by others or past school failure.
5. Aggressiveness due to conflicts with different cultures or disorganized home situations.
6. Unusual emphasis on rote memorization in the hope of success.
7. Underdeveloped language in English or the native language.
8. A tendency to follow, sometimes exacerbated by following the "wrong" group.

In some schools, students identified as having disabilities are also in bilingual programs. When this is the case, all involved must work together to meet the special needs of the students.

For speech disorders to be considered disabilities, they must be present in all of the languages that the student speaks (Baca & Cervantes, 1989). Some indicators of speech disorders in students who are bilingual are:

1. Omissions of initial or final consonants in both languages.
2. Substitutions. However, teachers must identify cultural substitutions and eliminate them from consideration.
3. Reluctance to participate in class discussions in their native language. Reluctance in English may be normal until students are proficient and feel comfortable.
4. Distortions of sound in both languages. Speaking too softly may be related to culture.
5. Disfluency in both languages. As students learn English, some disfluency is normal.

Teachers can provide a classroom atmosphere to enhance speaking opportunities and speaking skills. Following are some suggestions to help provide a supportive atmosphere:

1. Provide activities that have as their purpose the acceptance and appreciation of cultural diversity.
2. Present contributions of individuals from the ethnic groups represented in the class.
3. Use multicultural materials.
4. Organize instruction with a focus on multicultural education.

According to Polloway and Smith (1982), teachers can demonstrate support for culturally diverse students by:

1. Avoiding negative comments about the student's language. Statements such as "Can you say that in a way I can understand?" are more supportive than "I can't understand you."
2. Reinforcing language production. Students learn language by using it, and using it increases production. Reinforcement should be culturally appropriate.
3. Planning small-group activities. Students have more opportunities to speak in small groups and usually feel more confident. It is also possible for the teacher to prompt and reinforce students more frequently and in a more private setting.
4. Reducing the tension that will likely develop in classes where a high degree of oral participation is expected, thus allowing students to be more productive.
5. Encouraging discussions concerning language differences and comparisons of languages.
6. Involving persons from the ethnic groups represented in the community as guest speakers. All students benefit from this type of exposure.
7. Learning to understand nonstandard English dialects. Students who speak nonstandard dialects usually experience no difficulty in understanding what they hear, but teachers may not understand them. However, this is not necessarily

true of bilingual students, who may have significant difficulty comprehending oral English.

Many school districts provide teachers with such suggestions in a handbook or at in-service meetings. The time a teacher spends in recognizing cultural diversity and in understanding the individual needs of students from diverse cultural and linguistic backgrounds will pay great dividends in teacher satisfaction and in student well-being and achievement.

THE ROLE OF REGULAR CLASSROOM TEACHERS

Teachers must remain alert to make referrals of students who need special assistance in the area of speech or language. They should be particularly alert to possible voice disorders. Often, when arithmetic or reading skills are obviously quite low, teachers feel more secure in making referrals, for they feel confident in these areas and have considerable training. Many teachers have not had similar training with speech and language problems, and therefore the following guidelines may be of value. The guidelines may require revision to conform with local practices, but in principle, they are generally applicable.

1. For a teacher who is not experienced in evaluating potential speech problems, overreferral may be the best practice. With experience, the number of referrals may be reduced without the risk of overlooking students who require assistance.
2. If a speech specialist is available for conferences with teachers (and one should be, on either an informal basis or a formally scheduled basis), teachers should confer with the specialist to learn more about the type of information needed and who should or should not be referred. Such conferences usually turn

out to be informal in-service training sessions, and as such, they are of great value. The number of such conferences can be reduced as a teacher gains experience.

3. When it appears that a speech or language difficulty is related to other problems, such as hearing impairment or mental retardation, a teacher should check all records and talk with previous teachers (when possible) to determine if these possibilities have been investigated. Any recent audiological evaluation should receive particular attention in a case of possible hearing impairment.
4. In settings in which the speech specialist is overloaded with cases (a common situation), the teacher may expedite matters by describing the type and extent of the problem in detail. It is not enough to say that the child lisps. Many other factors can be considered, such as how consistently the problem occurs, whether it occurs mainly when the child is under pressure or is tired, and whether it is noticed by other children.

If the teacher's referral leads to speech evaluation and the speech specialist begins to provide assistance to the student, usually the specialist also provides specific suggestions to the teacher. The teacher's role depends on the type and extent of the problem. In general, the role of the classroom teacher relates to the following concepts:

1. Being sure the aims and objectives of the therapy program are fully understood.
2. Demonstrating acceptance of the student with a communication disorder and encouraging other class members to do the same.
3. Reinforcing good speech and language habits in all students, especially in the student with the impairment, so the importance of what is learned in the therapy sessions is transferred to other set-

tings. Modeling appropriate speech and language also communicates the importance of speech and language.

4. Attending to *what* the student is saying more than to *how* it is said.

5. Helping students follow medical instructions relating to vocal rest or other disorders for which there are medical instructions.

6. Recognizing that students with cleft lip or palate may require surgery and thus miss school. Help them either keep up or catch up.

7. Being aware of the strengths as well as the weaknesses of students with cerebral palsy.

8. Keeping records of the students' progress, following a system devised in collaboration with a speech-language specialist.

THE ROLE OF SPEECH-LANGUAGE PATHOLOGISTS

The speech-language pathologist is the orchestrator of school speech and language services. As such, the pathologist provides direct services to students with severe or difficult problems and advice to teachers who serve students with mild problems. Effective speech programs involve identification, evaluation, and remediation and depend on cooperative working relationships between speech specialists and regular classroom teachers. The American Speech-Language-Hearing Association and others

FIGURE 6–4
The comprehensive speech and language program continuum

Communicative development	Communicative deviations	Communicative disorders
Development and/or preventive programs carried out in class Speech specialist is involved in total curriculum to emphasize the value of attention to speech and language development Specialist serves as consultant and also provides some direct teacher training but essentially no *direct* service to students.	Mild to moderate problems (articulation, etc.) Specialist evaluates and provides instructions to regular class teacher, who implements major elements of program. Specialist monitors regularly and intervenes more directly as required.	Severe problems that require more intensive one-to-one service by specialist. Regular class teacher's efforts are quite important here, but most direct service comes from the specialist.

Service provided by regular class teacher

Service provided by speech specialist

recommend that speech and language programs be organized along a continuum extending from a communicative development component to a communicative disorders component (see Figure 6–4).

In respect to communicative development, a speech-language pathologist must make teachers and parents more aware of factors that help students develop good communicative skills, especially factors that can be part of a regular classroom or home environment.

Many of the suggestions provided in this chapter would be a part of any program of communicative development, along with efforts to construct a curriculum ensuring experiences that promote maximum communicative skills in all children. This program is primarily developmental and preventive in nature, and except for orienting teachers newly employed in a given school, the speech specialist has minimum visibility once the program is well established.

Communicative deviations are mild to moderate speech and language problems that require some assistance from the speech-language pathologist but with the regular classroom teacher providing much of the direct effort. Instructions, including original instructions and ongoing assistance, are provided by the specialist. If classroom efforts are not successful, the specialist intervenes more directly, as required in individual cases.

Communicative disorders include disorders that obviously require specialized help because of their severity and specific, one-to-one assistance on an ongoing basis. Even here, much cooperation between a regular classroom teacher and specialist is necessary, but this type of service requires much

Communication between the speech-language pathologist and the classroom teacher is essential.

greater time involvement on the part of the speech-language pathologist.

The speech-language pathologist must help teachers recognize situations in which various class proceedings, including certain standardized academic tests, are greatly affected by lack of speech or language ability. The speech-language pathologist must determine the most effective ways to improve a student's speech or language and must involve the teacher in such remediation, providing assistance in carryover activities for the classroom.

Speech-language pathologists serve in a variety of settings in public schools throughout the nation. Although the majority serve in a regular school setting, some are part of a special program for students with severe physical disabilities or multiple disabilities, in which cases, the day-to-day involvement of the pathologist is greater than this chapter describes. One or two speech-language pathologists may be assigned to a single building, but the more typical pattern is an itinerant assigned to several buildings. In a typical assignment, a speech-language pathologist is likely to have a caseload of 30 to 40 students, but in some areas, the load is greater.

As the services provided by speech-language pathologists have moved to the right side of the speech-service continuum (Figure 6–4), maximum caseloads have been reduced through state reimbursement regulations, meaning that regular classroom teachers must deal with many of the milder cases. When the speech-language pathologist and the regular classroom teacher develop a system through which cooperative efforts on behalf of individual students are possible, the program is successful and the students are the major beneficiaries.

SUGGESTIONS FOR REGULAR CLASSROOM TEACHERS

Students develop language as as an imitative function, so teachers have a special reason to model correct articulation, grammar, and language usage. Regular classroom teachers are regularly involved in promoting speech and language development for all students and may also be involved in individualized efforts for specific students. Reading to students from texts in content areas, fiction, and nonfiction is interesting to the student. Audiotapes also provide appropriate models of language. In addition, selected television programs that have been videotaped may provide language enrichment. Ideas such as these can easily be incorporated into the daily schedule at any grade level; will provide models of accurate articulation, phrasing, and appropriate speech; and will enhance language usage and comprehension.

In conjunction with a speech-language pathologist and consistent with the particular objectives for a student, structured naturalistic activities may provide opportunities for using the skills learned in therapy. Such activities for younger children may center around recess or involve role playing or puppetry. Language experience approaches in the beginning-to-read stage allow for expansion of vocabulary as well as assist in awareness of relationships between spoken and written language. For older students, activities may be based on clothing or grooming, food preparation, assembling or sorting of materials, and interviewing. Cognitive rehearsal strategies help students organize their thoughts before speaking. For some students, combining and recombining sentences in oral or written form provides linguistic awareness.

Instructions or oral directions in short,

simple sentences, with pauses and restatements of important information, provide appropriate models and help comprehension, which of course is a goal of communication. Discussing speech and language activities and what the student has learned may help reduce negative feelings about therapy. Responding to a student's efforts at communication in a positive manner will encourage the student and model acceptance for others.

Oral communication may be encouraged through activities like expression of feelings, oral reports, and problem solving. However, the teacher must be sensitive to situations that might be threatening to a student (Morsink, 1984).

Seating arrangement may facilitate opportunities for a student to use oral language in the classroom. Having the student near the teacher tends to restrict instead of enhance interactions (Lewis & Doorlag, 1991). Rather, the student should be surrounded by good speech models.

Discuss pronunciation and meanings of new words and provide opportunities for students to use new words orally and in written form. A structured format for teaching vocabulary includes demonstrating appropriate and inappropriate examples, asking for examples from students, providing examples by which students can assess their own performance, and providing definitions for students to identify (Schloss & Sedlak, 1986).

Students lacking conversational skills may be taught the pragmatics of conversation, which, according to Schloss and Sedlak (1986), include:

1. Taking turns
2. Initiating
3. Clarifying a point
4. Following the sequential organization

5. Making coherent contributions
6. Maintaining a reasonable social distance (p. 237)

In content areas requiring specific vocabulary (for example, science), quizzes may help ensure understanding of concepts that enhance comprehension of lectures or explanations. Explanations of the derivations of words may help some students comprehend a variety of words more fully. For example, a student who learns the meaning of *inter* as between or among may be able to infer the meanings of *intercolonial, intercultural, intercellular,* and *interdependent.*

Role playing in appropriate situations provides practice of skills in effective communication. An example that is applicable in almost any content area is having a student teach a particular concept or lesson. This requires planning what will be taught and how it will be taught. A student might explain the concept of osmosis with the aid of a chart, or the correct positioning of the body when holding a bat by using stick figures. Oral presentation might be rehearsed to ensure clarity.

Encouraging active participation in class may be of great value, especially if a student with some particular problem has notice. For example, the teacher might say, "Tomorrow I am going to ask you to comment on the basic differences between communism and democracy. Let's see if you can challenge the thinking of the rest of the class."

The Language Master, a machine providing visual and auditory information, may be a useful tool. This system uses cards with visual representations (words, pictures, or short phrases) on the top and a magnetic tape near the bottom. As a card is inserted in the machine, a verbal message (which the teacher has prerecorded) is played. The

The Language Master provides simultaneous auditory and visual information.

student receives simultaneous auditory and visual stimuli. The Language Master will record the verbal response of the student, allowing for playback. The student may, for example, see a picture of teeth and hear the auditory stimulus "The plural of *tooth* is _____?" The student's response, "*teeth*," is recorded. On the prerecorded message, the teacher may have left space for the student's response and provided the correct response so that the student receives corrective feedback or immediate verification of a correct answer. The Language Master also provides practice in a variety of other grammatical aspects, vocabulary, and reading enrichment exercises.

To combine oral language and sequenc-ing, the teacher may ask students to provide oral directions for certain activities. For example, the teacher might have a student direct the class as they construct a collage for a bulletin board or perform a specific dance. In order to practice verbal skills, ask students to interview another student for specific information, such as favorite sports or least favorite subject and the reasons for the choice. It is important for students to phrase their questions in ways that require more than one-word responses.

When targeted skills are being practiced, a tape recorder may be used, and a student allowed time to evaluate his or her performance. For example, when the use of adjectives is the targeted skill, provide an opportunity for a student to prepare and record a short presentation about a topic of interest. After recording, the student would evaluate his or her use of adjectives in the presentation. Videotaping conversations between two students will also allow students to replay the videotape and determine how well they used specific targeted skills.

Listening skills may be enhanced through the use of materials in a content area. The teacher can read a series of paragraphs from the text in a content area and ask the students to either write or provide an oral concluding statement. The statement should be a summary of the content of the paragraphs previously read. Skills related to evaluation and judgment may also be reinforced by asking the students to choose the most appropriate statement from a group of concluding statements. A similar activity related to listening skills is reading a short story, poem, or other selection, not reading the title, then asking the students to provide a title.

The teacher may show a movie or read a story that addresses a topic of interest to students and then provide a list of questions that follows the format of the movie or story. This provides guidance, structure, and practice for students who have difficulty staying on a topic in oral discussions.

Sample sentences may direct students to identify descriptive words (or any other class or words). Students can be asked to suggest other words that will change the meaning of a sentence, or for a more difficult exercise, to suggest words that alter the meaning without completely changing it.

Singing activities may be used to increase oral language and fluency. Choral reading has the same benefits. Time between classes or at the beginning of class may be used by having students tell jokes or ask riddles. Students may be told in advance that they will need to be prepared on a given day. Some ground rules about appropriateness of jokes or riddles may need to be discussed with the students to help them learn how to adjust what they say based on situations and listeners (pragmatics).

Students can be directed to work in pairs, with one the describer, who provides a verbal description of a simple picture, and the other the listener. The listener sketches the picture, based on the words of the describer. After completion of the drawing, the original picture and the sketch may be compared and the roles may be reversed.

Students may be provided with a map of the school building, local area, or the United States (depending on the students' abilities) and taken on an oral trip. The teacher gives directions that must be followed in order to arrive at the destination. A more complicated version of the same activity is to provide the students with a paper grid and give directions that they must follow to arrive at a specific square. Since a grid is more abstract than a map, it requires considerably more skill on the part of the students. Activities similar to these also provide students with practice in using terms such as *left, right, north,* and *south.*

Videotapes, stories, or another student telling a story provides for a variety of activities in which students must recall what they hear. Students may illustrate what they hear and retell it or sequence pictures that illustrate the major points. To make the task more difficult, allow time to elapse (a few minutes, hours, or days) before asking the students to respond. This emphasizes memory as well as listening.

Music such as "Peter and the Wolf," "The Nutcracker," "Sorcerer's Apprentice," or "2001: A Space Odyssey" provides students with a source for describing mental pictures. As an alternative, students can draw or paint pictures or develop creative

FIGURE 6-5
A cluster diagram (visual representation) about transportation

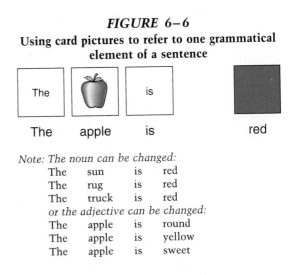

Motorcycles   Bicycles

2-wheeled

Gliders   Wagons

Transportation   4-wheeled

Flying

Blimps   Airplanes   Carts   Cars

movement activities related to music (Norton, 1989).

Teachers may provide oral information regarding a specific topic (from a content area) or use a story and develop a cluster diagram with students. A simple cluster diagram related to transportation is presented in Figure 6-5. A cluster diagram enables students to observe a visual representation of what they have heard and to note the organization of the various concepts. More complex cluster diagrams may be used as the students' skills increase. Prior to expecting the students to develop such diagrams, teachers must model the procedure for the students.

When students have difficulty with word order or exhibit certain consistent omissions in spoken language, the use of card pictures to make sentences more concrete may be of value. In this activity each card is used to refer to one grammatical function of a sentence (see Figure 6-6). Through lengthening the sentence or fading the visual cues, the students should be able to generalize the rules relating to word order.

A number of abstract concepts are uti-

lized at elementary levels of spoken language. Examples include (a) comparisons of size—big, bigger, biggest, longer, shorter; (b) spatial concepts—on, under, beside, in, in back of, top, middle; (c) ordinal concepts—first, second, third; and (d) directional concepts—left, right, north, west, southeast. When students have difficulty using such abstract concepts correctly, visual aids often provide the concrete experi-

FIGURE 6-6
Using card pictures to refer to one grammatical element of a sentence

| The | 🍎 | is | | 🟥 |

The   apple   is   red

Note: The noun can be changed:
The	sun	is	red
The	rug	is	red
The	truck	is	red

or the adjective can be changed:
The	apple	is	round
The	apple	is	yellow
The	apple	is	sweet

ences necessary for understanding. Physical activities relating to the concepts also develop understanding.

Enhance thinking skills and verbal exchanges by providing opportunities for teacher-student and student-student interactions. Present problems for which there are no "correct" answers, such as the following:

1. What would you do if you found a $20 bill on the floor? Why?
2. If you are driving somewhere and have a flat tire, what can you do?
3. What would you take along with you if you were going to spend 2 weeks on an island? Why did you choose those things?

Students with severe language disabilities may need visual cues (pictures cut from magazines) to elicit initial responses or to broaden responses. Such cues are removed as soon as possible.

Acting out scenes from daily life can provide opportunities for students to practice sequencing skills and to practice skills in communication. Such dramatic play may provide an incentive for some students who otherwise avoid self-expression to exercise spoken language. If the spoken language used in such play is limited, the activity may be expanded to include small-group brainstorming to list different words that might be used. For example, if part of the play concerns baking a cake, the cake might be described as *delicious, yummy, exquisite, super good, moist, dry, burned,* or *lopsided.* Dramatic play provides opportunities for spoken language similar to that provided by written-language experience stories. Topics relevant to the lives of the students provide the motivation. Dramatic play can be used in such content areas as literature and social studies. Students can develop skits related to *The Diary of Anne Frank* or the three branches of the U.S. government.

Puppets permit the transfer of the identity of students to the characters represented by the puppets. Such substitution encourages many shy students to participate in a variety of discussions, for they can hide behind the puppet. The use of puppets may relate to stories the students have read, stories the students have written, or stories read to the students. Even creation of the puppets is an opportunity for enhancing spoken language among students.

Role playing is a more structured form of dramatic activity. It is better suited to some students and some age-groups than puppetry. Problems of various types can be suggested by the students or the teacher. A discussion of the facets of the problem will provide motivation and time for the students to get into the character. The students assume roles and act out solutions to the problem. After each role-playing session is completed (sessions are brief), a discussion of the events as well as alternative solutions is conducted. The problem-solving aspect and the use of spoken language provide students with opportunities for growth. Some teachers use this type of activity to solve routine classroom discipline problems, such as waiting for others to finish speaking or respecting the property of others. Frequently, students who act, speak, and think as someone else in role playing use a broader range of vocabulary and greater sentence complexity.

Most students learn concepts through experiences—direct teaching of concepts may be quite difficult. Often, students use terms representing abstract concepts without fully understanding them. Concept teaching must include specific language training and use of the concepts in a variety of situations. The following steps are suggested to develop understanding of concepts:

1. Clearly identify the concept to be taught.
2. Identify and discuss critical and noncritical attributes. Take care to note that the critical attributes apply to that concept only.
3. Identify examples and nonexamples of the concept. After you complete several discussions of examples and nonexamples and you feel the students understand, ask the students to provide both examples and nonexamples.
4. After the students master critical and noncritical attributes and examples and nonexamples, discuss finer discriminations and distinctions.
5. Provide opportunities to use the newly acquired knowledge.

Interesting and unusual lost-and-found ads may be selected and brought to class. They may be read to the students if students have difficulty reading, or the students may read them. A discussion of what lost-and-found ads are and purposes for them should follow. Students may develop oral stories about the ads. Dividing the class into small groups should provide all students with opportunities to share their stories. The activity may be varied for older students, using want ads or apartment rental ads. The students might describe the type of person who would perform well at the job, what type of person would desire or would want to sell the objects listed, or who lived in the apartment or wants to live in the apartment described. Such oral discussions promote spoken language development, but the responses may also be written to develop written skills.

A discussion may be held regarding the differences between conversation and interviewing, and a list of purposes for interviewing may be developed. Appropriate and inappropriate factors relating to interviewing may be discussed, and interviewing skills may be practiced. When the students are proficient, assign various school personnel to be interviewed (the principal, custodians, other students, or teachers). In conjunction with content areas, students may interview individuals in the community. Prior to the interviews, the students should establish purposes for the interviews and develop lists of questions to ask. After the interviews take place, the students should report the results to the entire class. A variation of this activity is to use want ads and role-play the interviewer and the interviewee. Students may be required to do some reference work related to the job requirements. An activity such as this is easily incorporated into units on career opportunities or awareness.

In place of the usual written reports, students may design dioramas or television commercials that illustrate the main theme of a book. Dioramas or pictures may be used as visual aids in oral presentations. Television commercials may consist of enactment of portions of a book, with announcers describing the salient aspects. In addition to providing practice in oral language, such activities provide means of synthesizing for students who have difficulty in written expression.

In order to help students visualize figures of speech or metaphors, provide a list such as "I'll put a bug in his ear" and "She has a frog in her throat." Ask the students to illustrate the literal meanings. As an extended activity, students may illustrate their inferred meanings on the reverse side of the paper.

A series of questions, direct and indirect, such as those that follow, may be compiled. In a few instances, questions might be either direct or indirect requests, with other cues the determining factors. Teachers should read the questions with the students, indicating the real meaning of the question. Examples of questions are:

1. What day of the week is this?
2. Can you open the window?
3. Won't you stop talking?
4. When does your bus leave?
5. Must you stand there?
6. Is the door open?
7. Can't you sit still?

Students can record stories for younger students. While preparing tapes, they are learning to use appropriate voice inflection, which has benefits for oral language and reading. Rap songs relating to topics addressed in the content areas (safety, nutrition, or health) may be created by older students for younger students (Polloway, et al., 1989).

Teachers at all grade levels must attend to the manner in which they recognize language usage. This attention requires careful planning, but with practice, such planning becomes second nature and has positive effects on all students in the class. The key concepts in such planning and teaching are exposure, encouragement, variety, opportunity, and innovation. The interest of students must be stimulated and maintained. A reward system must be established, be it grades, praise, or privileges, to encourage students to maintain effort. McCormick

(1986) suggests that students with speech or language deficits are more alike than different from their peers in that they "need and can benefit from a range and variety of learning experiences; . . . are interested in and want to talk about the same general objects, events and relationships; and . . . seek the same control over their environment" (p. 124).

The preceding ideas and suggestions are samples of what may be done. They may be modified and thus provide a wide variety of options.

SUMMARY

This chapter included a discussion of various theories of language development and consideration of articulation, stuttering, voice, and language disorders. The importance of coordinating classroom remedial efforts with those of the speech-language pathologist was emphasized. Linguistic variations, and the need to recognize them for what they really are, were discussed. The role of the speech-language pathologist was reviewed, and a number of practical suggestions for regular classroom teachers were provided. Students use their speech and language skills throughout the school day, so the remedial and development efforts of regular classroom teachers are the most essential elements in any successful program of intervention.

- To what extent may an individual with a visual impairment further damage residual visual abilities?

- Which students with thick-lensed glasses fit the definition of visually impaired? Which do not fit the definition?

- What behaviors that can indicate impaired vision may be observed in school? What action should be taken when such behaviors are observed?

- How do you think common environmental scenes will appear to someone with glaucoma? cataracts? a detached retina?

- What electronic devices are available to help persons with visual impairments read normal print? What devices are available to help them with travel about the community?

- What is the difference between orientation skills and mobility skills? How can a blind student learn such skills?

- If a blind person needs travel assistance across the street and into a fifth floor office, would you know how to provide such assistance?

- How do dog guides communicate with their masters? What are their strengths and limitations?

TEACHING STUDENTS WHO ARE VISUALLY IMPAIRED

Most people are acquainted with someone who has a visual impairment, often an elderly person who can no longer easily read a newspaper, a menu, or the label on a medicine bottle. Yet, through some curious reasoning, people frequently assume that if individuals have some serious visual difficulty but are not elderly, they must be blind, that is, have no usable vision at all. In fact, only about 15% of the persons classified as legally blind have no usable vision. In the 1930s, the federal government defined legal blindness, and this definition may have contributed to the belief that all persons with serious visual impairment are blind. As a result, there is a great deal of confusion about the differences between blindness, low vision, visual impairment, and partial sight. This chapter clarifies the terminology and related issues, as well as provides suggestions for classroom teachers to assure that students with any type of visual impairment are fully participating members of the class.

Educating visually impaired students with their sighted peers was advocated by Dr. Samuel Gridley Howe in 1866.

Although some of the terminology he used seems strange, the concept he advocated was ahead of PL 94–142 by over 100 years. His statement also provides insight regarding how persons with visual impairment were treated at that time:

All great establishments in the nature of boarding schools, where sexes must be separated; where there must be boarding in common, and sleeping in congregate dormitories; where there must be routine, and formality, and restraint, and repression of individuality; where the charms and refining influences of the true family relation cannot be had—all such institutions are unnatural, undesirable, and very liable to abuse. We should have as few of them as possible, and those few should be kept as small as possible. . . .

. . . With a view to lessening all differences between blind and seeing children, I would have the blind attend the common schools in all cases where it is feasible (depend upon it, one of the future reforms in the education of the blind will be to send blind children to the common schools, to be taught with common children in all those branches not absolutely requiring visible illustrations, as spelling, pronunciation, grammar, arithmetic, vocal music and the like). We shall avail ourselves of the special institutions less and the common schools more. (quoted in Irwin, 1955, p. 128)

DEFINITIONS, MEASUREMENTS, AND CLASSIFICATIONS OF VISION

Barraga (1983) notes "a gradual trend to use blind and low vision to differentiate the population and to use visually handicapped as a generic term to refer to the entire population" (p. 21). The American Federation for the Blind (1987) suggests that terms such as *visually impaired, low vision,* and *partially sighted* be used when referring to individuals who have usable sight, reserving the term *blind* for those who have no usable sight.

When the government first defined legal blindness to determine who would be eligible for governmental benefits, it used the terminology of eye care specialists, which relates to acuity and visual field. A person is regarded as legally blind when the central visual acuity is 20/200 or less in the better eye after correction and the field of vision is no more than 20 degrees in diameter (American Federation for the Blind, 1987).

Ratios such as 20/20, 20/70, and 20/200 are used to express visual acuity. The first number is the distance in feet at which the test is made. The second number is the size of symbols or letters on the Snellen chart, expressed in terms of the distance at which a person with normal vision can comfortably read them. For example, if at 20 feet an individual can read the 20-foot-size symbol or letter on the chart, the measured acuity is 20/20, or normal vision. If an individual can read only the symbol representing the 70-foot-size letter or larger on the Snellen chart, then the individual's distance visual acuity is 20/70. If an individual can read only the largest, the 200-foot-size letter, then the individual's measured distance visual acuity is 20/200. These figures indicate distance visual acuity, but they do not provide information concerning near-point vision (the ability to see at close distances, as in reading), and there is considerable variance among individuals with the same measured acuity. For example, two students may have 20/200 measured acuity, but one may be able to read printed material, whereas the other may read braille.

The Keystone Telebinocular device may be used to assess near-distance vision and depth perception, factors that also affect the ability of students to use vision effectively. A complete evaluation of functional vision includes near vision, far vision, depth perception, and color discrimination (McLoughlin & Lewis, 1990).

The *Federal Register* (1977) defined a visual handicap as a "visual impairment which even with correction, adversely affects the child's educational performance. The term includes both partially seeing and blind children" (p. 42479). Also referring to an educationally oriented definition rather than a legal one, Barraga (1983) states, "A visually handicapped child is one whose visual impairment interferes with his optimal learning and achievement, unless adaptations are made in the methods of presenting learning experiences, the nature of the materials used, and/or in the learning environment" (p. 25).

The functional ability of the student is also important to consider. A student whose vision is unreliable, who finds it necessary to rely on other senses, and who cannot use print even with maximum magnification may be classified as functionally blind. A student who can perform visual tasks but does so with reduced precision and endurance and at reduced speed is likely to be considered as having low vision.

IDENTIFICATION OF STUDENTS WHO ARE VISUALLY IMPAIRED

Students with severe visual impairment are usually easily identified before enrollment in school. However, impaired vision in some students goes undetected for many years. Impairment may be detected by routine visual screening during the primary grades, or it may not be detected until fourth or fifth grade, when the subject matter requires extensive visual work, like increased reading and map study. Many screening programs are carelessly conducted, with the procedures carried out sloppily or not carried out on a routine basis. In addition, tests for near-point vision (ability to read at 12 to 16 inches) are required by only a few states. Most screening programs are concerned with distance vision (ability to see at 20 feet). Although vision screening procedures are improving, even at best, they do not identify all students with impaired vision.

When the problems associated with vision screening are considered, the role of regular classroom teachers in identifying students with vision problems cannot be overemphasized. Teachers have opportunities to observe students in a variety of settings and under a variety of conditions and may be in the best position to identify visual difficulties. Therefore, it may be helpful for regular classroom teachers to be aware of behaviors and observable signs that may indicate a visual problem.

Indicators of Possible Vision Problems

There are many indicators of possible vision problems, and teachers should watch for them. Following are some of the most common such indicators.

Rubbing Eyes. One behavior that may be an indication of a vision problem is eye rubbing. The rubbing may be observed in excessive amounts or during close visual work.

Shutting or Covering One Eye. A student who is having difficulty seeing may close one eye or tilt or thrust the head forward.

Light Sensitivity. Some students with an undetected vision problem may demonstrate unusual sensitivity to bright or even normal light by shutting their eyes or squinting.

Difficulty with Reading. An unusual amount of difficulty with reading or other work requiring close use of the eyes is another possible indicator of visual impairment. A student who has little difficulty with oral or spoken directions or tasks but experiences difficulty with visual work may have vision loss.

Losing Place During Reading. The student who has a tendency to lose his or her place in a sentence or page while reading may have a vision problem. Teachers should carefully observe to see if the student is demonstrating a mechanical reading problem or one related to a possible visual defect.

Unusual Facial Expressions and Behaviors. A student who demonstrates an unusual amount of squinting, blinking, frowning, or facial distortion while reading or doing other close work should be observed and possibly referred for further examination.

Achievement Disparity. A possible indication of visual loss is a disparity between expected and actual achievement. Obviously, there may be many reasons that a student does not achieve in a manner consistent with his or her ability, but teachers should be aware that one of the reasons may be visual loss.

Eye Discomfort. The student who complains of burning, itching, or scratchiness of the eyes may be experiencing a vision problem and should be referred to the school nurse for closer examination.

Holding Reading Materials at an Inappropriate Distance. Behavior that may indicate a student has a visual problem is holding reading materials too close or too far or frequently changing the distance from near to far or far to near.

Discomfort Following Close Visual Work. A student who complains of pains or aches in the eye, headaches, dizziness, or nausea following close visual work may have a visual problem.

Difficulty with Distance Vision. A student who experiences difficulty in seeing distant objects or who avoids gross motor activities may have visual loss. Such a student may prefer reading or other academic tasks to playground activities.

Blurred or Double Vision. A student who complains of blurred or double vision should be referred for a visual examination as soon as possible.

Reversals. A tendency to reverse letters, syllables, or words may be an indication of impaired vision.

Letter Confusion. A student who confuses letters of similar shape *(o and a, c and e, n and m, h and n, f and t)* may have impaired vision.

Poor Spacing. Poor spacing in writing and difficulty in staying on the line may be an indication of visual impairment.

Physical Indications. There are also several physical indications that teachers should not overlook. These include red eyelids, crusts on lids among the eyelashes, recurring styes or swollen lids, watering eyes or discharges, crossed eyes or eyes that do not appear to be straight, pupils of uneven size, eyes that move excessively, and drooping eyelids.

VISUAL DISORDERS AND IMPAIRMENTS

This discussion considers three major classifications of visual disorder/impairment. First, it considers refractive errors (which are more commonly corrected through the use of lenses). Next, it considers muscle disorders, and then a varied group of impairments that may result in such problems as a reduced field of vision, reduced visual acuity, and blurring of vision. Many of the following descriptions are more readily understood through reference to Figure 7–1, which is a diagram and condensed description of normal visual functioning.

Refractive Errors

Some of the common refractive errors are:

1. *Myopia, or nearsightedness.* An increased curvature of the eyeball (the eyeball is longer than normal from front to back), resulting in the focus of light rays in front of the retina, causing difficulty in seeing distant objects clearly.
2. *Hyperopia, or farsightedness.* A decreased curvature of the eyeball (the eyeball is shorter than normal from front to back), resulting in the focus of light rays beyond the retina, causing difficulty in seeing clearly objects that are near.
3. *Astigmatism.* Irregularities or unevenness in the cornea, causing light to be refracted differentially rather than at one point (part of the image is correctly focused; other parts are not), resulting in blurred or distorted vision.

FIGURE 7-1
Normal visual functioning and refraction

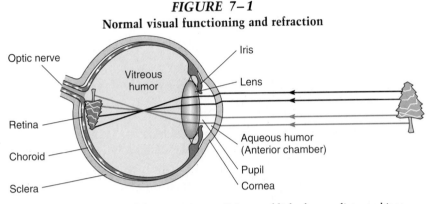

Note: In normal visual functioning, parallel rays of light from a distant object are refracted (bent) by the cornea, and again by the lens, bringing the object into sharp focus on the retina. The image is actually upside down on the retina, but the brain interprets it as right side up.

Muscular Defects

Disorders relating to the muscles around the eye include:

1. *Nystagmus.* A circular or side-to-side, rapid, involuntary movement of the eyeball.
2. *Strabismus.* An inability of the muscles to pull equally, resulting in crossed eyes (internal strabismus) or eyes pulled outward (external strabismus), usually requiring surgery for correction.
3. *Amblyopia.* A loss of vision due to a muscle imbalance that results in double vision. The brain attempts to reduce the confusion by suppressing the vision in one eye, and the unused eye may atrophy, resulting in a loss of sight. This may often be corrected by surgery or by wearing a patch over the unaffected eye to force the affected eye to focus.

Other Disorders

Among the more common conditions that result in reduced field of vision, blind spots, reduced visual acuity, or blurring of vision are glaucoma, cataract, retinal detachment, retinitis pigmentosa, macular degeneration, corneal pathological condition, and diabetic retinopathy. Figures 7-2 to 7-10 depict the results of myopia and hyperopia (previously discussed) plus a number of these other visual problems. Figure 7-2 shows a street as seen by someone with 20/20 visual acuity. The remaining figures represent the same scene as it might appear to persons with various serious vision problems. Below each representation is a brief description of the condition and its effects on what the individual sees. These figures are only illustrative of the various conditions; there may be considerable variance in any of the conditions represented.

REFERRAL

When any of the behaviors or signs of visual problems are observed, teachers should immediately refer the student to the school nurse, principal, or other individual in the school designated to receive such referrals. The parents should also be consulted. It is possible that there are refractive errors, which may be corrected by lenses, but it is also possible that more serious problems have developed, which require immediate medical attention.

Teachers may find it helpful to have information concerning the capabilities of the various eye specialists in the community in order to make the necessary referrals or provide information to parents. Occasionally, classroom teachers may need to confer with one of these specialists; therefore, a brief description is provided here:

1. *Ophthalmologist.* A medical doctor who specializes in the diagnosis and treatment of diseases of the eye. This physician is also licensed to prescribe glasses.
2. *Optometrist.* A highly trained person who specializes in eye problems but does not possess a medical degree. This individual is licensed to measure visual function and prescribe and fit glasses. If

disease is suspected, a referral will be made to an ophthalmologist.
3. *Optician.* A technician who makes glasses and fills the prescriptions of ophthalmologists and optometrists.
4. *Orthoptist.* A nonmedical technician who directs prescribed exercises or training to correct eye muscle imbalances and generally works under the direction of an ophthalmologist.

After assessment of vision is completed, if the student has impairments not correctable by lenses or surgery, a staffing meeting will likely be called to determine how to meet the needs of the student. At this time, reports from the vision specialists are consulted and an IEP is developed. The teacher, with the help of others in the school, must obtain information as complete as possible concerning the nature of the student's eye

FIGURE 7–2
Normal vision

FIGURE 7–3
Myopia (nearsightedness)

Note: With myopia, vision is clear when looking at near objects but blurred at far distances.

FIGURE 7–4
Hyperopia (farsightedness)

Note: With hyperopia, vision is blurred when looking at near objects but clear when looking at a distance.

FIGURE 7–5
Glaucoma

Note: With glaucoma, there is loss of peripheral vision while retaining most of the central vision.

FIGURE 7–6
Cataract

Note: With a cataract, there is diminished acuity caused by a density or opacity of the lens. The field of vision is not affected, and there are no significant blind spots. There is an overall haziness (denser in some spots), particularly in glaring light conditions.

FIGURE 7–7
Retinal detachment

Note: With retinal detachment, a hole in the retina (back of the eye) allows fluid to lift the retina from its normal position. This results in a field defect, seen as a dark shadow. It may be in the upper portion or lower part, as illustrated.

FIGURE 7–8
Retinitis pigmentosa

Note: Retinitis pigmentosa is a form of tunnel vision. Generally, only a small area of central vision remains.

FIGURE 7–9
Macular degeneration

Note: Macular degeneration is a breakdown of the central part of the retina that results in an area of decreased central vision called a blind spot or scotoma. Peripheral vision remains unaffected.

FIGURE 7–10
Corneal pathological condition

Note: With corneal pathological condition, the image may be distorted or clouded so that clear detail is not discernible. The field of vision is normal.

condition, functional vision, effects of diminished vision in other areas (such as motor development, social skills, intellectual capabilities), lighting needs, and travel limitations. An understanding of the variety of conditions that may affect vision and information relating to the specific abilities and the needs of the student should lead to the most advantageous educational programming.

EDUCATIONAL PROGRAMMING

For nearly three quarters of a century, educators have recognized that students with visual impairment could be educated with their sighted peers with only minor modifications and adaptations, and that the limitations imposed by visual disability do not require a special curriculum. Materials must be provided in different media or in modified or adapted form so that such students can learn through sensory channels other than vision. For example, if a student is not able to read material in printed form, the material may be provided through the tactile (touch) or auditory channels. If the student can read printed material but only with considerable difficulty, the material may be enlarged or the student may use magnification devices or reading machines. The primary nature of special education services for students who are visually impaired is modification and adaptation of educational materials.

Students who are blind or have low vision follow the same curriculum as their peers but need additional help. They study reading, math, and social studies but may need braille instruction, orientation and mobility (travel) training, typewriting, and training in the use of an abacus. Generally, compensatory skills are taught by a resource or itinerant teacher and are not a responsibility of regular classroom teachers.

CONTINUUM OF SERVICES

There is a definite need for a full continuum of services for students with impaired vision. The following variables should be considered when placement options are being studied: (a) age, (b) achievement level, (c) intelligence, (d) presence of multiple disabilities, (e) emotional stability, (f) nature and extent of eye condition, (g) wishes of students and parents, and (h) recommendations of the staffing team. Naturally, each student should be considered individually, but some general placement considerations should be taken into account. For example, there seems to be a relationship among the age of the student, the nature and extent of the visual impairment, the student's level of achievement, and the amount of special education service and instruction needed. If a child is a young braille reader (ages 5 to 9), resource or itinerant assistance is needed on a routinely scheduled daily basis to provide instruction in braille reading and other specialized areas. During early education, a child may spend 1 to 1½ hours each day with a resource or itinerant teacher. When the child has developed braille reading skills (Figure 7-11) and familiarity with the necessary tangible apparatus, he or she may attend regular classrooms for increasing amounts of time. If the student is able to read printed material with or without an aid, it is not necessary to spend as much time with a resource or itinerant teacher. A student at the secondary level may also require specific instruction from resource or itinerant personnel, but this student's needs are not the same as those of younger students. Special teachers may do more counseling relevant to adjustment to secondary school life or career opportunities, training in orientation and mobility, training in the use of advanced technological equipment, and instruction related to independent living skills.

FIGURE 7–11
Braille alphabet

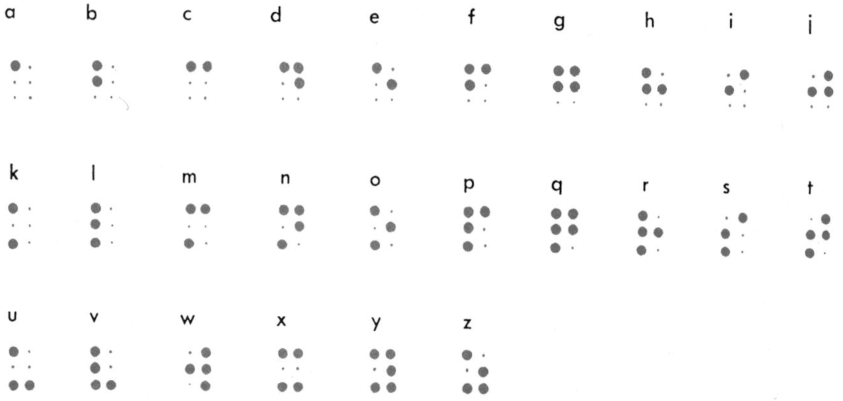

Note: Each letter of the braille alphabet is represented by a pattern of raised dots within a six-dot cell. Additional combinations include letter sequence, numbers, punctuation, and words.

SUGGESTIONS FOR REGULAR CLASSROOM TEACHERS

The suggestions that follow may be used for readers of either braille or print, because many techniques and modifications are the same for both groups. The suggestions fall into six categories: (a) adapted educational equipment, (b) educational environment, (c) orientation and mobility, (d) teaching strategies and adaptations, (e) general considerations, and (f) integration of special services. Although some suggestions are loosely categorized, grouping permits easier conceptualization of these techniques and modifications.

Adapted Educational Equipment

As mentioned, the primary nature of educational programming for students who are visually impaired is the modification and adaptation of educational materials. Most of these materials are available from private agencies at no cost to students. Over the many years of service to individuals who are visually impaired, an extensive array of helpful materials has been developed. It is not practical to review all of the adapted materials and special equipment available for students with impaired vision, for there are several hundred different types. Most of these materials are directed at increasing learning through sensory channels other than vision.

The following paragraphs briefly describe the most commonly used equipment. It is important that regular classroom teachers have a basic understanding of various kinds of tangible apparatus to ensure their proper use and thus maximize their value to students.

Braillewriters, Slates, and Styluses. A braillewriter is a six-key (corresponding to the six dots in the braille cell) machine that is manually operated and types braille. The slate is a metal frame with openings the size of the braille dots; the stylus is a pointed object used to emboss the dots. The slate and stylus can be carried in a pocket and are often used to take notes.

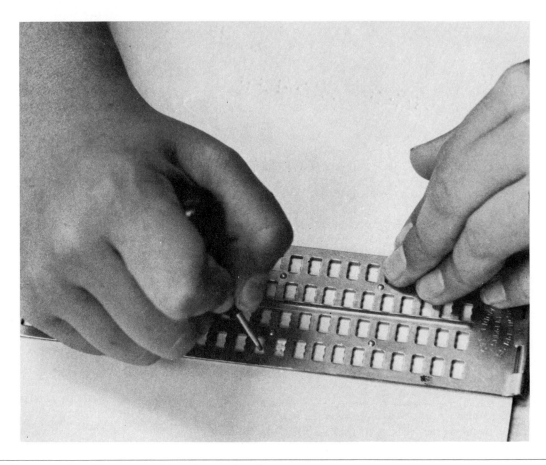

This person is taking notes with a slate and stylus.

Raised-Line Drawing Boards. A raised-line drawing board is a board covered with rubber. A piece of acetate is placed on the board and a pen or pointed object is used to "raise" the drawings so that the student may feel them. A teacher may use a raised-line drawing board to draw geometric shapes, script letters, or diagrams.

Raised-Line Paper. Special raised-line paper allows a student who is visually impaired to write script on a raised line. Also, raised-line paper may be used to draw a graph.

Cassette Tape Recorders. Tape recorders may be used to take notes, formulate compositions, listen to recorded texts, or record assignments.

Talking Book and Other Recorded Programs. Records or tapes recorded specifically for individuals who cannot use print as their primary means of reading are provided by the Library of Congress. A wide variety of textbooks and leisure reading is offered on disks and cassettes.

Variable-Speed Attachments. Variable-speed attachments can be used to vary the speed at which the student listens to a tape, allowing the student to listen to the material at a slower or a faster rate (speeding up the tape results in a higher pitch).

Portable Braille Recorders. A portable braille recorder may be interfaced with a computer that will convert braille to standard print and vice versa.

Speech Compressors. A speech compressor is a modified tape recorder. In a speech compressor, the pause between each recorded word is electronically removed, thereby compressing the material and speeding up the listening process without changing the pitch.

Optacons (Optical to Tactual Converters). The Optacon is an instrument that scans printed material electronically, transforming the print into vibrating letter configurations. This is accomplished through an array of 144 pins. The reader holds a scanner over the print material while placing the index finger of the opposite hand over the raised configuration.

Text Magnification Software. Software that is compatible with a variety of brands and types of computers magnifies the text on the computer screen from two to eight times the original width and height.

Braille Computers. Braille computers are laptop computers with braille keys and a braille display. Some models provide synthesized speech in place of or in addition to a braille display.

Lamps with Rheostats. Lamps with adjustable positions and variable light intensities can provide additional illumination, angled light, or dimmed light according to the needs of a student.

Paperless Braille Systems. A variety of equipment with braille input stores information on cassettes or computer disks and, upon demand, displays it on a braille display strip, provides voice output, or prints it in standard print. Students may take a paperless braille system to the library, take braille notes, print them out in standard print for a friend, and retrieve them with voice output to develop a paper for class.

Braille Printers. When interfaced with a computer, a braille printer will print in braille the information stored in the computer. With a standard keyboard, users may print in either braille or standard print, thus allowing class outlines, study guides, vocabulary terms, or tests to be easily provided to both students who use braille and those who do not.

Speech Synthesizers. Synthesizers are devices attached to computers that are able to read words or numbers displayed on the computer screen. They read at three times the normal rate of conversational speech.

Echo Commanders. The Echo Commander is a device that may be attached to the Apple II, II+, or IIe computer. It will convert visual representation to speech. There is provision for headphone listening, addition of a second speaker for stereo, and attachment to a tape recorder.

Talking Calculators. A talking calculator is an electronic calculator that presents results visually and auditorily.

Closed-Circuit Television. A closed-circuit television is a system that enlarges printed material on a television screen. It can be adjusted to either black on white or white on black. The Perkins Videoscope is an example of a closed-circuit system.

Kurzweil Reading Machines. The Kurzweil Reading Machine, a computer-based device, provides direct access to typed or printed material by converting it to synthetic speech. The speed and tone can be controlled, and the machine can spell a word letter by letter.

Other Aids. Often, students who have some remaining vision can use a number of optical aids. These aids may be used at all times or for specified tasks. Magnifiers that can be mounted on a desk, held by hand, or head mounted are frequently prescribed by low-vision clinics. Students may also use monoculars (telescopic aids for one eye) that may be mounted on glasses or held in the hand. With a monocular, a student may view the chalkboard, classroom demonstrations, or other distant objects. The following list of additional visual aids represents types available from various sources:

1. Geography aids
   a. Braille atlases
   b. Molded plastic, dissected and undissected relief maps
   c. Relief globes
   d. Landform models (a set of three-dimensional tactile maps illustrating 40 geographic concepts)
2. Mathematical aids
   a. Abacuses
   b. Raised clockfaces
   c. Geometric area and volume aids
   d. Wire forms for matched planes and volumes
   e. Braille rulers
   f. Talking calculators
3. Writing aids
   a. Raised-line checkbooks
   b. Signature guides
   c. Longhand-writing kits
   d. Script-letter sheets and boards
4. Miscellaneous aids
   a. Audible goal locators, which can be used as goal, base, or object locators or warning devices
   b. Special braille or large-type answer sheets
   c. Science measurement kits (containing such items as thermometers, spring balances, gram weights, and gravity specimens)
   d. Sports field kits (containing raised drawings of the playing fields or courts of various sports)
   e. Simple-machine kits, including working models of simple machines like pulleys and levers, including planes, wheels, and axles
   f. Games such as Rook, Rack-O, Scrabble, bingo, cards, checkers, Parcheesi, and backgammon
   g. Adapted sports equipment (like audible balls)
   h. Braille clocks, wristwatches, and timers

Occasionally, some students are self-conscious about their need for special equipment and are reluctant to use it. A teacher's openness and understanding can do a great deal to help students and classmates appreciate the benefits and need for special equipment.

The American Printing House for the Blind has an extensive offering of adapted materials and educational equipment. In addition, the American Foundation for the Blind has an *Aids and Appliances Catalog* from which materials may be ordered. Several other agencies also have special materials available.

It is generally not the responsibility of regular classroom teachers to obtain materials unless a resource or itinerant teacher is

A variety of magnification devices may be used by students with visual impairment.

not available. Resource or itinerant teachers are familiar with the agencies that provide adapted materials and equipment. In the event that materials are not available from any of the agencies, the resource or itinerant teacher will have to reproduce these materials or arrange for them to be prepared. For example, a particular reading text may not be available in modified form because it has been published only recently. After all agencies have been queried, the resource or itinerant teacher may have the text reproduced in large type, tape-recorded, or transcribed into braille.

In addition to textbooks and adapted materials available from an agency, there is always a need for teacher-made materials, such as teacher-made tests, work sheets, and special games or activities. These must be reproduced in the desired format by the resource or itinerant teacher or by specially trained aides, because it is essential that the materials be the same as the materials of the student's peers.

Planning and a special communication system must be implemented with resource or itinerant teachers to provide explanations of the nature of the materials needed and allow sufficient time for their reproduction. This is usually accomplished by leaving the desired materials in the resource or itinerant teacher's mailbox, establishing a routine conference with the resource or itinerant teacher, or sending the material with the student when he or she meets with the resource or itinerant teacher.

Occasionally, regular classroom teachers may have to modify materials. For example, if duplicated materials are being prepared for class distribution, it may be necessary to darken the letters or figures with a felt-tipped pen so that they can be seen more easily by the student who has only partial vision. Materials duplicated in purple usually cause considerable difficulty for individuals who are visually impaired; black stencils may provide the desired contrast. Yellow acetate placed over the printed page tends to darken the print itself as well as provide greater contrast. It may also be of value to consider preparing handout materials in primary or enlarged type for all students.

Educational Environment

Although not major concerns, several environmental or classroom modifications can facilitate the education of students with impaired vision. Preferred or open seating allows students to sit wherever they are most comfortable. When a teacher is using the chalkboard, when a movie or filmstrip is being shown, or when the teacher is demonstrating a particular concept using tangible materials, a student with impaired vision should be allowed to select the best visual location.

The student's seating should be arranged for the best possible lighting conditions, but this does not mean that all students with low vision should be in brightly lighted areas. Some visual impairments require no special lighting, whereas others require lower levels of illumination. Resource or itinerant teachers and reports from eye specialists should be of particular value in this matter.

Teachers should not stand in front of a bright light source, such as a window, because students are then looking directly into the light. Writing on a chalkboard where there is considerable glare should also be avoided. When a demonstration is given, a student with low vision should be encouraged to stand near the teacher or actually assist in the demonstration. It may also be helpful to allow the student to handle the demonstration materials before or after the demonstration.

Before the actual placement in the regular classroom, a formal orientation procedure should be conducted. The resource or itinerant teacher or an orientation and mobility specialist can provide additional guidance in structuring this experience. Initially, the student should be familiarized with the general layout of the classroom and be given guided and unguided opportunities to explore. Certain landmarks within the classroom should be established, such as (a) the student's desk, (b) the teacher's desk, (c) cabinets or bookshelves, (d) storage areas for paper and general classroom materials, (e) the wastebasket, (f) bulletin boards and chalkboards, (g) windows, (h) special interest centers, (i) doorways and restrooms, and (j) other classroom equipment.

After the student is oriented to the classroom and the general school building, other areas may be introduced, such as the school offices, gymnasium, cafeteria, auditorium, restrooms, recreation areas, locker rooms. Often, orientation to the school building and surrounding areas is taught formally by an orientation and mobility specialist or a resource or itinerant teacher.

Teachers who have students who are visually impaired are sometimes reluctant to change the classroom seating or position of desks, tables, and other items because they are afraid the student may become disoriented or sustain an injury. The physical arrangement of the room should be changed as often as normally necessary, but the student must be oriented to the changes. This should take only a few minutes of formal orientation and a few minutes of independent exploring by the student, followed by a brief question-and-answer session concerning the new arrangement. Other students in the class can be of assistance by directing the student who is visually impaired through the new arrangement or describing it.

Safety while traveling independently in the classroom can be a problem if classroom doors and upper cabinet doors are not completely open or closed. Often, a student may think the classroom door is open, because of auditory and other cues, to find it only partially open. Keeping the door completely open or closed is difficult to accomplish with 30 other students in the classroom, but it should be attempted.

The noise level of the classroom should be kept reasonably low, since the student who has low vision must depend on audi-

tory skills for much of his or her educational program. Braille-reading students need open space and shelves at the side of the room, since braille materials are large and bulky. Braille-reading students may also need room for braillewriters, typewriters, books, and other materials.

Orientation and Mobility

The ability of a student who is visually impaired to move about independently is one of the most important factors in the total educational program.[1] Programming efforts should be directed toward academic and social development, but if the area of travel is neglected, the student may be denied opportunities to move freely and independently in the school and community.

The concepts of orientation and mobility are interrelated because mobility cannot be achieved unless an individual is oriented. Orientation refers to an individual's use of the other senses to establish position and relationship to objects in the environment. Mobility refers to the individual's movement from one point in the environment to another. In other words, mobility is getting from point A to point B, whereas orientation involves knowing the location, the location of the objective, and the most efficient way to reach the objective.

Regular classroom teachers are not responsible for formal training in orientation and mobility. This training is specialized and should be conducted by an orientation and mobility specialist or in the case of pre-cane orientation and mobility, a resource or itinerant teacher whose background includes specific preparation in this area. It is

[1]Special acknowledgment is due David Kappan, associate professor of special education, University of Northern Colorado, for his critical evaluation and assistance in the development of the section on orientation and mobility.

important, however, that regular classroom teachers understand the nature of the training and the major methods or modes of travel. The five modes of travel used by persons who are visually impaired are (a) the sighted guide, (b) cane travel, (c) the dog guide, (d) the electronic travel aid, and (e) independent travel.

Sighted Guide. One of the most common techniques taught is use of a sighted guide. The student with low vision grasps the guide's arm just above the elbow, with fingers on the inside and thumb on the outside, and assumes a position approximately a half step behind the guide. The grip is just firm enough to maintain contact. The guide's arm is positioned next to the body. In effect, the person who is visually impaired is "reading" the sighted individual's arm or elbow, and any movement of the guide's body and arm is detected. By following approximately a half step behind, the individual with visual impairment knows when the guide is stepping up or down and turning left or right. This position provides the necessary reaction time.

When ascending or descending stairs, the guide should approach the stairs at a right angle and pause at the first step. The individual who is visually impaired can locate the beginning of the step with one foot and negotiate the stairway, remaining one step behind the sighted guide. The guide's arm position indicates when the landing or end of the staircase is reached. The classmates of a student with low vision can readily be taught how to serve as sighted guides. Additional methods related to efficient use of this technique would be taught by a resource or itinerant teacher or an orientation and mobility specialist.

All students should be acquainted with the proper procedures used in serving as a sighted guide. A resource or itinerant teacher or an orientation and mobility specialist may want to attend or actually conduct a brief in-service session. The students may want to wear blindfolds to gain a better understanding of traveling without sight. However, some caution should be exercised here, so that the students do not develop a pitying attitude but rather an understanding of travel techniques used by people who are visually impaired.

Cane Travel. Use of a cane is a common systematic method of travel. The age at which a student is introduced to a cane and provided formal training in its use depends on the student's maturity, need for independent travel, and physical and mental ability.

There are several types of canes, but the most common are made of aluminum or fiberglass and are approximately half an inch in diameter. The tip of the cane is usually made of steel or nylon. The length of the cane is prescribed by the orientation and mobility specialist and is determined by the user's height, length of stride, and comfort.

Cane travel is taught on a one-to-one basis by a specialized instructor. It initially involves fundamentals in restricted areas, and later training is applied in outdoor situations, such as residential and business districts. Extensive training is conducted in crossing streets, utilizing public transportation, and dealing with complex navigational situations.

Dog Guide. The third mode of travel uses a dog guide. Generally a dog guide is not recommended until a student is at least 16 years old. Before this age, the student may not have the maturity to handle a dog properly or the need for independent travel. Often, young students want to obtain a dog guide as a pet or companion, not necessarily for independence in traveling. For obvious reasons, a dog guide should not be considered a pet but rather a partner in achieving independent travel. Contrary to popular opinion, only a relatively small percentage of persons who are visually impaired use dog guides. Specific information concerning dog guide agencies, such as cost and nature of training, may be provided by either the resource or itinerant teacher or the orientation and mobility specialist. It is essential that potential dog guide users investigate the individual program offering dog guide training to ensure that the highest standards are maintained.

Electronic Travel Aid. The electronic travel aid is the fourth mode of travel used by individuals who have visual impairment. A number of devices are available, and most are used to supplement another method of travel. Although it is encouraging to see research being conducted in this area, it does not seem that any one device meets the needs of all individuals. Some of the devices enhance auditory feedback, some detect obstacles, others enable individuals to walk in a straight line, and still others are directed at revealing the specific location of obstacles in the environment.

A Mowat Sensor is a small hand-held device that uses a high-frequency elliptical sound beam to detect obstacles. If an object is present, the entire sensor vibrates, and the vibration rate increases as the person approaches the object. The sensor operates on a rechargeable battery and is small enough to be carried in a purse or coat pocket.

A Sonicguide™ emits a high-frequency sound. It converts detection echoes into audible stereophonic signals and provides information about the distance, position, and surface characteristics of objects within the travel path and immediate environment. The electronic system for the unit is built into special eyeglasses fitted for the individual user.

A Laser Cane emits invisible light beams that strike an object and are reflected back to the receiving unit of the cane. A sound or tone is emitted to warn the person of objects or dropoffs. In addition, a vibrating unit felt by the user's finger signals obstructions ahead. The three beams include upper-, lower-, and mid-range signals to provide basic protection for the user's entire body.

A Russell Pathsounder is a chest-mounted device that emits an ultrasonic signal. When an object is located, the device offers auditory feedback and/or tactile signals. It provides protection for the upper body and has possible value for a student with both vision and hearing impairments.

The mobility aids or device used, whether cane, dog, electronic aid, or some combination, should be given careful consideration by a student and parents after consultation with the resource or itinerant teacher or the orientation and mobility specialist. Numerous hours of instruction by an orientation and mobility instructor are prerequisite to successful use of these devices.

Independent Travel. A fifth mode of travel is independent, that is, with no aid. Generally, after a student with low vision has become familiar with the environment, he or she is able to move about without aid, for instance, in the classroom, short distances in the school building, to the bus, and perhaps on the school campus.

Protective Techniques. A number of protective techniques may be used by a student with visual impairment while traveling with or without the use of other aids. These protective techniques are routinely taught to young children and are normally used only in familiar areas. They may be used in combination with a cane or an electronic aid for additional protection. Three of the basic techniques taught by the resource or itinerant teacher or orientation and mobility specialist are:

1. *Upper hand and forearm technique.* For protection in familiar settings, a student may extend one arm in front of his or her body at shoulder height and parallel to the floor, with the palm outward (Figure 7–12).

2. *Lower hand and forearm technique.* When protecting the lower body, a student extends one arm down and forward toward the midline of the body with the palm of the hand facing him or her. The student may use the upper hand and forearm together with the lower hand and forearm to give both upper and lower body protection.

3. *Trailing technique.* Trailing enables a student to maintain orientation, determine his or her position in space, locate specific objects, and secure a parallel line of travel. The student positions himself or herself a comfortable distance from the surface to be trailed, extends one arm forward at hip level, and establishes contact with this surface with the outside of the little finger. The student can then walk along the object using the

FIGURE 7–12
Use of the upper hand and forearm for protection while traveling independently

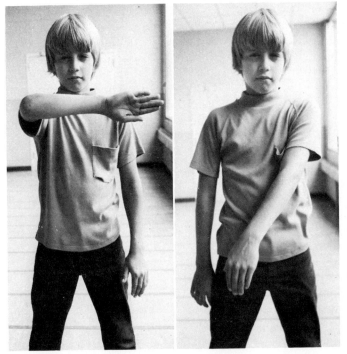

hand to maintain contact and detect information (Figure 7–13).

Teaching Strategies and Adaptations

It is generally not necessary for regular classroom teachers to significantly change teaching strategies to accommodate a student with visual impairment. However, it may be helpful to consider a few suggestions that have been found to be effective.

Concrete Materials. Whenever possible, instruction should be initiated at a concrete level. It should start with concrete materials, moving more to the abstract as students develop the concept. The use of manipulative, tangible, or auditory materials is preferred to totally verbal instructions or lessons. Hands-on learning should be emphasized as much as possible, and students may need repeated contact with objects. Although a model may be necessary, a real object or situation is much preferred. For example, if a science lesson is concerned with simple pulleys, an actual pulley shoud be provided, if possible. Local museums are valuable sources for such materials, and they often lend them to school personnel. Resource or itinerant teachers can also assist in obtaining actual objects or making models.

Experiences that are unified also help students form concepts. The small pieces of information that sighted students are able to unify into organized, meaningful concepts at a mere glance must be unified for students who are blind or have low vision. A trip to a clothing store provides a basis for reinforcing and unifying concepts related to quantity, percentages, money, sizes, shapes, and social skills. In a similar manner, trips to supermarkets, bowling alleys, record shops, and restaurants provide opportunities for integration of skills. When planning such trips, notify the staff in ad-

FIGURE 7–13
Trailing

vance. They will frequently allow the student who is visually impaired to go beyond normal barriers.

Physical Education. Lessons in physical education or gross motor activities should be demonstrated by physically moving visually impaired students through the activity. For example, if a particular tumbling routine is being taught, the instructor may want to actually move the student through the correct movements rather than merely explain the process.

Hands-On Learning. Learning by doing and teaching by unifying experiences are certainly not new concepts to regular classroom teachers. These concepts, however, are particularly important to students with impaired vision because such students may not have the same experiential background as other students of the same age. Whenever possible, a student with low vision should be allowed to explore physically rather than have the process explained verbally. Closely related is the need to integrate experiences and concepts as often as possible. A young child may not be able to relate one isolated concept to another because of lack of previous experience with the particular concept.

Chalkboard. When writing on the chalkboard, teachers should be certain to explain verbally the concept or actual writing being presented. In general, any highly visual instructions or lessons should be supplemented with verbal explanation. This can become routine with a little effort and practice. Some teachers have found it helpful to give a student who is visually impaired a copy of the notes written on the board. To be certain that the best possible dark-light contrast is provided, be certain that the chalkboard is as clean as possible. Allow the student to move as close to the chalkboard as necessary to see it comfortably.

Fatigue. A student who has impaired vision may become fatigued if tasks involving close visual examination are required for long periods of time. It may be helpful to vary activities as much as possible, as by alternating listening activities, close visual activities, and motor activities. The student should be encouraged whenever possible to take short breaks from activities requiring prolonged periods of visual work.

Fire Drills. As the class as a whole is being prepared for a fire drill, instruct a student who is blind or has low vision to take hold of the nearest student or adult and quickly and quietly follow the others. The princi-

ples are the same as those for using a sighted guide. Young students may need practice, especially if they are not used to having a student with visual impairment in the class. For older students, it is routine.

Giving Directions. Teachers should be as specific as possible when giving directions. For example, saying "Your science project is on the shelf in the back of the room, to the left of the sink, about 2 feet away from the sink" is clearer than "Your science project is on the back shelf." If giving directions relating to the building as a whole or to some area outside the school, say, for example, "The snack machine is to the left as you leave this room, down four doors, and the about three steps to the right" to provide precise directions. It may be necessary to give the directions slowly, to repeat them, or with a young student, even ask the student to repeat the directions.

Media. If a filmstrip being used has subtitles, ask another student to read the titles aloud to the entire class. When a film is used, another student may summarize the key visual concepts or briefly provide a running visual narrative.

Extra Time. A student with low vision may need extra time to complete assignments and examinations. Allowing time and a half is usually adequate. The work may be completed in a resource room or library or at home. If the student understands the concepts being presented, it may be a good idea to shorten the assignment.

Tactile Activities. For the approximately 20% of the visually impaired students who are blind, art activities should emphasize the tactile sense. Use activities such as clay modeling, finger painting, weaving, paper sculpture, and collage whenever possible. It is important that the students carry out the process involved in an art project; the end product should be deemphasized. By completing the process, in whatever medium, the students can achieve the same objectives as peers.

Note Taking. At the secondary level, students are often required to take notes or submit assignments. Naturally, students who have visual impairment should meet these requirements, but the ways in which they do so may be different. Students who are blind or have low vision may use a slate and stylus, braillewriter, or cassette tape recorder. After recording lectures, students may transcribe their notes into braille and finally type them to be handed in. Some teachers allow such students to provide a modified recording of their notes.

Raising Hands. If other students are expected to raise their hands to gain recognition or respond, the student with visual impairment should be expected to do the same. Since such students may not be able to see classmates raising their hands to respond, teachers may need to provide specific instructions on hand-raising procedures.

Test Taking. Testing procedures may have to be modified for students who are visually impaired. Reading braille or large type takes considerably longer than reading standard print, and it may be necessary either to extend the amount of time for completion of tests or reduce the number of test items. Students should not be penalized if they cannot finish tests because of the tools they are using. Of course, time modification depends on whether the purpose of the test is speed or power. If the purpose is speed, a student may have considerable difficulty.

The administration of a test may also have to be modified. For example, it may be necessary to (a) administer the test orally, (b) tape the test in advance and have the student record or type his or her answers, or (c) send the test home with the student and have a parent read the test while the student types or braillewrites his or her answers. If the examination is to be taped, the reader should state the total number and type of questions, the value assigned to each item, and time limitations. The examination should be read slowly and clearly. Sometimes, a student can braillewrite responses and give them to the resource or itinerant teacher, who in turn, writes in the student's responses and returns the test to the classroom teacher. Some students require few or no modifications and are able to take the tests with the other students.

Achievement tests are administered at the beginning or end of the school year. Because of their relative importance and the amount of time needed to complete them, they may have to be administered by resource or itinerant teachers or aides. Regular teachers should be certain to consult with resource or itinerant teachers in advance to consider the options for testing.

Braille. Teachers often express concern when informed that they will have braille-reading students in their classrooms. Actually, it is not necessary for teachers to learn braille, because resource or itinerant teachers can write or print whatever the student has written directly above the braille dots. If a student completes an assignment and turns it in to the classroom teacher in braille, the teacher should forward it to the resource or itinerant teacher, who can write the student's responses and return the assignment to the classroom teacher. At the upper elementary, middle school, and the secondary school levels, students may complete assignments on a conventional typewriter or use a paperless braille system, which provides materials in conventional print.

General Considerations

When speaking to students who are blind or have low vision, teachers should use normal volume unless distance warrants otherwise. Such students may become frustrated when people raise their voices unnecessarily.

During class discussion, the teacher should be certain to use the name of a student who is blind or has low vision in order to make sure that the student knows the teacher is looking at him or her. Likewise, when entering a room, the teacher should address the student by name and identify himself or herself.[2] Similarly, if the student enters a room where the teacher is alone, the teacher should speak directly to the student or use some other auditory cue.

If a student who is blind or has low vision drops an object, the teacher should allow sufficient time for the student to recover the item without help. If necessary, however, the teacher may use verbal guidance to help the student locate the item. When handing an object such as a book to the student, a teacher and other students should lightly touch the student's hand with the object to let the student know the location of the object.

Unless an eye specialist has indicated that a student should not use his or her vision, every effort must be made to increase the student's visual efficiency. There are several misconceptions concerning the use of residual vision. Contrary to myth, using

the vision will not decrease it. In fact, it is not unusual for a student's measured acuity to remain the same over a period of years while visual performance actually increases. Holding a book close to the eyes or reading with a dim light will not further damage the eyesight of a student with low vision. Some students may require a dim light to read more comfortably. Even at the secondary level, it may be necessary to tell other students about this, since they have probably been told by parents and teachers not to hold books too close or to read in dim light. Resource or itinerant teachers will be able to provide guidance relating to reading, postural, and lighting requirements.

Somewhat related to this matter is the use of low-vision or optical aids (such as magnifiers and special glasses). Students who use these aids should be encouraged to use them whenever appropriate. Regular classroom teachers should observe whether the devices seem to be helpful, how often they are used, and under what conditions they are beneficial. Frequent visual fatigue may be an indication of need for larger-print materials or reevaluation of the efficiency of the visual aids being used.

Generally, the length of time a student can use special aids can be determined only after careful classroom observation. Some students may perform well for a short time but tire after several hours of close visual work. Naturally, this information should be shared with resource or itinerant teachers, who in turn may share this information with physicians or specialists in low-vision aids.

Students with impaired vision often develop poor postural habits. This may result from poor muscle tone, lack of knowledge about preferred head or shoulder position, or continual close examination of printed material. Some system of gentle reminders

---

[2]Once it becomes clear that a student recognizes the teacher's voice, the teacher should *not* identify himself or herself, but simply address the student by name. Students who are blind or have low vision often pride themselves on voice recognition, and teachers should acknowledge this skill.

should be established to help students develop good postural habits. Students who are partially sighted may spend a great deal of time bent over, with their heads only a few inches from their desks. This position can obviously result in poor posture and considerable fatigue. Easels and bookrests can enable students to read much more comfortably. Resource or itinerant teachers can suggest specific postural training and adaptations for reading efficiency and comfort.

Established standards for grading or discipline should not be altered for students with visual impairment. When an assignment has been given or a classroom rule established, such students should be expected to adhere to the same procedures as the other students. If teachers employ a double standard, one for the class and another for students with visual impairment, the other students will be quick to recognize the difference and resent it. Such resentment may have an adverse effect on interpersonal relationships and cause other students to reject students who have impaired vision.

A student with impaired vision may not be able to see the teacher's positive facial expressions after completing an assigned task successfully or a look of displeasure when he or she has not. Verbal feedback, a pat on the back, or a touch on the arm may be necessary. Of course, the teacher should praise the student only when the job has been well done, not just because it was done by a student who is blind or has low vision.

Teachers may assign buddies to help with, for example, highly visual assignments, orientation to a new school building, physical education activities, and fire drills. The buddy system is a desirable approach to peer teaching or assistance, regardless of whether or not a student is disabled.

Students who are blind or have low vision often demonstrate unusual mannerisms, such as rocking, head movements, eye pressing, and hand waving. The mannerisms tend to occur when the students are tense or nervous or are listening intently. Although such students are usually unaware of these behaviors, other students notice them. To discourage such mannerisms, teachers should use systematic plans that they have worked out with resource or itinerant teachers.

Independence, freedom of movement, and play are as important for students who have impaired vision as for sighted classmates. More than 100 years ago, Samuel Gridley Howe, a noted educator of children who were visually impaired, offered the following general rules:

Never check the actions of the child; follow him, and watch him to prevent any serious accidents, but do not interfere unnecessarily; do not even remove obstacles which he would learn to avoid by tumbling over them a few times. Teach him to jump rope, to swing weights, to raise his body by his arms, and to mingle, as far as possible, in the rough sports of the older boys. Do not be apprehensive of his safety. If you should see him clambering in the branches of a tree be assured he is less likely to fall than if he had perfect vision. Do not too much regard bumps on the forehead, rough scratches, or bloody noses; even these may have their good influences. At the worst, they affect only the bark, and do not injure the system like the rust of inaction. (Buell, 1950, p. 37)

It is natural for a teacher who has not had experience with students who have visual impairment to be somewhat overprotective and to be concerned that these students might injure themselves on playground equipment or in traveling around the school building. However, every effort should be made *not* to underestimate the capabilities of students who have impairments. The teacher's responsibility to a student with impaired vision is the same as to other students—helping the student develop socially, emotionally, physically, morally, and intellectually.

Integration of Special Services

When several professionals work with a student, it is important that they consult with each other so that each is aware of the nature of the training provided by the others. It has been suggested that a case manager be named at the time of the development of the IEP to coordinate all of the efforts being made on behalf of the student (Kirk & Gallagher, 1989). The classroom teacher is generally able to observe the student in a variety of settings and under a variety of conditions, as well as provide the specialists with information concerning the transfer and maintenance of desired skills or concepts. Often, a student may be able (especially when first learning) to demonstrate a skill or understanding of a concept when working on an individual basis with a resource or itinerant teacher or an orientation and mobility teacher but be unable to transfer this understanding to classroom activities.

Coordination among the various teachers at the secondary level is also important, although unless visual impairment is newly acquired (by an accident, for example), the student will have learned many of the basic skills. It may be helpful for secondary teachers to know about various technological devices that a student may use to determine how much classroom adaptation is required. The importance of close communication with the parents of a student who is visually impaired cannot be overemphasized, and every effort should be made to work cooperatively with parents.

SPECIALIZED INSTRUCTION AND ASSISTANCE FROM RESOURCE OR ITINERANT TEACHERS

The amount and nature of specialized assistance from special educators varies from school district to school district and at times within a single district. The exact nature of assistance from special education resource or itinerant personnel depends on the following factors:

1. *Geographic distance to be traveled between schools.* Some teachers are responsible for only one school, whereas others have responsibilities extending to two or three schools. In some rural areas, a resource or itinerant teacher may travel to several communities.
2. *Number of students and teachers to be served.*
3. *Age of student.* Generally, the younger the student, the more need for direct service.
4. *The number of braille readers and print readers.* This can vary extensively. Generally, a braille-reading student requires many more direct services.
5. *Availability of orientation and mobility instruction.* If an orientation and mobility specialist is not available, a resource or itinerant teacher may be responsible for this instruction.
6. *Availability of paid or volunteer braille transcribers, large-print typists, and tape transcribers.*
7. *Availability of adapted and special materials.* In states where an instructional materials center for individuals who are visually impaired is available, the acquisition and distribution of educational materials can be greatly facilitated.

Resource or itinerant teachers may provide services directly or indirectly. Direct services involve working directly with students who have visual impairment on a one-to-one basis or in small groups. Indirect services involve working with individuals other than students such as teachers, administrators, medical personnel, and parents. Most resource or itinerant personnel provide both direct and indirect services. Although it is sometimes difficult to clearly establish that one service is direct and another indirect, the following discussion of specific responsibilities is based on these categories.

Direct Services

Compensatory skills, such as compensatory listening skills, use of a stylus and slate, and use of a braillewriter are taught by special education specialists. If academic lags are *directly attributable* to vision deficits, these are remediated by special education personnel.

Specialized Instruction in Reading. Resource or itinerant teachers provide instruction in braille reading and braillewriting, the use of a slate and stylus, and use of the reading devices like the Optacon or Kurzweil Reading Machine. The amount of time required for instruction in special skills depends on the age of the student. More time is required for young braille-reading students because they are developing these specialized skills, whereas secondary-level students may have already developed these skills. Braille instruction should be provided on a daily basis for the first 3 years of the student's education or until the student develops the necessary competency. After the student is relatively proficient at braille reading and braillewriting, it may not be necessary for the resource or itinerant teacher to work with him or her on a daily basis.

If a student is a print reader, the amount of instruction is usually not so great as for a braille reader. However, if the student uses low-vision aids (magnification devices or special reading machines), it may be necessary to provide specific instruction in their use.

Instruction in Listening Skills. It has been estimated that nearly one half of communication time is spent in listening activities and that approximately two thirds of a student's school day is spent in activities related to listening. Since listening is one of the most significant avenues of learning for students who have visual impairment, such students must rely on the auditory channel more than their sighted classmates do. As a result, systematic instruction in listening must be provided and incorporated into regular classroom instruction as much as possible. Instruction in listening should include a variety of listening situations, such as environmental situations, formal presentations, informal conversations, talking books, and tape-recorded materials.

Instruction in Techniques of Daily Living. Functioning as a responsible and contributing member of society requires more than being able to complete academic tasks such as reading and math. A student who has low vision or who is blind may not know how to carry out all of the activities of daily living, because many of these skills are learned by watching and with minimal instruction. For example, young children learn about combing hair or shaving by observing these activities carried out by their parents. Such skills, as well as housecleaning, cooking and serving of food, and home repair, must be taught to students who are blind or have low vision. School curriculums must include instruction regarding many of these skills. Other skills for independent living must be taught, too, such as handling money without seeing it and selecting clothing that matches. Teachers at both the elementary and secondary level are involved to some degree in either teaching the skills or reinforcing them. Resource or itinerant teachers can provide information regarding how to adapt or modify these activities and how to use the special equipment that is available for individuals who are blind or have low vision.

Instruction in Orientation and Mobility. The extent to which resource or itinerant teachers are responsible for direct instruction in orientation and mobility depends on whether orientation and mobility specialists are available and whether resource or itinerant teachers are also certified as orientation and mobility specialists. If available, a specialist is responsible for formal instruction; if not, a resource or itinerant teacher may assume some of this responsibility.

In addition, resource or itinerant teachers are responsible for familiarizing or orienting students to new classrooms or school buildings and supplementing the instruction of orientation and mobility specialists. Throughout the education program, orientation and mobility training should be systematically provided.

Student and Parent Counseling. Many resource or itinerant teachers assume responsibility for student and parent counseling and for seeking appropriate professional counseling when needed. These teachers may work with a student for several years, whereas a classroom teacher may be in close contact with the student for only one year. Resource or itinerant teachers are acquainted with the problems imposed by impaired vision and the relationship of those

problems to adjustment and social and emotional growth. Resource or itinerant teachers may also be in the best position to discuss personal problems, interests, and projected vocational plans.

Although the primary responsibility for reporting student progress rests with regular classroom teachers, resource or itinerant teachers should attend parent-teacher conferences to report progress in special areas. Often, it is necessary for a resource or itinerant teacher to meet separately with a student's parents to interpret special programming efforts or special problems related to the student's visual impairment.

Instruction in the Use of Adapted or Special Equipment and Aids. Instruction in the use of special equipment and aids, like tape recorders, tape players, speech compressors, the Optacon, talking calculators, closed-circuit television, and talking-book machines, is necessary for students who are visually impaired. Instruction in the use of special mathematical computation devices like the abacus and talking calculator and special maps is required. Generally, instruction in the use of such equipment is introduced as the need arises rather than systematically scheduled.

Development of Visual Efficiency. Through systematic instruction, the visual efficiency of a student with low vision can be increased. Special techniques and materials to determine the amount of visual efficiency and specific techniques to increase visual ability are available. Constant visual stimulation provided through a sequentially planned program can increase the visual efficiency of many students. This instruction should be provided by resource or itinerant teachers on a routine basis. Resource or itinerant teachers may also observe students in regular classrooms to determine if the students are using their vision as much as possible.

Instruction in Writing. Instruction in handwriting for a student who is partially seeing should be initiated at the same time as it is introduced to sighted classmates. It may be necessary, however, for a resource or itinerant teacher to provide supplemental assistance in this area. A student who reads braille must gain proficiency at handwriting so that he or she can provide a signature and make brief notations. Special handwriting aids and instruction are necessary.

Typing—with an electric or electronic typewriter if available—is routinely taught to students who are blind or have low vision. Since their handwriting may be difficult to read and braille writing can be read by only a few individuals, typing can boost their written communication skills. Instruction is generally initiated at about the fourth-grade level. Often, typing is taught along with spelling assignments because there is considerable repetition in both subject areas. As students increase their typing proficiency, they can complete more and more assignments with the aid of a typewriter. The adapted approach to instruction known as touch typing employs a special system that does not require vision. Naturally, accuracy is emphasized rather than speed, since it is difficult for students to check their work. Instruction in this area usually continues throughout the upper elementary and secondary school years.

Supplementary or Introductory Instructions. Because it may take longer for a student who is visually impaired to complete an assignment or because an assignment may be highly visual, it is often necessary for a resource or itinerant teacher to supplement the instruction of the regular classroom

teacher. For example, if the process of carrying in mathematical addition is being introduced, the resource or itinerant teacher may want to introduce the use of a special mathematics aid or supplement the regular classroom teacher's instruction by using a special mental mathematics technique.

Often, the resource or itinerant teacher may want to introduce a particular concept before its introduction in the regular classroom. For example, a unit on the solar system may have considerably more meaning to the student with low vision if the resource or itinerant teacher provides a model of the solar system and introduces the unit to the student first. In physical education, it is often necessary to orient a student to special equipment, games, and activities before the physical education period so that the student acquires a basic understanding of the concept and the physical education instructor does not have to take a disproportionate amount of time to introduce the concept to the class.

Indirect Services

Services other than those that involve face-to-face contact with students are considered indirect services. As mentioned, a number of variables determine the nature and extent of indirect services provided. The following discussion is an overview of indirect services that might be provided by special education personnel.

Preparation of Materials. If an educational material is not available from any agency in the desired format and all sources have been queried, it may be necessary to have a transcriber-reproducer prepare the material. Resource or itinerant teachers serve as liaisons between classroom teachers and transcriber-reproducers to ensure that materials are in the needed formats and that they are completed in sufficient time.

Many day-to-day materials, such as teacher-made tests, work sheets, and special projects, obviously are not available from outside agencies. Therefore, it is the responsibility of the resource or itinerant teacher to have these materials prepared or to prepare them. The materials needed may be varied, ranging from teacher-made mathematics tests to geologic survey maps.

Often, it is not practical or possible to have a text brailled on relatively short notice or for use only once. In this event, the resource or itinerant teacher can assist in arranging for the material to be read aloud by another person. Readers are used frequently for secondary school students. If used properly, they can be tremendous helps to students who are visually impaired.

Acquisition of Materials. The acquisition of educational materials such as braille or enlarged-type texts, tapes, and tangible apparatus is one of the primary responsibilities of resource or itinerant teachers. Such materials must duplicate the content of the materials being used by the other students and must be obtained in the shortest possible time. Several well-established procedures are used by resource or itinerant teachers to obtain materials in the needed formats without duplication of efforts. These procedures involve checking national and state agencies and volunteer groups before actual transcription or production of the desired materials.

In-Service Sessions. Resource or itinerant teachers may be responsible for in-service education of classroom teachers and administrators. They may be expected to acquaint building staffs with the rationales underlying integrated placement of students who are blind or have low vision. In some instances, the nature of in-service education

is general, relating only to the philosophy of integrated education. In other instances, in-service education is directed at small groups of teachers and specifically relates to techniques for modifying and adapting materials or teaching strategies. Another in-service role often assumed by resource or itinerant teachers is providing journal articles, readings, or films for regular classroom teachers. These materials are directed at providing the competencies needed to work effectively with students who are blind or have low vision.

To ready students for classmates who are blind or have low vision, resource or itinerant teachers may conduct short in-service sessions with students to acquaint them with the nature of blindness or low vision. At other times, student in-service sessions may relate to special materials and techniques.

Coordination of Outside Services. Resource or itinerant teachers often assume responsibility for providing and coordinating many services needed in addition to classroom activities. Resource or itinerant teachers may coordinate orientation and mobility services or therapeutic recreation and leisure activities. They may also assist in planning and implementing work-study or vocational education programs. In general, the role is one of student advocacy— providing the services and programs necessary for the complete educational and social development of students with disabilities.

Assistance in Adapting or Modifying Activities. Resource or itinerant teachers may assist physical education, art, music, home economics, or industrial arts teachers in adapting or modifying particular lessons or activities. If resource or itinerant teachers have established routine and ongoing communication with all teachers, it is relatively easy for them to anticipate activities that require modification or adaptation. Resource or itinerant teachers may offer specific suggestions on how to change activities so that students who are visually impaired can meet the objectives of lessons. Sometimes, it is desirable for resource or itinerant teachers to actually attend activities to assist students or teachers.

Interpretation of Medical Information. Often, resource or itinerant teachers are expected to serve as liaisons between medical personnel and regular classroom teachers. They may be asked to interpret medical reports and to explain the nature of eye conditions and the limitations imposed by them. In addition, resource or itinerant teachers must share information concerning seating arrangements, lighting requirements, and levels of visual expectation for students who see only partially. They may also be asked to evaluate the suitability of materials to be used, particularly clarity of pictures, type size, spacing, and margins.

In addition to the specific indirect services already mentioned, there is, of course, ongoing consultation with regular classroom teachers. This includes monitoring the progress of students who have visual impairment, additional vision assessments that may indicate change in the aids used, modifications in programs, and general support to regular classroom teachers.

SUMMARY

This chapter included the legal definitions of visual impairment, and information about how vision is measured and classified. Practical suggestions outlined how teachers may observe indications of visual impairment as students complete classroom tasks. Referral guidelines were also given. The major visual impairments (refractive errors and muscular defects of the visual system) were outlined, along with other, less common impairments.

Suggestions for educational programming, including the use of adapted equipment and modifications in the educational environment, were given. A discussion of orientation and mobility techniques and alternatives was also provided. The importance of specialized assistance from vision specialists was emphasized, and the types of help were outlined.

- How does an orthopedic impairment differ from a health impairment?

- How do the duties and responsibilities of an occupational therapist differ from those of a physical therapist? To what extent to they overlap?

- Why is cerebral palsy often considered a multiple disorder? How should educators prioritize goals for a student with multiple disorders?

- What actions should the teacher take if a student has an insulin reaction while in class?

- Why are absence seizures sometimes not recognized? If they are so minimal, why are they such a problem?

- What actions should the teacher take if a student has a generalized tonic-clonic seizure in class?

- What are the essential components of an official policy relating to medication in the schools?

- What conditions may likely result from maternal substance abuse?

C H A P T E R   8

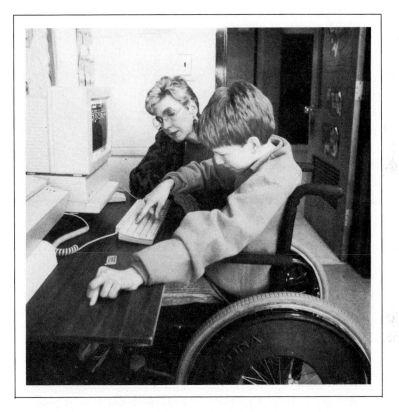

TEACHING STUDENTS
WHO ARE
ORTHOPEDICALLY OR
HEALTH IMPAIRED

ALTHOUGH CLASSIFIED UNDER A COMMON NAME, students with disabilities are as different from each other as students without disabilities are different from each other. The terms used in federal definitions, *orthopedic impairments* or *other health impairments*, indicate the heterogeneity of this population. Students grouped in this broad category range from those with asthma to those with cerebral palsy to those born without a limb or having lost a limb in an accident. One student may have limited use of hands but have good use of legs, or the opposite may be true. Another student may have good use of extremities but have difficulty breathing or have difficulty attending to learning tasks because of substance abuse by the mother prior to his or her birth. One student may be completely mobile in the classroom, but another may require crutches for mobility, and still another may need a wheelchair.

The focus of programming for students with orthopedic and health impairments is modification and, as much as possible, elimination of physical barriers. The phrase "least restrictive environment" in PL 94–142 is concerned with appropriate placement of students who have disabilities. Least restrictive environment has special meaning when applied to students with orthopedic and health impairments. The least restrictive environment for these students is appropriate academic placement in a carefully considered physical environment.

Several other factors should also be given serious consideration before students with orthopedic and health impairments are placed in regular classrooms. Of course, the willingness and ability of regular classroom teachers to accept and make changes for these students are of concern. The availability of support and ancillary personnel (resource teachers and therapists) is another factor. If a student needs daily therapy and must be bused to receive such service, provision must be made. Support from and a close working relationship with parents are essential elements for the success of a mainstreaming program. The degree of acceptance and positive interaction with nondisabled classmates is very important, too.

Specific student variables that should be considered are (a) modes of communication; (b) stamina; (c) intellectual ability; (d) achievement level; (e) personality, (f) relative independence in ambulation and mobility; (g) ability to profit from large-group instruction; and (h) personal interest, motivation, and commitment to being served in a regular classroom setting. These variables are not intended as criteria for placement or success in a regular class-room; they are provided as general guide-lines for professionals in making placement decisions.

If it is recommended that a student who is orthopedically impaired be placed in a regular classroom, a resource teacher or consultant must begin specific planning to determine the best possible educational placement and arrange for transportation and therapeutic services as required. The mere presence or placement of the student in a regular classroom and accomplishment of assigned academic tasks may represent only a small part of the total educational need for the individual.

Independent ambulation is an important factor in the total development of students, possibly more important to students than many of the academic challenges. Move-ment is essential for not only maintaining and improving motor function but also fa-cilitating important psychosocial interac-tions. Teachers should be aware of the ef-fects that lack of movement has on students and their interactions with peers. Schools and classrooms should be arranged to enable movement to all areas. Indepen-dent ambulation must be given priority if students are to be allowed equal opportuni-ties to grow socially, educationally, and emotionally.

Because of the diversity of problems pre-sented by students who are orthopedically or health impaired, a complete continuum of educational services must be offered, ranging from full-time special class place-ment for students who are multiply dis-abled or severely physically disabled to full-time regular class placement for those able to function and achieve in a regular class environment. Children temporarily dis-abled by infectious diseases or accidents may receive hospital or homebound instruction; however, the primary goal should be education in regular classrooms wherever possible.

Today, it is possible for more children to be educated in regular classes than in years past because of the reduction of architec-tural barriers, as required by the Rehabilita-tion Act of 1973 (Section 504). School build-ings built around the turn of the century typically had many stairs and second sto-ries, whereas today's schools are generally one-level structures, much more accessible or adaptable for students with limited mo-bility. However, even modern schools often require modifications. Some modifications include bathroom stalls made wider and deeper, sinks and water fountains lowered to enable individuals in wheelchairs to use them, classroom doors widened to accom-modate wheelchairs, and chalkboards low-ered and hinged to allow individuals in wheelchairs to write comfortably.

Many variables contribute to the number of students with physical disabilities who attend regular classes. Advanced medical and technological procedures may lessen the degree of disability. For example, chil-dren born with congenital heart defects may have these corrected surgically and live without serious restrictions. This was not possible in the past. Similarly, changes in treatment procedures for conditions such as asthma, diabetes, and heart defects allow students more complete participation in normal activities. Students may be fitted with artificial limbs at an early age, and congenital defects such as clubfoot may be corrected earlier, also allowing fuller partic-ipation in nearly all endeavors.

ORTHOPEDIC IMPAIRMENTS
This section discusses the most commonly found serious orthopedic impairments: (a) amputation, (b) arthritis, (c) cerebral palsy, (d) spina bifida, (e) muscular dystrophy, (f)

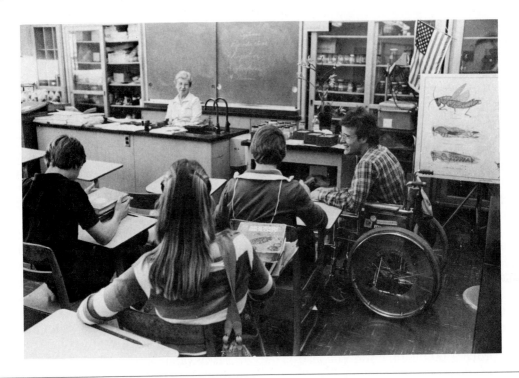

Advanced science is no problem for these students.

scoliosis, (g) hip disorders, and (h) osteogenesis imperfecta. More than two hundred possible conditions are included in the category of orthopedic impairments; however, this section discusses the conditions found most commonly in regular classrooms.

Amputation

Nature of Condition. A missing limb may be a congenital condition, or a result of amputation made necessary by trauma, disease, or infection. In nearly all instances, the student will have been fitted with an artificial arm or leg (prosthesis). Generally, the student with a congenital condition has been fitted with a prosthesis very early and has adapted to it by the time he or she begins school. A prosthesis may be made of wood, metal, or plastic. Plastic materials

are used more commonly today because of their light weight.

Educational Implications. Students with a prosthesis are usually able to function at nearly normal capacity and require very little educational modification. The extent of modification, however, depends on the age of the student, the site of the amputation (the higher on the extremity, the more severe), and the student's adjustment to the disability. Regular classroom teachers should be aware of the following factors to ensure the best educational programming:

1. Because of growth, a student's prosthesis rarely fits for more than a year. As a result, teachers must be certain the stu-

dent is using the prosthesis effectively and that it fits properly. The student visits a prosthetist for routine adjustments and fitting.

2. Teachers should have general information, particularly for a young student, concerning the basic mechanics, proper fitting, and maintenance of a prosthesis. This information may be obtained from the student, the student's parents, a resource or itinerant teacher, or a prosthetist. If the student feels comfortable in discussing his or her prosthesis, it would be of great social and psychological value for the student to explain its function to the entire class. Of course, this depends on the age of the other students and the extent to which the student has adjusted to the amputation.

3. The height of the student's working surface (such as a desk or table for a student with an upper extremity prosthesis) should be adjusted so that it does not interfere with the function of the prosthesis. With young children, a rim around a table or desk top may help prevent pencils or crayons from rolling off the working surface.

4. Students with a lower extremity prosthesis may need extra time to get to their classes and, if traveling a long distance or over rough terrain, may need a wheelchair.

5. Proper exercise is important for a child with a prosthesis, particularly in the joints around an amputation. Physical education activities and games may be adapted or individualized to ensure maximum fitness and exercise. One commonly reads or hears about individuals with amputations who not only participate but excel in competitive athletic events. Many individuals with lower extremity amputations participate and compete successfully in activities such

as bowling, snow skiing and water skiing, golf, and even football.

6. Postural habits must be carefully observed to ensure that the student does not develop a spinal curvature such as scoliosis, a lateral curvature of the spine resulting in a C-shaped curve. The student may develop habits such as using only one side of his or her body, causing postural problems. Postural problems can limit body mechanics and general functioning. If the student has a lower extremity amputation, the teacher must try to prevent unusual gait or ambulation problems.

7. Proper hygienic principles must be exercised in the care of a stump. It should be kept clean and allowed to air for brief periods. Although these practices are typically conducted at home, teachers should be aware of this need.

8. Some students with amputations use modified or adapted equipment, such as pencil holders and page turners. Many of these materials are available from commercial sources, and others may be easily adapted or made by teachers. Resource or itinerant teachers may be of assistance in modifying materials and equipment.

9. Curricular modifications may also be necessary. For example, typing may be taught using a one-handed method with very little modification. In general, typing may be a preferred means of communication for the student with an amputation because it saves time and requires less energy. Resource or itinerant teachers should have information concerning typing. Occupational therapists are valuable resources and should be consulted when questions arise. Occupational therapists can assist in modifying equipment and materials and can plan and initiate activities that facilitate maximum

functioning for the student. Amputations in children are generally not so troublesome as they are in adults, because children are more tolerant and adaptable. Children generally can participate in regular classrooms successfully with only minor modifications and adaptations.

Arthritis

Nature of Condition. Although arthritis is a condition that occurs primarily in adults, it can begin at any age. The most common form of arthritis in students is juvenile rheumatoid arthritis. It may have a sudden onset, or it may begin gradually. The effects and complications vary greatly. In some instances, arthritis may last only a few weeks or months and not seriously limit the student. In other cases, it may continue throughout the student's life, becoming worse as time goes on.

Rheumatoid arthritis attacks the joints of the body and may involve many organs, such as the heart, liver, and spleen. There may be a skin rash, inflammation of the eyes, retardation of growth, and swelling and pain in the fingers, wrists, elbows, knees, hips, and feet. As the disease progresses, the joints may stiffen, making movement difficult and painful. Osteoarthritis, or the wear-and-tear type of arthritis, is generally confined to one joint and does not affect the whole body.

Treatment Procedures. There are no cures for rheumatoid arthritis, only ways to control the inflammation and secondary effects. The majority of students with this condition are free of active disease after a period of about 10 years. The major aim of treatment is to allow the students to live as normally as possible. Many times, students with arthritis become "care-cripples." In other words, they are overprotected and not allowed to participate fully in the activities of home or school. Juvenile arthritis is self-limiting, and students ordinarily use good sense in determining whether they should participate in activities.

Treatment procedures are generally individualized, because no two cases are exactly alike. Because of the variance among patients and their individual response to drugs, the drugs prescribed by physicians may be different in each case. Generally, aspirin is the single most effective drug used in the treatment of arthritis because it reduces pain and inflammation of the joints and is among the safest drugs on the market. Usually, large amounts are prescribed on a routine basis, and dosage must be continued even after the swelling and pain have subsided.

Special exercises may be prescribed, involving putting joints through a full range of motion to prevent loss of strength in the muscles and joint deformity. Heat treatments may also be prescribed to enable joints to move more smoothly and with less pain. Heat treatments take a variety of forms. They may be carried out at home or in a clinic. Surgical procedures are also used to prevent and correct deformity caused by this disease. For some children, splints, braces, or plaster casts are prescribed to subdue inflammation and protect the joint or joints.

Educational Implications. The educational modifications necessary for the student with juvenile arthritis depend on the age of the student, severity of condition, independent travel ability, and range of motion in the arms, hands, and fingers. A student with juvenile arthritis probably does not need special methods or materials in the academic areas. If the joints in the upper extremities are severely involved, however, the student may need writing aids, adapted paper, or special pencils. The Arthritis Foundation publishes an illustrated "Self-Help Manual for Arthritis Patients." This manual describes aids and devices that may be helpful.[1]

It is likely that a student with arthritis has the most difficulty with walking. The knees, ankles, and hips may be more involved than the upper body, and walking may cause considerable pain. As a result, it may be well to consider somewhat limited movement for many such students. However, some students experience increased joint stiffness during prolonged immobility and may need to get up and walk to relieve the discomfort. Some students need an individualized physical education program or a program carried out by a physical therapist, whereas others need very little modification in their physical education program.

Teachers should watch for any changes in vision, because eye disease is commonly associated with rheumatoid arthritis. Inflammation of the iris (iridocyclitis) is a serious condition and may be found in association with some forms of juvenile rheumatoid arthritis. In particular, pain in the eyes or light sensitivity may indicate need to be seen by an ophthalmologist. It is generally recommended that students with arthritis be checked for changes in vision at least every 6 to 9 months.

Psychological and environmental factors may influence the manifestations of arthritis and its ultimate conclusions; however, they are not causes of arthritis (Hanson, 1983). Teachers need not modify academic and social standards. They should simply be aware of the general emotional climate and its possible effects on the student. Changes in mood or temperament are common for such students and may be related to the amount of pain. Teachers and school counselors can help students cope with the frustration, anger, and pain.

Teachers should be aware of other implications for students who have arthritis. For example, a student may miss a considerable amount of school during arthritic attacks. Faulty posture habits should be avoided, since good body alignment and posture are important in reducing the effects of arthritis. Activities such as extensive and prolonged writing may need to be avoided if they are painful. It may also be necessary to give the student extra time to get to and from classrooms and extra time for completing assignments. Students must learn to live with arthritis and accept the limitations imposed by it. Understanding teachers can do a great deal to help students develop acceptance.

Cerebral Palsy

Nature of Condition. Cerebral palsy is not a disease but a group of conditions that may seriously limit motor coordination. Of the serious crippling conditions, cerebral palsy is the most common. Several years ago, polio was the number one crippling condition among children; today, cerebral palsy is more common. Cerebral palsy is most commonly present at birth, but it may be acquired at any time as the result of a head injury or an infectious disease. It is characterized by varying degrees of disturbance of voluntary movements resulting from brain injury. Because of brain injury, the majority of students with cerebral palsy have multiple disabling conditions, such as mental retardation, hearing impairment, visual difficulties, language disorders, and speech problems. Depending on the severity, some students with cerebral palsy attend special schools or special classes that provide comprehensive educational and therapeutic ser-

---

[1]Arthritis Foundation, 3400 Peachtree Rd, N.E., Atlanta, GA 30326.

vices. However, a number of students with mild or moderate cerebral palsy attend regular classes for part or all of the school day.

The two most common types of cerebral palsy are spastic and athetoid. Spastic cerebral palsy is characterized by jerky or explosive motions when the student initiates a voluntary movement. For example, in a severe type, a student who is asked to draw a line from one point to another may demonstrate erratic or jerky movements such as this:

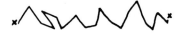

A student with athetosis also has difficulty with voluntary movements, but controlling movement in the desired direction is an added problem. In other words, this student demonstrates extra or purposeless movements. In drawing a line from one point to another, the student may have considerable uncontrolled movement, such as this:

Cerebral palsy and other conditions may be classified on the basis of limb involvement (topographical classification) as follows:

1. *Monoplegia.* One limb.
2. *Hemiplegia.* Both limbs on same side of body.
3. *Paraplegia.* Lower limbs only.
4. *Diplegia.* Major involvement in lower limbs and minor involvement in upper limbs.
5. *Triplegia.* Three limbs, usually one upper limb and both lower limbs.
6. *Quadriplegia.* All four limbs.

This classification is generally specified in the diagnostic information and in the student's school records.

Educational Implications. The severity of cerebral palsy dictates where a student would best be served, but the emphasis should be on providing as normal an educational environment as possible. Wherever practicable, students with cerebral palsy should attend regular classes with their nondisabled peers. Classroom modifications vary according to individual needs. Some students need no modifications, whereas others need some minor or major adjustments.

Often, an interdisciplinary approach is required in the care and treatment of individuals with cerebral palsy. It may be necessary for some students to be served on a routine and continued basis by a physical, occupational, or speech therapist or a combination of these. If such therapies are initiated early, they may not be needed as frequently during the upper elementary and secondary school years. Therapy sessions may be attended during the school day or after school hours.

Physical therapists are primarily concerned with the lower extremities and with posture, movements, and prevention of contractures (permanent muscle shortening because of lack of neurostimulation and muscle use). They are trained to evaluate physical development, ability, and movement. Physical therapists work under the direction of physicians in carrying out precise programs. Nonetheless, it is necessary for regular classroom teachers to have a basic understanding of treatment procedures so that they may reinforce desirable movements and postural habits.

Occupational therapists are primarily concerned with the upper extremities and with the routine activities required in daily living, such as buttoning, tying shoes, and eating. Many routine activities may be seriously limited for cerebral palsied students because of lack of muscle coordination. It is important that regular classroom teachers have information concerning the skills being taught so that they may reinforce them in the classroom. Often, occupational therapists assist in modifying and adapting educational materials to be used by students who have cerebral palsy.

In the past, there has often been a distinction between physical and occupational therapists. This role differentiation is not so distinct now, and many therapists share responsibilities or delineate them according to student needs. The services offered by speech therapists also need to be reinforced by teachers to ensure carryover and maintenance of desired speech habits.

Before actual placement of the student in a regular classroom, it is helpful for the regular classroom teacher to obtain as much information as possible about the student from the parents, resource or itinerant teachers, and therapists. It is helpful to obtain specific information concerning methods of communication, therapy needs and schedule, reading or writing aids used, and ambulation devices used. If time permits, actual observation of therapy sessions and a few brief meetings with the student are beneficial.

If the student with cerebral palsy is placed in the proper educational program, it should not be necessary to offer the student a curriculum different from that of his or her peers. However, it may be necessary to modify or adapt materials and equipment so that the student can participate more fully in classroom activities. The extent of the modifications necessary varies considerably. For example, some students have limited use of their hands and arms but have no difficulty getting around. As a result of the variance between individuals, it is difficult to offer specific suggestions.

The following list of materials and equipment provides examples of ways that modifications may be made:

1. Pencil holders made of clay, Styrofoam balls, or plastic golf balls may be helpful for students with fine-motor coordination difficulties.
2. Adapted typewriters may be useful for students with fine-motor coordination difficulties or students with very weak muscles. Electric or electronic typewriters are generally preferred. A pencil, rather than the fingers, may be used to strike the keys if the condition is very serious. Hand calculators may be used in arithmetic computations if the student has considerable difficulty writing.
3. Some students have conditions so severe that communication is seriously limited. These students may have average-to-high intellectual ability but because of poor motor coordination have considerable difficulty with speech. For these students, alternative communication systems may be necessary.
4. Positioning the student so that most of the body is supported may reduce uncoordinated movements, thus allowing the student to concentrate on only one or two body parts.
5. Page turners are useful for students with limited arm use. A turner may be attached to the head, elbow, or hand. A rubber thumb (used by office workers) may also make page turning easier.
6. Weights (such as small sandbags) placed on the wrist or hand can be used to eliminate random or uncontrolled

movements. Cursive writing may be easier than manuscript writing for some students with cerebral palsy.

7. Book holders that can be adjusted to any angle are helpful for some students.

8. Desks and tables should be at such height that the student's feet firmly touch the floor and the student's forearms rest on the working surface. Occasionally, the trunk of a student's body may need to be stabilized by straps or a harness.

9. Paper holders may be necessary for students who have the use of only one arm or very limited use of both arms. A clipboard to hold paper in position may be fastened to a desk, or a piece of unbleached muslin cloth may be attached to the desk and sprayed with nonskid fluid. It may be necessary to tape down the paper while the student is writing on it. A large rubber band may also be used to hold paper down.

10. A lip or rim around tables or desks may prevent pencils and other items from rolling off.

11. Some materials originally designed for use by individuals who are blind, such as talking books and cassette recorders, are helpful for students who have difficulty turning pages or balancing a book.

12. Stand-up tables are necessary for many students with cerebral palsy. Since a considerable amount of time is spent sitting, provisions should be made to allow students with cerebral palsy to stand for parts of the school day. Standing is often required to prevent muscle contractures, provide proper circulation, and maintain desired posture. Since standing unaided may be difficult, a stand-up table may be purchased or built inexpensively to provide support while the student is standing. An

individual stand-up table should normally include a tray for a work area approximately 2 feet square. The table should have a base of the same size so that it does not easily tip over. The height of the table can be changed by raising or lowering the foot platform.

Spina Bifida

Nature of Condition. Spina bifida is a serious birth defect in which bones of the spine fail to close during the 12th week of fetal development. As a result, a cyst, or sack, is present in the lower back when the child is born (Figure 8–1). This protrusion is generally surgically treated during the child's first 24 to 48 hours of life. The extent of the disability resulting from this condition varies enormously. Some individuals have little or no disability, whereas others have varying degrees of paralysis of the legs and incontinence (lack of bowel and bladder control). In addition to the degrees of paralysis and incontinence, the child may have

FIGURE 8–1
Spina bifida.

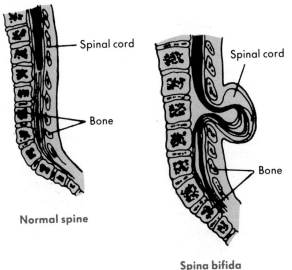

impaired autonomic nervous system functioning (absence of perspiration) and absence of sensation below the level of the spinal defect.

In some respects, spina bifida is similar to other crippling conditions that cause degrees of paralysis in the legs, but it is complicated by the lack of bowel and bladder control. Because of the deficiency of nerve fibers, a student may not be able to tell when his or her bladder is full. The bladder may overflow, and the student may not be aware of the situation until he or she sees the wetness through the outer clothing. There is a threat of infection from residual urine in the bladder, and the student may also have difficulty with bowel control.

Surgical procedures can assist in accommodating this condition, or artificial devices may be worn to collect urine. The student may also regulate fluid intake and adhere to a systematic voiding schedule. Generally, the student is able to take care of toileting needs, but young children may need some assistance from a classroom aide, volunteer, parent, or resource or itinerant teacher.

Educational Implications. It is important for teachers to work closely with medical personnel, especially the school nurses, to ensure proper health care. Teachers must also maintain a close working relationship with physical and occupational therapists. Last, but certainly not least, teachers should discuss the special needs and problems with the parents and should be aware of the symptoms of urinary infection—increased temperature, flushed skin, and excessive perspiration. The parents or the school nurse should be contacted if any of these symptoms occurs. Infections can generally be avoided with proper care, but in the event of infection, the student may have to be hospitalized, necessitating absence from school. Frequent urological, neurosurgical, and orthopedic consultations and procedures are also commonly required, necessitating careful planning between parents, resource teachers, consultants, and regular teachers. A schedule providing specific times for toileting needs should be implemented.

Teachers should be aware of problems associated with the lack of sensation in the legs. The lack of sensation can lead to skin or pressure sores. Teachers should also watch for injuries of which the student is unaware because of the lack of sensation. Problems imposed by wearing braces or using a wheelchair should also be considered. It may be necessary to reposition the student or ask the student to sit up straight during the school day to prevent pressure sores, postural problems, and muscle contractures.

If not handled properly, the psychosocial limitations imposed by spina bifida can be serious. The student may bear the brunt of laughter or joking because of odor or accidental urination. Teachers should also be aware that factors such as excitement or spicy foods can cause problems and should allow students with spina bifida to leave the classroom suddenly if an "accident" occurs.

The problems imposed by poor ambulatory skills must be taken into consideration by therapists and teachers. However, this factor is not any more significant for a student with spina bifida than for a student with cerebral palsy or any other major orthopedic impairment. Inasmuch as students with spina bifida have good use of their upper body, arms, and hands, the educational modifications necessary are minimal. Children with spina bifida can profit from regular classroom attendance and instruction with only minor modifications and adaptations.

Muscular Dystrophy

Nature of Condition. Muscular dystrophy is a progressive condition in which the muscles are replaced by a fatty tissue. Although there are several types, the most common and most serious type, Duchenne's disease, occurs in male children. Duchenne's disease, or childhood muscular dystrophy, is a generally fatal disease characterized by a slow deterioration of the voluntary muscles. The onset of the disease generally occurs between a child's first and sixth year and rarely occurs after the first decade of life. Early signs of the condition include a tendency to fall easily, clumsiness in walking, difficulty in climbing stairs, and difficulting in rising from the floor.

There is a progressive decline in the child's ability to walk. The child falls more frequently and eventually needs crutches to move about. As the child continues to lose strength, it is necessary to move from crutches to a wheelchair. Later, nearly all large muscles are involved and the child is bedridden. During the later stages, the child may be unable to raise his arms, sit erect, or hold his head up. Fortunately, the small muscles of the hands and fingers maintain some strength even during the most advanced stages.

Educational Implications. Regular classrooms offer obvious educational advantages as compared to special schools or classes for students with muscular dystrophy. In addition to the educational advantages, there are many recreational and social factors involved in regular school attendance. During the early stages of muscular dystrophy, very few modifications and adaptations are necessary, but as the condition progresses, some modifications are necessary. Eventually, the student may not be able to attend any educational program and may require homebound instruction; however, every effort should be made to maintain students with muscular dystrophy in regular classrooms as long as possible.

Muscular dystrophy imposes a contradiction in attitude. On the one hand, it is known that it is generally fatal, and on the other, students, parents, teachers, and others must carry on as though the students were going to live a rich and full life. This apparent contradiction must be dealt with. Guidance and counseling services can do a great deal to accommodate acceptance of this conflict. There is little question that if children and parents are to accept this contradiction, ongoing counseling must be offered.

Counseling programs should be conducted in cooperation with students, parents, brothers and sisters, therapists, teachers, and physicians. Counseling should center on acceptance of the condition, the best ways in which to utilize the time available, preparation for the inevitability of death, and related matters. Because of variations in age of onset, speed of deterioration, and other factors, all counseling must be individualized. There are currently nearly 200 clinics throughout the United States sponsored by the Muscular Dystrophy Association of America. These clinics provide no-cost services such as counseling, physical therapy, medical management, diagnostic services, and follow-up care.

It is important that students with muscular dystrophy attend adapted physical education classes and maintain a balance among diet, activity, and rest, since there is a tendency for such children to become overweight. They should be encouraged to participate as fully as possible in recreational and physical activities. Although the effects of the condition cannot be stopped by physical activity, there is some indication that such activity may delay some of the debilitating effects. Some caution must be exercised, however, because students with muscular dystrophy become very easily fatigued. They should be allowed periods of rest as needed.

Several studies have been conducted to determine whether mental retardation is associated with muscular dystrophy. There have been no indications that there is a greater incidence of mental retardation in students with muscular dystrophy than in the population as a whole. In addition, research studies have attempted to identify particular personality characteristics associated with muscular dystrophy. Although some researchers have found personality patterns unique to students who have muscular dystrophy, others have not been able to do so. Therefore, it is reasonable to assume that differences in personality may be attributed to something other than the muscular dystrophy. If there is no mental retardation or particular personality configuration associated with muscular dystrophy, then achievement and adjustment in school should be similar to that of other students. Perhaps, the most important role of teachers is to stimulate students who have muscular dystrophy academically, recreationally, and socially and to expect as nearly as possible the same of these students as of others.

Scoliosis

Nature of Condition. Scoliosis means lateral (side-to-side) curvature of the spine (Figure 8–2). The normal spine has several curvatures in a front-to-back direction but no curvature from side to side. The most common type of scoliosis, idiopathic (cause unknown), is most commonly but not exclusively found in young adolescent girls. The second most common form, *paralytic*, is often associated with conditions such as cerebral palsy, spina bifida, muscular dystrophy, or poliomyelitis.

FIGURE 8–2
Scoliosis

Scoliosis screening programs are usually conducte as part of physical education programming or by school nurses. Teachers should watch for a difference in shoulder height, differing contours of normal flanks, or a hump when a child bends over (Figure

FIGURE 8–3
Appearance of scoliosis when an individual bends forward

8–3). If curvature is suspected, teachers should inform the school nurse or family so that further testing may be conducted.

Educational Implications. Since there are strong hereditary tendencies for scoliosis, teachers should be alert to signs of the condition in siblings of a student with scoliosis.

Students with scoliosis should be expected to participate in all routine activities, including physical education. Students with other orthopedic impairments may have a more severe form of scoliosis. Often, a brace such as the Milwaukee or Boston brace, to be worn full-time, is prescribed to correct the condition. In very severe cases, surgery may be recommended.

Teachers should be particularly watchful for an improperly sized wheelchair, which may result in the student's leaning to one side, thus making scoliosis worse. If a student is wearing a brace, the teacher should also watch for an improper fit, which can cause discomfort, pain, or pressure sores. As indicated, students with scoliosis can be expected to participate in all school activities. A teacher in doubt should consult with the parents or medical specialist. Special care must be taken so that the treatment of the student with scoliosis does not become more of a disability than the condition itself.

Hip Disorders

Nature of Condition. The two most commonly found hip disorders in school-age children are congenital dislocation of the hip and Legg-Perthes disease. Congenital dislocation of the hip occurs as a result of an abnormally formed hip joint. The hip may be completely dislocated, partially dislocated, or generally unstable. Medical intervention is initiated at an early age by gentle reduction of the misalignment and maintenance in the realigned position through the use of casts or splints. In more severe cases, surgery is required to release tightened tendons in the hip area. Generally, a child with a congenital hip problem has had the condition diagnosed and treated before entering school. In some cases, however, it is not diagnosed until after the child enters school.

Like congenital dislocation of the hip, Legg-Perthes disease is a problem that can be corrected by bracing, casting, or surgery. It is a condition of unknown origin and results from a disruption of the blood supply in the head of the long bone of the thigh (the femur). The lack of blood supply to the growth center of the femur causes disintegration and flattening of the femoral head at the hip joint.

Legg-Perthes disease is more common among males than females and is seen during the elementary school years (3 to 11 years of age). Treatment is directed at reducing weight-bearing pressure on the head of the femur, allowing for bone restoration. The child may be involved with an extensive treatment for as long as 2 years. In some cases, surgery is required to reshape the hip socket or the head of the femur.

Educational Implications. Close communication between teachers and parents is essential in cases of prolonged hospitalization. Hospital and homebound instruction may be necessary to ensure that when the student returns to the regular classroom, he or she will not be significantly behind classmates.

During treatment, the student's legs are usually placed in a position spread wide apart and maintained in this position by a cast, brace, or splint (Figure 8–4). After the cast, brace, or splint is removed, the student may progressively bear weight on the legs. Occasionally, the student may use a creeper (a low platform on wheels, similar to what an automobile mechanic uses to work underneath an automobile) for a period of time. Naturally, the student should avoid physical activities that put weight-bearing stress on the affected hip. Other than this consideration, there need not be any significant modifications or adaptations for students with Legg-Perthes disease.

Osteogenesis Imperfecta
Nature of Condition. Osteogenesis imperfecta, commonly called brittle bones, is a defect in the development of bone structure. Because of structural weakness, the bones break very easily. In addition, af-

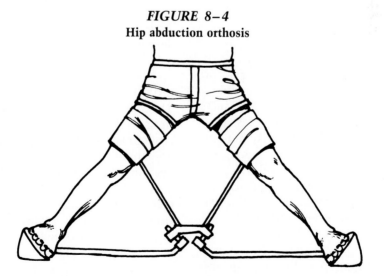

FIGURE 8–4
Hip abduction orthosis

Note: From *Atlas of Orthotics* (p. 93) by American Academy of Orthopedic Surgeons, 1975, St. Louis: C. V. Mosby. Adapted by permission.

fected individuals often have deformity, dwarfism, and hearing loss. During the early years, it may be necessary for a child to live in a protective environment to minimize breaks and fractures.

Educational Implications. Students with the less severe type of osteogensis imperfecta should be encouraged to attend regular classes. Since their intellectual ability is within the normal range, they may attend regular classes with only minor modifications. Naturally, they should be excluded from participation in all activities that might result in bone fractures. Braces and crutches may be used for support, and some students use wheelchairs to decrease falls and bumps. Other students should exercise caution when playing with children who have osteogenesis imperfecta because routine falls or bumps can mean serious fractures. Every effort must be made to maintain such students in regular classrooms to maximize the social and educational benefits of interaction with normal peers.

HEALTH IMPAIRMENTS

The next sections address several of the more common health impairments of school-age children—allergies, asthma, conditions resulting from maternal substance abuse, cystic fibrosis, diabetes, epilepsy, heart disorders, hemophilia, human immunodeficiency virus, and sickle-cell anemia. In each case, the discussion covers the nature of the condition and educational implications. Where applicable, the discussion also includes treatment procedures.

Allergies

Nature of Condition. An allergy is an adverse sensitivity or intolerance to a specific substance that may not be a problem to other individuals. When students who have

allergies come in contact with substances to which they are sensitive, they develop reactions, or irritations. Reactions may take many forms, such as sneezing, watering eyes, runny nose, tiredness, itching, or rash. The student may react to a number of different substances. Among the most common are inhalants (pollen, smoke, dust, and perfumes, for example), foods (eggs, chocolate, wheat, pork, strawberries, nuts and citrus fruits, for example), infectious agents (bacteria and fungi, for example), substances that come in contact with the skin (poison ivy, poison sumac, fur, leather, animal hair, and dyes, for example), and drugs (vaccines, serums, and antibiotics, for example).

Treatment Procedures. Physicians may prescribe medication for temporary relief, but generally they carefully examine medical history, home surroundings, eating habits, and so on to determine the allergens to which individuals are sensitive. They may conduct specific allergy tests, such as skin tests on the arm or back, to determine substances to which the individuals react. They may also suggest a series of shots to desensitize the individual to a particular substance.

A student with allergies can participate fully in nearly all educational programs. Teachers may, however, assist in identifying specific sensitivities, particularly if the student seems to have more difficulty when at school. If an allergic reaction is suspected, this should be reported to the parents or school nurse, since treatment can do a great deal to ease the effects of the condition. In addition, students with allergies tend to develop asthma, and this should be avoided if at all possible.

Educational Implications. Some students miss school because of their condition, particularly during early fall or in the spring, when pollen levels are highest. It is the responsibility of teachers to make certain that students complete missed assignments. It may also be necessary to provide additional instruction or establish a peer teaching arrangement.

Some students with allergies fatigue more easily than other students when participating in physical activities. As a result, they may withdraw during recess or physical education, while their classmates continue. This behavior must be observed very carefully, since withdrawal may have serious social and emotional results. Because physical fitness is an important component of treatment, teachers may assist by modifying or adapting activities and encouraging students who have allergies to participate as much as possible. Teachers should also carefully observe to see if there is any change in the condition as a result of activity and report this information to the parents or physicians. Students must learn how to live with the limitations caused by allergies and develop a life-style that allows a maximum amount of freedom.

Asthma

Nature of Condition. Asthma usually results from an allergic state that causes an obstruction of the bronchial tubes, the lungs, or both. When sensitivity flares into an attack, an excessive amount of mucus is produced and there is a spasm of the bronchial musculature. As a result, breathing becomes difficult, and a student may lose color, wheeze, and perspire excessively. The attack may last for minutes, hours, or days.

Asthma attacks may be frightening because of the labored breathing and other behaviors. An attack may be brought on by a specific sensitivity to an allergen or by excessive physical activity. Asthma attacks can cause emotional stress for the students

and those around them. The arousal of emotions may intensify the frequency and severity of asthma symptoms. The disease and emotional climate are so interrelated that they affect each other (Kraemer & Bierman, 1983).

Treatment Procedures. Treatment procedures are similar to those for allergic individuals. Adrenaline administered by injection or by inhalation usually gives relief for brief periods. However, since asthma is a chronic condition, long-term treatment procedures must be employed.

Educational Implications. Students with asthma should be treated as normally as possible. Caution must be exercised to avoid overprotection from routine classroom activities. If care is not practiced, students may become asthmatic or emotional cripples.

Teachers should be aware of the factors that precipitate asthma attacks and have information concerning the proper course of action should an attack occur. Although the severity of the asthmatic condition of each student is different and there are unique care and treatment procedures for each, teachers should consider some general factors. Mild attacks can sometimes be controlled by asking a student to sit down and breath easily. Medical personnel occasionally recommend drinking warm water as a way of stopping a mild attack. During an attack, a student may be more comfortable in a standing or sitting position rather than lying down. Teachers should encourage the student to sit forward in a chair, with hands on knees and shoulders forward, while breathing through the mouth.

Students may have to take medicine during school hours to keep mild asthma from becoming severe. If a pressurized aerosol is used, the teacher, after careful consultation with parents, should closely monitor its use to be certain it is not overused.

If a specific food being offered in a classroom party is an allergen, the teacher should check with the parents to see if a substitute may be used. It is also recommended that classmates be helped to understand this condition to avoid ridicule, which would only add to the problem.

Management of students with asthma should include attention to psychological factors that may aggravate the condition. Teachers should also be aware of possible side effects or behavioral changes related to prescribed drugs. Teachers are in a unique position to observe students during a variety of activities throughout the school day. They can provide an atmosphere that promotes growth, acceptance, and independence. Information provided by teachers may be helpful to parents or the physicians in determining subsequent treatment procedures.

For students who experience asthma attacks during periods of exercise, some general guidelines may be considered. Warm-up periods are helpful, as are short periods of moderate exercise. Certain types of exercise, such as gymnastics, wrestling, and swimming, are usually less likely to produce asthma attacks (Richards, 1986). Short sprints are also less likely to produce attacks than prolonged running. In addition, exercise in warm, humid conditions is generally less likely to induce attacks than that done in cold, dry air outdoors. With appropriate management (for example, medications taken prior to strenuous exercise), students may effectively compete in activities such as basketball, soccer, or track (Kraemer & Bierman, 1983). It is essential that teachers check with parents or physicians to determine specifically what students can and cannot do.

Conditions Resulting from Maternal Substance Abuse

Nature of Condition. The prenatal environment may seem safe and secure as compared to the more complex environment of childhood. However, with the increased use of a variety of substances by mothers during pregnancy, this is not always true. The use of alcohol, cocaine, crack (a form of cocaine), phenylcyclidine hydrochloride (PCP), heroin, hallucinogens, and other similar drugs during pregnancy has increased, resulting in a population of children experiencing a variety of disorders (Van Dyke & Fox, 1990). Prenatal development is affected by a variety of environmental factors called teratogens, which are agents that increase the likelihood of various malformations. Such factors affect a fetus in different ways at different times during pregnancy. For example, a critical time for the central nervous system is weeks 3 through 5, and teratogens ingested during this time affect the central nervous system in a more adverse manner at this time than any other. Similarly weeks 4 through 7 are important for the normal development of arms. Some teratogens can more easily be avoided, whereas others cannot—for example, medications required by a mother to control seizures or other diseases. The presence of other conditions, such as nutritional deficiencies or metabolic disorders, may intensify the impact of maternal substance abuse.

Children born to mothers who have ingested large amounts of alcohol may be born with fetal alcohol syndrome. Such babies may have distinguishing facial characteristics (including narrow eyelids, low nasal bridges, and short, upturned noses) and may be born with heart defects and joint and limb abnormalities that restrict movement (Leerhsen & Schaefer, 1989; Schiamberg, 1988). They may experience mental retardation from mild to severe, be hyperactive, and have short attention spans and emotional problems (Behrman, Vaughan, & Nelson, 1987; Creasy & Resnick, 1989; Pueschel, Bernier, & Weidenman, 1988; Van Dyke & Fox, 1990). Babies born to cocaine- or crack-addicted mothers may have already experienced a stroke or neurologic insult, and are likely to be born prematurely (Revkin, 1989). Crack babies, as they are frequently called, are increasing in number, and there is increasing concern regarding their ability to succeed in school.

Cocaine is derived from the leaves of the coca plant, in which it occurs naturally as an alkaloid. When it is sold, it is usually in the form of hydrochloride salt diluted with inert substances. Crack is manufactured by boiling the hydrochloride in water and baking soda, which converts the salt back into the alkaloid and precipitates out of the solution as pure cocaine crystals. Once either substance enters the body, neurons in the brain are stimulated to release the chemicals that carry messages across the gap from one neuron to the next (neurotransmitters). The results are an accelerated heart rate, raised blood pressure, a lower digestive rate, and a feeling of euphoria. Fetuses are particularly vulnerable to cocaine, because it readily passes through the placental barrier. It lingers much longer in fetuses than in adults because the liver in fetuses is insufficiently developed and thus cannot break down the cocaine as quickly. Cocaine use can have significant effects on the developing central nervous system, and the risk increases when cocaine is used frequently.

Cocaine or crack use by mothers may lead to two major negative effects. The first, neurologic insult, may affect learning ability and cognitive processing. Neurologic insult may result in poor organization, reading problems, difficulty in acquiring mathematical skills, and decreased social adjustment (Revkin, 1989; Van Dyke & Fox, 1990). A second effect is less direct and more difficult to determine. Frequent users of cocaine experience a period of euphoria followed by depression, paranoia, irritability, and loss of appetite, which increases the desire for more cocaine and the resultant high. This cycle becomes the norm, and getting cocaine becomes the most important goal (Morganthau, 1989). A parent who is experiencing this cycle often neglects or abuses the child (Revkin, 1989). Thus, neither the nutritional nor emotional needs of the child are being met, and the child suffers physical abuse as well (Berger, 1987). Additionally, there is some evidence that crack babies do not respond normally to their parents. Therefore, abnormal response on the part of the child may lead to absence of normal bonding even if the parents no longer use cocaine (Van Dyke & Fox, 1990).

Babies born to mothers who ingested phenylcyclidine hydrochloride (PCP) have characteristics different from those of newborns exposed to other drugs before birth. They exhibit sensitivity to touch, sensitivity to environmental sound, and abnormal eye movements. At a later age, they seem to be delayed in language and fine-motor abilities (Pueschel, Bernier, & Weidenman, 1988).

Children born to heroin-addicted mothers are generally slow in growth. They often experience behavior and perceptual problems and difficulties in organizational ability. In addition, they seem to be more susceptible to such complicating factors as infections, malnutrition, and acquired immune deficiency syndrome.

Mothers who are multiple drug users increase the risk for their children. Children born to multiple drug users tend to be more severely retarded, are more likely to have physical abnormalities, and are more likely to have severe neurologic disorders.

Educational Implications. Children born to mothers who have used drugs may require educational practices similar to those for children with mental retardation, learning disabilities, or other physical or health impairments. It is the needs of the individual student, not the cause of a disability, that dictates specific educational measures. The severity of the physical disability indicates the accommodations necessary. Sufficient longitudinal studies have not been completed to determine how such children will fare when they reach their teens and adulthood (Van Dyke & Fox, 1990).

Cystic Fibrosis

Nature of Condition. Cystic fibrosis is the most common potentially lethal hereditary disease. It is a recessive genetic disorder that results from an inborn error of metabolism. It affects the exocrine glands (outward-secreting glands of the body), often causing severe respiratory and digestive problems. Normal mucus is thin, slippery, and clear; however, in children with cystic fibrosis, the mucus is thick and sticky. This thick mucus clogs the bronchial tubes. If not removed, it can lead to recurrent lung infections, lung damage, digestive difficulty, and occasionally cirrhosis of the liver. As the condition progresses, more mucus remains and areas of the lungs become blocked.

Treatment Procedures. Inhalation treatments and chest physical therapy (patting the back in certain areas to loosen the thick mucus) are used to ease the breathing of children with cystic fibrosis. Parents and therapists may employ chest physical ther-

apy and postural drainage techniques several times a day.

In the past, children with cystic fibrosis often did not survive beyond the primary grades. Today, because of advanced medical treatment procedures, many live normal adult lives (Mangos, 1983; Schwartz, 1984).

Educational Implications. Teachers should consider several factors for students with cystic fibrosis:

1. Students may cough frequently. Cystic fibrosis is *not* contagious; therefore, there is no need to keep other students away during a coughing episode. In fact, students with cystic fibrosis should be encouraged not to try to hide the cough, because coughing clears the mucus from the lungs.
2. Students may need to go to the restroom more frequently than other students and should be allowed to do so.
3. Students may need to take medication during school hours, and as a result, a flexible schedule and arrangements with the school nurse may be helpful.
4. Physical stamina may be impaired because of lung involvement, but students with cystic fibrosis should be encouraged to participate in all activities as fully as possible. However, it may be necessary to prevent them from attempting to hide their condition and going beyond their limit. It may also be advisable to watch them during hot weather because they may perspire excessively and may need added salt.
5. Students with cystic fibrosis may have an increased appetite. Some students with cystic fibrosis may be on a low- or modified-fat diet, and if so, teachers should encourage adherence to the diet.
6. Because frequent absences may be common for students with cystic fibrosis,

teachers must work diligently with hospital and homebound personnel to ensure the best possible education.

Teachers should assume responsibility for knowing exactly what students can and cannot do. This is best accomplished by close communication among parents, resource personnel, and regular teachers.

Diabetes

Nature of Condition. Diabetes is a metabolic disorder wherein an individual's body is unable to utilize and properly store sugar. This condition is a result of inability of the pancreas to produce a sufficient amount of the hormone insulin. Although diabetes is most commonly seen in adults, it does occur in school-age children and can become a serious problem if the proper treatment procedures are not adhered to. Symptoms indicative of diabetes include unusually frequent urination, abnormal thirst, extreme hunger, changes in weight (generally a rapid loss), drowsiness, general weakness, possible visual disturbances, and skin infections like boils or itching. If a student shows any of these symptoms, the school nurse and the student's parents should be contacted as soon as possible. Prompt medical diagnosis and treatment are essential in the care of diabetic students.

Treatment Procedures. If diabetes is diagnosed, treatment procedures probably involve daily injections of insulin, adherence to a strict diet to maintain the correct sugar level, and a balance between exercise and rest. Generally, students with diabetes have normal childhood and adolescence and can do almost everything their peers do except fill up on sweets. They must maintain a balance between exercise and rest.

To most of us, daily injections seem a serious problem, but to the student with dia-

betes, they become routine. Injections are generally administered at home and become as routine as other hygienic practices, such as bathing or brushing teeth. Often, students and parents attend a clinic that teaches them how to manage daily activities, such as injections, diet, exercise, care of the feet (this can be a definite problem because of poor circulation), and the changes in life-style that are necessary to accommodate the condition. As a result of these clinics, students who have diabetes generally know a great deal about the condition and how to manage it.

Educational Implications. Classroom teachers should be aware of several potential problems, such as an insulin reaction (hypoglycemia) and diabetic coma. An insulin reaction may result from anything that increases the metabolic rate, such as too much exercise, too much insulin, too little food, or nervous tension. Reactions may occur anytime during the day, but most often, they occur before meals or after strenuous exercise. For instance, an insulin reaction may occur if a student refuses to finish breakfast and the usual dose of insulin becomes unbalanced by the reduced food intake. Emotional tension about school or personal problems may have variable effects. Occasionally, tension may cause the blood sugar level to fall below normal, resulting in an insulin reaction.

An insulin reaction may follow a typical pattern for each individual, and therefore it is important to consult with students or their parents to determine what these signs may be. Often, general irritability may be the first sign. One student may be despondent and cry readily, whereas another may be exuberant or belligerent. The student may be hungry, perspire excessively, tremble, be unable to concentrate, and complain of being dizzy. Symptoms vary in duration and often disappear after the student is provided with a sugar cube, soft drink, candy, raisins, fruit juice with sugar, or any other carbohydrate. Generally, the symptoms will disappear after 10 to 15 minutes. If they do not, the student's parents or physicians should be called.

The opposite of an insulin reaction is a diabetic coma. Although fairly rare, comas do occur and can be serious if not treated immediately. A diabetic coma is the result of failure to take insulin, an illness, or neglect of proper diet. An individual has too much sugar and must have an injection as soon as possible. Generally, a coma is slow in onset, and the following symptoms may be observed: thirst, frequent urination, flushed face, labored breathing, nausea, and vomiting. Such symptoms should be reported to the parents, school nurse, or physician as soon as possible. Treatment involves rest, injection of insulin, and possible hospitalization.

Table 8–1 is a summary of the indica-

TABLE 8–1
Summary of observable signs, causes, and actions to take for diabetic reaction and insulin reaction

	Insulin Reaction (Rapid Onset)	Diabetic Coma (Slow Onset)
Observable signs	Facial pallor Hunger Impaired vision Irritability Excessive sweating Personality change Headache Faintness Trembling Forceful heartbeat	Excessive thirst Abdominal pains Repeated urination Loss of appetite Nausea or vomiting General aches Weakness
Causes	Reduced intake of food Delayed meals Abnormal amount of exercise Too much insulin	Infections Fever Emotional stress Failure to follow diet Too little insulin
What to do	Call the parents, doctor, or school nurse Provide sugar or other food with sugar, such as orange juice, candy, or a sweetened soft drink	Call the parents, doctor, or school nurse immediately Allow the student to lie down Keep the student warm Provide fluids without sugar

tors, causes, and appropriate actions in cases of diabetic coma and insulin reaction. If in doubt over the symptom, administer sugar, since the body's reaction to an excess of sugar is slower and can be corrected later. However, the body's reaction to too much insulin is sudden and dangerous (Kleinberg, 1982; Winter, 1983). Specific instructions from a physician always take precedence over generalized instructions, but the guidelines in Table 8–1 may be of value until you consult with a physician or school nurse.

Several additional factors should be considered:

1. Check with the student's parents to see if the student should have a midmorning snack. If so, help the student be as inconspicuous as possible about it. It may also be advisable to schedule the student for an early lunch period.
2. Very active or strenuous physical activities should be avoided immediately before lunch. Since the goal in the management of diabetes is to maintain a balance among insulin, food intake, and energy expenditure, it might be well to encourage the student to establish an exercise routine at the same time each day.
3. Keep candy, raisins, or sugar handy in case the student needs them.
4. Be certain to inform special or substitute teachers that there is a student in the class with diabetes, and record in writing what substitutes should do in case of insulin reaction or diabetic coma. This suggestion is relevant not only in the case of the student with diabetes but for all health impairments.
5. Encourage the parents to have their child's vision routinely checked, because many individuals with diabetes develop retinal problems.
6. Allow the student who has diabetes the

flexibility to use the restroom whenever necessary, because students with diabetes may need to urinate more frequently. Inform the parents if there is a sudden increase in use of the restroom or the drinking fountain. Such an increase may be an indication of need for medical attention.

7. With permission of the student and parents, a teacher may present a unit of study concerning endocrine function and energy and their relationship to sugar consumption and nutrition.
8. Above all else, do not panic about having a student with diabetes. Proceed calmly if the student has an insulin reaction or goes into a coma. The vast majority of the time, the student can be treated like any other student in the class.

Students with diabetes should be expected to participate in all normal school activities unless a physician has advised specific restrictions. Students who have diabetes must learn to live with the condition and to accept the limitations imposed by it. They must develop a life-style that allows the greatest possible freedom and still maintains the necessary balance among diet, rest and activity, and medication.

Epilepsy (Seizure Disorders)

Nature of Condition. Epilepsy is a chronic disorder of the brain, accompanied by seizures. Epilepsy has been traditionally classified according to terms such as *grand mal, petit mal,* and *psychomotor.* These terms describe both the type and severity of the disorder and continue in common use; however, many doctors use a newer, alternate classification system. The following discussion uses the newer system, indicating the traditional terms parenthetically.

Convulsions, or seizures, are the main

symptoms in all types of epilepsy. Many individuals, especially young children, have one or two seizures in their life, but when several seizures occur unrelated to illness or fever, the diagnosis is likely to be epilepsy. Seizures are a result of excessive, uncontrolled electrical discharges in the brain cells. Actually, epilepsy is common, with many cases of seizures never recognized or reported. Estimates of occurrence range from 1 of every 50 to 1 of every 500 children, depending on the criteria established for the study. The most common types of seizures are (a) generalized tonic-clonic (grand mal) seizures, also known as generalized convulsive seizures or major motor seizures; (b) absence (petit mal) seizures; and (c) complex partial (psychomotor) seizures, also known as temporal lobe seizures.

Generalized Tonic-Clonic (Grand Mal) Seizures. Generalized tonic-clonic seizures are the most alarming to school personnel and other students. When such a seizure occurs, an individual loses consciousness, collapses, and has general convulsive movements. The individual may shout or produce a gurgling sound, and saliva may escape from the lips. The muscles first become rigid or stiff, and then there are jerky movements of the arms and legs. An individual may bite the tongue or lose bladder control. Breathing is often labored and at times seems to have stopped completely. The individual may have a bluish or pale complexion. The seizure may last for several minutes, and afterwards the individual may be confused or drowsy. The individual does not recall what happened during the seizure, and he or she may be very tired and want to sleep for a short time.

There are many misconceptions concerning epilepsy, including the presumption of mental retardation, brain injury, or insanity. But there is even more misinformation about what should be done when an individual has a generalized tonic-clonic seizure. Such a seizure can be frightening unless the teacher knows exactly what to do. The Epilepsy Foundation of America suggests the following steps in the event of a generalized tonic-clonic seizure:

1. Remain calm. Students tend to assume the same emotional reaction as their teacher. The seizure itself is painless to the student.
2. Do not try to restrain the student. Nothing can be done to stop a seizure once it has begun. It must run its course.
3. Help the student lie down, and put something under the student's head.
4. Clear the area around the student so that he or she is not injured on hard, sharp, or hot objects. Try not to interfere with the student's movements in any way.
5. Remove glasses and loosen tight clothing.
6. Do not force anything between teeth. Under no circumstances should a hard object such as a spoon, pen, or pencil be put in the student's mouth. More harm may result from such an action than from doing nothing. Do not put fingers into the mouth.
7. After the seizure, turn the student's head to one side for the release of saliva.
8. Do not offer the student anything to drink until he or she is fully awake.
9. It is not generally necessary to call a physician unless the attack is immediately followed by another major seizure or unless the seizure lasts more than 10 minutes.
10. When the seizure is over, let the student rest if he or she needs to.
11. Inform the student's parents of the seizure.

Absence (Petit Mal) Seizures. Absence seizures are generally short in duration, lasting from 3 to 30 seconds. They are most common in children and can occur between 50 and 200 times a day if untreated. Often a student who experiences absence seizures may be accused of being a daydreamer because he or she loses contact with what is happening in the classroom during the seizure. The student may become pale and may stare into space. The student's eyelids may twitch, or the student may demonstrate slightly jerky movements. After the seizure, the student continues with activities almost as though nothing has happened because he or she is probably not aware of a seizure. Absence seizures have a tendency to disappear before or near puberty but may be replaced by other types.

One of the most significant problems of absence seizure behavior is that it often goes undiagnosed. Teachers can play an important role in identification and should watch for a number of signs that might otherwise elude detection for some time. Repeated occurrences of two or more of the following signs may indicate the presence of this form of epilepsy: (a) head dropping, (b) daydreaming or lack of attentiveness, (c) slight jerky movements of arms or shoulders (ticlike movements), (d) eyes rolling upward or twitching, (e) a seeming inability to hear complete sentences or directions, and (f) dropping things frequently. If any combination of these signs is observed, be certain that the school nurse and the student's parents are contacted to ensure that a proper medical examination is obtained. Once diagnosed, absence seizures are almost always quickly brought under control with medication.

Complex Partial (Psychomotor) Seizures. Complex partial seizures affect not only the motor system but also mental processes. A seizure may last from a few minutes to several hours. Behavior during the seizure varies from person to person, but for any individual, generally the same behavior occurs during each seizure. During a seizure, an individual may chew or smack his or her lips or appear to be confused. In some instances, the individual may carry out purposeless activities, such as rubbing his or her arms or legs. The individual may pick at or take off clothing, or the individual may demonstrate a sudden arrest of activity along with staring. Although this is uncommon, some individuals experience fear, anger, or rage. After the seizure, the individual does not remember what happened and wants to sleep. A teacher who observes any of these behaviors should contact the school nurse and the student's parents.

Educational Implications. All of the three most common types of seizures can cause severe educational problems. Generalized tonic-clonic epilepsy is probably the most serious because of the possibility of bodily injury and because it is so widely misunderstood. Absence seizures can seriously limit a student's achievement because he or she misses the material being covered during a seizure and may be labeled a behavior problem. Although complex partial seizures are relatively uncommon in children, they impose serious limitations on school achievement and adjustment. All three types are serious, and minor modifications and adjustments may be necessary to accommodate a student with any of these conditions.

Special curricular modifications are not necessary for students with epilepsy. Their academic program and materials are the same. Several factors, however, should be considered by teachers. The extent to which a student's seizures are controlled determines the extent to which the following factors and suggestions should be considered. If the seizures have been controlled for several years, it is not necessary to make many special provisions. If the seizures are not well controlled or if epilepsy has only recently been diagnosed, however, many of these factors are important.

1. If a seizure occurs, a teacher may turn the incident into a learning experience for the entire class. Explain what a seizure is, that it is not contagious, and that it is nothing to be afraid of. Teach the class understanding of the student—not pity—so that classmates continue to accept the student as "one of the gang." After the seizure and a short rest, the student can generally carry on routinely. The way in which the teacher and students react to the seizure is very important. Overreaction by the teacher can have a negative effect on the student with epilepsy and on other students in the class. However, if the teacher has prepared and informed the students concerning what to do in the event of a seizure, a potentially traumatic and upsetting experience can be a routine matter.

    There is some controversy concerning whether a student's previous history of seizure behavior should be discussed with the class before a seizure occurs in the class. It is possible that seizure may never occur in class. On the other hand, education about the nature of epilepsy as a part of general education may reduce the stigma and provide information for everyday living.

2. A teacher may want to discuss the condition with the student and the student's parents to obtain more complete information concerning how the student feels about the condition, the extent of seizure control, and any individual aspects that need to be considered.

3. A teacher should not lower the level of expectation or set up protective devices that would single out the student with epilepsy. This attitude must be avoided if the student is to develop a feeling of self-worth and a healthy personality.

4. A teacher should inform special or substitute teachers that there is a student in the class with epilepsy and should record in writing what to do in the event of a seizure.

5. School personnel, including other teachers, should be educated about the nature of epilepsy and procedures to be employed in the event of a seizure.

6. In general, a student with a seizure disorder should participate in school sports or games with as few exceptions as possible. When a physician so indicates, sports that in the past were routinely denied to students with epilepsy, such as football, karate, or boxing, are allowed. Swimming is certainly allowed; however, it is recommended that the student not swim alone. The teacher must consult the parents and physician to determine if there are any activities that must be specifically avoided.

7. A teacher should obtain information from state and national agencies concerned with epilepsy. Free information is available from the Epilepsy Foundation of America.[2] Materials from a national agency such as the Epilepsy Foundation can familiarize the class with procedures to employ in the event of a seizure. Students can be assigned specific responsibilities so that care of the student with epilepsy becomes a routine matter. If the

---

[2]The Epilepsy Foundation of America has a program entitled "School Alert." This program presents a basic educational program for classroom teachers, school nurses, and others in recognizing epilepsy and techniques of management in the school and classroom (Epilepsy Foundation of America, 1828 L St. NW, Washington, DC 20036).

class is prepared for a seizure, it should not be a disturbing experience.

The greatest limitation imposed by epilepsy is not the condition itself but the misinformation, antiquated attitudes, and in many cases, consistent rejection in a society that fears what it does not understand.

Heart Disorders

Nature of Condition. There are two major types of heart disorders in children: congenital and acquired. Congenital heart disease may be the result of maternal rubella (German measles), chromosomal aberrations (such as Down syndrome), or structural abnormalities, including holes in the walls of the heart chambers and problems related to the flow of blood or the valves.

The most common acquired heart disorder in children is caused by rheumatic fever. Permanent heart damage resulting from rheumatic fever is called rheumatic heart disease. Rheumatic fever is brought on by a streptococcal infection, commonly known as strep throat or scarlet fever. This disease can affect many body organs but most commonly affects the valves of the heart. The incidence of heart disorders as a result of rheumatic fever is falling dramatically because of advances made in diagnosis, such as the use of throat cultures to detect strep throat.

Treatment Procedures. Advanced medical technology has significantly decreased the effects of congenital heart disorders. Most congenital heart problems can be corrected surgically, so that students with heart disorders can live normal lives. There are some students, however, who must live with the effects of their condition.

Students with rheumatic fever usually return to normal school activities after a period of hospitalization and home bed rest.

Not all attacks of rheumatic fever result in a heart disorder, but if there is a residual effect, it most often involves the heart. Frequent follow-up medical evaluations for such students are mandatory. Often, such students must receive prophylactic penicillin or other preventive antibiotics indefinitely to prevent a recurrence of strep throat, which might result in rheumatic fever.

Educational Implications. The degree of involvement for students with heart disorders is different in each situation, and therefore, it is difficult to provide specific recommendations for every student. However, some general principles or guidelines should be considered. Probably the most important consideration is close communication between teachers and parents. Parents can provide specific information concerning appropriate expectations and precautions. Health records should also be consulted to obtain more complete information. Occasionally, the records note that a student's heart condition is self-limiting, which means that the student is able to pace himself or herself, and may do so without teacher reminders.

If there is an indication that the student's activity should be limited, the student's physician should give specific information as to which physical activities may or may not be appropriate. Generally, students should not engage in competitive athletics unless their physicians specifically approve. Some students may require a shortened school day combined with home instruction, special rest periods, a modified physical education program, or a special diet. Teachers can help parents avoid overprotectiveness (an understandable reaction on the part of parents) by encouraging the student to participate in as many activities as possible. Good communication and a strong relationship between parents and teachers cannot be overemphasized.

Hemophilia

Nature of Condition. Hemophilia results from a hereditary deficiency in certain coagulation factors within the blood. It rarely occurs in girls. It is transmitted from mother to son in a sex-linked, passive pattern. It is generally recognized in boys in the first 3 or 4 years of life, when they seem to bruise easily, bleed easily from minor cuts and scrapes, or bleed in the joints or during surgery. There may also be bleeding under the skin without a cut or scrape, which destroys surrounding tissues. If the bleeding occurs in the joints, it eventually causes immobility through destruction of the lining of the joint, and it may result in permanent degeneration of the joints.

Treatment Procedures. In the early years of care for hemophiliacs, massive and frequent transfusions of whole blood were routinely provided. Today, because of advanced medical technology and the isolation of the clotting factor, a treatment for controlling and preventing the bleeding tendency is available. Home therapy programs, in which parents and children are taught intravenous self-administration to replace the deficient blood factor, are now widely practiced. Parents are also taught to recognize the early signs of bleeding, and children with hemophilia may be placed on a prophylactic program. Administration of the blood factor two or three times a week has significantly contributed to positive benefits for hemophiliacs.

Educational Implications. As with other health impairments, the key to successful programming is close communication among teachers, parents, and medical personnel. Students and their teachers must be aware of limitations in activity. Naturally, a student with hemophilia should not be involved with any contact sports, but he or she should be encouraged to participate in other activities that allow exercise of joints. The student should maintain good exercise and health practices. Swimming is an ideal, non-weight-bearing activity that can provide daily exercise.

Although home therapy programs have dramatically reduced frequent absences from school, absences must still be anticipated. School adjustment for students with hemophilia can be difficult. Frequent attacks can cause discontinuity of programming, changes in physical ability and interests, and fear of injury associated with the active games of boys. Hemophiliac students who want to participate in active games but realize the consequences of injury may withdraw, become self-protective, and shy. Some adolescent boys rebel against an overprotected life-style by indulging in alcohol or drug abuse, which can adversely affect medication. Students with hemophilia need considerable emotional support and understanding. A great deal of this support can be provided by informed and empathetic teachers.

Human Immunodeficiency Virus

Nature of Condition. Human immunodeficiency virus (HIV) is a condition wherein a microscopic-sized virus, introduced into the body, attaches itself to helper T cells, which are the coordinators of the body's immune system. Inserting itself into the chromosomes of the cells, the virus directs the cells to produce more viruses. The invaded cells swell and die, releasing many new viruses to continue the attack on other helper T cells. As this process repeats itself, the body's immune system is unable to fight off diseases as a healthy body can do. Various diseases then invade the body, producing a variety of symptoms, each of which makes the individual more ill. Persons infected with HIV are diagnosed as having acquired immune deficiency syndrome (AIDS) if they develop conditions such as Kaposi's sarcoma (a form of cancer), pneumocystis carinii, pneumonia, or other serious diseases. An individual may be infected with HIV for years before developing AIDS, which indicates the latter stages of HIV.

HIV can be spread through sexual intercourse, sharing contaminated needles, and exchange of infected blood. Some infected mothers infect their infants prior to or after birth (through breast milk). HIV cannot be spread through casual contact, such as handshaking, eating food prepared by an infected person, swimming in pools, drinking from fountains, sitting on toilet seats, or handling doorknobs. Students infected with HIV or AIDS are clearly included under the Rules and Regulations of PL 94–142 and an individualized education program must be designed to meet the needs of the student and updated in accordance with the annual review process or as warranted by the condition of the student. Particular care must be taken with regard to confidentiality (Fraser, 1989).

Educational Implications. Students infected with HIV may not require any modifications in expectations or assignments. Should the student develop AIDS, modifications related to the needs of the student may be required, depending on the complications relating to the conditions that develop. Then, students may have frequent absences or need less fatiguing activities.

The procedures for attending to body fluids of persons infected with HIV are not different from those of persons not infected. Teachers and other school personnel must exercise care in maintaining a healthy environment for all who are in school. Body fluids, such as saliva, nasal discharge, urine, blood, and vomit, can transmit a wide variety of infections, such as colds, hepatitis A, and flu, and should be cleaned up following accepted practices. Procedures for cleaning up any body fluids should be in place in the school and include disinfection of mops, brooms, dust pans, rugs, pails, floors, and disposal of infected towels and bandages. The same procedures should apply if a student who is infected with HIV attends the school.

According to the Centers for Disease Control (1989), all school personnel should be trained in preventing the spread of all infectious diseases. The centers suggest that the routine cuts and scrapes, which usually occur in schools, pose little problem and students can be encouraged to wash and bandage their own minor injuries. In case of larger amounts of body fluid, some barrier should be placed between the skin of a person who is in contact and the fluids, as plastic gloves or a thick layer of paper towels. Materials used in cleanup should be disposed of in plastic bags. Clothing and other nondisposable items that have fluids on them should be removed and placed in plastic bags until they can be washed in hot, soapy water. If direct contact with the skin has occurred, the skin areas should be washed. Every school should have liquid soap in dispensers, paper towels, and covered waste receptacles with disposable plastic liners in all bathrooms or classrooms in which there is a sink. Procedures for washing hands are:

1. Wet hands with warm running water.
2. Apply liquid soap and water.
3. Wash hands using a circular motion and friction for 30 seconds, including around the nails, between the fingers, and the wrist.

FIGURE 8–5
The Council for Exceptional Children's policy statement on managing communicable and contagious diseases

Controlling the spread of communicable and contagious diseases within the schools has always been a problem faced by educators, the medical profession, and the public. Effective policies and procedures for managing such diseases in the schools have historically been developed by health agencies and implemented by the schools. These policies and procedures were primarily designed to manage acute, temporary conditions rather than chronic conditions which require continuous monitoring and remove children from interaction with other children while the condition is contagious or communicable.

The increased prevalence of chronic communicable diseases such as hepatitis B, cytomegalovirus, herpes simplex virus, and acquired immune deficiency syndrome have raised public and professional concern, necessitating the reassessment of existing school policies and procedures. The Council believes that having a communicable/contagious disease does not in itself result in a need for special education. Further, the Council believes that in developing appropriate policies for managing communicable diseases, schools and public health agencies should assure that any such policies and procedures:

a. Do not exclude the affected child from the receipt of an appropriate education even when circumstances require the temporary removal of the child from contact with other children.

b. Provide that determination of a nontemporary alteration of a child's educational placement should be done on an individual basis, utilizing an interdisciplinary/interagency approach including the child's physician, public health personnel, the child's parents, and appropriate educational personnel.

c. Provide that decision involving exceptional children's nontemporary alterations of educational placements or services constitute a change in the child's Individualized Education Program and should thus follow the procedures and protections required.

d. Recognize that children vary in the degree and manner in which they come into contact with other children and school staff.

e. Provide education staff with the necessary information, training, and hygienic resources to provide for a safe environment for students and educational staff.

f. Provide students with appropriate education about communicable diseases and hygienic measures to prevent the spread of such diseases.

4. Rinse hands well under warm running water.
5. Repeat steps 2 through 4.
6. Wipe the surfaces around the sink with a paper towel, and discard the towel.
7. Repeat step 4.
8. Dry hands and dispose of the towel.
9. Apply lotion (lotion prevents chapping and serves as a barrier to infections).

Procedures to prevent the spread of infectious diseases should be practiced in all schools, whether or not a student with HIV is enrolled (see Figure 8–5). However, more critical for the inclusion and well-being of a student with HIV is the support of teachers and students.

Students with HIV, AIDS, or AIDS-related conditions may require alterations in

g. Provide, where appropriate, carrier children with education about the additional control measures that they can practice to prevent the transmission of the disease.

h. Enable educational personnel who are medically at high risk in regard to certain diseases to work in environments which minimize such risk.

i. Provide educational personnel with adequate protections for such personnel and their families if they are exposed to such diseases through their employment.

The Council believes that special education personnel preparation programs should:

a. Educate students about communicable and contagious diseases and appropriate methods for their management.

b. Counsel students as to how to determine their level of medical risk in relation to certain diseases and the implications of such risk to career choice.

The Council believes that the manner in which policies for managing communicable and contagious diseases are developed and disseminated is critically important to their effective implementation. Therefore, the following must be considered integral to any such process:

a. That they be developed through the collaborative efforts of health and education agencies at the state, provincial, and local levels, reflecting state, provincial, and local educational, health, and legal requirements.

b. That provision is made for frequent review and revision to reflect the ever-increasing knowledge being produced through research, case data reports, and experience.

c. That policies developed be based on reliable identified sources of information and principles endorsed by the medical and educational professions.

d. That such policies be written in content and format to be understandable to a variety of consumers including students, professionals, and the public.

e. That policy development and dissemination be a continual process and disassociated from pressure associated with precipitating events.

Note: From *Policies Manual* (p. 13) by Council for Exceptional Children, 1989, Reston, VA: Council for Exceptional Children. Copyright 1989 by Council for Exceptional Children. Reprinted by permission.

nutrition, physical activity, or intake of fluids due to physiological changes resulting from the condition. Such students may also have feelings of powerlessness due to the condition or experience family disturbances because of the disease. Students may also experience fear or diminished self-concept because they have a terminal disease. There may be a grieving process related to the loss of good health or a knowledge deficit regarding what HIV is, what AIDS is, the risk of transmission, or how HIV was aquired. If so, the students need strong acceptance from teachers and other students and reassurance, education regarding the illness, encouragement to maintain independence as far as possible, and self-management to maintain or build self-esteem.

Sickle-Cell Anemia

Nature of Condition. Sickle-cell anemia is an inherited disorder characterized by sickle-shaped red blood cells. The irregularly shaped blood cells become blocked in blood vessels. Blockage may result in decreased blood supply to some tissues, causing pain in the arms, legs, and abdomen. In addition to severe pain, effects are swollen joints, fatigue, and dehydration. This hereditary disorder is more prevalent among the black population.

The condition is characterized by periods of remission and periods of crisis that involve pain. Children under the age of 10 may have as many as 8 to 10 crises a year, with the number decreasing during adulthood (Kleinberg, 1982). Life expectancy for individuals with sickle-cell anemia is shortened—with an average mortality age of 40.

Treatment Procedures. Treatment during periods of crisis involves bed rest, antibiotics to prevent infections, pain relievers, and high fluid intake. During a serious crisis, blood transfusions may be necessary.

Educational Implications. Although learning problems are not associated with sickle-cell anemia, frequent absence from school may result in significant educational delay. Students who have sickle-cell anemia require frequent hospitalization and extensive convalescence. Close communication among the parents, hospital teachers, homebound teachers, and regular teachers is essential to reduce serious educational gaps and delays that may result. Special consideration must also be given to the concomitant psychosocial problems that result from absences, growth problems (such students may be smaller than age mates and puberty may be delayed), and the conflict between overprotection and independence.

Students with sickle-cell anemia should be allowed to participate in physical education classes and other motor activities unless the physician recommends otherwise. Lack of physical stamina prohibits such students from participation in most athletic events; therefore, such students should be encouraged to participate in activities that do not require physical activity. Teachers should be aware that sickle-cell anemia causes a need for frequent urination, and students with sickle-cell anemia should be allowed to go to the restroom as necessary. Teachers should also be watchful for changes in vision and should educate themselves as much as possible about this condition.

As with any chronic health impairment, it is essential that teachers be aware of the social limitations imposed by the condition and provide the necessary support to students and their parents. Close communication among parents, teachers, and medical personnel is of the utmost importance.

MEDICATION IN SCHOOLS

Often, students with health impairments must take medication as part of the treatment. For example, students with cerebral palsy may take Lioresal or Dantrium to relieve some of the spasticity associated with cerebral palsy or students with a seizure disorder may take Dilantin or phenobarbital to control the seizures. Sometimes, students with spina bifida experience bladder problems that result in urinary tract infections, and they take either antibiotics, acidifying agents, or anticholinergic medications or a combination of them. However, most medications have some side effects, such as dizziness, fatigue, lethargy, vomiting, or lack of appetite. Teachers must be aware of and monitor students for the presence of such side effects.

Few states have legislation or formal regulations regarding the administration of prescribed drugs in schools. The American Academy of Pediatrics (AAP) Committee on School Health has published guidelines for the administration of medication in school (1984). They may be summarized:

1. A physician must provide written orders, including the name of the drug, dosage, how often it is to be taken, why it is needed, and the approximate termination date.
2. The parents must request, in writing, that school personnel administer the medication according to the physician's instructions.
3. The medication for use in school must be in a container labeled by a pharmacist.
4. If a student is able to take the medication independently, he or she should be encouraged to do so with the written permission of the parents and physician.
5. If the medication is administered by school personnel, proper authorization must be obtained, the medications stored in a locked space, and a record kept (date, time of day, and individual who administered).

Forms that address the authorizations necessary and that are to be used to keep records in school may be developed if the school does not have them.

In order to avoid legal risks, teachers, principals, and school nurses should work together to ensure adherence to the recommendations of the AAP. The Committee on School Health of the AAP suggests that as school districts develop policies regarding the administration of prescribed medication, they seek the advice of an attorney and that they provide liability coverage for all staff members.

SPECIAL EQUIPMENT

Students who have orthopedic or health impairments may require special equipment, classroom aids, and adaptations in order to participate fully in classroom activities. The modifications necessary depend on the age of the student, the severity of the impairment, and the primary use of the classroom. Young students may need more specialized equipment, since they have not yet developed daily living skills or modes of ambulation. They may also require more assistance in the care of crutches, braces, or wheelchairs. The severity of the condition usually dictates the specialized equipment necessary, and the purpose of the classroom usually dictates the need for modifications. For example, if students are expected to move about frequently, as in a biology lab, modifications with regard to mobility may be necessary. However, if the classroom is used primarily for lecture and the students listen and take notes, minimal accommodations are necessary. The following sections describe the care and maintence of braces, crutches, and wheelchairs; specialized furniture and equipment; and classroom aids.

Braces, Crutches, and Wheelchairs

Many students with cerebral palsy, spina bifida, muscular dystrophy, and other orthopedic impairments need braces, crutches, or wheelchairs. Therefore, regular teachers should be acquainted with the purpose, care, and maintenance of this equipment. Braces are classified into three general types: (a) corrective, (b) control, and (c) supportive.

Corrective braces are used for prevention and correction of a deformity during a student's rapid growth. Often, during this period, the tendons (cords that attach muscles to bones) do not keep pace with the growth of the long bones. When this happens, the heel cords may tighten, and surgery may be required to lengthen them to keep up with the long-bone growth. Corrective braces may prevent or delay surgery. Control braces are used to prevent or eliminate purposeless movements of the type found in athetoid cerebral palsy or to allow movement in only one or two desired directions. Support braces are used to provide support for children who need assistance in standing. Often, students in a wheelchair do not have adequate muscle strength or control to support themselves. In this instance, a body brace may be used to support the spine and prevent serious scoliosis. Some students wear braces for only a short time, whereas others need them for many years and perhaps for their entire lives.

It is not the primary responsibility of regular classroom teachers to maintain this equipment. Teachers are assisted by therapists, resource or itinerant teachers, and the parents. However, classroom teachers may have more contact with students than the others do and may be able to spot-check equipment periodically. For example, teachers should be watchful for torn or worn leather pieces and should check to see that a brace is not rubbing against the body and causing pressure sores to develop. Teachers may also want to check periodically for loose or missing screws and the general condition of buckles, locks, and joints.

Crutches are used to stabilize the trunk and to provide support while standing and walking. Generally, crutches do not call for much care or maintenance, but they should be checked periodically for loose screws, worn rubber tips, and proper height adjustments.

Wheelchairs may be either manual or electric. Electric wheelchairs are powered by battery packs, which allow them to be operated by hand, mouth, chin, or breath. Wheelchairs are most commonly used by students who have severe crippling conditions, but some students who attend regular classes need a wheelchair for part or all of the school day because of slowness, fatigue, or lack of independent travel skill. Wheelchairs must be checked periodically for worn or broken parts, and teachers should be aware of posture, fit, and comfort. If a teacher notices any equipment in need of repair, a therapist, resource teacher, consultant, or parents should be notified immediately.

Specialized Classroom Furniture

Students in wheelchairs often need an adapted writing or work area (Figure 8–6). Tables that can be raised or lowered to different heights permit flexibility. A table with a pedestal base allows greater maneuverability and freedom than does a table with legs. Cutout desk tops attached to existing surfaces or portable lapboards are also beneficial. Traditional classroom arrangements of rows of desks are generally inconvenient unless some provision is made for wider aisles.

FIGURE 8–6

A cutout lapboard or desk top that may be fitted over wheelchairs to provide a work area

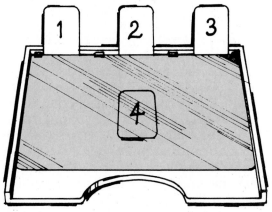

Chalkboards and bulletin boards may be lowered to be more accessible to students in wheelchairs. Relocating classroom items such as coat hooks, alarms, light switches, some doorknobs, plumbing fixtures, and pencil sharpeners may be advisable in some situations. The practicality of these modifications should be considered in view of cost and necessity.

Many schools built recently follow designs that incorporate modifications to reduce barriers for students who have disabilities. Modifications incorporated include:

1. Floors with nonskid surfaces, such as carpeting
2. Doors with automatic door checks that allow them to remain open for wheelchairs and crutch walkers (at the very least, doors should have a grasping bar rather than doorknobs)
3. Lowered chalkboards (about 24 inches from the floor)
4. Classrooms with two doors, one near the front and another near the back
5. Sinks accessible from three sides
6. Faucets that self-close
7. Toilet facilities near classrooms
8. Facilities for students who need additional rest
9. Sliding doors on storage spaces
10. A variety of equipment, such as standing tables, adjustable seats, and adjustable desks

Such modifications are not prerequisites for successful mainstreaming of students who are orthopedically impaired, but they may facilitate accessibility. When exit plans for fire drills or other emergencies are developed, care should be taken to make certain that students in wheelchairs or using crutches or braces are not left unattended or without assistance (if necessary).

Communication Devices

Some students who possess average or above-average intellectual ability and are otherwise capable of attending regular classrooms may not have the necessary communication skills to do well in regular classes. For example, many students with cerebral palsy have well-developed recep-

FIGURE 8–7
A student with cerebral palsy using a head pointer and communication board

FIGURE 8–8
AutoCom

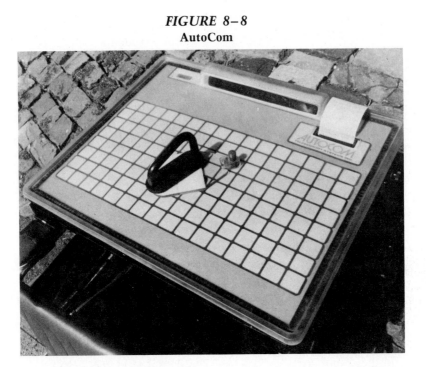

Note: AutoCom is a portable, microprocessor-based communication system operated by moving a magnetic handpiece across the surface of the board to make word, phrase, or sentence selections that may be read on a display or printout.

tive language skills but lack the fine-motor coordination needed to express themselves using writing or typewriting. Other students may have speech impairment severe enough to seriously limit their functional oral language. In years past, these students were often relegated to educational programs that seriously limited their academic, social, and emotional growth. Today, because of technological advances and alternative communication systems and devices, students with severe motor or communication problems can participate to a much greater extent in regular classrooms.

There are many different types of communication systems, ranging from direct-selection communication boards with the letters of the alphabet to highly sophisti- cated microcomputers. Communication boards are commonly used to help nonverbal students express themselves and answer questions (Figure 8–7). When using a manual communication board, a student points to numbers, letters, words, or phrases. Other boards employ a scanning procedure, in which a student moves a light to indicate the word selected. Boards may require changes as students develop new vocabulary or pursue new areas of study.

Electronic communication boards are available from several sources. AutoCom[3] displays students' comments and responses

---

[3]Prentke Romich Co, 8769 Township Road, #513, Shreve, OH 44676.

FIGURE 8–9
Two models of Phonic Ear HandiVoice

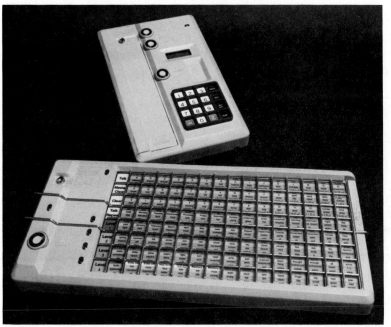

Note: Phonic Ear HandiVoice is a portable electronic voice synthesizer that enables individuals who are nonvocal to communicate.

on a television screen, enabling teachers to include the students in classroom discussions (Figure 8–8). HandiVoice[4] provides a voice output from a self-contained vocabulary of over 400 words (Figure 8–9). Express[5] is a microprocessor-based communication aid offering meaningful written and optional speech output. Entire thoughts may be programmed into its memory with a single or minimal number of selections. These are only a few examples from the array of devices available. It is exciting to think about

technological advances that greatly enhance the communication process for individuals with expressive or upper-extremity motor control difficulties.

Classroom Aids

Because of difficulty with movement, students who have orthopedic impairments may use a number of learning aids not typically found in regular classrooms. The aids may be very simple modifications, such as clay-wrapped pencils to assist with grasping and holding, four-fingered scissors, or clipboards or elastic tape to hold paper on writing surfaces. Page turners are useful for students with limited arm use; wrist or hand weights may assist students who have limited control. Teaching machines such as

[4]Phonic Ear, Inc., 250 Camino Alto, Mill Valley, CA 94941.

[5]Prentke Romich Co., 8769 Township Road, #513, Shreve, OH 44676.

magnetic-card machines are often used if they do not require complex motor movements. Conventional and modified typewriters are used extensively. Students who have difficulty with movement may use head wands to strike the keys. With light-operated typewriting machines, students use a light source fixed to the hand or head to project a light spot on the control panel.

Talking books, previously available for the blind only, are now available for individuals with impairments that prevent them from handling books comfortably. Talking books and talking book machines are distributed by the Library of Congress at no cost to the users.

Resource or itinerant specialists in consultation with physical and occupational therapists may recommend other ways to modify materials. They can observe the stu-

dents in regular classrooms and offer suggestions of ways to modify and adapt equipment and materials. Part of their responsibility is to keep abreast of new materials and equipment and share their recommendations with regular teachers.

ADAPTING PHYSICAL EDUCATION

Students with a crippling condition or health impairment can often successfully participate in nearly all curricular areas; however, one area that presents special problems is physical education. Physical educators who have had experience or special preparation in this area often adjust easily to accommodate such students. Physical educators who have not had experience or preparation in this area may have special

Physical education is important for all students.

problems adjusting to students with limited ambulation or health impairment. As mentioned, activity is essential for students who have disabilities, perhaps even more so than for nondisabled students, because nondisabled students routinely get the necessary activity, whereas students with physical problems may be overprotected and not afforded opportunities to be active. In general, physical education activities can be adapted in at least four ways to allow greater participation for students who have disabilities:

1. Change the way all students participate.
2. Change the way one player of each team participates.
3. Modify the equipment.
4. Make special allowances for students who have disabilities.

The following suggestions are not intended as comprehensive or a detailed program but should be considered when attempting to modify or adapt programs for students with crippling conditions or health impairments:

1. Consider minor rule modifications of games or contests.
2. Ask the students how to adapt a game or activity. Some physical educators have had considerable success in asking the students to identify ways to modify or adapt an activity.
3. Schedule opportunities for rest. Fatigue may be a factor for students who have disabilities. The number of points required to win a game can be reduced, quarters may be shortened, or distances may be reduced.
4. Use larger balls and pieces of equipment, use lighter balls and racquets, or lower baskets.
5. Use more players on a team, reducing

the individual responsibility and activity.
6. Change the way the entire class plays a game—all players on knees, sitting on the floor, using only one hand, or using scooter boards.
7. Have one person on each team assume a functional disability—using a wheelchair, crutches, or brace.
8. Create a special role for the student who has a disability and one other student on the other team, such as to hand out a baton at the end of a relay or catch a basketball after a goal is made and return it to the shooter.
9. Plan a backup activity in the event that the primary activity does not work.
10. Use as many activities as possible that the student with disabilities can do.

We are not advocating that activities be modified every day; daily modification may not provide the activity needed by nondisabled students. We are suggesting, however, that attempts be made to meet the needs of *all* students.

Participation in a regular physical education program can have many benefits and should be encouraged as much as possible. Regular physical education, however, should not preclude physical therapy provided by a physical therapist or individualized or adapted physical education provided by a specialist. Regular physical educators are also strongly encouraged to consult with adaptive specialists, special education resources, or itinerant teachers for additional suggestions.

RESOURCES OUTSIDE SCHOOLS

The families of students with orthopedic or chronic health impairments may need financial assistance, medical services, or social support systems. While it is not the role of classroom teachers to become or take the place of social workers or counselors, it may be helpful for classroom teachers to provide parents with information regarding services available to them. Teachers often have considerable contact with the parents and therefore know about their particular needs. Unusual financial needs may relate to costs of continued treatment, equipment, or transportation. In addition, families may need information regarding medical management of specific conditions. Social support systems address the issues of counseling, support groups, and recreational opportunities. Prior to contacting any source for assistance, teachers should be sure the family needs the assistance and that *the family is willing to use the resource.*

Resources available to assist families may be at the local, regional, state, or national level. Usually, it is best to begin at the local level; however, the resources may not be available locally, so regional, state, and national resources must often be contacted. Local resources for financial aid include various clubs, such as Lions, Rotary, and VFW; church groups; and businesses. Regional sources (a county or counties) include farm bureaus, clubs such as the Masons, and foundations. State and national resources include Shriners' hospitals, Services for Children with Handicaps, the March of Dimes, the Arthritis Association, and the National Kidney Association.

Resources for medical care at the local level include physicians, nurses, hospitals, and school health services. Regional resources include clinics, specialists, and community (usually county) health services. State and national resources include children's hospitals, university hospitals, and special-purpose clinics.

Social support groups at the local level

may include counselors, clergy, church groups, and social service groups such as the Boy or Girl Scouts and Boy's or Girl's Clubs. Many national groups have local chapters that can provide information about local support groups. Regional sources that provide support or information include mental health centers, county social services, and specialty camps. State or national organizations that provide support or information include United Cerebral Palsy, the Easter Seal Society, and the Association for the Aid of Crippled Children. (See Appendix B for a list of national organizations.) School nurses, public health nurses, referral agencies, clearinghouses, consultants, and social workers are other sources that can provide information about additional resources in a particular locality.

Resources such as those just described can also provide information to teachers about specific conditions and recommended practices. Although this text addresses many of the conditions students may experience, it is not all inclusive. It is the responsibility of professional teachers to continue to gain insights and information regarding the students who are in their classrooms.

SUMMARY

Students whose special needs were described in this chapter do not fit a classification in the same sense as those with hearing impairment or mental retardation. They were grouped together because many of them require medical supervision, adapted physical education, and the service of physical or occupational therapists. The following orthopedic impairments were considered: amputation, arthritis, cerebral palsy, spina bifida, muscular dystrophy, scoliosis, hip disorders, and osteogenesis imperfecta. Allergies, asthma, conditions resulting from maternal substance abuse, cystic fibrosis, diabetes, epilepsy, heart disorders, hemophilia, human immunodeficiency virus, and sickle-cell anemia were also discussed. Guidelines for administering medication in school and for managing communicable diseases were provided, along with general information about the maintenance of crutches, braces, and wheelchairs and information about adapting physical education.

- What is adaptive behavior? Why is it essential in consideration of mental retardation? Why is it difficult to measure?

- How can one differentiate between academic retardation without mental retardation and academic retardation associated with mental retardation?

- How do individuals with mental retardation differ from their peers who have normal mental abilities with respect to memory abilities and deficits?

- What can be done to correct or adjust for the potential bias in tests of intelligence?

- How does career education differ from vocational education? Why is it essential for students with mental retardation?

- Which environmental influences may have the greatest negative effects on intellectual development?

- How might a referral for suspected mental retardation lead to a permanent negative result? How can educators minimize the chance that this will occur?

C H A P T E R   9

TEACHING STUDENTS
WITH MENTAL
RETARDATION

ACROSS THE CENTURIES, PERSONS WITH MENTAL retardation have been sometimes feared, sometimes considered fools (even used as court jesters), and almost always misunderstood. Their treatment has been related to the perceptions of various societies and historic times. However, starting in the 18th century, more persistent efforts were made to understand mental retardation and more scientific methods were devoted to its study. Historically, individuals called mentally retarded (fools, mo-rons, imbeciles, or idiots) were primarily those recognized today as persons with severe or profound mental retardation, plus some persons with moderate mental retardation. Those called mildly mentally retarded were not considered part of this group. Have the historic misconceptions been laid to rest? What is known about mental retardation? Who is mentally retarded? Is it possible to determine the true potential of individuals with retardation? How can they be educated?

Many students with mild mental retardation disappear into the mainstream of adult society after completion of their formal education. When appropriate programs are provided, the percentage who become self-supporting, responsible citizens increases, and all of society benefits. As for those with moderate mental retardation, truly normal participation in society is unlikely, but many can become partially self-supporting. However, this goal can be achieved only if society provides the right opportunities during their formative year and monitors their work and living environments during their adult years. Note, too, that some students who were thought to be moderately retarded perform at higher levels than was earlier believed possible.

Since the early 1970s, there have been many changes in the ways in which indi-viduals with mental retardation have been educated. Before that time, most of the children with mild mental retardation were in separate special classes in the public schools, and many of the children who were moderately retarded or had severe/profound retardation were housed and educated, to some extent, in large residential facilities. Today, with many of the residential facilities closed and large numbers of individuals deinstitutionalized, more individuals with greater degrees of mental retardation are in local communities. Many of the separate special classes for children with mild mental retardation have been abandoned in favor of more integrated settings.

The main reason for abandoning most special class programs for students with mental retardation was that investigators could not prove that separate special classes were superior to regular classes (L. Dunn, 1968; Goldstein, Moss, & Jordan, 1965). Along with concerns about stigma and social development, this lack of proof concerning special classes played a significant role in the advent of mainstreaming. On the other hand, research evidence favoring placement in regular classes (indicating, for example, higher academic achievement or better social adjustment) is not clear-cut. Semmel, Gottlieb, and Robinson (1979) reviewed the research on this topic and found few, if any, meaningful differences. *We conclude that while all of the necessary evidence may not be available, at this point, many of the daily educational programs for students classified as mildly mentally retarded and some of the daily educational programs for individuals classified as moderately and severely mentally retarded can be provided in regular classrooms.*

A DEFINITION OF MENTAL RETARDATION

Mental retardation has been defined by various individuals and groups, for a variety of purposes, but in the schools, until the mid-1970s, students were commonly identified as mentally retarded based on IQ scores. There is little doubt that IQ-only identification led to inaccurate classification in some cases. In 1973, the American Association on Mental Deficiency (AAMD), now the American Association on Mental Retardation (AAMR), provided the following definition: "*Mental retardation* refers to significantly subaverage general intellectual functioning existing concurrently with deficits in adaptive behavior and manifested during the developmental period" (Grossman, 1973, p. 5).

This definition, developed and accepted by the AAMD, was reaffirmed in the AAMD's seventh manual on classification

(Grossman, 1977) and again in its *Classification in Mental Retardation* (Grossman, 1983). The AAMD/AAMR definition, supported by PL 94–142 and its accompanying regulations, requires substantial agreement between at least two measures before a diagnosis of mental retardation may be made. In the presently accepted AAMR guidelines, significantly subaverage intellectual functioning is suggested to be approximately 70 IQ or below. The 1983 manual notes that considering the IQ with some flexibility permits the provision of special education programs for persons with IQs higher than 70 in unusual circumstances. It is important to note that both the results of an IQ test and corroborating evidence on a measure of adaptive behavior are necessary for the diagnosis of mental retardation. If either indicates a higher level of functioning, the student may not be considered mentally retarded. In addition, the subaverage intellectual ability and adaptive behavior deficits must be manifested during the developmental periods.

A conceptual definition of mental retardation may be inferred from the cognitive developmental theories of Jean Piaget. Piaget, whose work has profoundly influenced education, provides a way to view the cognitive development of children that may be applied to individuals with mental retardation.

Inhelder (1968) interpreted Piaget's theories and their implications for individuals identified as mentally retarded and provided comparisons between Piaget's stages and three levels of retardation, plus a fourth level that Inhelder called borderline intelligence (see Table 9–1). Inhelder suggested that persons who have borderline intelligence do not attain the stage of formal operations, and persons with mild retardation do not usually reach the stage of concrete operations until midadolescence. This con-

TABLE 9–1
Mental retardation and Piaget's stages of childhood development

Levels of Retardation	Piaget's Stages
Borderline intelligence	Formal operations
Mild mental retardation	Concrete operations
Moderate mental retardation	Preoperational thought
Severe mental retardation	Sensorimotor

cept is valuable in planning educational programs for students with mental retardation, but it is not well suited to classification in mental retardation as required by most state regulations for eligibility for special education services.

Mental age (MA) is one term associated with the concept of IQ. It is used to varying degrees among educators and psychologists. The term became popular with the intelligence testing movement early in the 20th century and is still used to some extent. Mental age is a measure intended to indicate an individual's mental ability. It is expressed in terms of the average chronological age (CA) of others who answered correctly the same number of items on a test of mental ability. Thus, a student with a mental age of 12 would theoretically be able to answer correctly the same number of questions on a test of mental ability as the majority of 12-year-old students.

Mental age was originally associated almost exclusively with the formula that was part of the original concept of IQ, that is, MA/CA × 100 = IQ. Today, MA data, when used, may be derived in a variety of ways, depending on the test(s) used. But however used, mental age refers to pre-

dicted ability to correctly respond to items on a test purporting to measure mental ability.

Classification—Levels of Mental Retardation

When a student is classified as learning disabled or behaviorally disordered, there may be some indication of severity of disability, but there is no nationally recognized designation for level of disability. In the case of mental retardation, level (severity) is part of the classification, and two systems pertinent to educators are recognized nationally. Grossman's AAMD manual, *Classification in Mental Retardation* (1983) suggests levels and IQ ranges for classification purposes. Although the labeling of mental retardation requires the establishment of subaverage intellectual functioning (low IQ) and deficits in adaptive behavior existing concurrently, levels of mental retardation are almost always given in terms of IQ alone. The levels suggested by Grossman are given in Table 9–2.

Another system is often used by school districts. According to Polloway, Patton, Payne, and Payne (1989), these guidelines ordinarily specify three levels—educable, trainable, and severe/profound. Although there are no national guidelines for levels of mental retardation (each state may establish its own) our experience suggests the

TABLE 9–2
Levels of mental retardation and IQ (first system)

Level of Handicap	IQ
Mild	50–55 to 70
Moderate	35–40 to 50–55
Severe	20–25 to 35–40
Profound	Below 20–25

ranges in Table 9–3, with more national variation in the educable range guidelines than in the others.

For many years, public schools used guidelines and regulations allowing any student who scored below some specific IQ level on an individual test of intelligence to be eligible for a program for individuals with mental retardation. The two most commonly used tests were the Stanford-Binet (Terman & Merrill, 1973) and the Wechsler Intelligence scales (WISC–R) (Wechsler, 1974). In most states, parents were consulted, or at least informed before the tests were given, but in some cases, they were neither consulted nor informed. Now, both federal and state regulations require that parents or guardians give permission before individual testing can be initiated.

Until the mid-1970s, the most common upper limit for placement in a program for students with mental retardation was an IQ below 75 or 80. A few states even had an upper limit of 85. Some states included in guidelines a mention of evaluation of adaptive behavior (the way an individual functions in social settings, also sometimes called street behavior), but before the mid-1970s, this was an exception rather than the rule. PL 94–142 and its accompanying regulations required at least two measures for a diagnosis of mental retardation: (a) re-

sults of an individual IQ test and (b) corroborating evidence on a measure of adaptive behavior. In addition, school functioning in both academic and social areas should confirm these measures.

Adaptive Behavior

Although there are various concerns about the validity and reliability of tests of intelligence, level of adaptive behavior is even more difficult to determine, and measures of adaptive behavior are much less precise. Most public school students who are classified as mentally retarded have been referred for further evaluation due to significant problems in academic areas. The various intelligence tests and the IQ scores that they generate correlate highly with academic performance and apparent ability to perform academically. But what about social ability and behavior? What about practical, daily living skills? The AAMR refers to "personal independence and social responsibility" when discussing adaptive behavior.

Chinn, Drew, and Logan (1979) discuss differing adaptive behavior expectations for various age levels, reminding educators that deficits in adaptive behavior vary by age. Their list of areas of deficits by developmental stages, derived from the AAMD/AAMR classification system, includes the following:

1. Deficits during infancy and early childhood
   a. Sensory and motor skills
   b. Speech and language
   c. Self-help skills
   d. Socialization
2. Deficits during childhood and early adolescence
   a. Basic academic skills when applied in practical, daily activities
   b. Reasoning and judgment when applied in everyday activities

TABLE 9–3
Levels of mental retardation and IQ
(second system)

Level of Handicap	IQ
Educable (EMR or EMH)	50–55 to 70–75
Trainable (TMR)	25–30 to 50–55
Severe/profound	Below 25–30

  c. Social skills in group activities and in-
     terpersonal relationships
3. Deficits during late adolescence and
   adult life
  a. Vocational ability
  b. General social skills (both group and
     interpersonal)

Perhaps the most widely recognized measure of adaptive behavior is that developed
by the American Association on Mental
Deficiency (AAMD) and revised as a public
school version in 1981. This Adaptive Behavior Scale–School Edition (ABS–SE) includes the domains and subdomains shown
in Figure 9–1.

Patton, Beirne-Smith, and Payne (1990)
provide an excellent discussion of the
AAMD scale and several others. They also
provide a valuable review of major issues
relating to the use of adaptive behavior
measures in the identification and placement of students in programs for individuals with mental retardation. They conclude
that "although mandated by professional
guidelines and by law, the use of adaptive
behavior as a criterion for determining
mental retardation is clouded by confusion"
(p. 116).

What then, may educators conclude
about adaptive behavior and its importance
as a concept in mental retardation? Polloway et al. (1985) note a historical emphasis
on social concerns in both defining and understanding mental retardation. However,
they say, "throughout the middle of the
20th century the emphasis moved toward
intellectual and academic factors. The increased reliance on intelligence in defining
retardation is an example of how the initial
concept of social incompetence was replaced by one of intellectual subnormality"
(p. 365). They do not suggest a shift to some
exclusive personal-social focus but remind
teachers that "a total emphasis on academ-

FIGURE 9–1
Adaptive Behavior Scale–School Edition
(ABS–SE)

Domain 1. Independent functioning
  Eating
  Toilet use
  Cleanliness
  Appearance
  Care of clothing
  Dressing and undressing
  Travel
  Other independent functioning
Domain 2. Physical development
  Sensory development
  Motor development
Domain 3. Economic activity
  Money handling and budgeting
  Shopping skills
Domain 4. Language development
  Expression
  Comprehension
  Social language development
Domain 5. Numbers and time
Domain 6. Prevocational activity
Domain 7. Self-direction
  Initiative
  Perseverance
  Leisure time
Domain 8. Responsibility
Domain 9. Socialization
Domain 10. Aggressiveness
Domain 11. Antisocial vs. social behavior
Domain 12. Rebelliousness
Domain 13. Trustworthiness
Domain 14. Withdrawal vs. involvement
Domain 15. Mannerisms
Domain 16. Interpersonal manners
Domain 17. Acceptability of vocal habits
Domain 18. Acceptability of habits
Domain 19. Activity level
Domain 20. Symptomatic behavior
Domain 21. Use of medications

Note: The classifications are from *AAMD–ABS
School Edition* by N. Lambert, M. Windmiller, D.
Tharinger, and L. Cole, 1981, Washington, DC:
American Association of Mental Deficiency.

Teachers should understand how a child interacts at home.

ics can lead to isolated teaching of the 3 Rs with no relevance for the real world" (pp. 365–366).

We believe this point of view to be of great importance. Personal-social skills alone have limited value. Academic skills alone have limited value. Students with mental retardation require both if they are to function with maximum effectiveness as adults. Students with mental retardation will not learn personal-social skills as readily as other students; thus, they require specific instruction. This instruction, however, must be individualized, just as academic instruction must be individualized. Fortunately, the past decade has witnessed a resurgence in interest in the teaching of personal-social skills, and special education resource personnel should be able to provide specific suggestions for specific needs at specific age levels.

THE NATURE OF MENTAL RETARDATION

Definitions and systems of classification are important, but a concept of the nature of mental retardation may also be valuable. One of the best and most succinct introductions to the nature of mental retardation resulted from the efforts of a group of experts in mental retardation who were asked to prepare a report to guide the Steering Committee of the National Institute of Child Health and Development (NICHD) in developing a 5-year research plan. The members of this study group included national experts on mental retardation. Figure 9–2 contains the introductory remarks in their report.

With the NICHD conceptualization of the nature of mental retardation as a base, we would like to add our beliefs about mental retardation, focusing on programs that

FIGURE 9–2
Introductory remarks of the steering committee for the NICHD

Evidence today indicates that the causes of mental retardation are biological, psychological, and social in origin and that they occur frequently in combination in a single individual. Genetic factors, metabolic disorders, and prematurity or other disturbances during pregnancy are a few of its biological determinants, but infection or injury at birth or in early childhood may also underlie mental retardation. In addition, lack of stimulation, inadequate educational opportunities, and generally deprived living conditions may be causal or contributory factors. Whether such factors modify normal developmental processes or cause aberrant neurogenetic programs is not at all clear. The moderate and more severe conditions of retardation most frequently result from disorders or insults that can usually be traced to faulty genes, infections, accidents, diseases, and disorders that cause brain damage. Knowledge is needed from almost every branch of science in order to understand the interaction of these elements in the development and behavior of children and adults.

Mental retardation is identified clinically by the presence of several signs that include, but are not limited to, a significant impairment of intelligence and a concurrent deficit in adaptive behavior. Typically these impairments occur before age 18. The identification of mental retardation through the years has reflected with varying degrees of emphasis a mix of two factors. Before the beginning of the mental testing movement, the primary behavioral characteristic of those who were referred to as mentally retarded was inadequate social adaptation. With the rise of the mental testing movement, specifically with regard to intelligence testing, a greater reliance has been placed on measured intelligence as the primary characteristic in defining mental retardation. The term *intelligence* was used to refer to the ability of the individual to master verbal, visual, and mathematical symbol systems, and the concept of intelligence itself became defined by the instruments that purported to measure it. . . . Social systems, such as diagnostic clinics, public schools, and other service agencies, have created standards of definition that vary on the basis of different perceptions of individual and societal needs.

Note: From *Mental Retardation: An Evaluation and Assessment of the State of the Science* (pp. 1–2) by D. Purpura, J. Gallagher, and T. Tjossem (Eds.), 1981, Bethesda, MD: National Institute of Child Health and Development, U.S. Department of Health and Human Services.

should be offered in schools or the local communities. Our beliefs about students with mental retardation include the following:

1. Some students have been mislabeled on the basis of inappropriate or biased tests, insufficient data, or both.
2. Some students classified as having borderline mental retardation can be helped to approach the level of normal mental ability.
3. There is true mental retardation, and it

may be found in all races, ethnic groups, and socioeconomic levels.

4. Many students with mild mental retardation can be effectively educated in regular classes for the major part of the day if teachers receive assistance with materials and methods.
5. Students should be identified by multiple criteria, including (a) functioning in social situations, (b) level of language development, (c) functioning on an individual test of intelligence (full-scale or glo-

bal IQ, plus consideration of the patterns of the subtest scores), (d) emotional maturity, and (e) academic achievement. Ethnic, cultural, social, and economic background must be considered.

6. Most students with mild mental retardation benefit greatly from a program in which career awareness and information are emphasized, starting in the elementary grades. Such a career education program must be much more than vocational preparation.

7. Most secondary school students with mild mental retardation benefit from a special work experience program coordinated with a life skills and career education curriculum emphasis.

8. Community-based programs, operated jointly by public schools and other community or state agencies (as appropriate in the various states) should be provided for individuals (children and adults) with severe/profound mental retardation. Such programs should also be available for individuals with moderate mental retardation who cannot be served effectively by the public schools. (This is often due to the existence of multiple disabilities.) Such programs should not represent an abrogation of the responsibility of the public schools, but rather an effort to obtain the assistance of all appropriate governmental agencies.

CHARACTERISTICS OF MENTAL RETARDATION

This section describes characteristics commonly seen in individuals already classified as mentally retarded, emphasizing characteristics common to mild mental retardation.

Personal-Social Skill Deficits

If accepted definitions of mental retardation are applied as intended, a student cannot be classified as mentally retarded unless there are deficits in adaptive behavior. For individuals with mild mental retardation, such deficits may not be so great as to be evident every moment of the day, but they show up in various circumstances. For example, a student may not be able to deal with emotions as well as might be expected considering age and experience. There may be problems with self-directed activities and initiative. Behavior may lead to a general conclusion—usually based on multiple criteria—that the student is immature.

Students with mild mental retardation may be slow in interpreting social signals (for example, of acceptance or nonacceptance) and may have difficulty in getting along with peers, especially when any sort of dissension occurs. Such students may tend to socialize with younger children and when interacting with age peers, they may permit themselves to be blamed for behaviors that are really group initiated. They may also have unusual difficulty in understanding that others see and interpret situations differently than they do. In summary, their personal-social skills are more like those of a child several years younger.

It must be noted that personal-social deficits may also be seen in children with learning disabilities, but as compared with students with learning disabilities, students with mental retardation are more likely to have low personal-social skills in general, whereas students with learning disabilities are more likely to have some normal personal-social skills, with deficits in only certain areas.

General Academic Retardation

Students who are later classified as mildly mentally retarded are usually referred for evaluation because of lack of progress in academic areas and inability to learn when taught in the same manner as other students in class. In primary grades, this characteristic is more often first recognized because of poor progress in reading, but general academic retardation usually involves difficulty in all academic areas of the school program. A rule that generally, but not necessarily always, applies is that if a student is far behind the rest of the class and has serious academic difficulty in only one area (for example, reading) but is normal or above normal in achievement in another major area (for example, arithmetic), that student probably is not mentally retarded.

Some students may appear to be making satisfactory progress in first grade, and at that level this rule is somewhat less applicable. But if a third- or fourth-grade student is doing very well in either reading or arithmetic, he or she is likely not a student with mental retardation. The degree of symbolic and abstract thinking required for success at the third- or fourth-grade level (assuming the student is the appropriate age for that level) is simply not consistent with mental retardation as it is viewed today.

Academic retardation is also a characteristic of other conditions (for example, learning disabilities and hearing impairment). Academic retardation does *not* necessarily indicate mental retardation, but it is a major characteristic of students with mental retardation.

Memory Deficits

Memory may be defined as "the ability to store information and retrieve it on demand" (Polloway et al., 1989, p. 30). It has been heavily researched, and a variety of research efforts continue. However, such efforts do not necessarily target individuals with mental retardation. Considerable research over the years suggests that individuals with mental retardation are no less likely to forget information once they learn it than are individuals with normal intellec-

tual ability *if* what they learned is consistent with their mental abilities (Polloway et al., 1985). Thus, in general, the long-term memory of individuals with mental retardation approaches normal. (This does not reflect how long it may take to learn something in the first place.) On the other hand, short-term memory (information stored from a few seconds to a few hours) appears to be considerably less than that of normal learners (Borkowski, Peck, & Damberg, 1983; Ellis, 1970). Thus, the emphasis in teaching individuals with mental retardation must be on helping them originally learn (store) the information.

Below-Average Language Ability

Although language ability that is below average may indicate hearing impairment, learning disability, lack of opportunity to develop language, or other factors, students with mental retardation almost always have below-average (for age) language ability. The only exceptions to this generalization are borderline students in situations where well-informed, highly motivated parents have invested unusual efforts at the preschool level. In such cases, these children enter school with normal language ability. Usually, it slowly becomes lower than that of the normal peer group, as other children grow in this area.

Below-Average Ability to Generalize and Conceptualize

Below-average ability to generalize and conceptualize is at least partially measured by most individual tests of intelligence and thus is to be expected, since intelligence test results play a significant part in determining mild mental retardation. It is useful for classroom teachers to think in terms of the abilities of students in these areas, but care should be taken to avoid confusion between ability to generalize or conceptualize relating to what is read and ability to generalize or conceptualize in other settings. A student with a serious reading problem, for example, may appear to be unable to conceptualize if reading is the base for conceptualization. However, the student may be able to conceptualize quite well if initial information is provided verbally. In contrast, a student with mild mental retardation has a tendency to have difficulty with generalization and conceptualization in a variety of settings.

Characteristics in Total

In the case of students with mental retardation, no single characteristic alone is distinguishing. Rather, it is the total of the characteristics that distinguishes students with mental retardation. The preceding characteristics are of value to classroom teachers as clues that indicate the *possibility* that a given student is mentally retarded. They are of further value in indicating possible teaching methods or techniques. Note, however, that according to state and federal definitions and identification guidelines, a student may be classified as mentally retarded only if the results of *both* an individual test of intelligence and adaptive behavior measures indicate he or she is mentally retarded. Even then, if the results are borderline or there are conflicting data, the identification should be questioned.

In most cases, the composite effect of the preceding characteristics of mental retardation is that students with mental retardation develop a related set of tendencies that should be systematically considered in instructional planning. Patton et al. (1990) outline three tendencies that have significant influence on success in learning:

1. *An external locus of control.* As a result, students with mental retardation tend to believe that they have little personal control or influence over their environment or the consequences of their actions.
2. *A high expectation of failure.* Because of many, repeated failures, students with mental retardation tend to anticipate failure and after a time may refuse to attempt new learning tasks.
3. *Outerdirectedness,* including "a tendency to rely on external cues or instructions for behavior" (p. 328).

Patton et al. provide several suggestions for strategies to counteract these tendencies. For example, with respect to an external locus of control, instruction may deliberately associate actions with their consequences. Then, students may be taught to anticipate possible consequences, so that they choose appropriate behaviors. (Note here that most students with normal learning abilities learn this relationship in the process of daily living, *without* specific instruction. The key to effective instruction of students with mental retardation is understanding that such students often do not learn automatically from their environment as do most other students). Another suggestion is use of a social learning contract. In such a contract, which may be established in writing or in pictures, various behaviors may be linked to possible positive, negative, or neutral outcomes.

Expectations of failure may be reduced by establishing reasonable, reachable goals and utilizing very small learning steps. A system of positive rewards for the achievement of each step can help students develop confidence in their ability to succeed and, thus, overcome the failure syndrome.

The tendency to rely on external cues may be overcome in a variety of ways that reward inner-directed behaviors. For example, a student may be taught to try to find two or three ways to solve a problem and then to try them out. Eventually, the student may generalize this approach to new situations.

CURRICULA FOR INDIVIDUALS WITH MENTAL RETARDATION

Although all curriculum planning must be individualized, certain generalizations related to severe/profound, moderate, and mild mental retardation may be made with respect to appropriate planning. The following discussion is based on presently accepted educational practice related to these three levels. Various combinations of the instructional practices are common for students who are borderline with respect to these levels.

Curriculum for Individuals with Severe/Profound Mental Retardation

Individuals with severe/profound mental retardation are almost always identified at birth or very soon thereafter, and often, special provisions for their needs are instituted at an early age. A few years ago, such individuals were considered unable to learn, so education and training efforts were thought to be hopeless. Thus, individuals with severe/profound mental retardation were provided custodial care, which gave them protection and kept them away from other members of society.

Public Law 99–457 addressed the education of individuals with severe/profound mental retardation. Now, frequently, such individuals are educated in community facilities or separate, special classes in schools. Especially at the elementary school age, children with severe/profound mental retardation may spend part of each day in a regular class. Alternately, when programs are provided in school-based special classes,

students from regular classes may serve as peer tutors. Preparation for and supervision of such peer tutoring, sometimes called reverse mainstreaming, is usually handled by special class teachers, because the learning difficulties of individuals with severe/profound mental retardation dictate very specialized educational programming.

Curriculum for Individuals with Moderate Mental Retardation

Like individuals with severe/profound mental retardation, individuals with moderate mental retardation were seldom considered the responsibility of the public schools as recently as the 1960s. However, in most of the nation, the question today is how to most effectively serve the needs of these individuals in the public schools.

According to Patton et al. (1990), individuals with moderate levels of mental retardation "can benefit from multifaceted training that will eventually prepare them for semi-independent or supervised living and working situations. Self-care skills like toileting, dressing, self-feeding, and grooming are often worked on first, along with physical development and oral or signed communication" (p. 320). In most schools of the nation, most students with moderate mental retardation spend much of their time in special class programs, but some are in regular classes for a considerable part of the day. A few students at the upper levels of moderate mental retardation spend all day in regular classes; however, this is the exception rather than the rule. Almost always, classroom teachers who have students with moderate mental retardation receive special assistance and such students receive at least some special instruction outside the regular class.

Because the emphasis for education of students and adults with moderate mental retardation is ability to function successfully in the community, it is important that such individuals associate with nondisabled peers to the greatest extent possible consistent with meeting their more specialized educational needs. In other words, learning to function alongside nondisabled persons is a significant part of their educational program. Learning to read significant words such as *men, women, ladies room,* and *danger* is important, as is a basic understanding of money and use of the telephone. Skills such as counting, telling time, and basic cooking are also important. Memorizing home address, phone number, parent's name, and other significant words and facts, along with learning work skills (such as being on time and completing tasks) are essential parts of a specialized curriculum. In most instances, the curriculum is taught by a special teacher. *Yet, these skills are of limited value if the student with moderate mental retardation does not have sufficient contact with nondisabled students to prepare him or her to successfully function alongside a variety of adults later in life.* For this reason, providing experiences alongside students in regular classrooms is important. The manner in which such experiences are provided varies in relation to age of the student involved, the educational activities involved, and a host of other variables. In almost all instances, however, such activities are planned jointly by a special education teacher or consultant and the regular classroom teacher.

Curriculum for Individuals with Mild Mental Retardation

A variety of special education supportive services should be available to regular classroom teachers, regardless of the level of mental retardation of the students under consideration. The following discussion, which targets instruction of students with mild mental retardation, assumes the existence of at least a moderate range of services.

In the first and second grades, the provision of teaching suggestions and special materials may permit students with mild mental retardation to remain full time in regular classrooms. If the disability is greater (such as a lower level of intelligence, other disabling conditions, or inadequate experiential background), part-time placement in a resource room may be an essential part of the total educational plan. In resource rooms, students receive much more individual help in developing basic reading and number skills, and special teachers determine the approaches that best provide maximum growth when the students are in regular classes.

Many students with mild mental retardation are later able to return to regular classes on a full-time basis; however, some need to move into part-time special class programs if the resource room setting proves to be insufficient to provide for their educational needs. A few students may continue in a part-time special program throughout their school years, but every effort should be made to help students function successfully in regular classes.

When students continue to have significant academic difficulties, there is a growing discrepancy between their level of achievement and that of their age peers. The use of high-interest, low-vocabulary materials permits the teaching of many essential concepts, but some curriculum modification becomes inevitable if education is to remain meaningful. If a student receives the benefit of several years of special programming that helps others return to regular classes but is of much less help to him or her, by age 12 or 13 a more special program must be considered. Such a program should focus on social skills, habits, attitudes, and understandings that maximize the ability of the student to obtain and retain employment.

In conjunction with the emphasis on employability, special efforts to help the student become a knowledgeable consumer and a responsible parent and citizen must be initiated. Such programs are often called prevocational at the junior high level and vocational, work-study, or work experience at the senior high level. Students in such programs still have some involvement with regular class programs, with emphasis on classes like driver education, typing, metalwork, body and fender work, and various semiskilled trades that are deemed individually appropriate. Personnel from state rehabilitation service agencies may be able to assist in a number of ways, including making arrangements for special vocational school training and paying employers for training functions. In high school, a workstudy coordinator should arrange and supervise off-campus work activities.

Special educators always hope that a remedial effect will permit return to regular classrooms; however, this is not likely if the initial identification was accurate. The hope for a remedial effect was fueled by factors in the mid- to late 1970s that exist to a lesser extent now. At that time, when many students from special classes were being moved to more normal, less restrictive environments, a significant number of students in such classes had been classified and placed inappropriately. Some were minority students who were not actually mentally retarded, others were emotionally disturbed, and still others were learning disabled. A few of the students merely needed a good remedial program, but provision of special education services was less expensive for local districts because they received state funds for special education but not for remedial programs.

During this time, the upper IQ limits of mental retardation were lowered, the bor-

Appropriate models promote academic and social progress.

derline range was eliminated, and a measure of adaptive behavior was added to the requirement of subaverage IQ. These changes resulted in a decrease in the number of students identified as mentally retarded since they led to a more restricted concept of mental retardation. Therefore, it is now less likely that educators will inaccurately identify students as mentally retarded, and since the upper limits of mental retardation have been lowered, it is now more likely that students identified as mildly mentally retarded will need specialized assistance.

Commenting on this phenomenon, MacMillan and Borthwick (1980) note, "Mainstreaming is feasible for only a very small percentage of the mentally retarded population when a restrictive definition is employed, such as is the case in California today" (p. 158). Very little has happened since 1980 to lead to less restrictive guidelines. The restrictiveness of the definition of EMR presently varies greatly from state to state, and any discussion of mainstreaming of students with mental retardation must be undertaken with the understanding that this variation exists.

Although the purpose of this text is to help regular classroom teachers provide appropriate education in the least restrictive environment, we urge teachers to be aware of the need for special assistance and to demand such specialized assistance as part of the approved individualized education program (IEP) required by PL 94–142 and state regulations. To do less would contradict both the spirit and the letter of PL 94–142 and everything known about the needs of students who are disabled.

CAREER EDUCATION

Career education attained considerable national attention in 1974, when the Office of

Career Education was established within the U.S. Office of Education. Its purpose was to promote national awareness of the need for career education for all students. Kokaska and Brolin (1985) note that one of the major problems experienced with this terminology has been that too many educators have tended to consider *career* as synonymous with *occupation*, which is inaccurate. They indicate, "Career education is the process of systematically coordinating all school, family, and community components together to facilitate each individual's potential for economic, social, and personal fulfillment and participation in productive work activities that benefit the individual or others" (p. 43). They further note, "Career education does not de-emphasize the fundamentals. Rather, it brings meaning to the curriculum by making individuals more aware of themselves, their potentials, and their educational needs" (p. 43).

In 1976, in recognition of the importance of the concept of career education for individuals with handicapping conditions, the Council for Exceptional Children established a new division, the Division on Career Development (DCD). Since that time, special educators have evolved various curriculum models to guide the development of career education efforts for students with disabling conditions. One of the leading advocates of career education for students with disabling conditions, Donn Brolin (1978, 1982), began the development of the Life-Centered Career Education (LCCE) model in the early 1970s. This model, developed as a competency-based approach, specifies competencies shown in Figure 9–3. The LCCE model is referenced by many other authors, and apparently, it is widely accepted for its provision of 22 major competencies and 102 subcompetencies. It is obvious that to achieve these competencies, close cooperation must be main-

FIGURE 9–3

The life-centered career education model

Daily Living Skills

1. Managing family finances
2. Selecting, managing, and maintaining a home
3. Caring for personal needs
4. Raising children—family living
5. Buying and preparing food
6. Buying and caring for clothes
7. Engaging in civic activities
8. Utilizing recreation and leisure time
9. Getting around the community

Personal-Social Skills

10. Achieving self-awareness
11. Acquiring self-confidence
12. Developing socially responsible behavior
13. Maintaining adequate interpersonal skills
14. Achieving independence
15. Achieving problem-solving skills
16. Communicating adequately with others

Occupational Skills

17. Knowing and exploring occupational possibilities
18. Selecting and planning occupational choices
19. Exhibiting appropriate work habits and behaviors
20. Exhibiting sufficient physical-manual skills
21. Obtaining a specific occupational skill
22. Seeking, securing, and maintaining employment

Note: Adapted from *Career Education for Handicapped Individuals*, 2nd ed. by C. Kokaska and D. Brolin, 1985, Columbus, OH: Merrill.

tained between the school, the family, and the community.

White and Biller (1988) note that there are two major ways to approach planning for career education programming. These are: (a) separate content—perhaps a short unit to teach such competencies as money skills and check writing—or (b) infusion— that is, integrating career education concepts with other subject matter. They suggest that either approach has certain merits, but that a combination of the two may be best. Factors such as severity of disabling condition and age or grade level tend to favor one approach over the other. Whatever the approach they use, most educators agree that all students need some degree of career education, and special educators feel that students with disabling conditions have a particularly critical need. Educators also agree that unless the curriculum is specifically planned, important aspects may be missing from it. Regular class teachers should be aware of this emphasis and provide for development of career-related skills and understandings whenever possible.

SUGGESTIONS FOR REGULAR CLASSROOM TEACHERS

It is important that regular classroom teachers understand the learning problems often experienced by students with mental retardation, but it is equally important to know that not all students with mental retardation experience all of these different problems. It is altogether too easy to classify students on the basis of their IQ and the disabilities or academic difficulties supposedly automatically generated as a result of this IQ. About all that can be assumed is that such students have some difficulty with cognitive and academic learning and that some curricular adjustments and adaptations are necessary. The following discussion includes a number of generalized approaches that may be of value with students with mental retardation, but remember that each student must be considered individually. Note, too, that some of the suggestions effective with students with learning disabilities may also work with students with mental retardation.

Nonclassroom Settings

Although the major concern of regular class teachers may be how to more effectively teach and manage behavior in the classroom (academic) setting, such teachers must also consider nonclass settings, like the playground, cafeteria, and hallways. These are important in the total spectrum of opportunities for learning for students with mental retardation. These are also settings in which teachers may come in contact with and be responsible for students who are not enrolled in their academic classrooms.

Nonconforming behavior is a predictable concern for many teachers. Besides applying common sense, teachers should attempt to gain more information about the students who are of particular concern. This information may be available from the teacher who is responsible for the student for the majority of the day or from the special educator (resource room teacher or consultant). Information about management techniques that work in other settings may also be of great value here. Information about level of language, ability to understand rules, response to aggressive behavior on the part of other students, and similar aspects can be invaluable. Although the suggestions that follow this section are related more to academic learning, such suggestions as using concrete language may be of value in out-of-class settings also.

In addition to concerns about management of behavior, teachers should remem-ber that students with mental retardation have great need for social learning, that is, learning to act in a normal manner and react to problems so as to not appear different. Playgrounds, cafeterias, and halls are good places to learn normal behavior. Therefore, it is the responsibility of teachers to promote learning in these settings, regardless of the type of learning involved. Simply being aware of these opportunities may lead to effective use of learning situations as they develop.

Classroom Settings

Following are several suggestions to maximize classroom learning.

Build Motivation to Learn in All Possible Ways. Two major possibilities are (a) using specific reward systems (as with behavior modification) and (b) relating learning situations to students' areas of interest. Attempt to discover what things are really important to students and involve these interests in teaching whenever possible.

Be Aware of Skills, Information, and Concepts That Are Prerequisites to New Learning Tasks, and Do Not Attempt New Tasks Until These Prerequisites Are Part of the Learning Repertoires of the Students. It is likely that there will be gaps in skills or basic information not present with nondisabled students. These areas must be identified and when possible developed before initiating new learning tasks. In some cases, when such prerequisite learning cannot be accomplished in a reasonable amount of time, substitute assignments and modified goals must be established. In any event, just as learning long division in the traditional manner requires understanding of subtraction, there are prerequisites in other subject and skill areas. In some cases, the prerequisite is a specific skill; in others, it is information; and in still others, it is a concept. Prerequisites may be particularly important in science and social studies, because most students learn many concepts in these areas in the course of daily living. However, students with mental retardation may require specific teaching, and it is important that teachers be aware of this possibility.

Use Concrete Rather Than Abstract Examples Whenever Possible. For example, in teaching that 4 plus 3 equals 7, it would be better to ask, "How many oranges would I have if I had four oranges in this hand and three oranges in this hand?" This approach helps students visualize the situation and the adding process, making it easier to visualize the answer. The student might have

Concrete objects may be helpful in the learning process.

much more difficulty with the question in the abstract, but after learning the process with concrete objects, the student may find it easier to learn on the abstract level. Making learning concrete also includes the principle of relating new learning to familiar experiences.

Be Aware of a Variety of Possible Readiness and Ability Levels, Both Across and Within Subject Areas. Modify Assignments as Necessary in Recognition of These Variations. The use of multiple reading groups at the elementary level is common, and most elementary teachers have learned to manage this instructional practice. Students with mental retardation may require adjustments for some aspects of reading instruction beyond the traditional three groups but may be able to participate in many reading group activities if other facets of their reading assignments are modified. Similar modifications may be necessary in other subject or skill areas. The nature of such modifications varies among students. Teachers must be alert to the likelihood that students may benefit from the content of group reading (what they hear other students reading) and group discussion even if their own reading ability does not permit fluent reading of the material.

At the secondary level, particularly in senior high, it is more likely that students with mental retardation are in specially scheduled class groupings, but for classes in which there is no special grouping, the same principle applies. In some schools, simplified versions of reading materials (similar concepts and content, but simplified written form) are used. In other instances, it is a matter of maximizing the learning that can take place through group work. In all cases, if students can learn *without* modifications and adaptations, this approach is most desirable. Yet, if learning without modifications is possible in most areas of the school curriculum, it is likely that the student has been misclassified.

Make Maximum Use of Group Experiences as Vehicles for Learning. This suggestion is included in the discussion of reading assignments but should also be followed in all areas of the school curriculum. Good readers sometimes learn more efficiently when left alone to read new material, but students with mental retardation are more likely to benefit from oral input when learning new concepts or basic information. This does *not* mean that individualized planning and individual efforts in respect to basic skills may be overlooked or shortchanged. It means that teachers must involve students in group experiences whenever possible, especially when covering basic information or introducing new concepts.

Create Opportunities for Verbal Expression. Students with mental retardation are often less adept at self-expression than are nondisabled students. The effects of below-average learning ability are cumulative and are readily seen when students attempt broad verbal expression. Some teachers may be concerned about negative effects on self-concept or become discouraged and thus avoid attempts to encourage students to engage in further self-expression, but teachers must use both structured, individually planned experiences and incidental opportunities to encourage students to improve language development. Language development requires experience, and students with mental retardation require more experience with language to develop a given level of language ability than do students with average or above-average intellectual ability.

Finally, if earlier school experiences and provisions have been inconsistent with the level of readiness, students may be even more retarded in language development than their intellectual level would indicate. A further complication is the effect of bilingual or bicultural influences. Teachers must be alert to provide all possible opportunities for verbal expression and general language development and to make these opportunities interesting and appropriate to the present level of development. Such opportunities are important at both the elementary and the secondary level.

Be Alert to Special Needs in the Abilities to Generalize and Conceptualize. Two abilities, generalization and conceptualization, are among the more significant factors in learning as measured by individual intelligence tests. Therefore, by definition, students with mental retardation have lower than average ability in these two important areas. A young student may recognize the plus sign in a mathematical equation but have difficulty understanding that the word *and* (as in "6 and 7 equals 13") has the same meaning as the plus sign. The student may understand and follow the rules governing behavior in the cafeteria line but have difficulty relating the same rules to another situation, such as the recess line. Teachers must specifically point out how one principle may apply in other academic or social situations.

Through practice with generalization and conceptual skills, students acquire repertoires of experiences that promote maximum development of these abilities. Ability to generalize and conceptualize is the basis for skills related to successful employment and participation in the adult world, but such skills are regularly overlooked or underemphasized in favor of specific facts or improvement in basic skills such as reading. It is doubtful whether, for example, an increase of 1 year in a student's basic reading level will be as important to the student as development of the ability to generalize in social situations or conceptualize the requirements of various job-related tasks. It is difficult to demonstrate that any specific area of learning is more important than any other, but generalization and conceptualization are certainly among the most important for students with below-average intellectual ability.

Use a Variety of Techniques to Support or Simplify Learning Tasks. Following are several suggestions:

1. Reduce distractions in the learning environment whenever possible.
2. Provide for frequent review.
3. Simplify instructions.
4. Introduce new vocabulary words *before* making new assignments (experience indicates which words are more likely cause difficulty—there is no rule or list of difficult words applicable to all students).
5. Assign problems in smaller clusters.
6. When practical, use peer tutors (the viability of peer tutors varies considerably from subject to subject, grade to grade, and student to student).
7. Whenever possible, use filmstrips or films to introduce broad new concepts, such as the tropics or the polar regions, or to introduce topics such as novels or classics that the class will discuss for a considerable period of time.
8. Provide an outline of important points of reading assignments.
9. Use color coding when appropriate.
10. Use pictures and arrows on direction sheets or other written assignments.
11. Avoid true-false tests that require an understanding of language that the student may not have (otherwise, the test results reflect the language level of the student rather than actual knowledge of the subject).

These general suggestions are a brief sample of ideas that have worked with some students. Resource room specialists should be able to provide many more, including ideas that have developed out of the more individualized work taking place in the resource room. In many instances, alternate approaches are a part of the IEP or the extended ideas that grow out of the IEP. Especially in the lower grades, activities used with other students in regular class work also with only minimal modifications for students with mental retardation.

The preceding suggestions are applicable at the elementary level, and many are applicable at the secondary level, but education in regular classrooms at the secondary level remains more difficult. This greater difficulty may occur because educational retardation is cumulative—students fall farther and farther behind their peers as they go through their school program—or because secondary curriculum planners tend to assume basic reading, language, and mathematics skills when they plan course goals and content. In any event, it is likely that the secondary curriculum planned for students with mental retardation will be more separate than it is for students with most other disabling conditions.

SECONDARY SCHOOL PROGRAMS

It is possible that some students with mental retardation can complete an adapted version of the secondary school program with minimal assistance from special education personnel. When a student can achieve at least modest success, such programming may be the best possible alternative. It certainly is consistent with the concept of education in the least restrictive environment. On the other hand, as long as the student is having educational difficulties and is classified as a student with a disabling condition, programming decisions must be made by the IEP committee, and social, educational, and career goals must be carefully considered.

If students are ready for more normal school programs, enrollment in one or two special class sections taught by the special education teacher may still be necessary, but the best or more appropriate program is strictly an individual matter. Sometimes, in large high schools, class sections are taught by nonspecial educators for students who are academically less ready than other students. Such classes may include some students who are considered part of the special education program and some who are not. The major common characteristic of students in such classes may be, for example, reading competency at the third- or fourth-grade level. Therefore, adapted materials may be used with the entire class.

In other programs, central, vocational training facilities are established primarily for nondisabled students but include students with mental retardation. In some such programs, a special education coordinator helps students learn specialized or technical vocabulary or complete reading assignments that are too difficult. This coordinator also usually provides assistance to students with learning disabilities or hearing impairment and others who are the responsibility of the special education staff of the school district.

When adaptations of existing programs do not meet the needs of students who are disabled, more specialized programs must be provided. Morsink (1984) suggests that a work-study or work experience program is "an excellent way to provide a transition for the student from the sheltered school environment to the competitive world of work" (p. 336). For many students with mild mental retardation, complete self-support (as adults) is possible if appropriate work training is provided. The work-study approach was originally outlined by Kolstoe

and Frey in 1965 and has been used in various forms since then.

Regular classroom teachers may play roles in secondary programs primarily oriented to work-study by providing instruction in areas such as typing, home economics, driver education, and other practical secondary school subjects. Assignment to such classes is ordinarily determined on an individual basis, though all students with mild mental retardation may take the driver education course. Special education teachers try to ensure the maximum readiness of students for certain programs. Special education teachers need guidance from regular classroom teachers who receive the students for these classes.

Work-study coordinators, often working in conjunction with vocational rehabilitation counselors, find employment sites and supervise students on the job. With guidance from work-study coordinators, teachers may play significant roles in remedying difficulties that students experience in the workplace (Morsink, 1984).

As described by Mercer and Payne (1975), the five major phases of a work-study program are vocational exploration, vocational evaluation, vocational training, vocational placement, and follow-up. In this sequence, students (a) become familiar with the nature of the required skills, (b) are provided guided experience with job skills, thus permitting instructors to determine abilities and preferences, (c) receive broad training in a wide variety of vocational areas, (d) are assisted with placement in an actual job, and (e) are assisted with on-the-job difficulties. Vocational rehabilitation personnel employed by rehabilitation services agencies are important in this process, especially in the last two steps.

Work-study programs vary widely, but the goal is the same in all instances. The role of regular classroom teachers varies with the ability level of the students and

FIGURE 9–4
Susan and MariAnn, two 16-year-old students

Susan
Age: 16 years
Program: first year in senior high special program,
  with limited enrollment in adapted regular classes
Years in school: 11
Physical health: good
Full-scale WISC–R IQ: 65

MariAnn
Age: 16 years
Program: first year in senior high special program,
  with limited enrollment in adapted regular classes
Years in school: 11
Physical health: good
Full-scale WISC–R IQ: 66

Based on these data, Susan and MariAnn might be expected to be relatively similar in school performance. Each was referred as a result of significant academic problems near the close of the third year in school (second grade). At that time, Susan's IQ was recorded as 62, MariAnn's as 68. Measures of adaptive behavior supported identification of both girls as educable mentally retarded. Each was placed in a special program at the start of third grade. During their elementary school years, each spent approximately 2 hours each day in a special resource room and the remainder of the day in the regular class.

Susan and MariAnn have lived in the same city throughout their 11 years of school attendance and have been in the same school and same resource room program since they moved to middle school. Other information indicates that the program quality in the two different elementary schools that they attended was essentially the same.

There are no known serious family problems in either family, and parents have been generally cooperative with school officials through the years. Both girls are from white, middle-class families.

But here the similarity ends.

Susan is reading at the upper fourth-grade level, according to standardized achievement tests. She can recognize the words included in the special program reading curriculum (relating to employment, voting, family responsibility, and practical, daily living skills), and next year will move into phase one of the work experience program with excellent preparation. She is successful in the adapted vocational education program taught by a regular class teacher and is as skilled as most other students in her school, including nondisabled students, in interpersonal relations. She has learned that she will be rejected or ignored by some students but does not make an issue of their behavior. Susan's speaking vocabulary is somewhat below that of other students her age but not notably so in most normal social situations. (This discrepancy would be noticeable if she were enrolled in some of the advanced classes in her school, but she is not.) In most respects, in the large school Susan attends, she does not appear different.

MariAnn is reading at the middle second-grade level, according to standardized achievement tests. She has difficulty in reading approximately 50% of the words included in the special program reading curriculum, and she will not likely be ready for phase one for the work experience program for at least 2 years. MariAnn experiences her greatest difficulty in the adapted vocational education program, where the teacher says, "She has difficulty reading our low vocabulary materials, but her biggest problem is understanding the concepts involved." MariAnn socializes with a few students in the special program but is not well accepted, even by many of the special program students. She has essentially no acceptance by nondisabled students. MariAnn's speaking vocabulary is very limited, and she has often attempted to become part of a conversation only to be rejected because her comments make her appear different. Even with specific suggestions from her teacher, she cannot seem to anticipate such situations.

Perhaps the most important understanding to be gained from the comparison of Susan and MariAnn is that students classified as EMR may perform very differently in regard to both academic achievement and social competence, regardless of similarity of test scores or other variables generally recognized as important. As such students progress through their educational program, projections of educational and social ability and success may become more reliable, but at ages 6, 7, and 8, predictions of future success may be inaccurate. Certain generalizations may be made based on valid test results and environmental and sociological data, but these are only generalizations. Variations in performance are undoubtedly just as great among students diagnosed as EMR as they are among the so-called normal student population.

the availability of special education and rehabilitation personnel, but for the most part, the teachers of vocationally related subjects are most involved. Although special educators and rehabilitation personnel retain primary responsibility for these programs, regular classroom teachers in the secondary schools may have increasing contact with students with mental retardation.

In concluding this consideration of programs for students with mental retardation, we feel it is essential to call to attention the great variations that can exist between students who look very similar on paper. We have chosen to do this through a comparison of Susan and MariAnn, two 16-year-old students classified as educable mentally retarded (EMR) (Figure 9–4). The likelihood that such differences exist makes it imperative that educators plan programs on an *individual* basis, not on the basis of some generalization based on classification.

SUMMARY

In this chapter, mental retardation was defined, levels of mental retardation were described, and the role of measurement of adaptive behavior in identifying mental retardation was explained. Characteristics usually associated with mental retardation—personal-social deficits, general academic retardation, memory deficits, below-average language ability, and below-average ability to generalize and conceptualize—were discussed.

Curriculum planning for individuals with mental retardation was outlined at three levels: severe/profound, moderate, and mild. Career education program guidelines were also provided. Suggestions for the regular classroom teacher were provided, including those related to learning in the classroom and those related to nonclassroom settings. A separate discussion of work-study programs applicable at secondary school levels was also provided.

- Why were learning disabilities identified and named so much later in history than was mental retardation?

- What definitional disputes continue in the field of learning disabilities? What differences would it make if the definition required proof of a central nervous system disorder?

- Can a learning disability be caused by inappropriate teaching practices? If so, how might this happen?

- How can the assessment team differentiate between learning disabilities and behavior disorders when the student's behavior is common to both diagnoses?

- In how many ways may attention deficits affect learning? What can teachers do to reduce the negative effects of attention deficits?

- Can you describe your own cognitive learning strategies? How might a better understanding of your learning strategies help you learn more efficiently?

- Why have several authorities felt positive conditioning to be so important? How will positive reconditioning methods vary in application with an 8-year-old as contrasted with a 16-year old?

C H A P T E R   1 0

TEACHING STUDENTS WITH LEARNING DISABILITIES

LEARNING DISABILITIES WERE NOT RECOGNIZED AS a specific, separate exceptionality until the 1960s, and more than 30 years later, they remain a topic of discussion and disagreement regarding definition and cause. Different disciplines associated with the study of learning disabilities use different terminology. For example, doctors discuss *brain injury* and *minimal brain dysfunction,* psychologists refer to *perceptual disorders* and *hyperkinetic behavior,* and speech-language specialists discuss *dyslexia* and *aphasia.* These terms may refer to different conditions, but all fall under the umbrella term *learning disabilities.* This chapter provides information to help regular classroom teachers understand the nature of learning disabilities and work with consulting teachers or learning disabilities specialists in providing the best possible educational programs. Although some students with severe learning disabilities are in self-contained programs, most are in regular classrooms for most of the school day and, therefore, are served primarily by regular classroom teachers.

LEARNING DISABILITIES, DEFINITION AND DISCUSSION

Learning disabilities can best be understood as a broad, general term that includes a number of conditions or disabilities historically recognized as separate and distinct. The commonality is that students have difficulty in learning. The following definition, developed at the federal level as a result of the passage of PL 94–142, is used with variations in all 50 states:

Specific learning disability means a disorder in one or more of the basic psychological processes involved in understanding or in using language, spoken or written, which may manifest itself in an imperfect ability to listen, think, speak, read, write, spell, or to do mathematical calculations.

The term includes such conditions as perceptual handicaps, brain injury, minimal brain disfunction, dyslexia, and developmental aphasia. The term does not include children who have learning problems which are primarily the result of visual, hearing, or motor handicaps, of mental retardation, of emotional disturbance, or of environmental, cultural, or economic disadvantage.

Dissatisfaction with the federal definition led to a number of other definitions, including the following:

Learning disabilities is a general term that refers to a heterogeneous group of disorders manifested by significant difficulties in the acquisition and use of listening, speaking, reading, writing, reasoning, or mathematical abilities. These disorders are intrinsic to the individual, pre-

Teaching Students with Learning Disabilities

sumed to be due to central nervous system dysfunction, and may occur across the life span. Problems in self-regulatory behaviors, social perception, and social interaction may exist with learning disabilities but do not by themselves constitute a learning disability. Although learning disabilities may occur concomitantly with other handicapping conditions (for example, sensory impairment, mental retardation, serious emotional disturbance) or with extrinsic influences (such as cultural differences, insufficient or inappropriate instruction), they are not the result of those conditions or influences. (National Joint Committee on Learning Disabilities, 1989, p. 1)

The essential difference between this proposed definition and the federal definition is the emphasis placed on the selectivity of learning disabilities, that is, how learning disabilities affect some abilities but not others, are variable in their manifestation, and influence individuals in a broad range of activities, not just in academic areas. However, several problems result from the proposed definitions: (a) the ambiguity of the definitions, (b) the exclusive rather than inclusive aspect of the federal definition, and (c) the lack of guidelines for identification of individuals with learning disabilities. Lerner (1989) suggests that a definition to satisfy all disciplines and professionals may not be possible and that several definitions, one for researchers, one for identification, and one for instructional or remediational purposes would solve the dilemma. Whatever the decision, the federal definition is the only one with national legal stature and therefore the one that all states must take into account as they develop their own definitions.

Among the problems faced by the states is the lack of guidance that the federal definition provides about the degree of educational discrepancy required to identify an individual student as learning disabled (see

Figure 10–1). Various attempts have been made to correct this problem by indicating either a percentage of educational lag or deficit (for example, 40% or 50%) or a grade-equivalent discrepancy (for example, that a fifth-grade student must score below the 2.5-grade-equivalent level in one of the academic areas if the student is to be consid-

FIGURE 10–1
Criteria for determining the existence of a specific learning disability

(a) A team may determine that a child has a specific learning disability if:
  (1) The child does not achieve commensurate with his or her age and ability levels in one or more of the areas listed in paragraph (a) (2) of this section, when provided with learning experiences appropriate for the child's age and ability levels; and
  (2) The team finds that a child has a severe discrepancy between achievement and intellectual ability in one or more of the following areas:
    (i) Oral expression;
    (ii) Listening comprehension;
    (iii) Written expression;
    (iv) Basic reading skill;
    (v) Reading comprehension;
    (vi) Mathematics calculation; or
    (vii) Mathematics reasoning.
(b) The team may not identify a child as having a specific learning disability if the severe discrepancy between ability and achievement is primarily the result of:
  (1) A visual, hearing, or motor handicap;
  (2) Mental retardation;
  (3) Emotional disturbance; or
  (4) Environmental, cultural, or economic disadvantage.

Note: From the Federal Register, December 29, 1977, p. 65083.

ered learning disabled). In some instances, the primary purpose of such regulations or guidelines has been to reduce confusion. In others, it has been to reduce an unusually high percentage of children identified as learning disabled in a particular state. Whatever the reason, this specification appears to be the major form of state-imposed addition to the federal definition.

The federal definition and identification criteria plus the description of characteristics exhibited by some students who are learning disabled (provided in the following section) should provide a basis for understanding learning disabilities. However, because of the diverse nature of learning disabilities, it may always be necessary to try out various approaches that seem to fit the assessment data and information available about a given student.

CHARACTERISTICS OF STUDENTS WHO HAVE LEARNING DISABILITIES

Students who have learning disabilities display a significant discrepancy between learning potential and actual level of learning, as well as deficient learning processes. In addition, they may display hyperactivity, lack of coordination, memory disorders, attention fixation, perceptual disorders, and poor self-concept. Screening devices for learning disabilities look for significantly different classroom behavior, significantly below-average performance in auditory comprehension and listening, significantly below-average performance in spoken language, significant academic problems, orientation difficulties, and motor disabilities or significant underdevelopment for age.

Significant Discrepancy

The discrepancy between learning potential and actual level of learning is one of two characteristics that are found in *all* stu-dents who have learning disabilities. At first glance, this may seem easy to verify, but in fact, it is confounded by several factors: (a) opportunity to learn (sometimes referred to as amount of meaningful exposure to education), (b) level of intellectual potential (IQ), and (c) motivation to learn. In turn these factors are related to racial and ethnic language considerations, economic considerations, and a host of other, less obvious influences. Therefore, although significant discrepancy is an accepted requirement for identification as learning disabled, significant discrepancy is not simple to verify.

Deficient Learning Processes

Deficiencies or developmental delay in some of the mental processes through which most individuals learn is the second characteristic found in all students who are learning disabled. This characteristic overlaps with or includes many other characteristics and is related to concepts about which authorities do not fully agree. According to DeRuiter and Wansart (1982), research indicates that "the study of learning processes in the learning disabled can be organized under five major areas: attention, perception, memory, cognition, and encoding" (p. 15). They further note that a deficiency in any one of these areas "may be involved in the development of inaccurate or incomplete mental structures in the learning disabled" (p. 15). The result is that a student with a learning disability may be described by the teacher as not able to think as well as other students. The teacher may further indicate that the activities and explanations that work with other students do not work with this student or that the logic that other students of the same age exhibit is not seen in the student with a learning disability. In fact, the student with a learning disability may not assimilate new information in the same manner as age peers because his or her thinking abilities have evolved differently, with adaptations related to partially inaccurate perceptions and memory. The student may not have the strategies to learn that age peers have or may not be able to use them efficiently (Reid, 1988). In some ways, a 10-year-old student may think more like a typical 10-year-old student and in some others like a typical 6-year-old student.

Other Indicators

A number of other indicators are evident in students who have learning disabilities. No single characteristic is seen in all students with learning disabilities, but each is more often associated with students who have learning disabilities than with the population as a whole. Therefore, although such indicators are clues to the possible presence of learning disabilities, their presence does not mean that a given student has a learning disability. However, such indicators may provide insights into the formulation of a concept of learning disabilities.

Hyperactivity. The *Diagnostic and Statistical Manual of Mental Disorders* (American Psychiatric Association, 1987) uses the term *attention-deficit hyperactivity disorder* (ADHD) in place of the 1980 term *attention deficit disorder* (ADD), while much of the popular press and most persons in ordinary conversations use *hyperactivity*. All of these terms refer to difficulty in working or playing quietly, waiting for turns, following through on instructions, and sustaining attention to a task. In addition, students may talk excessively without saying anything of substance; intrude on the conversations or activities of others; lose books, papers, assignments, or toys; and act without considering the consequences. Since all students exhibit some of these actions at times, the frequency or the degree with which students demonstrate these actions causes concern. In adolescents, the behav-

ioral characteristics may also be manifested in low self-esteem, oppositional behavior, or even depression (Shaywitz, 1987).

The relationship of ADD or ADHD to learning disabilities is the subject of considerable discussion. Shaywitz (1987) suggests that from 33% to 80% of the students with learning disabilities also demonstrate some of the symptoms of ADHD. Such a wide range results from ambiguity related to the symptoms, the frequency of occurrence, and the source of the diagnosis (such as parent, teacher, or psychologist). It seems that greater than expected numbers of students who have learning disabilities are also diagnosed as having an attention-deficit hyperactivity disorder, but neither the terms nor conditions are synonymous.

Lack of Coordination. Below-average (for age) coordination is another characteristic commonly mentioned. Some highly coordinated students have learning difficulties, but by and large, students who are identified as learning disabled according to multiple criteria are below average in coordination for their age. Students with learning disabilities are often slower to develop the ability to throw and catch a ball, to skip, or to run; are likely to have difficulty in writing and other fine-motor skills; may be generally clumsy; and stumble or fall frequently. Some coordination problems are related to inability to assess position in space properly, problems with balance, or both. Other coordination problems may be related to physical or medical conditions, but such problems should be discovered during the physical examination required as a part of the assessment process.

Memory Disorders. Memory disorders include those related primarily to short-term memory or long-term memory. They may include either auditory or visual memory. Memory is a complex process, and it is not fully understood, although various individuals have established theories that seem to explain most of the observable facets of memory. Case studies describe individuals who cannot remember where their window is or on which side of the room their bed is placed, even though it has been there for months. Other reports describe students who cannot repeat a simple sequence of three words immediately after hearing them. Such memory deficits seriously affect the learning process.

Attention Fixation. Students who cannot shift their focus of attention in a normal manner have just as much difficulty in learning as do students who cannot focus on any object or activity long enough to learn new material. Such students may regularly focus on some object in the room or outside the window and literally be unable to respond to the attempts of a teacher to attract their attention. They shut out other sensory signals, even those that call attention to something they would very much like to do. It is not a matter of *choosing* to shut out other signals, but rather a matter of involuntary overattention. This problem and hyperactivity often overlap.

Perceptual Disorders. Perceptual disorders include disorders of visual, auditory, tactile, or kinesthetic perception. Students with visual perceptual problems may not be able to copy letters correctly or perceive the difference between a hexagon and an octagon. They may reverse letters or produce mirror writing. Students with auditory perceptual problems may not perceive the difference between different consonant blends or between the ring of a doorbell and the ring of a telephone. Because of these perceptual problems students may at first seem to be lacking in sensory acuity (that is, seem to have visual loss or be hard of hearing), but when acuity is normal, the possibility of

perceptual disorder must be considered.

There are generally accepted theories of how perceptual abilities develop through the normal developmental paths of learning, but there is much less consensus on what happens—or what to do about it—when perception does not develop normally. There is, however, evidence to suggest that significantly below-average perceptual ability often results in educational retardation.

Another View of Indicators

A more systematic way to look at characteristics of students with learning disabilities is to look at the factors referenced in screening devices. The following outline reflects the types of difficulties often observed in students who have learning disabilities:

1. Significantly different classroom behaviors
   a. Difficulty in beginning or finishing tasks
   b. Difficulty in organizing
   c. Inconsistent in behavior
   d. Difficulty in peer relationships
2. Significantly below-average performance in auditory comprehension and listening
   a. Difficulty in following directions
   b. Difficulty in comprehending or following class discussions
   c. Inability to retain information received aurally
   d. Difficulty in understanding or comprehending word meanings
3. Significantly below-average performance in spoken language
   a. Use of incomplete sentences or an unusual number of grammatical errors
   b. Use of immature or improper vocabulary or very limited vocabulary
   c. Difficulty in recalling words for use in self-expression

d. Difficulty relating isolated facts; scattered ideas

e. Difficulty in relating ideas in logical sequence

4. Significant academic problems
   a. Difficulty in reading fluency
   b. Difficulty in associating numbers with symbols
   c. Incorrect ordering of letters in spelling
   d. Confusion of manuscript and cursive writing
   e. Avoidance of reading
   f. Confusion of math concepts—addition, multiplication

5. Orientation difficulties
   a. Poor time concept, no grasp of meaning of time
   b. Difficulty in "navigating" around building or school grounds
   c. Poor understanding of relationships (big, little, far, close, under, on, near)
   d. Inability to learn directions (right, left, north, south)

6. Motor disabilities or significant underdevelopment for age
   a. Poor coordination, clumsiness
   b. Very poor balance
   c. Awkward, poorly developed manipulative or manual dexterity
   d. Lack of rhythm in movements

This list provides an appropriate conclusion to a discussion of characteristics of students who are learning disabled. Note that although observable behaviors may lead teachers to suspect problems, these behaviors do not actually identify students as learning disabled.

THE NATURE OF LEARNING DISABILITIES

Teachers often comment that the characteristics of students who have been identified as having learning disabilities are similar to those of other students who have not been so identified. Alternately, they indicate that students with hearing impairment or mental retardation also have similar characteristics. They further note that students who do not have a command of the English language may exhibit some of these characteristics, but below-average performance in spoken language is not surprising in bilingual students, environmentally deprived students, and culturally diverse students.

Mental retardation and learning disabilities may be confused because there are some similarities, but they are different. For example, learning disabilities may remain "hidden" for many years, especially if a student is above average in intelligence. In such cases, the student is apparently able to compensate through intact learning channels for a disability that exists in other learning channels. Such a student might have serious difficulties in accurately gaining information through the auditory channel, but with a high level of intelligence and effective learning through the visual channel, the student may be able to learn and appear to be normal in most respects.

One might ask, "Why interfere if the student is learning normally?" Part of the answer is that learning that places a student within the average for age is not necessarily normal or optimum learning for the student. If a student's ability is such that he or she should be in the top 5% of the class, then achievement at the 50th percentile is not normal. Teachers may be tempted to leave well enough alone, but a 12-year-old student with an IQ of 140 may be learning disabled if he or she is doing only as well as 12-year-olds with average intelligence. With proper assistance, the student's achievement may improve dramatically. Of course, the student may *not* be learning disabled. The student may have adequately developed learning abilities and simply be unmotivated or may have well-balanced basic abilities that are severely underdeveloped because of poor educational opportunities.

Figure 10–2 compares Jim and Mark, two 9-year-old boys whose educational difficulties at first seem the same. This comparison should help clarify the differences between mental retardation and learning disabilities, and it is just one example of the differences that may be found through a more complete evaluation of the learning problems of students.

DYSLEXIA

The following true story illustrates a great deal about the nature of learning disabilities and the ways in which they may affect the learning of an otherwise capable individual. Dyslexia is just one of the conditions included under the umbrella term *learning disabilities,* so it should not be assumed that all students with learning disabilities are dyslexic. However, this story illustrates various characteristics of learning disabilities, how they affect some abilities and not others, how they can persist into adulthood, what teachers should *not* do, and how the spirit and determination of an individual with learning disabilities can influence the outcome. We believe that study of this story will make the rest of the chapter more meaningful.

LIVING AND LEARNING WITH SALLY[1]

Sarah Levine and Sally Osbourne

I remember kindergarten being a lot of fun, but school wasn't fun from the first grade on. My first-grade teacher used to walk by our house

[1]From "Living and Learning with Sally" by S. Levine and S. Osbourne, April 1989, *Phi Delta Kappan, 70,* pp. 594–598. Reprinted by permission.

every week to drop off a bunch of flash cards. My mother was supposed to go over them with me until I learned the words. But it was so hard. I'd look at a word and wouldn't know it. When my mother told me what it was, I would repeat what she said. But then we'd go to the next word, and I'd forget the first one. It was frustrating.

I was in the seventh grade when my teacher asked me to stand up and read. I stood up, but I couldn't recognize even one word on the page. After what seemed an eternity, the teacher got angry and told me to go into another classroom where I was to write, again and again: "I am stupid because I cannot read."

I didn't say a word. But I couldn't do what the teacher wanted, because I couldn't spell. So I just sat and waited until a friend came in at the end of the day to collect the assignment. After she had spelled it out for me, I wrote it over and over again. Then I gave it to the teacher and went home.

That was the end of it. The teacher never helped me with my reading or writing before or after that time.

*   *   *   *   *

Students with learning disabilities often become frustrated with their inability to learn in school. Some become behavior problems to divert attention from their academic performance; others try to behave perfectly and hope that adults won't notice them. Sally adopted the latter strategy, always smiling and pretending that she was happy. "It was much easier to make believe that everything was fine than it was to admit that I did not understand," she says.

Sally knew very early in her school career that something was wrong. There had to be a reason why she couldn't learn when all her friends were learning. She decided there was something wrong with *her.* She decided that she was *dumb.*

In elementary school, when one of Sally's friends asked to have Sally sit near her, she was told that Sally was retarded and needed to sit next to the teacher.

FIGURE 10–2
Jim and Mark: A study of similarities and differences

Jim	Mark
Age: 9 years	Age: 9 years
Grade: 3	Grade: 3
Years in school: 4½	Years in school: 4½
Reading achievement: 1.6 (grade equivalent)	Reading achievement: 1.6 (grade equivalent)
Group IQ score: 75	Group IQ score: 75

The preceding descriptions of Jim and Mark are obviously identical until the IQ as indicated by an *individual* test of intelligence is considered:

Full-scale WISC IQ: 68	Full-scale WISC IQ: 102

Through the individual test of intelligence, it is found that Jim may have mild mental retardation, whereas Mark may have learning disabilities. Additional data are then gathered:

Arithmetic: 1.8 (grade equivalent)	Arithmetic: 3.2 (grade equivalent)

Generally, a student with mild mental retardation has basic skills in mathematics that are at about the same level as his or her reading skills, although sometimes they are higher if they involve rote memory. In contrast, many students who have learning disabilities may have severe problems in reading but do near-grade-level work in mathematics as long as reading is not required. The reverse may also be true of a student who is learning disabled. The student may do satisfactory work in reading but have significant problems in mathematics. The inconsistency in performance among various academic areas and various types of activities characterizes a student who is learning disabled. Additional information about the boys' abilities in classroom interaction, abilities to learn from peers, and abilities to conceptualize follows:

In classroom interaction regarding relationships of planets and the sun, Jim had real difficulty following the idea of relative movement. Jim can follow class discussion as long as concepts are simple but has difficulty making generalizations. Jim's speaking vocabulary is better than his reading vocabulary, but it is still far below the class average.

In classroom interaction regarding relationships of planets and the sun, Mark was one of the first in the class really to understand. In most topics related to science, if no classroom reading is involved, Mark does very well. On a verbal level, he conceptualizes and generalizes well. Mark's reading vocabulary (words he can recognize in print) is no better than Jim's; however, his spoken vocabulary is up to the class average in all respects and is above average in science areas.

Often a student with learning disabilities has a performance profile (in such areas as reading, arithmetic, vocabulary, ability to generalize, and ability to conceptualize) that is characterized by many ups and downs. Sometimes (or in some academic areas), the student seems average or perhaps above average, but in some areas, the student may be less able than some students with mild mental retardation. It is possible for a student who is learning disabled to be low in *all* areas of achievement and class interaction, but this is unusual. In contrast, the performance profile of the student with mild mental retardation is usually relatively flat.

What seems strange to Sally today is the fact that most adults in the schools simply ignored her. Once, when she was called on to read and couldn't, the teacher told her mother that Sally needed glasses. When that didn't work, the teacher moved Sally from the lowest reading group to the highest reading group—and never asked Sally to read again. Of course, Sally couldn't even read the book in the lowest group, but, wherever the teacher told her to sit, Sally sat and continued *not reading*.

In high school, Sally's guidance counselor told her that she was "not college material." But Sally's mother insisted that she was. After a heated argument, Sally was placed in the vocational track, to satisfy the guidance department—*and* in the college-preparatory track, to satisfy her mother. She had no free periods, she had twice as much work, and she was under a lot more pressure to hide her differences.

From first grade through high school, Sally did not experience academic success. For the most part, teachers returned her smile but were content to ignore her learning problem. Always, her mother encouraged her. And Sally kept wondering what was wrong. Gradually, she became convinced that she was not stupid. The way she was treated and the results of all her efforts in school, however, offered powerful evidence to the contrary.

*   *   *   *   *

College was a struggle from the start. I remember fighting my way through freshman registration lines, asking other students where to go. I felt ashamed because I couldn't read the signs posted on the walls or the forms I held tightly in my hand. Had anyone asked why I was having so much trouble, I was prepared to say that I was a foreign student.

When I did register, it was for classes that had oral tests, projects, or papers. I could not take a written exam.

Four years later, I earned a bachelor's degree—or perhaps I should say my mother and I earned one. She read many of the textbooks to

me; she transcribed the ideas from my head onto paper; she pushed me to accept new challenges. I remember how she smiled when I received an A in a class in which she had once received a B. She danced with delight when she saw my first grade report with a B+ average. She cried when my name appeared on the dean's list.

*   *   *   *   *

Sally graduated from college with a teaching certificate and found a job teaching first and second grades in a rural school. Sally's ingenuity paid off in the classroom. She had second-graders teach first-graders, even though some of the children refused to believe her when she said she didn't know the answers to their questions. When she read a book and came to a part she couldn't remember, she would close the book and ask the class, "What might happen next?"

Sally and her students did a lot of hands-on learning. Since they were out in the country, they could go for long walks. She used these times to demonstrate, and this is how they did math and science. Inside, they also learned by doing; they did a lot of cooking, for instance. Parents were frequently invited to visit and help with the class, and Sally had an aide who could teach the children phonics.

The test scores of Sally's students improved. And it is interesting that her alternative and expanded strategies for teaching and learning were the products of her ostensible *limitations*. Perhaps all teachers could do more for students by doing less traditional teaching. Certainly, most teachers could profitably expand their repertoire of teaching methods.

A year later, Sally agreed to take over a friend's special-needs classroom in another state. Her friend, a teacher of the learning disabled, suspected that Sally had learning difficulties and encouraged her to take the position, which would also require Sally to enroll in an intensive summer course. As Sally learned about teaching dyslexic children, her own reading and writing abilities gradually improved. For

Sally, both the learning experience and the discovery that she had a learning disability were revelations.

One of Sally's enduring qualities is her tendency to set high personal standards. She is bent on proving her capabilities to the world (and to herself). After years of teaching kindergarten, she wanted a new challenge. She began by taking several graduate courses. Then she decided to go back to school full-time. She applied to the Harvard Graduate School of Education, and she was accepted.

At Harvard, Sally's insecurity about her disabilities resurfaced with fierce intensity. She did not want anyone to know that she was dyslexic, to make concessions for her, or to decide that she didn't belong. She lived by herself in a dormitory room, telling no one of her learning disabilities for the entire first term. One can only imagine how difficult it must be for someone with severe dyslexia to cope in such a highly conceptual environment, in which reading and writing are so important.

Sally started her papers months before they were due. In one course, she joined every available study group, so she could hear the readings discussed over and over again. She repeatedly turned down opportunities to go out. Her friends were limited to the students who could help her learn. She slept an average of four or five hours a night. By the start of winter, she was on the brink of exhaustion.

Only a marginal grade on a term paper drove Sally to seek help. Thinking she had failed, Sally went to an office at the university that was specially designed to help students with reading and writing. Even then, she initially told the counselor that she was seeking information to improve her teaching. Desperation— more than courage—finally motivated Sally to tell her story and agree to be tested. Two weeks later, Sally received the first official description and diagnosis of her learning disabilities: she was the most severely dyslexic student that the specialist had seen in his many years at the university. . . .

She was referred to an office for student services in the Harvard Graduate School of Education, where she learned that the university would pay for someone to tape her assignments, read to her, and edit her written work. She also discovered other resources: a university support group for learning-disabled students and a student organization that sponsored monthly speakers on learning disabilities.

During her second semester at Harvard, Sally told her story—to teachers, to classmates, and to friends. To her surprise, most of them were empathic. None lowered their expectations for Sally's performance, but many developed a new appreciation for diverse learning needs. Several teachers were especially helpful. One offered the services of his teaching assistants as well as his own time to read assignments, to review papers, and to discuss the readings. Sally took advantage of this offer and talked to the teacher about specific readings. Understanding Sally's preference for visual learning, this teacher made a point in class of drawing figures and diagrams on the chalkboard and pausing after a question to give students time to formulate their responses.

Not all of Sally's teachers were comfortable with her disclosure. Sally noted in one class that her fast-paced instructor consistently overlooked her raised hand, which Sally interpreted as an effort to protect her. In fact, it exaggerated her sense of isolation, of being different.

Today, Sally believes that the services she received from the university markedly strengthened her ability to read and write, but she is convinced that the most critical factor in her growth was her enhanced feeling of self-worth. "Once I began to feel good about myself," she says, "I could start learning. And now that I'm learning, I never want to stop."

Sally's story raises some important questions: How is it possible for a student to go through school without learning to read and write with proficiency? How can educators pass over, ignore, or deny learning difficulties? Why are there so many schools in which only a very narrow range of learning styles is rewarded?

Sally's story also teaches many lessons— some of them painful, but most of them promising. Sally's gains have not been without cost. In order to keep up with her schoolwork and to keep her disability a secret, Sally distanced herself from the activities and friendships that most of us take for granted. A person who likes people, Sally found it especially difficult to maintain this social isolation.

Sally's story dramatizes the essential role of parents in personal development and in schooling. Sally's mother contributed to Sally's success in tangible and intangible ways. Without her support and encouragement, Sally would not have believed in herself or experienced success.

Sally's story also dramatizes the power of individual initiative, courage, and resilience. Despite constant obstacles, Sally refused to accept defeat. In fact, the obstacles only sparked her desire to triumph.

Sally's experience at Harvard illustrates the importance of special services for learning-disabled students. It shows the positive influence of knowledgeable and understanding teachers, as well as the need to reeducate those teachers who may be unfamiliar or uncomfortable with learning handicaps.

Finally, Sally's story reminds us that learning disabilities may be constructively thought of as learning *differences.* Children and adults with dyslexia and other learning handicaps often demonstrate talents in the visual arts, athletics, music, and math. Rather than dismiss learning-disabled students, teachers can identify their strengths and can capitalize on them.

PREREFERRAL

Identification of learning disabilities is probably the most subjective identification procedure involved in special education, except perhaps for identification of behavior disorders. At first glance, the criteria for identification may seem relatively clear, but in fact, they are ambiguous in many respects.

When a classroom teacher suspects that a student has a learning disability, a prereferral meeting should be held. At this meeting, the regular classroom teacher may pro-

vide documentation regarding modifications already made or interventions already tried. Then, a specialist may suggest additional modifications or interventions. After a reasonable period of time, if the interventions suggested at the prereferral meeting have been tried with little apparent success, the teacher may make a formal referral.

RESPONSIBILITIES OF SPECIAL EDUCATION PERSONNEL

The specialists with whom regular classroom teachers will likely be working in the case of learning disabilities may be called learning disabilities consultants, consulting teachers, LD teachers, resource room teachers, or teachers of the mild and moderately disabled. The titles vary from state to state and sometimes within a given state; however, the roles and responsibilities are quite similar. In general, the specialist conducts some part of the assessment required for identification purposes and coordinates the assessment process. After the staffing team determines that a student has learning disabilities, the specialist provides direct or indirect services, depending on the needs of the student and the IEP (see chapter 2 for the continuum of services).

For most students who are learning disabled, the services provided by the resource teacher or consultant take place in either a resource room or a regular classroom. If the student receives the services of a resource room teacher in the resource room, the amount of time the student is out of the regular classroom and the specific time of day the student goes to the resource room is stipulated as the IEP is developed. If the student is to receive services in the regular classroom, the responsibilities of the specialist are delineated as the IEP is written. At the secondary level, the time that the student is in a separate setting (more often called the resource room) is usually one or more of the regular class periods during the school day. In either case, it is a matter of joint planning and service by a regular classroom teacher and learning disabilities specialist or consultant. Each must work cooperatively to ensure that the needs of the student are being met.

THE ROLE OF REGULAR CLASSROOM TEACHERS

The first and foremost responsibility of any teacher is to help each student in class achieve the recognized goals of instruction in that class to the fullest extent possible. This responsibility extends equally to students who are learning disabled, and much of the instruction for such students is little different from that of other students in the class. For decades, good teachers have been applying somewhat different methods and techniques for certain students. In fact, it appears that some students who might have turned out to be among those considered mildly learning disabled have been successful because they have had a sequence of teachers who understood the need for individualization, took the time to provide specialized instruction, and helped the students overcome their learning difficulties. We hasten to add, however, that students with serious, specific learning disabilities are not likely to achieve remediation in this manner. They are much more likely to require specialized assistance from the resource room teacher and coordinated efforts from regular classroom teachers.

Although it is difficult to generalize to fit all situations, it is likely that regular classroom teachers will proceed as follows in dealing with the students who are learning disabled. The most important step is to modify the program in the manner suggested by the consultant or resource room teacher. This often involves just one or two subject or skill areas, and the consultant should provide concrete examples of what to do, including materials to use. However, the regular classroom teacher remains responsible for the program in class and should apply suggestions, ideas, and materials as they are possible and practical. The role of the resource teacher or consultant is to suggest and assist, not to dictate to the regular classroom teacher. This principle is important, and it places the responsibility for classroom management squarely where it belongs—with the teacher in charge of that class.

Basic Principles for Program Planning

The needs of any group of students who are learning disabled are sufficiently unique to make it impossible to say that all must receive some specific type of instruction or that some established set of instructional goals always apply, but it is possible to outline certain principles. This approach to program planning is necessary because of the umbrella definition of learning disabilities. The following principles do not tell *what* to teach. Instead, they provide a *basis for deciding what to teach*. They also provide guidance as to *how* to teach, but they must be related to the needs of each student.

The principles that follow may be successfully applied by teachers with a variety of teaching styles. There is, in fact, only one type of teacher who cannot use these principles: the teacher who believes that all children learn in the same way and that he or she knows the only successful way to teach. When students with learning disabilities are assigned to such a teacher, no set of principles will help.

If the usual teaching method—that used with most other students in a regular class—works, then that method should be used. Teachers must not use different methods just to be able to say they are doing something different, but teachers should initiate different methods when the usual methods are not achieving results commensurate with the apparent ability of students to learn. The following principles should provide concrete assistance in determining how to modify the educational program, but they must be used in conjunction with specific information about the abilities, areas of weakness, and past educational experiences of students. For students who are diagnosed as learning disabled, this information should be available as part of the summary of assessment results; however, it should be further verified through informal assessment and day-to-day observation.

Principle 1 ■ ***There is no single "right" method to use with students who are learning disabled.***

Students are referred for assistance in learning disability programs because they are *not* learning effectively through the approach used in the classroom with the general population of students. Of course, teachers who know they are working with a student who is deaf would not use an approach that is primarily auditory in teaching word-attack skills, but many regular classroom teachers continue to use methods that rely heavily on hearing sounds accurately with students who do not have the ability to discriminate between the sounds. A student may hear sound as well as others but be unable to discriminate between phonemes that are similar. An analogous situation exists with a student who has good visual acuity but who cannot accurately discriminate between certain letters and thus does not do well with approaches based primarily on visual recognition.

Acknowledgment of individual problems forms the basis for trying a number of alternate approaches. It is a major step in understanding that there is no one right method for dealing with learning disabilities. The idea that there is one right method that works for all children with learning disabilities violates common sense. Educators must realize that they may need to try a number of methods in difficult cases.

Principle 2 ■ ***All other factors being equal, use the method newest for the student.***

When gathering data about educational history and background, teachers should make every attempt to determine which approaches and materials have been used with each student. These may not be significant in all cases, but they are in many. Analysis of this information can have several applications. If certain approaches have been used with little or no success, such approaches may be inappropriate. This is not always the case, however, for such approaches may have been poorly implemented or the student may have acquired certain requisite abilities that he or she did not possess earlier. Nonetheless, educational background provides a starting point for further investigation.

An equally important point, and one too often overlooked, is that many students develop a failure syndrome. Teachers may feel it necessary to continue to attempt to help students learn to read or to read more effectively, but the teachers should try to use methods that look and feel different to the students. The more severe the learning problem and the longer it has been recognized and felt, the greater the need for this procedure. This principle dictates that when a variety of approaches are possible and all other factors are approximately equal, the approach that is most different from earlier methods is likely to be the most effective.

Principle 3 ■ *Implement positive reconditioning.*

Pioneers in the field of learning disabilities, Fernald and Gillingham (see Gearheart & Gearheart, 1989, pp. 172, 186) recognized the value of this principle, a value that remains today. The newest possible method (principle 2) is part of this positive reconditioning effort, and additional attempts should be directed toward convincing students with learning disabilities that their inability to develop adequate reading (or arithmetic or language) skills is not their fault. Rather, it is caused by the failure of the school and teachers to recognize that the students need to learn by methods different from those used for other children. The obvious points of this effort are to convince children that they are OK and to boost their self-esteem to the point that they will approach the learning task with confidence and thus maximize their chances of success.

Unfortunately, most schools are organized in such a way that students with learning difficulties are reminded daily, sometimes hourly, that they are failures. There is a scarcity of research on the effects of planned positive reconditioning, but the

Most students with learning disabilities are in a regular class for most of the day.

experience of a number of teachers with whom we have worked, the historical testimony of Fernald and Gillingham, and common sense indicate that *success must be planned.*

Principle 4 ■ **High motivation is a prerequisite to success, so consider the affective domain.**

Attempts to maximize motivation are difficult to measure or monitor and may seem unglamorous, except as related to some unusual behavior modification system. Principles 2 and 3 are a part of the overall attempt to maximize motivation, but deliberate efforts beyond these two principles must be planned. In the case of older students who have developed the basic learning abilities necessary for academic success but developed them several years late, a program to promote higher motivation may be particularly important. The fact that various behavior modification techniques are in common use, many with apparent success, attests to the validity of this principle.

This principle also dictates some sort of planned investigation of the affective domain—a look at how students feel about themselves, both in general (in the world outside the academic boundaries) and in respect to the school setting. Some students with learning disabilities have emotional problems that can scarcely be overlooked. In this case, the best approach is to initiate attempts to counteract, remedy, or otherwise attend to these problems. Many of the other principles have the effect of attending to the problems of low self-esteem, and improved academic achievement automatically has a positive effect. But beyond these positive vectors, it is imperative that the affective components be deliberately considered to maximize the potential of other remedial efforts and to prevent the growth of

negative emotional components. This investigation of the affective domain, even when there are no overt behavior problems, must be a part of evaluation and planning for students who are learning disabled.

Principle 5 ■ **Recognize the possibility of nonspecific or difficult-to-define disabilities, particularly with older students.**

A serious educational problem in reading or arithmetic can be defined, but if, for example, a secondary student experienced significant visual perceptual problems at an early age and did not have the visual perceptual skills necessary for success in reading at 8 years of age but developed them later, it may be almost impossible to pinpoint the specific disability. In most cases, significant educational retardation may exist along with a negative attitude toward school. For example, there may be a need to develop second- or third-grade reading skills in a 15-year-old student who has learned many ways to circumvent his or her reading problem. Remediation for such a student must use materials appropriate for the student's age and interests. Principles 2 and 3 are critical for this type of student.

Principle 6 ■ **Be concerned and involved with both process- and task-oriented assistance and remediation.**

This principle must be followed for the most effective use of time and effort. Many of the earliest efforts to help students overcome learning disabilities centered on remediation of process skills and paid little attention to helping students carry these skills over into the actual task of learning to read or understand arithmetic. Experience indicates that it is generally best to teach students in the context of the work they will be doing as they use the skill. If a student cannot visually discriminate between *ad* and *ab*, he or she must learn to do so in the context of using the skill. Similarly, if a student must learn to outline, then outlining should be taught in the content areas in which it will be used. In all cases, meaningful practice as opposed to drill is critical. If teachers are aware of the need for skills to be taught in context and plan for meaningful practice, they can apply this principle in a variety of situations.

Principle 7 ■ ***Attempt to determine how students who have learning disabilities approach cognitive learning, and then help them develop better learning strategies.***

In many instances, this final principle is the most important. All individuals establish ways in which they learn. In essence, they develop ways in which to organize the information at hand. Precisely how each individual develops his or her personal learning system is not known. However, it is known that some individuals are much better organized, more systematic, and more effective learners than others. It is also known that students with learning disabilities appear to approach many learning tasks in a disorganized manner.

Organization for learning applies to all learning—motor learning, basic language learning, and concept formation. Teachers must pay as much attention to *how* students learn as they do to *what* students learn. They must analyze how the students think—how students approach cognitive learning—and help the students improve their learning strategies. Applications of this principle include cognitive training and the teaching of specific study skills.

Behavior Management Approaches

Behavior management approaches may be well known to some readers and new to others. But it is doubtful that any reader of this text has not *experienced* behavior management techniques, either as the recipient of such efforts or a user of them, perhaps unknowingly. One often thinks of the term *operant conditioning, behavior modification,* or *applied behavior analysis* when thinking of this topic, but regardless, the term refers to changing behavior. Although one may first think of behavior as acting out or withdrawing, listening and reading are also behaviors. Alberto and Troutman (1990) point out that behavior management approaches can be used to teach academic subjects as well as manage students' social behavior.

Behavior management involves procedures whereby educators specify behavioral goals, establish ways to reach these goals, and then attempt to help students maintain whatever desirable changes have taken place. Often, some type of contract (a written agreement) is involved and positive reinforcement is used. However, at other times, students are unaware that behavior modification (shaping or management) is taking place. Obviously, teachers must establish realistic objectives, consistent with the overall learning program for students.

Behavior management that relates to highly distractible students (often referred to as hyperactive by teachers, although a clinical diagnosis has not been made by a psychologist or psychiatrist) or those with intense sensitivity to visual, auditory, or tactile stimuli includes the following environmental modifications:

1. When differentiated assignments are possible, assign activities that involve fewer potential distractions. Be careful in the assignment of group activities for

the student, considering the size of the group, other students in the group, and similar factors.

2. Change the student's seating assignment according to possible sources of distraction. If this change does not provide enough environmental control, assign the student to a study carrel. (For young students, this may be called an office, which may be temporarily constructed out of large packing boxes.)

3. Limit the amount and type of materials at the student's desk through the use of a tote tray or a storage and checkout procedure that you control.

4. Use some sort of device, such as a headset, to cover the student's ears (used only at selected times).

5. Move the student to another classroom. This is more likely to be necessary if the classroom has an open setting.

Implementation of some of these suggestions will require permission from the parents or principal. For example, when suggesting that a student use a study carrel or headset to muffle sound, parents and other students should understand the reason for the modification so that they don't view it as a punishment. Moving a student to another classroom ordinarily requires permission of both the parent and the principal.

Tactile, Kinesthetic, and Multisensory Approaches

The tactile and kinesthetic senses are too often overlooked by teachers as channels for learning, perhaps because the auditory and visual channels appear more effective. This discussion considers the tactile and kinesthetic senses as channels for effective learning and discusses their use as part of a multisensory, visual-auditory-kinesthetic-tactile approach.

For students who cannot see, the sense of

touch—the ability to feel shapes and forms and configurations—provides an effective substitute for sight when applied to developing the ability to read. In various ways, the tactile and kinesthetic learning channels can also be used help some other students read:

1. Ask students to identify objects placed in a cloth bag so that they cannot see them.

2. Blindfold students and ask them to identify objects.

3. Use sandpaper letters or numbers to promote tactile and kinesthetic learning of these symbols.

In each of these activities, the major purpose is to provide tactile and kinesthetic support for visual learning, either to help develop skills that have been slow in developing or to attempt to straighten out previously scrambled reception and interpretation of visual signals. In some cases, it is helpful to have children feel a letter or word while looking at it, thus providing simultaneous signal reception through the visual and tactile senses. In other cases, it is more effective to block the visual signal to be certain that the student is completely accurate in tactile sensing before adding the visual. The important principle is the use of more than one sensory modality. This principle commonly supports the visual sense with the tactile sense.

In a somewhat different application of this principle, a teacher or helping student traces out letters or sometimes words on the arm or back of a student who needs help. This approach is significantly different in that the student receives no kinesthetic input, only tactile. The student may be looking at letter cards on a desk and attempting to find one matching the letter traced out on his or her back or may keep eyes closed and concentrate on feeling the letter or word. A whole variety of games or activities may be developed using this type of assistance when the evidence indicates that the student needs it. Note, however, that this type of activity might be misused or overdone if not carefully monitored.

The preceding activities and approaches are most appropriate with primary-age children who show evidence of developmental or remedial needs in the visual-perceptual abilities required for reading. The kinesthetic and tactile modalities are currently used in a wide variety of learning activities in kindergarten and first grade. They may not be emphasized as such, but experienced primary-grade teachers regularly verify their use and general acceptance. These two modalities may also be a part of an organized teaching approach more often used for remedial purposes with students having unusual difficulties in learning to read.

When used along with the visual and auditory channels, kinesthetic and tactile approaches are sometimes called VAKT (visual-auditory-kinesthetic-tactile) approaches, and sometimes they are simply called multisensory approaches. One of the best known of such approaches is that first advocated by Grace Fernald over 50 years ago and still in use today. In 1943, Fernald provided an account of her methods, and although many variations of her approach have since been proposed, they retain the basic ideas outlined in her original text. The following review of her work illustrates the basic thrust of this approach.

The Fernald approach has been called a multisensory approach, a tracing approach, or a kinesthetic method. The terms *tracing* and *kinesthetic* have been applied because those are unique features of the approach, but the most accurate name for this method is simultaneous VAKT, which differentiates her approach from most other approaches called multisensory or VAKT.

Before the remedial program is actually started, the Fernald procedure strongly recommends positive reconditioning. This recommendation is based on the assumption that almost all students who have experienced school failure have developed a low self-concept, particularly in relation to anything associated with school or formal education. The following suggestions involve conditions to be avoided.

1. *Avoid calling attention to emotionally loaded situations.* Attempts by either teachers or parents to urge the student to do better generally have negative effects. Reminding the student of the future importance of academic success or telling the student how important it is to the family should be avoided. If the student is already a failure and knows it, these admonitions or urgings are at best useless and sometimes result in a nearly complete emotional block.

2. *Avoid using methods that previous experience suggests are likely to be ineffective.* This is important during both remediation and reentry to the regular classroom. If the student is experiencing success in a temporary, out-of-class remedial setting (after school or for a set time period each day) and then must return to class and to methods by which he or she was previously unable to learn, the remedial program may be negated.

3. *Avoid conditions that may cause embarrassment.* Sometimes, a new method used in the new setting is effective and satisfactory, whereas in the old setting, unless some special provisions are made, it may seem childish or silly. For example, the tracing involved in the Fernald approach may seem so unusual in the regular classroom that the student feels out of place there. The reward, that is, the learning, may not be worth the feel-

ings of conspicuousness and embarrassment.

4. *Avoid directing attention to what the student cannot do.* This problem is really an extension of the first condition.

Regardless of what is required, attempting to bring about positive reconditioning and avoiding emotional reversal after the reconditioning has taken place are of prime importance.

The first step in each remedial case in the actual classroom or clinic procedure is to explain to the student that there is a new way of learning words that really works. The student is told that others have had the same problem he or she is having and have learned easily through this new method.

The second step is to ask the student to select any word he or she wants to learn, regardless of length, and then to teach the student to write and recognize (read) it, using the following method:

1. Write the word chosen by the student, usually with a crayon in plain, blackboard-size cursive writing. In most cases, regardless of age, cursive writing is used rather than manuscript because the student tends to see and feel the word as a single entity rather than a group of separate letters.
2. Have the student trace the word with his or her fingers in contact with the paper, saying the word at the same time. Repeat this step as many times as necessary, until the student can write the word without looking at the copy.
3. Have the student write the word on scrap paper, demonstrating to himself or herself mastery of the word. Teach several words in this manner, taking as much time as necessary for the student to completely master them.
4. When the student has internalized the fact that he or she can write and recog-

nize words, encourage the student to start writing stories. Let the student's stories be whatever the student wishes them to be at first, and give the student any words (in addition to those mastered) necessary to complete the story.

5. After the story is written, type it and ask the student to read it in typed form while it is still fresh. It is important that this reading be done immediately.
6. After the story is completed and the new words have been used in a meaningful way, have the student write the new words on cards that the student files alphabetically in an individual word file. In addition, use this word file to teach the alphabet without undue emphasis on rote memory.

This procedure is often called the Fernald tracing method because the tracing is an added feature in contrast to the usual methods of teaching reading or word recognition. However, note that the student is simultaneously *feeling, seeing, saying,* and *hearing* the word. Thus, the approach is truly multisensory.

Carefully observe the following points for maximum success:

1. Each word should be selected by the student.
2. Finger contact is essential. The student may use either one or two fingers.
3. The student should write a word, after tracing it several times, without looking at the copy.
4. In case of error or interruption in writing, the word should be crossed out and a new start made.
5. Each word should be used in context.
6. The student must always say each word aloud or to himself or herself while tracing it and writing it.

Although many additional details could be given, the preceding points outline the essence of the Fernald approach. This approach has been used with various students having a variety of problems, including problems in the auditory channel. However, the approach is probably most beneficial for students with visual channel problems, particularly problems of visual sequential memory or visual imagery.

Cognitive Training Techniques

A variety of techniques—cognitive training, metacognition, and cognitive behavior modification—involve training students to monitor and modify their cognitive strategies. Such approaches are applicable from elementary grades through high school. The premise underlying these approaches is that some students do not produce effective strategies for learning; therefore, their learning processes are ineffective and disorganized. The strategies that tend to require remediation are the plans, actions, steps, and processes that result in inefficient learning or problem solving.

Meichenbaum (1983) suggests that teachers examine their own cognitions before attempting to teach thinking skills to students. His guidelines follow:

1. *Try out* target behaviors yourself to determine all of the steps. Ask students who perform well, and those who don't, to help analyze the task.
2. *Tune in* to students as they perform tasks. Be especially attuned to hesitation or confidence expressed verbally and nonverbally.
3. *Choose as a training task an actual task the students perform* (or something similar). Otherwise, the students will be unable to generalize.
4. *Ask for students' advice* in devising the training. Use the actual words of the students whenever possible.
5. *Train subtasks and metacognitive skills at the same time;* otherwise, the students may develop separate skills. Subtasks are the skills needed to perform the task, and metacognitive skills include skills such as self-questioning.
6. *Provide specific feedback,* indicating how the use of the strategy leads to improvement. The goal is not to use the metacognitive skills but to improve performance.
7. *Teach generalization* by using the strategy under new circumstances. Use a variety of persons in a variety of settings.
8. *Provide a coping model* by demonstrating what happens when the strategy is not used and how to cope with that failure.
9. *Review the strategy* on a planned basis. Provide for reteaching specific skills.

After thinking through these guidelines, teachers may want to begin to use some of the strategies. Remember above all that changing or modifying thinking processes is a long-term task.

A self-questioning strategy (Wong & Jones, 1982) that may help reading comprehension consists of the following steps:

1. Ask, Why am I reading this?
2. Locate main ideas and highlight them with a marker.
3. Write down a question about each main idea.
4. Think about an answer for each question.
5. Read the passage or chapter.
6. Reexamine the questions and compare your mental answers with the answers in the passage just read.

Divide lengthy chapters into sections for this strategy to be effective.

Schumaker, Deshler, Alley, Warner, and Denton (1982) devised a multipass comprehension strategy. Each of the three passes through the reading material recommended in this strategy has specific purposes.

The survey pass requires the student to gain as much information from the chapter as possible, using the chapter title, illustrations and captions, major subtitles, the summary, and so on. Paraphrasing of the information gathered leads to a beginning level of comprehension.

The size-up pass requires the student to collect as much information from the chapter as possible without reading it word for word. Questions at the end of the chapter are used to guide the finding of dates or italicized words. Cues such as italics, colors, and bold print are changed into questions. For example, if the word *ecosystems* is in bold print, the student may ask, "What does *ecosystem* mean?" or "How is ecosystem related to environment?" The student then skims the section around the word and paraphrases an answer.

The sort-out pass enables the student to evaluate his or her own knowledge of the material. The student tries to answer the questions at the close of the chapter. The student places a mark by any question he or she can answer immediately. If the student is unsure of the answer, he or she locates the answer by skimming the appropriate section of the chapter and then places a mark by that question until all questions are marked.

A number of teachers have found that many students who have difficulty with academic tasks tend to respond impulsively (for example, with wild guessing) to problem solving, virtually ignoring various clues or cues that more reflective students use to advantage. Since cognitive style is apparently learned and impulsive students have not learned to employ their cognitive pro-

cesses effectively, it seems logical to provide assistance through specific cognitive training. One training technique provided by Meichenbaum and Goodman (1971) includes teaching specific verbalizations in the following modeling and rehearsal sequence:

1. The teacher models the task to be learned, talking aloud while the student watches and listens.
2. The student performs the task, verbalizing (self-instructing) in a manner similar to that demonstrated by the teacher in step 1. The teacher assists as needed.
3. The student performs the task, self-instructing as in step 2 but with no assistance from the teacher.
4. The student performs the task, self-instructing in a whisper.
5. The student performs the task, thinking the self-instruction that was formerly verbalized.

Self-instructional cognitive training may involve questions, such as "What must I look at before I decide the answer?" In addition, the student may be trained to supply self-reinforcement by verbalizing statements such as "That was good—I got the right answer."

Another approach that relates to problem solving and learning to think about alternatives has been suggested by Buser and Reimer (1988). They suggest using activities to help students who have difficulty with planning and organization and who believe that there can be only one correct answer, which only the teacher knows. The overall goals of these activities include:

1. To introduce children to different problem-solving strategies and give them practice using these strategies
2. To encourage the deduction of solutions through reasoning rather than by purely guessing

3. To aid children in developing their *own* schema for organizing and synthesizing information into more usable forms
4. To investigate the relationships between logical problem solving in a situational context and problem solving in the academic area (p. 22)

Such problem-solving activities take 15 to 20 minutes and can be enjoyed by students of all ages if teachers choose problems appropriate for the age and interests of the students. The general steps are:

1. The teacher presents a problem that has no right or wrong answers (for example, "We have all of these cans and boxes of food to put on kitchen shelves. How can we place them so that we can easily find them?").
2. The teacher and students briefly discuss the problem to make sure all understand what they are to do.
3. The students provide possible solutions and tell *why* they think their solutions are workable. Discussion follows each proposed solution, with students suggesting the positive and negative aspects of each and their reasons for thinking as they do.
4. After various solutions have been suggested and perhaps even tried out, the students select what they think is the best solution.
5. The teacher and students then enagage in a brief discussion designed to promote application in academic or social areas. In our example, the principle of organizing food on shelves can easily be applied to organizing school materials the night before or putting things in a locker for easy retrieval just before class.

Problem-solving activities can be especially meaningful when the students can actually carry out and check their proposed solutions (actually placing the food in some

order and timing another student to see how long it takes that other student to find it). A variety of activities can be used—individual puzzles, ways to carry a number of articles (such as books, comb, lunch money, homework, note to the principal, and jacket), or the sequence to follow in performing a specific task (such as washing the car, cleaning off the table after dinner, making a phone call or taking a shower). The purpose of generating alternatives to such problems is for students to think about their actions, the strategies they use to solve the problems, and the many possible solutions. Through discussions, teachers provide the assistance that students need to generalize problem-solving skills to academic and school-related tasks.

Study Strategies

The teaching of study strategies is closely related to cognitive training and may be approached in a number of ways. Direct, systematic teaching of essential study strategies has been recommended by a number of authorities (Alley & Deshler, 1979; Mercer & Mercer, 1989). What is involved is directly teaching students to improve specific study skills, and use of this method with students who are learning disabled is suggested by the fact that many such students appear to have very poor study skills.

Educators who advocate the teaching of specific study skills believe that there are specific "techniques, principles or rules that will facilitate the acquisition, manipulation, integration, storage, and retrieval of information across settings and situations" (Alley & Deshler, 1979, p. 13). The focus is teaching students how to study and learn, not on specific content. The specific techniques or skills should help students learn in content areas as diverse as literature and mathematics.

Students with academic problems relating to learning disabilities may be gifted in other areas.

The rationale for teaching study skills is that students with learning disabilities often do not know how to study effectively. However, once students fully learn a particular skill, they may generalize it and use it in a variety of content areas. For example, skimming can help students manage increasing amounts of text materials, focus on key points, and discriminate essential information. Similarly, students can learn how to determine essential information and how to organize, sequence, and condense information. All of these skills are useful in the content areas.

Sheinker and Sheinker (1989) have developed an approach to teaching the skills of skimming, summarizing, note taking, and outlining. The strategies are hierarchic in nature, each building on the strategies learned previously. The method of teaching the skills follows Meichenbaum's (1983) suggestions for teaching thinking skills and is generally applicable in all content areas. A summary of some of these teaching strategies follows:

1. Collect baseline data to determine existing abilities and brainstorm with students to detect thinking that impedes learning the strategies. This activity may also provide motivation to learn more effective and efficient techniques for dealing with reading material.

2. Collaborate with students in the development of effective strategies. Continual use of self-questioning and self-search for the thinking processes provide more student input than do many teacher-directed activities.

3. Work to enable students to internalize

how, when, where, and why to use specific strategies. Repeat demonstrations and detailed explanations of which strategies work, when they work, and why they work. The emphasis is collaboration in trying out a variety of strategies and determining the effectiveness. The key is *why*. Knowledge of why provides the ability to choose or reject a strategy in future reading assignments.

4. Provide practice in using newly acquired strategies. When students master a particular skill, provide repeated opportunities for generalization and internalization. The skills of scanning and skimming, for example, should be demonstrated in such diverse content areas as science, mathematics, social studies, health, government, and economics. Carefully monitor practice sessions and emphasize why specific strategies do or do not work. In this way, generalization of the skills is taught as conscientiously as the skills themselves.

In addition to teaching the skills mentioned, the program teaches self-direction, self-monitoring, self-evaluation, and self-correction. The program contains practice sheets that can be duplicated for class use and step-by-step guidelines for teachers.

Listening is related to language development in young students but remains important as students begin to experience more lectures in their progress through school. Students who have learning disabilities often have difficulty recalling and organizing information presented to them auditorily. Suggestions for training or guided practice include:

1. *Rehearsal.* Students summarize, in their own words, the information they have just heard. This might be a passage that is read to them or commercials taped from the radio.

2. *Prediction.* Students listen to a portion of a story or newspaper article and guess what comes next. Then, they confirm their predictions.

3. *Details.* Students listen for specific details as stories, newspaper articles, or magazine articles are read to them.

4. *Main idea.* Students listen to a passage, story, newspaper article, or magazine article and provide the main idea. Alternately, students compose headlines for newspaper or magazine articles that were read to them. Using reviews of the latest musical albums, articles about movie stars or sports heroes, movie reviews, or other similar motivating materials can help students practice skills that are difficult for them.

5. *Details–main idea.* In combination with suggestions 3 and 4, the class is divided into groups, and some students in each group listen for details. Others listen for the main idea. Then, as a group, all of the students reconstruct what they heard. Longer stories or passages may be used for this activity.

6. *Absurdities.* Students listen for words, phrases, or sentences that do not fit the passage or story being read to them.

7. *Propaganda.* Students listen to recorded advertisements for phrases that are meant to entice listeners into buying the product. Students should also separate fact from opinion.

Some students with learning disabilities have difficulty preparing for classes and spend little or no time at the close of class reflecting on what they have learned. Ellis (1989) suggests a set of strategies to help students learn skills related to class preparation (PREP):

1. *Prepare materials.* Think about what is needed for class: Get your notebook, pencil, text, etc.

2. *Review what is known.* Read over key points from the previous class; page through the text, examining graphs and pictures; read study questions from the previous class; and think about what was learned.

3. *Establish a mind-set.* To get ready to learn something new, do self-talk about positive aspects of learning.

4. *Pinpoint goals.* Think about what you will learn. Page ahead in the text and decide what you want to know. Think about questions to ask, and make some notes about what you want to know.

Students can be taught to take time to reflect on what they learned during class using the following steps (WISE):

1. *Were your goals met?* Were your questions answered? Did you learn what you wanted to learn?

2. *Itemize important information.* Review class notes, highlight important information, clarify what you don't understand, and reexamine the text graphs, pictures, and bold print.

3. *See how information can be remembered.* Make a vocabulary list, make a visual outline, or list three or four things that are important.

4. *Explain what you learned.* Put into your own words what you learned. Discuss key points with others.

Teach these two strategies, explaining just what students are to do in each step as it is relevant to a particular subject, perhaps modifying some of the steps to make them more applicable to specific content. Devote a few minutes at the beginning and closing of classes to teaching the skills. As the students become more proficient in their use, 3 to 5 minutes at the beginning for PREP and 5 to 10 minutes for WISE at the close is usually sufficient time for the students to employ the strategies. By allowing time at the beginning of class, teachers communicate the importance of what is being taught and do not take for granted that the students know it. Time at the beginning of class also enables students to begin thinking about the content of the class, recall information from previous classes, and set learning goals. Such time is critical for students who have difficulty with transitions from one class to another or who have memory problems. When students set learning goals for themselves, they tend to participate more and become more responsible for their own learning. Time at the close of class allows students to reflect on what they learned, think about the information in a manner that matches their learning style, and prepare for the next class by noting key information.

A broad-based approach suggested by Deshler and Schumaker (1986) stresses appropriate diagnosis of the skills students do not use consistently or efficiently and the skills they do use effectively. Then, teachers can examine the various content areas to determine what skills students must have to function effectively in each area. With the knowledge of what students already know and use and what demands will be made on them, teachers may design a specific curriculum. The skills required are then taught in a structured, systematic fashion. They are taught across a variety of content areas, so as to promote generalization. If teachers develop long-range goals concerning skills to teach, they can maximize progress. Deshler and Schumaker suggest that three to four learning strategies per year are appropriate.

SUGGESTIONS FOR REGULAR CLASSROOM TEACHERS

After the assessment process is completed and an IEP is written, a teacher should have a clear picture of how learning disabilities affect a particular student. The following sections include teaching suggestions to stimulate the thinking of teachers. The question that teachers must ask is, How do I best facilitate learning? The key to the usefulness of suggestions is the selection of methods. Teachers should base their teaching methods on knowledge of particular students and the learning problems that the students are experiencing.

Reading

Following are a number of teaching suggestions to help students with reading. Also, see Figure 10–3, which includes teaching suggestions for letters and words.

When reading stories aloud, stop and ask the students to predict what will come next. In the early stages, monitor the students so that their predictions are related to the passage. To monitor comprehension,

ask students to identify words or phrases that provided the clues they used to make their predictions.

Provide activities before, during, and after students read to help them interact with the print. Before reading, discuss the story or poem to help the students activate their knowledge about the topic. Teach vocabulary words and key concepts so that the students are able to read without unnecessary interruptions. Above all, generate a purpose for reading. During reading, ask relevant questions and provide assistance when needed. After reading, determine with the students whether or not they accomplished their purpose for the reading. Condense the information that they read, and integrate the new information with prior knowledge. Finally, when appropriate, apply the information.

When students, especially older ones, have difficulty with basic sight vocabulary

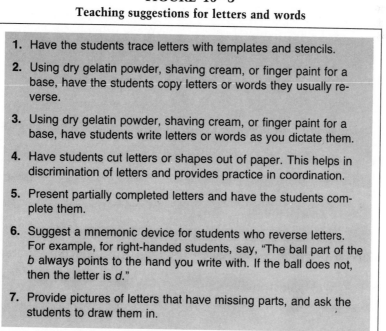

FIGURE 10–3
Teaching suggestions for letters and words

1. Have the students trace letters with templates and stencils.

2. Using dry gelatin powder, shaving cream, or finger paint for a base, have the students copy letters or words they usually reverse.

3. Using dry gelatin powder, shaving cream, or finger paint for a base, have students write letters or words as you dictate them.

4. Have students cut letters or shapes out of paper. This helps in discrimination of letters and provides practice in coordination.

5. Present partially completed letters and have the students complete them.

6. Suggest a mnemonic device for students who reverse letters. For example, for right-handed students, say, "The ball part of the b always points to the hand you write with. If the ball does not, then the letter is d."

7. Provide pictures of letters that have missing parts, and ask the students to draw them in.

words, such as *and, if, from, was,* and *going,* prepare audiotapes of stories or selections. Choose short and interesting passages (about 15 minutes each) at the listening level of the students and record the passages on tape. Be sure to include cues such as page numbers and times to turn pages. (Either teachers or good readers can prepare tapes.) Then, have the students listen to the tapes while following the printed versions of the passages, listening and simultaneously reading as many times as necessary to recognize all of the words. When the students recognize all of the words within a passage, listen to them read the passage without the tape. The purpose of this activity is to help students recognize the printed versions of words in their speaking vocabularies. In addition, the activity provides appropriate models for oral reading. Hargis (1982) suggests that this activity reduces the failure aspect of poor readers. Note, however, that although the activity helps students recognize words, it does not help them use context clues. It also slows the rate of silent reading. Hargis suggests using this activity only as supplementary, because it can easily lead to boredom with overuse.

Using newspaper clippings, list questions that are answered in either the articles or captions. To provide practice in skimming, time the students. To provide practice in critical thinking, have the students seek possible bias or opinions. To provide practice in synthesizing, have the students read articles and tape record or write one-paragraph summaries.

Teach students about words that indicate chronology and sequential or causal relationships. History books usually provide practice in chronological arrangement. Science and math books frequently illustrate sequential arrangement. In addition, newspaper articles use cue words, such as *when,*

then, because of, and *therefore.* Similar words indicate that ideas are being compared, such as *in contrast, parallel to, on the other hand,* and *in relation to.* Words that signal main ideas include *in summary, basically,* and *in essence.* Words that alert students to important information include *categories, characteristics, parts, stages,* and *steps.*

Teach students how to use a story map to note common elements among narrative stories and relate prior information to new information (Idol, 1987). A story map can categorize the story components and provide a purpose for reading. To help students discover common elements, give them a set of questions, such as the following, to answer for several stories.

1. Who was the major character? Who were the other essential characters?
2. When and where did the story take place?
3. What problem did the characters need to solve in the story?
4. How did they solve the problem?
5. What other ways could the story have ended?
6. Did you learn something from the story? What?

After the students complete the reading, have them give oral responses to the questions or ask them to write their responses individually. Then, write the responses on a large chart to compare the stories. Help the students apply the new information to what they learned previously.

Figure 10–4 is a modification of the mapping approach. Note, however, that either of these mapping strategies requires adaptation for young students. The stories that young children read are simple, so some of the elements of the map may be irrelevant. Maps may be more complex for

FIGURE 10–4
A visual display mapping strategy

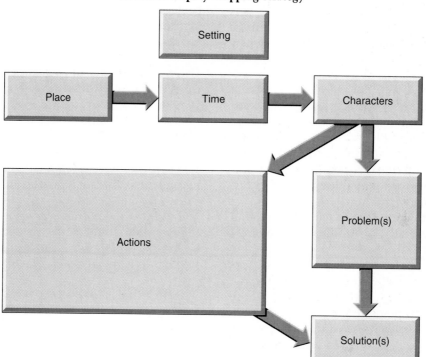

Note: Reprinted with permission of Merrill, an imprint of Macmillan Publishing Company, from *Learning Disabilities: Educational Strategies* (p. 330) by B. R. Gearheart and C. J. Gearheart. Copyright © 1989 by Merrill Publishing Company.

older students. If the purpose of reading is comprehension and writing is difficult for the students, concentrate on oral responses or let another student write the responses of students on the chalkboard, a chart, or an overhead projector.

To help students with ordering, put each step for a recipe on individual cards. Use directions for building a model or playing a well-known game, and have the students put the steps in the proper sequence. If the students have difficulty with this task, ask them to talk through the procedure, or if possible, allow the students to attempt to determine their errors.

Some teachers object to spending time teaching strategies to students. They feel that such teaching takes time away from the content of the class. However, teaching reading strategies provides dividends in motivation, interest, and prevention of behavior problems. Because inefficient readers may become discouraged and want to give up when expected to read independently to acquire information, they may benefit from the following reading strategies. Simplify the strategies for young students or combine them for older ones. Be sure to *teach* these strategies, that is, give the students information regarding how and why to use them. In addition, guide the students as they practice the strategies.

SQ3R. SQ3R is a reading strategy that many teachers recall as being taught when they were in school. The steps of this strategy are:

1. *Survey* the material, including the headings, introduction, and summary to grasp the main ideas.
2. *Question.* Formulate questions based on the information grasped during the survey. Questions may relate to who, what, where, why, and how.
3. *Read.* Students should read the material with the questions in mind to provide a purpose.
4. *Recite.* Students should recite the answers to the questions, paraphrasing the author's words without looking at the material, if possible.
5. *Review.* Students should then review the material as well as any notes they took during the reading.

Note that the 3R in SQ3R refers to steps 3 to 5—read, recite, and review.

PQ4R. PQ4R is a variation of the SQ3R method (Cheek & Cheek, 1983). The steps of this strategy are:

1. *Preview the material.* This step is similar to the survey step in SQ3R.
2. *Question.* This step is the same as the question step in SQ3R.
3. *Read.*
4. *Recite.*
5. *Review.* Note that the first 3 r's are the same as found in SQ3R.
6. *Reflect.* In reflection, students reread any portions of the material that were unclear or find answers to questions that they could not answer from memory.

Some students benefit especially from techniques similar to those used in the preview stage, as rereading the introductory and summary statements and attending to visual displays in the context of the material.

Other Variations of SQ3R. Other variations of the SQ3R method add or delete certain steps, so they may be easier or more meaningful to some students. Variations include OARWET (Norman & Norman, 1968). In OARWET, the steps are (a) *overview*, (b) *achieve*—refers to positive self-statements, (c) *read*, (c) *write*, (d) *evaluate*—refers to self-checking written responses, and (e) *test.* Another variation is OK5R (Pauk, 1984). In OK5R, the steps are (a) *overview*, (b) *key ideas*, (c) *read*, (d) *record*, (e) *recite*, (f) *review*, and (g) *reflect.*

The Reading Visual Aids Strategy. Teach students to use the visual aids provided in texts by using the reading visual aids strategy (Barry, 1986). Self-questioning strategies are reinforced as part of the overall strategy. The strategy follows:

Read until the written material indicates a visual aid, then:
1. *Clarify* what you read and what was illustrated in the visual aid.
2. *Locate* major concepts and details.
3. *Uncover/find* cue words in captions or within the visual aid.
4. *Examine* what you see and determine the congruence with what you read.

Question yourself:
1. *Fit.* Does the written material fit with the visual aids?
2. *Understand.* How do the visual aids help you understand the written material?
3. *Remember.* How do the visual aids help you recall the material you read?

Summary: Either write or verbalize all of the information presented in the written material and the visual aids.

Writing

When verbal ability seems much greater than writing ability, students may be avoiding words that they cannot spell and substituting words that they can spell. Such substitutions often result in stilted, awkward, and immature grammatical constructions. Tell students to write just as they talk or think in order to tell what they know. Tell the students to not worry about spelling but to underline the words that they are unsure how to spell. Tell them that no points will be deducted for underlined words, so they should express what they actually know. This approach may be especially helpful in essay exams.

Similarly, some students frequently erase because they can't spell or want to avoid the writing task. Tell such students that they must stop erasing. They may, however, draw a line through whatever they want deleted and continue with their work. This allows teachers to note what struggles students are experiencing and plan appropriate remediation. It also allows students to spend more time in actual writing.

Teach the TOWER strategy (Mercer & Mercer, 1989) to provide a framework for students to use in developing written themes and reports. Use the TOWER strategy in connection with the COPS strategy (Schumaker, Nolan, & Deshler, 1985). The steps for TOWER are:

1. *Think.* This is the prewriting stage of putting ideas down on paper and using ideas from notes from previous research.
2. *Order ideas.* This is the outlining or organizational stage of writing. Students may use any form of outlining they have previously learned.
3. *Write.* This is the drafting stage of writing, which consists of writing all or portions of the theme or report, but some students may need to go back to the or-

dering, or outlining, step. It is helpful if students write on every other line during the drafting stage.
4. *Edit.* Students should use COPS at the editing stage.
5. *Rewrite.* A rewriting stage should follow the editing.

Use the COPS strategy to teach students to ask specific questions regarding their written work. The steps for the COPS strategy are:

1. *Capitalization.* Students should ask themselves, Have I capitalized all first words, names, and proper nouns? Relate the level of questioning to the age and skill of the students.
2. *Overall.* How does this paper look? Students should ask themselves, Did I indent? Did I use correct spacing? Is my writing legible?
3. *Punctuation.* Students should ask themselves, Did I use correct punctuation?
4. *Spelling.* Students should ask themselves, Did I spell all of the words correctly? If not, do I know how to find the correct spelling?

When students are editing their papers, it is helpful if they use different colored pens or pencils. Thus, teachers can see the types of corrections the students make and students can more easily find their changes during the rewriting stage.

Following are additional teaching suggestions for writing:

1. Teach common punctuation marks, such as the comma, question mark, and exclamation mark. Explain that punctuation marks constitute a symbol system that aids the communication process in writing and reading. For example, have the students demonstrate what they would say if they saw a building on fire or someone fall off a bridge and how

they would write these exclamations ("Fire!" or "Help!"). Arrange other hypothetical situations. Provide many opportunities to observe how these punctuation marks translate to daily speech.

2. Tape a favorite record with vocals. Have the students listen to the tape and transcribe the lyric. Earphones prevent distracting other students and being distracted by them, and a tape recording allows students to stop when necessary to take time to write.

3. Provide students with one or two paragraphs that have all of the nouns, adjectives, or verbs omitted. Then have the students fill in the missing words. Alternately, have the students fill in the missing words to make humorous paragraphs.

4. Cut comic strips or books apart and cover the captions. Adjust the difficulty to the ability of the students. Have the students write their own captions. If you wish, let the students compare their captions with the originals.

Language Development

Some students have limited oral vocabulary. Thus, they fail to comprehend what they read. Teachers may use a variety of activities to help students develop their speaking and reading vocabulary.

On field trips, point out objects and simultaneously name them. Using simple sentences, explain the functions of objects or relationships. Have the students repeat important words and functions or relationships. Repetition helps focus attention. After field trips, show pictures of objects and have the students name them and tell about their functions. Have the students describe similarities or differences between the pictures and the objects.

Use activities that provide practice with synonyms, antonyms, suffixes, and prefixes.

Play a game called old and new. Write words that the students frequently use on the chalkboard under the old column. Then, ask the students to find as many ways as possible to say the same thing. Place these words under the new column. For example:

Old	New
am done	am finished
	have completed
want	desire
	wish
am good	am expert
	am efficient

Keep laminated copies of the *Reader's Digest* "It Pays to Enrich Your Word Power." ("It Pays to Enrich Your Word Power" is a monthly feature of the *Reader's Digest*, consisting of a one-page list of vocabulary words with multiple-choice responses that indicate possible meanings of the words. Answers are provided on the reverse side of the page.) Let the students use the laminated copies as self-checking exercises. For additional practice, ask the students to write stories that include most of the words in context.

Spelling, too, is a difficult subject for many students (Vallecorsa, Zigmond, & Henderson, 1985). However, research over the years has provided some effective methods for teaching spelling. Be sure to consider the learning style of the student when deciding on the methodology. It is possible to use more than one method in a classroom at the same time. For some effective and ineffective methods of teaching spelling see Table 10–1.

Difficulty in spelling correctly may be the result of not clearly understanding the relationship between oral and written sounds. Help in recognizing this relationship benefits some students. For other students, point out the similarities in words

TABLE 10–1
Effective and ineffective methods of teaching spelling

Effective Teachers	Ineffective Teachers
1. Test-study-test.	1. Study-test.
2. Test words that are part of the student's listening and speaking vocabulary, focusing on high-frequency words first.	2. Require repetitious writing of words to improve the student's memory regarding correct spelling.
3. Use high-interest and motivational games.	3. Assume that students know the meaning of a word because it was introduced in the context of a sentence or paragraph.
4. Have students correct their own spelling with teacher guidance.	4. Permit students to develop their own methods of learning how to spell.
5. Teach spelling as a component of writing and developing skill in proofreading.	

they know. For example, if they know *could*, teach the words *should* and *would* as part of a word family or as variations of a word they already know. Help students see small words in larger words, such as *major* in *majority* and *science* in con*science* to provide clues regarding correct spelling (Roswell & Natchez, 1989). Illustrate relationships by using root words, suffixes, and prefixes, such as *nation, national, nationality,* and inter*national*.

Place pictures on the bulletin board and have the students find and write as many words as possible that relate to the picture. Dictionaries and thesauruses are useful in this activity, and they provide additional practice for students who are having difficulty with locational skills.

Mathematics

The following ideas for mathematics are samples of methods that help students who have difficulty learning, whether or not they have been identified as having learning disabilities. (Figure 10–5 contains teaching suggestions for basic mathematical con-

cepts.) With inventiveness and ingenuity, effective teachers may develop many additional activities to enhance the learning of students.

The attitudes of teachers toward mathematics is often reflected in the teaching practices that they employ. Research regarding the teaching of mathematics to both elementary and secondary students indicates differences between the teaching practices of teachers who are effective and those who are ineffective (Driscoll, 1983). See Table 10–2 for examples of teaching practices that seem to be more effective and those that are less effective.

In order to teach students who are not efficient readers how to gain knowledge of the content areas, teachers must be aware of the demands of each area. Each of the content areas has its own vocabulary. In addition, the different content areas have different typography, different organization, and different uses for illustrations. In some books, the illustrations are supplementary. In others, they are essential to understanding the text. It is imperative that teachers

FIGURE 10–5
Teaching suggestions for basic mathematical concepts

1. Using a piece of masking tape, make a number line by marking even spaces and numbering (much like a ruler with only inch marks). Place the number line on the desks for referral when the students work on computational tasks.

2. To reinforce the association between numbers and sets, have students put clothespins on a hanger as they count. Alternately, have the students close their eyes and count the taps on a drum or piano. Have able students work with students who are having difficulty.

3. Provide many experiences of putting together and taking apart concrete objects to familiarize students with the concepts of addition and subtraction before you introduce them to the symbols for plus and minus.

4. Allow students to verbalize what they are writing as they complete arithmetic assignments if they find it helpful. Often, hearing themselves helps them understand the task.

5. Teach the words *plus* and *minus* as part of a separate mathematical language.

6. Encourage students to use objects or materials when completing computation assignments. Usually, when students are ready to proceed without manipulative materials, they will stop using them.

7. Use ordinary playing cards to match numbers or to practice addition and subtraction. (The jack, queen, and king can be zero or wild, or students can decide each time the numerical value of such cards.)

8. Teach multiplication as a faster, more efficient way of adding. Provide opportunities for students to add. Then, time the students and demonstrate how multiplication shortens the time required to solve the problem. Repeat the process many times with some students who are learning disabled.

9. Prepare ditto sheets of multiplication tables. Encourage the students to use the ditto sheets when tasks involve multiplication. In this way, students who are having difficulty memorizing the multiplication tables are not penalized in learning other concepts.

10. Prepare charts that visually represent the relationship of fractions to the whole. Allow students to use these charts until they no longer need them.

TABLE 10-2
Effective and ineffective methods of teaching mathematics

Effective Teachers	Ineffective Teachers
1. Ask questions requiring explanations. 2. Provide reinforcement for thinking processes. 3. Model problem solving in daily school life. 4. Use vocabulary words that students understand or provide systematic explanations. 5. Expect students to do well and provide support for their efforts.	1. Ask product questions, which require correct answers. 2. Look only for correct answers. 3. Treat mathematics as a content area having relevance only during that class. 4. Follow only the teacher's manual, without innovation or accommodations. 5. Record grades and tell students that they must work harder to get better grades.

thoroughly analyze the texts that students use. After analyzing them, teachers must instruct students how to manage them. Smith and Smith (1980) have compiled a list of subject matter reading features that detail the variety of skills needed in several content areas. Following are several special considerations in relation to mathematics:

1. *Special vocabulary.* In mathematics, a special vocabulary consists of words or phrases that determine operations, such as *total, sum, difference, minus,* and *product.* Words and signs may be used interchangeably (for example, *plus* and +; and *percent* and %). Also, certain terms have meanings different from general conversation, such as *mean, square,* and *product.* Finally, many terms must be memorized, such as *diameter* and *radius.*

2. *Types of reading.* Students may be required to skim to gain overall understanding. They may be required to do detailed reading to determine what is asked. They may be required to reread to determine whether or not all of the data they collected lead to the correct solution.

3. *Problem organization.* Problems gener-

ally follow a pattern, depending on the level. Usually, a situation is provided, a numerical question is asked, and an equation must be designed to arrive at the solution.

4. *Special considerations.* Sometimes, the same vocabulary may indicate different operations. For example, *altogether* may mean to add or multiply.

Word Problems. Word problems seem to present unusual difficulty for students with learning disabilities. Sometimes, students do not see the relationship between the problem solving that they do as part of everyday life and word problems. Teachers inadvertently foster this type of thinking by relating word problems to mathematics and not to daily activities. Cawley, Miller, and School (1987) provide *do's* and *don'ts* for teachers to consider. Following are some suggestions (*do's*) based on Cawley et al.

1. Make problem solving a priority from the first day of school, and use it regularly. Include problem solving in your long-term curriculum, planning and sequencing it carefully.

2. Present problems that deal with daily living activities of the students, and gen-

eralize problem solving to other subject areas. Provide opportunities for students to develop problems or modify them.

3. Be certain that students understand the difference between process and knowledge, that is, between problem solving in its broadest sense and computation. Remember that problem solving is a daily activity in the lives of students, but computation is not necessarily so. Do not treat problem solving as less important than computation. Likewise, do not make assumptions about students' problem-solving abilities based on their computational skill (that is, do not assume incorrect answers are problem-solving deficits).

4. Involve all of the modalities of the students in problem-solving activities.

5. If necessary, make accommodations for students. For example, be sure that word problems are at the independent reading level of the students. If the reading level is too difficult, tape record the problems, pair students so that one student is able to easily read the problems, or rewrite the problems. In particular, avoid passive verb tense. (Wood, 1989). Monitor and adjust problems to meet the needs and abilities of the students.

Examine errors in order to develop an understanding of the thinking of students and to provide remediation (Gable & Hendrickson, 1990). Some of the common errors that students make are inappropriate operations, inaccurate computations, incomplete or incorrect procedures, regrouping, and randomness. After noting the errors that students are making, ask the students to verbalize the procedures that they used in solving the problems, and devise teaching methodologies to remedy the errors. Note that word problems that have irrelevant information often confuse students. Also, beware of

word problems that contain more than one operation. Until students have been taught to look for and deal with multiple operations, they frequently make errors related to incomplete solutions.

Introduce various aspects of word problems and provide students with practice before presenting more complex problems. Teach students a step-by-step approach to solving word problems. Modify the steps and complexity of the problems to accommodate young or older students (Salend, 1990). Enright and Beattie (1989) suggest a simple, five-step plan appropriate for young students: (a) study the problem, (b) organize the facts, (c) form a plan, (d) compute, and (e) examine your answer. Salend suggests a plan appropriate for older students:

1. Read the problem for the general idea. Note any unknown words, and get help regarding them.
2. Reread the problem. Pay attention to key aspects. Highlight key words and numbers and hypothesize about the operation(s) to use.
3. Draw a visual representation of the problem.
4. Write the steps to the problem and label the steps with the correct operational symbols $(+, -, \times, \div)$.
5. Estimate your answer.
6. Solve the problem using your hypothesis, previously planned operations, and estimation.
7. Check your answer by comparing it to the estimate and the visual representation. Check each step. Was the step necessary? Did you complete the problem in the correct order? Did you use the correct operation(s)? Were your calculations correct?

Automaticity. Researchers theorize that persons have limited capacity for information processing. They believe that if much of one's processing capacity is used for figuring correct answers to simple facts, then less of the capacity is left for developing higher-level concepts, such as multiple-digit multiplication or long division (Resnick, 1983). An example is three-digit multiplication, which is a multistep process. Therefore, students must monitor the process and their place in it. If they must stop to compute the facts, they may forget where they are. The processing required to compute the facts takes away from the higher-level processing required for the complex problem. Thus, automaticity is beneficial.

Automaticity is automatic recall of facts such as addition, subtraction, multiplication, and division facts. Hasselbring, Goin, and Bransford (1987) suggest a procedure for helping students develop automaticity for arithmetic facts. First, they suggest thorough assessment of the specific facts to determine which facts students know, that is, which facts the students can provide answers to within one second. They consider answers taking longer than one second as not known. Keep precise records in the case of older students, giving separate emphasis to addition, subtraction, and multiplication.

Second, teach the students to build on what they know. For example, 5 + 4 = 9 (which is known) is the same as 4 + 5 = 9 (which may be unknown). Generally, students quickly learn facts that have an addend of 1 (for example, 7 + 1, 8 + 1, and 9 + 1). If students already know these facts, then select facts with a minimum addend of 2 (for example, 7 + 2, 8 + 2, and 9 + 2). After students automatize addends of 2, teach addends of 3, 4, 5, and so on.

Third, concentrate on facts that are difficult for the students, commonly addends that are larger than 5 (for example, 7 + 6, 8 + 6, and 9 + 6). At any one time, direct

concentrated practice to small numbers of facts until the students achieve automaticity. Use only 5 or 6 minutes of the total time allotted for instruction. To increase motivation, use games and charts to record progress during the acquisition stage.

Finally, determine whether or not automaticity has been achieved by using either flash cards or oral presentations and timing responses. Consider responses within 1 second to be automatized. If facts are not automatized, then repeat the second and third steps. The procedure is based on the premise that students already understand the concepts of addition, subtraction, or multiplication. Otherwise, they develop a skill entirely dependent on memory.

Before introducing a particular mathematical concept, provide problems that relate to it. For example, before a study of probability, have the students write the numbers 1, 2, 3, and 4 on paper and direct them to ask people to circle a number. Collect all of the papers and tally the number of times each number was circled. The theory of probability suggests that one out of four people will circle the 3. Ask the students if their experiment confirms this. Several such activities encourage students to think about the concept. Such activities also provide meaning when the concept is introduced.

For motivation, arrange hopscotch, ladder climbing, river crossings on rocks, or other similar games on the floor. Have the students complete the game by adding, subtracting, multiplying, or dividing. Alternately, list assignments and provide a time limit in which to complete each assignment. If the students complete the work during the specified period, provide a reward (such as 5 minutes to listen to a record or 3 minutes to watch a filmstrip).

Provide replications of money and set up a store, amusement park, or other business.

TABLE 10–3
Percent table

Item	Price	Reduction	Actual Cost
Potato chips	1.69	30%	
Sugar	2.49	50%	
Paper towels	.78	15%	

Have the students buy items and receive change. Older students can shop from advertisements in the newspaper. They can prepare budgets, plan meals, purchase foods, and buy clothes. They can also compute the savings from advertisements, as for 30% off or half price (see Table 10–3). Provide experience that clarifies the difference between 25% off and $0.25 off or a 30% reduction and a $0.30 reduction in price (see Table 10–4).

Using either actual restaurant menus or menus constructed by the students (have the students affix pictures of food and assign prices to them), direct the students to choose what they will eat, indicate how much it will cost, and if paying without exact change, indicate the change that they

TABLE 10–4
Percent and cent table

Item	Price	Reduction	Actual Cost
Milk	1.40	25%	
Milk	1.40	$0.25	
Frozen pies	1.90	30%	
Frozen pies	1.90	$0.30	

should receive. Make this activity more complex by charging for substitutions, adding tax, and computing tips.

Other Content Areas

When a content area lends itself to simulations, role playing, or dramatic improvisations, use these techniques to help students understand critical concepts. Many students who have learning disabilities are passive or inactive, but such techniques force them to become active in their learning. Figure 10–6 contains additional suggestions for content areas.

Combine visual displays with content materials to help comprehension and memory skills. For example, for a chapter of a science text on temperatures and climate zones, prepare a display that illustrates a concept and discuss this display immediately upon reading the paragraph or section that explains the concept. Alternately, divide the students into groups and have each group prepare a display related to a particular concept and then discuss the display and concept in class.

If students are learning to read maps, combine map reading skills with locational skills in travel books by developing a student travel bureau (Ekwall, 1985). Plan real or imaginary trips using maps and travel books, emphasizing the use of indexes. Have the students identify famous landmarks on the maps and additional information in travel books or textbooks. As a variation, organize teams and see which team can most quickly plan a trip and locate the most information regarding the destination. This variation emphasizes speed and should be used only after the students have acquired sufficient skill.

Study Skills

Organize classes or sessions in study skills to help students explore alternate ways to identify, analyze, categorize, and recall in-

FIGURE 10–6
Teaching suggestions for content areas

1. Use a large manipulatable clock and provide individual clocks by which to plan the activities of the day. Change the time as the activities change. Call attention to the time that has elapsed since the last activity. Say, for example, "It is now 9:40, or 20 minutes until 10:00. When we began the reading lesson, it was 9 o'clock. Forty minutes have gone by." This helps students conceptualize short time periods and associates the concept of time with the clock.

2. Have students bring television schedules to school. Have them look up their favorite programs and arrange the hands of their individual clocks to show the times that these programs are on. Bus, plane, and train schedules can be used in the same manner.

3. Have students compile time lines of the activities for each day. Display the time lines on an overhead projector and compare them for overlapping and events that run concurrently. Make reference to the time lines throughout the day to help students learn time concepts. Lengthen the time lines to include weekly or monthly activities.

4. Have the students develop time lines of their own lives. These can be pictorial, or they may include narrative. Students can use these time lines as demonstrations for parents or other classes. As an added dimension, ask the students to extend their time lines into the future in 5- or 10-year segments (for example, what do they expect to be doing in 5, 10, 15, 20 years?). Such activities help students gain such time concepts as past, present, future, months, years, and seasons.

5. On a tiled floor, use each block as a unit of measure. For example, say that one block equals one foot, one mile, or one city block. Construct a room, building, or town. For students with unusual difficulty, begin with the replication of a room. Then, let them refer to the model of the room for larger projects.

6. Provide scaled diagrams of the school or campus. Have the students follow a map to get to specific locations. After they can do this efficiently, provide directions without the map and ask the students to tell you where they will be if they follow them.

7. When teaching the states, have the students trace them first and then draw them from memory and compare the results. The comparisons are especially effective if the drawing paper is transparent and is laid over the original or if both are held up against a window.

8. Collect a variety of natural objects, such as birds' nests, acorns, leaves, and pinecones. Discuss the properties of each. Measure height, width, or circumference of each. Arrange the items from smallest to largest or shortest to tallest. Have the students illustrate the patterns, lines, and shapes of the objects. Such activities can help students understand measurement, balance, and visual-spatial properties.

formation. Alternately, a resource teacher or consultant may teach these skills to a small group or use several class sessions during regular class time, providing support and practice as required. Many students who have not been identified as special needs students will benefit from learning such skills. Teach the need for different reading rates. Content area reading materials differ considerably from literature.

To help students with note taking, divide 5-by-8-inch cards into three spaces as in

Figure 10–7. Alternately, direct the students to divide each notebook page into four columns going down the page. Tell the students to label the columns "Vocabulary," "People," "Places and Dates," and "Ideas and Discoveries." At the top of the notebook pages, have the students write the headings that are in bold print or color. (Several notebook pages may be necessary for each chapter.) Teach the students to fill in the columns as they read the chapter. The labels for the columns may be modified to reflect the relevant aspects of the various content areas or the particular chapters within a specific book.

Some students require specific teaching regarding the use of organizational aids and cues. Teach students the names and uses of the specific parts of a book, such as the index, glossary, and table of contents. Also teach students how to identify and use headings, subheadings, italics, color, and bold print. In addition, content area materials often depend on graphics and illustrations to present important information. Because such characteristics of content area materials can be problematic for students, teach students to recognize such organizational cues.

When students are beyond the initial teaching stages but do not know how to use organizational aids, merely telling them is insufficient, so provide practice. Ekwall (1989) provides a number of useful ideas. He suggests copying a paragraph or two from various textbooks that the student uses and has immediately available. Be sure the paragraphs contain clues regarding the type of text from which they are taken. For example, factual information about the seasons would come from a science text. Also, be sure the paragraphs contain hints that will allow the use of an index. In addition, choose tables or graphs. Place each item in an envelope, and have the students select an envelope and find the exact location in the text of the same paragraph, table, or graph by using the index or a list of tables and graphs. When students locate the same piece of information, have them note the page and source they used to find the information.

Indrisano (1982) developed a method called SEARCH to help students realize that learning involves a specific process. Each letter in SEARCH stands for a step in the process:

1. *Set goals.* With the students, select a topic to be researched and determine the questions that the students must answer to know about the topic. Possible questions and activities are listed in Table 10–5. Clarify the questions until they are answerable, and identify persons, films, books, and another sources to provide clear goals as well as means to achieve them. The section of Table 10–5 labeled "Where Do I Find Out" is a composite of the myriad sources available, including print, films, and persons.

FIGURE 10–7
Diagram for note taking

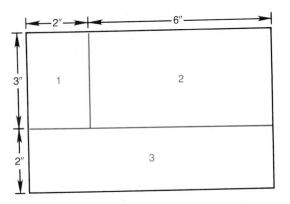

Note: Space 1 is for major ideas and topics, space 2 is for supporting information, and space 3 is for a summary or questions.

TABLE 10-5
Sample table of questions and activities for use with SEARCH method

What Do I Want to Know?	How Do I Find Out?	Where Do I Find Out?	What Did I Find?
Rabbits What do they eat? Where do they live? What kinds are there?	Read books Interview Mr. Jones who raises rabbits Preview film on rabbits	Names of books on rabbits Mr. Jones Films on rabbits, ask media specialist	

Note: Reprinted with permission of Merrill, an imprint of Macmillan Publishing Company, from *Learning Disabilities: Educational Strategies,* 5th ed. (p. 324) by B. R. Gearheart and C. J. Gearheart. Copyright © 1989 by Merrill Publishing Company.

The choice is determined by the abilities of the students. Note that not all of the sources require reading.

2. *Explore the sources.* Have the students answer all of the questions by examining the proposed sources. In the initial stages at least, most students need guidance in recording the information that they collect. They may use card files, sheets of paper with questions at the top, or other forms of recording.

3. *Analyze and organize the information.* At this stage, students should organize the information and indicate the answers to the questions on the chart. Stress the interrelatedness of the information. Explain why some of the information collected may be extraneous, and help the students find the best place to incorporate useful information that they did not initially ask for.

4. *Refine and rehearse.* To provide opportunities to use the newly acquired information, help the students plan ways to share the information. Select the mode of presentation and the audience. Written reports are possible, but there are other possibilities, too. Let the students give short oral introductions to the ques-

tions and answers on the chart. Alternately, let the students present taped commentaries or oral discussions with friends or younger students. Once the mode of presentation and audience are decided, have the students prepare and rehearse the presentations.

5. *Communicate with others.* Either before or soon after the students share the information with the intended audience, discuss the successes and problems that occurred to this point. Make notes that will be available during the next search. Evaluation enables students to recognize which methods and materials were most helpful, which were not helpful, and most importantly, if a method or material was not helpful, why not. Aspects that were not helpful may become the topic of additional discussion. For example, the student didn't take complete notes, couldn't read his or her writing, or the sources selected were at too high a reading level.

6. *Help yourself.* The last step is a culmination of the assessment procedure. Utilizing the information from the assessment of what was helpful and what was not, the student and teacher begin an-

other search. This may be an extension of the topic just investigated or an entirely new one.

After a few repetitions of the steps, students may begin working somewhat independently.

SECONDARY SCHOOL PROGRAMS

Secondary school programs for students who have learning disabilities are likely to be considerably different from elementary school programs. At the elementary level, programs for students who are learning disabled tend to build the basic academic skills of reading and arithmetic. In the upper elementary grades, the focus shifts toward synthesis, generalization, and conceptualization but continues to include basic skills. When programs are successful, students who were formerly learning disabled no longer require special programming. For such students, the only evidence of learning disability may be some slightly unusual learning or memory techniques.

Yet, many students need special assistance at the secondary level. Among such students are those who have learning disabilities that were not recognized at the elementary level and those for whom earlier efforts were not sufficient. Such students may be helped in a number of ways, and regular classroom teachers play an important role in many of the approaches.

The emphasis most likely to involve regular classroom teachers at the secondary level is accommodation, or compensatory teaching. The following description may clarify the change in emphasis:

Accommodation and compensatory teaching refer to [approaches] whereby the learning environment of the student, either some of the elements or the total environment, is modified to promote learning. The focus is on changing the

learning environment or the academic requirements so that the student may learn in spite of a fundamental weakness or deficiency. This may involve the use of modified instructional techniques, more flexible administrative practices, modified academic requirements, or any compensatory activity that emphasizes the use of stronger, more intact capabilities or that provides modified or alternative educational processes and/or goals.

Remediation or remedial teaching refers to those activities, techniques, and practices that are directed primarily at strengthening or eliminating the basic source(s) of a weakness or deficiency that interferes with learning. The focus is on changing the learner in some way so that he or she may more effectively relate to the educational program as it is provided and administered for all students. The presumption is made that there is something wrong with the learner that can be identified and corrected. (Marsh, Gearheart, & Gearheart, 1978, p. 85)

Accommodation, adaptation, and the various approaches that may be called compensatory have the same basic goal as the remedial orientation at the elementary level, but in secondary schools, it is more practical and efficient to emphasize content learning as opposed to improvement of basic skills. Remedial efforts and further development of reading or arithmetic skills remain important goals, but they often become secondary to acquisition of important understandings and concepts.

For example, encourage students who are deficient in note-taking skills to tape record all or portions of lectures or other class presentations. When students can express themselves orally but cannot prepare orderly, well-conceived written reports, permit them to tape their responses to assignments and evaluate the oral responses. Thus, you avoid situations in which inability of students to express themselves in writing masks information and knowledge. If you cannot accept taped reports, address the content of reports without regard to mechanics. Devise a grading or evaluation system that, in effect, does not lead to failure because of mechanics. Note, however, that students and parents must understand and agree to such an arrangement. To prevent later claims by students or parents that students were not provided effective education, inform the parents and students—preferably in writing—that you are deliberately not evaluating the student's writing skills, and explain why.

Modifications may take a variety of forms, including course content, presentation of information, and form of student response. Teachers are challenged to develop teaching approaches that enable otherwise bright and capable students to demonstrate their understanding of the content of specific subject areas even though disabilities inhibit their performance in some ways.

Develop a close working relationship with resource teachers or consultants. These individuals can provide additional suggestions regarding your content area. Teachers who remain open to new ideas, observe individual learning patterns, and strive to understand the nature of learning develop teaching styles that match the needs of the students in their classrooms. The following list illustrates these principles and provides a starting point for helping secondary school students who have learning disabilities.

1. Be well organized. Provide verbal or written overviews of units or chapters and review key points after the completion of chapters or units. Begin each class period with a short overview of that class period and its relationship to the whole unit. Review important information at the close of the class.

2. Break tasks into subparts. For example, visualize an oral or written report on energy problems as follows: (a) traditional energy resources, (b) cost of energy, (c) alternative forms of energy. Demonstrate how to take notes for each of the main ideas and how to organize them prior to writing or orally presenting the report. Likewise, shorten reading assignments. Secondary school students who have learning disabilities may read less than one third as much as their peers in the same amount of time.

3. Whenever possible, obtain texts that have been written at a lower reading level but address the same concepts. Several textbook companies provide such texts as part of their regular offerings.

4. Use direct questions when you give both reading and writing assignments. Emphasize and review key questions until they become automatic. Vary questions according to subject area, but try to include the following: Who is important? What has happened? When did it happen? Where did it happen? Why did it happen? What will happen next?

5. Type assignments, tests, advance organizers, vocabulary lists, and similar materials that you give to students—typing is much easier to read than handwriting. Provide clear, well-spaced materials. Leave space to write directly on the page, and draw lines for responses. Some students may need wide spaces in which to write.

6. Model or demonstrate the use of preview, self-questioning, and review techniques. For consistency, modify commercially prepared work sheets or handouts to reflect the same techniques.

7. Whenever possible, provide information using more than one sense. For ex-

ample, use diagrams, pictures, or slides as you discuss a concept. Provide tapes for the students to listen to while they are reading, so that the students receive the information auditorily as well as visually. Such dual presentation helps slow or otherwise inefficient readers. Likewise, use films and visuals to reinforce key concepts.

8. Use peer tutors in many ways and in a wide variety of subject areas. Alternately, use computer tutorials to allow students to repeat the critical information addressed in class. Use cooperative learning groups or practice tests to provide opportunities to study and review for tests.

9. Provide wait time for students to formulate responses, and provide informational and motivational feedback to allow students to modify their responses.

10. For students with poor writing ability, allow other options for demonstrating knowledge, such as oral reports, artwork, photographic essays, and dioramas.

11. Arrange tests sequentially from easiest to most difficult, and test major concepts rather than details. Use visual cues, such as diagrams, on the test paper itself or on the chalkboard.

12. Allow more time for the completion of tests, or give one section one day and another the next day. Give students a choice regarding the place they will take tests—in the resource room, in a carrel, or in the library (if there is supervision). Alternately, allow students to take their tests on a computer.

SUMMARY

In this chapter, several definitions of learning disabilities were reviewed. Characteristics often correlated with students identified as having learning disabilities include hyperactivity, lack of coordination, memory disorders, attention fixations, and perceptual disorders. The major characteristic, difficulty in learning despite apparently adequate intellectual ability, was also discussed.

The prereferral and referral processes were outlined, and the role of regular classroom teachers was described. Basic principles for educational planning, behavior management approaches, multisensory approaches, cooperative training techniques, and study strategies were discussed. Practical teaching suggestions were given for use in the teaching of reading, writing, language development, mathematics, other content areas, and study skills. Suggestions related to secondary school programming were also provided.

- Under what conditions might unacceptable behavior be an indication of behavior disorders? When might it not be an indication of behavior disorders?

- Why might some students be considered to have a behavior disorder in one school and not considered to have a behavior disorder in another school? How are such decisions made?

- Why is there such variety in approaches to treatment of behavior disorders?

- What is the ecological approach to the treatment of students with behavior disorders? How does it differ from the behavioral approach? How does it differ from the psychodynamic approach? Which might you more likely use to deal with a 10-year-old boy who is exhibiting acting out behavior and identified as having a behavior disorder?

- How do logical consequences and punishment differ? How are they similar?

- How are juvenile delinquency and behavior disorders related? To what extent are they synonymous?

- How may child abuse be related to behavior disorders?

CHAPTER 11

TEACHING STUDENTS WHO HAVE BEHAVIOR DISORDERS

IN THE AREA OF EMOTIONAL DISTURBANCE, CONtroversy regarding a definition, the terminology, and even the name of the condition abounds. Terms such as *aggressive, disruptive, withdrawn, immature, delinquent, hyperactive,* and *shy* are used in association with the disorder. The federal definition uses the term *seriously emotionally disturbed* but professional organizations advocate use of the term *behavior disorders* (Huntze, 1984). We use the term *behavior disorders,* but the literature uses a variety of terminology in reference to the same population of students.

DEFINITIONS OF BEHAVIOR DISORDERS

Although there is general agreement on the existence of a condition relating to emotional or behavioral problems that handicap individuals, no definition is satisfactory to all. The federal rules and regulations governing the implementation of PL 94–142 define the *term seriously emotional disturbed* as follows:

The term means a condition exhibiting one or more of the following characteristics over a long period of time and to a marked extent, which adversely affects educational performance.

An inability to learn which cannot be explained by intellectual, sensory, or health factors;
An inability to build or maintain satisfactory relationships with peers and teachers;
Inappropriate types of behavior or feelings under normal circumstances;
A general pervasive mood of unhappiness or depression;
Or a tendency to develop physical symptoms or fears associated with personal or school problems.

The term includes children who are schizophrenic or autistic.[1] The term does not include children who are socially maladjusted unless it is determined that they are seriously emotionally disturbed. (*Federal Register,* August 23, 1977, p. 42478.)

The federal definition uses the term *seriously* but does not elaborate on how to measure severity. Bower (1981) restated his earlier conceptualization of five levels of severity on a continuum of behavior ranging from least severe to most severe:

1. Students who experience the usual problems of growing up, testing limits, and exploring alternatives
2. Students who develop some of the characteristics of emotional problems because of usual but difficult stresses of life, such as death of a parent or serious injury

---

[1]In 1990, in Public Law 101–476, autism was listed as a separate disability.

3. Students who demonstrate a persistence of some or all of the characteristics beyond normal expectations but are able to manage their lives
4. Students who experience continuous or persistently recurring characteristics but with support can maintain school attendance and develop some personal relationships
5. Students who experience more continuous and persistent characteristics, are unable to profit by regular school attendance, and may be served best in residential settings

The difficulties of students in the last three categories are not temporary, and many of the methods that are sufficient for most students are not effective for these. Kauffman (1977) includes the concept of remediation, or correction. In his definition, students who have behavior disorders "are those who chronically and markedly respond to their environment in socially unacceptable and/or personally unsatisfying ways but who can be taught more socially and personally gratifying behavior" (p. 23).

Psychological, psychiatric, and other health care workers use the *American Psychiatric Association Diagnostic and Statistical Manual of Mental Disorders* (1987), which provides a classification system that includes the terms *disruptive behavior disorders, oppositional-defiant behaviors, overanxious disorder, gender identity disorder,* and *elective mutism,* none of which is mentioned in the federal definition. However, students falling within any of these classifications would likely receive services under the provisions of PL 94–142 because they would demonstrate one or more of the characteristics listed in the federal definition. Other authors and sources use classification systems that include the terms *conduct disorders, aggressive conduct disorders, antiso-*

cial behavior, social isolation, compulsive, depression, psychotic, and *personality disorders* (Hardman, Drew, Egan, & Wolf, 1990; Kauffman, 1989; Von Isser, Quay, & Love, 1980).

While other professionals debate the merits of definitions and terminology, teachers have "little difficulty identifying the student with emotional problems" (McDowell, Adamson, & Wood, 1982, p. 3). Rather than attempting to find a universally acceptable definition for behavior disorders, it is more positive to focus on students as learners. Teachers do not need precise definitions or levels, but rather solutions to the learning and behavioral difficulties of students.

Normal behavior is often considered a range of behaviors along a continuum that is comparable to Bower's. The limits of normal or acceptable behavior are subjective. They are based on environmental, cultural, and situational factors. However, as behaviors begin to be noticed by teachers, they may be considered similar to Bower's level 2 (some of the characteristics of emotional problems, which may be triggered by some unusual event in the student's life). As the number and severity of the characteristics increase (levels 3 through 5), teachers note the discrepancy between this behavior and the behavior of the other students. Teachers observe a range of behaviors each day and are, therefore, in the best position to note variation from normal behavior for their grade level and school.

On the other hand, teachers should not determine that a student has a behavior disorder based on arbitrary or capricious factors. The behavior must be present over a period of time, be of sufficient intensity (clearly different from normal), and occur frequently. All students experience emotional crises that may be minor or severe; however, they are usually transitory. The frequency of occurrence, duration, and degree of severity form the guidelines for teachers in determining which students to refer for special assistance.

PREREFERRAL

Teachers who are aware of behavior that is sufficiently different from normal and that occurs frequently over a period of time may request assistance. Many school districts hold a prereferral meeting before actual referral is made. A prereferral conference usually includes the classroom teacher, special education or consulting teacher, principal, and school counselor. It may also include the parents. The purpose of this conference is to examine the factors having a bearing on the behavior (such as a death in the family, separation of the parents, possible sexual abuse, or other traumatic events), to determine what techniques or methods have been tried, and ascertain their effectiveness. At this conference, the decision may be made to try other management techniques, in which case the meeting is adjourned with the understanding to provide opportunities for change in the behavior. If the decision is to initiate a referral, the teacher completes a referral form accord-

FIGURE 11–1

Sample items from a specialist's behavior disorder checklist

Behaviors	Date	Length of Observation	Mark Each Time Behavior Occurs	Comments
Student uses profanity.				
Student must be told more than once to begin work.				
Student destroys property.				
Student talks out inappropriately.				
Student makes inappropriate noises.				
Student moves around aimlessly.				
Student is out of seat.				
Student does not follow teacher directions.				
Student interrupts others.				
Student is verbally abusive to others.				
Student becomes angry with little provocation.				

ing to the practice of the school district, and forwards the form to the appropriate personnel.

Depending on state and local requirements, the specialist who teaches students with behavior disorders observes the student in the regular classroom to complete a checklist or rating scale of classroom interactions (Figure 11–1) or asks the regular classroom teacher to complete a checklist (Figure 11–2). More formal checklists may also be used, such as the *Walker Problem Behavior Identification Checklist* (Walker, 1983), which lists observable behaviors; *Burks Behavior Rating Scales* (Burks, 1977),

which requires ratings by the teacher; the *Behavior Rating Profile* (Brown & Hammill, 1983), for which teachers, peers, and parents provide ratings; the *Hahneman High School Behavior Scale* (Spivak & Swift, 1972), which measures ability to cope with the pressures of the secondary school system; the *Woodcock-Johnson Scales of Independent Behavior* (Woodcock & Johnson, 1983), which measure independent and adaptive behavior in social and communication skills, personal-living skills, and community-living skills.

The special education or consulting teacher observes the student in the regular

FIGURE 11–2

Sample items from a regular classroom teacher's behavior-disorder checklist

Student's name: _____ Date:_____

Birth date: _____ School:_____

Please check the areas that are applicable. If you wish to make comments, please do so.

Behaviors	Frequency			Under what circumstances does the behavior occur?	Comments
	Daily	Weekly	Monthly		
Needs close supervision.					
Destroys property.					
Throws temper tantrums.					
Displays erratic, unpredictable behavior.					
Indicates poor self-concept.					
Appears angry or hostile.					
Isolates self.					
Appears out of touch with reality.					
Does not achieve at expected academic level.					

Continued.

FIGURE 11–2—cont'd

Sample items from a regular classroom teacher's behavior-disorder checklist

Behaviors	Frequency			Under what circumstances does the behavior occur?	Comments
	Daily	Weekly	Monthly		
Seeks inordinate amount of attention.					
Interferes with learning of others.					
Makes inappropriate noises.					
Threatens to injure self or others.					
Does injure self or others.					
Verbally assaults others.					
Physically assaults others.					
Avoids eye contact.					
Cries inappropriately.					
Refuses to talk with teacher.					
Refuses to talk with others.					
Seems to daydream.					

classroom or asks the teacher to complete a checklist or rating scale as a preliminary means of objectifying or quantifying the student's behaviors. The school psychologist (or psychiatrist, as required in some states) assesses the intellectual ability (IQ) of the student as well as personality factors. The IQ measurement is required because by federal definition, the inability to learn must not be the result of intellectual factors (*Federal Register*, August 23, 1977, p. 42478). Intelligence tests such as the *Wechsler Intelligence Scale for Children—Revised* (WISC—R) (Wechsler, 1974) or the *Stanford-Binet Intelligence Scale* (Thorn-

dike, Hagen, & Sattler, 1986) may be administered.

Emotional, motivational, interpersonal, and attitudinal characteristics are measured by various personality tests. Specific tests are chosen according to state or local guidelines or by the psychologist or psychiatrist. These assessment tools were designed to present relatively unstructured stimuli with the intent of examining the manner in which students perceive and interpret test materials. Examples are the *Thematic Apperception Test* (Murray, 1943) and the *Rorschach Inkblot Test* (Rorschach, 1942). Presumably, this type of measurement reflects underlying aspects of psychological functioning (Anastasi, 1982). Other evaluation tools used by the psychologist or psychiatrist may include a diagnostic interview, play, questioning, observation, or paper-and-pencil tasks. Whatever devices are used, the major purpose is to gain insight into the personality of the student.

In addition to these evaluations, various academic achievement tests are administered by either the psychologist or the specialist in behavior disorders. The nurse may screen the student for vision or hearing impairment, and the social worker considers the student's developmental history.

After all of the information is gathered, a conference is held, including the personnel involved in testing the student, as well as the classroom teacher, parents, and others (see chapter 2 for a list of persons required by law to attend). At this conference, the most appropriate plan is developed for providing assistance to the student. An individualized education program may be written and a placement designated.

For some students with behavior disorders, the least restrictive alternative may be a special class or even a residential school. This type of placement may be necessary when the student is self-injurious, suicidal, completely out of touch with reality, or injurious to others. Most students remain in regular classes with support from consulting or special education teachers.

RESPONSIBILITIES OF SPECIAL EDUCATION PERSONNEL

If students are to be in regular classrooms for any part of the day, consulting teachers should be available to provide whatever assistance is necessary. The assistance varies, depending on the needs of the student and the teacher. Special education teachers provide suggestions relating to management of behavior problems and remedial academic assistance. They also teach social skills to small groups of students, provide a place for students to cool off, and temporarily remove students from the regular classroom for intense discussions relating to behavior. In general, the assistance occurs in response to requests or mutually agreed upon plans. In some cases, psychologists, psychiatrists, or counselors provide therapy for students on a regular basis.

Teachers may individualize instruction for students who have learning disabilities and feel successful in meeting their academic needs, or make accommodations for students who have hearing impairment or low vision and feel successful. However, the same teachers may implement a variety of modifications to address the needs of students who have behavior disorders and feel as if they are making little or no progress. The disruptive nature of behavior disorders may lead teachers to discouragement and doubt about their teaching ability. Therefore, a mutual support system between consulting teachers or teachers of students who are behaviorally disordered and classroom teachers may be necessary. By sharing frustrations, disappointments, and successes, teachers can regain perspective and renew their enthusiasm for the challenges ahead.

COOPERATION AMONG TEACHERS

It is essential that teachers of regular classes and specialists discuss what methods are to be used. Because there is such a variation in theories about the causes of behavioral disorders and, therefore, a wide variation in treatments, the teachers involved must agree theoretically and personally how best to proceed. Students who have behavior disorders are often manipulative. They use ambiguities on the part of the teachers to their fullest advantage. For example, if a specialist believes that the student's difficulties are caused by internal hostility and pent-up anger and thinks the way to deal with them is to provide a warm, accepting environment and to allow acting out or aggression so that the student can work through them, then treatment is based on this premise. If, on the other hand, the regular classroom teacher cannot allow such acting out in the classroom or cannot tolerate barrages of obscene language, the two different approaches will lead to ambiguity or dissension.

A second example involves a specialist who believes in counting and observing every behavior. The specialist also believes that the student has learned inappropriate behaviors and therefore must learn new behaviors to function successfully in regular classes. This philosophy is reflected in the specialist's suggestions for treatment. However if, in this scenario, the regular classroom teacher believes in allowing students to express themselves freely and personally believes in "flowing with the students," allowing them many choices in what and how to study, both teachers will be frustrated and the student will take advantage of the situation.

Regular class teachers and specialists must arrive at some general agreement, and each must be somewhat comfortable with the other's approach to the treatment. Few teachers are able to teach consistently in manners inconsistent with their personalities. For example, teachers who are extremely creative, take almost all their cues from the students, and plan on a minute-by-minute basis are not usually comfortable with a structured, precise behavior modification approach. This is not to say that either approach is better or more effective but only that they are different. Both teachers must recognize and acknowledge their

unique teaching styles and know how they teach most comfortably and effectively. Then, during the writing of the IEP, each style must be considered when developing the best educational plan for the student. This cooperation requires discussion and compromise, but it is at this point—the writing of the IEP—that various potential conflicts must be resolved.

MAJOR THEORETICAL APPROACHES

Rather than attempting to find a universally acceptable definition for behavioral disorders, it is more positive to focus on students as learners. Teachers do not need precise definitions, but rather solutions to the learning and behavioral difficulties of students. There are several major theoretical approaches to teaching students who have behavioral disorders. Table 11–1 and the following discussion indicate the key aspects of the major approaches and provide insight into ways in which teachers may modify these approaches for classroom use.

Behavior Modification

In the early 1960s, the term *behavior modification* was introduced (and later the same decade, the term *applied behavior analysis* was used) to emphasize the application of behaviorist principles to real-life settings. Usually, the term *applied behavior analysis* refers to a more stringent relationship between the behavior changed and the intervention (Alberto & Troutman, 1990). Applied behavior analysts use the principles of specific data collection, reinforcement, and observation of change in a manner similar to that of behaviorists (Ysseldyke & Algozzine, 1984). In the interest of simplicity, this chapter uses the term *behavior modification*. As a general rule, in journal articles or other books, *behavior modification* is de-

TABLE 11–1
Theoretical approaches to behavioral disorders

Approach or Conceptual Model	Causes of Behavioral Disorders	Treatment Indicated
Biophysical	Internal causes, such as chemical imbalances, genetic deficiencies, poor nutrition, disrupted sleep patterns, brain injury.	Use medication like tranquilizers, stimulants, or antidepressants and/or apply behavior modification.
Behavioral	External causes, such as inappropriate behavior learned, reinforced, and maintained by others in the environment.	Remove reinforcers that maintain inappropriate behavior, reinforce appropriate behavior, teach acceptable behavior.
Psychodynamic	Internal causes, such as unsuccessful negotiation of psychological stages, internal conflicts, guilt feelings.	Allow free expression of feelings, provide accepting warm environment, avoid too many demands.
Sociological	External causes, such as society's labeling as deviant, factors "forcing" rule breaking, lack of social rules that serve as behavior inhibitors.	Modify society, teach alternate behaviors, help the individual establish rules for himself or herself.
Ecological	Internal and external causes, that is, interaction between feelings, needs, and desires and society's norms, demands, and responsibilities.	Aid adjustment of the individual, the environment, or both; manipulate either the individual or the environment for the benefit of both.

fined more generally and *applied behavior analysis* somewhat more rigorously, but both deal with behavior change.

With students who are verbally or physically aggressive, some variation of behavior modification is ordinarily attempted first. Many educators believe it to be the quickest, most efficient technique to reduce or eliminate inappropriate behaviors (Alberto & Troutman, 1990; Walker & Shea, 1991).

As noted in Table 11–1, behaviorists assume that inappropriate behaviors have been learned and are being maintained by reinforcement. The keys to this approach are determining the nature of the reinforcement and eliminating it or using a more powerful reinforcer to bring about desired

behavior. Teachers become manipulators of the environment of students, and by such manipulation, they systematically plan changes in behavior.

In practice, teachers observe students, count the inappropriate behaviors (which have been stated specifically), and attempt to determine what precedes and follows the behaviors. Observing and counting provide information regarding how frequently the behaviors occur, as well as show the seriousness of the behaviors. By noting what precedes and follows behaviors, teachers may gain clues concerning what reinforces them. After obtaining a count and noting possible reinforcers, teachers carefully select reinforcers to apply when students exhibit desired behaviors after a given time period or a given number of appropriate responses.

For example, a student uses obscene language at the slightest provocation. The teacher defines the behavior precisely. Then, the teacher counts the number of times this behavior occurs during a class period, during a particular time of the day, or during an entire day. This count is usually taken for 3 to 5 days to establish a baseline (Figure 11–3). The teacher may also note that after each occurrence, some or all of the class laughed or that she said something about the language to the student.

At this point, the teacher selects an intervention. In this example, if the student seems to enjoy the attention and social rewards of attention from the class and the teacher, the teacher may decide to provide attention when the student does not use obscene language. This, then, is the intervention. Watching for times when the student is working or paying attention, the teacher may praise the student at least three times during every hour. During this period of intervention, the teacher keeps careful records to note whether the obscene language is decreasing, increasing, or remaining the same (Figure 11–3). If the behavior is decreasing, the positive comments may be considered successful.

If the behavior is not decreasing, the reinforcer is not powerful enough and another must be selected. This new reinforcer is

FIGURE 11–3
Sample teacher record of frequency of a student's verbal abuse

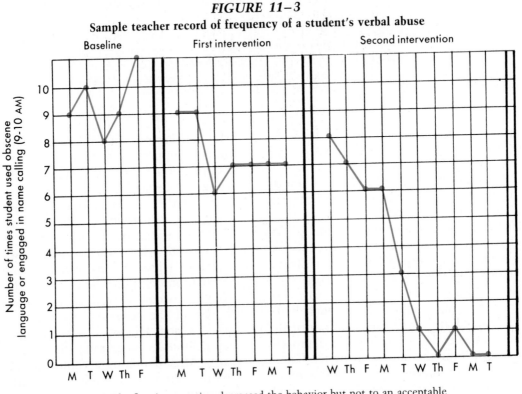

Note: The first intervention decreased the behavior but not to an acceptable level, and another intervention was attempted.

then tried, records are kept to determine whether the behavior is decreasing, and if necessary, still another reinforcer is selected. The process continues until the appropriate reinforcer is found and the behavior is decreased to an acceptable level or eliminated; then the reinforcers are phased out.

In other situations, the objective may be to increase a desirable behavior. For example, the objective may be to increase the number of times the student volunteers a response during a class discussion. The same principles of obtaining a baseline, attempting an intervention, and noting the results apply, except that in this case, the teacher notes whether the behavior is increasing. Completion of work, time spent on tasks, cooperative efforts with peers, and effective use of study time are other behaviors that teachers ordinarily want to increase.

Reinforcers. There are a variety of ways to find out what is reinforcing, such as by observing what students do during free time or asking what they would enjoy doing. Reinforcers can be tangible items, tokens, social reinforcers, or special privileges (Figure 11–4).

The goal of teachers should be to choose reinforcers that are useful with all students. For example, a teacher should not give cookies to a ninth grader to eliminate tardiness if providing 10 minutes at the end of the class period to begin homework is sufficient reinforcement. If the principal of a school does not allow students on the playground or in the student lounge except at designated times, then the teacher cannot use free time in such locations as reinforcers. If the teacher has a personal aversion to using food, free time, or any other particular reinforcer, these obviously should not be used.

FIGURE 11–4
Reinforcers

1. *Tangible reinforcers.* Peanuts; personal grooming aids; special materials, such as felt pens and colored pencils; toys; models.

2. *Token reinforcers.* Individual behavior charts; achievement charts; checks; points; happy faces; stars; trading stamps.

3. *Social reinforcers.* Verbal praise; clapping or cheering from others; display of work or projects; helping the librarian, school secretary, nurse, cooks, custodian, or counselor; tutoring younger children.

4. *Special privileges.* Exemption from an assignment, homework, or a test; extra time before or after recess; taking class roll; distributing or collecting materials; serving as secretary for class meetings; operating the slide, movie, or filmstrip projector; leading or organizing an event, such as a class raffle or auction; reading a message over the intercom; washing the blackboard; watering the plants; feeding the fish or other animals.

Note: Based on *Behavior Management: A Practical Approach for Educators* (pp. 98–99) by J. E. Walker and T. M. Shea, 1991, Columbus, OH: Merrill.

Tape recording may enhance interest and promote motivation.

Time-Out. Sometimes, students who have behavior disorders require a period of time during which they are separated by some physical space in the room. When this separation seems advisable, the teacher can physically move the desk of a student to the front, back, or side of the room to provide physical space between the student and the rest of the class. The purpose of the removal varies. Sometimes, it is to reduce the amount of reinforcement from other students (if the student is in the back of the room or over to one side, antics are not so visible). Being very near the teacher often prevents the student from annoying others. However, a student may refuse to move, thereby creating a new problem for the teacher—a test of wills. Alternately, the

student may create more commotion as he or she moves than the move is worth. The student may bang desks; knock books, pencils, or papers off desks; and move slowly to lengthen the time of the chaos. The teacher must determine whether asking the student to move is advisable.

In another form of time-out, a specific place is physically marked (for example, bookcases arranged to form an enclosed corner). In this area, a rug or pillows may be available along with reading materials or anything else the teacher and students arrange. A class discussion should be held about the purpose of such a space. The teacher may suggest that a student go to the space to gain control, or the student may go independently for the same reason.

Be sure that this place is seen as a safe haven, not punishment, so that time-out is a way to reduce tensions that arise from having to deal with pressing problems.

Regardless of whether the teacher suggests that a student go to the space or the student selects it, the student should come out only when he or she chooses to. It is important that the teacher explain that using this space does not absolve the student from responsibility for assignments or homework. This explanation should prevent abuses and misunderstandings. If a student does abuse the privilege, and it is to be expected that students who are behaviorally disordered will try, discuss the guidelines with the offending student—and discuss them again and again.

Contracts. No discussion of behavior modification, however brief, should omit the principle of contracting. Contracts are agreements that specify in exact terms what the student must do and what the teacher will do *after* the student has completed his or her portion of the agreement. This sequence is essential, particularly with students who have behavior or academic problems. The teacher would be in an untenable position if the student were to receive the reward before performing his or her portion of the contract, an approach analogous to saying, "You can have the ice cream first if you promise to eat your spinach afterward."

Contracts may be informal verbal agreements, simple written statements, or sophisticated written and witnessed agreements (Figures 11–5 and 11–6). Which is most useful depends primarily on the needs of the student. Secondary students often respond more favorably to written agreements. Sometimes, a teacher may want the parents to sign the contract, especially if the task being negotiated is one involving homework. By asking the parents to sign, the teacher is ensuring their awareness. Of course, teachers must realize, particularly with the parents of disruptive students, that the parents' awareness does not ensure follow-through or cooperation.

The following contract guidelines are based on Homme, Csanyi, Gonzales, and Rechs (1979). The guidelines provide a useful summary of the characteristics of proper contracting.

1. Performance should come before rewards.
2. Rewards should immediately follow performance in the beginning.
3. Rewards should be provided frequently and for each approximation.
4. Rewards should be provided for accomplishment rather than obedience. The tone of the contract should be, "When you do this, you can . . ." rather than "If you do this, then I will allow you to . . . ."
5. Contracts should be fair and honest. Teachers and students must agree that the rewards are appropriate for the tasks completed. After completion of the tasks, teachers must follow through with the rewards. If for some unforeseen reason teachers cannot provide the rewards, students should be allowed to choose alternate rewards or be given the rewards specified at the earliest possible time.
6. The terms of the contract should be clear. A statement like "if you behave during class" is not clear. Teachers may have definite standards in mind, but students may interpret *behave* in an entirely different manner.
7. Contracts should be positive. This quality is especially important for students who have a history of conflict with authority figures. Positive statements

FIGURE 11–5
Sample contract

CONTRACT

This contract is between _____ and

_____ .

I (student) agree to do the following:

_____

_____

_____

When I do I will be able to:

_____

_____

_____

And I (teacher) agree to help by:

_____

_____

_____

_____   _____
Student signature   Teacher signature

Date signed_____   Date to be renegotiated _____

---

avoid the threat of punishment and contribute to positive educational experiences.

8. Contracts should be used systematically. Teachers might ask themselves what the payoff is for the student. Does the student achieve a sense of satisfaction from appropriate behavior, or will the student gain satisfaction from being able to have free time? Will this change become the first of a series of small but ever closer approximations to the desired goal of appropriate behavior in the classroom?

For teachers unfamiliar with negotiating contracts, it may be best to begin with a simple format. Teachers should use the following contract checklist when first making contracts.

1. Explain contracts and contracting.
2. Show an example of a contract.

FIGURE 11–6
Sample contract

Look At Me

And if that's not enough here is what I plan to do next:

_____

_____

_____

When I do, I'll be able to _____

_____

And I will have it done by _____

| date | student | witness | Teacher |

Note: From *It's Positively Fun* (p. 27) by P. Kaplan, J. Kohfeldt, and K. Sturla, 1974, Denver: Love. Reprinted by permission.

3. Discuss possible tasks and list student-suggested and teacher-suggested tasks.
4. Agree on a task.
5. Suggest reinforcers or ask the student to suggest them.
6. Negotiate the ratio of the task to the reinforcer.
7. Identify the time allotted for the task.
8. Identify the criterion or achievement level for a task completion.
9. Agree on the method of evaluation.
10. Negotiate the delivery of the reinforcer.
11. Set a time or date for renegotiation.
12. Sign the contract and have the student sign it.

Once familiar and comfortable with contracting, teachers may omit or combine various steps.

Combinations of contracts, point systems, or tokens can also be used. Students and teachers should negotiate the items and the possible points or tokens to be earned. The points or tokens can then be traded for free time or other reinforcers (Figure 11–7). By arranging the value of the reinforcers with students (the three cards alluded to in Figure 11–7) some allowance is made for students who find it extremely difficult to perform the tasks required. They have goals for which to strive yet receive something for less successful efforts. There should be a lower limit (145 points in Figure 11–7) below which no reinforcement is given.

There is an element of risk in using this type of contract and point system. If a student views something on card 2 as desir-able, the student may reach exactly the points necessary to receive it and thereafter be uncooperative, knowing that he or she will still receive the reward. If teachers anticipate this problem, they should not use the varying reinforcer system. However, if students discuss the issue in good faith but manipulate it to advantage, teachers should point out the change and use a more direct system of contracting.

Modeling. Research indicates that children imitate the behavior they observe; however, they are not always discriminating in what they imitate. Thus, teachers may want to seat certain students in close proximity to students who model specific behaviors (such as seating a student behind one who

FIGURE 11–7
Points or tokens that can be traded for reinforcements

Name: _____ Date: _____						
5 points possible for each	**Mon.**	**Tues.**	**Wed.**	**Thurs.**	**Fri.**	**TOTAL**
Promptness Preparedness (book, paper, pencil) Completed homework Use of time Effort Cooperation Attitude						
Bonus points for extra effort, extra neat home-work						
					GRAND TOTAL:_____	

175 points or above: Choose from card 1

160–174 points: Choose from card 2

145–159 points: Choose from card 3

usually does raise his or her hand and waits to be called on). Yet, teachers must keep in mind elements that can affect the results. In its simplest form, modeling perhaps works best with young students. Still, for a variety of reasons, some students do not receive sufficient reinforcement merely in the example of a model. In addition, the mere fact that a teacher sees a student as a model does not mean that other students view him or her in the same manner. To them, a model may seem too good, too bright, the teacher's pet, or simply obnoxious. Thus, it may be a violation of peer-group norms to imitate this student in any manner whatsoever. When such is the case, the model may be subjected to taunts and ridicule outside of class, and more aggressive students may not wait until after class to begin their jeers.

Peer Pressure. At the secondary level, guiding students in discussion of problems is generally more productive than is modeling. In discussion, help students (a) define a problem precisely, (b) establish appropriate goals, and (c) find solutions to the problem. With this approach, peer pressure may be a powerful influence on students who have behavior disorders.

Ethics. One additional concern related to behavior modification must be addressed—the ethical aspects of manipulating another person's behavior. The following guidelines for teachers who are considering the use of behavior modification are loosely based on Walker and Shea (1991):

1. Consider why you want or feel a need to change the behavior of another person. Is it to create a positive learning environment for all students? Or is it some inner need to exert control or demonstrate power?
2. Attempt to understand the problems of

students, not merely control. Discuss the behavior you deem inappropriate to gain insights with regard to the behavior. If you learn through such discussions that the student throws a pencil because he or she observes a parent throwing dishes when angry or frustrated, you can better decide if or how to use behavior modification.
3. Determine whether the behavior change will help the student better understand himself or herself or the environment. Manipulating behavior merely for the sake of conformity is not defensible.
4. Be aware that your knowledge of human behavior is in a continuous stage of development and that students change and develop. Keep abreast of developing information in regard to how and why people behave as they do.

Teachers should also consider the following questions with respect to the use of behavior modification:

1. Will intervention help this student be viewed as more normal in this environment?
2. Will a change in the student's behavior lead to greater acceptance by peers?
3. Is this intervention fair to the student?
4. Does the intervention demonstrate respect for the student as an individual?
5. Does this intervention allow the student to maintain dignity?

Psychodynamic Approach

As a treatment for mental illness, psychodynamic therapy is used in mental health settings such as hospitals (Rich, 1982). In schools, psychologists and psychiatrists may use it in conjunction with other types of therapy or may adapt it to meet the needs of students. Ethical considerations that relate to required training and expertise with guidance from qualified supervisors contraindicate use of the psychodynamic approach by teachers, but regular classroom teachers may find some variations and adaptations useful. As noted in Table 11–1, the psychodynamic approach includes certain basic assumptions in regard to the cause of inappropriate behavior.

If a student is extremely angry with himself or herself, peers, the teacher, the school, and the whole world, then expressing the anger in an acceptable manner may serve as a release to the student. Drawing, painting, or writing may be used as a medium for expression of feelings, as may dance, drama, or role playing. Teachers must decide how and when to use this method. Often, the medium depends on the age of the student, the structure of the classroom, and the school system. In lower grades, because the classrooms are essentially self-contained, teachers have more latitude in the selection of the time and means of implementation. In the upper grades, when teachers have each group of students for only a relatively short time (a 40- to 50-minute period), implementation is much more difficult.

In primarily self-contained rooms, a portion of the room can have an easel, paints, phonograph, or whatever else is necessary for various types of therapy. After the teacher knows the student well enough and thinks that one or more of the expressive media may be helpful, the teacher can discuss with the student when, how, and under what conditions the student may use the materials. When the school system is departmentalized and students move from room to room, it is usually necessary to make arrangements with the specialist. In the resource room, the materials may be readily available. Again, it is necessary to determine the guidelines for the use of the materials.

The emphasis with art, music, or dance is conveying feelings in a nonverbal manner, not the production of masterpieces. Teachers should not be shocked at the pictures or gestures that may result in therapeutic activities. Sometimes, the intent is to shock, and on other occasions, confusion, anger, or guilt is reflected.

Puppetry and role playing may also be used to help students express their feelings. Puppetry allows for verbal expression without face-to-face contact. Sometimes, shy or withdrawn students participate in this form of expression while hiding behind the stage. Depending on the age of the students involved, puppet shows may be given to other class members or to younger students. Beginning with nonthreatening materials such as fairy tales usually enables students to gain sufficient self-confidence to attempt shows that depict situations more true to life.

Often more successful with older students, role playing is very similar to puppetry. Again, by beginning with nonthreatening situations, students gain the motivation they require and can later attempt sensitive forms of dialogue. Generally, it is necessary to discuss the feelings that specific roles engender. The use of situations that are part of life can teach students alternate coping strategies. During both the role playing and the discussion that follows, the student can learn new strategies concerning effective ways to handle this problem.

The psychodynamic approach has many variations. It cannot be overemphasized, however, that teachers must not experiment with the emotions of students. It is a wise policy to discuss with the school psychologist, psychiatrist, or specialist what is best for each student before implementing the psychodynamic approach in the classroom.

Biophysical Approach

As noted in Table 11–1, the biophysical approach assumes the cause of behavior problems to be internal, that is, the result of genetic defects, chemical imbalances, brain injuries, nutritional deficiencies, and so on. Obviously, diagnosis of such causes of behavioral disorders is out of the realm of education; therefore, a physician is involved. The medical role is dominant in the biophysical approach to behavioral disorders. Parents and teachers must work in cooperation with the medical professionals to ensure the best possible results.

Medical doctors may prescribe medications, and if so, teachers may have to help monitor the results. The task is not to be taken lightly. Teachers should be aware of what medications students are receiving, possible side effects, and behavior changes to expect. Because the best method of determining the correct dosage of such medications is trial and error, reports to the parents or physician are extremely important. With too much medication, students may be lethargic or sleepy. With too little medication, students show no effect. Therefore, reports from teachers and parents can help physicians adjust dosages (Barkley, 1981).

Sociological and Ecological Approaches

From a sociological and ecological perspective, behavior disorders are a result of rule breaking, social disapproval, and lack of harmonious interaction between individuals and the environment. Regular classroom teachers must be aware of the various backgrounds of their students and of the powerful influence of background. This awareness is even more important with students who are behaviorally disordered.

The unacceptable behavior of a student may be the result of the socialization process taking place in the home. When youngsters are taught by their elders that stealing is not wrong but getting caught is, they may demonstrate this belief in school. It is not surprising to discover such youngsters stealing coats, books, assignments, and lunches with extraordinary finesse. Teachers certainly cannot allow stealing; however, knowledge about what is taught in the home provides insight into the problem.

Students who have behavior disorders are frequently in conflict with school, home, neighborhood, and various other social environments. In school, they may be in conflict with teachers, the principal, cafeteria workers, and others. It is possible that a major part of the conflict is caused by a mismatch between the student and one particular environment in the school. For example, lack of structure plus noise level plus horseplay with other students may lead to conflict in the cafeteria. A careful analysis of the subenvironments in school may indicate major trouble areas. Discussion and scheduling adjustments may alleviate major stress areas and lead to improved behavior.

Within a classroom, conflict may result from a mismatch between the student's skills, the teaching style, and peer relationships. Careful analysis of all of the factors pertinent and adjustment (as required and possible) may reduce stress and improve behavior.

A word of caution is necessary: the solution is not always an adjustment on the part of teachers and the school. Students must develop coping skills, which will be important not only in the school and during school years, but also for the rest of life. The ecological approach leads to an examination of interaction between a student and the various environments that exist in school. Whenever possible, this examination should be expanded to include other environments, but educators must focus first on the school environment. To apply this approach effectively, educators must be careful to arrive at a solution that will lead to a reduction of conflict, not place blame.

The sociological approach seeks to provide assistance in all parts of the environment. The dynamics of the family may need to be examined and supportive therapy provided. Teachers may be the most effective persons for this task, or individuals more skilled in counseling techniques may need to intervene.

When a student's behavioral problems are sociological or ecological, it is essential that all appropriate personnel (social worker, parole officers, principal, and so on) be involved. Because the sociological and ecological causes of behavior problems involve the values and mores of society and changing interrelationships, a wide range of expertise must be involved in effecting behavior changes. Working with allied professionals, classroom teachers may be the catalysts to change and improve the environments of students who have behavior disorders.

Other Approaches

Some approaches that may be valuable to teachers but are not readily categorized under the other major approaches follow.

Rudolf Dreikurs. Dreikurs and Cassel (1972), noted psychiatrists, identify several goals of students that are generally at cross-purposes with those of teachers. Students who have behavior disorders often demonstrate behaviors associated with one or more of these goals. Dreikurs suggests various methods of counteracting these undesirable behaviors. Table 11–2 indicates

these goals, the behaviors that students demonstrate in attempting to reach the goals, and possible alternatives for teachers.

Dreikurs believes that in attempting to achieve these goals, students operate with faulty logic. With attention getting, students feel worthwhile only if people pay attention to them; therefore, the students extract that attention at any price. Students must be made to feel worthwhile when not seeking attention so as to realize that they are valuable.

With power, the faulty logic is "Unless I win or get you to do what I want, I am not worthwhile." Any teacher soon recognizes that students do have power and that if they are determined, they can "win." One need teach only a few months to realize that a teacher seldom can force a student to do anything he or she does not want to do. When a student is seeking power, the best, most disarming device is simply to give it. There are many legitimate ways to do this: give the student the power to choose what and when she will study, enlist the student's cooperation (power) in formulating rules, or provide the student with leadership positions.

One of the most disarming statements a teacher can make is simply "I know I can't *make* you do anything, I know you don't *have* to do anything, but I'm asking you to please do this." Often, after such a statement, the teacher can observe in the student physical changes, such as a reduction of tension in the shoulders and a less defiant stance. At this time, one can make use of the student's willingness and quickly move on to the task at hand; it is *not* the time for the teacher to flaunt his or her power!

To some students, the world and all the people in it seem so hurtful that students feel the only thing to do is to gain revenge. Such students feel disliked by all, distrusted

TABLE 11–2
Counteracting student goals associated with behavior disorders

Goal	Behavior Demonstrated	Teacher Alternative
Attention getting	Attempts to get teacher's attention, shows off, asks useless questions, disturbs others	Ignore misbehavior if possible, do not show annoyance, give much attention for appropriate behavior, select student as a helper
Power	Contradicts teacher and other students, deliberately disobeys rules, dawdles, lies, has temper tantrums	Recognize student's power, give power as much as possible, give student choices, do not argue, avoid struggle for power, ask student for help, make contracts with student.
Revenge	Steals, hurts others, acts sullen or defiant, makes others dislike him or her, retaliates	Apply natural consequences, persuade student that he or she is liked, enlist a buddy to befriend the student, do not show the student that you are hurt or disappointed, enable other students to support him or her.
Display of inadequacy or hopelessness	Demonstrates inferiority complex, will not try, is discouraged before attempting new activity, gives up too easily, refuses to get involved	Do not support inferiority feelings, be constructive, get class cooperation, praise student, provide ways for student to demonstrate ability.

by all, and vulnerable. Such students see the world as unfair. Teachers must attempt to help such students see that there are persons who can be trusted, that there are places in which one can be safe, and that people can care. This process is difficult to accomplish because students often view such attempts with suspicion and lack of trust.

When a student displays vengeful behavior, the teacher must take care that the remainder of the class does not turn against the student, thus confirming the student's belief in the absence of goodness. Punishing a student may further entrench this belief, so the application of logical consequences can be a valuable procedure with this student. At times, it may help to encourage a

promising friendship between a vengeful student and another student.

Some students become so discouraged that they seem to give up all hope—they no longer attempt to get even. Their faulty logic may lead to display of inadequacy or hopelessness, which includes the building of a protective shield of despair. The shield is reinforced by a display of ineptitude, so that nothing is expected of the student. When confronted with this type of behavior, teachers may also be tempted to give up. Usually, such students are not disruptive, do not demand anything from teachers or classmates, and can easily be allowed to "vegetate." However, such students may have the greatest need for attention. Attempts to achieve in any arena must be encouraged, and highly motivating activities must be used. Students who are demonstrating hopeless behavior must receive much praise—but it must be honest praise. Mistakes must be handled as learning experiences. At times, it is helpful for teachers subtly to admit mistakes that they make in the presence of the entire class, saying, for example, "Did you see how I spelled that today? Didn't I spell it differently yesterday?" and then correcting the error.

Young children usually easily reveal their behavior as goal seeking. The older the students, however, the more effective they are in camouflaging their goals. Often, these goals are also intermingled with desire for excitement, behaviors resulting from drug use, or other contaminating factors. In short, it may be fairly difficult for teachers to sort out just which goal or combination of goals students are seeking.

Since Dreikurs discussed logical consequences as early as 1964 (Dreikurs & Saltz, 1964), the term has often been used in suggestions for classroom discipline. This concept involves teacher attitudes more than actual disciplinary measures. Teachers must believe the basic tenets of this philosophy before they can make the method of logical consequences workable in the classroom.

The first of these tenets is that the classroom is a replica of the democratic system that is an essential aspect of life in the United States. A democratic classroom implies that both teacher and students are working toward a common goal and that no one has more power than anyone else. This principle rules out punishment, because punishment is meted out by someone in authority. Clearly, the teacher is the adult in the classroom, the teacher does have various responsibilities to ensure learning, and the teacher is not just another child or adolescent. However, even though the teacher has responsibilities and is not another child, according to this philosophy, the teacher does not have the right to sit continually in judgment, to hand out punishments, or to be a dictator. (The teacher *can* do these things but will pay the price with students who retaliate.)

The democratic classroom consists of teacher and students who choose rules for the common good and goals to be pursued. Within this context, the method of natural or logical consequences can become appropriate. If the natural flow of events is allowed to take its course, natural consequences become learning tools. For example, if a student forgets his or her lunch money, the natural flow of events is that with no lunch money the student gets no lunch; therefore, the teacher does not rescue the student, does not scold, does not discuss it. The natural consequence of going without lunch will teach the student to remember to bring lunch money.

At times, of course, the safety of a student does not permit the teacher to allow natural consequences to occur. There are also times when natural consequences simply are not present, so the method of logical consequences may be useful. Logical consequences are structured and arranged by the teacher and *must be experienced by the student as logical*; that is, the student must see the relationship between his or her actions and the consequences. This awareness is absolutely necessary—it is not enough for the teacher alone to see the relationship.

Logical consequences can often be arranged through the manner in which the teacher makes a statement. For example, the statement "when you are finished with your assignment, you may leave for free time" provides for logical consequences. The responsibility is placed on the student. A student who does not finish in time may miss free time. This approach does not set the teacher up as the authority, handing out privileges or punishments, as the student may perceive in the statement "I will let you go for free time when you finish the assignment."

In another example, if two students engage in a fight, the teacher can step in to settle the fight or simply say, "We decided in this room that fights are not allowed and that whoever fights will not be able to go to the gym," and then walk away. Of course, the teacher cannot allow students to be hurt, but a reminder of the consequences chosen by the group along with the lack of attention given the inappropriate action often defuses the situation. If not, and if the students are in danger of being hurt, the teacher may need to ask the rest of the class what was decided about fighting. When they state the consequences, much of the punitive aspect and imposition of authority by the teacher are removed from the consequences. The teacher may need to step between the students to stop the fight. Again, this action should be performed with as little imposition of authority as possible. When it is time for the class to go to the gym, the students who were fighting are asked, "What are the consequences for fighting?" When they answer, the rest of the class can be taken to the gym.

The purpose of the use of logical consequences is to help students be responsible for their own actions with a minimum of conformity for the sake of conformity. The teacher first asks, "What is likely to happen if I don't intervene?" The answer is usually the natural or logical consequence. The teacher then asks, "What consequence would the student most likely see as a result of his or her actions?" That consequence is the one to use.

Dreikurs and Cassel (1972) suggest several reasons for considering the use of logical consequences: they are learning processes, they are related to inappropriate behavior, they involve distinctions between the student and deeds of the student, and they reflect the reality of social order rather than the whim of an adult. Teachers must be educators who are sympathetic and understanding, who are interested in situations and the outcomes, who are objective, and who provide a choice of continuing a behavior or experiencing the consequences.

A thorough understanding and acceptance of the principles of natural and logical consequences may provide imaginative teachers with a variety of methods to promote a cooperative attitude. Interested readers may refer to the references to locate more of Dreikurs's valuable suggestions concerning discipline in the classroom.

William Glasser. William Glasser (1965) developed a type of individual therapy or counseling that with modification may be useful in classrooms. The basic tenet of this therapy is that all persons attempt to fulfill various needs even though it may be difficult to interpret the need when the behavior appears irrational or inadequate. The basic needs are (a) to love and (b) to feel worthwhile to others—to be loved. Glasser believes that all races and cultures have these two needs in common and that all people strive to meet them. How an individual behaves is often the key to whether or not that person elicits love from others. Being loved by others is the result of appropriate behavior. When an individual acts in a manner that causes discomfort in others, they find it difficult to demonstrate their love.

Glasser suggests that only by taking responsibility for one's actions can one be lovable. The key to his therapy therefore is to cause persons to be responsible for their actions. In other words, the right way is to help individuals gain self-respect and the closeness with others by saying in essence, "I care enough about you to force you to act in a better way, a way whereby you will learn through experience to know what I already know" (p. 19).

Glasser is a firm believer in the rightness or wrongness of actions—for instance stealing is always wrong, regardless of the reasons for doing it—and this moral value must be taught to students. Only when students behave "rightly" do they develop self-respect. Readers interested in further information regarding reality therapy as well as specific techniques for classroom meetings and helping students develop more responsibility for their actions should consult Glasser's text, listed in the references.

Lee and Marlene Canter. In the mid-1970s, an assertive discipline approach was developed and advocated by Lee and Marlene Canter (1976). The basic premise of the approach is that students learn more effectively when teachers are clearly in charge and the students clearly understand what is expected of them. The Canters believe that their approach provides teachers with effective means of managing inappropriate behavior constructively while providing a warm, caring atmosphere.

The Canters suggest that many teachers labor under several misconceptions regarding discipline, such as the notion that firm control is stifling rather than liberating, that students neither need nor deserve firm discipline, and that teachers who are assertive are necessarily authoritarian and dogmatic in their approach. According to the Canters, teachers must believe that they have rights, like the right to determine what behaviors are appropriate, to expect those behaviors from students, and to provide consequences when students do not exhibit appropriate behaviors. These rights provide teachers with opportunities to es-

tablish environments most conducive for learning. On the other hand, students have basic rights also. They have the right to a teacher who supports them when their behavior is appropriate, to receive assistance in controlling inappropriate behavior, and to choose their behaviors with full knowledge of the consequences of their choices.

The basic needs of the students and teachers are met through the use of assertive discipline. Teachers never violate the needs of students or the best interests of the entire class, but they do communicate unequivocally their expectations in relation to behavior and consistently follow through with the predetermined consequences.

Teachers following the assertive discipline approach:

1. Clearly identify expectations; that is, they go over the day and determine the acceptable and unacceptable behaviors related to each activity (for instance, the amount of talking appropriate when small groups are working as differentiated from working at an interest center or the computer). They discuss these expectations with the students more than once. Students learn these expectations by repetition and practice, just as they learn multiplication or correct letter-writing form.

2. Understand the difference between nonassertive, hostile, and assertive responses to the behavior of students. Nonassertive teachers are generally unable or unwilling to place demands on students, or if they do, they retreat at the first sign of opposition. In general, they accept the decisions of the students. This is clearly not a situation conducive to learning. Hostile teachers usually feel out of control and resort to threats and irrational punishments that infringe on the right of students to have

teacher assistance in limiting their behavior and to choose their behavior with complete knowledge of the consequences.

Assertive teachers clearly indicate expectations and insist on compliance. The teachers' words are always backed up by actions, appropriate behaviors are supported, and inappropriate behaviors are quickly and efficiently followed by predetermined consequences. Canter and Canter suggest that teachers practice assertive responses until they come naturally. Following are examples of the three types of responses in two different situations.

1. *Behavior: not paying attention*
   Nonassertive: "Won't you please listen?"
   Hostile: "Are you ever going to learn to pay attention? I've asked ten times already this morning!"
   Assertive: "Listen to what I say since I won't repeat it."
2. *Behavior: fighting on the playground*
   Nonassertive: "It would be better if you tried not to fight anymore."
   Hostile: "You always pick on someone. Why don't you grow up!"
   Assertive: "The rule is we don't fight.

Stand here until you are ready to obey the rule."

These examples illustrate clear disapproval of the action, unambiguous statements of what consequences follow, and the behaviors expected of the students. Assertive responses deliver the expectation that students can and will choose appropriate behavior. It is essential that teachers recognize the appropriate behavior in the same assertive manner: "You did listen and now you know what to do" or "You did stand here. Are you ready to join the group and follow the rules?"

Canter and Canter also suggest that teachers make assertiveness plans in much the same manner as they do lesson plans for reading, history, or math. This planning is to be accomplished prior to the beginning of the school year and repeated as often as necessary during the school year. The guidelines for assertiveness planning include (a) determining inappropriate behaviors that are occurring or the potential for them, (b) identifying the specific behaviors that students are to engage in, and (c) determining positive and negative consequences and deciding on implementation of consequences.

TABLE 11–3
Assertiveness planning table

Activity	Acceptable Behaviors	Consequences	Unacceptable Behaviors	Consequences
Music class (large group)	Playing instruments	At least four comments per class recognizing good behavior	Playing instruments while I'm talking	Saying to the student, "We don't play when I'm talking, so I'll take the drumsticks" and taking them until I'm finished

An aid for assertiveness plans may be constructed, duplicated, and used for as many activities as necessary (see Table 11–3). This type of planning requires visual and mental preparation for both appropriate and inappropriate behaviors, as well as consequences for both (Charles, 1981). Some teachers may wish to rehearse verbally what they will say so that when the need actually arises, assertive responses will feel natural.

The assertiveness approach borrows from several other approaches. For more information on this and other models of discipline, see the Canter and Canter reference and the Charles reference for additional insights.

STRESS

Regular classroom teachers may easily succumb to feelings of inadequacy, frustration, and even despair when it seems that all attempted interventions are useless. It can be helpful, however, to reflect on the various aspects of behavior that are not under the control of teachers. Students may be experiencing stress from the normal developmental stages, such as separation from home for the first time, not knowing what to do about bodily changes that are taking place, and approaching graduation with its pressure for deciding a career. Economic stresses, including poor diet, inadequate housing, lack of privacy, and limited opportunities to participate in social activities may also affect students. Some students experience psychological stress, such as being told they were or are unwanted, that they will be kicked out if they misbehave, or that they are dumb, troublemaking, or useless. Others live with abusive or psychotic parents. Still others endure stress that may seem minor to teachers but is significant to the students, such as severe acne just at the time of an important date, a friend's acci-

dentally spilling soda on the English assignment due next period, or a trusted friend's telling someone something that was to have been a secret.

Any one of these types of stress can lead to what Long and Fagen (1981) refer to as a stress cycle. The student experiences a stressful situation that leads to a variety of feelings. The student may feel uncomfortable with these feelings, thinking that they are unacceptable or wrong. Attempting to deal with the feelings, the student engages in some sort of behavior that is an honest reflection of the feelings or an attempt to cover these up. A student who verbally attacks the teacher because of an incomplete assignment may have strong feelings of inadequacy or inferiority because of lack of study time or of a place to study or because the student was fighting with a drunk parent when he or she should have been finishing homework. The behavior that the student demonstrates leads to an environmental reaction. Other students observe the outburst, and the outburst evokes feelings in the teacher. At this point, a power struggle may be initiated. The teacher may feel threatened by the student's verbal abuse and react in an authoritarian manner: "You will not speak to me that way!" or "Take your things and go to the principal's office immediately!" In such cases, there is no winner. Rather, both the teacher and student are acting immaturely. The teacher must be the responsible professional and attempt to interpret the student's actions.

Long and Fagen (1981) suggest a series of guidelines for teaching students how to cope with various kinds of stress:

1. Be attentive to nonverbal communication. Many students learn early that what they say can be held against them and that speaking evokes angry responses from adults. Therefore, they

may refrain from verbal communication. However, tense muscles, clenched fists, rapid breathing, jerky body movements, and looks in the eyes can tell observant teachers much about the anger or frustration students are experiencing.

2. Attend as much to *how* students speak as to *what* they say. The tone or short, clipped statements may be more important than what is actually said. A *yes* or *no* said through clenched teeth indicates far more than agreement or disagreement.

3. Label and accept the feelings of students. As teachers hear what is really being said through nonverbal and verbal communication, they can label the feelings for students: "You are really angry about this, aren't you?" As teachers reach out to students in this way, the first hesitant step toward a relationship is made. For students, labeling feelings is one matter, but accepting those feelings is far more complex. Teachers must indicate that the feelings are legitimate even though acting them out is not always acceptable: "I know you are angry, but I cannot allow you to hit another student" or "You have a right to be upset about what she said, but you cannot destroy her property." The process of labeling and accepting feelings while rejecting specific behaviors is difficult for students to learn. Teachers need to repeat this process time and time again.

In providing students with a supportive, helping environment, teachers must be certain that the students take responsibility for changing their behavior. Sometimes, teachers become too sympathetic and actually support or contribute to inappropriate behavior. Students may begin to feel put upon and feel that because of stress, they have a right to act inappropriately. The questions or comments of teachers should lead students to examine the behaviors that contributed to problems and what they can do to change the situations. Teachers must be aware of and support the students' attempts—however feeble or unsuccessful—to change situations. Most students do not suddenly begin to have behavioral problems; therefore, changing behavior for the better is also generally slow and painful. Teachers who understand this difficulty can provide encouragement as students develop the skills necessary to change their behavior.

SUGGESTIONS FOR REGULAR CLASSROOM TEACHERS

Teachers who have students with behavior disorders perhaps find this particular disability the most difficult to accept. The difficulty certainly is not surprising, because by definition this behavior is *not normal.* Other students in the class also find it difficult.

Whenever inappropriate behavior occurs in the classroom, teachers must decide quickly whether it is an individual problem or a group problem. At times, a problem in class dynamics, such as a lack of unity, low morale, or negative reactions, contributes to the difficulties of students who have behavior disorders. It is mandatory for regular classroom teachers to examine the dynamics of the class as a whole and take effective steps for correction if they find problems. However, it is also mandatory that individual problems receive prompt attention. It is a matter of correcting both areas of concern simultaneously, not one first and then the other. Johnson and Bany (1970) list a number of observable behaviors that teachers may use for determining whether the general atmosphere of the classroom is a factor further compounding the problem of a student who is disruptive (Table 11–4).

TABLE 11-4
**Observable behaviors when the classroom atmosphere compounds
disruptive behavior**

Classroom Problems	Observable Characteristics
Ease of distraction	Undue attention to visitors, noises, movements outside windows, etc.; inability easily to return to task when distracted, almost as if looking for diversions; frequent squabbles over books, pencils, chairs, etc.
Lack of cohesion	Division into subgroups: boys vs. girls, minorities vs. majority, various cliques; frequent arguments between subgroups over usual competitive aspects of classroom, such as grades, games, differentiated assignments
Lack of conformity to normal standards	Excessive noise and talk in routine situations, between classes, going to assembly, etc.; more than usual noise in activities such as handing back papers, correcting work, and completing assignments; nonadherence to rules of quiet talk when in small groups, committees, or ability groups
Put-down of individuals	Active hostility or aggressiveness toward one or two students; ridiculing, ignoring, criticizing, or refusing to work with certain students, hiding books or papers of disliked students and attempting to trip them or make them appear clumsy, dumb, different
Resistance and hostility toward teacher	Slow-downs or work stoppages created by certain groups' "losing" things, asking for assignments to be repeated, or asking obviously irrelevant questions; accusations of other students that are clearly a challenge to the teacher
Rigidity	Unusual restlessness, argumentativeness, or disagreeability when schedules are changed, when a substitute is present, or when different types of assignments are given or classroom activities are varied.
Support for misbehavior	Encouragement of acting out, talking back, or clowning around; suggesting disruptive activities to individuals; attention to any misbehavior

Note: Adapted from *Classroom Management: Theory and Skill Training* (pp. 46–47) by L. Johnson & M. Bany, 1970, London: Collier-Macmillan.

Some techniques can temporarily address the needs of a student or prevent further problems among other students as a result of contagion. Long and Newman (1980) describe several:

1. *Hurdle lessons.* Provide individual attention to the student's academic needs in order to get past some difficult hurdle. Be alert to determine when to provide this assistance.
2. *Restructuring the classroom routine.* Although students generally benefit from routine, a sensitive teacher may see that the students need a change of pace. For example, a student has just had an emotional outburst, which the entire class has witnessed. Break the class into groups instead of continuing with the lecture or vice versa.
3. *Direct appeal to values.* Get students to thinking by asking questions as Do you realize that if you don't finish this, you will not be able to go to cheerleader practice? or What do you think _____ (best friend) will say? Long and Newman

suggest that the trick is to learn how to say *no* without being angry and how to say *yes* without feeling guilty.

4. *Removal of seduction object.* It is often easier to remove an object from sight than it is to manage the behaviors related to the object. For example, place a toy or pencil on a shelf or in a container. An interesting science project does not have to lose its appeal just because the bell rings for another class. Discuss the project for a few minutes and then remove all equipment related to it in order to reduce the seduction it might continue to produce.

5. *Tension reduction by humor.* Many potentially explosive situations are defused by a humorous comment; however, such comments must never be at the expense of a student. Teachers who are self-confident are able to use humorous comments at their own expense.

Most teachers practice a number of variations of these techniques, having learned them through experience. However, if teachers understand the principles, when to use them, and how to use them, the principles are far more powerful.

As a former regular classroom teacher and later a teacher of students with behavior disorders, one of the authors found it essential to know and understand himself and his teaching style, to think creatively, to borrow ideas from all sources, and to adapt, modify, and keep trying. The suggestions that follow are offered in this spirit. According to teaching style and personality, teachers may use these suggestions to create dynamic new beginnings for students who are behaviorally disordered.

Examination of Feelings

To allow students opportunities to identify their own moods or feelings and to indicate them to others, a "feelings board" may be developed with or by the students. Teachers can hold a discussion of the wide variety of emotions, such as disappointment, happiness, excitement, and anger. Students can then make cards with appropriate descriptions on them. Each day, as the students come into the classroom, they choose the cards that best express their feelings and place them on the bulletin board. For some students, this choice is difficult, because they are unaware of their feelings. As frequently as desired by the teacher or students, hold discussions to explore why students feel the way they do, whether these reasons are under their control, and so on.

Sometimes, students do not want to publicize their emotions; therefore, alternately, allow them to place their cards on their desks or in their notebooks. Some students find that their moods change during a class period or during the day, in which case they may change their cards to indicate the current mood. The overall guiding purpose is to help students recognize their feelings and, when appropriate, consider why they feel as they do. When students recognize the how and why of their emotions, they can explore alternative solutions to problems and ways to change moods or to gain control over them.

Students who are disruptive and withdrawn often find it difficult to describe or evaluate their own behavior. Teachers may find it helpful to discuss their behavior with them on a daily basis, usually at the close of the day or the close of a class. Recalling specific circumstances or events one at a time in a factual manner and asking students to monitor them is often effective. If students find this method too threatening, describing real events in imaginary settings can objectify them.

For example, the teacher may describe an incident this way: "There was a fourth-grade boy who cheated in the ball game. He did not follow the rules of the game, so everyone else got mad and made him get out of the game. He then called them names and they began hitting him. There was a big fight and the teacher had to come over and tell them all to stand by the wall. What really started the fight? Why did the others get so mad? If this boy had played by the rules, how would the story end? If the boy didn't like the rules, what two things could he have done?"

With students who have sufficient writing skills, ask them to write what took place in a particular situation. After an angry student has written his or her account of the event, the anger may be sufficiently diffused and the entire matter can be dropped. At other times, written accounts can be matters for discussion. Discussion can be used to teach alternative behaviors rather than to argue concerning the accuracy of perceptions.

Figure 11–8 illustrates an end-of-the-school-day evaluation that includes clearly positive and potentially negative aspects.

FIGURE 11–8
Behavior self-evaluation

Note: From *It's Positively Fun* (p. 29) by P. Kaplan, J. Kohfeldt, and K. Sturla, 1974, Denver: Love. Reprinted by permission.

The student may not be able to make truthful positive statements concerning the first two items; however, the next three are stated so that the student's response is positive. The last space can be used by the teacher to include an item to which the student responds, or it can be filled in with a positive statement of something the teacher observed. This evaluation, too, may be used for discussion, taken home, or placed in the "good deeds" scrapbook.

Stories. Creating stories may serve as an outlet for a variety of feelings and emotions. The emphasis should be on expression rather than grammar, spelling, or punctuation; however, these aspects of communication should be taught and reinforced in other writing activities. Allow students to explore a range of feelings and to examine alternatives for problem solving. If stories often repeat similar themes, an atmosphere of openness and acceptance can encourage exploration of other, perhaps more sensitive, issues of concern to students.

If students find the whole blank sheet of paper intimidating, have them fold it into fourths. The first block is for the beginning, the two middle blocks are for elaboration, and the final block is for an ending. At times, students need to be prompted. Suggest, for example, "Write a story with a car as the main character" or "Using these words, write a story" or "Using this picture, describe what happened before and what you think will happen next." Encourage students to use one-word sentences or pictures if their writing skills are insufficient to permit them to do more.

After the stories are written, discuss them. However, allow individual students to decide whether or not to discuss their stories. Some students are reluctant or unable to verbalize the feelings about which they have written.

When students become secure and proficient in writing stories, introduce the concept of alternative solutions. Have one student write the beginning and middle of the story while two or three classmates write endings. When all are completed, have the students discuss the various solutions or outcomes. Gradually, students may generalize to other areas of life the reflective thinking and understanding of choices and consequences that they applied in writing (Dehouske, 1982).

Drama. Using facial expressions, pantomime, or charades is a nonthreatening form of releasing feelings or emotions (Necco, Wilson, & Scheidemantal, 1982). When students are comfortable with these techniques, let them act out original skits, stories, and real-life events, such as what happened on the playground or on a date. Hold a discussion of the emotion, story, or event with all members of the class. This provides an opportunity for reflection and careful consideration of all facets of the situation. As the discussion progresses, ask for volunteers to take the part of certain characters or to discuss with individuals what they would do. When there are volunteers to play the part of each character, let reenactment take place. If the drama begins to deteriorate or when it has served its purpose, hold another discussion. The entire class should participate, emphasizing the critical feelings, solutions, and alternatives demonstrated. Gradually, as the students are able, guide the discussion in such a manner that reenactment can be applied to real-life situations. The purpose is to enable the students to recreate feelings and emotions while exploring a variety of solutions to their own problems in a nonthreatening atmosphere.

Recognition

Certificates of recognition for working co-operatively with another student may positively influence the behavior of a student who has behavior problems (Figure 11–9). The opportunity to share a reward may be an incentive for some students (Figure 11–10). "Renting" popular playground balls, bats, gloves, or areas like a basketball court or softball field is also a powerful incentive for some students (Figure 11–11). However, take care in arranging such rentals so that only objects that can be replaced are used and that the students demonstrate some responsibility for the property of others. Realize that some students are much too destructive to be entrusted with the property of others.

Another incentive is free class time, that is, time in which a student has no specific assignment (Figure 11–12). In addition, gaining cooperation of members of the class can be a method of reducing the frequency of disruptive behaviors. Certificates such as that in Figure 11–13 may be used to recognize the effort of members of the class when they demonstrate cooperative behavior or ability to accommodate difficult situations.

FIGURE 11–9
Certificate of recognition

_____ and _____
have shown that

2 HEADS ARE BETTER THAN 1

in

_____
ON THIS MEMORABLE DAY   AS WITNESSED BY

_____   _____

Note: From *Positive Pitches* (p. 27) by P. G. Kaplan and A. G. Hoffman, 1981, Denver: Love. Reprinted by permission.

FIGURE 11–10
Rental card to share

Note: From *It's Positively Fun* (p. 16) by P. Kaplan, J. Kohfeldt, and K. Sturla, 1974, Denver: Love. Reprinted by permission.

FIGURE 11–12
Free-time card

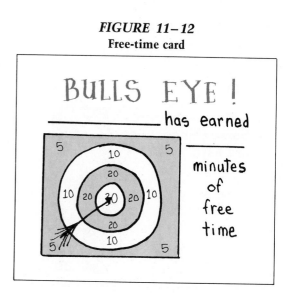

Note: From *It's Positively Fun* (p. 18) by P. Kaplan, J. Kohfeldt, and K. Sturla, 1974, Denver: Love. Reprinted by permission.

FIGURE 11–11
Rental card

Note: From *It's Positively Fun* (p. 16) by P. Kaplan, J. Kohfeldt, and K. Sturla, 1974, Denver: Love. Reprinted by permission.

Because students with behavior problems often receive minimal praise, certificates similar to those illustrated in Figures 11–9 to 11–13 can be used to provide significant positive recognition. Some students attempt to moderate their behavior to receive them. Other students do not actually work *for* them but are exceptionally pleased if teachers surprise them with certificates after situations that are particularly trying. Depending on the reaction of parents to such reinforcement, students may want to take certificates home for additional praise. In other situations, students may not take certificates home, but they are additionally rewarded if the certificates receive prominent placement on a bulletin board or in a scrapbook.

Disruptive students are commonly unaware of the progress they have made, perhaps because after the students have not demonstrated a particular behavior for a time, teachers select another behavior that

FIGURE 11–13
Certificate for cooperation

TO:

_____

Some things
are hard
to ignore. . .

By turning
your back
you were a . .

SUPER
HELP

Many thanks for

_____

_____

_____
Official Appreciator

_____
Special Day

Note: From _Positive Pitches_ (p. 27) by P. G. Kaplan
and A. G. Hoffman, 1981, Denver: Love. Reprinted by
permission.

is disruptive and begin working on it. Thus, students may be deprived of opportunities to enjoy their success. The perception may be that they are always working at something (this may be true in regard to academic areas also) and are not making progress.

To provide opportunities for students to note their successes or achievements, keep a "good-deeds" or "good-work" scrapbook. The scrapbook may be purchased or made of construction paper together with a cover. Achievement certificates awarded to students may be glued into it along with math, handwriting, or any other academic work sheets. When appropriate, a student may page through and recall the reasons for different awards and note the progress he or she has made. Such books can stimulate positive discussions between teachers and students, which can be rewarding in and of themselves. Scrapbooks can also be used at parent-teacher conferences.

Structuring

The academic needs of students must receive attention along with the behavioral needs. A variety of suggestions related to academic help described in other chapters may be useful with students who have behavior disorders. For example, some of the materials designed for use with students who have low vision may provide sufficient tactile stimulation to capture and maintain the attention of students who have behavior disorders. Similarly, materials developed for use with students who are hearing impaired may provide visual representations helpful in presenting concepts related to various content areas. Many of suggestions for academic remediation provided in chapter 10 are appropriate for students with behavior disorders, since many such students are not successful in academic arenas. Erickson (1987) suggests that for some students, success in academic work must precede any expectations for behavior change.

Generally, if teachers are organized, they can help students structure or organize their day. (On the secondary level, this process is accomplished to some extent by the existing organization of the school day.) Simple cards or sheets on which assignments are written by either students or teachers provide a minimum of organization (see Figure 11–14). The use of columns allows for a record of what is not yet begun, what is begun but not completed, and what is completed. Either teachers or students may use the comments column. Teachers

FIGURE 11-14
Format for organizing a student's day

Name:		Date:	
Activities, assignments, or page numbers	**Started**	**Completed**	**Comments**

may peruse the work and make comments, or students may make notes, such as "need history book" or "ask about this."

In addition to organizing the day or week, teachers may call attention to specific goals or qualities (see Figure 11–15). During the time allotted for completion, teachers monitor behavior according to the attributes listed. At the end of the period or class, teachers can quickly indicate either a grade or the points received. Such records help students note the progress they are making. If students do not make progress, the reasons for lack of progress may be the basis for discussion. Rating cards or sheets may be useful for either upper-elementary

FIGURE 11-15
Format for rating specific goals or qualities

Name:			Week:		
Assignments	**Good attitude**	**Showed effort**	**Used time wisely**	**Completed work**	**Comments**
Mon.					
Tues.					
Wed.					
Thurs.					
Fri.					
			Teacher's signature:		

or secondary students. The students use one card for each class. Some specialists want to collect the cards so that they, too, may understand the progress.

At times, the assignment given to a student may seem overwhelming, either because of the task itself or because the student lacks organizational skills. Figure 11–16 illustrates one way that a task can be subdivided to make it more manageable. Subdividing is especially appropriate for assignments like themes, because the various elements of research, outlining, writing, proofreading, editing, and revising can be slices. Indicating intermediate dates for completion also helps students organize long-term assignments. Likewise, an hour period to work on assignments may be sliced into 5- or 10-minute portions.

Most students with behavior problems need help in structuring their day, assignments, and activities. The need for structure is indicated by their inability to begin a task or to make the transition from one task to another (for example, science to history or physical education to math) or from one type of activity to another (small-group work to individual work or lecture to independent work). Some students even have difficulty moving from one type of response to another within the same task or class (subtraction to multiplication or written response to verbal).

Another common difficulty with students who have behavior problems is their inability to wait quietly for teacher assistance when they encounter a problem and the teacher is not able to assist them immediately. A sign as in Figure 11–17 can be attached to the top of a pencil or dowel, which may be placed in a spool or a mound of clay. Such a sign serves as a silent signal that the student requires assistance. By using such a nondisturbing system, the teacher also reinforces the idea that study

or independent activity time is a time to be quiet. Note, however, that it is unrealistic to place a restriction such as being quiet on a student simply because he or she tends to be disruptive and not impose the restriction on the entire class.

Alternative Assignments

Incentives that may be extremely motivating are modified assignments based on recognition of the feelings of the student. The teacher may say, for example, "I see you are really angry about the fight you had and that you still think it wasn't your fault. For now, why don't you write the answers to only these two rows of problems, skip this one, and do the last. As soon as you are finished, you can paint. That will cheer you up, won't it?" In this scenario, the teacher is acknowledging the student's feelings and his or her right to them and is demonstrating a flexibility in assignments and an alternative for changing the feelings. After an exchange such as this, the student often begins the assignment. The student hears the lesson about redirecting feelings, but being excused from a part of the assignment provides incentive to complete the task instead of dwelling on the unfairness of the fight and its aftermath.

The method of crossing out some problems or exercises may be useful. When a student is finding it extremely difficult to work, explain why the modifications are made ("I can see that you are having trouble concentrating today" or "I realize that you are upset because Tom said some awful things to you") and with a magic marker or red pen boldly cross out some portion of the assignment. Alternately, tell the student, "Do only the even-numbered questions at the end of the chapter in your science book." Used sparingly, this technique helps students begin what seemed to be an insurmountable task.

FIGURE 11–16
Subdividing a task

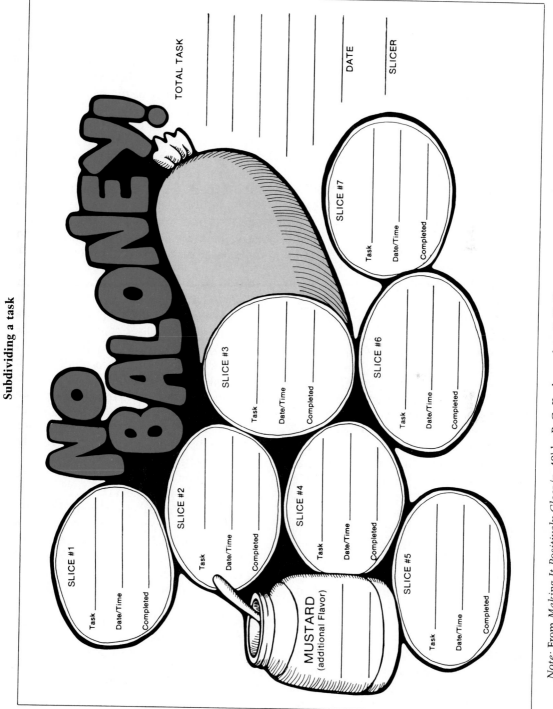

Note: From *Making It Positively Clear* (p. 40) by P. G. Kaplan and A. G. Hoffman, 1981, Denver: Love. Reprinted by permission.

FIGURE 11–17
Need-help sign

Note: From *It's Positively Fun* (p. 7) by P. Kaplan, J. Kohfeldt, and K. Sturla, 1974. Denver: Love. Reprinted by permission.

Figure 11–18 illustrates a more complex variation of this concept. When a student is having a particularly difficult time following through on assignments on a given day, such an assignment sheet makes the work seem more manageable to the student and need not be time consuming for the teacher. At the secondary level, the same principle may be applied either for a class period or for an entire day. Although some teachers object to this procedure, arguing that every problem or exercise is necessary, other teachers argue that not every exercise is essential and that they can determine the competency of the student with fewer exercises. All teachers must decide this matter for themselves. If daily homework is required or expected in a particular school, allowing one free night as a reward is a powerful reinforcer for some students (Figure 11–19).

Variations of obtaining baseline data, as in the behaviorist approach, can often be useful with disruptive students. Discussing the behaviors that are inappropriate and

having students who are disruptive keep a card tally of each time they call out or engage in unacceptable behavior often reduces the behavior immediately. Such students may cheat and not mark the card, but they are still aware of their behavior. After class, discuss the number of marks on a card and point out how disruptive the behavior has been, the effect it has on the class, and some possible solutions to the problem.

The same system can be associated with a contract or reward system; for example, say, "If there are no more than two marks, you do only the even-numbered math problems." If a reward is contingent on no marks or a certain number of marks, then students must keep accurate counts.

Commercial Programs

Commercial programs may be of value if they are carefully selected. Such programs can be used by teachers alone or in conjunction with consulting or resource teachers to teach social skills and help students learn to accept or label feelings. Such programs may use puppetry, sociodrama, role playing, group discussions, or art. Programs may be used as complete curriculums for affective needs or to address specific needs. Many such programs are available in most schools. Some examples are:

1. *Contract Maturity: Growing Up Strong* (1972). This program is written for junior and senior high school students with a low reading level. It uses posters, pictures, short stories, and open-ended stories to stimulate discussion and help clarify values.
2. *ACCESS* (Walker, Todis, Holmes, & Norton, 1988). This program may be used to develop relationships with peers or adults, and self-management skills with students of middle school or high school age. It provides suggestions for

FIGURE 11-18
Assignment priority schedule

Name:		Date:	
Must Do	**Should Do**	**Do If There's Time**	**Do Not!**
Reading workbook, p. 37, nos. 1, 3, 5, 7, 8	Use colored pencils to circle the correct answers.	Nos. 6 and 9	Do nos. 2 and 4 on p. 37
Math, pp. 142–143, all even numbers		The odd-numbered ones that have a 4 in them	Do numbers that have a 3 in them
Take 10 minutes and listen to your favorite record.	Use the earphones so no one knows you are doing it.		Let anyone know you are taking a break
Write 2 paragraphs about your hobby.	Read the rules for a good paragraph before you begin. Write neatly.	Draw a picture that illustrates your hobby.	Write more than 2 paragraphs
Work on the mural for social studies.	Take time to think about where you finished last time. Decide what you want to put on it today.	Color what you drew.	Do any more than you want
Read pp. 105–110 in your reader.	Read carefully. Watch for the new words. (They are on the chalkboard.) Write down any word that gives you trouble.	Write *your* ending to the story.	Read more than 5 pages or write more than 1 sentence for your ending

grouping students, procedures for teaching, and teaching scripts.

3. *The Coping With Series* (Wrenn & Schwarzrock, 1984). This series contains four sets of five books, each addressing concepts related to such themes as personal identification, human relationships, facts and fantasies, and teenage problems. The program is designed for use with students in upper elementary and early senior high school.

4. *Social Skills and Me* (Crane & Reynolds, 1983). This program contains 100 lessons, which focus on skills in communication, responsibility, assertiveness, and problem solving for the first through sixth grades. It includes individual and group activities.

5. *Developing Understanding of Self and Others—Revised (DUSO—R)* (Dinkmeyer, 1982). This program includes DUSO I, which is for students in kinder-

FIGURE 11-19
No homework permit

Note: From *It's Positively Fun* (p. 17) by P. Kaplan, J. Kohfeldt, K. Sturla, 1974, Denver: Love. Reprinted with permission.

garten through third grade, and DUSO II, which is for third and fourth graders. The program contains discussion, poetry, music, and stories relating to independence, choices and consequences, stress, and personal motivation.

Commercial materials intended for use by teachers are also available. An example is *Choices* (National Information Services Institute, 1989), which provides a description of such behaviors as fighting, truancy, talking out, and substance abuse; abstracts of current research relating to the problems; and "Outlines of Action" (which include suggestions for alleviating the problems). *Choices* is produced on disks for IBM, IBM Compatible, Macintosh, Apple IIE, and Apple IIGS computers.

Communication with Parents

Communication with parents is important when working with students who have behavior disorders. McCarney (1986) con-

ducted a study that determined the types of communication preferred by parents are:

1. Notes sent home (from the teacher)
2. Work sent home by the teacher
3. PTA meetings or open house at the school
4. Homework assignments requiring parental supervision or signature

It would seem that this surprisingly simple list of preferences could be followed with relative ease by most teachers.

Things to Think About

There are a number of principles regarding discipline and management of behavior problems. If properly applied, these principles may provide a classroom atmosphere that prevents many inappropriate behaviors. These may be formally stated as principles or more simply stated as things to think about, that is, ideas for teachers to consider. Twenty-seven such ideas are provided in Figure 11-20.

Suspensions

We have deliberately placed this discussion last in the consideration of suggestions for the regular classroom teacher, because although such measures may be required, they take place under only certain conditions and as a last resort. In general, suspensions relate to the safety of a student or the safety of others. All other methods and techniques must be used first. No teacher would suggest suspending a student because the student could not see or hear, because these are conditions for which the student is not responsible. However, it seems there is no such clear recognition in relation to behavior disorders, which relate to interactions with others and beliefs regarding the ability of students to become socialized and to control their behavior. Many people think that behavior disorders are merely the result of a lack of self-discipline, lack of discipline on the part of parents, poor parenting, or such factors as poverty, culture, broken homes, and drug abuse. Such factors may be related to behavior disorders, but designating cause-and-effect relationships is too simplistic.

Historically, schools have used suspension from school to coerce students into modifying their behavior (Barnetti & Parker, 1982). Students may be truant, do something that is prohibited (such as smoke), or fail to do something required (such as hand in homework). In accordance with school policy, they are suspended, meaning not allowed to come to school for a specified number of days. The underlying assumption is that students want to be in school and will change their behavior so that they can attend. The procedure is valid if students want to be in school, but it is not if students do not value school attendance. Not being allowed

FIGURE 11–20
Things to think about

The following "things to think about" list provides ideas and principles that may help prevent unacceptable or inappropriate behaviors, help teachers understand the origins of certain behaviors, and prevent situations from becoming unmanageable:

1. Know the background and both personal and academic problems of each student. Knowledge will aid in prevention.
2. Cultivate a demeanor that is friendly, but demands respect.
3. Disciplinary actions are most effective when they are quick, fair, consistent, and inevitable. If punishment is necessary, make it fit the individual, not the crime.
4. Group punishment for inappropriate behavior generates ill will among all students.
5. Look at the situation from the student's point of view. What were his reasons and motivations?
6. Model effective, cooperative working relationships with co-workers: fellow teachers, secretaries, maintenence personnel, the principal, kitchen employees.
7. Redirection, diversion, and provision of alternatives are nonpunitive ways of addressing minor misbehavior.
8. Be aware that students have bad days just as adults do, and have constructive, alternative activities or tasks available for such days.
9. Actively "listen" to students, especially to the nonverbal messages.
10. Well-planned lessons with a variety of activities (group work, lecture, independent work, research, problem solving, etc.) allow the teacher to concentrate on teaching and behavior, rather than on what or how to teach.
11. Understand fads and phases, even if they seem silly. They are part of growing up and developing a self-identity.
12. Don't make deals or compromise your standards but be fair and remember that students are in your class to learn how to be authoritative and how to live with authority.
13. Avoid anything that humiliates a student. No matter how angry you are, allow yourself time to cool off.
14. Recognize that some discipline problems are related to situations beyond your control. If appropriate, discuss these with the student, even if it is just to show that you understand.
15. Strike a balance between encouraging students to make decisions and you making all the decisions.

Continued.

FIGURE 11–20—cont'd
Things to think about

16. All persons in the class are human. Recognize that teachers also err, and be mature enough to admit it. This also provides the students with a positive model.
17. Repeated discussions about the student's past mistakes or failures rarely accomplish anything except make the teacher feel better.
18. Recognize that undisciplined, aggressive behavior is rarely directed at the teacher personally, but is directed at the symbol of authority.
19. If there is a disturbance, try to stop it immediately. Usually, the longer you wait, the more difficult it is for the student to remove him/herself from the disturbance.
20. Try to help students feel liked and appreciated. Make a conscious effort to find reasons to praise students. Most students with behavior problems receive a great deal of negative interaction with the teacher. Reward the absence of disturbing behavior; reward for not swearing, hitting, or interrupting. Try to "catch students" being good.
21. Be consistent. Don't make threats if you don't plan to carry through. It may take only three or four times of being consistent and following through for the student to know that you mean what you say.
22. Videotape or audiotape students so you can show them their behavior. Turn on the recorder (without their knowing) when they are noisy or disruptive. Later, play it back to them. Many students don't realize how noisy and disturbing they are.
23. If a student uses abusive language, refuse to be shocked. Ask the student to define the term. Let the student know that you don't approve of his/her language.
24. Don't tell a student that an assignment or required behavior is "easy," and that you know he/she can do it. It may not be easy for the student—and if the student does complete it, you have belittled the task.
25. Begin each day with a clean slate—for yourself, and for each student.
26. Remember that students will not likely treat you any better than you treat them.
27. Look into the mirror each day and say something good about yourself and your teaching.

Note: The authors wish to thank Dr. Clifford Baker for these "Things to Think About." From "257 Things to Do About Behavior Problems" by Clifford Baker. Selected portions are reprinted by permission.

to be present in a place in which one does not want to be in the first place does not likely motivate change in behavior. Thus, suspension may not be effective in all cases. Furthermore, if a student has a condition or a disability identified as a behavior disorder, to prevent the student from receiving services by suspension from school seems to be punishing the student for something for which he or she is not entirely responsible.

In-school suspensions consist of removal of the student from the classroom to another room, usually the resource room, the counselor's room, an unused room, or a similar place in the school building. Supervision of the student is provided and the length of time spent in the room must be a previously specified, short duration. Specific behaviors that lead to in-school suspension are discussed with the student and with the parent (usually during the development of the IEP). Counseling by the special education teacher, counselor, or consulting teacher should be provided at some time during the in-school suspension so that the student is learning and gaining insight regarding the behavior, the consequences, or other factors necessary to reduce the likelihood of additional need for this type of suspension. Most schools have policies regarding in-school suspensions, and teachers should be fully informed about them.

In-school suspensions are used for only extremely serious problems. If a student is frequently being placed in an in-school suspension, it would seem that the placement of the student might need to be reconsidered. The authors of PL 94–142 recognized that the needs of students range from all services being provided in regular classrooms to hospital services, homebound services, and 24-hour care (see chapter 2). The principle of least restrictive environment must be followed, but the fact remains that for some students, self-contained classrooms or even more restrictive placements are the least restrictive possible. Such changes of placement require reconvening of the staffing team and parental consent.

RELATED CONSIDERATIONS

Several factors are often associated with behavior disorders but are separate issues. Adolescence may be a time of disruptive behavior that exacerbates minor behavior disorders, or it may be completely unrelated. Students who commit illegal acts are referred to as juvenile delinquents and may or may not be identified as behaviorally disordered. Similarly, students who abuse substances may or may not be identified as behaviorally disordered. Depression is a characteristic of behavior disorders and is often associated with suicide. In general, students who are severely depressed are considered behaviorally disordered, but they may not be identified, because the depression has not been noticed. Students who are behaviorally disordered may commit suicide; however, not all students who

commit suicide are identified as behaviorally disordered or considered so by friends, parents, or teachers. Students who have been abused or neglected may sometimes exhibit behaviors similar to those associated with behavior disorders. The following discussion is provided to help teachers note relationships which may exist between these factors and behavior disorders.

Adolescence

As with learning disabilities, most programs for adolescents who are behaviorally disordered were developed at the elementary level and were adapted for the secondary level (Brown, McDowell, & Smith, 1981). Because of a variety of factors, an acceptable definition of what constitutes behavioral disorders in adolescents has been even more elusive than has a definition for younger students. One factor in this definition problem is the lack of a clear definition of what is acceptable behavior in normal adolescents. It is generally agreed that adolescence is a time of transition (Jones, 1980; McDowell, 1981; Schiamberg, 1988). It involves the passage of an individual from a position of dependence to one of independence. This passage may be initiated at various chronological ages and lasts a varying number of years. The transition involves both physiological and psychological stages.

Physiological changes include the production of hormones that lead to the development of secondary sex characteristics and the ability to reproduce. During these changes, adolescents begin to look more to peers than parents for approval and have increasing concern for physical appearance. At the same time that adolescents look at peers for approval, peers seem to seek some indefinable standard of how one should look and act. Any deviations are subject to taunting by peers. Being too tall, too short, too thin, or too fat is a relative characteristic, but for many adolescents, these factors have great significance. Rarely are adolescents satisfied with their physical appearance, but such dissatisfaction does not always lead to severe crisis.

Psychological changes take place as a result of the expectations by society as well as individuals for new standards of behavior. No longer are childhood manners acceptable. Adolescents must find separate identities and become increasingly independent. These psychological changes are likely to cause considerable consternation for adolescents, school personnel, and parents. McDowell (1981) describes several issues related to the new expectations, which should be viewed as closely interwoven. Difficulty in any of these areas is usually a reflection of problems in other areas, too:

1. *Status.* Status involves how one is perceived by others. For adolescents, how one is perceived by peer groups is far more important than how one is perceived by parents or relatives. This perception by others is closely allied with self-concept. Status may be conferred by others, as in the case of a class clown, who is designated after one or two incidents and then accepts the role as a way to gain status.

2. *Identity.* Identity is generally developed in two areas: (a) identity with a group such as a gang, club, or team and (b) self-identity, which is reflected by a knowledge of who one is, what one believes in, and what one represents. The development of an identity usually involves an element of breaking away from family ties.

3. *Independence.* The degree to which an individual is self-sufficient reflects the independence of the individual. Striving for independence involves testing limits, establishing an identity, and redefining

relationships. Perhaps one of the most difficult aspects of gaining a sense of independence is being expected to act as an adult but enjoying few of the privileges of the adult. In attempting to solve the dilemma, adolescents may disregard authority, resulting in conflicts in school as well as at home.

4. *Relationships.* Although they vary from interactions with strangers to intimate interactions, relationships are a vital part of life. Early adolescence involves seeking out of a same-sex best friend or friends. Later, this interaction expands to include members of the opposite sex. As adolescents strive for identity, independence, and status, they gradually grow away from family support systems, which are replaced by other relationships. Unless various other relationships are developed, adolescents suffer from alienation and feelings of loneliness and inadequacy, which adversely affect development in other areas.

5. *Sex.* Although much has been written recently concerning sex-role stereotypes, the development of a sexual identity is a major issue that adolescents must resolve. Any interference with the development of a sexual identity may have lifelong effects. Adolescents must learn about the potential functions of their bodies and how to use them. Religious beliefs, parental attitudes, and peer knowledge affect this development in a positive or negative fashion.

6. *Values.* One's identity generally reflects one's values, which often become the criteria by which one is judged. Often, adolescents seem to reject the values of their parents as they strive for independence and identity. Because they may be unwilling to live by the values taught by their parents, required by religion, or expected of younger individuals and yet

have not developed workable, consistent values of their own, adolescents find themselves in a dilemma. The inconsistency in judgment and behavior of adolescents often reflects this seemingly unsolvable puzzle.

7. *Decision making.* The ability to examine alternatives, choose among them, and live with the consequences is important for successful adult living. Objectively examining alternatives is often difficult for adolescents. As a general rule, adolescents are more concerned with immediate goals than long-range ones, and this concern often leads to decisions that may be seen as not appropriate in hindsight. Effective, appropriate decision making is a skill that must be developed and practiced. Often, adults significant to adolescents are impatient with the inability to make effective decisions. Peers, a lack of acceptable models, and need for independence may influence adolescents to make poor decisions that have lifelong effects.

One or any combination of the seven psychological changes to which adolescents must adjust may cause short-term or lifelong crises. For a variety of reasons, which usually can be determined only on a case-by-case basis if at all, some adolescents experience problems far beyond those considered normal. Such adolescents may turn to drugs, alcohol, crime, or in extreme cases, suicide. This is not to say that every adolescent who experiments with drugs, alcohol, sex, or criminal acts is suffering from a behavior disorder. The problem depends on the frequency, the severity, and the dependence of the behavior.

Teachers of adolescents must be aware of the normal behaviors of adolescents to be able to help students with special needs. Teachers can employ a variety of approaches that enhance the opportunities of adolescents for successfully negotiating this important stage in life:

1. An open, honest, respectful relationship with their students
2. Challenging, motivating activities
3. Frequent and positive attention
4. Fair and firm limits
5. Involvement in goal setting in both academic and behavioral areas
6. Acceptance of students as individuals while not reinforcing inappropriate or self-defeating behavior
7. Learning environments that ensure considerable success

Juvenile Delinquency

Delinquency may seem difficult to define precisely. Its use in ordinary conversation gives it a variety of meanings. It does, however, have a specific legal definition. In common usage, any act by a juvenile considered inappropriate by another person may be labeled delinquency; however, legal definitions relate specifically to acts that are against the law. These include criminal offenses such as stealing, destruction of the property of another person, deliberately causing injury to another, and killing. These are called index crimes. Other offenses are illegal only if the offender is within a specific age range, for example, running away from home, truancy, buying alcoholic beverages, or cigarettes, and sexual promiscuity. These are called status crimes. If the individual is convicted, both types of crimes carry penalties.

Students who have been convicted of either type of crime and are attending school may be on probation and be considered juvenile delinquents. A probation officer may be involved with the school if the terms of the probation relate to attending school or maintaining certain grades. The role of teachers may vary widely. Students convicted of a crime may be model students in every other way. In such cases, the role of teachers relates to the provisions of the IEP and the provisions of the probation. Usually, an individual at school is designated to be the contact person for the probation officer—the counselor, special education teacher, social worker, principal, or homeroom teacher. The role of that person is determined by the provisions of the probation and the circumstances of the student in school.

Substance Abuse

Substance abuse includes the use or abuse of either legal or illegal substances, including alcohol, nicotine, glue, paint thinner, heroin, cocaine, crack, LSD, PCP, and marijuana. Use induces a psychological or physiological change that has a therapeutic purpose. Abuse may cause health risks, psychological dysfunction, or other adverse consequences. Abuse of substances does not seem to be associated with a particular disability, since many "normal" persons abuse drugs (Wolman, 1987). Because of the numbers of students involved in the abuse of substances, it would not be uncommon for a class to include a number of students who are at least experimenting with drugs and other substances subject to abuse (Miksic, 1987; Wong, 1979).

Teachers must be aware of the possible progression from experimentation to dependency, although they must remember that not every student who experiments eventually becomes dependent. A brief description of the increased involvement that can occur follows. Experimentation is trying out or infrequent use, often with a variety of substances. Situation-specific, or social, use reflects attempts to conform. The individual feels "I can handle it—no big deal" but experiences some guilt. Such use varies from

once to several times per week. With habitual use, the individual looks for or needs the euphoria, feels guilt and depression when not using, and uses or tries to use the substance daily. With dependency, the individual feels uncomfortable if drugs are not available, committing other crimes to get them. The individual demonstrates erratic, disorganized thought processes or behavior, sometimes suicide. Such an individual uses several times daily if possible.

Miksic (1987) describes the changes in behavior often associated with substance abuse. At the experimental stage, little change is noticeable; however, by the social stage, teachers may note more association with others who use drugs, a withdrawal from productive activities outside school, or a decrease in academic performance. If students reach the habitual stage, teachers may notice decreased interest in school, frequent unexplained absences, family problems related to usage, and mood swings or impulsiveness. When students are dependent on drugs, there is usually only sporadic school attendance, a change in physical appearance through weight gain or loss, and a somewhat unkempt look due to a loss of concern regarding personal appearance. There may also be aggressive behavior, betrayal of friends, lying or stealing to obtain drugs or money for them, and depression, paranoia, or suicidal thoughts.

Most schools have drug awareness and prevention programs and policies and procedures to follow in cases of suspected drug use, actual use, intoxication, or withdrawal crisis. Teachers must be aware of such policies and procedures, and depending on their own knowledge, they may offer to teach or otherwise participate in awareness or prevention programs. Primarily, however, teachers should know the procedures indicated by the school, effectively manage students during a crisis, maintain a calm and nonjudgmental attitude, and refer students to proper authorities in accordance with school policy.

Depression and Suicide

Only recently has childhood depression become a topic of study, especially as it is differentiated from depression in adults (Forness, 1988). The *Diagnostic and Statistical Manual of Mental Disorders* (American Psychiatric Association, 1987) describes several problems that must be exhibited frequently over a 2-week period before a clinical diagnosis of depression can be made. They include changes in appetite and weight; irregularities in sleep patterns; physical agitation or lethargy; inability to experience pleasure; inordinate feelings of guilt or inadequacy; lack of ability to concentrate or make decions; and thoughts, threats, or attempts of suicide. The reasons that students may become depressed are unclear, although there are several theoretical views. Forehand, McCombs, and Brody (1987) suggest that depression in the family can be a factor; however, the distinction between genetic predispositions and the family relations that develop because of depression is not clear. Depressed parents may set unrealistic goals for their children, lack effective parenting skills, be unable to provide sufficient support, and overly emphasize punishment. Depression may also be caused by low self-esteem, low social competence, lack of self-control, or a belief that all bad things that happen are one's own fault (Harris & Howard, 1987).

When a psychologist or psychiatrist makes a diagnosis of depression, several interventions are possible. Antidepressant drugs may require careful monitoring of behavior changes. Training in social skills may also be indicated on the IEP. Such training is usually implemented by consulting teachers or specialists and may be directed toward the student in question or a small group. It is critical that classroom teachers be fully aware of the goals and provide support for newly emerging social skills. Interventions may also center on cognitive modification, which is designed to alter negative beliefs. Classroom teachers are expected to provide support and encouragement as students modify their manner of thinking.

Suicide and depression are closely related, but not all students who threaten or attempt suicide are depressed. Although PL 94–142 recognizes "a general pervasive mood of unhappiness or depression" as a characteristic of severe emotional problems, it does not specifically include threats of suicide. School administrators are divided in their beliefs about providing suicide prevention programs. Some schools do, while others fear that discussions and awareness programs create a climate in which students are tempted to think about or attempt suicide (Guetzloe, 1989).

The problem of suicide cannot be ignored. Suicide rates have steadily increased over the past 20 years even though many actual suicides are not reported (Muse, 1990). Researchers have noted higher rates of suicide in exceptional students than in the normal population. The highest rates of suicide among exceptional individuals are among those identified as having behavioral disorders or as being gifted (Blumenthal, 1985; Hawton, 1986; Willings & Arsenault, 1986).

Causes of suicide may be general genetic predisposition, genetic predisposition to schizophrenia, alcoholism, or substance abuse (all of which are associated with suicide), birth trauma, or extreme stress (Fowler, Rich, & Young, 1986; Hawton, 1986; Pfeffer, 1986; Salk et al., 1985).

Most authorities believe that it is impossible to identify with precision the students who might attempt suicide (Muse, 1990). There are, however, warning signs and risk factors that should receive attention:

1. Behavior or emotional problems
2. Depression, including expressed feelings of unhappiness, helplessness, inadequacy, or sadness
3. Drug or alcohol abuse, including intoxication, which decreases inhibitions
4. Familiarity with suicide, including suicide threats or attempts, attempted or completed suicide in the family, or recent, publicized suicide in the community
5. Severe stress from any of a variety of sources, such as death in the family, loss of friends, family violence, parental divorce, parental loss of employment, public humiliation, poor achievement, sexual abuse, or other physical abuse
6. Severe mood changes
7. Poor concentration
8. Frequent accidents
9. Unusual fatigue or anxiety
10. Poor self-esteem, including inability to tolerate any flaws in oneself or to accept compliments or negative comments
11. Sudden changes in friends
12. Preoccupation with death as evidenced by actions that have an aspect of finality, including giving away prized possessions, notes of farewell, repeated apologies, plans for the future that do not include the individual, or frequent discussions about the desirability of death

Teachers who become aware of such indicators should immediately report such information to the proper authorities. Because of controversy related to the contagion factor (students who discuss suicide or know of someone who committed suicide may be tempted), many schools do not have established policies or procedures related to the prevention of suicide. As a result, teachers may be unsure of appropriate actions. In the absence of established policies, teachers should contact the principal, counselor, psychologist, nurse, or social worker. Some schools have incorporated assessment of potential for suicide in the overall assessment completed prior to staffing for students who have behavior disorders. The results of such assessment are incorporated into the IEP, and resources for the family, including agencies outside the school, are identified so that the interventions available can be incorporated into the plan (Minneapolis Public Schools, 1986). The goal in relation to suicide is prevention. Teachers should always take threats or talk about suicide seriously, attempt to maintain or establish communication, provide emotional support, and seek immediate help from other professionals.

Child Abuse and Neglect

With the passage of federal legislation in 1974 and the growing national concern reflected by the passage of similar laws in every state about child abuse and neglect, it is imperative that teachers be aware of what constitutes abuse or neglect in their particular state as well as the procedures for reporting suspected cases. All 50 states have legislation that requires citizens in general and school personnel in particular to report suspected child abuse. Each state has specific directives regarding what types of abuse *must* be reported and what *may* be reported as well as the specific procedures for reporting suspected abuse or neglect. Teachers should consult the appropriate school personnel to determine the procedures mandated in their state.

Since a number of characteristics of children who have behavior disorders are similar to those of children who are abused, identification of abused children must be made carefully. The two problems are not synonymous, but they are closely related, and assistance required by abused children is often similar to that for students who have behavior disorders. Halperin (1979) suggests a number of characteristics that may indicate a child who has been mistreated. The following eight classifications indicate some of the various personality patterns that may result from maltreatment:

1. *The aggressive child.* This child is quarrelsome and bullying. He or she may have a pattern of behavior learned from parents who express themselves with physical punishment when they are displeased.
2. *The show-off.* This child is an extreme extrovert, identified by clowning in class and inability to wait, both behaviors masking insecurity and feelings of inferiority, feelings that may be the result of little or no warmth or attention from the parents.
3. *The disobedient child.* This child is an insolent, disrespectful child, who never seems to hear directions and who engages in a continuing power struggle with authority. A lack of recognition in the home may lead to the child's extreme attempts at gaining attention. Parental attitudes toward authority, especially school, may also influence the child's attitudes toward teachers.
4. *The child who cheats, lies, or steals.* Infrequent occurrence of such behavior, especially in young children, is usually not a cause for alarm, but repeated activities of this nature often reflect hostility to-

ward family or authority. They can also indicate a need for attention or may result from modeling behaviors in the home.

5. *The child nobody likes.* This child is often listless, sometimes destructive, seemingly incapable of forming satisfying relationships. Commonly, this student is absent from school or is a dropout. The home environment may lack warmth or satisfying relationships. Family members may live isolated lives; therefore, the child has not learned the skills necessary for productive interactions.
6. *The unkempt child.* This child's dirty face, matted hair, and soiled clothing may result from a lack of proper facilities for bathing or laundering clothing but also from carelessness of the parent. Such a child does not feel valued and feels little or no personal pride. Both feelings are reflected in the child's work.
7. *The shy or fearful child.* Whether a child is fearful or is shy can be determined by becoming aware of what and whom the child fears. The fearful child is usually afraid or fearful of many persons and things; the fear is generalized. The shy child differs in that the fear is related more to contact with people. The shy child usually speaks in a low voice, sits with head lowered to avoid eye contact, and declines participation in group activities. The shy child may be modeling parental behavior or may be the victim of excessively critical parents, who expect perfection. Since the child cannot meet this standard, he or she hesitates to attempt any task.
8. *The careless child.* Messy papers, desk, and physical appearance are hallmarks. Often, the teacher is unable to decipher the work of the child to evaluate it.

Other children trip over the books, papers, and boxes strewn around the child's desk. The child seems to stumble through life. This careless attitude may be the result of parents who place little value on orderliness or organization, or the child may adopt this pattern of behavior because of excessive demands made by the parents.

Alert teachers may discern many forms of mistreatment (Halperin, 1979), including abandonment, emotional abuse or neglect, physical abuse and neglect, and sexual abuse. Abandonment occurs when children are simply left behind. Even when children are left with an adult but no provisions are made for their continued support, they have been abandoned.

Emotional abuse and neglect often result in extremely low self-concept and inappropriate attempts to seek attention. Young females may turn to promiscuous behavior in efforts to receive love and attention. Young males may turn to vandalism, drugs, or gangs to feel of value to others or themselves. Emotional abuse may take the form of ridicule for failing to achieve the goals parents set. In such cases, the normal parent-child relationship of unconditional caring is either absent or destroyed. Some children withdraw from contact with others because their normal family relationships have been so devastating. Others are so convinced that they are worthless that they begin to act out behaviors that confirm their worthlessness. Emotional neglect reflects lack of involvement by parents. It is a fault of omission rather than commission. The parents may provide the basics of food, clothing, and shelter, but seem unable to provide any of the warmth and caring essential for the development of children.

Physical abuse and neglect are other forms of child abuse. Physical neglect occurs when the physical needs of food, clothing, general care, supervision, or shelter are not met. The actions of children, such as stealing food or articles of clothing, may seem inappropriate, but they may be the attempts to meet basic needs. In cases where poverty causes the neglect, social agencies are usually available to assist. Yet, poverty is not the reason some parents neglect their children. Some parents are barely able to meet their own emotional needs and have little time or concern for their offspring.

Physical abuse is the most often reported and most easily recognized form of maltreatment. The various forms of physical abuse can generally be observed by teachers. Signs of possible physical abuse include (a) abrasions in various stages of healing; (b) burns shaped like objects such as cigarettes or utensils or burns that indicate immersion in hot water or of having had water poured on parts of the body; (c) injuries that suggest an imprint of belts, clothes hangers, hose, hand, teeth, or rope; injuries on parts of the body inconsistent with a fall; injuries of peculiar sizes or shapes; or injuries around the head; and (d) bruises of different colors, indicating they were received over time. Children are often reluctant to discuss why or how they received injuries that result from physical abuse. Victims of physical abuse show fear of adults that is manifested when they protect their heads with their hands or use other forms of apparent self-defense when approached suddenly or unexpectedly by adults. Sexual abuse involves a range from exposure, to fondling, to rape, to incest and may occur from infancy through adolescence. Generally, it is not a one-time event except in the case of strangers. Because a sexually abused child generally exhibits no physical signs, the abuse is frequently undetected. Sometimes, teachers observe a sudden change of behavior that occurs at the onset of the abuse or

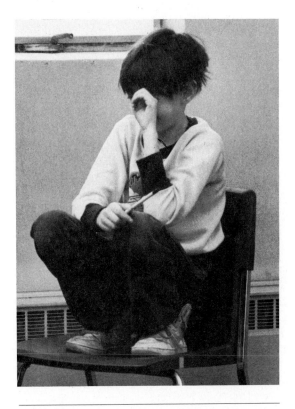

Major behavior changes may be indicative of child abuse.

when the child becomes aware that such treatment is not normal among peers. Many sexually abused children attempt to hide the mistreatment because they recognize they are participants in activities that are unacceptable in society. They submit to abuse because of fear of punishment or withdrawal of love, because of desire for some promised reward, or because they are physically forced to submit. At times, the burden of undeserved guilt becomes so great that the child turns to a trusted adult. This confidence must not go unheeded. Although extremely personal, the matter must be investigated. Teachers need to be aware of the proper procedures for reporting suspected sexual abuse.

SUMMARY

Definitions, terminology, and much of the discussion of the nature of behavior disorders are characterized by disagreement and controversy. This chapter provided the federal definition of *seriously emotionally disturbed*. In addition, it provided a listing of characteristics of behavior disorders as outlined by various authorities. Four major theoretical approaches and teaching strategies that grow out of these approaches were discussed, and various behaviorally oriented techniques were emphasized. The chapter also considered stress.

A variety of suggestions for classroom teachers were provided, including a discussion of the use of in-school suspension as a last resort. Consideration of adolescence, juvenile delinquency, substance abuse, depression and suicide, and child abuse completed the chapter, because many of these problems are related to behavior disorders and may be difficult to distinguish in actual cases.

- How are giftedness, creativity, and talent interrelated? How are they different? Can one exist in the absence of the others?

- Why is it difficult to discover giftedness among some students from culturally diverse populations? How might the situation be remedied? What are the pitfalls in any attempted remedy?

- Under what conditions might separate schools for students who are gifted be justifiable? How would opponents of such schools support their position?

- How may a future studies program benefit students who are gifted? How might the benefits be expanded beyond the students enrolled in the program?

- What is Bloom's taxonomy? How is it useful in planning programs for students who are gifted?

CHAPTER 12

TEACHING STUDENTS
WHO ARE GIFTED

OTHERS WHO HAVE WRITTEN TEXTS ON MAIN-streaming and exceptional students have elected not to address students who are gifted (Wood, 1989, p. 5). Programs for students who are gifted may or may not be part of special education, depending on the organization of the state department of education or public instruction. Special educational programs for students who are gifted are not mandated by the federal government (as is the case for students who have disabilities), and in most states, programs for students who are gifted receive considerably less special funding from state-level sources than do programs for students with disabilities. In some states, students who are gifted receive no special support except for a part-time, state-level consultant.

Yet, despite this apparent lack of support, parent and advocacy groups have kept programs alive, and "worldwide, interest in the education of the gifted and talented is steadily growing" (Clark, 1988, p. 181).

Whatever the influences that have contributed to the wide variation in the breadth and depth of programs, we believe that students who are gifted have special needs. In addition to inconsistency in degree and type of programming for students who are gifted, there is only limited consensus concerning which students to include in the special programs. In part, this relates to disagreement in definition of the terms *gifted*, *talented*, and *creative* and the means whereby such students should be identified.

DEFINITIONS

Definitions of giftedness (or talent or creativity) may be categorized in a variety of ways, and the structure of a definition greatly influences the type of special programming provided. IQ-based definitions relate to intelligence. They are relatively popular because they provide definite cutoff points for determination of giftedness. Students who score at or above some established point are gifted; those who score be-low are not. However, such definitions ignore artistic or creative gifts (unless the student who is artistic or creative also has a high IQ) and tend to discriminate against individuals who are poor, who are from culturally diverse populations, or who underachieve on tests of intelligence for any reason.

Percentage-based definitions are preferred by some educators because on the surface, they provide a definite line of demarcation between individuals who are gifted and individuals who are not. Percentage-based definitions are based on some factor or factors, which may be overall academic achievement, intelligence test scores, or scores in one or two academic areas (such as mathematics or science). However, percentage-based definitions present problems, too. For example, in one school district, the top 5%, based on composite achievement test scores, were included in programs for the gifted. A considerable controversy quickly developed. When the percentage was applied systemwide, some schools (in more affluent areas of the city) had as many as 11% or 12% of their total student population eligible, while others (in low socioeconomic neighborhoods) had less than 1%. So, the criteria were interpreted to mean the top 5% of each school. Using this interpretation, there were many students from lower socioeconomic area schools included in the program who had much lower achievement scores and IQs than other students in the school district who were not considered gifted, according to these guidelines. What had appeared simple and objective when the board of education authorized the program became a public relations nightmare.

Talent-based definitions consider demonstrated talent in one or more areas. This might mean talent in music, art, dance, or—in a few cases—unusual talent in science or mathematics. Although this differentiation is not universally accepted, *talented* more often means talent demonstrated for the age of the student under consideration in one or just a few areas. *Gifted* more often means intellectually gifted. An increasing number of school programs seem to be using *gifted and talented* or *gifted/talented* to describe their programs, indicating that both are recognized as important. Talent-based

definitions can use achievement test scores if the talent under consideration is in mathematics or science. They must use some type of expert-opinion procedure if the talent under consideration falls in an area such as music, dance, or art. Giftedness and talent are nebulous concepts. They are officially determined by those who develop state or local program guidelines. There is only one common element—being significantly above (or *potentially* significantly above) average in intellectual ability, achievement, or some particular talent.

Among the most widely recognized definitions of giftedness are those provided at the federal level. The first such federal definition, which has had considerable impact, was provided by Marland in 1972 in his report to the U.S. Congress on the status of education of the gifted and talented (Marland, 1972). In this definition, six areas of special ability are recognized: (a) general intellectual ability, (b) specific academic aptitude, (c) creative or productive thinking, (d) leadership ability, (e) visual and performing arts, and (f) psychomotor ability. This definition notes that the classification of gifted should include individuals who have demonstrated achievement and individuals with potential ability. It also notes that children who are gifted or talented require differentiated curriculums. However, the Marland definition has been revised by succeeding federal pronouncements. For example, Public Law 97–35, the Education Consolidation and Improvement Act (1981), refers to "children who give evidence of high performance capability in areas such as intellectual, creative, artistic, leadership capacity, or specific academic fields, and who require services or activities not ordinarily provided by the school in order to fully develop such capabilities" (Sec. 582). This definition is consistent with earlier modifications of

Marland's original definition in that it does not mention psychomotor ability.

A second, widely recognized definition of giftedness is provided by Renzulli and Smith (1980) and Renzulli, Reis, and Smith (1981). Their definition, which they consider an operational definition of giftedness, reflects their belief that the categories in the federal definition often overlap to a considerable extent. Renzulli et al. suggest three generalizations. First, three traits are common to all truly gifted individuals: (a) above-average intellectual ability, (b) task commitment, and (c) creativity. They suggest that no single trait should be used to identify giftedness, since it is the interaction of these traits that leads to what we commonly call giftedness. The second generalization is that giftedness should be recognized in relation to all socially useful areas of performance. The third generalization is that there is great need to increase efforts to mea-

There is some debate regarding the inclusion of athletic abilities within the classification of gifted/talented.

sure or assess a broad range of abilities or potential abilities in addition to those of general intellectual ability.

A third definition, which has received increasing attention, is proposed by Clark (1988). Her definition is based on her interpretation of brain research and the belief that in gifted individuals, there is advanced, or accelerated, brain function development. Her definition is:

Giftedness is a biologically rooted concept, a label for a high level of intelligence that results from the advanced and accelerated integration of functions within the brain, including physical sensing, emotions, cognition, and intuition. Such advanced and accelerated function may be expressed through abilities such as those involved in cognition, creativity, academic aptitude, leadership, or the visual and performing arts. Therefore, with this definition of intelligence, gifted individuals are those who are performing, or who show promise of performing, at high levels of intelligence. Because of such advanced or accelerated development, these individuals require services or activities not ordinarily provided by the schools in order to develop their capability more fully. (p. 7)

Many states recognize these definitions or derivatives of these definitions in their guidelines for determining which students are gifted. At the very least, these definitions influence those who provide or direct programs for gifted and talented students in our schools.

CHARACTERISTICS

Because nomination for further inclusion in a program for students who are gifted and talented plays such an important role in the identification process, teachers should be aware of various characteristics of giftedness and talent, particularly in cases where students do not give evidence in their academic work. Figure 12–1 indicates three

general categories for students who are intellectually gifted: (a) general behavioral characteristics, (b) learning characteristics, and (c) creative characteristics. In compiling this list, Whitmore (1985) used characteristics suggested by many authors. A student who is intellectually gifted usually displays several (but not *all*) of the characteristics. Yet, clusters of characteristics do not necessarily identify students as gifted—more comprehensive assessment is necessary. Therefore, classroom teachers should use such lists to nominate students for further consideration for programs for students who are gifted. Remember, though, that these characteristics are for students who are *intellectually* gifted. The major characteristics of students who have an unusual talent in a specific area of the arts is unusual ability (for age and experience) in that particular area.

"She certainly is creative!" or "Doesn't that really reflect his creativity!" are phrases often heard from both teachers and parents, but according to Clark (1988), "Creativity is a very special condition, attitude, or state of being that nearly defies definition" (p. 46). Although there are a number of aspects to what is broadly called creativity, the two most commonly recognized relate to what Clark calls the "rational thinking aspect" and the "talent aspect." The rational thinking aspect is potential for creative thinking or performance that may be measured by existing tests of creativity. The talent aspect is creativity in products, most often recognized in relation to a jurying process, carried out by experts in the field of endeavor. Many authors in the field of giftedness, talent, and creativity seem to feel that although some children retain their giftedness as older children or adults, many seem to lose their creativity as they grow older. This appears to be reflected with respect to

FIGURE 12–1
Characteristics of intellectually gifted children

General Behavioral Characteristics

- Many typically learn to read earlier with a better comprehension of the nuances of the language. As many as half of the gifted and talented population have learned to read before entering school. They often read widely, quickly, and intensely and have large vocabularies.
- They commonly learn basic skills better, more quickly, and with less practice.
- They are better able to construct and handle abstractions than their age mates.
- They are frequently able to pick up and interpret nonverbal cues and can draw inferences which other children have to have spelled out for them.
- They take less for granted, seeking the "hows" and "whys."
- They display a better ability to work independently at an earlier age and for longer periods of time than other children.
- They can sustain longer periods of concentration and attention.
- Their interests are often both wildly eclectic and intensely focused.
- They frequently have seemingly boundless energy, which sometimes leads to a misdiagnosis of "hyperactive."

- They are usually able to respond and relate well to parents, teachers, and other adults. They may prefer the company of older children and adults to that of their peers.
- They are willing to examine the unusual and are highly inquisitive.
- Their behavior is often well organized, goal directed, and efficient with respect to tasks and problems.
- They exhibit an intrinsic motivation to learn, find out, or explore and are often very persistent. "I'd rather do it myself" is a common attitude.
- They enjoy learning new things and new ways of doing things.
- They have a longer attention and concentration span than their peers.

Learning Characteristics

- They may show keen powers of observation, exhibit a sense of the significant, and have an eye for important details.
- They may read a great deal on their own, preferring books and magazines written for youngsters older than themselves.
- They often take great pleasure in intellectual activity.

both the production of creative products and scores on tests of creativity. The reasons for this apparent loss have not been established through research, but speculation includes an educational system that rewards convergent thinking and conformity above other factors. Another possible reason is the structure and content of creativity tests.

Torrance (1974) developed one of the leading measures of creativity (Tests of Cre-

ative Thinking). He noted that creativity can be defined in terms of (a) product (invention and discovery), (b) process, and (c) characteristics of the individual who is considered to be creative. His concept of creativity includes many elements that others ascribe to intelligence but also includes sensitivity to deficiencies, gaps in knowledge, and disharmonies.

A more traditional concept of creativity relates to bringing something new into ex-

- They have well developed powers of abstraction, conceptualization, and synthesizing abilities.
- They generally have rapid insight into cause-effect relationships.
- They often display a questioning attitude and seek information for the sake of having it as much as for its instrumental value.
- They are often skeptical, critical, and evaluative. They are quick to spot inconsistencies.
- They often have a large storehouse of information regarding a variety of topics which they can recall quickly.
- They show a ready grasp of underlying principles and can often make valid generalizations about events, people, or objects.
- They readily perceive similarities, differences, and anomalies.
- They often attack complicated material by separating it into its components and analyzing it systematically.

Creative Characteristics

- They are *fluent* thinkers, able to produce a large quantity of possibilities, consequences, or related ideas.
- They are *flexible* thinkers, able to use many different alternatives and approaches to problem solving.
- They are *original* thinkers, seeking new, unusual, or unconventional associations and combinations among items of information. They also have an ability to see relationships among seemingly unrelated objects, ideas, or facts.
- They are *elaborative* thinkers, producing new steps, ideas, responses, or other embellishments to a basic idea, situation, or problem.
- They show a willingness to entertain complexity and seem to thrive in problem situations.
- They are good guessers and can construct hypotheses or "what if" questions readily.
- They often are aware of their own impulsiveness and the irrationality within themselves and show emotional sensitivity.
- They have a high level of curiosity about objects, ideas, situations, or events.
- They often display intellectual playfulness, fantasize, and imagine readily.
- They can be less intellectually inhibited than their peers in expressing opinions and ideas and often exhibit spirited disagreement.
- They have a sensitivity to beauty and are attracted to aesthetic dimensions.

Note: From "Characteristics of Intellectually Gifted Children" by J. R. Whitmore, 1985, *ERIC Digest*, 344.

istence, literally creating something new. This concept recognizes that creative individuals work with given physical or mental materials but shape these materials into something new. Common-use definitions relate creativity to inventiveness and seem to view creativity primarily as the making of a product. However, most authorities agree that creativity, like intelligence, is a good thing, even if the general population has widely varying concepts.

If the concept of creativity is limited to creativity resulting in a product, there is a degree of agreement that invention of such things as the electric light bulb, the telephone, and the zipper reflects creativity. Yet, is it possible to predict that a child will later become such a creative inventor? How can educators and parents encourage such potential creativity in children? The answers are not clear-cut, but there are possible indicators of creativity and ways to encourage creativity if the potential is present.

A potentially creative individual might have any of the following characteristics:

1. Unusual curiosity
2. Unusual persistence
3. Unusual imagination
4. Originality

A fifth characteristic is sometimes included with these four: restlessness. This may not be seen until after the child's entrance into school and is usually a reaction to meaningless, repetitive tasks, which are not challenging to creative students.

Most children show some degree of curiosity, persistence, and imagination. Potentially creative children, however, have an unusually high degree of these characteristics compared to age peers. Originality may be the distinguishing characteristic, but originality is easy to overlook, probably because originality in children generally does not produce products as obvious as the light bulb, the telephone, and the zipper. Originality in children relates to their age and experience. It involves something that would not be expected from an individual of that age or level of experience.

For example, a very young child might use a self-constructed lever arrangement to lift something when the child has had no specific experience that would lead to understanding the lever and has not observed someone using a lever. Of course, many people use levers, but most have seen someone else do so or have had a sequence of experiences that led to understanding the mechanical properties of levers. Whatever the child might demonstrate, the question of originality is a matter of whether it is usual or normal for someone of that age and experience to demonstrate that ability, understanding, or insight.

The efforts of J. P. Guilford deserve special mention in any discussion of creativity. In fact, Guilford deserves equal mention for his efforts related to understanding general intelligence, giftedness, and creativity. He developed a three-dimensional conceptual model called the "structure of intellect," with which he predicted the existence of at least 120 distinct types of intellectual ability (Guilford, 1959). This model played a major role in triggering debate and research related to "convergent" and "divergent" thinking.

It has undoubtedly been reproduced in textbooks, dissertations, and scholarly articles more often than any other conceptual model in the history of the study of intelligence. Guilford's consideration of divergent thinking, now usually related to creativity, has led to continuing speculation about the true nature of creativity, but unanswered questions still exceed those that have been definitively answered. Guilford's continued personal research and the research of others relating to his concept of the structure of intellect have been essential in the development of interest in the field of creativity.

Facilitating the development of creativity is the teacher's responsibility. Such facilitation requires both an accurate general concept of the nature of creativity and some specific ideas and skills. Table 12–1 provides a brief sample of factors and conditions that may facilitate or inhibit creativity. Teachers who want to encourage creativity should think in terms of both "what should I do" and "what I should avoid doing," since many schools encourage teachers to follow practices that may inhibit creativity. Although there is disagreement in the identification of creativity, most teachers indicate an interest in promoting it. With continuing attention to the behavior of individual students, regular

TABLE 12-1
Factors and conditions that may facilitate or inhibit creativity

Facilitating	Inhibiting
Spontaneous participation and expression	Requirement of unquestioning obedience to authority
Encouragement of many questions and acceptance of divergency from plan	No deviation from preestablished lesson plan
Openness to unevaluated practice and experimentation	Evaluation of all student work—a grade for everything
Encouragement of imagination, make-believe, fictional discussion, and writing	Discussion of real, practical ideas only
Encouragement of problem solving at all age levels	Emphasis on memorizing "correct" answers
Openness to new ideas and a self-concept relatively independent of student comment and behaviors	Requirement that students recognize teacher "rightness" regularly

classroom teachers can become facilitators rather than inhibitors of creative efforts.

FORMAL MEASUREMENT OF INTELLIGENCE

Because the basic criterion in many programs for students who are gifted is above-average intelligence, it is appropriate to discuss briefly how intelligence is measured. A major problem in measuring intelligence is that it has many possible meanings. Like size, intelligence has many dimensions. In addition, the measures of various aspects of intelligence are less specific than are measurements of physical aspects. Intelligence contains many factors lumped together and referred to as IQ.

Still, educators attempt to determine whether a child is intellectually gifted by administering an individual test of cognitive ability, or intelligence. According to Witt, Elliott, Gresham, and Kramer

(1988), one test, the Wechsler Intelligence Scale for Children—Revised (WISC—R), is "the standard against which other measures of cognitive abilities have been judged for the last three decades" (p. 168). McLoughlin and Lewis (1990) indicate that the WISC—R is "the individual test most often used to assess general intellectual performance of school-aged individuals" (p. 192). Although *all* tests of intelligence have been criticized as biased as applied to certain groups of individuals, the WISC—R is as near a standard as exists. Therefore, individuals who score significantly above average (for their age) with respect to the knowledge, skills, or mental abilities that the WISC—R attempts to measure apparently reflect what educators have come to recognize as intellectual giftedness.

A brief description of the subtests of the WISC—R illustrates what this highly respected test assesses. The WISC—R has 12 subtests—6 verbal scale subtests and 6 performance scale subtests. Following is a list of the 6 verbal scale subtests in the WISC—R:

1. *Information subtest.* Thirty questions require general, factual knowledge. This subtest includes questions that subjects might answer correctly through general experience and questions that relate closely to formal educational experience.
2. *Similarities subtest.* Seventeen word pairs require an indication of how the two words in each word pair are similar. This may indicate logical thinking ability, and like the information subtest, it may be influenced by formal schooling.
3. *Arithmetic subtest.* Eighteen practical arithmetic problems require response without paper and pencil computation. Although intended to avoid dependence on reading skill and general verbal ability, school experience may play a role in this subtest.
4. *Vocabulary subtest.* Thirty-two words require synonyms or meaningful definitions. This subtest requires subjects to indicate the meaning of words taken from a master list arranged in order of increasing difficulty. It directly reflects school experience and, particularly with young children, the range of vocabulary used in the home.
5. *Comprehension subtest.* Seventeen problem situations are posed for solution. Subjects must possess practical information and have the ability to evaluate past experiences to be successful on this subtest.
6. *Digit span subtest.* This is an alternate test. It may be used as a substitute for any other verbal scale test, when necessary. In this subtest, subjects must repeat series of digits forward and backward after hearing them only once.

Following is a list of the 6 performance scale subtests in the WISC—R:

1. *Picture completion subtest.* Twenty-six drawings of common objects require subjects to identify missing elements in incomplete pictures. It is designed to measure ability to differentiate the essential from the nonessential. In some respects, it might be considered a test of visual memory.
2. *Picture arrangement subtest.* Twelve sets of pictures require placement of the pictures in each set in logical sequence. This subtest involves arranging sets of cartoon-style panels into a sequence that tells a story. It requires interpretation of social situations and is intended to measure ability to comprehend a total situation in relation to its parts.
3. *Block design subtest.* Eleven designs are to be copied using two-colored blocks. This subtest requires arranging sets of blocks, colored red and white, so that they match pictures of designs shown by the examiner. As required in this subtest, the ability to perceive and analyze forms is believed to reflect ability to analyze and synthesize information.
4. *Object assembly subtest.* This subtest requires the assembly of four jigsaw puzzles so as to complete pictures of commonly known objects. This involves visual and motor functions but also permits examiners to observe general task approach and reaction to mistakes.
5. *Coding subtest.* Symbols are to be copied by matching them to numbers. This requires the matching of numbers and symbols through referral to a code that the subject keeps in view. This subtest is scored for both speed and accuracy. Motor speed is probably more important than motor coordination.
6. *Mazes subtest.* Eight mazes require the subject to find the way out without being blocked. This subtest is an alternate for the coding subtest and involves trac-

ing on a paper maze. Success depends on planning and ability to follow a visual pattern.

If an individual is significantly above average (as compared to age peers) on the tasks included in the WISC—R, that individual may be considered intellectually gifted. State or local educational agency guidelines or regulations dictate how much above average the individual must be. However, regardless of guidelines or regulations, students who are significantly above average in intellectual ability need special provisions in educational planning and programming if they are to develop to their maximum potential. They are, truly, students who have special needs.

IDENTIFICATION OF STUDENTS

The first question to ask when initiating identification procedures is, What type of program is planned or available? If the program is for students who have demonstrated high levels of academic achievement, the identification procedure is considerably different from that for a program for students with talent in music or art or a program for intellectually gifted students who are underachieving. According to Reis and Renzulli (1985), the most frequently used sources of information in the identification process are test scores, completed products and performances, anecdotal records, observational reports, teacher ratings, peer ratings, self-ratings, parental ratings, unstructured self-expressions, and classroom performance.

In *A Handbook for Identifying the Gifted/Talented*, Platow (1984) describes six specific identification instruments: (a) teacher nomination, (b) autobiography and self-rating scales, (c) children's drawings, (d) peer nomination, (e) parental nomination,

and (f) standardized tests. With respect to teacher, peer, or parental nomination, Platow emphasizes guidelines and assistive materials to make the nominations meaningful. He provides a variety of forms, inventories, and questionnaires. He also provides guidance regarding the use of autobiographies, self-rating scales, children's drawings, and standardized tests.

Most authors who discuss identification of students who are gifted or talented recommend collecting data, following a case study procedure, and allowing a committee that is responsible for evaluation and placement to make the final identification. Much of the data collected should be similar to that collected for identification of other exceptional students, such as students who are hearing impaired or learning disabled. The data should include family history, teacher reports, and standardized test data. Exceptions to this general identification procedure include students who are referred or nominated with respect to unusual talent in art, music, or dance. In such instances, although the various types of information are valuable, the actual identification of unusual talent should be the responsibility of one individual or panel of three or four individuals who are recognized authorities in that area.

Given the present conceptualizations of giftedness and methods for identification, some students are extremely difficult to identify as gifted. The first group, sometimes called gifted disabled, have disabilities but are also gifted in some way. The second and third groups, students who are economically disadvantaged and students who are from culturally diverse populations, do not have disabilities in the traditional sense, but due to differences from the majority of students, they are unlikely to be identified as gifted. In *Intellectual Giftedness in Disabled Persons*, Whitmore and

Maker (1985) discuss the emerging field of education of students who are gifted and disabled. They illustrate difficulties inherent in this area through case studies, examining the lives of persons who have obvious disabilities but are also intellectually gifted. Most of their suggestions relating to students who are gifted and disabled also apply to students who are gifted and economically disadvantaged and students who are gifted and culturally diverse.

Students Who Have Disabilities

Whitmore and Maker believe that there are four major obstacles to identifying children with disabilities as being intellectually gifted. These are (a) stereotypic expectations, (b) developmental delays, (c) incomplete information, and (d) lack of opportunity to evidence superior intellectual abilities. First, according to Whitmore and Maker, stereotypic expectations that present major problems include absence or retardation of normal spoken language skills, lack of ability in physically active investigation (which is typical of many gifted children), and an assumption that gifted children "look bright." Stereotypic expectations involve expectations of individuals with disabilities (or who are economically deprived or culturally diverse), and individuals who are gifted. Whitmore and Maker say that in order to increase ability to identify giftedness, "professionals must be trained to stimulate productive and creative thought to observe the manifestation of those traits in atypical forms" (p. 21).

Second, developmental delays often occur when a disabling condition limits a child's ability to receive and respond to cognitive stimulation. Educators should compare the child to others having similar disabilities when completing assessment and evaluation, because reduced opportunity for normal, meaningful interaction with the

environment may conceal great potential. Third, incomplete information about a child is always a potential source of inaccurate assessment. When a child has obvious disabilities, educators sometimes do not search further for signs of giftedness. Making certain that information is received from all possible sources is essential. Finally, lack of opportunity to demonstrate superior intellectual abilities may result from the nature of programming for a disability. For example, if the program emphases are self-help and basic skills (due to the disability), then opportunities to demonstrate higher-level intellectual abilities are likely to be significantly reduced, particularly if a student is in a self-contained, special program but also if a student is in an integrated setting.

Whitmore and Maker believe that two factors are critical to identification of giftedness in children who have disabling conditions. They say, "First, opportunities must be provided that will elicit indicators of mental giftedness" (p. 21). Such opportunities are best provided in settings specifically designed to be stimulating. Such settings encourage performance in tasks that do not require the use of skills that are underdeveloped due to a disabling condition. Whitmore and Maker caution that formal tests of intellectual ability "must be appropriately adapted and scores adjusted for severe disabilities where there is reason to believe cognitive functioning exceeds performance capabilities on that measure" (p. 21). The second factor is careful, deliberate gathering and pooling of information from a wide variety of settings, including professionals and parents or caregivers.

Minority Students

The various problems related to providing appropriate programs for children who are economically disadvantaged and children who are culturally diverse require differing solutions with different subgroups. For example, identification of giftedness in students for whom English is a second language must be somewhat different from identification of giftedness in students for whom English is the first and only language. Programs in which inclusion is based primarily on academic achievement tests require provisions different from those using multiple criteria. There are no simple answers, but the first step is widened awareness of the problem. The second step is acceptance of the principle of flexibility in determining which students should be provided the opportunities available in programs for students who are gifted.

One way to provide flexibility and to avoid some of the limitations imposed by percentage figures in state guidelines is a system similar to that advocated by Reis and Renzulli (1982) and Delisle, Reis, and Gubbins (1981), the revolving door identification and programming model. The model is based on the premise that "a relatively large proportion of persons manifest gifted behaviors at certain times, in certain areas of study, and under certain circumstances" (Delisle, Reis, & Gubbins, 1981, p. 152) and involves selecting a large (15% to 25%) talent pool for each grade level and then providing regularly scheduled enrichment activities "designed to capitalize on their existing interests" (Reis & Renzulli, 1982, p. 619). Research in Connecticut led to the conclusion that with this approach, students who scored in the top 5% on standardized tests of intelligence or achievement did no better in terms of various abilities than did those who were above average but below this top 5% group.

Until a definition of giftedness permits accurate identification, the best answer is the use of multiple criteria, paying careful attention to students who are not moti-

vated and utilizing a revolving door identification and programming model. While educators should provide for students who are readily identifiable as gifted, they must also remain alert to students not presently motivated by traditional cognitive learning and the formal education process.

Cummins (1984) suggests that in assessment designed to identify gifted students among bilingual populations, knowledge of the cultural background is a prerequisite to valid interpretation of either observational or test data. He further suggests that until schools are organized to reward culturally specific talents, nondiscriminatory assessment will be difficult at best. (In other words, abilities and talents valued in a specific subculture may provide the best basis for determining which students are gifted or talented.) If educators completing assessments of bilingual and culturally diverse students are not fully aware of what giftedness means in another subculture, observations may be essentially useless.

Davis and Rimm (1985) believe that "because of cultural bias in test instruments and other identification methods, many typical procedures actually obscure students' giftedness by 'proving' these children are *not* gifted" (p. 259). Cummins (1984) outlines three requirements that must be met if observational procedures are to effectively identify minority students who are gifted and talented. He believes that teachers or psychometricians must:

1. Have access to the child's linguistic and cultural world outside the school;
2. Be knowledgeable about research findings on bilingualism and second language learning;
3. Ensure that curricular and extra-curricular activities encourage the display and development of a diverse range of talents. (p. 219)

Often, actual programs for minority students who are gifted and talented must be different from those provided for other gifted and talented students. The variations and modifications must be specifically tailored for the students under consideration. Sensitivity to the problem and sincere desire to find such students are the responsibilities of regular classroom teachers. We hope this brief consideration will help build such sensitivity and interest.

SCHOOL ORGANIZATION

Gifted students are not served consistently throughout the nation. Some regular classroom teachers receive essentially no assistance or guidance from specialists; some receive only limited consultative help; and others have both consultative assistance and special materials for students who are gifted. Still other teachers work with gifted students in some some type of ability grouping. When regular classroom teachers have the advantage of continuing consultation with a specialist in the education of students who are gifted, their role is primarily that of cooperative planning and implementation of ideas. Day-to-day modifications of instructional activities are required, but most teachers soon develop the ability to meet the educational needs of students who are gifted.

The instruction provided by regular classroom teachers is greatly influenced by the local organizational plan for education of students who are gifted. The three major organizational plans utilized on behalf of gifted students are (a) ability grouping, (b) enrichment, and (c) acceleration.

Ability Grouping

Grouping in separate, special classes or special schools means that regular classroom teachers are involved only in relation to

identification and referral of students who are gifted. Alternately, some schools provide special classes but integrate students into several regular classes. Still other schools supplement regular classes with special, pullout programs for part of the school day. Clustering several gifted students in one regular class allows interactions between students who have a broad range of abilities. Various combinations of ability grouping are utilized, and any groupings in which regular class teachers are active may be valuable, but in each arrangement, teachers must recognize and plan to meet the needs of students who are gifted.

Enrichment

Enrichment may be the most utilized program for gifted students. At least, it is among the most often mentioned when school administrators are asked how they serve gifted students in their district. In the ability groupings mentioned in the preceding section, it is assumed that enrichment is taking place. However, school district practice with respect to serving students who are gifted is often enrichment with no special grouping. This means differentiated learning opportunities for gifted students, but authorities disagree as to the effectiveness of enrichment without ability grouping.

Acceleration

Acceleration moves students who are gifted more rapidly through the regular program of the public schools. This may mean early school entrance, the skipping of grades, early or advanced placement in college, or a combination of procedures that lead to completion of the regular school program in less time than is normally required. Although perhaps not so popular today as in past decades, a variety of research seems to support the general effectiveness of acceleration on an individual basis (Kulik & Kulik, 1984).

CURRICULUM

Students who are gifted or talented are similar to students who have disabilities in that both groups have special needs and both groups should be educated with students in the mainstream as long as this education achieves the desired results. Teachers must modify their teaching methods to meet the needs of all exceptional students, and to do so, most teachers need assistance from individuals who have specialized training and skills.

A basic tenet of this text is that exceptional students should be educated in the most normal way possible, consistent with meeting established educational goals. To the extent that educators can help exceptional students become more effective learners in the mainstream, the efforts are successful. Most authorities in the education of students who are gifted or talented accept the idea that students who are gifted should be educated along with students who are not gifted as long as this achieves the desired results. However, most of these same authorities recognize that the unusual abilities of students who are gifted increase the likelihood that such students will require different learning environments and different teaching approaches. Educators of students who are gifted and talented endorse the goal of development of normal social skills and competence in interpersonal relationships, but in the learning arena, educational success accentuates differences. In some instances, such differences dictate removal from the mainstream.

A number of other factors make any consideration of education of students who are gifted or talented different from that of students with disabilities. For example, educators must be careful about *over*inclusion of economically deprived or culturally diverse students in some programs for students with disabilities. In contrast, educators must be alert to the possibility of *under*inclusion of gifted students in these groups. In addition, educators may initially provide quite different programs for economically deprived and culturally diverse gifted students than for gifted students from the middle-class and above. Because there is less certainty about identification of students who are gifted than there is for students with disabilities, a specific educational practice may be appropriate for students identified as gifted in one area but inappropriate for as many as 70% to 80% of the students identified as gifted in another area.

Figure 12–2 is a brief set of guidelines for developing a curriculum or evaluating an existing one for students who are gifted. These guidelines are provided by Clark (1988), who also cautions that while these (or other) guidelines are useful, "you will always need to assess your gifted learners for their particular needs. They are your very best guide to an appropriate curriculum" (p. 278).

SUGGESTIONS FOR REGULAR CLASSROOM TEACHERS

Benjamin Bloom (1956) provides a conceptualization of the various levels of thinking. Bloom's conceptualization, known as Bloom's taxonomy, describes six levels. From low to high, these levels are (a) knowledge, (b) comprehension, (c) applica-

FIGURE 12-2
The shoulds and should-nots of an appropriately designed differentiated curriculum

1. The curriculum *should* be planned and sequentially organized to include specific expectations for the acquisition of subject matter, mastery of skills, creation of products, and development of attitudes and appreciations related to self, others, and the environment.

   The curriculum *should not* be a potpourri of learning activities that are disjointed and haphazardly selected without reference to specified criteria.

2. The curriculum *should* place emphasis on the interdependence of subject matter, skills, products, and self-understanding within the *same* curricular structure.

   The curriculum *should not* focus on the attainment of cognitive competencies in isolation from the development of affective competencies. Nor should the curriculum focus on affective development without concern for cognitive growth.

3. The curriculum *should* include provisions to meet the need for some type of instructional pacing by any or all of the following means:
   a. Making it possible to accomplish a range of learning experiences in a shorter span of time using a continuous progress curriculum
   b. Assigning students to curricula at levels beyond those expected at the students' age/grade level
   c. Eliminating from the curricula what is already learned and substituting curricula more appropriate to student interest, abilities, and needs.

      The curriculum *should not* penalize students for being gifted or talented, through restricting their opportunities to learn by ignoring those characteristics that define their giftedness.

4. The curriculum *should* allow for the expression of some aspect of the individual's interests, needs, abilities, and learning preferences. The curriculum *should* be organized to allow for some individualization and self-selection.

   The curriculum *should not* be without defined expectations and clearly expressed opportunities for teacher-directed as well as student-selected learning activities.

tion, (d) analysis, (e) synthesis, and (f) evaluation. Bloom's taxonomy addresses the needs and characteristics of all students, and educators regularly use it to help them plan curriculum for individuals and groups. In a single classroom, a teacher may work with one or two gifted students, normal learners, and one or two students with disabilities. Still, the teacher may use Bloom's taxonomy to differentiate instruction.

Teachers can display the levels of thinking and verbs associated with each level to remind themselves and their students to use higher levels of thinking and to help structure thinking activities. (Table 12-2 lists key verbs and classroom products related to Bloom's taxonomy.) To display the levels of Bloom's taxonomy, make a clothesline and hang from it "bloomers" that represent the six levels. Then, highlight verbs associated with the levels on the ruffles of the legs. Make each level a different color, and code the levels consistently through learning centers and other areas of

5. The curriculum *should* provide opportunities to learn to reconceptualize existing knowledge, to perceive things from various points of view, and to use information for new purposes or in new ways.

   The curriculum *should not* stress the accumulation of knowledge or reinforce mastery without simultaneously encouraging students to be productive thinkers.

6. The curriculum *should* provide learning experiences for students to address the unresolved issues and problems of society and apply personal and social data to analyze, clarify, and respond to such issues and problems.

   The curriculum *should not* focus only on knowledge of the world as it is, but should encourage the development of perceptions of the need to invent in order to restructure the world into what it ideally could be.

7. The curriculum *should* incorporate learning experiences that foster the development of the complex thought processes that encourage the creation of unique products and develop strategies of productive thought. The curriculum *should* teach both fundamental and higher-level thinking skills as integral parts of every learning experience.

   The curriculum *should not* overemphasize mastery of fundamental basic skills, nor should it exonerate gifted/talented students from mastering these. The curriculum *should not* ignore the development of fundamental or basic skills for the mastery of higher-level thinking skills.

8. The curriculum *should* provide opportunities for students to practice leadership and followership skills and appropriate and varied forms of communication skills and strategies.

   The curriculum *should not* be based on the assumption that gifted/talented students can assume positions of leadership without the development of skills and understandings that promote this end.

Note: Reprinted with permission of Merrill, an imprint of Macmillan Publishing Company, from *Growing Up Gifted*, 3rd ed. (pp. 276–278) by Barbara Clark. Copyright © 1988, 1983, 1979 by Merrill Publishing Company.

the classroom. Figure 12–3 contains additional ways to display the levels. Teachers should use their imagination and creativity in developing other displays.

Clark (1988), Maker (1982), Sisk (1987), and many others have used Bloom's taxonomy in various ways in planning for students who are gifted and talented. For example, Leiker (1980) created the questions in Figure 12–4 about Maurice Sendak's (1963) *Where the Wild Things Are*, a popular book for young readers. To develop higher-level cognitive skills, write story questions such as Leiker's on an appropriate figure form (a monster for *Where the Wild Things Are*) that is laminated.

Reading

According to Baskin and Harris (1985),

Reading is the single most important component in any curriculum for gifted children. Not only is that skill essential for the mastery of all other subjects, but it allows youngsters to pursue their

TABLE 12–2
Verbs and classroom products related to Bloom's taxonomy

Areas	Definition	Key Verbs	Classroom Products
Knowledge	Knowing and remembering facts	Match, recognize, identify, list, describe, name, define, show, record, select	Report, worksheet, chart, map
Comprehension	Understanding	Explain, locate, inquire, demonstrate, discover	Diagram, model, game, picture, teach a lesson, diorama, time line
Application	Doing, making use of what is known	Model, apply, code, collect, organize, construct, report, experiment, sketch, paint, draw, group, put in order	Survey, diary, mobile, scrapbook, photographs, stitchery, cartoon, model, illustration, sculpture, learning center, construction
Analysis	Explaining what is known	Categorize, take apart, analyze, separate, dissect, compare, contrast	Graph, survey, report, questionnaire, time line, family tree, commercial, fact file
Synthesis	Putting together the known into something new	Add to, create, imagine, combine, suppose, predict, role-play, hypothesize, design, [ask] what if . . ? invent, infer, improve, adapt, compose, change	Story, poem, play, song, pantomime, news article, invention, radio show, dance, mural, comic strip
Evaluation	Judging the outcome	Justify, debate, solve, recommend, judge, criticize, prove, dispute	Editorial, survey, panel, self-evaluation, letter, conclusion, recommendation, court trial

Note: From *An Affordable Gifted Program That Works* (p. 39) by M. Leiker, 1980, Denver: Coronado Hills School, Adams School District No. 12. Adapted by permission.

intellectual interests both inside and outside the classroom. Researchers continue to report reading as an activity of singular importance in the lives of gifted youth who, through books, can control the depth, pacing, direction, sequence, quantity, quality, and complexity of their learning. Books remain the most accessible, affordable, and pleasurable tool for fostering cognitive growth and independence. Reading surpasses even direct experience in this task since such knowledge is obviously limited by time, place, accessibility, and the like.

Many activities depend on reading for successful completion. Although gifted students are usually competent in reading (as

FIGURE 12–3
Examples of mobiles and displays of Bloom's taxonomy

compared with age peers), their reading abilities require continued analysis, and their selection of reading materials requires guidance. Students should develop skimming strategies, meaning-related strategies (such as making predictions and drawing inferences from materials read), and reasoning-related strategies (such as generalizing). Gifted students may develop these competencies on their own, but if they do not, teachers should help them. A second-grade teacher, for example, may need to obtain assistance from a fifth- or sixth-grade teacher with respect to strategies that are not ordinarily considered with respect to second-grade students.

Because students who are gifted may be ready and able to grasp relatively complex concepts for their age, teachers must remember that their reading materials must be qualitatively different from that used with age peers. Ordinarily, the basal reading series at grade level is inappropriate, and basal reading books several grade levels above placement may not be appropriate, since they are designed for another purpose and based on assumptions that may not apply to the particular students. Gifted chil-

FIGURE 12–4
Story questions related to Bloom's taxonomy

WHERE THE WILD THINGS ARE

Knowledge
Where did Max go?
What grew in Max's room?
Where did Max really want to be?

Comprehension
What did Max tame the "wild things" with?
How did the "wild things" act when they first saw Max?
What did Max want from his mother?

Application
Show how Max felt when he was sent to his room.
Draw a picture of the "wild things."
What could Max have done differently?

Analysis
Why did Mother send Max to his room?
What probably happened to Max when he was just sent to his room?
What did Max do to frighten the "wild beasts"?

Synthesis
What would have happened if Max had missed the boat home?
How would you have changed the story to make it better?
Create a new monster of your own for the story.

Evaluation
Which ending to the story do you like best?
Would Max have been happy if he had missed the boat?
How did the new monster change the story?

Note: Questions from *An Affordable Gifted Program That Works* (p. 111) by M. Leiker, 1980, Denver: Coronado Hills School, Adams School District No. 12. Reprinted by permission.

dren are often interested in topics that are usually considered inappropriate for their chronological age. For example, a third-grade student interested in paleontology may demonstrate advanced reading ability and understanding of complex vocabulary plus understanding of concepts far beyond the readiness of other third graders. If there is no readily available consultative help from a specialist, the school librarian may be of assistance. Parents can also help in relation to areas of interest.

Education of students who are gifted requires a differentiated, individualized program. Modifications or adaptations of the standard reading program at the elementary school level are often inadequate, and the normal wide reading program at the secondary level may be unchallenging. If there is a nearby college or university, or a major library, include it in the planning for secondary school students.

Learning Centers

Learning centers may address any subject or topic, and teachers may use learning centers in the classroom to individualize instruction and better serve students who are gifted. Thus, teachers may develop activities and materials based on student needs and objectives, and they may use learning centers to introduce, reinforce, review, or enrich concepts.

Programs for the gifted should have many dimensions.

Bloom's taxonomy may be used in the development of learning centers. For example, teachers may code file folders by color and develop questions for each of the six levels of thinking. Numerous books on the market offer ideas and patterns for learning centers; however, teachers must exercise creativity and originality in the development of learning centers to meet the needs of specific situations.

Story Questions

Teachers may write specific questions relating to the six levels of Bloom's taxonomy to correspond to specific books, general questions to correspond to specific books, or general questions to be used with a number of books. Questions may cover the general categories of humor, adventure, science, fiction, animals, distant lands, historical fic-

tion, fantasy, tall tales, biography, folktales, fairy tales, and myths. Leiker (1980) lists generic questions corresponding to the six levels of Bloom's taxonomy. Figure 12–5 provides examples of this type of questioning.

Autonomous Learning

The autonomous learner model is based on the belief that students who are gifted should become responsible for the development, implementation, and evaluation of their own learning. This, of course, is the eventual goal of the program. Figure 12–6 illustrates the five dimensions of the autonomous learner model: (a) orientation, (b) individual development, (c) enrichment activities, (d) seminars, and (e) in-depth study. Figure 12–7 illustrates the individual development dimension of the model. Figure

FIGURE 12–5
Generic literature questions

Science Fiction

Knowledge: 1. What is the *setting* of the story? List the main characters.
Comprehension: 2. What was the main idea or theme of the story?
Application: 3. Draw a picture of the *setting* of the story.
Analysis: 4. Compare the environment *(setting)* in this story to your own *setting*. List the things that are the same and different.
Synthesis: 5. Choose one thing from the story that you feel could benefit our world if it existed. Write a short story explaining how you would make it a part of life today.
Evaluation: 6. Anticipate problems. List the major hurdles you would encounter in selling the idea to others.

Adventure

Knowledge: 1. Locate by page number a place in the book that shows *action, conflict, suspense.*
Comprehension: 2. What was the *main bold idea* in the story? What was one exciting event that made you nervous until you knew the ending?
Application: 3. List in order what happened in the story. Put a star next to the most exciting event.
Analysis: 4. In adventure stories, there are *usually two forces* (people or things) *working against each other.* What were they in this story?
Synthesis: 5. Write an adventure story about an event in your life. Be sure to include action, conflict, suspense, and two forces working against each other.
Evaluation: 6. Evaluate your story. Give one point for each of the points in Question 5. How did you score?

Fantasy

Knowledge: 1. Who are the main characters in the story? Where did it take place?
Comprehension: 2. What *extraordinary* thing happened in the story?
Application: 3. In fantasy STRANGE things happen. List 4 things that could never *really* happen.
Analysis: 4. Choose the one thing out of the 4 above that you feel shows the *greatest imagination.*
Synthesis: 5. Write down the thing in your life that you feel is an example of your own imagination at work.
Evaluation: 6. What effect does your imagination have on your life?

Biography

Knowledge: 1. Whose life is the book about? What type of work did the author have to do before writing the book?
Comprehension: 2. *What makes you feel you really know what the person in the book was like?*
Application: 3. Make a diary of the person's life. List only major events.
Analysis: 4. *What emotions did you feel toward the person in the book?* When did you feel these emotions?
Synthesis: 5. How could the author have improved this book? Be specific.
Evaluation: 6. Do you feel biographies are important types of books? Should they be published before or after a main character's death? Why?

Note: From *An Affordable Gifted Program That Works* (p. 63) by M. Leiker, 1980, Denver: Coronado Hills School, Adams School District No. 12. Reprinted by permission.

FIGURE 12–6
The autonomous learner model

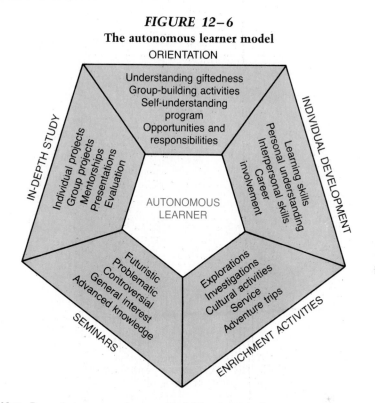

ORIENTATION

Understanding giftedness
Group-building activities
Self-understanding
program
Opportunities and
responsibilities

INDIVIDUAL DEVELOPMENT

IN-DEPTH STUDY

Individual projects
Group projects
Mentorships
Presentations
Evaluation

Learning skills
Personal understanding
Interpersonal skills
Career
involvement

AUTONOMOUS
LEARNER

Futuristic
Problematic
Controversial
General interest
Advanced knowledge

Explorations
Investigations
Cultural activities
Service
Adventure trips

SEMINARS

ENRICHMENT ACTIVITIES

Note: From *Autonomous Learner Model for the Gifted and Talented* (p. 2) by
G. T. Betts, 1985, Greeley, CO: Autonomous Learning Publications & Specialists (ALPS). Copyright 1985 by ALPS. Reprinted by permission.

12–8 is Betts's (1985) description of the five dimensions of the model.

Mentors

The use of mentors to provide learning opportunities for gifted students has proved successful in many programs. Mentor programs may use interested professionals from the community, high school students with special talents (to mentor gifted students in grade school), and senior citizens who have had successful careers, as appropriate. Such programs may be essentially informal, as when a student is linked with a resource person on an individual basis (observing proper cautions, orientation, parent involvement, and so on) or part of formal,

planned enrichment programs. Runions and Smyth (1985) discuss the significance of mentorships and provide guidelines for developing them in local school districts (Figure 12–9). Although mentorship can be a valuable part of an enrichment program, it should not be considered *the* program. Mentorships involve unique, meaningful, experientially based learning opportunities, but like all successful educational program components, they require consistent monitoring and involvement by responsible educators.

Bibliotherapy

Bibliotherapy has been advocated as a procedure to help improve self-concept, modify

FIGURE 12–7
Individual development dimension

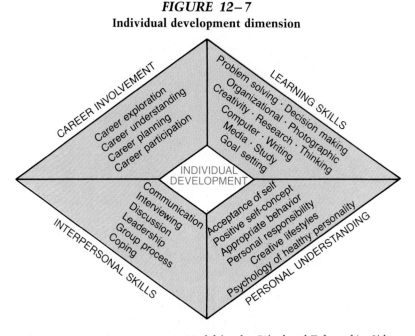

Note: From *Autonomous Learner Model for the Gifted and Talented* (p. 3) by G. T. Betts, 1985, Greeley, CO: Autonomous Learning Publications & Specialists (ALPS). Copyright 1985 by ALPS. Reprinted by permission.

attitudes, and contribute to better mental health, but the concept also has applicability to enriching the educational program. In bibliotherapy, individuals use books and other reading materials to help in problem solving. Clark (1988) believes that the technique has special advantages in use with gifted students. Through bibliotherapy, abilities that are usually strengths (ability to conceptualize, generalize, and deal with abstractions) can be used to promote areas identified as targets for additional development. Like most strategies, this one must be highly individualized and should be part of an overall educational plan.

Biographical Research

It is important for gifted students to understand their attitudes, needs, and drives. Biographical (or autobiographical) research can

help develop understandings of the characteristics, attitudes, needs, and motivations of various eminent persons, and thus provide insight regarding personal attitudes, needs, and drives. This may be particularly valuable if students can research the lives of persons who have followed paths or professions of personal interest. Initial teacher guidance is important in biographical research, but once started, students may go a long way on their own.

Individual Projects

Individual projects are units of learning designed by students who are aided by teachers as facilitators. Individual projects may take on a variety of forms and be applicable to many areas. Thus, each student is afforded the opportunity to pursue individual interests and use his or her own learning.

FIGURE 12–8
The five dimensions of the autonomous learner model

The Orientation Dimension of the model provides students, teachers, administrators and parents the opportunity to develop a foundation of information concerning the program. Emphasis is placed on understanding the concepts of giftedness, creativity and the development of potential. Students learn more about themselves, their abilities and what the program has to offer. Activities are presented to give students an opportunity to work together as a group, to learn about group process and interaction, and to learn more about the other people in the program.

During the Orientation Dimension of the program, a series of inservices are presented for teachers, administrators, parents and involved community resource people. Again, emphasis is placed on the opportunities possible for students, the responsibilities for students and involved personnel, and information given regarding the overall format of the program.

The Individual Development Dimension of the model provides students with the opportunity to develop the cognitive, emotional and social skills, concepts and attitudes necessary for life-long learning: in other words, to become autonomous in their learning.

The Enrichment Activities Dimension of the model was developed to provide students with opportunities to explore content which is usually not part of the everyday curriculum. Most content in the schools is prescribed. Someone beyond the student is deciding what is to be learned, when it is to be learned, and how it is to be learned. Within the Enrichment Activities Dimension students are able to begin explorations into their major area(s) of emphasis, related areas of interest, and new and unique areas. Students decide what they want to pursue, how it is going to be arranged, and where and when the learning will take place. Gifted and talented students need responsibility in selecting what they are going to study and how they are going to learn.

The Seminar Dimension of the model is designed to give students, in small groups of three to five, the opportunity to research a topic, present it as a seminar to the rest of the group and other interested people, and to evaluate it by criteria selected and developed by the students. A seminar is essential because it allows students the opportunity to move from the role of a *student* to the role of a *learner*. If students are to become learners, they must have an opportunity for independent individual and group learning, which means having a structure which allows and promotes the development of knowledge by the individuals.

The In-Depth Study Dimension of the model allows learners to pursue areas of interest through the development of a long-term small group or individual in-depth study. The learners determine what will be learned, how it will be presented, what help will be necessary, what the final product will be and how the entire learning process will be evaluated. In-Depth Studies are usually continued for a long period of time. Plans are developed by learners, in cooperation with the teacher/facilitator, content specialists, and mentors. The plans are then implemented and completed by the learners, with presentations being made at appropriate times until the completion of the project. A final presentation and evaluation is given to all who are involved and interested.

Note: From *Autonomous Learner Model for the Gifted and Talented* (pp. 3–4) by G. T. Betts, 1985, Greeley, CO: Autonomous Learning Publications & Specialists (ALPS). Copyright 1985 by ALPS. Reprinted by permission.

FIGURE 12–9
Mentorships

Why Are Mentorships Significant in the Education of the Gifted and Talented?

Mentorships provide a creative and viable means of differentiating programs for gifted and talented learners:

- By creating opportunities for learner access to professional expertise in the community to pursue in-depth career and academic interests at competent levels.
- By offering real-life experiences that support the growth of the learner's self-concept through the acquisition and application of life skills.
- By facilitating the cooperative use of community resources in more effective and efficient ways.
- By establishing a network of community resource people available to all members of the school community.
- By offering the learner more responsibility in the learning process.
- By providing an experientially-based framework for enriching the curriculum.
- By involving the learner in the application of networking skills necessary for an information society.
- By providing leadership opportunities through cross-age tutoring between and among elementary and secondary school students.
- By presenting traditional and nontraditional role models of competence in the pursuit of and commitment to excellence.
- By supporting the development of independent and interdependent learning skills in real life situations.

How Are Mentorships Developed?

In selecting the strategy for your school and community to use in developing a mentorship program, the following suggestions may be helpful:

- Select students who have the intensity of interest and commitment to explore learning beyond the classroom.
- Select school and community resource people interested in pursuing mentorships.
- Develop program and curriculum guidelines flexible enough to accommodate mentorships.
- Orient all participants (student, teacher, mentor) to their redefined roles—students as co-learners, teacher as facilitator, mentor as networker.
- Develop communication skills—telephone skills, interview skills, small group process skills, letter writing skills, contract learning skills, and journal writing skills.
- Develop community research skills—data collection, analysis, and presentation.
- Develop self-directed learning skills—decision making, problem solving, critical thinking, creative thinking, effective communication, and self-evaluation.
- Establish a community-based component of linking agencies (volunteer bureaus) that can facilitate access to available and receptive people and print resources.
- Make evaluation a shared process among the learner, the mentor, and the teacher, with clear and precise guidelines mutually agreed upon. Both the program and process should be evaluated on an individual and group basis, using the techniques of quantitative and qualitative evaluation, as well as summative and formative evaluation. Because mentorships are a personal learning experience, self-evaluations can play an important role in communicating the value of the experience.

Note: From "Mentorships for the Gifted and Talented" by T. Runions and E. Smyth, 1985, *ERIC Digest, 346.*

For example, a student interested in computers planned and participated in a project to investigate computer applications in the field of art. After learning the techniques of programming, the student created a cartoon using the graphic capabilities of the computer.

On the other hand, a student may earn specific course credit for developing new fields of interest. In this case, the student, a facilitator, and a content area teacher negotiate a project that fulfills the objectives and requirements for a particular course. Then, the student goes beyond the regular classroom activities and independently pursues an interest in depth. As an example, a student was interested in the study of anatomy. After consulting with a biology instructor, the student produced a comparative anatomy study of a shark, a cat, a pig, and a snake, making evolutionary comparisons and highlighting contrasts. The student presented the results in a formal paper and gave a slide presentation to diversified audiences, including biologists, college students, and persons in the medical field.

Group Projects

Group projects differ from individual projects. In a group project, two or three students develop the project rather than a single individual. The project is broader in scope but still reflects the interests of each student involved. For example, three students were interested in working together on a project. One student wrote poetry and short stories; another enjoyed working with lasers and photography; and still another was proficient in computer programming. The result of combining these three talents was an original planetarium show, controlled by a computer and incorporating photographs, poetry, and laser techniques.

Futuristics

Future studies (futuristics) are part of the curriculum in many school districts. Aspects of future studies have often become parts of the sciences and social sciences, but they may be integrated with almost any subject. Futuristics is based on the concept that students will live in a future quite different from the world as it exists today and even more different from the world as it existed when their parents and teachers were children. According to Clark (1988), "A futurist must deal comfortably with uncertainties, open-ended situations, and vastly divergent possibilities" (p. 597). It would seem that gifted individuals would be uniquely able to help forecast events and needs, and prepare members of society to live in the world as it will exist in the future. Sisk (1987) believes that a futuristic point of view must be adopted as a teaching philosophy and applied in teaching all subject areas. She feels that this philosophy is particularly essential in education of students who are gifted "if gifted students are to use their ability to help create the future" (p. 118).

In recognition of this need, Torrance et al. (1980, 1981) initiated the Future Problem Solving Program for gifted students in grades 4 through 12. This project involves 80,000 students throughout the United States and consists of a variety of curriculum activities, group and individual involvement, and state and national competition. (To learn more about this program, write to Future Problem Solving Program, Nebraska Department of Education, Lincoln, Nebraska 68508.)

Established programs such as the Future Problem Solving Program can be valuable to regular classroom teachers in planning for gifted students, but other strategies may be of equal value. For example, teachers may develop and write scenarios as starting points for thinking about the future: "As I was unplugging the overnight regenerator on my nuclear hovercraft, I realized that someone or something must have used it last night. The trip odometer, which is automatically reset each night as it regenerates, read 125,310 ergometers. And the seat had been readjusted to be closer to the steering control, and much higher than I had left it. I sensed a strange sickly-sweet odor, and felt a prickly sensation at the back of my neck. Then, it happened. . ." Teachers can then encourage students to develop the next scenes and discuss alternatives. This may be accomplished as individual projects or small-group efforts. Either way, futuristic scenarios promote creative thinking and the use of creative language. Develop similar scenarios about environmental concerns, space stations, and world conflicts.

Simulation

When properly developed and focused, simulation can be a powerful learning tool for all students, but it may be particularly stimulating to students who are gifted. Sisk (1985) believes that simulation builds on curiosity, requires keen observation skills, affords opportunities for the use of inquiry skills, and requires the use of problem-solving abilities. Use simulation to lead to better understanding of the feelings of others, such as a student who has AIDS, or some real-life process, such as a meeting of the state senate.

Brainstorming

Brainstorming may be of particular value to gifted students, but it requires careful handling by the facilitator (usually the teacher). In the initial stage, warn against judgmental comments, such as "that doesn't make sense," "that wouldn't work," or "that's been done before." The goal is to solicit ideas without evaluation. Terms such as *free-wheeling* (relating to the way in which individuals contribute suggestions) and *hitchhiking* (relating to the building on the ideas of others) are often used in characterizations of successful brainstorming.

In a typical brainstorming session, the facilitator establishes a problem and members of the group suggest solutions. In most cases, the facilitator records the solutions on the chalkboard so that others can see them. This encourages hitchhiking on the suggestions made by others. Only after the collection of ideas is complete (some suggest a time limit of 15 to 20 minutes for the initial collection of ideas) are the ideas evaluated or discussed in any manner. Even at this point, avoid having any student feel put down by another student, or this may influence the manner in which students contribute at the next brainstorming session.

Social Development

Schneider (1987) believes that "two types of myth impede objective reasoning about social relations of the gifted" (p. 1). The first is that they are destined to be social outcasts; the second is that they are "destined to succeed in all areas of functioning" (p. 3). Schneider makes the case that both ideas are myths. Often, they are based on case histories of a limited number of gifted individuals, without proper attention to all of the others who do not fit these stereotypes. Schneider reviews a number of studies of the social development of gifted students and concludes that although sometimes special programming for students who are gifted seems to correlate with the establishment of parallel social systems, one that includes primarily gifted students and one that includes primarily nongifted students, this is certainly not always the case. He concludes that although "insensitivity to, and outright rejection of, young gifted peers are not unknown . . . such treatment cannot be seen as the prevalent state of affairs" (p. 102).

Meaningful, satisfying social development of students who are gifted appears to be specific to the type and structure of special programming (if it exists) and the personality of individual students. Teachers must understand that peers may be threatened by students who are gifted and may not understand the near-adult-level concern that gifted students express with social causes, environmental concerns, and so on. On the other hand, gifted students may ignore social learning and the social rules of age peers, and thus become outcasts. Alternately, they may be unusually sensitive to the feelings of age peers and attempt to hide their cognitive abilities, so they will be like other students, and thus be accepted. In either case, teachers must nurture the characteristics essential to the social development of students who are gifted.

SUMMARY

Giftedness was described as having three definitional categories: (a) IQ-based, (b) percentage-based, and (c) talent-based. Three widely recognized definitions of giftedness were presented, along with procedures for identifying students who are gifted or talented. Formal measurement of intelligence (IQ) was discussed and the subtests of the WISC—R were reviewed. Creativity was discussed as a related but separate area of ability. Students who are gifted may have disabilities, be economically disadvantaged, or be culturally diverse.

Guidelines for the development of a differentiated curriculum for gifted students were presented, and three administrative plans—ability grouping, enrichment, and acceleration—were discussed. A variety of suggestions for regular classroom teachers were provided, including ideas for academic and social development.

APPENDIX A

BOOKS ABOUT EXCEPTIONAL INDIVIDUALS

This appendix contains two sections of books about exceptional individuals: (a) books for children and youth and (b) books for adults. The section on books for children and youth is divided into the following classifications (listed alphabetically): behavior disorders, giftedness and talents, hearing impairment, learning disabilities, mental retardation, orthopedic and health impairments, and visual impairment. The books within the individual classifications are listed alphabetically according to author.

BOOKS FOR CHILDREN AND YOUTH

Written for children and youth, the following books provide information about exceptional individuals. The annotated listing is based on areas of exceptionality. Age ranges are provided to help in determining the approximate reading level; however, some books for older students may still be profitably read to younger students.

BEHAVIOR DISORDERS

Please Don't Say Hello by Phyllis Gold, Human Sciences Press, 1975.

A boy who is autistic and his family move into a new neighborhood and face the problems of acceptance by their new neighbors. This is a sensitive story of real experiences, written by the mother of a severely disturbed, autistic boy. Ages 10 and up.

GIFTED/TALENTED

Daniel's Duck by Clyde Robert Bulia, Harper & Row, 1979.

Daniel, a Tennessee mountain boy of the early 1900s, learns about creative talent, pride, and false pride. Ages 5 to 8.

No Good in Art by Miriam Cohen, Greenwillow Books, 1980.

Jim, a talented boy, learns to overcome the negative kindergarten experience that convinced him he was "no good in art." Ages 5 to 8.

Carol Johnston: The One-Armed Gymnast by Pete Donovan, Children's Press, 1982.

This is the true story of a Canadian gymnast who won All-American honors despite the fact that she was born with just one arm. This is more a story of talent than an account of disability. Ages 8 to 12.

The Gifted Kids Survival Guide for Ages 10 and Under and *The Gifted Kids Survival Guide for Ages 11–18* by John Galbraith, Free Spirit, 1983 and 1984.

These books are not *about* exceptional students in the usual sense of the word but are *for* gifted students to read in order to learn more about themselves. The ages are in the titles.

Jemmy by Jon Francis Hassler, Atheneum, 1980.

Jemmy, a half-Chippewa high school senior, is told by her father to quit school in October of her senior year. Initially, she accepts this situation, but through a series of experiences, she discovers both her Native American heritage and great artistic talent. Ages 12 and up.

HEARING IMPAIRMENT

The Secret in the Dorm Attic by Jean Andrews, Gallaudet Univ. Press, 1990.

This mystery involves strange happenings in the attic of a school for the deaf. As the story proceeds, readers learn about the deaf culture in addition to enjoying an exciting mystery story. Ages 8 and up.

My Sister's Silent World by Catherine Arthur, Children's Press, 1979.

Heather's eighth birthday as told by her older sister. Heather has a hearing aid and can distinguish sounds but not words. Ages 5 to 9.

The Waiting Game by Anne Evelyn Bunting, J. B. Lippincott, 1981.

Three high school seniors (one of them deaf) anticipate possible offers of college football scholarships. Ages 10 and up.

Burnish Me Bright by Julia Cunningham, Pantheon Books, 1970.

This is a story of friendship between Auguste, who is deaf and mute, and Monsieur Hilaire, who is a mime. Through mime, Auguste is accepted by the village and becomes very close to Monsieur Hilaire. Ages 8 to 12.

Gallaudet, Friend of the Deaf by Etta DeGering, McKay, 1964.

This is a biography of a man who was instrumental in the education of the deaf in America. Ages 9 to 11.

Meet Camille and Danille: They're Special People by Margaret H. Glazzard, H.&H. Enterprises, 1978.

A very simple book explains how people who are deaf communicate and understand others. It also explains how people who can hear should communicate with those who have hearing impairments. Ages 8 to 12.

What Is the Sign For Friend? by Judith E. Greenberg, Franklin Watts, 1985.

This is a story of a boy who is deaf. The text is "real" and includes signs. Ages 8 and up.

Breakaway by Ruth Hallman, Westminster, 1981.

Rob, a 17-year-old who is almost totally deaf as a result of a diving accident, has many difficulties in adjusting to his situation. His overprotective and domineering mother is one of his major problems. Ages 12 and up.

The Swing by Emily Hanlon, Bradbury Press, 1979.

This books tells how two children—one deaf—learn from each other. Their bonds are their mutual love of animals and the swing that stands between their two houses. Ages 10 to 12.

Silent Dancer by Bruce Hlibok, Julian Messner, 1981.

A youngster who is deaf finds pleasure and confidence in her ballet school classes, which have been adapted to accommodate students who are deaf. Ages 8 to 11.

Child of the Silent Night by Edith Fisher Hunter, Dell Publishing, 1963.

This is the story of Laura Bridgman, who suffers an illness that leaves her blind and deaf. She is sent to the Perkins Institute, where she is taught to see and hear. Ages 7 to 12.

Lisa and Her Soundless World by Edna A. Levine, Human Science, 1984.

This book teaches nondeaf children about their peers who are deaf and shows children who are deaf how they can successfully participate in the social environment around them. Ages 8 to 13.

Annie's World by Nancy Smiler Levinson, Gallaudet Univ. Press, 1990.

A 16-year-old girl is mainstreamed after 9 years in a private school for the deaf. This story includes elements of mystery and romance, along with valuable understandings about deafness. Ages 12 and up.

Words in Our Hands by Ada Bassett Litchfield, Whitman, 1980.

Three children with normal hearing communicate with their parents who are deaf. In addition to building understanding of communication with individuals who are deaf, there is a good deal of specific information, such as the alphabetic, fingerspelling symbols. Ages 12 and up.

Albert Whitman & Company by Ada B. Litchfield, Whitman, 1982.

Michael has two sisters and a mom and dad. There is only one difference between Michael's family and other families. Michael's parents are deaf. He explains what their family life is like and the special gadgets used in their house to help his parents function better. The book also provides a fingerspelling chart. Ages 8 to 12.

I Have a Sister: My Sister is Deaf by Jeanne Whitehouse Peterson, Harper & Row, 1977.

This story is about a little girl whose sister is deaf. The girl believes her sister is exactly the same as anyone else except she cannot hear and explains the similarities instead of the differences. Ages 8 to 12.

Apple is My Sign by Mary L. Riskind, Houghton Mifflin, 1981.

An interesting, historically pertinent story about a boy who is deaf at the turn of the century. This story includes factual material about various sign languages and shows the evolution of sign language. Ages 10 to 14.

David in Silence by Veronica Robinson, J. B. Lippincott, 1966.

David, born deaf in a small town in England, is harassed by children of his own age. His efforts to make friends result in disaster. David proves his competence and courage in a hair-raising trip through an abandoned tunnel and then finds acceptance and friendship. Ages 9 to 13.

Just Like Everybody Else by Lillian Rosen, Harcourt Brace Jovanovich, 1981.

This is the first-person story of a teenager who loses her hearing. This book contains factual information but also manages to maintain interest and promote understanding of the considerable affective needs of individuals who are deaf. Ages 11 and up.

Child of the Arctic by Hubert C. Woods, Follett Publishing, 1962.

A child's deafness makes other Eskimos suspect him until he becomes hero of the village. Ages 8 to 12.

LEARNING DISABILITIES

Do Bananas Chew Gum by Jamie Gilson, Lothrop, Lee & Shepard, 1980.

A boy has repeated failures in school until he is diagnosed as learning disabled and is provided the special help he needs. Ages 9 to 11.

Will the Real Gertrude Hollings Please Stand Up? by Sheila Greenwald, Little, Brown, 1983.

This is the story of Gertrude, a teenage girl who has learning disabilities, and her cousin Albert, a straight-A overachiever. Albert learns a great deal from Gertrude. Ages 11 and up.

Tuned In-Turned On by Marvell Lo Hayes, Academic Therapy, 1974.

This is a book for kids with learning disabilities

about kids with learning disabilities. Ages 7 to 11.

Sue Ellen by Judith Fisher Hunter, Houghton Mifflin, 1969.

Sue Ellen has a learning disability and is surprised and happy with her new special class. This is the touching story of a child who is finally given the opportunity to learn. Ages 8 to 12.

He's My Brother by Joe Lasker, Whitman, 1974.

This is a simplified explanation of a little boy who has learning disabilities. Ages 5 to 8.

Putting Up with Sherwood by Ellen Matthews, Westminster, 1980.

Diane, a fifth grader who feels sorry for herself, is asked to tutor Sherwood, who has a learning disability. Sherwood helps her toward a happier life. Ages 9 to 11.

Running Scared by Jane Morton, Elsevier/Nelson Books, 1979.

This is the straightforward story of a boy's frustration with his inability to achieve in school. Ages 10 to 14.

The Whales to See by Glendon & Kathryn Swarthout, Doubleday, 1975.

A special class of students who have learning disabilities goes out to sea to watch the semiannual whale migration, and a class of "normal" students happens to be on the same ship. This story provides an interesting view of attitudes. This was written before mainstreaming but still has validity. Ages 10 and up.

MENTAL RETARDATION

Love Is Like Peanuts by Betty Bates, Holiday House, 1980.

A 14-year-old girl takes a summer job caring for a girl who is brain-damaged and mentally retarded and has a handsome 18-year-old brother. This story mixes romance with understanding of the condition of mental retardation. Its value is enhanced by characterizations of the manners in which different persons respond to mental retardation. Ages 11 to 14.

Nancy and Her Johnny-O by Bianca Bradbury, Washburn, 1970.

An adolescent girl and her family respond in different ways to 5-year-old Johnny, who is mildly retarded. Ages 9 and up.

For Love of Jody by Robbie Branscum, Lothrop, Lee & Shepard, 1979.

This story, which takes place during the Depression on an Arkansas farm, presents an interesting picture of how Jody, a child who is severely mentally retarded, changes the life of one family. Age 9 to 12.

The Child Who Never Grew by Pearl Buck, John Day Co., 1950.

This is a moving account of a parent's personal experience in rearing a child who is severely retarded. Miss Buck has successfully portrayed the problems of many parents. Ages 15 and up.

Our Jimmy by Ruth K. Doorly, Service Associates, 1967.

A father talks with his two children about their younger brother, who is retarded, explains the special needs, and explains ways in which they can help him learn. This is a warm and loving book for parents and children. Ages 5 to 13.

One Little Girl by Joan Fassler, Behavioral Publications, 1968.

Because she is somewhat retarded, grownups call Laurie a slow child, but Laurie learns that she is slow in doing only some things. Ages 6 to 12.

Alice with Golden Hair by Eleanor Means Hull, Atheneum, 1981.

Alice, who is nearly 18 years old, has been in institutions for individuals who are mentally retarded since early childhood. This book provides a rare, interesting insight into the thinking of individuals who are mildly mentally retarded. Ages 11 and up.

Deep Search by Theodore Koob, J. B. Lippincott, 1969.

A 16-year-old girl finds herself in the midst of her parents' disagreement about the future of her

10-year-old brother, who is mentally retarded. Ages 9 to 13.

She's My Sister: Having a Retarded Sister by Jane Claypool Miner, Crestwood House, 1982.

A 16-year-old has great difficulty with the fact that her sister, who is retarded, is coming home from her special school and that they will be attending the same public school. Ages 11 and up.

Clunie by Robert Newton Peck, Alfred A. Knopf, 1979.

A teenage girl who is retarded, overweight, and poorly accepted by many of her peers has a variety of difficulties and a generally unhappy life. This story tells a great deal about "how it really is" for many persons who are retarded. Ages 12 and up.

Show Me No Mercy: A Compelling Story of Remarkable Courage by Robert Perske, Abingdon Press, 1984.

Twins, one with Down syndrome, share their lives and discuss some of the unique challenges they face. Ages 10 and up.

In My Sister's Eyes by Grace Posner, Beaufort Books, 1980.

The story is about a sister who has mental retardation who is at times considered the "skeleton in the closet." Ages 12 and up.

My Brother Is Special by Maureen Crane Wartski, Westminster, 1979.

A teenage girl loves her brother, who is retarded. She can't understand people who think of individuals who are retarded as "creatures from another planet." Ages 10 to 13.

My Sister Is Different by Betty Ren Wright, Raintree, 1981.

Carlo has a sister who is retarded. Sometimes he resents her greatly and sometimes he loves her. This is a realistic picture for young readers. Ages 6 to 9.

A Racehorse for Andy by Patricia Wrightson, Harcourt, Brace, 1968.

This is a sensitive portrayal of the desire of a boy who is retarded to be included in his friend's games. Ages 8 to 15.

ORTHOPEDIC AND HEALTH IMPAIRMENTS

Anna Joins In by Katrin Arnold, Abingdon Press, 1982.

Anna, who has cystic fibrosis, deals with peer influence regarding the taking of her medicine. She visits a doctor and participates in many activities. This is a descriptive and frank discussion of Anna's illness. Ages 9 and up.

Crazylegs Merril by Bill J. Carol, Steck, 1969.

This is the story of a lad who has had polio and his success with friends and football. Ages 12 to 14.

Angie and Me by Rebecca Castaldi Jones, Macmillan, 1981.

A girl with severe juvenile rheumatoid arthritis has a terminally ill roommate. Ages 9 to 11.

Accident by Hila Crayder Colman, William Morrow, 1980.

The first date between two teenagers leads to a tragic motorcycle accident. The story provides a look at the slow rehabilitation process and related feelings of anger, hopelessness, and guilt. Ages 11 and up.

Darlene by Eloise Greenfield, Methuen, 1980.

A 6-year-old girl confined to a wheelchair has problems with attitudes. Ages 5 to 7.

Alesia by Eloise Greenfield, Philomel Books, 1981.

Entries in Alesia's diary provide an intimate look at the daily activities of a teenage girl who overcomes her physical limitations with courage and good spirit. Ages 10 to 14.

Circle of Giving by Ellen Howard, Atheneum, 1984.

Marguerite learns more about a neighbor with cerebral palsy and becomes friends with her in the process. Through this process, Marguerite learns to overcome some of her own fears. Ages 9 and up.

Laura's Gift by Dee Jacobs, Oriel, 1980.

This is a story about twins and muscular dystrophy. Ages 11 and up.

Karen by Maria Killilea, Dell Publishing, 1952.

This book tells what can be done for a child who has spastic cerebral palsy and the emotional trauma involved. Ages 13 and up.

With Love from Karen by Marie Killilea, Dell Publishing, 1963.

This is the continuing true story of Karen. It tells how Karen grew up. Ages 9 to 12.

Wren by Marie Killilea, P. H. Dell Publishing, 1968.

This is the story of a child born with cerebral palsy. She is helped by the patience, love, work, and faith of her family. Ages 8 to 12.

You Can't Catch Diabetes from a Friend by Lynne Kipnis, Triad, 1979.

This is a well-done presentation of the problems of juvenile diabetes. It emphasizes the problems of the family. Ages 7 to 12.

Nick Joins In by Joe Lasker, Whitman, 1980.

This is the story of a 7-year-old in a wheelchair, his fear of school, and the growing ability of his classmates to make him a part of the group. It provides a hopeful look at mainstreaming. Ages 5 to 8.

It's a Mile from Here to Glory by Robert C. Lee, Little, Brown, 1972.

Early MacLaren, the school's star runner, is temporarily disabled by a freak accident. His struggles and what he learns about being a person versus being a star makes this book valuable. Ages 9 to 13.

Go Toward the Light by Chris Oyler, Harper & Row, 1988.

This is an account of the experiences of a child who has AIDS. This real-life story may help students better understand the feelings of children who have AIDS. Ages 10 and up.

Only Love by Susan Diana Sallis, Harper & Row, 1980.

This story has sorrow and reality. All does not end on a happy note. It's the first-person narrative of an English girl, a paraplegic who has lived in institutions since she was abandoned as a child. It's a sad love story that may be of value in special circumstances. Ages 12 and up.

On the Move by Harriet M. Savitz, John Day Co., 1973.

After becoming involved with other disabled youths, a formerly sheltered paraplegic girl realizes that she can also learn to lead an independent life. Ages 8 to 12.

Run, Don't Walk by Harriet Savitz, Watts, 1979.

After Samantha is told that she cannot enter the marathon because she is confined to a wheelchair, she realizes why Johnny Jay, another wheelchair student, is determined to fight for what he wants. Ages 8 to 12.

Shutterbug by Lou & Zena Shumsky, Funk & Wagnalls, 1970.

An eighth-grade boy becomes stricken with rheumatic fever. Ages 7 to 11.

Martin Rides the Moor by Vian Smith, Doubleday, 1965.

Gail is struck down by polio, and her recovery is almost halted until a horse brings back her desire to walk. Together, the girl and the horse triumph over fear and pain. Ages 10 to 12.

Let the Balloon Go by Ivan Southall, Bradbury Press, 1985.

This book tells of the decision of a boy with spastic cerebral palsy to no longer accept the words "you can't do that." Ages 9 to 16.

About Handicaps by Sara Bonnet Stein, Walker, 1974.

An interesting story explains "extraordinary ways that ordinary children between 3 and 8 years of age attempt to make sense of difficult events in their lives." The story is about a boy and his friend with cerebral palsy. It is well written, and the photographs are excellent. Ages 12 and up.

My Name Is Jonathan (and I Have AIDS) by Jonathan Swain and Sharon Schilling, Prickly Pair Publishing, 1989.

This is a first-person account of the experiences of a child who has AIDS. It is an excellent way to help build understanding of the unusual emotional impact of AIDS. Ages 10 and up.

Be Not Afraid by Robin White, Berkley Medallion, 1972.

This is the true story of Checkers, who at 8 years of age received a blow on the head that led to incapacitating epilepsy. The story, told by the father, tells much about severe epilepsy but even more about a family's love and compassion. Ages 9 and up.

Marathon Miranda by Elizabeth Winthrop, Holiday House, 1979.

Miranda tells her story and explains some of the problems experienced by children who have severe asthma. Ages 9 to 11.

VISUAL IMPAIRMENT

The Blind Connemara by G. W. Anderson, Macmillan, 1971.

A beautiful white pony is going blind. Rhonda knows that a sightless horse is dangerous to himself and his rider. She cannot stand the thought that he might have to be put away. When Pony is given to her, she is overjoyed. With patience and devotion, she begins to gain his trust and to teach him to move with confidence again. Ages 8 and up.

Gift of Gold by Beverly Butler, Dodd, Mead, 1973.

A young girl is determined to prove she can succeed as a speech therapist despite her blindness. Ages 9 to 15.

Light a Single Candle by Beverly Butler, Dodd, Mead, 1964.

A girl finds she must face a very different way of living when she loses her sight at age 14. The greatest challenges are in the attitudes of other people rather than in her physical disability. Ages 8 to 12.

A Girl and Five Brave Horses by Sonora Carver, Doubleday, 1961.

A young lady is injured riding stunt horses and learns to ride again even though blind. Ages 11 and up.

See You Tomorrow, Charles by Miriam Cohen, Greenwillow Books, 1983.

A boy must learn to cope with his blindness after an accident. Ages 8 to 11.

Finding My Way by Borgheld Dahl, E. P. Dutton, 1962.

In an autobiography, a well-known author gives a gripping account of her day-to-day experiences learning to live with total blindness, continuing her career, and leading a full life. Ages 12 to 15.

Helen Keller by Margaret Davidson, Hastings, 1970.

This excellent book tells the courageous story of Helen Keller and her teacher, Anne Sullivan. Ages 7 to 10.

Seeing Finger, Louis Braille by Etta DeGering, McKay, 1963.

This book tells how the French inventor of a system of reading for the blind adjusted to his own disabilities. Ages 9 to 12.

About Glasses for Gladys by Mark K. Ericsson, Melmont, 1962.

After getting glasses that are just right, Gladys no longer is teased by her classmates about her nearsighted way of reading. Ages 7 to 12.

The Seeing Summer by Jeanette Hyde Eyerly, J. B. Lippincott, 1981.

A 10-year-old is upset when her new neighbor turns out to be blind, but she eventually adjusts to the situation. A kidnapping and adventure are wrapped into this fast-paced story. Ages 8 to 10.

Follow My Leader by James Garfield, Viking Press, 1967

This story of an 11-year-old boy who is blinded in an accident describes how he overcomes this blindness and uses a Seeing Eye dog. Ages 9 to 12.

Half the Battle by Lynn Hall, Charles Scribner's Sons, 1982.

An 18-year-old who is blind and his sighted brother make a grueling, 100-mile trip on horseback. The trip highlights their conflict and their genuine affection for each other. Ages 11 and up.

Mary Lou and Johnny: An Adventure in Seeing by Mildred Hart, Watts, 1963.

When Mary Lou befriends her young neighbor, who is blind, he helps her with her problems. They brighten life for each other and for their friends in a story that emphasizes the importance of not feeling or expressing pity for individuals with disabilities. Ages 8 to 11.

Sound of Sunshine, Sound of Rain by Florence Heide, Parents' Magazine Press, 1970.

With feeling and sensitivity, this book communicates the world of a child who happens to be blind. Ages 5 to 7.

What's That? by Virginia Jensen, Collins, 1979.

This book is about the adventures of imaginary characters. The book can be used with all children, but it is especially designed for children who are visually impaired or blind. The design of the book is tactual, so children can use the sense of touch to actually feel the characters of the story. Ages 5 to 7.

The Rose-Colored Glasses by Linda Leggett and Linda Andrews, Human Sciences Press, 1979.

Melanie loses most of her vision in a car accident and must wear "ugly" glasses to aid her vision. The story describes the initial reaction of her classmates and tells how the teacher, Melanie, and a friend help the class understand Melanie's situation. Ages 7 and up. *Note:* this book is a bit harsh and sarcastic.

Through Grandpa's Eyes by Patricia Maclachlan, Harper & Row, 1980.

This book can be used to help children understand the aging process or to help children understand the world of someone who is blind. In this story, Grandpa is blind and his grandson John attempts to understand the world as his grandpa does—through using his other senses. Ages 8 to 12.

Stevie's Other Eyes by Lois Eddy McDonnell, Creative Educational Society, 1962.

A boy who is blind learns about the outside world and teaches something to his sighted companions. He proves that he can do many of the things they can do and earns their respect and admiration. Ages 7 to 11.

"Seeing" in the Dark by Elizabeth Rider Montgomery, Garrard, 1979.

A young girl who is blind moves to a new home and must adjust to a new teacher and new classmates. This mainstreaming success story emphasizes her strengths and the generally helpful attitudes on the part of classmates. Ages 5 to 7.

Jennifer Jean, the Cross-Eyed Queen by Phyllis Naylor, Lerner Publications, 1967.

This story is about a cross-eyed girl and how she avoids ridicule even when her eyes are in the process of being straightened (she has to wear glasses and a patch). Ages 5 to 12.

Triumph of the Seeing Eye by Peter Putnam, Harper & Row, 1963.

A man who is blind writes of the history and workings of the Seeing Eye and explains the great love between a Seeing Eye dog and his master. Ages 12 and up.

My Mother Is Blind by Margaret Reuter, Children's Press, 1979.

In this story, a family must adjust to a parent's blindness. Ages 5 to 8.

Blind Outlaw by Glen Harold Rounds, E. P. Dutton, 1981.

A blind horse and a teenager who cannot speak respond to each other and form a lasting bond. Ages 9 to 12.

To Catch an Angel by Robert Russell, Vanguard, 1962.

This autobiography was written by a man who was blinded at the age of 5 yet proceeded to become a great scholar, fine wrestler, and finally an associate professor, all through his determination. Ages 8 to 13.

The Road to Agra by Aimee Somerfelt, Criterion, 1961.

A village boy walks nearly 300 miles with his 7-year-old sister to a hospital where her blindness may be cured. Ages 8 to 12.

The Cay by Theodore Taylor, Doubleday, 1969.

This story is about Phillip, who loses his sight from a blow to the head. He and Timothy find themselves cast on an island after the freighter on which they were traveling is torpedoed. The book tells of their struggle for survival and of Phillip's effort to adjust to his blindness and overcome learned prejudice. Ages 12 to 15.

The New Boy Is Blind by William E. Thomas, Julian Messner, 1980.

This books tells what individuals who are blind and individuals who are nondisabled can learn from each other. Ages 6 to 10.

Window for Rosemary Marguerite Vance, Harcourt Brace, 1965.

Blind from birth, Rosemary enjoys all of the ordinary childhood activities because her parents' loving, unsentimental attitude toward her gives her a sense of security and independence. Her sighted brother is a good friend. Ages 8 to 12.

Run with the Ring by Kathryn Vinson, Harcourt Brace, 1965.

This book tells the painful struggles of an intelligent boy to accept the limitations imposed by sudden blindness. Ages 13 and up.

The Lake Is on Fire by Maureen Crane Wartski, Westminster, 1981.

An auto accident blinds Ricky and kills his best friend. Ricky is deeply depressed and attempts suicide. This story outlines his comeback and includes adventure. Ages 10 to 13.

Dead End Bluff by Elizabeth Wetheridge, Atheneum, 1965.

Despite his blindness, Quig wants to be as much like other boys as he can be, but an overprotective father prevents it. A summer job tests and proves Quig's capabilities and shows his father that Quig can climb and swim like other boys. Ages 9 to 11.

Second Sight for Tommy by Regina J. Woody, Westminster, 1972.

This is a story of bravery, discovery, blindness, life, death, love, and loneliness. Ages 10 to 14.

BOOKS FOR ADULTS

The following books were written primarily for adults, but they are about children and youth who have severe behavior disorders and may be of value to teachers and high-school-age youth who have an interest in behavior disorders. The books in this section are listed alphabetically according to author.

Dibs: In Search of Self by Virginia Axline, Ballantine Books, 1976.

This is an account of a young autistic-like child, Dibs, who is involved in play therapy sessions. It provides insight into the nature of autism and the process of play therapy. Ages 14 and up.

I Never Promised You a Rose Garden by Hannah Green, Signet, 1964.

This is a novel about Deborah, a 16-year-old who spends 3 years in a mental hospital. This classic work provides valuable insights into the world of a girl who is psychotic, life in a mental hospital, and the difficult road back to reality.

A Child Called Noah by Josh Greenfeld, Pocket Books, 1970.

This true story of raising a child who is autistic provides a realistic picture of the anger and despair of parents who find little real help in their quest for understanding of Noah's condition.

A Place for Noah by Josh Greenfeld, Pocket Books, 1978.

The continuing story of Noah is told by his father, who rejects the term *autistic* in favor of *brain damaged*. Noah is 11 years old, and his father feels even more anger in the lack of viable programs and services for Noah. This story provides additional insight into the relationships between Noah, his parents, and his brother.

One Child by Torey Hayden, Avon Books, 1980.

This is the story of 6-year-old Sheila, who was placed in a class for individuals who are mentally retarded after she committed a serious act of violence against a 3-year-old. Sheila had been abused by her father, abandoned by her mother, and was apparently without emotion. This is another story of the triumph of a teacher's persistence and love.

Lovey: A Very Special Child by Mary Mac-Cracken, Signet, 1976.
This is the story of Hannah, a child who is behaviorally disordered, and a teacher who was able to reach her. This true story provides a glimpse of the success that may be found with some children who are behaviorally disordered.

Lisa, Bright and Dark by John Neufeld, Signet, 1969.
This is a novel about a 16-year-old who thinks she is crazy, and three friends who try to serve as her therapists when her parents choose to ignore her plea for help.

A P P E N D I X   B

ADDITIONAL SOURCES OF INFORMATION

Administration on
  Developmental Disabilities
200 Independence Avenue, S.W.
Washington, DC 20201

Alexander Graham Bell
  Association for the Deaf, Inc.
3417 Volta Place, N.W.
Washington, DC 20007

American Academy for Cerebral
  Palsy and Developmental
  Medicine
2405 Westwood Avenue
P.O. Box 11083
Richmond, VA 23230

American Association on
  Mental Retardation
1719 Kalorama Road, N.W.
Washington, DC 20009

American Association of
  Psychiatric Services for
  Children
1133 Fifteenth Street, N.W.,
  Suite 1000
Washington, DC 20005

American Association of School
  Administrators
1801 North Moore Street
Arlington, VA 22209

American Bar Association Child
  Advocacy Center
1800 M Street, N.W., Suite 200
Washington, DC 20036

American Cancer Society
777 Third Avenue
New York, NY 10017

American Council for the Blind
1010 Vermont Avenue, N.W.,
  Suite 1100
Washington, DC 20005

American Diabetes Association
1819 H Street, N.W., Suite 1200
Washington, DC 20006

American Epilepsy Society
179 Allyn Street, Suite 304
Hartford, CT 06103

American Foundation for the
  Blind
15 West 16th Street
New York, NY 10011

American Juvenile Arthritis
  Organization
1314 Spring Street, N.W.
Atlanta, GA 30309

American Occupational
  Therapy Association
1383 Piccard Drive, P.O. Box
  1725
Rockville, MD 20850

American Physical Therapy
  Association
1111 N. Fairfax Street
Alexandria, VA 22314

American Printing House for
  the Blind
1839 Frankfort Avenue
Louisville, KY 40206

American Psychiatric
  Association
1400 K Street, N.W.
Washington, DC 20005

American Psychological
  Association
1200 Seventeenth Street, N.W.
Washington, DC 20036

American Speech-Language-
  Hearing Association
10801 Rockville Pike
Rockville, MD 20852

Apple Computer's Office of
  Special Education Programs
20525 Mariani Avenue
Cupertino, CA 95014

Association for the Education
  and Rehabilitation of the
  Blind and Visually Impaired
206 North Washington Street,
  Suite 320
Alexandria, VA 22314

Autism Society of America
1234 Massachusetts Avenue,
  N.W., Suite 1017
Washington, DC 20005

Braille Circulating Library
2700 Stuart Avenue
Richmond, VA 23220

Clearinghouse on the
  Handicapped
Office of Special Education and
  Rehabilitation Services
330 C Street, S.W., Switzer
  Building
Washington, DC 20202

Clearinghouse and Research in
  Child Abuse and Neglect
P.O. Box 1182
Washington, DC 20013

Council for Disability Rights
343 South Dearborn, #318
Chicago, IL 60604

Council for Exceptional
  Children
1920 Association Drive
Reston, VA 22091

Cystic Fibrosis Foundation
6931 Arlington Road
Bethesda, MD 20814

Disability Law Center, Inc.
11 Beacon Street, Suite 925
Boston, MA 02108

Disability Rights Center, Inc.
1616 P Street, N.W., Suite 435
Washington, DC 20036

Epilepsy Foundation of America
4351 Garden City Drive, Suite
  406
Landover, MD 20785

Gifted Child Society, Inc.
190 Rock Road
Glenrock, NJ 07452

Gallaudet University Press
800 Florida Avenue, N.E.
Washington, DC 20002

IBM National Support Center
  for Persons with Disabilities
P.O. Box 2150
Atlanta, GA 30055

Juvenile Diabetes Foundation
  International
60 Madison Avenue
New York, NY 10010

Learning Disabilities
  Association of America
4156 Library Road
Pittsburgh, PA 15234

Leukemia Society of America
733 Third Avenue, 14th Floor
New York, NY 10017

Muscular Dystrophy
  Association
810 Seventh Avenue
New York, NY 10019

National Aid to the Visually
  Handicapped
3201 Balboa Street
San Francisco, CA 94121

National Association of the
  Deaf
814 Thayer Avenue
Silver Spring, MD 20910

National Association for the
  Deaf-Blind
12573 S.E. 53rd Street
Bellevue, WA 98006

National Association for Down
  Syndrome
P.O. Box 4542
Oak Brook, IL 60521

National Association of Parents
  of the Deaf
814 Thayer Avenue
Silver Spring, MD 20910

National Association for
  Parents of the Visually
  Impaired
P.O. Box 180806
Austin, TX 78718

National Association for
  Retarded Citizens
2501 Avenue J
Arlington, TX 76006

National Association of School
  Psychologists
1511 K Street, N.W., Suite 716
Washington, DC 20005

National Association for Sickle
  Cell Disease
3460 Wilshire Boulevard, Suite
  1012
Los Angeles, CA 90010

National Association of State
  Directors of Special
  Education
2021 K Street, N.W., Suite 315
Washington, DC 20006

National Association for the
  Visually Handicapped
305 East 24th Street
New York, NY 10010

National Braille Press
86 St. Stephen Street
Boston, MA 02115

National Center for Stuttering
200 East 33rd Street
New York, NY 10016

National Council for the
Handicapped
800 Independence Avenue, S.W.
Washington, DC 20008

National Down Syndrome
Congress
1640 West Roosevelt Road
Chicago, IL 60608

National Easter Seal Society for
Crippled Children and
Adults
2023 West Ogden Avenue
Chicago, IL 60612

The National Foundation for
Ileitis and Colitis
444 Park Avenue South
New York, NY 10016

The National Hemophilia
Association
The Soho Building
110 Greene Street, Room 406
New York, NY 10012

National Information Center for
Handicapped Children and
Youth
P.O. Box 1492
Washington, DC 20013

National Kidney Foundation
2 Park Avenue, Suite 908
New York, NY 10016

National Library Services for
the Blind and Physically
Handicapped
Library of Congress
1291 Taylor Street, N.W.
Washington, DC 20542

National Multiple Sclerosis
Society
205 East 42nd Street
New York, NY 10017

National Retinitis Pigmentosa
(RP) Foundation, Inc.
1401 Mount Royal Avenue
Baltimore, MD 21217

National Tay-Sachs and Allied
Diseases Association
92 Washington Avenue
Cedarhurst, NY 11516

The Orton Society (Dyslexia)
724 York Road
Baltimore, MD 21204

Recording for the Blind, Inc.
215 East 58th Street
New York, NY 10022

Scoliosis Research Society
444 North Michigan Avenue
Chicago, IL 60611

Spina Bifida Association of
America
1700 Rockville Pike, Suite 540
Rockville, MD 20852

Telecommunications for the
Deaf, Inc.
814 Thayer Avenue
Silver Spring, MD 20910

United Cerebral Palsy
Association, Inc.
66 East 34th Street
New York, NY 10016

GLOSSARY

AAMR The American Association on Mental Retardation. An organization of individuals from many professional disciplines, concerned with mental retardation. For the most part, the AAMR is an organization of professionals. (Most other groups organized on behalf of individuals who are mentally retarded include primarily parents and laypersons.)

absence (petit mal) seizures Epileptic seizures of short duration (5 to 20 seconds) that may occur as many as a hundred times a day. An individual may become pale and stare into space, his or her eyelids may twitch, and he or she may demonstrate jerky movements.

academic planning meeting Group meeting in which the students and teacher plan the academic program.

acceleration A process leading to a student's accelerated movement through the various grade levels, including early entrance to school, skipping grades, and early or advanced college placement.

acuity Acuteness or keenness, as of hearing or vision.

adaptive behavior Ability to meet standards set by society for a cultural group. The American Association on Mental Retardation considers three areas of performance in assessing adaptive behavior: maturation, learning, and social adjustment.

adaptive physical education Physical education programs designed to meet the specific needs of students who have disabilities.

Adlerian theory Theory suggesting that schools must become truly democratic, with students playing an active role in the process of their education. One advocate is Rudolph Dreikurs.

ambulation Walking without assistance from others. It may include the use of crutches, a cane, or other mechanical aids.

aphasia Loss or impairment of the ability to use oral language.

articulation problems Most common type of speech problem including addition (*buhrown* for *brown*, *cuhow* for *cow*), distortion (*shled* for *sled*), omission (*pay* for *play*, *cool* for *school*, *ift* for *lift*), substitution (*dat* for *that*, *wabbit* for *rabbit*, or *thum* for *some*).

assertive discipline An approach to classroom management that encourages teachers to be in control of classrooms through clear identification of expectations plus an understanding of how to respond to student behavior assertively but without hostility. Lee and Marlene Canter are leading advocates of this approach.

athetoid cerebral palsy A type of cerebral palsy that involves recurring, slow wormlike movements of the hands and feet.

audiogram Graph on which results of audiometric evaluation are charted to indicate the ability to hear each tone at each of the presented frequencies.

audiologist Hearing specialist who administers an audiometric examination.

audiometer Instrument that produces sounds at varying intensities (loudness) and varying frequencies (pitch) for testing purposes.

audiometric evaluation A hearing test using a series of carefully calibrated tones that vary in loudness and pitch. This evaluation assists in determining the extent and type of hearing loss so that proper remedial or medical steps can be taken to overcome the problem.

aura, epileptic Subjective sensation that precedes and marks the onset of an epileptic seizure.

autism Disorder rendering an individual noncommunicative and withdrawn.

behavior modification Techniques offering

tools and systematic procedures that teachers may implement to change or modify unacceptable or defiant behavior and encourage more acceptable and appropriate behavior.

brainstorming A problem-solving process in which a group of individuals attempt to find solutions to a specified problem. Brainstorming sessions typically involve verbalizing and recording in some brief written form a variety of solutions. No judgment or initial evaluation of solutions is made by either the facilitator or participants, thus encouraging innovative ideas. After a preset time period (15 to 20 minutes in many settings), evaluation and discussion take place.

cane technique Use of a cane as an aid to mobility.

career education The combination of experiences through which one acquires the attitudes, knowledge, and skills required for successful community living and employment. *Career education* is much broader than a series of courses in vocational or occupational areas.

CEC The Council for Exceptional Children.

central nervous system (CNS) That part of the nervous system to which the sensory impulses are transmitted and from which motor impulses originate. In vertebrates, the brain and spinal cord.

cerebral palsy A group of conditions that may seriously limit motor coordination. Cerebral palsy is commonly present at birth but may be acquired any time as the result of head injury or infectious disease. The conditions are characterized by varying degrees of disturbance of voluntary movement.

class-action suit Litigation instigated on behalf of a group of individuals in a common situation (such as students with similar disabilities).

classification Indicating, as a matter of written record, that a committee of professionals has determined a specific type of disability, based on the use of appropriate testing, data gathering, and group consideration and discussion. Traditional classification categories were established by PL 94–142 and reaffirmed in later legislation and regulations; however, the various states may use somewhat different classification categories.

cleft lip or palate Congenital fissure of the palate or lip that can cause articulation errors and problems with nasality. Normally corrected by surgery.

cognition The process of comprehending and understanding information. The term *cognitive development* is perhaps more often used than cognition and includes efforts to learn new facts and develop new understandings and concepts. Most cognitive development is believed to be a result of relating new experiences to previously developed knowledge and understandings.

colostomy Surgical procedure in which an artificial anal opening is formed in the colon.

complex partial (psychomotor or temporal lobe) seizures Complex seizures that affect motor systems and mental processes and are manifested by peculiar behavior, such as licking or chewing of lips or purposeless activities. May last for a few minutes or several hours.

conductive hearing loss Hearing loss caused by interference with the transmission of sound from the outer ear.

congenital Present in an individual at birth.

consent decree Formal approval by the court of an out-of-court agreement reached by plaintiffs and defendants. It ends litigation, thus saving time and cost.

continuum of alternative placements Full spectrum of services that may be tailored to the needs of each student at any time during the student's educational career.

contracture Condition of muscle characterized by fixed high resistance to passive stretch and generally caused by prolonged immobilization.

control braces Braces to prevent or eliminate purposeless movement or to allow movement in only one or two directions.

cooperative plan Plan in which the student is enrolled in a special class but attends a regular classroom for part of the school day. The student's homeroom is a special class.

corrective braces Braces for prevention and correction of deformity during a child's rapid growth.

crisis, or helping, teacher Teacher who provides temporary support and control to troubled students when they are unable or unwilling to cope with the demands of the regular classroom.

cystic fibrosis Hereditary disease resulting from a generalized dysfunction of the pancreas.

decibel (dB) Unit of measurement of the loudness of sound.

defiant behavior Stubborn or aggressive behavior resulting from forces within a student or the environment, including interactions with significant others.

delayed speech Condition wherein a child does not talk by the time when normal developmental guidelines would indicate that he or she should be talking.

diabetes Metabolic disorder wherein the individual's body is unable to utilize and properly store sugar. It is the result of the inability of the pancreas to produce a sufficient amount of the hormone insulin.

diabetic coma Condition caused by too much sugar (too little insulin), resulting from failure to take insulin, illness, or neglect of proper diet.

diagnosogenic theory Theory that sees the cause of stuttering as the labeling of normal disfluencies by individuals in a child's early environment.

direction taking Travel method employed by individuals who are visually impaired. It involves using an object or sound to establish a course of direction toward or away from an object.

disability Objective, measurable lack of function; lowered capacity or incapacity.

Down syndrome A clinical type of mental retardation related to an abnormal arrangement of chromosomes.

Duchenne (childhood) muscular dystrophy Generally fatal disease characterized by slow deterioration of the voluntary muscles and ending in a state of complete helplessness.

due process Procedures and policies established to ensure equal educational opportunities for all children. PL 94–142 contains due process procedures specific to students who have disabilities.

dyslexia Severe reading disability accompanied by visual perceptual problems and problems in writing, such as reversals and mirror writing.

educable mentally retarded (EMR) Term used to describe a student who displays mental retardation and has an IQ of 50 to 70 and similarly retarded adaptive behavior. The concept of mild or educable mentally retarded implies that the student can be educated and that with proper educational opportunity, he or she can be a self-supporting, participating member of society.

efficacy studies Research specifically established to determine the extent to which given educational practices or procedures achieve the desired effects.

electronic mobility devices Devices to enhance hearing efficiency, detect obstacles, enable an individual to walk in a straight line, or reveal specific location of obstacles in the environment.

environmental factors Variables such as poverty, racial discrimination, school pressures, and deteriorating families considered when evaluating students.

epilepsy Not a disease in itself but a sign or symptom of some underlying disorder in the nervous system. Convulsions or seizures are the main symptoms related to this term.

etiology The study of causes or origins of a disease or condition.

Flanders classroom-interaction analysis Teacher evaluation tool that takes into consideration the verbal behavior of teachers and students. The interactions are analyzed on the basis of categories.

frustration theory Theory about the cause of stuttering, based on the idea that a student may have an unusual need to be listened to. In the drive to keep the listener's attention, normal disfluencies cause the speaker to become more and more frustrated.

Galloway nonverbal system Teacher evaluation system that contains a procedure for decoding nonverbal cues associated with six of the seven teacher behaviors of the Flanders category system.

glad notes Notes given to students or parents by teachers for positive actions by students which help overcome social or academic difficulties.

generalized tonic-clonic seizures Major seizures, usually involving loss of consciousness, general convulsive movements, and at times, frothy saliva from the mouth. The individual may also lose control of his or her bowel and bladder.

handicap Subjective or environmental limitation associated with disability.

hearing loss Inability to perceive sounds.

hemophilia Hereditary blood disorder resulting in insufficient clotting.

hertz (Hz) Unit of measurement used to express frequency of sound.

hospital-bound and homebound Terms used for students who have conditions requiring long-term treatment in a hospital or at home. Such students receive special instruction from homebound or itinerant special education personnel.

hostile aggressiveness Behavior characterized by violence toward teachers, peers, and parents, including kicking, hitting, biting, and fighting.

humanistic approach Approach that involves the acceptance of a student's behavior and the reflection of that behavior back to the student. This direct and uncomplicated framework encourages the student to learn, to express, and to better understand his or her feelings in a caring, reflective environment.

hyperactivity Condition characterized by incessant motion or activity that interferes with learning.

hypoglycemia A condition in which there is an unusually low level of circulating glucose in the blood. This may lead to lethargy and learning disabilities.

incontinence Lack of bowel or bladder control.

individualized education program (IEP) Tool to assure that each student has an educational plan that has been developed on the basis of his or her individual needs.

In-school suspension A procedure in which a student is removed from his or her assigned classroom to another room (such as an unused room or the counselor's room) on a temporary basis. Ordinarily, such suspensions are the result of certain specified behaviors. Such suspensions must be supervised and should be for specified time periods.

insulin Protein hormone produced by the pancreas and secreted into the blood, where it regulates carbohydrate (sugar) metabolism. Used in treatment and control of diabetes mellitus.

integrate To include and educate in the regular classroom. Implies joint effort on behalf of special and general educators.

itinerant teacher Traveling teacher who works with a student on a regularly scheduled basis depending on the student's needs at a particular time.

kinesthesis The sense by which movement, weight, position, and so on are perceived.

kyphosis Curvature of the spine; hunchback.

language nonfluency General lack of smoothness in language production.

learning disabled Displaying the following characteristics: (a) significant discrepancy between achievement and apparent ability to achieve or perform, (b) normal or above-average intelligence, and (c) normal sensory acuity.

learning lab Diagnostic and prescriptive center designed to meet the needs of each student.

legally blind Category of individuals having central visual acuity of 20/200 or less in the better eye after correction, or visual acuity of more than 20/200 if there is a defect in which the widest diameter of the visual field subtends an angle no greater than 20 degrees.

listening helper or buddy Peer in the classroom who helps a student who is hearing impaired in such things as turning to the correct page, taking notes, or adjusting to a new class or school.

litigation Carrying on a suit in a court of law.

magic circle Technique used by elementary

school teachers to help students dispel the feeling that they are significantly different from those around them. The teacher attempts to foster an atmosphere of warmth and honesty, in which each student contributes his thoughts and feelings and listens respectfully to peers.

mainstreaming Maximum integration of students who are disabled into regular classrooms, coupled with concrete assistance for non-special education teachers.

manual communication A method of communication in which fingerspelling or sign language is used in place of speech.

mental retardation Significantly subaverage general intellectual functioning existing concurrently with deficits in adaptive behavior and manifested during the developmental period.

misclassification Inaccurate classification (see *classification*). Misclassification of many minority students was a major factor in the litigation against school districts that contributed to the move toward mainstreaming.

mobility Individual's movement from one point in his or her environment to another.

muscular dystrophy A progressive condition in which the muscles are replaced by fatty tissue.

myelomeningocele Type of spina bifida in which a sac containing part of a malformed spinal cord protrudes from a hole in the spine.

near-point vision Ability to see at close range, as in reading.

neurotic-tendencies theory Theory that portrays stuttering as the outcome of such needs as satisfaction of anal and oral desires, infantile tendencies, and other Freudian-theory regressions.

occupational therapy Therapy directed at upper extremities, emphasizing activities of daily living, such as tying shoes and eating.

ophthalmologist Medical doctor specializing in the diagnosis and treatment of diseases of the eye; licensed to prescribe glasses and contact lenses. Also called an oculist.

Optacon Device that converts printed material to either a tactile or auditory stimulus.

optician Technician who makes glasses and contact lenses and fills the prescriptions of ophthalmologists and optometrists.

optometrist Specialist in eye problems who does not possess a medical degree. Licensed to measure visual function and prescribe and fit glasses and contact lenses.

oral communication Approach to teaching students who are hearing impaired. Communication is carried on through spoken language, such as speechreading, listening, and writing without sign language or fingerspelling.

orientation Blind individual's use of the remaining senses to establish position and relationship to objects in the environment.

orthopedic impairments Physical impairments related to disorders of the joints, skeleton, or muscles. Students with orthopedic impairments make up one major part of the more general classification *physically disabled*; the other major part relates to health impairments, such as asthma, and diabetes.

orthoptist A nonmedical technician who directs prescribed exercises or training to correct eye-muscle imbalances and generally works under the direction of an ophthalmologist.

osteoarthritis Degenerative arthritis usually confined to one joint.

otologist Medical doctor specializing in diseases of the ear.

overattention Condition in which an individual focuses on one particular object and seems unable to break the focus.

paralysis Loss or impairment of function in a part of the body.

paraplegia Paralysis of the lower limbs or lower section of the body.

partially sighted Category of individuals whose visual acuity is better than 20/200 but is still significantly impaired.

pedagogy The art, science, or profession of teaching.

perceptual disorders Disorders involving visual, auditory, tactile, or kinesthetic perception.

perfectionism Extreme fear of failure or criticism, sometimes seen in students who are troubled.

perseveration   Persistent repetition without apparent purpose.

physical therapy   Therapy directed at the lower extremities, emphasizing posture, gait, movements, and the prevention of contractures.

plus factors   Additional instruction that students who are visually impaired might need in nonacademic areas, such as braille, orientation and mobility, and typewriting.

poliomyelitis   Acute viral disease characterized by involvement of the central nervous system. Sometimes results in paralysis.

postlingual deafness   Deafness occurring after the development of speech and language.

prelingual deafness   Deafness that is present at birth or develops in early life, before the development of speech and language.

prereferral intervention   A system in which special consultive help is requested, with the hope that formal placement within the framework of special education services might never be required. Prereferral intervention is based on the principle of prevention.

pressure theory   Theory that views the cause of stuttering as developmental pressure that promotes disfluency.

problem-solving meeting   Group meeting in which students learn to examine situations, propose solutions, and evaluate the results.

prosthesis   Artificial arm or leg to replace an amputated part of the body.

psychoanalytical approach   Approach to troubled students in which teachers provide ways for the students to bring into consciousness their unconscious repressions. All program cueing comes from the students. Used in residential schools and not readily adaptable to public schools.

quadriplegia   Paralysis affecting both arms and both legs.

readability level   Indication of the difficulty of reading material by the grade level at which students might be expected to be read it successfully.

referral   In most cases, a formal request for assistance in planning a more meaningful educational program for a specific student. This usually means completing a form providing certain basic information on the student, including reason(s) assistance is required. (See also *prereferral intervention.*)

Regular Education Initiative (REI)   The name given a movement to promote restructuring of the special education-regular education relationship. The REI has been defined and interpreted differently by various special educators.

rehabilitation   Restoring to a former capacity. For example, a student may suffer damage to a limb and, through therapy, the limb may be restored to good condition and use. The term is commonly applied to a variety of services that are designed to help individuals overcome disabilities, especially in preparation for employment—such services are referred to as vocational rehabilitation services.

remediation   Correction of a deficiency. Often refers to correction of academic deficits, such as problems in reading.

residential, or boarding, school   School established for students who are visually or hearing impaired, emotionally disturbed, or mentally retarded because local school districts did not offer the services needed. Usually provides 24-hour care and treatment.

residual hearing   Individual's remaining hearing after some hearing loss.

resource room teacher   Teacher who provides supplemental or remedial instruction (usually daily) to a child enrolled in a regular classroom. The assistance is regularly scheduled in a room that has been specifically designated for that purpose.

responsibility-oriented classroom   Classroom in which students are responsible for their own behavior, academic success, and failure. They cannot blame the environment, parents, or peers; they have the ability to choose. The classroom is neither a teacher-dominated nor a student-controlled room, but rather is a joint effort to learn, relate, and experience. One advocate is William Glasser.

rheumatoid arthritis   Systemic disease characterized by inflammation of the joints and a broad spectrum of other manifestations involving destruction of the joints and resultant deformity.

rubella   German measles.

scoliosis Abnormal lateral curvature of the spine (C curve).

seizures Excessive electrical discharges released in some nerve cells of the brain, resulting in loss of control over muscles, consciousness, senses, and thoughts.

sensorineural hearing loss Hearing loss associated with damage to the sensory end organ or a dysfunction of the auditory nerve.

sighted-guide technique Technique in which an individual who is visually impaired grasps the arm of a sighted person just above the elbow, enabling him or her to "read" any movement of the guide's body.

Snellen chart Chart consisting of letters, numbers, or symbols of graduated sizes to be read at a distance of 20 feet to determine field visual acuity. A special Snellen chart to be read at a distance of 14 inches may be used to measure near vision.

sociometry A technique used to measure the social structure of a group or class.

spastic cerebral palsy A condition characterized by jerky or explosive motions when an individual initiates a voluntary movement.

special education A subsystem of the total educational system for the provision of specialized or adapted programs and services or for assisting others to provide such services for exceptional youth and children.

special educator One who has had specialized training or preparation for teaching children who are disabled. May also work cooperatively with regular classroom teachers by sharing unique skills and competencies.

speech disorder Speech that (a) interferes with communication, (b) causes the speaker to be maladjusted, or (c) calls undue attention to the speech as opposed to what is said.

speechreading A highly important skill for individuals who are hearing impaired. Individuals learn to observe lip movements, facial gestures, body gestures, and other environmental clues, to supplement whatever degree of residual hearing is present. The term *speechreading* has, for the most part, replaced the term *lipreading*, which emphasized only one part of this skill.

spina bifida Serious birth defect in which the bones of the spine fail to close during the 12th week of fetal development, resulting in a cyst or sac in the lower back that is generally surgically treated during the child's first 24 to 48 hours of life. Varying degrees of paralysis in the lower extremities are generally observed.

tactile Pertaining to the sense of touch.

task analysis Breaking a skill into smaller parts.

taxonomy A classification system.

teacher-move analysis Tool that evaluates interaction between teacher and student by placing teacher behavior into eight categories, called teacher moves.

tinnitus Hearing noises within the head.

total communication Total-language approach for individuals who are hearing impaired, in which there is equal emphasis on speech, auditory training, and a system of visual communication.

trailing To follow lightly over a straight surface with back of fingertips to locate specific objects or to get a parallel line of direction.

visual acuity Measured ability to see.

visual-auditory-kinesthetic-tactile (VAKT) approach Multisensory approach to teaching reading. Designed by Grace Fernald to assist children with severe reading disabilities.

voice problems Disorders of pitch, intensity, quality, or flexibility of the voice.

REFERENCES

Alberto, P. A., & Troutman, A. C. (1990) *Applied behavior analysis for teachers* (3rd ed.). Columbus, OH: Merrill.

Alcorn, P. (1986). *Social issues in technology: A format for investigation.* Englewood Cliffs, NJ: Prentice-Hall.

Alley, G., & Deshler, D. (1979). *Teaching the learning disabled adolescent: Strategies and methods.* Denver: Love.

American Academy of Pediatrics (1984). Administration of medication in school, *Pediatrics, 74,* 433.

American Federation for the Blind (1987). *Low vision questions and answers.* New York: American Federation for the Blind.

American Psychiatric Association (1987). *Diagnostic and statistical manual of mental disorders* (3rd ed., revised). Washington, DC: author.

American Speech-Language-Hearing Association (ASHA), Committee on Language. (1983). Definition of language. *ASHA, 25,* 44.

Anastasi, A. (1982). *Psychological testing* (5th ed.). New York: Macmillan.

Anthony, D. (1971). *Seeing essential English.* Anaheim, CA: Anaheim School District.

Apter, S. (1982). *Troubled children/troubled systems.* New York: Pergamon.

Aronson, E. (1978). *The jigsaw classroom.* Beverly Hills, CA: Sage.

Asher, S. R., & Hymel, S. (1981). Children's social competence in peer relations. In J. D. Wine & M. D. Syme (Eds.), *Sociometric and behavioral assessment.* New York: Guilford.

Asher, S. R., Oden, S. L., & Gottman, J. M. (1981). Children's friendships in school settings. In L. G. Katz (Ed.), *Current topics in early childhood education* (Vol. 1). Norwood, NJ: Albex.

Asher, S. R., & Taylor, A. R. (1982). Social outcomes of mainstreaming: Sociometric assessment and beyond. In Phillip Strain, *Social development of exceptional children.* Rockville, MD: Aspen.

Baca, L. M., & Cervantes, H. T. (Eds.). (1989). *The bilingual special education interface.* Columbus, OH: Merrill.

Baker, C. (1990). *257 things to do about behavior problems.* Greeley, CO: Univ. of Northern Colorado. Unpublished list.

Ballard, J., & Zettel, J. (1977). Public Law 94–142 and section 504: What they say about rights and protections. *Exceptional Children, 44,* 177–185.

Barkley, R. (1981). *Hyperactive children: A handbook for diagnosis and treatment.* New York: Guilford.

Barnetti, S. M., & Parker, L. G. (1982). Suspension and expulsion of the emotionally handicapped: Issues and practices. *Behavioral Disorders, 7*(3), 173–179.

Barraga, N. (1983). *Visual handicaps and learning* (rev. ed.). Austin, TX: Exceptional Resources.

Barry, M. (1986, December). *An exploratory study of how college level students construct schemata from pictures.* Paper presented at the American Reading Forum. Longboat, FL.

Baskin, B., & Harris, K. H. (1985). Reading for the gifted. *ERIC Digest, 362,* Reston, VA: Council for Exceptional Children.

Beez, W. (1970). Influence of biased psychological reports on teacher behavior and pupil performance. In M. Miles & W. Charters, Jr. (Eds.), *Learning and social settings: New readings in the social psychology of education.* Boston: Allyn & Bacon.

Beez, W. V. (1972). Influence of biased psychological reports on teacher behavior and pupil performance. In A. Morrison & D. McIntyre

(Eds.), *The social psychology of teaching.* Baltimore: Penguin Books.

Behrman, R. E., Vaughan, V. C., & Nelson, W. E. (1987). *Nelson textbook of pediatrics* (13th ed.) Philadelphia: W. B. Saunders.

Bennett, R. (1982). Applications of microcomputer technology to special education. *Exceptional Children, 49,* 106–113.

Berger, G. (1987). *Crack, the new drug epidemic.* New York: Impact.

Berko Gleason, J. B. (1985). *The development of language.* Columbus, OH: Merrill.

Bernstein, D. K., & Tiegerman, E. (1989). *Language and communication disorders in children.* (2nd ed.). Columbus, OH: Merrill.

Betts, G. (1985). *Autonomous learner model for the gifted and talented.* Greeley, CO: Autonomous Learning Publications and Specialists.

Betts, G., & Knapp, J. (1981). Autonomous learning and the gifted: A secondary model. In *Secondary programs for the gifted/talented.* Ventura, CA: National/State Leadership Training Institute on the Gifted and Talented.

Bigge, I. L. (1982). *Teaching individuals with physical and multiple disabilities* (2nd ed.). Columbus, OH: Merrill.

Bloom, B. (Ed.). (1956). *Taxonomy of educational objectives: The classification of educational goals: Handbook 1: Cognitive domain.* New York: McKay.

Bloom, B. S. (1971). Mastery learning. In J. H. Block (Ed.), *Mastery learning: theory and practice.* New York: Holt, Rinehart & Winston.

Bloom, L. (1970). *Language development: Form and function of emerging grammars.* Cambridge: MIT Press.

Blumenthal, S. (1985, April 30). *Testimony before the United States Senate on juvenile justice.* Washington, DC: U.S. Department of Health and Human Services.

Borkowski, J. G., Peck, V. A., & Damberg, P. R. (1983). Attention, memory, and cognition. In J. L. Matson & J. A. Mulich (Eds.), *Handbook of mental retardation.* New York: Pergamon.

Bornstein, H. (1974). Signed English: A manual approach to English language development. *Journal of Speech and Hearing Disorders, 3,* 330–343.

Bower, E. M. (1981). *Early identification of emotionally handicapped children in school* (3rd ed.). Springfield, IL: Charles C. Thomas.

Brolin, D. (Ed.). (1978). *Life-centered career education: A competency-based approach.* Reston, VA: Council for Exceptional Children.

Brolin, D. (1982). Life-centered career education for exceptional children. *Focus on Exceptional Children, 14*(7), 1–15.

Brophy, J. E. (1983). Expectations: An update. *Journal of Educational Psychology, 75,* 631–661.

Brophy, J., & Good, T. (1974). *Teacher-student relationships—causes and consequences.* New York: Holt, Rinehart & Winston.

Brown, G., McDowell, R., and Smith, J. (Eds). (1981). *Educating adolescents with behavioral disorders.* Columbus, OH: Merrill.

Brown, L. L., & Hammill, D. (1983). *Behavior Rating Profile.* Austin, TX: Pro-Ed.

Brown, N. (1982). CAMEO: Computer-assisted management of educational objectives. *Exceptional Children, 49,* 151–153.

Bruininks, R., Rynders, J., & Gross, H. (1974). Social acceptance of mildly retarded pupils in resource rooms and regular classes. *American Journal of Mental Deficiency, 78,* 377–383.

Bruner, J. (1974). The organization of early skilled action. In M. P. M. Richards (Ed.), *The integration of a child into a social world.* London: Cambridge Univ. Press.

Bruner, J. (1975). The ontogenesis of speech acts. *Journal of Child Language, 2,* 1–19.

Bryan, T. (1974). Peer popularity of learning disabled children. *Journal of Learning Disabilities, 7,* 621–625.

Buell, C. (1950). *Motor performance of visually handicapped children.* Unpublished doctoral dissertation, University of California, Berkeley.

Burks, H. F. (1977). *Burks Behavior Rating Scales.* Los Angeles: Western Psychological Service.

Burns, N. (1982). *Math for smarty pants.* Boston: Little, Brown.

Buser, K. P., & Reimer, D. (1988). Developing cognitive strategies through problem solving. *Teaching Exceptional Children, 20*(2), 22–25.

Canter, L., & Canter, M. (1976). *Assertive disci-*

pline: A take-charge approach for today's educator. Seal Beach, CA: Canter & Associates.

Cartledge, G., & Milburn, J. F. (1986). *Teaching social skills to children* (2nd ed.). New York: Pergamon.

Cartwright, G. P., Cartwright, C.A., & Ward, M. E. (1984). *Educating special learners*. Belmont, CA: Wadsworth.

Cawley, J. F., Miller, J. H., & School, B. A. (1987). A brief inquiry of arithmetic word-problem-solving among learning disabled secondary students. *Learning Disability Focus, 2*(2), 87–93.

Centers for Disease Control (1989). Guidelines for prevention of transmission of immunodeficiency virus and hepatitis B virus to health-care and public-safety workers. *Morbidity and Mortality Weekly Report, 38.*

Charles, C. M. (1981). *Individualizing instruction*. St. Louis: C. V. Mosby.

Cheek, E. H., Jr., & Cheek, N. C. (1983). *Reading instruction through content teaching*. Columbus, OH: Merrill.

Chinn, P., Drew, C., & Logan, D. (1979). *Mental retardation: A life cycle approach*. St. Louis: C. V. Mosby.

Chomsky, N. (1957). *Syntactic structures*. Houston, TX: The Hague.

Chomsky, N. (1965). *Aspects of the theory of syntax*. Cambridge: MIT Press.

Cicchelli, T., & Ashby-Davis, C. (1986). *Teaching exceptional children and youth in the regular classroom*. Syracuse, NY: Syracuse Univ. Press.

Clark, B. (1988). *Growing up gifted* (3rd ed.). Columbus, OH: Merrill.

Cleary, M. E. (1976). Helping children understand the child with special needs. *Children Today, 5,* 24–31.

Coleman, M. C., & Gilliam, J. E. (1983). Disturbing behaviors in the classroom: A survey of teacher attitudes. *Journal of Special Education, 17,* 121–129.

Collier, C. (1989). Mainstreaming and bilingual exceptional children. In L. M. Baca and H. J. Cervantes (Eds.), *The bilingual special education interface*. Columbus, OH: Merrill.

Combs, A. W., & Avila, D. L. (1985). *Helping relationships: Basic concepts for the helping professions* (3rd ed.). Boston: Allyn & Bacon.

Commission on the Education of the Deaf (1988). *Toward equality: Education of the deaf*. Washington, DC: U.S. Government Printing Office.

Contact maturity: Growing up strong (1972). Englewood Cliffs, NJ: Scholastic Book Services.

Conture, E. G. (1990). *Stuttering* (2nd ed.). Englewood Cliffs, NJ: Prentice-Hall.

Costa, A. L. (1987). Thinking skills: Neither an add-on nor a quick fix. In M. Heiman & J. Slomianko (Eds.), *Thinking skills instruction: Concepts and techniques*. Washington, DC: National Education Association.

Council for Exceptional Children. (1978). *Position paper on career education*. Reston, VA: author.

Crane, J. C., & Reynolds, J. (1983). *Social skills and me*. Houston, TX: Reynolds.

Creasy, R. K., & Resnick, R. (1989). *Maternal-fetal medicine: Principles and practices* (2nd ed.). Philadelphia: W. B. Saunders.

Culatta, R., & Culatta, B. K. (1985). Communication disorders. In W. H. Birdine & A. E. Blackhurst (Eds.), *An introduction to special education* (2nd ed.). Boston: Little, Brown.

Cummings, C. (1980). *Teaching makes a difference*. Edmonds, WA: TEACHING.

Cummins, J. (1984). *Bilingualism and special education: Issues in assessment and pedagogy*. San Diego, CA: College-Hill.

Davis, G., & Rimm, S. (1985). *Education of the gifted and talented*. Englewood Cliffs, NJ: Prentice-Hall.

Dehouske, E. (1982). Story writing as a problem-solving vehicle. *Teaching Exceptional Children, 1*(1), 11–17.

Delisle, J. R., Reis, S. M., & Gubbins, E. J. (1981). The revolving door identification and programming model. *Exceptional Children, 48,* 152–156.

Delquadri, J., Greenwood, C., Whorton, D., Carta, J., & Hall, R. (1986). Classwide peer tutoring. *Exceptional Children, 52,* 535–542.

DeRuiter, J., & Wansart, W. (1982). *Psychology of learning disabilities*. Rockville, MD: Aspen.

Deshler, D., & Schumaker, J. (1986). Learning

strategies: An instructional alternative for low-achieving adolescents. *Exceptional Children, 52,* 583–590.

Devine, T. G. (1987). *Teaching study skills: A guide for teachers* (2nd ed.). Boston: Allyn & Bacon.

DeVries, D. L., & Slavin, R. E. (1978). Team games tournament: A research review. *Journal of Research and Development in Education, 12,* 28–38.

Dinkmeyer, D. (1982). *Developing understanding of self and others—Revised.* Circle Pines, MN: American Guidance Service.

Donaldson, J. (1980). Changing attitudes toward handicapped persons: A review and analysis of research. *Exceptional Children, 46,* 504–512.

Donaldson, R., & Christiansen, J. (1990). Consultation and collaboration: A decision-making model. *Teaching Exceptional Children, 22*(2), 22–25.

Dreikurs, R., & Cassel, P. (1972). *Discipline without tears.* New York: Hawthorn Books.

Dreikurs, R., & Saltz, U. (1964). *Children: The challenge.* New York: Hawthorn Books.

Driscoll, M. (1983). *Research within reach: Secondary school mathematics.* St. Louis: Research & Development Interpretation Service.

Dunn, L. M. (1968). Special education for the mildly retarded: Is much of it justifiable? *Exceptional Children, 35,* 5–22.

Dunn, R. (1983). Learning style and its relation to exceptionality at both ends of the spectrum. *Exceptional Children, 49*(6), 496–506.

Dunn, R., & Dunn, K. (1978). *Teaching students through their individual learning styles.* Reston, VA: Reston Publishing Co.

Dunn, R., & Price, G. (1980). The learning style characteristics of gifted students. *Gifted Child Quarterly, 24*(1), 33–36.

Dusek, J. B. (1985). *Teacher expectancies.* Hillsdale, NJ: Lawrence Erlbaum.

Dusek, J. B., & Joseph, G. (1983). The basis of teacher expectation: A meta-analysis. *Journal of Educational Psychology, 75,* 326–346.

Dworkin, N. (1979). Changing teachers' negative expectations. *Academic Therapy, 14,* 517–530.

Ehly, S. W., & Larsen, S. C. (1980). *Peer tutoring for individualized instruction.* Boston: Allyn & Bacon.

Ekwall, E. (1985). *Locating and correcting reading difficulties* (4th ed.). Columbus, OH: Merrill.

Ellis, E. S. (1989). A metacognitive intervention for increasing class participation. *Learning Disabilities Focus, 5*(1), 36–46.

Ellis, N. R. (1970). Memory processes in retardates and normals. *International Review of Research in Mental Retardation, 4.*

Enright, B., & Beattie, J. (1989). Problem solving step by step in math. *Teaching Exceptional Children, 22*(1), 58–59.

Erickson, M. T. (1987). *Behavior disorders of children and adolescents.* Englewood Cliffs, NJ: Prentice-Hall.

Esposito, B., & Reed, T. (1986). The effects of contact with handicapped persons on young children's attitudes. *Exceptional Children, 53,* 224–229.

Evans, R. J. (1984). Fostering peer acceptance of handicapped students. *ERIC Digest, 1406.* Reston, VA: Council for Exceptional Children.

Executive Committee of the CCBD (1989). Best assessment practices for students with behavioral disorders: Accommodation to cultural diversity and individual differences. *Behavioral Disorders, 14*(4), 263–268.

Federal Register (1977, August 23). Rules and regulations for the implementation of part B of PL 94–142. Washington, DC: U.S. Government Printing Office, 42474–42515.

Fernald, G. (1943). *Remedial techniques in basic school subjects.* New York: McGraw-Hill.

Fink, A., & Semmel, M. (1971). *Indiana behavior management system 2.* Bloomington, IN: Center for Innovation in Teaching the Handicapped.

Flanagan, J. (1960). *Test of general ability: Technical report.* Chicago: Science Research Associates.

Flanders, N. (1965). *Teacher influences, pupil attitudes, and achievement.* Washington: U.S. Department of Health, Education and Welfare, Office of Education.

Fletcher, D. G. (1986). Language of bilingual-bicultural children. In V. Reed (Ed.), *An introduction to children with language disorders.* New York: Macmillan.

Forehand, R., McCombs, A., & Brody, G. H. (1987). The relationship between parental depressive mood states and child functioning. *Advances in Behavior Research and Therapy, 9,* 1–20.

Forest, M., & Lusthaus, E. (1989). Promoting educational equality for all students. In S. Stainback & W. Stainback (Eds.), *Educating all students in the mainstream of regular education.* Baltimore: Paul H. Brookes.

Forest, M., & Lusthaus, E. (1990). Everyone belongs with the MAPS action planning system. *Teaching Exceptional Children, 22*(2), 32–35.

Forness, S. R. (1988). School characteristics of children and adolescents with depression. In R. B. Rutherford, C. M. Nelson, & S. R. Forness (Eds.), *Bases of severe behavioral disorders of children and youth.* Boston: Little, Brown.

Foster, G., Algozzine, B., & Ysseldyke, T. (1980). Classroom teacher and teacher-in-training susceptibility to stereotypical bias. *Personnel and Guidance Journal, 59,* 27–30.

Fowler, D., Rich, S., & Young, P. (1986). San Diego study II: Substance abuse in young cases. *Archives of General Psychiatry, 43,* 962–965.

Fraser, K. (1989). *Someone at school has AIDS.* Alexandria, VA: National Association of State Boards of Education.

Gable, R. A., & Hendrickson, J. M. (1990). *Assessing students with special needs.* New York: Longman.

Galloway, C. (1968). Nonverbal communication. *Theory into Practice, 7,* 172–175.

Gaylord-Ross, R. (Ed.). (1989). *Integration strategies for students with handicaps.* Baltimore: Paul H. Brookes.

Gearheart, B. (1974). *Organization and administration of educational programs for exceptional children.* Springfield, IL: Charles C. Thomas.

Gearheart, B., & Gearheart, C. (1989). *Learning disabilities: Educational strategies* (5th ed.). Columbus, OH: Merrill.

Gearheart, B., DeRuiter, J., & Sileo, T. (1986). *Teaching mildly and moderately handicapped students.* Englewood Cliffs, NJ: Prentice-Hall.

Gearheart, B. R., & Litton, F. (1979). *The trainable retarded: A foundations approach* (2nd ed.). St. Louis: C. V. Mosby.

Gearheart, C., & Gearheart, B. (1990). *Introduction to special education assessment: Principles and practices.* Denver: Love.

Glasser, W. (1965). *Reality therapy.* New York: Harper & Row.

Goldstein, A., Sprafkin, R., Gershaw, N., & Klein, P. (1980). *Skillstreaming the adolescent: A structured learning approach to teaching prosocial skills.* Champaign, IL: Research Press.

Goldstein, H., Moss, J., & Jordan, L. (1965). *The efficacy of special class training on the development of mentally retarded children* (U.S. Office of Education Cooperative Project No. 619). Urbana, IL: Univ. of Illinois.

Good, T. (1970). Which pupils do teachers call on? *Elementary School Journal, 70,* 190–198.

Goodman, H., Gottlieb, J., & Harrison, R. (1972). Social acceptance of EMRs integrated into a nongraded elementary school. *American Journal of Mental Deficiency, 70,* 412–417.

Gottlieb, J., & Budoff, A. (1973). Social acceptability of retarded children in nongraded schools differing in architecture. *American Journal of Mental Deficiency, 78,* 15–19.

Gottlieb, J., Cohen, L., & Goldstein, L. (1974). Social contact and personal adjustments as variables relating to attitudes toward educable mentally retarded children. *Training School Bulletin, 71,* 136–148.

Gresham, F. M. (1982). Misguided mainstreaming: The case for social skills training with handicapped children. *Exceptional Children, 48,* 422–433.

Gronberg, G. (1983). *Attitude responses of nonhandicapped elementary students to specific information and contact with the handicapped.* Unpublished doctoral dissertation, Univ. of Northern Colorado.

Grossman, H. (Ed.). (1973). *Manual on terminology and classification in mental retardation.*

Washington, DC: American Association on Mental Deficiency.

Grossman, H. (Ed.). (1977). *Manual on terminology and classification in mental retardation.* Washington, DC: American Association on Mental Deficiency.

Grossman, H. (1983). *Classification in mental retardation.* Washington, DC: American Association on Mental Deficiency.

Guetzloe, E. C. (1989). *Youth suicide: What the educator should know.* Reston, VA: Council for Exceptional Children.

Guilford, J. P. (1959). Three faces of intellect. *American Psychologist, 14,* 469–479.

Gustason, G., Pfetzing, D., Zawolkow, E., & Norris, C. (1972). *Signing exact English.* Rossmore, CA: Modern Science.

Guttman, J., & Bar-Tai, D. (1982). Stereotypic perceptions of teachers. *American Educational Research Journal, 19,* 519–528.

Hagen, D. (1984). *Microcomputer resource book for special education.* Reston, VA: Reston Publishing Co.

Haisley, F. B., Christine, A. T., & Andrews, J. (1981). Peers as tutors in mainstream: Trained "teachers" of handicapped adolescents. *Journal of Learning Disabilities, 14,* 224–226.

Hallahan, D., & Kauffman, J. (1978). *Exceptional children: Introduction to special education.* Englewood Cliffs, NJ: Prentice-Hall.

Halperin, M. (1979). *Helping maltreated children: School and community involvement.* St. Louis: C. V. Mosby.

Hammill, D. D., & Bartel, N. R. (1990). *Teaching students with learning and behavior problems* (5th ed.). Boston: Allyn & Bacon.

Hanson, V. (1983). Juvenile rheumatoid arthritis. In J. Umbreit (Ed.), *Physical disabilities and health impairments* (pp. 240–249). Columbus, OH: Merrill.

Hardman, M. L., Drew, C. J., Egan, M. W., & Wolf, J. B. (1990). *Human exceptionality* (3rd ed.). Boston: Allyn & Bacon.

Hargis, C. H. (1982). Word recognition development. *Focus on Exceptional Children, 14*(9), 1–8.

Haring, N. (1990). Overview of special education. In N. Haring & L. McCormick, *Exceptional children and youth: Introduction to special education.* Columbus, OH: Merrill.

Haring, N., & McCormick, L. (1990). *Exceptional children and youth: Introduction to special education.* Columbus, OH: Merrill.

Harris, F. C., & Howard, K. I. (1987). Correlates of depression and anger in adolescence. *Journal of Child and Adolescent Psychotherapy, 4,* 199–203.

Harris, J., & Aldridge, J. (1983). Three for me is better than two for you. *Academic Therapy, 18,* 361–365.

Harris, M. J., & Rosenthal, R. (1985). Mediation of interpersonal expectancy effects: Thirty-one meta-analyses. *Psychological Bulletin, 97,* 363–386.

Hasselbring, T. S., Goin, L. I., & Bransford, J. S. (1987). Developing automaticity. *Teaching Exceptional Children, 19*(3), 30–33.

Hawton, K. (1986). *Suicide and attempted suicide among children and adolescents.* Beverly Hills, CA: Sage.

Heiman, M., & Slomianko, J. (Eds.). (1987). *Thinking skills instruction: Concepts and techniques.* Washington, DC: National Education Association.

Heller, H. W., & Schilit, J. (1987). The regular education initiative: A concerned response. *Focus on Exceptional Children, 20*(3), 1–7.

Hersh, R. H., & Walker, H. M. (1983). Great expectations: Making schools effective for all students. *Policy Studies Review, 2,* 147–188.

Homme, L., Csanyi, A. P., Gonzales, M. A., & Rechs, J. R. (1979). *How to use contingency contracting in the classroom.* Champaign, IL.: Research Press.

Hoover, J. J. (1988). *Teaching handicapped students study skills* (2nd ed.). Lindale, TX: Hamilton Publications.

House Ear Institute. (1985). *So all may hear.* Los Angeles: author.

Howell, K. W., & Morehead, M. K. (1987). *Curriculum-based evaluation for special and remedial education.* Columbus, OH: Merrill.

Hunter, M. (1982). *Mastery teaching.* El Segundo, CA: TIP Publications.

Huntze, S. (1984). *Council for Children with Behavioral Disorders position paper.* Adopted November 14, 1984. Personal communication with Sharon Huntze.

Iano, R., Ayers, D., Heller, H., McGettigan, J., & Walker, V. (1974). Sociometric status or retarded children in an integrative program. *Exceptional Children, 40,* 267–271.

Idol, I. (1987). Group story mapping: A comprehension strategy for both skilled and unskilled readers. *Journal of Learning Disabilities, 20*(4), 196–205.

Idol, L., Paolucci-Whitcomb, P., & Nevin, A. (1986). *Collaborative consultation.* Rockville, MD: Aspen.

Idol-Maestas, L. (1981). A teacher training model: The resource/consulting teacher. *Behavioral Disorders, 6,* 108–121.

Indrisano, R. (1982). An ecological approach to learning. *Topics in Learning and Learning Disabilities, 1*(4), 11–15.

Inhelder, B. (1968). *The diagnosis of reading in the mentally retarded.* New York: John Day.

Irwin, R. B. (1955). *As I saw it.* New York: American Foundation for the Blind.

Itard, J. M. G. (1962). *The wild boy of Aveyron.* New York: Appleton-Century-Crofts.

Jackson, G., & Cosca, G. (1974). The inequality of educational opportunity in the Southwest: An observational study of ethnically mixed classrooms. *American Educational Research Journal, 11,* 219–229.

Jackson, N. F., Jackson, D. A., & Monroe, C. (1983). *Getting along with others—teaching social effectiveness to children.* Champaign, IL: Research Press.

Johnson, D., & Myklebust, H. (1967). *Learning disabilities: Educational principles and practices.* New York: Grune & Stratton.

Johnson, D. W., & Johnson, R. T. (1975). *Learning together and alone: Cooperative, competitive, or individualized.* Englewood Cliffs, NJ: Prentice-Hall.

Johnson, D. W., & Johnson, R. T. (1978). Mainstreaming: Will handicapped students be liked, rejected, or ignored? *Instructor, 87,* 152–154.

Johnson, D. W., & Johnson, R. T. (1986). Mainstreaming and cooperative learning strategies. *Exceptional Children, 52,* 553–561.

Johnson, D. W., Johnson, R. T., Nelson, D., & Read, S. (1978). *Mainstreaming: Development of positive interdependence between handicapped and nonhandicapped students.* Minneapolis: Univ. of Minnesota, National Support System.

Johnson-Dorn, N., Stremel-Campbell, K., & Toews, J. (1984). *Developing effective integration between students with severe handicaps and their peers: A teacher's manual.* Washington DC: Office of Special Education.

Jones, V. (1980). *Adolescents with behavior problems: Strategies for teaching, counseling, and parent involvement.* Boston: Allyn & Bacon.

Jose, J., & Cody, J. (1971). Teacher-pupil interaction as it relates to attempted changes in teacher expectancy of academic ability and achievement. *American Educational Research Journal, 8,* 39–49.

Kameenui, E. J., & Simmons, D. C. (1990). *Designing instructional strategies.* Columbus, OH: Merrill.

Kanner, L. (1964). *A history of the care and study of the mentally retarded.* Springfield, IL: Charles C. Thomas.

Kauffman, J. M. (1977). *Characteristics of children's behavior disorders.* Columbus, OH: Merrill.

Kauffman, J. M. (1989). *Characteristics of behavior disorders of children & youth.* Columbus, OH: Merrill.

Kelly, B. W., & Holmes, J. (1979). The guided lecture procedure. *Journal of Reading, 22,* 602–604.

Keogh, B. K. (1988). Improving services for problem learners: Rethinking and restructuring. *Journal of Learning Disabilities, 21,* 19–22.

Kester, S., & Letchworth, G. (1972). Communication of teacher expectations and their effects on achievement and attitudes of secondary school students. *Journal of Educational Research, 66,* 51–55.

Kirk, S. A., & Gallagher, J. J. (1989). *Educating exceptional children.* Boston: Houghton Mifflin.

Kleinberg, S. (1982). *Education of the chronically ill child.* Rockville, MD: Aspen Systems.

Kokaska, C., & Brolin, D. (1985). *Career education for handicapped individuals* (2nd ed.). Columbus, OH: Merrill.

Kraemer, M. J., & Bierman, C. W. (1983). Asthma. In J. Umbreit (Ed.), *Physical disabilities and health impairments* (pp. 159–166). Columbus, OH: Merrill.

Kretschmer, R. R., & Kretschmer, L. N. (1978). *Language development and intervention with the hearing impaired.* Baltimore: University Park.

Kulik, J. A., & Kulik, C. C. (1984). Effects of accelerated instruction on students. *Review of Educational Research, 54*(3), 409–425.

Lambert, N., Windmiller, M., Tharinger, D., and Cole, L. (1981). *AAMD-ABS school edition.* Washington, DC: American Association on Mental Deficiency.

Leacock, E. (1969). *Teaching and learning in city schools.* New York: Basic Books.

Leerhsen, C., & Schaefer, E. (1989, July 31). Pregnancy + alcohol = problems. *Newsweek,* 57.

Leiker, M. (1980). *An affordable gifted program that works.* Denver: Adams School District No. 12.

Lerner, J. W. (1989). *Learning disabilities: Theories, diagnosis and teaching strategies.* Boston: Houghton Mifflin.

Levine, J. (1986, Nov. 3). The toughest virus of all. *Time,* 76–78.

Levine, J. M., & Wang, M. C. (1983). *Teacher and student perceptions: Implications for learning.* Hillsdale, NJ: Lawrence Erlbaum.

Lewis, B. L., & Doorlag, D. (1991). *Teaching special students in the mainstream* (3rd ed.). Columbus, OH: Merrill.

Lilly, M. S. (1988). The regular education initiative: A force for change in general and special education. *Education and Training in Mental Retardation, 23,* 253–260.

Long, N., & Fagen, S. (1981). Therapeutic management: A psychoeducational approach. In G. Brown, R. McDowell, & J. Smith (Eds.), *Educating adolescents with behavior disorders.* Columbus, OH: Merrill.

Long, N. J., & Newman, R. G. (1980). Managing surface behavior of children in schools. In N. J. Long, W. C. Morse, & R. G. Newman (Eds.), *Conflict in the classroom* (4th ed.). Belmont, CA: Wadsworth.

MacMillan, D., & Borthwick, S. (1980). The new educable mentally retarded population: Can they be mainstreamed? *Mental Retardation, 18*(4), 155–158.

Maker, C. J. (1982). *Teaching models in education of the gifted.* Rockville, MD: Aspen.

Mangos, J. A. (1983). Cystic fibrosis. In J. Umbreit (Ed.), *Physical disabilities and health impairments* (pp. 206–213). Columbus, OH: Merrill.

Marland, S. (1972). *Education of the gifted and talented: Report to the Congress of the United States by the U.S. Commissioner of Education.* Washington, DC: U.S. Government Printing Office.

Marsh, G., Gearheart, C., & Gearheart, B. (1978). *The learning disabled adolescent: Program alternatives in the secondary school.* St. Louis: C. V. Mosby.

Marsh, G., Price, B. J., & Smith, T. E. (1983). *Teaching mildly handicapped children: Methods and materials.* St. Louis: C. V. Mosby.

McCandless, B. (1973). *Children and youth: Behavior and development.* New York: Dryden.

McCarney, S. B. (1986). Preferred types of communication indicated by parents and teachers of emotionally disturbed students. *Behavioral Disorders, 11*(2), 118–123.

McCarthy, J. M. (1987). A response to the regular education/special education initiative. *Learning Disabilities Focus, 2*(2), 75–77.

McCartney, B. (1984). Education for the mainstream. *The Volta Review, 86*(5), 41–52.

McCormick, L. P. (1986). Keeping up with language trends. *Teaching Exceptional Children, 18*(2), 123–129.

McDaniel, T. (1986). A primer on classroom discipline: Principles old and new. *Phi Delta Kappan, 68,* 63–67.

McDowell, R. (1981). Adolescence. In G. Brown, R. McDowell, & J. Smith (Eds.), *Educating adolescents with behavioral disorders.* Columbus, OH: Merrill.

McDowell, R., Adamson, G., & Wood, F. (1982).

Teaching emotionally disturbed children. Boston: Little, Brown.

McLoughlin, J. A., & Lewis, R. B. (1990). *Assessing special students* (3rd ed.). Columbus, OH: Merrill.

McTighe, J. J. (1987). Teaching for thinking, of thinking, and about thinking. In M. Heiman & J. Slomianko (Eds.), *Thinking skills instruction: Concepts and techniques.* Washington, DC: National Education Association.

Mehring, T. A., & Colson, S. E. (1990). Motivation and mildly handicapped learners. *Focus on Exceptional Children, 22*(5), 1–15.

Meichenbaum, D. (1983). Teaching thinking: A cognitive behavioral approach. In *Interdisciplinary Voices in Learning Disabilities and Remedial Education.* Austin, TX: Pro-Ed.

Meichenbaum, D., & Goodman, J. (1971). Training impulsive children to talk to themselves: A means of developing self-control. *Journal of Abnormal Psychology, 77,* 115–126.

Mendels, G., & Flanders, J. (1973). Teacher expectations and pupil performance. *American Educational Research Journal, 10,* 203–212.

Mercer, C., & Mercer, A. (1985). *Teaching students with learning problems* (2nd ed.). Columbus, OH: Merrill.

Mercer, C., & Payne, J. (1975). Programs and services. In J. Kauffman and J. Payne (Eds.), *Mental retardation: introduction and personal perspectives.* Columbus, OH: Merrill.

Miksic, S. (1987). Drug abuse management in adolescent special education. In M. M. Kerr, C. M. Nelson, & D. L. Lambert, *Helping adolescents with learning and behavior problems.* Columbus, OH: Merrill.

Milburn, J., & Cartledge, G. (1976). *Build your own social skills curriculum.* Unpublished manuscript, Cleveland State Univ.

Minneapolis Public Schools (1986). *Student suicide prevention guidelines.* Minneapolis, MN: School Social Work Services.

Minner, S. (1982). Expectations of vocational teachers for handicapped students. *Exceptional Children, 48,* 451–453.

Morganthau, T. (1989, September 11). Children of the underclass. *Newsweek,* 16–24.

Morrison, A., & McIntyre, D. (1969). *Teachers and teaching.* Baltimore: Penguin Books.

Morsink, C. (1984). *Teaching special needs students in regular classrooms.* Boston: Little, Brown.

Morsink, C., Soar, R., Soar, R., & Thomas, R. (1986). Research on teaching: Opening the door to special education classrooms. *Exceptional Children, 53,* 32–40.

Murray, H. A. (1943). *Thematic apperception test.* Cambridge: Harvard Univ. Press.

Muse, N. J. (1990). *Depression and suicide in children and adolescents.* Austin, TX: Pro-Ed.

National Information Services Institute (1989). *Choices, a classroom management and discipline system.* Phoenix, AZ: Classroom Management Systems.

Necco, E., Wilson, C., & Scheidemantal, J. (1982). Affective learning through drama. *Teaching Exceptional Children, 15*(1), 22–25.

Nessel, D. (1987). Reading comprehension: Asking the right questions. *Phi Delta Kappan, 68*(6), 442–444.

Norman, M. H., & Norman, E. S. (1968). *Successful reading.* New York: Holt, Rinehart & Winston.

Norton, D. (1989). *The effective teaching of language arts* (3rd ed.). Columbus, OH: Merrill.

Owens, R. E. (1984). *Language development.* Columbus, OH: Merrill.

Panda, K., & Bartel, N. (1972). Teachers' perception of exceptional children. *Journal of Special Education, 6,* 49–58.

Patton, J., Beirne-Smith, M, & Payne, J., (1990). *Mental retardation* (3rd ed.). Columbus, OH: Merrill.

Pauk, W. (1984). *How to study in college.* Boston: Houghton Mifflin.

Payne, J., Polloway, E., Smith, J., & Payne, R. (1981). *Strategies for teaching the mentally retarded* (2nd ed.). Columbus, OH: Merrill.

Pfeffer, C. R. (1986). *The suicidal child.* New York: Guilford.

Pfeiffer, S. (1982). The superiority of team decision making. *Exceptional Children, 49,* 68–69.

Phillips, V., & McCullough, L. (1990). Consultation-based programming: Insituting the collaborative ethic in schools. *Exceptional Children, 56,* 291–304.

Piaget, J. (1952). *The origins of intelligence in children*. New York: International Univ. Press.

Piaget, J. (1954). *The construction of reality in the child*. New York: Basic Books.

Piaget, J. (1962). *Play, dramas, and imitation in childhood*. New York: W. W. Norton.

Platow, J. A. (1984). *A Handbook for identifying the gifted/talented*. Ventura, CA: National/State Leadership Training Institute on the Gifted/Talented.

Polloway, E., Payne, J., Patton, J., & Payne, R. (1985). *Strategies for teaching retarded and special needs learners* (3rd ed.). Columbus, OH: Merrill.

Polloway, E. A., Patton, J. R., Payne, J. S., and Payne, R. A. (1989). *Strategies for teaching learners with special needs* (4th ed). Columbus, OH: Merrill.

Polloway, E. A., & Smith J. E. (1982). *Teaching language skills to exceptional learners*. Denver: Love.

Prillaman, D. (1981). Acceptance of learning disabled students in the mainstream environment: A failure to replicate. *Journal of Learning Disabilities, 14*, 344–346.

Pritchard, D. G. (1963). *Education and the handicapped: 1760–1960*. London: Routledge & Kegan Paul.

Public Law 94–142 (Education of the Handicapped Act of 1975). *Federal Register, 42*, 163 (August 23, 1977).

Pueschel, S. M., Bernier, J. C., & Weidenman, L. E. (1988). *The special child*. Baltimore: Paul H. Brookes.

Purpura, D., Gallagher, J., & Tjossem, T. (Eds.). (1981). *Mental retardation: An evaluation and assessment of the state of the science*. Bethesda, MD: National Institute of Child Health Development, U.S. Department of Health and Human Services.

Quigley, S., & Paul, P. (1984). *Language and Deafness*. San Diego, CA: College-Hill.

Rakes, T. A., & Choate, J. S. (1989). *Language arts: Detecting and correcting special needs*. Boston: Allyn & Bacon.

Reid, D. K. (1988). *Teaching the learning disabled: A cognitive developmental approach*. Boston: Allyn & Bacon.

Reis, S. M., & Renzulli, J. S. (1982). A case for a broadened conception of giftedness. *Phi Delta Kappan, 63*, 619–620.

Reis, S. M., & Renzulli, J. S. (1985). Identification of the gifted and talented. *ERIC Digest, 360*. Reston, VA: Council for Exceptional Children.

Renzulli, J., Reis, S., and Smith, L. (1981). *The revolving door identification model*. Mansfield, CT: Creative Learning.

Renzulli, J., & Smith, L. (1980). An alternative approach to identifying and programming for gifted and talented students. *Gifted/Creative/Talented, 15*, 4–11.

Resnick, L. B. (1983). A developmental theory of number understanding. In H. P. Ginsburg (Ed.), *The development of mathematical thinking*. New York: Academic Press.

Revkin, A. C. (1989). Crack in the cradle. *Discover, 10*, 62–69.

Reynolds, M. C., & Birch, J. W. (1982). *Teaching exceptional children in all America's schools* (rev. ed.). Reston, VA: Council for Exceptional Children.

Rich, H. L. (1982). *Disturbed students*. Baltimore: University Park.

Richards, W. (1986). Allergy, asthma, and school problems. *Journal of School Health, 56*, 151–152.

Rorschach, H. (1942). *Rorschach Inkblot Test*. New York: Grune & Stratton.

Rosenthal, R., & Jacobson, L. (1968). *Pygmalion in the classroom*. New York: Holt, Rinehart & Winston.

Rosenthal, R., & Rubin, D. G. (1978). Interpersonal expectancy efforts: The first 345 studies. *Behavioral & Brain Science, 3*, 377–415.

Roswell, F. G., & Natchez, G. (1989). *Reading disability: A human approach to evaluation and treatment of reading and writing difficulties*. New York: Basic Books.

Rubovits, P., & Maehr, M. (1971). Pygmalion analyzed: Toward an explanation of the Rosenthal-Jacobson findings. *Journal of Personality and Social Psychology, 19*, 197–203.

Rudman, M. K. (1984). *Children's literature: An issues approach* (2nd ed.). New York: Longman.

Runions, T., & Smyth, E. (1985). Mentorships

for the gifted and talented. *ERIC Digest, 346.* Reston, VA: Council for Exceptional Children.

Russell, S. J., Corwin, R., Mokros, J. R., & Kapisovsky, P. M. (1989). *Beyond drill and practice: Expanding the computer mainstream.* Reston, VA: Council for Exceptional Children.

Salend, S. J. (1984). Factors contributing to the development of successful mainstreaming programs. *Exceptional Children, 50,* 409–416.

Salend, S. J. (1990). *Effective Mainstreaming.* New York: Macmillan.

Salend, S. J., & Johns, J. (1983). Changing teacher commitment to mainstreaming. *Teaching Exceptional Children, 15,* 82–85.

Salk, L., Lipsitt, L. P., Sturner, W. Q., Reilly, B. M., & Levat, R. H. (1985). Relationship of maternal and perinatal conditions to eventual adolescent suicide. *The Lancet, 1,* 624–627.

Salvia, J., & Hughes, C. (1990). *Curriculum-based assessment: Testing what is taught.* New York: Macmillan.

Scheffers, W. L. (1977). Sighted children learn about blindness. *Journal of Visual Impairment and Blindness, 71,* 258–261.

Schiamberg, L. B. (1988). *Child and adolescent development.* New York: Macmillan.

Schlesinger, H. S. (1985). Deafness, mental health, and language. In F. Powell, T. Finitzo-Hieber, S. Friel-Patti, & D. Henderson (Eds.), *Education of the hearing impaired child.* San Diego: College-Hill.

Schloss, P., & Sedlak, R. (1986). *Instructional methods for students with learning and behavior problems.* Newton, MA: Allyn & Bacon.

Schneider, B. H. (1987). *The gifted child in peer group perspective.* New York: Springer-Verlag.

Schumaker, J., Deshler, D., Alley, G., Warner, M., & Denton, P. (1982). Multipass: A learning strategy for improving reading comprehension. *Learning Disability Quarterly, 5,* 295–304.

Schumaker, J., Nolan, S., & Deshler, D. (1985). *Learning strategies curriculum: The error monitoring strategy.* Lawrence, KA: Univ. of Kansas.

Schwartz, L. L. (1984). *Exceptional students in the mainstream.* Belmont, CA: Wadsworth.

Semmel, M., Gottlieb, J., & Robinson, N. (1979). Mainstreaming: Perspectives on educating handicapped children in the public schools. In D. Berliner (Ed.), *Review of research in education* (Vol. 7, pp. 126–130). Washington, DC: American Educational Research Association.

Shames, G. S., & Wiig, E. H. (1990). *Human communication disorders* (3rd ed.). Columbus, OH: Merrill.

Sharon, S., & Sharon, Y. (1976). *Small-group teaching.* Englewood Cliffs, NJ: Educational Technology.

Shaywitz, B. (1987). *Hyperactivity/attention deficit disorders in learning disabilities: A report to the U.S. Congress* (pp. 194–218). Washington, DC: U.S. Government Printing Office.

Sheare, J. (1978). The impact of resource programs upon the self-concept and peer acceptance of learning disabled children. *Psychology in the Schools, 15,* 406–412.

Sheinker, J., & Sheinker, A. (1989). *A metacognitive approach to study strategies.* Rockville, MD: Aspen.

Simpson, R. (1981). Further investigation and interpretation of the expectancy effect generated by disability labels. *Diagnostique, 17,* 101–108.

Siperstein, G., Bopp, M., & Bak, J. (1978). Social status of learning disabled children. *Journal of Learning Disabilities, 11,* 98–102.

Sisk, D. (1987). *Creative teaching of the gifted.* New York: McGraw-Hill.

Skinner, B. (1957). *Verbal behavior.* New York: Appleton-Century-Crofts.

Slavin, R. E. (1978). Student teams and comparison among equals: Effects on academic performance and student attitudes. *Journal of Educational Psychology, 70,* 532–538.

Slavin, R. E. (1980). Cooperative learning. *Review of Educational Research, 50,* 315–342.

Smith, C., & Smith, S. (1980). Study skills in the content areas. In P. Lamb & R. Arnold, *Teaching reading: Foundations and strategies.* Belmont, CA: Wadsworth.

Smith, G., & Smith, D. (1989). Schoolwide study

skills program: The key to mainstreaming. *Teaching Exceptional Children, 21*(3), 20–23.

Smith, M. (1980). Meta-analysis of research on teacher expectation. *Evaluation in Education, 4*, 53–55.

Soar, R., Soar, R., & Ragosta, M. (1971). *The Florida climate and control system*. Gainesville, FL: Institute for Development of Human Resources, College of Education, Univ. of Florida.

Social integration of handicapped students: Cooperative goal structuring. (1988, September) (Brief T1, ERIC Clearinghouse on Handicapped and Gifted Children). Reston, VA: Council for Exceptional Children.

Sorenson, A. B., & Hallinan, M. (1984). Effects of race on assignment to ability groups. In P. L. Peterson, L. C. Wilkenson, & M. Hallinan (Eds.), *The social context of instruction*. New York: Academic Press.

Spivak, G., & Swift, M. (1972). *Hahneman High School Behavior Scale*. Philadelphia: Department of Mental Health Sciences, Hahneman Medical College & Hospital.

Stainback, S., & Stainback, W. (1987). Integration versus cooperation: A commentary on educating children with learning problems, a shared responsibility. *Exceptional Children, 54*, 66–68.

Stainback, S., Stainback, W., & Forest, M. (1989). *Educating all students in the mainstream of education*. Baltimore: Paul H. Brookes.

Stephens, T. (1978). *Social skills in the classroom*. Columbus, OH: Cedars.

Strain, P. S. (1982). *Social development of exceptional children*. Rockville, MD: Aspen.

Strickland, B. B., & Turnbull, A. P. (1990). *Developing and implementing individualized education programs* (3rd ed.). Columbus, OH: Merrill.

Taylor, R., Smiley, L., & Ziegler, E. (1983). The effects of labels and assigned attributes on teacher perceptions of academic and social behaviors. *Education and Training of the Mentally Retarded, 18*, 45–51.

Terman, L., & Merrill, M. (1973). *Stanford-Binet intelligence scale*. Boston: Houghton Mifflin.

Thorndike, R. L., Hagen, E., & Sattler, J. (1986). *Stanford-Binet intelligence scale* (3rd ed.) Chicago: Riverside.

Tiedt, I. M., Carlson, J. E., Howard, B. D., and Watanabe, K. S. O. (1989). *Teaching thinking in K–12 classrooms: Ideas, activities, and resources*. Boston: Allyn & Bacon.

Torrance, E. P. (1974). *Torrance tests of creative thinking technical manual*. Lexington, MA: Personnel.

Torrance, E. P., Blume, B., Maryanopolis, J., Murphey, F., & Rogers, J. (1980). *Teaching scenario writing*. Lincoln, NE: Future Problem Solving Program, Nebraska Department of Education.

Torrance, E. P., & Torrance, J. P. (1981). Educating gifted, talented and creative students for the future. *American Middle School Education, 4*(1), 39–46.

Turnbull, H. (1986). *Free appropriate public education: The law and children with disabilities*. Denver: Love.

Tymitz-Wolf, B. L. (1982). Extending the scope of in-service training for mainstreaming effectiveness. *Teacher Education and Special Education, 5*, 17–23.

Unruh, D., Gilliam, J., & Jogi, A. (1982). Developing concept analysis skills. *Directive Teacher, 4*(2), 26–31.

U.S. Department of Education (1986). *What works: Research about teaching and learning*. Washington, DC: U.S. Department of Education.

U.S. General Accounting Office (1981). *Disparities still exist in who gets special education*. Washington, DC: U.S. Government Printing Office.

Vallecorsa, A. L., Zigmond, N., & Henderson, L. M. (1985). Spelling instruction in special education classrooms: A survey of practices. *Exceptional Children, 52*, 19–24.

Van Dyke, D. C., & Fox, A. A. (1990). Fetal drug exposure and its possible implications for learning in preschool and school-age populations. *Journal of Learning Disabilities, 23*, 160–163.

Van Riper, C., & Emerick, L. (1990). *Speech correction: An introduction to speech pathology and audiology.* Englewood Cliffs, NJ: Prentice-Hall.

Vargas, J. (1986). Instructional design flaws in computer-assisted instruction. *Phi Delta Kappan, 67,* 738–744.

Vaughn, B. E., & Langlois, J. (1983). Physical attractiveness as a correlate of peer status and social competence in preschool children. *Developmental Psychology, 19,* 517–567.

Von Isser, A., Quay, H. C., & Love, C. T. (1980). Interrelationships among three measures of deviant behavior. *Exceptional Children, 46,* 272–276.

Walker, H. M. (1983). *Walker Problem Behavior Identification Checklist* (rev. ed.) Los Angeles: Western Psychological Service.

Walker, H. M., Todis, B., Holmes, D., & Norton, N. (1988). *Walker social skills curiculum: The ACCESS program.* Austin, TX: Pro-Ed.

Walker, J. E., & Shea, T. M. (1991). *Behavior management: A practical approach for educators.* Columbus, OH: Merrill.

Wallace, G., Cohen, S. B., & Polloway, E. A. (1987). *Language arts: Teaching exceptional students.* Austin, TX: Pro-Ed.

Wallace, G., & Kauffman, J. M. (1986, 1990). *Teaching students with learning and behavior problems* (3rd & 4th eds.). Columbus, OH: Merrill.

Wang, M. C., & Wahlberg, H. J. (1988). Four fallacies of segregationism. *Exceptional Children, 55,* 128–137.

Wechsler, D. (1974). *Wechsler Intelligence Scale for Children—Revised.* Cleveland: Psychological Corporation.

Wechsler, H., Suarez, A., & McFadden, M. (1975). Teachers' attitudes toward the education of physically handicapped children: Implications for implementation of Massachusetts Chapter 766. *Journal of Education, 157,* 134–141.

White, W. J., & Biller, E. (1988). Career education for students with handicaps. In R. Gaylord-Ross (Ed.), *Vocational education for persons with handicaps.* Mountain View, CA: Mayfield.

Whitmore, J. R. (1985). Characteristics of intellectually gifted children. *ERIC Digest, 344.*

Reston, VA: Council for Exceptional Children.

Whitmore, J. R., & Maker, C. J. (1985). *Intellectual giftedness in disabled persons.* Rockville, MD: Aspen.

Will, M. (1986). Educating children with learning problems: A shared responsibility. *Exceptional Children, 52,* 411–415.

Willings, D., & Arsenault, M. (1986). Attempted suicide and creative promise. *Gifted Education International, 4*(1), 10–13.

Winter, R. J. (1983). Childhood diabetes mellitus. In J. Umbreit (Ed.), *Physical disabilities and health impairments* (pp. 195–205). Columbus, OH: Merrill.

Witt, J. C., Elliott, S. N., Gresham, F. M., & Kramer, J. J. (1988). *Assessment of special children.* Boston: Scott, Foresman/Little, Brown.

Wolfgang, C. H., & Glickman, C. D. (1986). *Solving discipline problems: Strategies for classroom teachers.* Newton, MA: Allyn & Bacon.

Wolman, B. B. (1987). *The sociopathic personality.* New York: Brunner/Mazel.

Wong, B., & Jones, W. (1982). Increasing metacomprehension in learning disabled and normally achieving students through self-questioning training. *Learning Disability Quarterly, 5,* 228–240.

Wong, M. R. (1979). Drug abuse and prevention in special education students. In D. Cullinan & M. Epstein (Eds.), *Special education for adolescents: Issues and perspectives.* Columbus, OH: Merrill.

Wood, J. (1984). *Adapting instruction to the mainstream.* Columbus, OH: Merrill.

Wood, J. (1989). *Mainstreaming: A practical approach for teachers.* Columbus, OH: Merrill.

Woodcock, R. W., & Johnson, M. B. (1983). *Woodcock-Johnson Scales of Independent Behavior.* Allen, TX: DLM Teaching Resources.

Wrenn, C., & Schwarzrock, S. (1984). *The coping with series.* Circle Pines, MN: American Guidance Service.

Ysseldyke, J. E., & Algozzine, B. (1982). *Critical*

issues in special and remedial education. Boston: Houghton Mifflin.

Ysseldyke, J. E., & Algozzine, B. (1984). *Introduction to special education.* Boston: Houghton Mifflin.

Zilboorg, G., & Henry, G. W. (1941). *A history of medical psychology.* New York: W. W. Norton.

Zirkel, P. A. (Ed.). (1978). *A digest of Supreme Court decisions affecting education.* Bloomington, IN: Phi Delta Kappa.

NAME INDEX

SUBJECT INDEX